Telecommunications Law

Edited by

Ian Walden

and

John Angel

 Blackstone Press

Published by
Blackstone Press Limited
Aldine Place
London
W12 8AA
United Kingdom

Sales enquiries and orders
Telephone +44-(0)-20-8740-2277
Facsimile +44-(0)-20-8743-2292
e-mail: sales@blackstone.demon.co.uk
website: www.blackstonepress.com

ISBN 1-84174-121-3
© Ian Walden and John Angel, 2001
The contributors hold the copyright for their respective chapters
First edition, 2001

The rights of the contributors to be identified as authors of this work have
been asserted in accordance with ss. 77 and 78 of the Copyright, Designs
and Patents Act 1988.

British Library Cataloguing in Publication Data
A CIP catalogue record for this book is available from the British Library

Typeset in 10/11 Plantin by Style Photosetting Ltd, Mayfield, East Sussex
Printed and bound in Great Britain by Antony Rowe Limited,
Chippenham and Reading

Contents

Preface

As with our previous collaboration, the *Telecommunications Law Handbook* (Blackstone Press, 1997), this book arose from our involvement in the University of London's LLM course in Telecommunications Law offered by the Centre for Commercial Law Studies (CCLS), Queen Mary, University of London.

One problem faced (bravely) by our students on the course has been the lack of an affordable textbook. Existing textbooks have been targeted at the professional adviser market and are priced accordingly. Whilst there is no lack of material in the area, both library-based and online, there was a perceived need for a single work designed specifically to meet the needs of our students.

Although an edited work, nearly all the contributors to the book have taught, at one time or another, on the course. As editors, we are extremely grateful to the authors for agreeing to extend their commitment to us from the odd lecture to the provision of a fully referenced chapter.

Despite the recent stock market troubles faced by the telecommunications sector, its strategic economic importance remains. Rapid technological and market developments are matched by changes to the legal and regulatory framework. This book attempts, but inevitably fails, to keep up with such developments. Whilst the law should be correct up to December 2000, the issues discussed will continue to occupy law students and professional advisers in the coming years.

We would specifically like to acknowledge the very considerable assistance given to us by Anne Flanagan during the editing process, a past student who has not been allowed to go; and Lorraine Mulpeter, the Unit Administrator, who efficiently co-ordinated the process and kept up the requisite bullying.

Finally, this book is dedicated to students, past and present, who never believed they would live to see its eventual publication — we hope it helps!

Dr Ian Walden
Head of the IT Law Unit
CCLS, Queen Mary
Consultant, Baker & McKenzie

John Angel
Head of Online Legal Services
Clifford Chance
Senior Visiting Fellow at CCLS

April 2001

Contributors

The Editors

John Angel is a solicitor and Head of Online Legal Services at Clifford Chance. He is also a Senior Visiting Fellow at the IT Law Unit, Centre for Commercial Law Studies, Queen Mary, University of London, and lectures on the University of London's LLM Telecommunications Law, Information Technology Law and Internet Law courses. He is joint editor of *Telecommunications Law Handbook* with Ian Walden and *Computer Law* with Chris Reed (both Blackstone Press, 1997 and 2000 respectively). John is general editor of *Outsourcing Practice Manual* (Sweet & Maxwell) and consultant editor to *Electronic Business Law* (Butterworths).

Dr Ian Walden is Head of the IT Law Unit in the Centre for Commercial Law Studies, Queen Mary, and Director of QM's Computer-Related Crime Research Centre. He is editor of *EDI and the Law* (Blenheim Online, 1989), and joint editor of *Information Technology and the Law* (Macmillan, 1990), *EDI Audit and Control* (NCC Blackwell, 1993), *Cross-border Electronic Banking* (Lloyds of London, 1995), *Telecommunications Law Handbook* (Blackstone Press, 1997) and Sweet & Maxwell's *Encyclopedia of Data Protection*. Ian is vice-chair of the e-centre UK's legal advisory group and a member of the European Commission's Legal Advisory Board. Ian is a consultant to solicitors Baker & McKenzie.

The Authors

Camilla Bustani holds a BA (Hons) from Harvard University and a Masters in International Affairs from Columbia University, as well as a BA (Hons) in Jurisprudence from Oxford University. She joined Clifford Chance in 1998, where she is presently a lawyer in the Telecommunications Group, focusing on telecommunications sector regulatory reform in emerging markets and developing countries and public international law aspects of telecommunications regulation and sector liberalisation. E-mail: camilla.bustani@cliffordchance.com.

Lisa Correa is a researcher in telecommunications regulatory economics at Queen Mary, University of London. Additionally, she operates as an independent consultant on regulatory issues and is a speaker at Cable & Wireless Coventry College as well as on the LLM Telecommunications Law course organised by the Centre for Commercial Law Studies at Queen Mary. She is involved in other regulated industries and has worked with OFGAS and OFGEM on the development of the Gas Trading Arrangements and the New Electricity Trading Arrangements. Prior to her current roles, she worked as an economist at Mercury Communications, now called Cable & Wireless Communications, investigating key issues affecting the industry. Some of the projects she has been involved with include the Retail and Network Price Cap, the UK Labour Party proposals for Regulation, Mobile Interconnection, Fixed/Mobile Convergence, Number Portability and Numbering where she was the Chair of the Industry Steering Group for Numbering Change Implementation.

Rohan Kariyawasam holds a BSc (Hons) in Communications Engineering from the University of Kent and qualified as a telecommunications engineer with Marconi. He has worked as a telecommunications analyst for McGraw-Hill in Hong Kong and Singapore, and is presently a solicitor and research consultant to the Media Computer and Communications Group at Clifford Chance. He lectures on the LLM in Telecommunications Law at the University of London and is also researching for a doctorate in international telecommunications trade law at the Centre for Commercial Law Studies, Queen Mary, University of London. E-mail: r.kariyawasam@qmw.ac.uk.

Jonathan Kembery is Legal and Business Affairs Director at Open Interactive. Open is an innovative television company, offering a range of interactive games, shopping, information and e-mail services to viewers via digital satellite. In terms of reach, Open is the UK's largest electronic commerce platform with availability to 13 million people and approximately 4 million weekly users. Jonathan joined Open prior to its commercial launch in 1999 having previously been an IT/broadcasting lawyer in private practice. He is a recognised leader in the area of e-commerce and writes and speaks on a variety of issues related to e-commerce and the convergence of broadcasting, telecommunications and IT.

Karen Lee is a US- and UK-qualified lawyer specialising in all aspects of UK and European telecommunications regulation, including fixed, mobile and satellite, and commercial agreements. She was seconded to OFTEL (Compliance Directorate) in 1998–99 where she advised on competition and licensing issues. Her recent experience includes advising the Radiocommunications Agency on the award of FWA licences; Energis on Local Loop Unbundling and its recent £350 million acquisition of EnerTel; and bidders in the UK's 3G and BFWA spectrum auctions. Karen is also a member of the Illinois bar and a former Senior Managing Editor of the *Federal Communications Law Journal*. She joined Denton Wilde Sapte in 1996.

Timothy Leeson is a senior solicitor in the Communications Group at Bird & Bird specialising in e-commerce, telecommunications, broadcasting and IT-related matters. Prior to qualification, Tim spent three years working in the satellite manufacturing and broadcasting sections of a major international company. During this time, he worked on the establishment of a major international consortium which made a successful application to the DTI for a 2G mobile operators' licence. He then spent a further four years working for a major international telecommunications company. Much of his work since qualification spans the entire communications and multimedia sectors. This ranges from dot-com seed fundings to commercial agreements, joint venture agreements and other general corporate and commercial work in this area. This work involves working with clients (whether start-ups or otherwise) in the B2B and the B2C marketplace. Tim is a regular conference speaker and writes many articles for the firm.

Christopher Millard (LLB, MA, LLM) is a Partner in the Media, Computer and Communications Group at Clifford Chance. His practice is focussed on e-commerce, e-business and data protection compliance projects. He was responsible for the launch in May 1998 of NextLaw®, a Clifford Chance online service providing guidance on e-business law and regulation in 36 jurisdictions (information about the service is available at http://www.nextlaw.com). As a Visiting Professorial Fellow of Queen Mary, University of London, he teaches on LLM courses in Internet Law, Information Technology Law and Telecommunications Law. He is a frequent speaker at international conferences and is a visiting lecturer at several universities. He is a past Chairman of the Society for Computers and Law and a past President of the International Federation of Computer Law Associations. He is author of *Legal Protection of Computer Programs and Data* (Sweet & Maxwell), Joint Editor of *Data Protection Laws of the World* (Sweet & Maxwell), is on the editorial boards of many IT, Internet and communications law journals and is a General Editor of the *International Journal of Law and Information Technology* (Oxford University Press).

Edward Pitt is a partner in the Competition and Regulation Group at Theodore Goddard. He has spent more than 20 years in private practice in both London and Brussels. Edward joined Theodore Goddard from the Office of Telecommunications (OFTEL), where he was Senior Legal Adviser. In this role he was particularly involved with licence enforcement and the control of anti-competitive practices by licensed telecoms operators, and also advised on reform to the UK telecoms regulatory regime. During this time he spent a period of secondment to the UK Department of Trade and Industry, advising on competition policy and on the new UK Competition Bill. In addition to telecommunications, Edward's experience lies primarily in the sphere of EC and UK competition and international trade law, as well as in general commercial law. He has represented multinational clients in cases before the EU Commission, both in major EC competition investigations and in many EC joint venture and merger clearances, and has handled cases before the UK competition authorities – the Monopolies and Merger Commission and the UK Office of Fair Trading. Edward is an active member in several legal professional associations and he serves on the editorial board of *International Trade Law and Regulations*.

Jamison Prime is an attorney with the US Federal Communications Commission in Washington, DC, where he specialises in land mobile, personal radio, microwave and other wireless services, as well as regulations pertaining to antenna towers. A 1996 graduate of the Indiana University School of Law, he served as a managing editor on the *Federal Communications Law Journal* and authored 'A Double-Barreled Assault: How Technology and Judicial Interpretations Threaten Public Access to Law Enforcement Records'. He received a BA in History from DePauw University in 1993.

David Satola received his BA and MA from The Johns Hopkins University and his JD from the University of Wisconsin, and has also studied at the London School of Economics and the Hague Academy of International Law. He is a member of the State Bars of Wisconsin and Georgia as well as the Union Internationale des Avocats. Having been an attorney with the Bell-South Corporation and in private practice (specialising in European telecommunications joint ventures, privatisations and regulatory reform projects), he is now Senior Counsel in the World Bank's legal department, focusing on legal and regulatory reform and privatisation across the Bank's regions. E-mail: dsatola@worldbank.org.

Tim Schwarz holds a BA (Hons) degree in Jurisprudence and a BCL degree from Oxford University, and was a Wiener-Anspach Scholar at the Université Libre de Bruxelles, Belgium, where he studied European law. He joined Clifford Chance in 1987, spent two years at the World Bank as its main telecommunications lawyer, and prior to that had been seconded to OFTEL. Since 1997 he has been a partner at Clifford Chance where one of his areas of focus is privatisation and regulatory reform in the telecommunications sectors of emerging markets and developing countries. He also lectures on the LLM in Telecommunications Law at the University of London. E-mail: tim.schwarz@cliffordchance.com.

Dr Michael Sinclair is a partner in Tarlo Lyons, a UK specialist technology and communications law firm, and specialises in outsourcings, telecommunications and technology. He is co-author of Sweet & Maxwell's *Outsourcing Practice Manual* and has a PhD from Cambridge University. Michael can be contacted at michael.sinclair@tarlolyons.com.

Lisa Suits joined Cable & Wireless plc in November 1997. Her current position is Vice President, Public Policy, Cable & Wireless IDC Inc. Japan, with overall responsibility for corporate policy development and advocacy before the Japanese government, trade, and regulatory authorities. Prior to joining Cable & Wireless, Lisa spent five years with AT&T Asia/Pacific's

International Public Affairs group, which had responsibility for corporate regulatory relationships with 15 Asian governments. Her AT&T experience was preceded by a stint in the US government at the Commerce Department's National Telecommunications and Information Administration (NTIA) doing Executive Branch policy formulation for telephony, cable and broadcasting. Lisa has a Master of Science degree from MIT in Telecommunications, Technology, and Public Policy, a Bachelor of Science degree from the Georgetown School of Foreign Service, and a post graduate diploma in Asian Arts from the School of Oriental and African Studies at the University of London.

Abbreviations

2G	second generation
3G	third generation
ACA	Australian Communications Authority
ACCC	Australian Competition and Consumer Commission
ADC	access deficit charge
ADSL	asynchronous digital subscriber line
AOL	America Online
API	application programming interface
Art.	Article
Arts	Articles
AS	autonomous system
ASP	application service provider
ATM	asynchronous transfer mode
AUP	acceptable use policy
B2B	business-to-business
B2C	business-to-consumer
BOT	build operate transfer
BT	British Telecom
CAT	Communications Authority of Thailand
CATV	community, antenna television
CCF	China-China-Foreign
CDR	call detail record
CLI	calling line identification
CPS	carrier pre-selection
CUG	closed user group
DGFT	Director-General of Fair Trading
DGT	Director-General of Telecommunications
DMSU	Digital Main Switching Unit
DoJ	Department of Justice (US)
DOS	denial of service
DSB	dispute settlement body

DTH	direct to home
DTI	Department of Trade and Industry
ECO	effective competitive opportunities
ECPR	efficient component pricing
EDI	electronic data interchange
EEA	European Economic Area
EPG	electronic programming guide
ETNS	European Telephony Numbering Space
ETSI	European Telecommunications Standards Institute
EU	European Union
FCC	Federal Communications Commission (US)
FPS	fax preference service
FRIACO	flat-rate Internet access call origination
FTC	fair trading condition
GATS	General Agreement on Trade in Services
GATT	General Agreement on Tariffs and Trade
GPO	General Post Office
GSM	Global System for Mobile
IA	indirect access
IBP	Internet backbone provider
ICANN	Internet Corporation for Assigned Names and Numbers
ICB	International competitive bidding
ICC	Internet commerce companies
IETF	Internet Engineering Task Force
IFI	International Financial Institutions
IFL	international facilities licence
ILEC	incumbent local exchange company
interLATA	inter-local access and transport area
IP	Internet protocol
IPC	Internet portal companies
IPLC	international private leased circuit
IPO	initial public offering
IPR	intellectual property rights
IRU	indefeasible right of use
ISDN	integrated services digital networks
ISDR	international simple data re-sale
ISP	Internet service provider
ISVR	international simple voice re-sale
IT	information technology
ITC	Independent Television Commission
ITU	International Telecommunications Union
JFTC	Japan Fair Trade Commission
KCC	Korean Communications Commission
KFTC	Korean Fair Trade Commission
LAN	local area network
LATA	Local Access and Transport Area
LEC	local exchange carrier

LEO	low Earth orbit
LINX	London Internet Exchange
LLU	local loop unbundling
LRAIC	long-run average incremental costs
MCIT	Ministry of Communications and Information Technology (Singapore)
MEO	medium Earth orbit
MMC	Monopolies and Mergers Commission
MFJ	Modification of Final Judgment
n.	note
NAP	network access point
NRA	national regulatory authority
NTIA	National Telecommunications and Information Administration
NTP	network termination point
NTS	Number Translation Services
NTT	Nippon Telegraph and Telephone
OECD	Organisation for Economic Cooperation and Development
OFCOM	Office of Communications
OFT	Office of Fair Trading
OFTEL	Office of Telecommunications
ONP	open network provision
p.	page
PABX	private automatic branch exchange
para.	paragraph
PC	personal computer
PCS	personal communications services
PLDT	Philippine Long Distance Telephone Company
POI	point of interconnection
POP	point of presence
PPIAF	Public–Private Infrastructure Advisory Facility (World Bank)
PSTN	public switched telephone network
Pt	Part
PTO	public telecommunications operator
PTT	posts, telegraph and telecommunications
PUC	Public Utility Commission
PVC	permanent virtual circuit
RBOCs	Regional Bell Operating Companies
RCS	relevant connectable system
reg.	regulation
ROA	recognised operating agency
RPI	Retail Price Index
RSF	Reporters Sans Frontieres
s.	section
Sch.	Schedule (in legislation)
SME	small business end-user *or* small- to medium-sized enterprises
SMP	significant market power
SNA	special network access

SPL	self-provision licence
TAS	Telecommunications Authority of Singapore
TCP	transmission control protocol (UK); tariffed components pricing (US)
TCP/IP	Transmission control protocol/Internet protocol
telcos	telecommunications companies
TOT	Telephone Organization of Thailand
TPS	telecommunications preference service
TQM	total quality management
TRIPS	Trade-Related Aspects of Intellectual Property Rights
TSL	telecommunications services licence
TSP	transit service provider
UMTS	univeral mobile telecommunications system
UNE	unbundled network element
USO	universal service obligation
USP	Uniform Settlements Policy
USTR	United States Trade Representatives Office
VAT	Value Added Tax
VoIP	voice over the Internet protocol
VPN	virtual private network
VSAT	Very Small Aperture Terminals
WAN	wide area network
WAP	wireless application protocol
WTO	World Trade Organization
WTSA	World Telecommunication Standardization Assembly
WWW	World Wide Web

Table of Cases

Table of Legislation

CHAPTER ONE

Telecommunications Law and Regulation: An Introduction

Ian Walden

1.1 THE TELECOMMUNICATIONS SECTOR

There is no doubting the dynamic nature of the telecommunications sector within the global economy. World stock markets currently rise and fall on perceptions of the health and wealth of this sector. Indeed, such is the dependency that financial regulators have recently expressed concern over the exposure of the banking system to the fortunes of the telecommunications companies bidding for the third generation mobile licences within Europe.[1] The World Trade Organisation's (WTO) 'Basic Agreement on Telecommunications', in 1997, can be seen as a definitive moment in the international community's commitment to the structural evolution of the sector, from a monopolistic to a competitive marketplace. Such acceptance has been driven by a recognition that telecommunications is a strategic economic sector, in terms of its being both a tradable service in its own right and the infrastructure via which other goods and services are traded and (in an age of electronic commerce) delivered.

This book is primarily concerned with the rules and regulations governing the provision of telecommunications equipment, networks infrastructure and services (e.g., the carriage of voice and data traffic), rather than the law governing the content of the traffic being sent across telecommunication networks. The latter is the domain of 'communications law' or 'media law' rather than 'telecommunications law', although content-related issues are addressed in a number of chapters. Indeed, one recurring issue in telecom-

---

[1] See Financial Services Authority Press Release, 'Telecoms lending – firms must remain vigilant', FSA/PN/153/2000, 7 December 2000.

munications law is the problem of distinguishing clearly between issues of carriage and issues of content, particularly with the emergence of new services such as Internet telephony (see 8.2.4). Even the categorisation of carriage as a service is evolving, with the development of commodity markets for trading carriage in terms of telecommunication minutes (e.g., Band-X (www.band-x.com)). Such economic re-categorisation is likely to have profound implications for policy makers and regulators.

The various aspects of telecommunications law addressed in this book can be broadly separated into competition issues and non-economic public policy issues. Competition law is primarily concerned with establishing and ensuring the sustainability of competitive markets at a national, regional and global level. Telecommunications as a sector capable of establishing a comparative advantage in international trade was recognised by the UK Government at the outset of liberalisation, in the early 1980s. In the Telecommunications Act 1984, four of the ten general duties imposed upon the regulators address trade aspects of telecommunications, from encouraging the provision of transit services, traffic being routed through the UK, to the supply of telecommunications apparatus (see s. 3(2)). For developing countries, the prospect of becoming a regional hub in the emerging information economy is promoted as an opportunity arising from market liberalisation. Non-economic public policy issues centre on the provision of telecommunication services to the population as a whole: the issue of universal service. Current concerns about the growth of a 'digital divide' between the information rich and poor, are the latest manifestation of such political imperatives.

It is inevitable that the seismic shifts in the structure of the telecommunication sector are reflected in a complex and rapidly changing legal framework. The liberalisation of the sector has usually required significant legal intervention, the classic exception to the rule being New Zealand. In parallel with the pursuance of liberalisation, the telecommunications sector has experienced rapid and dramatic developments in the technology, which have compounded the problems faced by policy makers, legislators and regulators when trying to establish legal clarity and certainty for an industry undergoing convergence with other industries.[2] The Internet, with services such as voice telephony and web-casting, is the classic example of this phenomenal technological development. The existence of a clear legal and regulatory distinction between issues of carriage, the primary focus of the book, and issues of content is also dissolving in the face of such technological change (see Chapter 12).

This chapter introduces some of the key themes present within the field of telecommunications law. These themes are then considered in greater detail in one or more of the following substantive chapters.

1.2 LIBERALISATION AND REGULATION

The telecommunications industry has been undergoing a fundamental change in structure, from that of monopoly to one of competition. Many of

---

[2] However, see also Standage, T., *The Victorian Internet* (London, Weidenfeld & Nicolson, 1998), which describes the revolutionary impact of the telegraph.

the laws and regulations examined in this book are concerned with this process of change – regulating for competition. However, the notion of what type of competition is being sought has sometimes distinguished the responses of legislators and regulators. The telecommunications market can be very crudely divided into equipment, networks and services. Liberalisation of the market for telecommunications equipment has been subject to the broadest consensus among policy makers, reflecting conditions in the broader information technology (IT) products market. The provision of telecommunications services has experienced similar general consensus.

It is at the level of the network, constructing the physical communications infrastructure, that debate over liberalisation continues to be heard. Historically, it was argued that telecommunications networks were natural monopolies, that replicating the physical infrastructure was inevitably uneconomic. While such arguments seem arcane in most developed economies, there continue to be those who argue that some form of single network platform is a feasible policy alternative, particularly for developing countries and increasingly driven by environmental concerns.[3] In addition, the natural monopoly position continues to have relevance in the provision of broadcasting networks and wireless telecommunication services, e.g.: 'In a country with a low population density such as Finland, the broadcasting network might constitute a natural monopoly.'[4] Although technological developments are continually improving our exploitation of the radio frequency spectrum, the market for wireless services is likely to remain oligopolistic, if not monopolistic, with associated competition concerns.

One of the historic myths of telecommunications liberalisation was that it would arise through market deregulation, a feature prominent in the related IT industry. To date, however, the reality has been quite the opposite. The telecommunications sector has become heavily regulated in order to ensure the transition to competition, as manifested in part by this book. Such regulation has focused primarily on controlling the activities of the incumbent operator in order to facilitate market entry for new providers. However, public policy concerns in respect of universal service and quality of service issues have also been present.

As markets become fully competitive, deregulation has reappeared as a policy objective, sometimes embodied in legislation. Again, as with the sector as a whole, the shift towards deregulation has arisen not only because competitive markets are maturing, but also because of technological developments, such as the Internet. In the US, for example, the Telecommunications Act 1996 imposed a general obligation upon the Federal Communications Commission both to forbear from the imposition of regulations under certain conditions and to engage in biennial reviews of the existing regulatory framework to remove those regulations identified as 'no longer necessary in the public interest as the result of meaningful economic competition between providers of such service' (47 USC §§ 160–161). Similarly, in the UK, specific

---

[3] See, for example, www.piazze.telematiche.it.
[4] Commission Communication, 'Sixth Report on the Implementation of the Telecommunications Regulatory Package', COM (2000) 814, 7 December 2000, at 24.

provision has been made for the modification of operator licences where the purpose is 'deregulatory', which is defined as meaning not only that an existing burden may be removed from the operator, but also that the removal of that burden does not remove any necessary protection (Telecommunications Act 1984, s. 12A(3), (7)).

Complementing the move towards deregulation, some jurisdictions have also given statutory recognition to the role of industry self-regulation in certain areas. In Australia, for example, the Telecommunications Act 1997, s. 4 states: 'The Parliament intends that telecommunications be regulated in a manner that . . . promotes the greatest practicable use of industry self-regulation.' The technical complexity of the telecommunications market has always meant that much of the regulatory input on particular issues, such as interconnection, simply consisted of the convening and oversight of particular industry groups, intervening only in the event of impasse. However, as regulators reduce or withdraw from market intervention, increasingly reliance is likely to be placed upon industry to regulate itself.

1.3 LIBERALISATION AND PRIVATISATION

A third concept often linked in the past with liberalisation and deregulation was privatisation – the conversion of the incumbent operator from being a state-owned public body to a privately-owned entity. As with deregulation, the nature of the relationship with the process of liberalisation has been far from straightforward. The policy drivers behind privatisation of the incumbent have tended to be based around state revenue concerns rather than the objective of liberalisation. The provision of a modern telecommunications infrastructure requires massive capital investment, a funding burden which governments are no longer prepared to shoulder. Attracting some degree of private sector finance is generally seen as the only feasible mechanism for meeting the policy objective of modernising this strategic economic sector.

Worries that a state-owned incumbent might inhibit market entry have come a clear second to such revenue-raising concerns. Nevertheless, the process of privatisation has, itself, sometimes acted as a barrier to the process of liberalisation. In the UK, for example, the divestiture of British Telecom (BT) occurred in three stages – in 1984, 1991 and 1993. However, at the time of the second sale, the Government was also undertaking a comprehensive review of the market, the 'Duopoly Review', in order to promote further liberalisation (see Chapter 3). During this process, it was generally perceived that BT used the need to maintain share price for the forthcoming sale as an effective tool in its negotiations with the Government. Government stakeholdings in incumbent operators have also become an international trade issue. In the US, for example, concerns have been raised in the legislature about Deutsche Telekom's proposed merger with Voicestream, on the basis that the German Government continues to have a stake in its incumbent. After privatisation, a government may continue to be concerned about the performance of the incumbent, particularly where, as in the UK, a significant proportion of the shares are held by the general public, who represent future voters. Although privatisation has been an important feature of the telecommunications market, governments remain remarkably attached to the 'national champion', with 21 OECD countries continuing to have some stake in the incumbent.

In many countries, the need to attract international investment into the telecommunications sector – through the sale of a strategic stake in the incumbent, through build-operate-transfer schemes, or through financing new entrants – has actually driven the adoption of a comprehensive legal framework for the provision of telecommunications networks and services. A lack of legal certainty is seen as a significant barrier to market entry (see Chapter 14).

1.4 POLICY, LAW AND REGULATION

The shift from monopolistic telecommunications markets to liberalised competitive markets arose due to a number of different policy drivers, from the need to modernise existing infrastructure, to extending the reach of the national network. In addition, the process of liberalisation was made subject to certain other public policy objectives, such as maintenance of universal service, protection of consumer interests and individual privacy (see Chapter 11).

Universal service is concerned with making available a certain, defined set of telecommunications services as widely as possible, both geographically and socially. Historically, such provision was seen as lying with the incumbent, however successful it was perceived to be in terms of meeting its obligation! In a liberalised market, such service provision needs to continue to be guaranteed through a mechanism that will not distort the competitive conditions under which providers operate. The scope of universal service will also inevitably evolve over time, as politicians try to ensure that the benefits of the new technologies are made available to society as a whole.

Governments generally set the broad policy objectives governing the telecommunications market. These objectives are then enshrined in law (primary and secondary legislation) which a new entrant may rely on and hold up for reference and examination in the case of dispute. Such legislative instruments may impose obligations directly upon operators to address the policy objectives, or lay down principles to which the regulator should have reference when intervening in the market.

Another aspect of telecommunications law concerns the legal relationships that exist between licensor and licensee, between operators and between service providers and their customers. An operator's licence may be used to provide for legal certainties absent in the statutory framework, or contain detailed obligations controlling every aspect of an operator's activities (see Chapters 4 and 14). Some commercial agreements, such as interconnection agreements and those involving consumers, are often subject to significant regulatory intervention; while others, such as outsourcing agreements, are substantially left to the freedom of the parties (see Chapters 5 and 6).

The third component of the governing framework is the establishment of a regulatory authority with a specific remit to intervene in the operation of the telecommunications sector and which is independent from vested interests (operators or the Government, where it is a shareholder in the incumbent). Most countries have adopted such an institutional approach to the telecommunications sector.

In the long term, the sustainability of a sector-specific regulator is likely to come under examination. The phenomenon of convergence is already leading to a reassessment of the appropriate regulatory structures for issues of carriage and content. In 1999, the European Commission proposed that there be a single regulatory framework for all forms of communications infrastructure, whether voice telephony, data or broadcasting (see the '1999 Communications Review'). At the same time, it can be argued that once a fully competitive market matures then the need for intervention may simply rest upon traditional competition law principles, enforced by the national competition authority rather than a telecommunications-specific regulator.

1.5 REGULATORY FRAMEWORK

The regulatory framework for the telecommunications sector is heterogeneous, both horizontally and vertically. At a national level, states will often divide the regulation of the sector between different authorities. In the UK, for example, the Telecommunications Act 1984 devolves concurrent jurisdiction upon the Secretary of State for Trade and Industry and the Director General of Telecommunications (s. 3), while responsibility for managing the radio frequency spectrum rests with the Radiocommunications Agency. In addition, there is jurisdictional overlap with related regulatory bodies, such as the Independent Television Commission on broadcasting issues and the Office of Fair Trading in respect of competition issues. In federal legal systems, such as the US, such jurisdictional complexities are multiplied (see Chapter 9). Regulatory multiplicity, with regulators exercising concurrent as well as exclusive jurisdiction, may in itself constitute a barrier to market entry, as operators try to work their way through the maze of procedures and peculiarities presented by each of the various institutions.[5]

Vertically, an operator may also need to look to regional organisations, whether acting as legislative bodies to whom representations may be made (such as the European Commission, Parliament and Council), or in terms of standards-making, where participation in the decision-making process may be a commercial imperative (such as the European Telecommunications Standards Institute (ETSI)). At an international level, there exists another layer of laws and regulations under the WTO's multilateral trade agreements and the regulations, recommendations and standards of the International Telecommunications Union (ITU) (see Chapter 11).

The construction of global communication systems, such as ICO Globalstar's satellite network, will require regulatory activity at both a national and an international level. Applications for appropriate orbital slots will need to

---

[5] See generally Coates, K., 'Regulating the telecommunications sector: Substituting practical co-operation for the risks of competition', in McCrudden, C. (ed.), *Regulation and Deregulation* (Oxford, Clarendon Press, 1998), at 249–74.

be made through the ITU, while operating licences may have to be obtained in every jurisdiction into which the services are provided. In contrast, a service provider can offer global Internet telephony services without needing to acquire any regulatory approval.

Such a layering of regulatory bodies inevitably raises important questions of legal order – the applicability and enforceability of the rights and obligations arising under various legal instruments, before national and supranational judicial or dispute settlement bodies, and against either governments or market competitors.

In less developed countries, much developmental assistance from organisations such as the World Bank or the European Bank of Reconstruction and Development is directed towards the telecommunications sector, as a strategic economic resource. Usually these lending institutions will impose conditions upon any such financial assistance, which may require the recipient jurisdiction to adopt a pro-competitive legislative and regulatory framework for the telecommunications market (see Chapter 14).

1.6 REGULATORY POWERS

What powers does a regulatory authority have to intervene in the operation of a telecommunications market? The key authority is that of authorisation of licensing, granting the right to construct, operate and supply telecommunications equipment, networks and/or services. Liberalisation is about the entry of competitors into a market, so that the process by which a new entrant can obtain the necessary authorisations may be critical to the liberalisation process.

Most jurisdictions distinguish between authorising those wanting to provide telecommunications services and those wanting to provide the networks or infrastructure for the carriage of such services. The nature of the activities associated with the latter category, such as digging up the streets to lay cables, has tended to mean more substantial legal obligations being placed upon such operators. In addition, the incumbent will fall into this category. It is also generally the case that barriers to market entry are greater for the provision of networks than for services, and therefore there is often more scope to engage in anti-competitive practices.

With regard to telecommunications equipment, regulatory intervention tends to be limited to procedures ensuring that such equipment is unlikely to cause harm either to the user, or to the networks to which it is connected.

Allied to the issue of authorisation is that of access to scarce resources. Where scarce resources are an element of the service provision, such resources need to be distributed on an appropriate basis that will not unduly restrict or distort competition. The key scarce resource in telecommunications is the radio frequency spectrum. Historically, the spectrum was distributed between the incumbent, the military and various related public service providers, such as the police and emergency services. With liberalisation, access to the spectrum available for commercial usage becomes a key regulatory control. As a scarce resource, spectrum is also usually seen as a public asset that should be utilised and managed in the best interests of society as a whole.

One current trend is to auction spectrum on the basis that this is the most economically efficient mechanism for distributing such scarce resources. In the UK and Germany, auctions for the third generation mobile spectrum have already netted the Governments US$30 billion and US$50 billion respectively; while in the US, similar auctions have been held for both the broadcasting and the telecommunications markets (see Chapter 9). However, as with much economic theory, rational actors often act irrationally, with the result that serious questions have been raised about whether the benefits in terms of public revenue will be achieved at the expense of the development of the market itself, through delayed roll-out and higher charges for third generation services.

Another important scarce resource is telephone numbers. Access to a number and the right to control access to numbers need to be subject to regulatory control in order to facilitate market liberalisation. However, as experienced by OFTEL in the UK, strategic national planning for the use and distribution of telephone numbers in the future can be an extremely difficult task and one which, if mistakes are made, can generate substantial adverse public feeling towards the national regulatory authority. The domain name and Internet protocol (IP) addressing scheme utilised for Internet-based communications has also generated legal and regulatory issues, relating to its management, scarcity and trademarks.[6]

The right to access or utilise the private property of another for the provisioning of networks and services is an issue that has sometime been viewed as similar in nature to the use of a scarce resource. While the granting of rights of way need not be limited, the exercise of a statutory right to interfere with another's property has such potentially significant consequences for the owner and/or occupier of the property that regulatory controls are inevitably necessary. Not least, the exercise of such rights interferes with an individual's right of privacy under the European Convention on Human Rights, Art. 8:

> 1.   Everyone has the right to respect for his private and family life, his home and his correspondence.
> 2.   There shall be no interference by a public authority with the exercise of this right except such as is in accordance with the law and is necessary in a democratic society in the interests of national security, public safety or the economic well-being of the country, for the prevention of disorder or crime, for the protection of health or morals, or for the protection of the rights and freedoms of others.

As telecommunications networks proliferate in a competitive market, it is possible that such human rights concerns may be raised to challenge the exercise of statutory rights by operators constructing their networks across

---

[6] See generally Reed, C., *Internet Law: Text and Materials* (London, Butterworths, 2000), at 3.2.

private land. The exceptions recognised under Art. 8(2) above, specifically the 'economic well-being of the country', may be sustainable as a basis upon which to interfere during the process of liberalisation, but would seem less 'necessary' once a market is fully competitive.

The construction of international telecommunications networks also raises issues of access to public resources, both state-based and those recognised under public international law as the 'property of all mankind', specifically outer space and the high seas (see Chapter 10).

Public policy makers and regulators are also giving environmental concerns – such as the siting of transmitters for wireless communications systems – greater consideration. Co-location and facility-sharing obligations address environmental as well as competition issues.

One critically important area of regulatory intervention is that of dispute resolution. Disputes may arise between service providers and their customers and between competing providers. In the former situation, a regulator is essentially redressing an inevitable imbalance that exists between the two parties, providing easier access to justice and redress for the customer. Intervening in disputes between providers, however, would seem important only while a market is undergoing liberalisation, primarily because of the position of the incumbent. Once the market is fully competitive, such regulatory intervention may be seen as an unnecessary use of public money when the parties have equal recourse to traditional legal processes.

The manner in which a regulator exercises its powers will be of relevance to a telecommunications lawyer. As with any public authority, the regulator will be continuously required to exercise its discretion in respect of when, where and how it intervenes in the operation of the market. Such intervention will then be subject to judicial review along traditional administrative law grounds, e.g., irregularity, irrationality and illegality. However, the complex nature of such decisions in the telecommunications sector may require that operators have the right to appeal against decisions on substantive as well as procedural grounds.

The frequency and manner in which decisions are challenged will also impact on the operation of the whole regulatory framework. Legal activism by operators, frequently challenging the decisions made by the regulator, may effectively slow down the decision-making process, as regulators become cautious and excessively procedural in order to stem legal challenges and the associated commitment of public resources. However, to mitigate this, some jurisdictions allow a regulatory decision to stand until the result of an appeal.[7] Legal interventions in regulatory decision-making are generally of benefit to the incumbent, rather than to new entrants.

1.7 REGULATORY MODELS AND METHODS

The importance of the regulatory authority in the telecommunications market requires consideration to be given to the structure and the manner of working

---

[7] For example, Denmark, Germany, Greece, Italy, Ireland, The Netherlands and Austria. See Commission Communication, *op. cit.* n. 4, at 14.

of the authority being established. Generally, regulatory authorities can be divided into one of four models:

(a) an autonomous quasi-judicial commission (e.g., the US Federal Communications Commission);

(b) an independent official or office outside a government ministry (e.g., the Director-General of Telecommunications (DGT) in the UK and the Autorité de Régulation des Télécommunications in France);

(c) an independent official or office inside a government ministry (e.g., PTS in Sweden); or

(d) a government ministry (e.g., Romania).[8]

Regulatory authorities often experience a number of problems in the telecommunications sector. First, the inevitable lack of expertise amongst the regulator's staff, particularly in the early years, may render the authority excessively dependent on information (and even personnel) supplied by the incumbent operator. Such dependency obviously gives rise to accusations of regulatory capture from new entrants. Secondly, as with any dynamic sector of the economy, the large difference in remuneration rates between public authorities and private sector operators means that staff retention can be a significant concern for a regulator trying to build and maintain institutional experience.

Personalities are always likely to influence the prevailing regulatory environment and the manner in which policies are pursued. Where the regulatory authority is invested in a single individual, the influence of personality is likely to be greater. Some countries vest authority in a committee, sometimes representative of the perceived interest groups involved, such as consumers, operators and general business. In the UK, the background and interests of the DGT have been seen as important in setting the overall direction of regulatory policy. For example, Don Cruickshank (DGT 1989–97) came from the airline Virgin Atlantic and was therefore often perceived as being pro-new entrant and naturally untrusting of BT as the incumbent.

The tools of regulation policy are various, but a feature of a liberalising market is the need to direct regulatory controls towards the activities of the incumbent operator and other operators with similar market influence, such as in the mobile sector. Within Europe, a range of *ex-ante* controls are applicable to organisations designated as having 'significant market power', a concept currently distinct from the traditional competition law concept of dominance (see Chapter 8). At an international level, similar regulatory focus can be seen in the use of the term 'major supplier' in the WTO's Reference Paper (see Chapter 10).

Establishing the costs associated with the provision of telecommunications networks and services is key to their effective regulation. Interconnection charges can represent nearly a third of a new entrant's costs, therefore regulatory control over such charges through 'cost-orientation' requirements

---

[8] See generally Gillick, D., 'Telecommunications policies and regulatory structures: new issues and trends', in *Telecommunications Policy*, December 1992, at 726–31. See also Chapter 14, at 14.7.

is critical to enabling competition (see Chapter 5). Likewise, universal service policy requires the identification of those service elements that are 'provided at a loss or provided under cost conditions falling outside normal commercial standards',[9] before regulators provide appropriate financial support mechanisms (see Chapter 8). However, determining and verifying such cost-based obligations is often an extremely controversial regulatory process in terms of attribution, calculation methodology (e.g., whether historical or forward-looking) and the establishment of appropriate cost accounting systems by incumbent operators (see Chapter 2).

Tariff controls are present under most regimes, whether at retail, wholesale or interconnection level, or all three. Such controls are generally perceived as being the most appropriate mechanism for ensuring that the incumbent is controlled while providing sufficient incentives to encourage economic efficiency. Such controls are, however, notoriously difficult to get right in terms of balancing the interests of customers, new entrants and the incumbent.

Related to tariff controls are requirements upon the incumbent to disclose information about various aspects of its business activities, either to the regulator, to competitors or to consumers, e.g., tariff filings and technical standards for interconnection. Such transparency is designed to remove the likelihood of anti-competitive practices and to provide a certain degree of legal certainty; for example, through an obligation to publish standard contractual terms and conditions. The publication of information also helps to develop international regulatory best practice in the sector, by enabling regulatory authorities to use benchmarks based on figures made available from comparative jurisdictions.

1.8　REGULATION AND COMPETITION LAW

In its 1999 Report, 'A new Federal Communications Commission for the 21st Century', the US Federal Communications Commission stated that 'competition should be the organizing principle of our communications law and policy'. Competition law is inevitably an important component of telecommunications law, but a distinction needs to be made between the reactive application of traditional competition law principles to activities in the telecommunications sector, and proactive regulatory intervention in the operation of the telecommunications market to achieve a competitive market (see Chapter 7). Both are of interest to a telecommunications lawyer and are examined in this book; however, it is the latter aspect that comprises much of the unique terrain of telecommunications law.

The only example of a jurisdiction that has pursued market liberalisation through reliance solely on the application of traditional competition law is New Zealand. It is generally recognised that such an approach has simply led to delays in the process of liberalisation through the need for lengthy recourse

---

[9] Directive 97/33/EC of the European Parliament and of the Council on Interconnection in Telecommunications with regard to ensuring Universal Service and Interoperability through Application of the Principles of Open Network Provision, OJ L 199/32, 26 July 1997, at Annex III.

to judicial intervention (see, e.g., *Telecom Corporation of New Zealand Ltd* v *Clear Communications Ltd* [1995] 1 NZLR 385). Competition law is generally effective against blatant anti-competitive practices, such as a refusal to supply, but it is less effective against minor but persistent obstructive tactics, such as delaying negotiations or the carrying out of innumerable tests. In such circumstances, *ex ante* regulatory intervention has proved critical. (It is interesting to note that in the European Commission's review of the regulatory framework for the telecommunications sector, the '1999 Communications Review', significant emphasis was placed on shifting from the current *ex ante* controls to a more hands-off *ex post* competition law regime. However, during the consultation exercise, new entrants expressed strong reservations that such a move was premature and would enable incumbent operators to entrench their existing positions.[10] As a result, the Commission's latest legislative proposals retain many of the *ex ante* controls present in the current regime (see Chapter 8).)

The interest of competition authorities in the telecommunications market can be subdivided into anti-competitive agreements and practices, mergers and joint ventures, and abuses of a dominant position. A feature of the telecommunications sector is clearly the last category, due to the position of national incumbent operators. Notification procedures imposed upon certain types of agreements and mergers enable the authorities to exercise prior restraint over players in the market. In addition, the nature of the telecommunications industry as a 'networked' industry, with parallels in industries such as airlines and power, gives rise to certain characteristics that raise particular competition concerns, such as issues relating to 'essential facilities', 'network effects' and 'collective dominance'.[11]

Lastly, it is important to note that in many jurisdictions, such as the Asian 'tiger' economies, competition law is a relatively underdeveloped discipline (see Chapters 13 and 14). As a consequence, domestic operators, regulators and the courts have little experience of the application of competition principles and practices. In such jurisdictions, foreign operators will often be more reliant on telecommunications specific regulations, whether statutory or licence-based, for the protection of their commercial rights.

1.9   REGULATION AND STANDARDS

In our information society, more and more technical standards are used in formulating laws, regulations, decisions etc. . . . standards are becoming more important in drafting contractual obligations and interpreting the meaning thereof, whether or not in the courtroom.[12]

---

[10] Communication from the Commission, 'The results of the public consultation on the 1999 Communications Review and Orientations for the new Regulatory Framework', COM (2000) 239, Brussels, 26 April 2000.
[11] See generally Shapiro, C. and Varian, H., *Information Rules: A Strategic Guide to the Network Economy* (Harvard, Harvard Business School Press, 1999).
[12] Stuurman, C., 'Legal aspects of standardization and certification of information technology and telecommunications: an overview', in Kaspersen, H.W.K. and Oskamp, A., *Amongst Friends in Computer Law* (Deveuter, Kluwer, 1991), at 75–92.

The nature of the communications process requires that the various parties adhere to a certain agreed standard, whether in terms of language, protocol, numbers or physical connection. The need for standardisation to communicate across national boundaries gave rise to the establishment of the ITU, one of the oldest inter-governmental organisations. As the extract above highlights, there is proliferation of standards within the laws, regulations and agreements governing the telecommunications market.

Standards are critical to the process of liberalising a market. New entrants will be as dependent on the technical certainty that arises from the existence of published standards, as they are on legal certainty upon which to base their investments. The absence of appropriate standards has been used by incumbents to delay the introduction of competing services. Within the European Union, standards have been vital in the establishment of an internal market for telecommunications equipment, networks and services (see Chapter 8).

Numerous standards-making bodies operate in every aspect of the telecommunications market, as well as at a national, regional and international level. Historically, such bodies have tended to operate in accordance with complex bureaucratic procedural mechanisms, which lead to inevitable delays in decision-making. With the appearance of new technologies and environments, such as the Internet, such institutions have increasingly faced competition from new entities, such as the Internet Engineering Task Force, operating under more flexible and rapid processes. Participation in the work of such bodies can require operators to devote significant financial and management resources, while failure to participate may effectively hand control over the development of a particular market to competitors.

One important aspect of standards in the technology field is the possibility that a particular standard may constitute the intellectual property of a company, such as a patented process. In 1999, a dispute arose between Ericsson and Qualcomm over the ownership of certain patents related to Code Division Multiple Access (CDMA) technology, which underpins third generation mobile telephony. In such circumstances, competition law principles may be applicable, particularly the 'essential facilities' doctrine (e.g., Cases C-241 and 242/91, *RTE* v *Magill* [1995] 4 CMLR 718). However, regulators may be concerned to ensure that *ex ante* measures are in place to prohibit such practices. The European Telecommunications Standards Institute (ETSI) addressed the potential conflict between intellectual property and standardisation in a 1992 draft policy. The policy detailed a procedure by which companies could be required to license their intellectual property, where required for the adoption of a standard in a particular area. The policy was subsequently withdrawn, although the European Commission recognised the need to achieve an appropriate balance in this area.[13]

1.10 REGULATING IN THE GLOBAL ECONOMY

As discussed above, the inherently global nature of telecommunications has meant that the sector has been the subject of international agreements since

---

[13] Commission Communication on 'IPR and Standards', COM (92) 445 final, 27 October 1992.

its beginnings. It is also worth noting, however, that the transnational nature of the industry is reflected at various levels in national regulatory policy. Mention was made at 1.7 above of the use of benchmarks as a mechanism for regulating the behaviour of the incumbent in areas such as tariffing, by reference to prices available under prevailing market conditions. Such benchmarks may be based on figures obtained within the national market, but regional or international figures may equally be utilised.[14] Through such mechanisms, the national regulatory framework can come to reflect and embody international 'best practice', particularly where the benchmark reference sites are those markets considered most advanced or liberalised.

Conversely, the imposition of benchmarks on national operators may be used as a tool to encourage further liberalisation in other national markets, raising issues relating to the exercise of extraterritorial jurisdiction. The classic example of this is the Federal Communications Commission's 1997 Benchmark Order for International Settlements, which required US licensed operators to pay only international settlements rates laid down by the Commission, on the basis of country-by-country benchmarks, rather than those reached through normal commercial negotiations between operators (see Chapter 10). The objective of the Order was to prevent operators from non-liberalised markets leveraging their domestic monopolistic position to the detriment of the US consumer.

Another feature of the telecommunications market is the amount of joint venture and merger activity taking place, as companies try to position themselves to take advantage of the increasingly global economy. Such agreements inevitably give rise to competition concerns, at a national and regional level. To address such industry globalisation, competition authorities have entered into their own agreements in order to coordinate their responses to such developments (e.g., between the United States and the European Community[15]). Such regulatory cooperation has already proved effective in a number of telecommunications cases, such as the WorldCom/MCI merger and the BT/AT&T joint venture.

National concerns about the impact of transnational merger activity on the national incumbent have also been the subject of regulatory intervention. For example, during BT's abortive attempt to merge with MCI, in 1997, the DGT in the UK expressed concerns that one of the potential consequences (were the merger to be successful) was that BT might end up with a substantial proportion of its assets residing overseas (as well as its investments) at the expense of the domestic market.[16] To address this concern, BT's licence was modified to include an annual reporting requirement whereby BT would effectively guarantee that sufficient resources were maintained to meet its domestic obligations.

---

[14] See, e.g., Commission Recommendation, 'On leased lines interconnection pricing in a liberalised telecommunications market', C (1999) 3863, 24 November 1999.

[15] See Agreement between the European Communities and the Government of the United States of America on the application of positive comity principles in the enforcement of their competition laws, OJ L 173/28, 18 June 1998.

[16] See OFTEL, 'Domestic Obligations in a Global Market', July 1997.

1.11 CONCLUSION

For many countries, the pursuance of a policy of market liberalisation coupled with the pace of technological development has meant that the telecommunications sector has evolved from an environment of scarcity to one of relative or actual abundance. The legal framework governing such abundance should become less complex than that required during the process of transition from a monopolistic environment. Indeed, a number of jurisdictions are currently addressing the problem of scaling-down the regulatory framework for telecommunications. Competition law is likely to provide the core principles upon which this 'second generation' of telecommunications law will be based.

Nevertheless, the pace of change in some sectors of the market, such as the local loop, has proven more stubborn to competition than anticipated, which has required renewed regulatory intervention. Oligopolistic markets also seem a defining feature of a mature telecommunications industry, whether through spectrum limitations imposed on mobile telephony or through the impact of globalisation on merger activity, which may require traditional competition law principles to be reconsidered.

At the same time, governments are examining the implications of convergence, which raises important issues of content regulation, on which little international consensus has been reached. Regulating content may become an increasingly prominent aspect of a telecommunications lawyer's work, when compared to issues of establishment and operation.

Telecommunications law is evolving rapidly in parallel with the market it purports to govern. Any book on the subject is therefore destined to date quickly in respect of many details. However, the process of liberalisation in Europe and the US, as well as in many other countries, is sufficiently well advanced to provide us with a clear outline of some of the key aspects of international best practice in law and regulation for the telecommunications sector over the next five to ten years.

CHAPTER TWO

The Economics of Telecommunications Regulation

Lisa Correa

2.1 INTRODUCTION

This chapter provides an overview of the economics of telecommunications regulation and summarises the key economic regulatory concepts of the industry. While the focus is mainly on economic regulatory developments in the UK, the conclusions and discussion should be relevant to all countries which are embarking or have embarked on telecommunications liberalisation.

Before describing the system of economic regulation, it is useful to place it within a basic analytical framework. While it is clearly essential for those who work in regulation – whether in companies, government or the regulatory bodies themselves – to be familiar with the content of telecommunications law and licences, it is also important that practitioners should understand the concepts of telecommunications economic regulation, and in particular what it is intended to do.

2.2 RATIONALE FOR REGULATION

Traditionally, throughout the world telecommunications services were provided in each country by one monopoly carrier. Such carriers were almost always owned by the government and operators as state agencies, often as part of the postal service. Beginning in the 1980s and continuing into the 1990s, the telecommunications industry in almost all countries experienced privatisation, or at least some degree of corporatisation. This was generally accompanied by the newly privatised companies being exposed to market pressures and being forced to become more efficient and competitive. The privatisation of these large, previously state-owned carriers involved, however, serious problems of remaining monopoly power or market failure due to the accreted advantages conferred upon them by their history and position as compared with those of potential competitors. In particular, these newly privatised companies benefited from having:

(a)   100 per cent share of the market at the time of privatisation, and thus 100 per cent control of customers;
(b)   the accumulated assets and economies of scale[1] and experience of the telecommunications market;
(c)   ownership of vital networks, or privileged use of public rights of way to which competitors must have access if they were to be able to compete.

In this situation, it was therefore recognised that without efficient entry (or the threat of entry), and growth of new rivals, competitive disciplines on the newly privatised incumbent firms would not be exerted. Thus, these firms would be able to exploit their dominant position at the expense of consumers. Given the extent of the accreted advantages conferred upon these carriers, it was however acknowledged that there could be a difficult transition period before the privatised company could become competitive, and during this time it could use its substantial power to charge customers monopoly prices as well as engage in strategic games to deter new entrants. For this reason, it was essential that economic regulation of the incumbent be implemented so as to prevent monopolistic abuse and anti-competitive behaviour.

2.3   THE PRINCIPLES OF ECONOMIC REGULATION

Before discussing the alternative forms of economic regulation and their subsequent implementation in the UK, the basic principles of such regulation need to be addressed. Different emphases are possible, but the following list is normally considered when evaluating different forms of economic regulation:

(a)   *Prevention of possible abuse of monopoly power.* Such abuse might arise if prices were very high in relation to costs so that super-normal profits were earned. Super-normal profits relate to the concept of monopoly profits. In a competitive situation, it is assumed that there should not be an excess profit as this will be competed away. However, in a monopoly environment this is not the case, and so super-normal or excess profit is earned.) Abuse may also arise if costs were higher than they ought to be or were likely to be in a competitive situation.

(b)   *Economic regulation should not distort business decisions.* Only where there is a demonstrable competitive or market failure is there a need for

---

[1] This is where an increase in output is associated with a less than proportionate increase in costs.

regulatory intervention, as economic regulation will always be inferior to effective competition.

(c) *Costs of regulation should be limited to what is essential.* Given the presumed disadvantages in practice of excessive control of nationalised industries by government departments, an important part of the rationale for privatisation is to reduce the detailed control over what are essentially business decisions. Therefore, economic regulation should ensure that the excessive control exerted over a nationalised industry is not replicated.

(d) *Regulation should try to 'mimic' the likely operation of a competitive market.* If this can be achieved, it means that resources will be used as efficiently and as well in one case as in the other.

2.4   FORMS OF ECONOMIC REGULATORY CONTROL

2.4.1   Rate-of-return and price cap regulation

In the light of the above principles, at the time of privatisation the favoured form of economic regulation outside the UK was Rate-of-return regulation. This offered the solution that prices should be such that an allowed 'fair' rate of return on capital could be earned. In other words, a ceiling would be placed on the profits that a company could keep from its regulated business, which would be based on the company's required rate of return on capital. (The required rate of return on capital can be considered as a hurdle rate for capital budgeting decisions.) However, as Averch and Johnson[2] revealed, setting a rate of return on the capital base distorts firms' business decisions by encouraging them to expand their capital base so as to achieve a greater absolute level of profit while remaining within their regulatory constraints. Thus, the Rate-of-return regulation rule proved to be fundamentally flawed since the firm, although it has no direct benefit from cost inefficiency, achieves a strategic gain by influencing the permitted price. In addition, this rule covered the whole business and so did not allow regulation to be focused explicitly on the particular services where monopoly power and public concern were greatest. The result, therefore, is the worst sort of regulation – both shareholders and customers are worse off!

To address the failings of the Rate-of-return rule and to meet the objectives of economic regulation more accurately, Professor Stephen Littlechild developed the now well known 'RPI − X' formula. This formula capped a selected basket of the incumbent's prices for a period of four to five years during which these prices could increase annually by the Retail Price Index (RPI) minus the X factor, with the latter being set by the regulator in the light of the presumed movement of productivity and costs within the industry. Within this four- to five-year period, the regulated company could then keep any extra profits generated by increased efficiency. And at the end of the review period, new price controls could be implemented which took account of the efficiency gains in the previous period.

---

[2] Averch, H. and Johnson, L., 'Behaviour of the Firm under Regulatory Constraint' (1962) 52 *American Economic Review* 1052.

The rule was deemed extremely attractive by many economists because it was easy to implement, it encouraged cost-reducing activities and it could be used to target those aspects of the business where regulation was most needed. Furthermore, it was viewed as a regulatory tool that could be decreasingly used as effective competition developed. (Effective competition can be considered as being in operation when a customer can make a decision independent of any operator across the whole telecommunications industry, or when a customer can choose from a multitude of services and/or deal directly with a large number of service providers without regard to the infrastructure that carries the chosen service from the service provider to the customer.) This last point was a key argument used by Littlechild. He believed:

Competition is indisputably the most effective means – perhaps the only effective means – of protecting consumers against monopoly power. Regulation is essentially a means of preventing the worst excesses of monopoly; it is not a substitute for competition. It is a means of 'holding the fort' until the competition arrives. Consequently, the main focus of attention has to be on securing the most promising conditions for competition to emerge, and protecting competition from abuse. It is important that regulation in general . . . does not prejudice the achievement of this overall strategy.[3]

Littlechild's vision was, therefore, that competition rather than regulation should be the main goal in developing a regulatory framework.

2.4.2 Setting the price cap

Although price cap regulation has achieved a considerable positive response, the setting of a cap requires a large amount of information about the future structure of the market. Setting an appropriate price cap in a monopoly environment requires not only the regulatory authority to have a good understanding of the future output and pricing structure of the company, but the regulator also need to know about the company's movements of costs and productivity over the life of the price cap. Forecasting growth and efficiency rates in an industry, such as telecommunications, driven so strongly by technological and regulatory developments, is however a highly complex exercise. Nonetheless, due to the importance of these parameters in setting X, it is imperative that the regulator ensures that assumptions are robust.

The complexity of this operation is further magnified when competition is introduced into the market, as the regulator then needs to take into account the impact of competitors' outputs and pricing strategies on the incumbent's output and prices and *vice versa* (see Figure 2.2).

---

[3] 'Regulation of British Telecommunications' Profitability', Report by Stephen C. Littlechild, Professor of Commerce, University of Birmingham, to the Secretary of State for Industry (London, HMSO, 1983), para. 4.11.

Figure 2.1   The financial model for setting the cap – monopoly

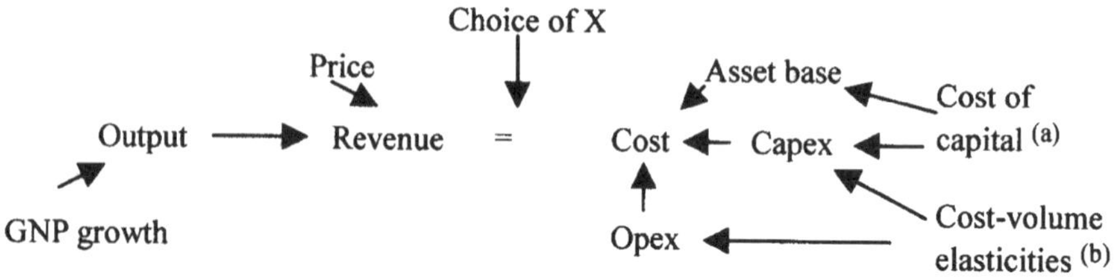

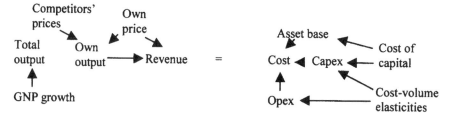

[a] The cost of capital, like the rate of return on capital, is a hurdle rate for capital budgeting decisions.
[b] Cost-volume elasticities indicate how costs increase when volume of calls increases.

Figure 2.2   The financial model for setting the cap – competitive

The *asymmetry of information problem* that exists between the regulator and the firm adds further difficulty to this exercise. If the regulator has as much knowledge about industry conditions and behaviour as the regulated firm, it could simply direct the firm to implement its chosen plan. But, of course, decision-makers within the firm are far more knowledgeable than regulators can be about circumstances facing them, and the regulator can neither observe nor infer all aspects of the firm's behaviour. In this situation, the regulator can therefore condition its policy only on what it knows and try to design an incentive mechanism so that the firm can be induced to act in accordance with the public interest.

Besides the factors discussed above, it is also important for the regulator when designing a price cap to consider whether there is need for additional price control, where the emphasis is not to force prices down but to provide a regulatory safety net for customers in case competition does not deliver for them. There are a number of possibilities, such as a median residential bill control which focuses on the customer's total bill and a limit on the change in the bill for those customers on a light user scheme (i.e., a specialised package that caters to the needs of uneconomic customers).

Another factor that needs to be considered is related to capital costs. Given the importance of capital costs in setting the price cap, the measurement of this plays a key role in the modelling exercise. In particular, the manner in which the asset base is valued can have a major impact on the cost structure of the incumbent. For example, assets can be measured either historically (i.e., what the assets cost in the first place, minus depreciation) or using current costs (i.e., what it costs to replace old assets with modern equivalent assets of equal remaining life; this reflects general inflation, plus specific effects such as technical progress). Generally, on a total cost basis the two measures do not differ significantly. The construction costs of trenches and ducts measured in current terms indicate that these costs have gone up, but the price of electronic equipment such as switches has declined substantially due to technological progress. One could perhaps, therefore, conclude that either measure is appropriate. This is incorrect, though, because if prices were set using historic costs, there is a risk that wrong entry signals would be provided to firms in the industry. Given this, therefore, from an economic perspective, there is a preference for the use of current costs because it ensures that correct and efficient entry signals are provided to all market players.

The duration of the cap is another issue that needs to be reflected on as it can have an enormous impact on the workings of the price control. In particular, if it is set for too short a period, it delivers inappropriate incentives for the incumbent to undertake activities which pay back within the designated time-scales. On the other hand, if the control is set for too long a period, the incumbent could benefit from too lax a control and consumers could suffer as a result.

Designing an appropriate price cap is thus an extremely difficult operation; an inappropriate price cap could have a significant negative impact on the development of competition. An erroneous segmentation of industry services and customer segments that need to be covered by the price cap could impose substantial distortions on the market through its impact on other operators. This will be discussed further in 2.9 and 2.10 below. Getting the price cap right is therefore crucial if regulatory control is to be effective.

2.5 STRUCTURE OF THE REGULATED INDUSTRY

The implementation of economic regulation has taken various forms in different industries and countries. This is partly because each industry/ country has an individual regulator, allowing personal differences to manifest themselves. More fundamental, however, are the underlying differences in the structure of the regulated industry. For 'effective' regulation to occur, it is important that an appropriate model or industry structure is developed so as to enable effective competition to emerge. As mentioned in 2.2 above, a newly privatised company could retain its dominance because the underlying structure of the market flowing from the history of privatisation could preclude the development of effective competition. To address this issue, the regulator might therefore at the outset intervene in the market to address the underlying structural obstacle. There are two ways in which the regulator can minimise the asymmetry of information problem, regulate dominance and promote effective competition:

(a) structural separation of the incumbent; and
(b) accounting separation of the incumbent.

Restructuring of this kind can enhance the effectiveness of competition and regulation by altering incentives and information conditions in such a way that private motives are directed more towards social ends.

In the United States, for example, the US authorities conceived that if AT&T was allowed into the marketplace as a vertically integrated player, it would, through its 'bottleneck' control of the relationship with customers, be able to erect barriers to prevent competition developing naturally. Moreover, based on the structure of costs of a telecommunications network within a static equilibrium framework, the view was that there would be wasteful duplication if households had telephone wires from several suppliers.[4] As a consequence, the US authorities in 1982 concluded their study of the US telecommunications market with a divestiture decree which resulted in the structural separation of the Regional Bell Operating Companies (RBOCs – which handled local telephone networks and services) from AT&T (which handled the long-distance network and services).

This type of structural adjustment, dividing the incumbent into smaller, supposedly more manageable organisations, proved, however, to be a radical measure to regulate dominance and break the monopoly of information. It increased the debate about whether structural separation actually solves the inherent problem of dominance. In most cases, experience appeared to indicate that the answer to this question was negative.

Separated parts of the business can still be dominant, and hence still require a high degree of regulatory scrutiny to ensure that monopolistic abuse does not occur. In the case of the US, the division of AT&T from the RBOCs created competition in long-distance traffic but left a monopoly in the local network. So the arguments about interconnection continue, with incorrect signals being provided to long-distance entrants, which has resulted in efficient entry into the marketplace being discouraged, inefficient bypass being encouraged and short-term arbitrage opportunities being created.

Moreover, it was subsequently recognised that the implementation of structural separation in the US ignored the potential for competition in the local loop. In particular, as cited by Peter Huber,[5] by 1984, the techno-economic rationale for divestiture was already obsolete given the technological changes within the industry. In other words, the dominance of a fully integrated AT&T could have been effectively challenged by technological innovation, by (for example) the use of radio-based technology. However, because of structural separation, technical innovation in providing competition to the local loop was essentially constrained by the regulatory authorities managing the market, thereby impeding the development of effective competition. (To address this issue, the US authorities recently introduced the 1996 Telecommunications Act which aims to introduce competition into the local network. Unfortunately, arcane rules have been put in place, making achievement of this objective difficult.)

---

[4] This implies that the local loop will not become sufficiently competitive. In other words, it was believed that it was a natural monopoly.

[5] Huber, P.W., Kellogg, M.K. and Thorne, J., *The Geodesic Network II: 1993 Report on Competition in the Telephone Industry* (Washington D.C., The Geodesic Company, 1993).

As a consequence, over time, structural separation may have an adverse impact on the development of effective competition. Structural separation institutionalises a structure that could become obsolete, as is the case in the US, due to technological advances, regulatory changes and differing trading patterns.

Accounting separation, in contrast, is much less Draconian and comparatively simple to implement. This method of structurally differentiating the business components of a company by simulating separation via accounting structures is responsive to technological and regulatory change. It provides a means by which relevant costs can be identified for interconnect charging purposes, and the presence of separated accounts means that the reconciliation of costs to financial accounts is much easier to implement. Moreover, for purposes of identifying cross-subsidies, and the use to which they are being put, the separated accounts can prove to be invaluable to regulatory authorities. Nonetheless, accounting separation still suffers (though decreasingly so) from the asymmetry of information problem.[6] For this reason, it is imperative that detailed regulatory involvement is included in the preparation and setting up of these accounting procedures.

2.6 THE ECONOMICS OF TELECOMMUNICATIONS

Before discussing the actual implementation of economic regulation in the UK telecommunications industry, it is worthwhile for purposes of economic policy analysis to consider briefly the important economic features of the industry. These include its multi-product nature, the non-storability of its services, stochastic time-varying demands, capacity constraints and sunk costs,[7] the existence of externalities between users, natural monopoly elements and the complex vertical structure of the industry. The first five factors deserve discussion because they influence the tariffing procedures of the industry, while the last three factors merit particular attention because externalities and natural monopoly elements are the market failures that provide the main rationale for policy intervention and vertical issues affect the ease with which regulation is carried out.

On the supply side, the telecommunications industry provides many products and services. These include customer premises equipment, ranging from telephones to private automatic branch exchanges (PABXs), and services provided by the network, which range from the supply of telephone calls to various locations at various times of the day, to the monthly leasing of dedicated private lines. The nature of telecommunications is such however, that there is a lump-sum cost of providing the consumer's connection or access to the network, a cost that is independent of the number of call minutes

---

[6] The asymmetry of information problem relates to the fact that the regulator has less information than the regulated firm, and therefore it is possible for the regulated firm to manipulate the regulatory situation so that it is able to benefit. This problem does, however, decrease in importance as the regulator gains experience of the environment.

[7] Sunk costs are defined by the US merger guidelines as 'the acquisition costs of tangible or intangible assets that cannot be recovered through redeployment of these assets outside the relevant market'. Clearly, large portions of the telecommunications infrastructure should, by this definition, be considered sunk. Not only that, there are also the intangible sunk costs of building a brand and customer acquisition which are no less significant.

used, and a variable cost representing the actual usage of the network. Given this cost structure, it is thus convenient and justifiable to charge customers a two-part tariff comprising a lump-sum and a variable component.

The setting of this two-part tariff can, however, have huge implications for competitive activity. The reason is that access and usage are complementary. There are cross-price effects in both directions, which means that the price for access to the telephone network has an influence on the number of telephone users. If the number of users increases, usage is likely to rise. Similarly, changes in usage charges heavily influence access demand. If the usage charges increase to a level where an individual's utility of using the network is lower than the costs of the phone calls made and the price of access, access demand is likely to decrease. There is therefore a significant level of interdependence in telecommunications between access and usage.

On the demand side, although it appears that telecommunication users' demands are random, customers' demands exhibit strong regular and weekly patterns. For example, business users only want to make calls during business hours, and therefore their demands are relatively insensitive to price; whereas residential users prefer to make calls during evenings and weekends and have more elastic demands. Given these variations in demands, there is therefore much opportunity for various kinds of price discrimination. The degree to which this is possible will, however, be highly constrained, and will in any event reflect each operator's individual constraints, its customers and its knowledge. Despite what economic theory may say,[8] competition in telecommunications appears to encourage increased price discrimination, as is evidenced by the proliferation of different pricing packages.

The preponderance of sunk costs in a dominant incumbent's overall cost base means that short-run variable costs are small. The non-storability of services coupled with low short-run variable costs means that up to the available capacity, additional output can thus be produced at nearly zero marginal cost.[9] Conversely, when demand exceeds capacity levels, output must be rationed, which results in a negative externality as additional call attempts cause some high-valued demands not to be served.[10] This factor, together with the above-mentioned systematic variation of demand over time, makes the use of peak-load pricing[11] schemes prevalent and justifiable for many services.

---

[8] Price discrimination features in economic theory as a manifestation of monopoly power. In theory, therefore, the more competitive the market becomes, the less scope there should be for it to take place.

[9] Marginal cost refers to the increase in the total cost of an enterprise when the output of a product or service that it supplies increases by one unit. In other words, it is the increase in the firm's total cost caused by the single-unit output expansion.

[10] The likelihood that a given call is made successfully is an important aspect of the quality of the service. If demand exceeds capacity and the network is therefore congested, a negative externality prevails.

[11] Firms that deal in markets with fluctuating demands such as peak and off-peak periods will incur some costs that are common to both periods and other costs which are separable to whichever is served. In the case of telecommunications, due to the level of sunk costs in the network, costs are low in off-peak periods resulting in low prices, while in peak periods costs are high due to lower capacity being available and prices are high.

Although, as mentioned above, capacity constraints can result in negative externalities, the two-way nature of telecommunications demand also gives rise to an important positive network externality. A fundamental characteristic of telecommunications is that new customers joining a network not only benefit themselves, but they also create extra opportunities for existing customers. There is evidence, moreover, of dynamic benefits for the economy arising from the development of the telecommunications sector.[12] The relationship between economic development and the development of telecommunications infrastructure appears to be reciprocal, with growth in one encouraging growth in the other.

The presence of these externalities, coupled with the fact that telecommunications has economies of density,[13] means that the marginal cost of adding one more customer to the network is much less than the average cost. This, therefore, has important policy implications for pricing structures as it provides a justification for subsidising line rentals so as to encourage new users to join the network. Moreover, it also has important implications for policy on interconnection between rival networks, for without interconnection, a small network would be severely disadvantaged relative to the larger one. Even if there is competition for attracting customers to operators' networks, with a great deal of choice over the network on which their call terminates, that choice is made by the called party. There is no incentive for the called party to be connected to more than one network operator; and in the unlikely event that this did occur, it would entail wasteful duplication. In essence, the called party network has control over a bottleneck monopoly, in which it can gain monopoly profits by inflating the call termination fees. As a consequence, there is a strong case for regulation of this service and its charges not only today, but for some considerable time to come on those operators with significant market power (i.e., operators with over 25 per cent of the market who can influence market conditions by their actions).

The vertical structure of the industry means that in order for a call to be made, a customer must be linked to a local exchange; and in order to complete a call, a customer's call must terminate on a local exchange. As discussed above, local termination of a call is a bottleneck monopoly, but what of local origination of a call? In the past, policy makers generally assumed that because call termination was an essential facility, call origination was also an essential facility. In other words, the view has been taken that the local loop comprising a home connected to a local exchange is a natural monopoly. In fact, for this reason, as discussed at 2.5 above, the US authorities decided structurally to separate the RBOCs from AT&T. However, as has also been discussed above, telecommunications technology is evolving rapidly, so that the concept of the local call origination network component being a natural monopoly is being challenged.

The diffusion of new technologies down to and including the local loop has considerable implications for the development of competition, in particular

---

[12] ITU World Telecommunications Development Report 1994.
[13] An industry exhibiting economies of density is one where the more closely packed together the customers are, the lower the unit costs. This is far from being unique to telecommunications – it exists in any industry where geographic location of customers is significant.

.iamic efficiency and innovation. Innovation lies at the core of the compet-
i.,ve process. With a number of firms competing to meet the needs of
customers, innovation is essential if they are to remain financially viable in
the long run. Innovation is multifaceted, including process developments,
product developments and technical and technology developments. Although
it can lead to lower prices, it can also bring about improved service quality,
new products and services, and complete shifts in the technical paradigm of
an industry.

Given the above and the fact that competition and regulatory policies have
an important influence on the incentive structure of operators, it is therefore
important that any policies implemented are flexible, unlike the US example
mentioned above, so as to allow dynamic efficiency and innovation to prevail.

2.7 ECONOMIC REGULATION IN THE UK

2.7.1 The privatisation of BT

The early debate on liberalisation in the UK began with customer premises
equipment, followed by services, and quickly spread to the beginnings of
network competition in response to intense demand for leased circuits in the
UK. Cable & Wireless and Barclays Bank were exploring this market and
joined together, with subsequent financial support from British Petroleum, in
response to the Government's offer to license network competitors in this area.
The consortium quickly decided that leased circuits alone did not provide a
viable business and sought extension of its remit, under its original 1982
licence, to the provision of national and international switched services. The
very large investment required for this purpose persuaded the group that it
needed a period as the single alternative switched network if it was to develop
as an effective competitor to BT. This duopoly policy was adopted by the
Government in the autumn of 1983 ahead of the sale of the second tranche of
shares in the (by then) privatised Cable & Wireless and the reintroduction of
what became the Telecommunications Act 1984 under which BT would be
privatised and OFTEL set up as the independent regulatory body.

The duopoly policy, to which the Government committed itself for seven
years from the date of its announcement, thus set the tone for the subsequent,
comparatively slow and cautious development of network competition in the
UK. The Government, right from the start, however, was determined to
introduce competition into all segments of the market and to foster development of broadband cable television networks in the UK to open up the
possibility of local network competition, licensing cable operators to provide
all forms of telecommunications services in addition to television programme
services.

In 1984 BT was privatised. Given extensive debate about the structure of
the industry encompassing the arguments discussed at 2.5 above, the Government shunned the vertical separation policy adopted in the US and instead
privatised BT as a vertically integrated company. BT's dominant position
throughout the industry meant, however, that there was a clear need for
a framework of regulation to contain BT's market power. In particular,

regulatory intervention was necessary to ensure that Mercury – and any other subsequent licensed telecommunications operator – had access to actual and potential customers via BT's local circuits at a non-monopolistic price, in order to be able to mount any effective competition. Herein, therefore, lies the eternal debate on call origination and termination charges, otherwise known as *interconnection* (see 2.15 for more detail).

In addition to the requirement for regulation over interconnection, though, there was also a requirement to protect consumers against BT's monopoly power. As such, considerable discussion occurred as to the appropriate vehicle for price control in the UK. Given the substantial arguments against rate-of-return regulation (see 2.4.1 above), Littlechild's proposal of RPI – X was adopted.

2.7.2   Retail price regulation in the UK

As recorded at 2.4 above, the presumption of the Littlechild doctrine was that the need for, and intensity of, price cap regulation would wither away in those elements of the telecommunications industry particularly amenable to the opening up of effective competition. Given the Government's determination in introducing competition into all segments of the market, it is worthwhile reviewing how, in reality, the price cap regime in UK telecommunications has evolved since its inception.

In 1984, the first price cap was set at RPI – 3%, and the basket of controlled services included rental of local exchange lines and tariffs for directly dialled local and national calls (except for phone boxes). In addition, BT volunteered not to increase residential line rentals by more than RPI + 2%. These controls covered approximately half of BT's revenues and were set for five years.

In the subsequent Price Review of 1988, OFTEL tightened the price cap to RPI – 4.5%, and added operator assisted UK calls to the basket. BT maintained its voluntary cap on residential line rentals, and connection charges were also made subject to the RPI + 2% restriction but kept outside the basket.

New controls over domestic private circuits were, implemented however, and were subject to a separate price cap of RPI – 0, with the basket including connection and rental charges for digital and analogue private circuits. This price cap was deemed necessary to increase BT's efficiency in the domestic private circuit market, as Mercury's competition alone was insufficient. In addition to the RPI – 0 price cap, BT committed to improving the quality of its service here, backed up by a customer compensation scheme.

These arrangements were supposed to stand for four years, but the Duopoly Review in 1991 meant that these commitments were jettisoned and new arrangements were substituted. The result was that the cap was tightened further, from RPI – 4.5% to RPI – 6.25%. Furthermore, due to routine monitoring of BT's international calls showing that profits were rising sharply instead of being eroded by Mercury's competition, the Review brought out-going international call charges under control by adding them to the price cap basket for the first time. BT also agreed to reduce its international prices on a one-off basis by 10 per cent, and to an increase of the line rental and connection charge restraint to RPI + 5% (from RPI + 2%) on multi-line business exchange lines only.

Some greater flexibility, subject to certain OFTEL-monitored conditions, was also allowed to BT in setting its tariffs, enabling it to offer the option of quantity discounts (with a higher rental charge) to larger users of its services. Moreover, international resale constraints were relaxed in order to put additional pressure on international call charges and settlement rates. To achieve this effect, however, International Private Leased Circuit (IPLC) prices were restrained. In 1991, therefore, IPLCs were incorporated into BT's domestic private circuit basket, subject to the RPI − 0 cap, due to expire in July 1993.

While the greater flexibility in setting tariffs, could be viewed as a movement in the direction of greater regulatory freedom for BT, the overall verdict on the direction of change in telecommunications price cap regulation resulting from the review indicated both a tightening of the main price cap and an extension of the coverage and complexity of UK telecommunications price cap controls. In fact, OFTEL itself calculated that the controls emanating from the review resulted in about 70 per cent of BT's revenues being subject to regulatory scrutiny as compared with around 50 per cent in 1989.

OFTEL's review of the BT price cap, in 1993, resulted in the limit on average price increases for switched services being tightened further from RPI − 6.25% to RPI − 7.5%, with individual price caps of RPI − 0 on most services included in the basket (except exchange line rentals, which remained subject to RPI + 2% for residential and most business customers, and wholesale exchange lines, subject to RPI + 5%). And for the first time connection charges were added to the basket. A price cap of RPI − 0 was also placed on three separate private circuit baskets: national analogue private circuits, national digital private circuits and international private circuits.

This further evolution of UK price cap controls thus represented a strengthening of regulation. This evolution dramatically changed in 1997, however, when OFTEL, after conducting a study of the extent of competition in the marketplace, decided that retail control should be implemented only where consumer protection was required. The impact of this view was that it limited the price cap to the lowest spending 80 per cent of residential customers and loosened the cap from RPI − 7.5% to RPI − 4.5%. This meant that 26 per cent of BT's group revenues would now be subject to retail price caps compared with nearly 70 per cent previously.

It therefore appears that Littlechild's doctrine is finally being pursued, and that Littlechild's vision of a regulatory framework based on the view that the dynamics of competition will eventually render regulation redundant appears still valid today.

2.7.3 The operation of price caps in the UK

As detailed in 2.7.2 above, excluding the current price cap, the workings of the price cap regime within the UK telecommunications industry have tended to intensify over time. First, the coverage of the price cap, in terms of the goods and services that are subject to regulatory control, has tended to expand and, secondly, the severity of X (the deduction factor) has typically tightened at successive review periods. This has led, therefore, to an enforced decline in real prices, which in the short term is of immediate benefit to consumers. A questionmark, however, hangs over the matter of whether such increasingly tightening price caps are to the benefit of consumers in the longer term.

Over the longer term, the competitive process forces efficiency on operators and leads to lower prices, particularly through longer-term dynamic efficiency gains.[14] This process has, however, wider dimensions. Competition leads to choice for customers, both between operators and in the range of services that are available to them. An effectively competitive market would therefore be characterised by a rich choice of differentiated services that meet the needs of each customer segment.

Given the true benefits of the longer-term competitive process, it is therefore important that any regulatory actions taken do not undermine inter-firm competition or its resultant technological and service innovation. If competition is to flourish, operators will have to extend their investments in the development of new services and their deployment of lower-cost technologies. The question that therefore needs to be asked is whether the price cap regime of increasing deduction factors weakens this process.

Price caps imply a particular view of the market. With their focus on lower prices and improved efficiency, they are consistent with a 'utility' view of the telecommunications market which emphasises a position of lowest-cost operator providing highly efficient *but* undifferentiated basic utility services. A price cap based on a utility model, therefore, imposes distortions on a competitive market. These are enshrined in the market through the influence of the price cap on other operators, with the result that these operators will be constrained from offering new service packages and possibly from moving their existing prices in line with their costs. In addition, entry signals will be distorted by regulatory definitions of markets. The shape of the market is by its very nature difficult to predict. Regulatory definitions therefore inevitably lead to arbitrarily defined markets and industry segments.

In a monopoly environment, the setting of a price cap is a relatively simple exercise. The regulator sets X commensurate with an efficient operator level of profit. The regulated firm then sets prices according to the RPI $-$ X formula, and the resultant profit level is then greater or less than forecast depending on cost control and volume changes.

In contrast, in a potentially competitive environment, designing an appropriate cap is an extremely difficult operation. In the UK telecommunications market BT is the dominant operator, and prior to the current price cap was the price leader within the industry. Increasingly severe price caps imposed on BT by OFTEL and the arbitrary regulatory definitions of the market thus

---

[14] Dynamic efficiency gains result from the degree of rivalry that exists as well as the technological dynamism that is generated by firms within the industry in their competitive struggles.

had the consequence of also forcing competitors such as Mercury to parallel any BT-led price cuts in order to gain and penetrate the market. However, due to BT's dominance, BT had significant freedom to target its required price cuts to hurt competitors in a potentially predatory and anti-competitive manner. The result might therefore be that the distortionary impact of the price cap could perversely retard the very development of competition that the regulatory structure is supposed to promote over the longer term.

2.8   OTHER FLAWS IN THE PRICE CAP APPROACH

Although the use of price caps is appropriate in a monopoly environment, when there is potential competition in the marketplace, for the reasons outlined at 2.7 above, it is imperative that the regulator takes deregulatory actions. Prolonging a broad price cap beyond the stage at which competition could become effective is extremely dangerous to nascent competition.

The price cap approach considers only one variable: price. In ignoring or failing to capture properly the other issues, while tightly constraining one variable, all the others are inevitably distorted. Some of the issues that need to be considered are:

- quality;
- evolution of competition;
- 'dynamic efficiency';
- differentiation;
- diversity;
- choice;
- consumer 'irrationality'; and
- innovation.

2.8.1   Quality

Quality is the scale by which each characteristic of the service is measured. In setting a price cap, the regulator is implicitly making an assumption about quality. If, through the regulatory regime, the regulator is emphasising or focusing solely on the price variable, this is inevitably at the sacrifice of quality. Examining past performance of BT's quality of service, Table 2.1 reveals that it appears to decline the tighter the price cap. The only exception

Table 2.1   BT's quality of service under price caps

Service Indicator	'X' < 4.5%	'X' > 6.25%
Call failure	Improved	Improved
Network/customer reported faults	Improved	Flat
Fault repair	Improved	Declined
Installation time	Improved	Declined
Operator services	Improved	Declined
Payphone serviceability	Improved	Declined

has been network services, where quality has generally improved. This, though, is due to network modernisation and digitisation, which would happen regardless of the level of X.

2.8.2 Evolution of competition

A dominant firm, as discussed above, will focus price cuts on those sectors of the market where competition is greatest, while attempting to earn monopoly profits in sectors where there is the least amount of competition.

Under a broad cap that eliminates monopoly profits on average, it is obvious that it would be profit-maximising behaviour for the dominant firm to cut prices below the level which earns normal profits in the competitive sector while keeping them above the normal profit level in the less competitive sector. Such behaviour would, however, completely destroy existing competition and foreclose the market and would be, of course, predatory.

Predatory pricing can occur in both a capped and an uncapped market, but the point here is that under a broad cap, there is an additional incentive for the dominant firm to engage in predation. If a broad cap is therefore to be implemented, measures will need to be designed to prevent this from occurring.

2.8.3 'Dynamic efficiency'

The focus of price cap regulation on the price variable assumes a static view of the industry cost structure. As discussed at 2.6 above, competitive industries improve unit costs over time by companies trying to better each other. In the telecommunications industry, however, due to the preponderance of sunk or fixed costs in running the network, a static analysis would conclude that the existence of fixed costs in each company is 'wasteful'. Costs of the industry could be lowered, at a given point in time, by reducing the industry to a monopoly environment. This one-off gain would, however, be at the expense of the dynamic efficiency of the market.

2.8.4 Differentiation, diversity and choice

Another fundamental characteristic of a competitive market is the product and firm-specific differentiation that evolves, as competing firms strive to meet the needs of consumers. In relegating competition to the simple role of price competition and via the arbitrary nature of regulatory definitions of the market, no value is attributed to differentiation, diversity or choice.

2.8.5 Consumer 'irrationality'

While a consumer's failure to behave as predicted can always be justified after the event by some new factor,[15] the regulator must recognise that customers are not always rational. In a regulated utility environment, it is the regulator's

---

[15] For example, a failure to buy a product at lowest available price could be rationalised by inventing a 'search cost' parameter that varied over time.

role to protect consumers from this. In a normal environment, there is no such protection. The regulator should not therefore continue with justified concerns from the old monopoly world and use them to prevent the transition to a competitive world.

2.8.6 Innovation

Innovation is a key element in the development of effective competition, but is also the most intangible as it is impossible to predict the nature of the market. This therefore highlights a stark choice for the regulator between:

(a)   the dynamic, diverse, innovative but risky world of a competitive market; or
(b)   the simple, featureless, basic but predictable world of a regulated utility.

2.9   KEY ISSUES – PRICE CAPS

Given the discussion above, in summary, one can conclude that the asymmetric nature of a price cap – in that it prevents price rises but allows price decreases – while being irrelevant in a monopoly market becomes a critical failing when potential competition is prevalent. A price cap designed to simulate competition could prevent that very competition from emerging. The dominant operator will make a commercial virtue out of a regulatory necessity and target any required price cuts against the competition. The regulator must thus decide whether he or she wants real competition or perpetual price control. Running both together for any period of time is unsustainable.

Price caps and competition do not mix: price caps must be removed to give nascent competition a chance. As outlined in 2.2, regulatory intervention should be initiated only if there is a demonstrable competitive or market failure. As a consequence, when reviewing a price cap regime, the regulator must examine the competitiveness and potential competitiveness of the market; and should then ensure that if the price cap regime is to continue, it does not impede the development of an effectively competitive market.

This is exactly what occurred in the UK for the 1997 review of BT's price controls. A report prepared for OFTEL by an economic consultancy, National Economic Research Associates (NERA), estimated that by the start of the new price cap period, 62 per cent of all business customers would have a choice of three or more direct access operators and 39 per cent would have a choice of five or more. It also estimated that 51 per cent of residential customers would have a choice of two or more direct access operators. Given the coverage of indirect access throughout the country, this meant that there would be considerable choice for an increasing range of customers.

In the light of these estimates and the fact that the industry has economies of density, OFTEL decided that retail control should be implemented only where consumer protection was required. The impact of this view was that it limited the price cap to the lowest-spending 80 per cent of residential customers and loosened the cap from RPI − 7.5% to RPI − 4.5%.

2.10 REBALANCING

In 2.6 above, the economic characteristics of the telecommunications industry were briefly discussed. In particular, the interdependence of access and usage meant that BT, in setting the two-part tariff for customers coupled with the price cap restrictions, could influence, through its balance of charges, the social aspects of telecommunications as well as the level of competitive activity in the marketplace.

The pricing structure of dominant operators, inherited from the public sector era, has been driven by history, politics and social policy. Governments generally feel it desirable, on political grounds, that individuals have access to communications facilities, so as to exercise their political rights; and on social grounds, to avoid a gulf emerging between 'information-rich' and 'information-poor' groups. This, combined with the existence of externalities and dynamic benefits for the economy, as discussed in 2.6, means that dominant operators have been encouraged in monopoly environments to subsidise line rental and local call charges so as to stimulate demand, funding this via long-distance and international call charges. This has, however, led to tariffs being out of balance with costs which, with the introduction of privatisation and liberalisation policies, has meant that competitive activity has been influenced wherever these imbalances have occurred.

In terms of economic efficiency, an unbalanced price structure has a number of adverse effects. First, it sends incorrect signals to potential entrants and may thus result in inefficient entry. Secondly, it results in a loss of economic welfare. Where the price of a service is in excess of long-run marginal cost, potential customers, whose valuation of the service exceeds the cost but not the price, are deterred from using it. Where the price is below long-run marginal cost, there will be consumers whose valuation of the service falls below its cost, but who nonethless use it because price is below cost. The potential economic welfare benefits from rebalancing can thus be substantial.

Before discussing rebalancing in more depth, it is worthwhile considering exactly what is meant by the concept. Tariffs for two services can be said to be balanced if they are set at levels which give equal returns on capital for the supply of the services. This generally means price changes in the direction of balanced tariffs, and in terms of telecommunications applies to line rental prices and call charges. But within this concept of rebalancing lie substantial complications. The first relates to the difficulty of separately defining costs where two services are closely linked. The second, and more significantly important, relates to the political aspects of rebalancing. Rebalancing of charges comprises the reduction of long-distance and international charges and the increase of local and line rental charges. Given that the majority of businesses and the better-off are typically the big spenders on long-distance and international calls, rebalancing would mean that these people would pay less while the majority (the voters) would pay more.

The issue of rebalancing became prominent in the UK when BT made its first price changes as a private company. It was keen to rebalance quickly, as having tariffs out of balance exposed it to competition targeted exclusively at the high-margin calling business. It argued that pricing line rentals below cost 'distorts the market and encourages inefficient and misplaced investment'.[16] It was, however, limited in its actions due to a restriction on line rentals of RPI + 2%. Nonetheless, BT managed to carry out some rebalancing although this tended to favour large users and involved price cuts in areas where competition was prevalent and price increases where it was not. (The incentives for BT to rebalance are therefore similar to those produced from price regulation, as discussed in 2.7 and 2.8.)

Rebalancing, if pursued too vigorously, could therefore undermine the liberalisation process. As a consequence, OFTEL investigated this and concluded in 1986 that no further rebalancing between local and long-distance charges should occur. The view was that the liberalisation process needed to be protected, which, if effective, would lead to natural cost reductions and rebalancing over a number of years. This would mean that in any one year no one would actually face price rises, while the economic welfare benefits of rebalancing would continue to be protected.

2.11   ACCESS DEFICIT CHARGES

In 1991, as mentioned at 2.7.2 above, the Duopoly Review occurred. This marked an end to the fixed-link Duopoly, and opened up the UK market to competition. With the advent of competition and the network-externality characteristic of telecommunications, this meant that each telecommunications operator needed access to the networks of other operators so that calls made to customers of those networks could be delivered. Given the resultant increase in new entrants and the fact that BT retained an effective monopoly over local access, BT claimed that due to the restriction on rebalancing via the RPI + 2% price cap on line rentals, user subscriptions would be inadequate to cover the costs involved. It argued that interconnecting operators should therefore contribute toward the resultant loss – the 'access deficit'. BT reported the size of this loss through its 'Financial Results by Service' publication, moderated by OFTEL under condition 13.5A of BT's licence, and claimed that it cost approximately £1.5 billion per annum.

It is in the consumer's interest to use the most efficient (least-cost) operator for each component part of its call. At the time, BT claimed that it needed to earn super-normal profits on calls in order to fund the deficit. This would, however, effectively enable a higher-cost or less efficient operator to carry the long-distance or international component of a call and still make a profit. In order to avoid this inefficiency, BT claimed therefore that some contribution must be made by competing operators to cover the access deficit.

As a consequence, in the Duopoly Review, BT's licence was amended. The provision was added that interconnection payments must include an 'access

---

[16] BT's response to OFTEL's Statement: *'Effective Competition: Framework for Action'* (London, BT, 1995), para. 7.1.

deficit charge' (ADC) in addition to covering BT's cost of conveyance. Effectively, this meant that the industry was economically rationalised by the rule of 'efficient component pricing' (ECPR).[17] Opportunity cost is included here as a business cost to BT, and so if BT loses retail revenue in allowing local access to competitors, it must be compensated. Consequently, the argument went that less efficient operators would be unable to enter the market.

In the first phase of the ADC introduction, OFTEL deemed that the deficit should be funded equally by all competitors in proportion to their traffic volume. This presented a huge barrier to entry, though. In the second phase, therefore, OFTEL was given the power to waive ADCs wholly or partially, using its own discretion and a set of rules relating to market share rates of entrants.

The imposition of ADCs in the UK market led, however, to severe distortions that acted as a reinforcement of BT's dominance in the market-place. As stated above, ADCs are strongly based on the ECPR. The ECPR is a controversial concept which is far from being universally accepted in the world of economics, let alone in telecommunications. It derives from the theory of contestable markets and is only relevant in this framework. Contestable market theory hinges on three elements:

(a)   market entry is free and without limit;
(b)   entry is absolute, so that the entrant can establish itself before the incumbent can make any price response;
(c)   entry is perfectly reversible so that the firm can leave the market and recoup all the costs of entry.

It is clear that each of these assumptions is invalid in the case of telecommunications, and therefore the use of the ECPR in this industry is inappropriate.

Under the ECPR, market entry would occur only when the entrant can provide service more efficiently than the incumbent, who, through the interconnect rate, is able to charge the entrant the 'opportunity cost' of business it has lost to the entrant. In a contestable market, the incumbent is assumed to be perfectly efficient, because an efficient entrant will always be able to drive out an inefficient incumbent. However, it is possible that the entrant could be more efficient than the incumbent, but not by enough to ensure that its total cost of supplying the product is lower than the incumbent's incremental cost. If this were the case, under the ECPR, market entry would not occur. The product would therefore not be provided by the most efficient producer, which the ECPR is supposed to guarantee. The ECPR therefore turns out to be internally inconsistent, because although it is supposed to ensure production by the most efficient carrier, it generates conditions under which this is unlikely to hold.

---

[17] The application of ECPR to telecommunications in the UK was originally advocated by William Baumol. A detailed exposition appears in Baumol, W.J. and Sidak, J.G., *Towards Competition in Local Telephony* (Cambridge, Massachusetts, MIT Press, 1994).

A further major problem with the theory relates to dynamic efficiency gains. Because the incumbent firm in a perfectly contestable market is assumed to be perfectly efficient before a competitor enters the market, it follows that market entry will not have an impact on the incumbent's costs which are supposed to be already minimised. There is, however, a great deal of evidence to show that incumbent monopolists are inefficient. Competition should be expected to cause the incumbent to become more efficient, improve its quality of service, bring its prices more into line with its costs and develop more innovative services, which would increase demand for telecommunications services. However, because the ECPR takes no account of these potential dynamic effects of competition, it undervalues the benefits of entry and reinforces the incumbent's inefficiency.

Given that, the ECPR/ADC regime:

(a)   enabled the incumbent operator to carry a substantial margin of inefficiency;

(b)   failed to take account of the dynamic gains brought about by competition, thereby leading to interconnect charges that distorted the make or buy decision faced by entrants; and

(c)   encouraged firms to behave in other ways that misallocated resources.

The Director-General thus concluded in 1995 that the regime was at odds with the policy objective of obtaining 'the best possible deal for the end user in terms of quality, choice and value for money'.[18] As a result, in 1996, BT's licence was modified and the RPI − 2% line rental constraint was lifted, resulting in the access deficit regime being removed. It was envisaged that given BT had claimed for so long the efficiency of rebalancing, it would raise line rentals accordingly so as to collect the extra £1.5 billion to finance the 'access deficit'. In practice, it did not increase them by the 80 per cent required to collect this extra amount. This, therefore, confirmed the viewpoint that it would not be in BT's interests to make a large rebalancing price change; instead it would be better to price to maximise its long-term value and profit.[19]

2.12 SOCIAL OBLIGATIONS AND FURTHER CONSTRAINTS ON RETAIL PRICES

As detailed above, BT, in setting its prices, is subject to a combination of regulatory constraints. In 2.10 and 2.11, the issues surrounding the

---

[18] OFTEL Consultative Document, *Interconnection and Accounting Separation*, (London, HMSO, June 1993), para. 1, p. 1.

[19] Even if the line rental constraint is removed, it is not in BT's interest to rebalance quickly. In a competitive marketplace, a company's products and services are often deliberately priced out of balance, especially when the sale of one service is linked to the sale of the other. An example of this is mobile telephony, where handset subsidies help to establish the customer and secure future revenue. It could be argued that this is not strictly comparable to fixed telephony, as a BT access customer can choose to send long-distance and international traffic via an indirect supplier. However, in attracting the line rental customer, the local call and interconnect revenue at least is also secured, so the principle is fundamentally the same.

rebalancing constraint were discussed. A further restriction on BT and on most incumbent operators relates to the non de-averaging of geographical tariffs and the requirement to provide service to all customers demanding service (otherwise known as the universal service obligation, or USO). This constraint, like that on rebalancing, has the effect of making access unprofitable, although the uncertainties in the demand for telecommunications services make it difficult to ascertain how a profit-maximising operator would set prices.

Under the averaging constraint, it is normally claimed that due to the economics of density of the industry, certain classes of customers become profitable to serve while others become unprofitable. In a pure competitive market, if this occurred, it would mean that those customers who were unprofitable would be excluded from the feasible market for service. However, the fact that the incumbent has a USO means that this cannot occur and therefore, to fund this, there is cross-subsidisation between profitable and unprofitable classes of customers. This subsidisation, like that by long-distance and international call charges to line rental and local call charges, has historically been encouraged by governments. The rationale for imposing a USO is both social and economic. The social policy goal, as discussed at 2.10 above, is to provide individuals with access to communications facilities so as to avoid a gulf emerging between 'information-rich' and 'information-poor' groups. The economic rationale, on the other hand, relates to the presence of externalities, not taken into account by individuals in their private decision-making. New customers joining a network not only benefit themselves, but also create extra opportunities for existing customers. There is, moreover, evidence of dynamic benefits for the economy arising from the development of the telecommunications sector.

The presence of these externalities and the social and political considerations mentioned above thus creates a case for imposing a USO-sharing mechanism as long as it can be proven that costs outweigh benefits. However, it is likely that the main aim of the obligations will differ at different periods. More precisely, at the time of network build-out and mass-market take-up, the objective of USOs is likely to be primarily economic. Once the network is completed, however, the goal of universal service will shift to being primarily a social one. In the former stage, it is desirable to keep installation prices, etc. low so as to stimulate demand. In the latter stage, the emphasis is likely to be upon targeting subsidies to ensure that the telephone is affordable to all and adapted to those with special needs.

Traditionally, in a monopoly environment, as mentioned above, the costs of USO have been covered by a cross-subsidy. When competition has been introduced, however, the incumbent has asserted, as with rebalancing, that having a USO exposes it to competition targeted exclusively at the profitable business, thereby resulting in it having inadequate funds to cover the costs of serving unprofitable customers. As a consequence, it claims that the costs of this should be shared amongst operators in order to ensure competition on equal terms.

2.12.1 Costing the USO

The costs of meeting the USO should comprise the sum of the losses incurred by the USO operator in serving customers whom it is obliged to serve but whom it would not otherwise serve had it not been a USO operator. The calculation must be made on the basis of the costs of an efficient operator, as it is imperative that operators do not subsidise embedded inefficiencies within the USO operator.

The computation of the cost of the USO therefore involves detailed examination of the costs and revenues associated with customers. Given that only a few customers are likely to impose net USO costs, the method for estimation should be focused on the costs of provision to loss-making customers on an avoidable basis. In other words, the calculation should ascertain how much would be saved (i.e., costs) and how much would be lost (i.e., revenues) if those loss-making customers were detached from the network.

The calculation of the cost side of the equation comprises detailed economic modelling which should aim to determine the maximum number of customers that can be served economically. Once this has been identified, it should then be possible to derive and cost the shortfall or the cost of serving loss-making customers using avoidable costs.

Once the avoidable costs of delivering universal service have been identified, any commercial benefits, such as good public relations, reduced customer churn, simplified credit procedures arising from serving remaining customers, must be quantified. All incremental revenues emanating from loss-making customers must also be included in the revenue calculation. This should comprise call charges and line rental charges, as well as revenue of incoming calls to loss-making customers. This is of key importance to the calculation, as this would be lost to the operator if the customer left the network.

The cost of delivering universal service is then the amount by which the cost of serving loss-making customers exceeds the benefits and incremental revenues associated with serving these same customers.

2.12.2 Funding the USO

As detailed above, if costs outweigh benefits, there is then a case for imposing a sharing system so that competition occurs on an 'even playing field'. A number of mechanisms exist for funding and sharing the costs of meeting the needs of unprofitable customers or services. If it is deemed that the rationale for the USO is social policy, so that the cost of funding the USO ultimately represents a tax on customers to fund extended services for others, it is appropriate for the costs to be met by general taxation. Governments generally, however, find this option unpalatable, and therefore it is usually the case that the costs of USOs are financed from within the telecommunications sector. This can be done in several ways. The first method relates to a fund or virtual fund, where the costs of the universal service are shared out between carriers according to the size of each operator's traffic share, as is the case in Australia. Alternatively, costs could be divided to reflect service revenues minus payments to other operators. A further method involves tampering with interconnection charges, such that there is a surcharge on interconnection which covers USO costs.

It is important that the way in which USOs are allocated and financed minimises market distortions. It should be recognised that the mode of implementation can influence longer-run resource allocation decisions, such as entry and exit, investments in networks and technology choices, thus resulting in losses in dynamic efficiency. In the case of a specific USO interconnection surcharge, the distortions would be similar to those of ADCs (see 2.11) and would inevitably result in tariffs being further unbalanced from underlying costs, as the interconnecting operator would undoubtedly recover the surcharge from the generality of its customers and not only those making calls to uneconomic areas and customers.

In the UK in 1996[20] the USO was costed at less than £0.05 billion. In this instance, since the cost of delivering universal service was more or less insignificant, while the transaction cost of administering and funding the mechanism and the costs flowing from the market distortion any mechanism will create exceeded the delivery cost, it was decided that the delivery of the USO should not be funded by the industry as a whole. This is periodically reviewed by OFTEL, however, and so change is possible.

If change is imminent then funding the USO could be carried out using the methods outlined above. Funding via a fund or virtual fund could, however, be further enhanced by the fact that alternative providers of service are present in the market. In other words, permitting the incumbent to contract out the USO to the most efficient service provider, or equally franchising the USO to the most efficient service provider and then making the appropriate transfers, could also potentially improve efficiency of USO delivery.

2.12.2.1 Competitive tendering Competitive tendering could operate by segmenting the market into different customer classes and/or regions, and auctioning the obligation to supply each of these. Under one possible competitive franchising arrangement, operators would be invited to bid to supply a USO in a particular region subject to satisfying minimum quality of service standards. Contracts would then be awarded to the lowest-cost operators. This would potentially ensure that the costs of providing universal service were minimised, thus also minimising the contributions required. It would also avoid the need to measure the costs of the USO, since these would be determined by a competitive bidding process.

An alternative would be to limit the franchise award with estimates of the current cost of USO provision in a particular region or for a customer class. This may be one way of ensuring that lack of competition does not lead to increases in the costs of providing USOs.

The efficacy of employing a particular competitive franchising scheme will, however, depend upon the extent of potential competition for each USO.

---

[20] OFTEL Statement, *Universal Telecommunications Services* (London, OFTEL, 1997).

This will partly depend upon the form of auctioning mechanism used and the incentives provided by it. However, no franchising scheme will work well where the incumbent or another operator is the only bidder, or where it is uniquely advantaged by virtue of its ownership of the network.

2.12.2.2 Subcontracting An alternative to franchising would be to allocate USOs to different operators, perhaps on the basis of their market shares or some other criterion, making them responsible for USO provision in a particular area. This scheme has the advantage of avoiding the need to levy other operators. It also has the potential to ensure that the overall costs of providing universal service are minimised. Each operator would then have an incentive to seek to meet its USO at the lowest possible cost, and to subcontract the supply of customers to other operators when they are more efficient.

However, like a franchising scheme, this scheme suffers from problems where there is a lack of potential competition. Moreover, and perhaps equally important, since different parts of the country are more profitable than others, the initial allocation process could not be conducted fairly without first calculating the costs of the USO in each region.

2.12.2.3 'Pay or play' Another method that could be used is 'pay or play'. In the UK, BT is obliged to provide a special service – the 'light user scheme' – which caters to the needs of loss-making customers. Under 'pay or play', competing carriers in loss-making areas could offer a special package or packages on terms similar to those offered by BT and agreed by OFTEL. If loss-making subscribers chose to take service from the alternative operator, that operator would then be credited with the net cost of providing universal service, payable from the fund or virtual fund.

All the alternative mechanisms discussed above have some merit, but it is important for any regulator (should it be necessary to fund the USO) to ensure that the way in which the obligation is allocated and financed minimises market distortions. The regulator should also try to secure the introduction of competition in USO provision so as to achieve the USO at minimum cost.

2.13 THE NEED FOR AN EFFECTIVE INTERCONNECTION REGIME

2.13.1 Introduction

As detailed in 2.6 above, a defining characteristic of all network industries, of which telecommunications is one, is that the value of belonging to or being connected to the network increases with the number of people on that network. This means that competition between separate networks is unlikely to be sustainable – the larger any one network becomes, the greater its advantage over the others.

The solution to this problem is for networks to interconnect, in effect forming one single network. While this is in the overall interests of society, if the market is characterised by one dominant network, it will be in that individual network's interest not to interconnect, in order to defend its position. An obligation to interconnect must therefore be imposed by regulators.

There is substantial confusion as to what the term 'interconnection' refers. The true definition is members of one network calling members of another. The obligation referred to above is therefore call completion, so as to attain the 'any-to-any' principle of a competitive telecommunications system. In the UK, however, BT is obliged to provide many other network services at a regulated price, and these are also treated as 'interconnection' services.[21] While this is the correct response to a market failure, it is not the interconnection market failure that has made this necessary, and these services come under the banner of interconnection only because of the way OFTEL's powers have been expressed in condition 13 of BT's licence.

Nonetheless, if the market is characterised by a dominant network, the effectiveness of an entrant's competitive challenge to the incumbent will depend crucially on the agreed terms of interconnection. Interconnection charges are a key cost component of entrants' tariffs; if high interconnection charges are set so that the incumbent is favoured, new entrants, in evaluating their entry business case, will conclude that business is not viable and will therefore not enter the market. The very development of competition that the regulatory structure is supposed to promote could therefore be perversely retarded. This distortionary impact will be further compounded by the fact that the incumbent will not only be insulated from competition, but will also be allowed to prolong its cost inefficiencies thereby adversely impacting consumers via continued higher tariffs. Existing entrants' behaviour, with regard to future investment decisions, will also be affected. In particular, the decision about whether entrants should continue to purchase network services from the incumbent or whether they should build them themselves, bypassing the incumbent's charges, will be strongly influenced by inflated interconnect charges. If interconnect is kept at such levels, existing entrants in the marketplace are likely to try to minimise costs by bypassing the incumbent's network and building their own network components to compensate. However, if these network components have natural monopoly properties,[22] this duplication of network may be inefficient and consumers could therefore suffer further.

---

[21] In the case of the UK, because BT held a monopoly over virtually all aspects of network operation and service provision, OFTEL obliged BT to provide call origination services to competitors at regulated prices. So, for instance, in the early years of Mercury's competition with BT, if customers connected to BT's local network wished to use Mercury's long-distance services, they could either dial an access code or use a pre-programmable telephone ('blue-button' telephone) to dial automatically into Mercury's network. This type of access thereby allowed customers connected to BT's network at the local end to benefit from competition, albeit in a limited form, while at the same time enabling Mercury to gain presence in the marketplace as well as 'incentivising' it to continue its network build-out.

[22] A natural monopoly is defined by economists as an activity which exhibits economies of scale throughout the entire stretch of its unit cost curve. Such a condition could make but one firm – the largest and lowest-cost one – the inevitable winner and only survivor in any competitive contest with others in that line of activity which exhibits natural monopoly features. It is important to note that it is quite possible for a firm to exhibit natural monopoly properties in one activity but not in others. See Vickers, J. and Yarrow, G., *Privatisation: An Economic Analysis* (Cambridge, Massachusetts, MIT Press, 1988) for further discussion of this issue in relation to UK privatisation and utility regulation.

In contrast, if interconnect charges are set too low, inefficient entry will be enabled, which in the long term will be detrimental to consumers and the industry. Moreover, if charge levels are too low, it is likely that the incumbent will not be able to recover its network costs efficiently. If this is the case, it will result in investor uncertainty and, in consequence, a corresponding decrease in investment and innovation in the industry. Future network build-out may be less robust because capital funding that might otherwise have been used for network and service construction is not readily available. In addition, technology choices may be driven by a short-term focus on recovery of network costs rather than by a long-term focus on overall industry growth. This may thus have potentially irreversible consequences for service provision and the development of competition in the industry.

Given the complexities in setting interconnect charges, as outlined at 2.13.2 below, getting the appropriate balance of interconnect charge levels right is crucial to ensure the efficient development of competition and of the industry. The role of the regulator in setting these charges is vital in establishing a sustainable interconnect regime. To prevent the dominant operator from abusing its position, the regulator must have the appropriate powers and penalty mechanisms to exercise control. The importance of these powers cannot be overstated. They are vital, both for creating the conditions for effective competition and for a system of minimum regulatory intervention.

2.13.2   Interconnection cost methodologies

Establishing the right arrangements for setting interconnection charges is probably the most important element in the competitive framework in telecommunications. Economic principles of telecommunication pricing to ensure the efficient use and development of the network dictate that prices should be set in relation to costs. Given that effective development of a competitive telecommunications environment is heavily reliant on the agreed terms of interconnection, it is imperative that the regulatory regime ensures that interconnecting operators pay for the specific services they use, and only for those specific services. The underlying costs of the network are therefore of utmost importance in setting these charges, and for the emergence of viable competition, detailed cost of service information is required.

2.13.2.1   Fully allocated costs   Historically, regulators and telecommunication operators have used fully allocated costs, valuing assets at historic prices (see 2.4 above), when setting interconnect charges. Fully allocated costs are calculated by attributing to any service whatever costs are directly determined or caused by that service. So, for example, large parts of the local loop can be associated with the provision of access to customers, or an international switch can be associated with the provision of international calls. There are, however, a number of costs that are 'common' to various services that cannot be allocated on a causative basis. For example, switching exchange costs are influenced by the number of subscribers attached to the exchange as well as by the usage which each subscriber makes of the telephone. To ensure recovery of these common costs, they are thus normally allocated to the respective service on the basis of the output, or the gross revenues or the direct costs of each service.

Although the use of fully allocated costs for the purposes of interconnect charging appeared to be relatively simple to implement and ensured that all costs were recovered, the procedures for deriving the costs were subject to difficulties. The first related to the asymmetric information problem, discussed at 2.4.2. The derivation of fully allocated costs is heavily reliant on information that the incumbent dominant operator supplies to the regulator. 'Strategic' cost allocations, on the part of the incumbent operator, can thus allow it to raise competitors' costs and so keep them at a permanent cost disadvantage. These 'strategic' cost attribution procedures can be highly complex and their scrutiny by the regulator can prove to be difficult. Another criticism of the use of fully allocated costs was the fact that many costs cannot be allocated on a causative basis and so must be attributed using some arbitrary rule. The arbitrariness of this rule structure means, however, that changing the rule can change the results.

The above arguments relating to fully allocated costs appeared to indicate that the use of these costs for the purposes of interconnect charging was likely to be inefficient. Because costs of assets were valued at historic prices, the charges set would not reflect the true replacement cost of the assets and so would not signal to buyers the costs that their actual demands would impose on suppliers. As a consequence, the discussion about cost information for the purposes of interconnection charges has shifted towards incremental or marginal costs.

2.13.2.2 Marginal and incremental costs Marginal costs represent the forward looking costs associated with the provision of an additional unit of output of any particular good or service. Thus the marginal cost of access would be the costs associated with attaching a new subscriber to the local loop, and the marginal cost of a long-distance call would be the marginal costs of local conveyance at both ends – the marginal cost of switching and the marginal cost of long-distance conveyance.

In a perfectly competitive market, economic theory states that setting price equal to marginal or incremental cost is a necessary requirement if resources are to be allocated in an economically efficient way. The reason for this is that if price was above marginal cost, it would always be profitable for firms to enter the market. Excess profits would thus be bid away by the new entry, so that eventually price equal to marginal cost would prevail. If, however, price was below marginal cost, firms would be making a loss and would exit the market, so that only efficient and sustainable competition would prevail. Marginal costs thus represent the costs of the marketplace, which will emerge if effective competition develops successfully.

The notion of marginal cost, as discussed above, provides a measure of the costs of producing a single unit of output. In contrast, incremental cost provides a measure of the costs per unit of producing a larger increase in service. So, for example, the incremental cost of long-distance calls could be computed on the basis of the extra costs of providing all long-distance calls given the availability of access, and would be expressed on a per unit basis.

Marginal and incremental costs can be calculated in two ways. The first, known as 'bottom-up' cost modelling, involves the construction of an engineering/economic model of an optimal telecommunications network. The idea is to try to design and cost an efficient and optimal network which can meet any given set of demands.[23] By changing certain demand parameters for individual services, it is then possible to calculate the marginal or incremental costs of that service. The alternative approach is known as 'top-down' cost modelling and starts from the incumbent's management accounts or fully allocated costs. The first step involves re-valuing the assets on the basis of their replacement costs. The non-incremental costs, such as non-attributive 'common' costs, are then removed from the accounts and the resulting costs are used to calculate the incremental costs of service on a per unit basis.

It is normal for both methods to be used in determining incremental or marginal costs. The reason for this is that each model acts as an auditing mechanism for the others as each has strengths and weaknesses that ensure that the reconciliation between the two models allows for only efficient costs to be recovered. If the regulator relied exclusively on the top-down model, derived from the fully allocated costs of the incumbent, the resulting incremental costs could include significant asymmetric information effects, thereby leading to a heavily skewed outcome in favour of the incumbent where inefficiencies in the incumbent's cost structure could be passed on to competitors in interconnection charges. The bottom-up model, in contrast, has the important advantage of being derived in an open and transparent way so that the confidence of the entire industry can be gained. However, because the model uses a theoretically efficient network rather than the actual network in place, it may be that the assumptions made in deriving the model may be unrealistic. As a consequence, the use of both models yields advantages and allows the regulator to scrutinise more closely the cost structure of the dominant operator.

2.13.2.3 Mark-ups The use of pure incremental costs in an industry in transition towards competition will rarely cover the total cost of service of even an efficient operator. Examples of this include the costs of access and the costs of geographic averaging. This, therefore, raises three important issues:

(a)   whether or not mark-ups on incremental costs to cover these 'common' costs are justified;
(b)   if so, which costs should be included in any mark-up system; and
(c)   how should the mark-ups be implemented?

It is already recognised that in a competitive market, the costs of interconnect would simply be incremental costs; there would be no need for a system

---

[23] The bottom-up model, in designing an optimal telecommunications network rather than using the actual network in place, removes the margin of inefficiency implicit in most incumbents' networks, thereby allowing only efficient costs to be recovered through the interconnect charges.

of mark-ups. Where the market is less than fully competitive, however, this issue needs to be considered further. The key criterion for judging the case for or against mark-ups should be the impact they would have on the development of effective competition. Mark-ups should be justified only when it can be demonstrated that this regulatory action is of benefit and where it can be shown that unintended consequences are avoided. Nevertheless, distortionary effects are likely to result as all the methodologies for calculating mark-ups entail significant problems. The ECPR is one such method. The flaws with this approach have already been discussed in 2.11 with regard to ADCs. The use of this rule for the imposition of ADCs resulted in a situation where the dominant operator was given substantial scope for inefficient production without the threat of market entry, as it encouraged firms to behave in ways that misallocated resources.

Another method for calculating mark-ups is Ramsey pricing. Ramsey pricing entails marking-up services where demand is not responsive to price. In other words, it involves varying the price to incremental cost ratio in inverse proportion to the elasticity of demand. The principle generally implies, therefore, the highest mark-up for access charges followed by local, national and international calls.

The typical Ramsey pricing formula for calculating the extent of the mark-up depends strongly on the type of competition between the incumbent operator and its competitors, the relative sizes of the firms, the differences in the costs of supplying the final output and the cost of interconnection. The complexity of the information required to put Ramsey prices into practice means, however, that it is impossible to see them being used at a practical level. The problems of estimating the various elasticities which are required in the Ramsey approach are considerable, if not insuperable, particularly when dynamic effects have to be factored in somehow. Whatever appeal the approach has at a theoretical level, therefore, in practice Ramsey pricing has little to commend it.

The practical problems which make it virtually impossible to use either the ECPR or Ramsey pricing to calculate mark-ups means that sometimes the short- to medium-term alternative might be to use equal mark-ups. These are effectively used in the calculation of fully allocated costs to cover 'common' costs. In the incremental cost case, these are calculated by type of service, with the ratio of mark-up to incremental cost being the same for each service. The immediate problem with this approach is that it lacks any of the theoretical economic justifications which, despite the practical problems associated with their implementation, the ECPR and Ramsey pricing at least partly possess. The rules governing equal mark-ups are completely arbitrary and take no account of customers' preferences. This means that the charges for interconnect would not be the cost of interconnect; instead, operators would be in a position where price signals would be distorted so that inefficient behaviour could be encouraged. In essence, an interconnection system comprising incremental costs plus equal mark-ups could be deemed to constitute little more than the fully allocated regime. Since it is generally acknowledged that the fully allocated regime has failed to engender effective competition, it is thus difficult to see how such a replacement would fare any better.[24]

2.14 INTERCONNECTION REGULATION IN THE UK

2.14.1 Background

In the light of the above theoretical discussion on interconnection and the importance of an effective interconnection regime, how has the UK regulatory regime dealt with this requirement?

The need for a clear interconnection policy became pressing when Mercury was licensed for operation. As discussed at 2.13 above, BT had no incentive to provide interconnect to Mercury, but its licence stated that it had an obligation to interconnect. Nonetheless, the licence did not specify how the interconnect charges should be set. Since the effectiveness of an entrant's competitive challenge depended crucially on the level of charges agreed, from 1982 to 1984, BT played out an effective series of interconnection negotiations with Mercury to meet its regulatory requirements while at the same time postponing Mercury's effective entry into the market. Given these obstacles, in early 1985 Mercury sought determination from OFTEL. The determination delivered in October 1985 included the following main elements:

(a)   A stipulation that any customer of one system should be able to call any customer of the other, whether or not this involved a choice of network operator by the calling customer (call termination services).

(b)   Interconnection at local and trunk level (call origination services). At the local level the interconnecting links between the systems were to be provided by BT on the basis of full tariff business exchange lines; for trunk interconnections, Mercury was given the right to take its system up to the BT exchange.

(c)   Re-structuring of call and connection payments as follows:

(i)   national call charges were time and distance related, mirroring the basic BT customer tariff structure;

(ii)   international calls were based on full published BT tariffs;

(iii)   connection payments payable by Mercury for system interconnection were to be wholly cost related and comprise two components–

(1)   direct costs of material and labour, and

(2)   a portion of BT's 'consequential incremental costs' (i.e. all costs increased or expected to increase because of the provision of the point of connection).

The 1985 Interconnection Determination, which provided the basis for the March 1986 Interconnection Agreement between BT and Mercury, was essentially a successfully pragmatic effort to facilitate market entry into an overwhelmingly dominated marketplace.

---

[24] OFTEL, *A Framework for Effective Competition* (London, OFTEL, 1994), at 16.

Interconnect prices were set with an RPI − 3% index, the same as the basket of BT's regulated retail prices at the time (see 2.7.2). BT had already adopted the economic principle of peak-load pricing coupled with distance-related pricing, to win maximum utilisation of its network. It thus seemed logical to transfer this rationale to the pricing of interconnect. At the time, margins were very high and the prospect of their erosion received little contemplation. There was thus no reason for Mercury to question this interconnect pricing structure, and it was keen to settle negotiations quickly since it was reliant upon the interconnect in order to commence business.

BT's pricing structure of interconnection with its network effectively placed it, however, in full control over the structure of retail prices offered by its competitors. The use of distance-related pricing meant that interconnect was not cost related to the number of network components involved in the call; instead, it depended on an arbitrary distance factor. The impact of this was that any form of competitor pricing innovation was effectively constrained to mimic BT's pricing structure. Furthermore, interconnect prices had not fallen in line with BT's costs. Competitors were thus essentially overcharged for their interconnection.

BT's retail prices fell in accordance with its price controls, which in turn eroded the differential with its wholesale interconnect prices leading to margin squeezes. If this had continued *ad infinitum*, competitors (whose prices were materially affected by the underlying wholesale prices) would not have been able to provide a price competitive alternative service.

Over the period, BT had little interest in reaching agreement over the interconnect. It was only when forced to do so by the regulator on an annual basis, following the breakdown in commercial negotiations, that BT reluctantly supplied minimum access to its interconnect 'bottleneck'. It did not, however, ask Mercury for interconnect to enable BT customers to call those directly connected to Mercury's network. This, therefore, added an additional obstacle for Mercury's market entry, as it meant that, given BT's dominance of the market, directly connected customers had to have the continuing inconvenience of separate BT incoming lines if they wanted to receive calls.

Given these difficulties, in June 1992, OFTEL issued a statement concluding that in the case of BT, detailed 'accounting separation' between its different businesses was necessary – for the continuing development of competition, and for public confidence that BT was not abusing its dominant position.[25] The application of accounting separation to BT's business was in the form of BT's 'retail' and 'network' arms. BT-Network was responsible for the sale of wholesale network services to all retailers, including BT-Retail, at non-discriminatory regulated prices, determined on an annual basis using the fully allocated cost approach outlined above. BT-Retail, in contrast, was responsible for selling on these services to final customers. Other results of the accounting separation process were a set of standard interconnection charges and methodology for determining undue discrimination (in terms of

---

[25] This policy is to be contrasted with the more radical policy in the US of structural separation of the RBOCs from AT&T. See 2.5 for a discussion of structural separation versus accounting separation.

BT's retail prices *versus* interconnection prices). Via this approach to accounting separation, BT's costs were therefore expected to be exposed to ensure transparency, non-discrimination and the revelation of unfair pricing.

It is of course debatable quite how transparent any system based on BT's own accounts can be given the asymmetric information effects in the provision of information. This is one of the reasons why Mercury lobbied hard for a move to incremental costing.

In 1996/97, the change in network costing from fully allocated costs (based upon historic cost accounts) to a system of forward-looking incremental costs (reflecting the replacement cost of capital assets) finally got under way. In addition, OFTEL proposed to move away from the need for annual interconnection determinations and instead opted for a more flexible approach based on a network price cap.[26]

Traditionally, price caps were used only for retail services; OFTEL, however, felt that the methodology for the setting of retail price caps could also be applied to network and wholesale prices (see 2.4 above for further discussion). This new approach marks a significant departure from the norm, since in other countries, regulators are getting more deeply involved in the direct regulation of interconnection. In the UK, in contrast, OFTEL is pulling back from regulation as competition develops and is transforming its role from a prescriptive regulator more to that of a competition authority.

In setting the network price cap, OFTEL stated that it intended to allow BT to recover in its wholesale prices the incremental costs of providing the relevant service, which would include an appropriate return on capital and a proportion of common costs. The requirement for incremental cost measures thus provoked OFTEL to undertake, in conjunction with the industry, work to develop the incremental cost models – the bottom-up model based on an economic/engineering approach to the costs of the network, and the top-down model based on costs derived from BT's current cost accounts. A detailed analysis of differences between the models then led to a reconciliation between them which produced 'hybrid' figures as the best measure of the relevant incremental costs.

2.14.2 New network charge controls

Given that under the new network charge controls, charges would no longer be determined annually but would be set by BT within the confines of network price caps, it was important that OFTEL produced a new framework of rules. If BT was to set the charges, the extent of its flexibility needed to be dependent upon the competitiveness of the relevant interconnection market, so that abuse of dominance could be avoided and so that the Littlechild rule of minimum regulatory intervention could be pursued.

In the event, this is exactly what occurred, with OFTEL proposing the following arrangements to commence from 1 October 1997 and ending in September 2001:[27]

---

[26] OFTEL Consultative Document, *Network Charges From 1997* (London, OFTEL, 1996).
[27] OFTEL Statement, *Network Changes from 1997* (London, OFTEL, 1997).

(a) For competitive services, BT would be free to set the charges, subject only to general competition legislation and the conditions of BT's licence, including the fair trading condition and the non-discrimination condition.

(b) For prospectively competitive services, BT would set charges subject to a safeguard cap of RPI + 0% on each discrete charge, in addition to the general competition legislation and the conditions of BT's licence.

(c) For non-competitive services, BT would set charges within three network baskets, each subject to a charge cap formula of RPI − 8%, calculated as discussed in 2.4 above, in addition to the general competition legislation and the conditions of BT's licence.

To allay fears of BT's ability to manipulate charges, OFTEL further proposed that reasoned complaints that the charges set by BT were anti-competitive, unduly discriminatory or unfair would be investigated by OF-TEL. Anti-competitive behaviour investigations would normally involve the comparison of the tariff for a particular service with its cost estimates, with the use of price floors and ceilings playing a significant role in the investigation. If prices were below price floors, set at incremental costs, it would be justifiable to assume that prices were predatory. In contrast, if prices were above price ceilings, set at the stand alone cost of providing the particular service in question, it could be assumed that monopoly profits were being earned at the expense of consumers.

2.14.3 The level of competition of services

In the case of the services that fell into the competitive, prospectively competitive and non-competitive service categories, OFTEL concluded that they should be grouped as shown in Table 2.2 below.

The requirement to judge the competitiveness of the services provided meant that the classification of conveyance services under the new regime needed to be more disaggregated than under the old. There are now two local exchange segment services: one for call termination and one for call origination. A single tandem segment is now composed of two services: a local exchange segment (either call origination or call termination) and local to tandem conveyance. A double tandem segment is made up of three services: a local exchange segment (either call origination or call termination), local to tandem conveyance, and inter-tandem conveyance. These services are shown in Figure 2.3 below.

The local exchange segment involves the use of the concentrator, the local switch and transmission between the concentrator and local switch known as remote-local conveyance. Local-tandem conveyance comprises the use of the tandem switch and transmission between the local and tandem switches, known as local-tandem transmission. Inter-tandem conveyance involves the use of a tandem switch and transmission between two tandem switches, known as inter-tandem transmission, and is subdivided into three distance bands.

All these components form the basis of inland conveyance interconnection services and are used in varying degrees by operators for the provision of

Table 2.2   Categorisation of services

Competitive services	Prospective competitive services	Non-competitive services
• Operator assistance	• Long-distance conveyance • International calls • Directory enquiry service • Phonebooks	• Call termination basket — Local exchange segment • General network basket — Call origination — Local to tandem conveyance (origination and termination) — Single transit • Specific interconnection services — Connections and rental of circuits — Certain data amendments

Figure 2.3   Main inland conveyance interconnection services

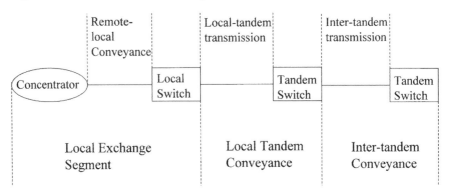

service. For those interested in obtaining more information, details are provided in OFTEL's May 1997 Statement, *Network Charges From 1997*, at Annex C.

OFTEL's attempt to judge the level of competition which currently exists and/or will exist in respect of the provision of each of the services provided by BT raised a substantial level of debate. In particular, the view that directory enquiries is prospectively competitive raised significant objections.

BT has control of access to the numbering database required for directory enquiries. In the industry's view this represents a substantial barrier to entry and so it was felt that it was inappropriate to categorise directory enquiries as a competitive service. Nonetheless, in spite of this opposition, although OFTEL acknowledges that there are barriers, it continues to hold this view and feels that the use of ceilings and floors will act as sufficient triggers to avoid anti-competitive behaviour.

2.15   KEY ISSUES – INTERCONNECTION

The effectiveness of the development of a competitive telecommunications environment is heavily reliant on the agreed terms of interconnection. Establishing a sustainable interconnect regime is thus probably the most important task in developing a competitive framework for telecommunications.

The role of the regulator in setting these charges is critical in ensuring that the industry has confidence in the interconnect charge levels. To prevent the dominant operator from abusing its position, the regulator must have the appropriate powers and penalty mechanisms to exercise control. The importance of these powers cannot be overstated. They are vital, both for creating the conditions for effective competition and also for a system of minimum regulatory intervention.

Economic theory states that prices should be set in relation to costs. The traditional use of fully allocated costs, although simple to implement, meant, however, that interconnecting operators received the wrong price signals since the charges did not reflect the true replacement costs of the assets. Thus, distortionary incentives were allowed to develop with respect to the efficient allocation of resources. The general shift towards the use of incremental costs consequently represents an improvement on the *status quo*, although it is difficult to implement and to monitor.

The UK interconnection regime has gone through several stages of development and the liberalisation of the market has necessitated the need for a fresh approach. This has been provided by the landmark introduction of the new network charge controls. These have a number of potential advantages for operators and for the market as a whole. The system could be considered to serve the industry better as it maximises the degree to which markets decide charges and thus reduces as far as possible the inevitable distortionary intervention by the regulator. The effectiveness of these new controls is as yet untested, though, and we will have to wait until September 2001 to ascertain exactly how they have operated and whether efficient behaviour has been encouraged.

2.16   CONCLUSIONS

This chapter has provided an overview of the economics of telecommunications regulation, encompassing the economic theory of regulation as well as the application of this theory to the UK telecommunications industry.

In years to come, there is little doubt that the 1980s and 1990s will be seen as a landmark era in the history of telecommunications. This is not because of the important technological changes that occurred, or the growing number of services and applications now available to consumers, noteworthy though these are, but because of the steps taken along the road to liberalisation. Where once telecommunications was seen as the monopoly preserve of state-owned enterprises, it is now recognised as an industry in which competition can and should be allowed.

Through liberalisation there has been a constant changing force on the UK telecommunications industry and a constant force on price. As we begin the twenty-first century there is a multitude of pricing packages on the market offering consumers more choice than ever before. Competitors will enter and exit and the fight for market share will continue.

The evolutionary forces of competition and technological developments, alongside the emergence of innovative economic regulatory policies, means that the future is very exciting!

CHAPTER THREE

The Telecommunications Regime in the United Kingdom[1]

John Angel

3.1 EARLY HISTORY

In a sense, the beginning of telecommunications in England occurred in 1660, when King Charles II was restored to his thrones in England and Scotland. He was acutely mindful that his father had lost his head in painful circumstances and wanted to retain his throne. To maintain his position as King he needed to forestall a new Great Rebellion. Therefore, he needed to know who was writing letters to whom, what people were saying about events and what people were saying about him. His reaction was to nationalise postal services and create a monopoly. This was the General Post Office (GPO). The decision to establish a monopoly over the conveyance of communications was taken for reasons of state. There was no consideration of 'economic efficiency' or 'natural monopolies'. As far as can be determined, the original GPO was not based on legislation or a Charter. It was a Government organ, which would now be called a Department of State, and seems to have been established under the Royal Prerogative. The monopoly appeared to have been taken by the King and was not conferred by Parliament or legislation.

Other monopolies were conferred in the sixteenth and seventeenth centuries, so there was nothing unusual about the postal monopoly. The basic GPO monopoly was over 'letters', but for over 300 years there was no definition of this term. It was only in 1981 that s. 66(5) of the British

---

[1] The first part of this chapter is based on a lecture given by Ian Ellison to LLM students at the University of London. The author is also grateful for the research assistance of Fiona McCrindle, soon to be trainee at Clifford Chance.

Telecommunications Act introduced a definition, under which a 'letter' was deemed to constitute:

> . . . any communication in written form which—
> (a)   is directed to a specific person or address;
> (b)   relates to the personal, private or business affairs of, or business affairs of the employer of, either correspondent; and
> (c)   neither is to be or has been transmitted by means of a telecommunication system,
> and includes a packet containing any such communication.

Until the second quarter of the nineteenth century there was no doubt that a letter was a tangible thing containing words written or printed on pieces of paper. There was a challenge, however, when newspapers began to come into circulation. As far as King Charles was concerned, these were kinds of letters, in the sense that they were written on paper and might contain opinions which were dangerous. So the GPO found itself in the newspaper distribution business. When the GPO conveyed the newspaper, it knew what was in it and who was committing sedition and seditious libel; and of course seditious newspapers could be impounded before they were delivered. Until relatively recently, most newspapers still carried a notice in small print that they were 'registered at the GPO as a newspaper'. More recently registration has been for postal tariff purposes, because newspapers are conveyed at a concessionary rate. However, it was not always so innocent, and only a combination of public and political opinion plus economics ensured later that newspapers fell outside the letter monopoly.

3.2   THE TELEGRAPH

The first real difficulty with the old letter monopoly arose with the 'telegraph'. Telegraph messages are conveyed over distances, but for most of the way they are not in written form – they are non-material.

Early telegraphs relied on flashes of light from heliographs, or on the movement of flags or signalling arms on telegraph towers. Chains of telegraph towers seem to have been established by the time of the Napoleonic wars. Where a telegraph was run on a formal or organised basis, a message which started out as a written letter (or signal) was conveyed over a distance in code and then converted back into written format at the far end. This was a letter in all but name.

In the beginning, the expense of establishing a chain of telegraph towers and its inflexibility meant that most (if not all) early telegraphs were under military or naval control. Apart from special cases like Lloyds (which early on established signalling stations), only the army and navy had the money to support telegraph systems, and only they had the requirement of the speed of communication conferred by telegraphs. Also, in those days companies with more than one office premises were rare; only the military had the organisational structures capable of setting up and running telegraphs.

In economic and regulatory terms, the early telegraphs were not important and the GPO did not seem to have worried about them. Then came the railways in 1825. These were large organisations conveying things over distances with a need for communications. Their signalling systems were a specialised form of telegraph, and they were initially large generators of written messages conveyed by hand of guards on trains.

Meanwhile electricity had been discovered, and with it the electromagnet. Between 1835 and 1844 the electric telegraph was introduced,[2] as was the Morse Code. Letters suddenly left their infancy and the years of telecommunications began. The railways had a need for telegraphs, and their expanding national networks gave them the physical wayleaves over which to convey messages for others (the introduction of Railway Regulation Act 1844 brought electric telegraphs within the legislative domain).

Electric telegraphs made it possible to send letter-like objects in non-material form, and the technology enabled 'telegrams' to be sent on a commercial and affordable basis. These developments threatened to move control away from the Government and into commercial hands, thus the Telegraph Act 1863 was introduced as a means of controlling the activities of these privately owned companies. The result of the Telegraph Acts of 1868 and 1869 was that those telegraph services originally conferred by private companies were nationalised.

3.3   REGULATION OF TELEGRAPHS

The regulatory reaction to the electric telegraph was to treat telegrams as a form of letter.[3] This was justified in part because the messages which were conveyed were written and delivered on paper. The fact that the messages were opened, coded into Morse Code, conveyed over a telegraph and transcribed back into writing was irrelevant to the sender or recipient. Telegrams started out as letters and finished as letters. This is what the Postmaster General concluded, and telegrams thereby came within his monopoly and commercial developments were not allowed except under his control.

The Telegraph Acts were not motivated by pure reasons of state. Britain in the mid-nineteenth century was remarkably secure, prosperous and confident. The modern postal service was being created, and it was based on ideas which are now described as standard charging, universal public service, cross-subsidies of remote areas by urban areas and economies of scales.

---

[2] Wheatstone and Cooke patented their invention in 1837 based on electromagnetic impulses travelling over wires.
[3] The Telegraph Act 1868, s. 3, defined 'telegram' as a 'message or other communication transmitted or intended for transmission by a telegraph'. Under the Telegraph Acts 1863 to 1962, a 'telegraph' included '(1) any wire, cable, tube, pipe or other thing whatsoever used or intended to be used for the purpose of transmitting telegraphic messages or maintaining telegraphic communication; and (2) any casing, coating, tube, pipe or other thing whatsoever enclosing or intending to enclose the same; and (3) any apparatus connected with anything falling within head (1) above and used or intended to be used for the purpose there mentioned'. It should be noted that the Telegraph Act 1869, s. 3, also stipulated that telegraph included communications conducted by means of electrical signals.

In the infancy of telecommunications technology, when networks were being installed, there were powerful arguments for monopoly, with a set of reasons for concentrating resources in one organisation, using its revenues to develop the business extensively and intensively and sharing overheads. The infant telegraph business shared facilities with the postal business, and each benefited from the economies it generated by using common investment and personnel. Also, the concept of a 'public service' took a powerful hold in the minds of those who thought about telecommunications. Not surprisingly the GPO took a monopoly of telegraphs and set up its own telegraph network.[4] A few organisations, such as Lloyds and the railways, seem to have run their own telegraphs under strict GPO supervision.

The early Telegraph Acts were largely codified in 1863 and 1868, with a series of amendments over the years. However, the key points which arise from this early legislation are:

(a)   the Acts were founded on the principle that telegrams were letters over which the GPO had a monopoly;

(b)   companies and individuals were allowed to run their own telegraph systems on their own land for their own internal purposes, but not to provide services to others;

(c)   there were arrangements for licensing companies and individuals to run their own telegraphs;

(d)   there were rules about the conduct of telegraphs, including confidentiality of what was conveyed, interference with telegraphs, etc.;

(e)   there were provisions about the construction and installation of telegraphs (especially telegraph poles), compulsory acquisition of land, arrangements for digging up streets, provision for running wires over private land, rights to cross railways and canals, etc.

The Telegraph Act arrangements for the construction and installation of telegraphs were to endure. Until as late as 1984, the British legal system recognised no concept of a 'telecommunication system' or of a 'telephone network'.[5] The public switched telephone network was installed on the basis that it was a telegraph. Ground stations communicating with satellites in synchronous orbits 22,000 miles above the earth were legally no different

---

[4] The Telegraph Acts of 1868 and 1869 granted the Postmaster General the authority to purchase those commercial companies conducting telegraph business within the UK. In addition, the 1869 Act granted the Postmaster General exclusive privilege in the transmission of telegrams.

[5] This lack of definition caused problems as long ago as the 1880s. At this time private companies developed telephone exchanges, and a dispute arose as to whether these telephone systems were infringing upon the exclusive telegraph monopoly of the Post Office. In *AG* v *Edison Telephone Company of London* (1880) 6 QBD 244, the Edison Telephone Company failed to show that the telephone and telegraph were technically different. The 1869 Act stated that telegraph extended to apparatus which could transmit messages by electrical signals without a wire, and the court held that this meant telegraph extended to electric signals, if such a thing were possible, from place to place, through the earth or the air. This statement has meant that the statute covered technology which was not invented at the time of the Act.

from a person with a Morse key tapping away in the back office of an 1840s post office. Even to this day, it is possible to find a manhole (or inspection) cover marked 'Post Office Telegraphs', concealing, in all probability, fibre optic cables.

In 1984 the UK codified the Telegraph Acts. Most of the principles remained as before, although the language needed to be changed to bring it into the twentieth century. It was also necessary to alter the references to the 'Post Office' to cover any 'operator of a telecommunications code system', because, in 1984, the crucial thing was to confer on other operators powers to dig up streets, etc., which had been possessed by the Postmaster General and then by the GPO and the Post Office alone.

3.4 THE TELEPHONE

In 1876, Alexander Graham Bell invented the telephone. It revolutionised telegraphy. Bell took telecommunications out of the hands of specialist operators with Morse keys and made telecommunication available universally to all who could speak and hear.

So how did the UK react to this revolutionary change? To begin with the Postmaster General did not regard it seriously. In regulatory terms it seems to have had two faults:

(a)   a telephone call was not a letter and was therefore outside the scope of the GPO monopoly; and

(b)   telephony was a passing phase for the rich few which would never be taken seriously.

In the late 1870s and the 1880s, the GPO licensed others to run telephone systems (Telegraph Act 1869, s. 5). As discussed at 3.3 above these were, legally speaking, telegraphs and needed a licence under the Telegraph Acts. The GPO retained its monopoly of telegraphs and the telegram business, but allowed others to construct and run telephone systems. Many telephone systems were developed. In some towns there were competing systems, but these were inevitably on a small scale and the economies dictated mergers and consolidation. The principal player at the time was the National Telephone Company.

3.5 RADIO AND MOBILE TELECOMMUNICATIONS

The early part of the twentieth century saw the introduction of radio. This important and technological change significantly expanded the scope of telecommunications activities. Nevertheless, it had minimal regulatory impact. UK law knows radio as 'wireless telegraphy', and to the GPO radio was just another form of telegraphy. It therefore fell inside the GPO monopoly and, apart from specialised regulatory requirements, for example to deal with frequency allocation, the GPO treated radio like any other form of telecommunications.

The legislation regulating radio was consolidated into the Wireless Telegraphy Act 1949, as later amended. That conferred licensing powers on the GPO which then licensed the use of radio for entertainment and allocated frequencies for national purposes, for example the police and the armed forces. The GPO retained for itself a monopoly over the uses of radio frequencies for third-party communications.

The special merit of radio is that it makes mobility possible. With radio, telecommunication users can move around. Various transport operators, in particular the large nationalised industries and also smaller firms like taxi operators, were licensed to run radio links. Some of these developed into 'closed user groups', where one operator handled communications on behalf of several different people and took messages on their behalf. Paging was also authorised. All the licensed operators were on a small scale and the GPO ran the main national radio and telephone networks.

Some of these radio licences permitted connections into the public switched telephone network, but these were normally indirect connections through human operators to private 'call handling' services. By 1979 the GPO woke up to the fact that these small operators were threatening its own operations and started to develop its own telephone systems. The GPO systems began to enjoy the economies of scale by using facilities installed for 'telegraphs', and as a result the competition struggled.

3.6 NATIONALISATION

Returning to the earlier years of the twentieth century, there were several private telephone networks. The Government saw the expansion of these as a threat to the viability of its own telegraphy services. It also saw the importance of telephones to national administration and defence. The Government realised the economies of scale of combining telephone and telegraphy networks, and thought it desirable to use telephone revenues earned in towns and cities to cross-subsidise less profitable rural services. These were the classic arguments which had been used at the time of the 'Penny Post' and there was discussion of 'postalising' telephone charges by having uniform nationwide tariffs. In the end, the Government decided that the original letter monopoly, as expanded in the nineteenth century to cover telegraphy, telegrams and (later) radio, should include telephony.

The GPO implemented the policy of nationalisation by the expedient of not renewing telegraph licences granted to telephone operators. As licences came to the end of the periods for which they were granted, the GPO took over the assets of the disenfranchised operators and absorbed their systems into its network. By the beginning of the twentieth century the process of remonopolisation was complete, with one interesting exception. The last decades of the nineteenth century saw an explosion in municipal capitalism. The main example was Joseph Chamberlain in Birmingham, but there was a host of municipal gas, lighting, electricity, tramway and other undertakings. Telephones were added to the list. The Telegraphy Act 1899 empowered local authorities to run telegraphs, and six were licensed to do so. One of these was Hull City Council. Some of the systems prospered, but the municipal systems fell victim to the GPO policy of not renewing licences. Eventually the licences fell and were abandoned, except for Hull's licence which was due to expire in about 1914, two years or so after the main nationalisation in 1912. For some reason, most likely the war, but also local pride, Hull's licence was renewed, and this continued successfully until in 1984 it was granted a 25-year licence very similar to BT's.

Hull was very important to telecommunications regulation in two ways:

(a)   It showed that a small operation that did not enjoy economies of scale could provide an efficient and cost-effective service.

(b)   Hull had a working interconnect which enabled messages sent via one company's system (i.e., Hull's) to be conveyed by another company's system (i.e., BT's), and this provided the critical precedent for the Mercury/BT interconnect which is discussed elsewhere in this book.

Hull no longer has a monopoly and the system was recently privatised.

3.7   EVOLUTION OF THE GPO

The first half of the twentieth century saw the development of the GPO Public Switch Telephone Network (the PSTN) and the steady atrophy of the original GPO's telegraphs business. Technology advanced significantly, with automatic switching, i.e. mechanical telephone exchanges in place of people with earphones putting plugs in holes, long-distance conveyance, undersea cables and the application of radio. In the 1950s it became apparent that the position of the GPO as a Government department headed by a political Postmaster General was unsatisfactory. Decisions were being taken for political reasons, money was controlled by the Treasury on a public expenditure rather than a business basis, and there were no proper accounts, only records on what public money had been collected as call charges and when that money had been spent.

In the mid-1960s the GPO as a whole was converted into a Government 'trading fund', which meant that it produced rudimentary commercial accounts, a balance sheet, etc. This produced a radical change within the organisation, but there was no legislation as such to implement the change. In 1969, the GPO was converted into a nationalised industry called the 'Post Office', under which the position of Post Master General was abolished. The new Post Office was set up under a special Act of Parliament.

The Post Office Act 1969 established the GPO as a statutory corporation headed by a chairman appointed by the Government. The independence of the GPO in 1969 could be viewed as the start of the long process of liberalisation which continued until the end of the century. The Act formalised the telecommunications monopoly by giving the new Post Office 'exclusive privilege'. It defined this exclusive privilege in terms of the 'running' of 'telecommunication systems'. The word 'running' was never defined, but 'telecommunication systems' was defined as:

. . . a system for the conveyance through the agency of electric, magnetic, electromagnetic, electro-chemical or electro-mechanical energy of—
    (a)   speech, music or other sounds;
    (b)   visual images;
    (c)   signals serving for the impartation (whether as between persons and persons, things and things or persons and things) of any matter otherwise than in the form of sounds or visual images; or
    (d)   signals serving for the actuation or control of machinery or apparatus.

This definition was introduced in 1969 but remains in s. 4(1) of the Telecommunications Act 1984, and the concept of running a telecommunication system is the foundation of the regulatory system.[6]

The 1969 Act was innovative in attempting to define what the running of a telecommunication system meant. But the Government did not take what now seems to be a logical next step of thinking through the licensing function and taking it over from the business which ran the public networks. Instead, it appears to have regarded licensing not as a regulatory issue, but as an aspect of the exclusive privilege. It surrendered all licensing powers to the new Post Office which, although essentially a commercial organisation, was given powers to license and run other telecommunication systems. The Post Office therefore had at least the theoretical power not to renew Hull's licence when its term expired (see 3.6 above).

The labour-intensive, low-tech and traditional postal business had little in common with the high-tech, capital-intensive and dynamically expanding telecoms business. The only cement was a shared history, common pool of employees and vested interests protecting its position. In July 1980, the Government announced its intention to restructure the Post Office and relax the monopoly over terminal equipment and value-added services. The British Telecommunications Act 1981 formalised the split in the Post Office. It also established new responsibilities for the British Standards Institution (BSI) and set up the British Approvals Board for Telecommunications (BABT), a subsidiary of the British Electro Technical Approvals Board. This was the necessary infrastructure to facilitate the opening of competition to terminal equipment. BT began operating under a licence and independent suppliers of telephones were permitted.[7]

3.8   BRITISH TELECOMMUNICATIONS ACT 1981

The 1981 Act also authorised the licensing of customer premises, or branch systems. Unfortunately the Act did not include a power to limit BT's

---

[6] See OFTEL's guidance notes to the telecommunications services licence (TSL) for further clarification of the meaning of 'running' a telecommunication system.

[7] Terminal equipment or apparatus liberalisation is concerned only with customer premises apparatus. For regulatory purposes the boundary has been drawn at the socket, or test jack frame, where a connection can be made between the chain of apparatus on a customer's premises and the chain of apparatus back to the telephone exchange and beyond the telephone networks. Apparatus liberalisation is concerned with the customer side of this boundary.

exclusive privilege, the Post Office having previously run all systems on customer premises under its exclusive privilege. As a result, the 1981 Act powers were never exercised.

The 1981 Act also allowed the licensing of the second fixed network, Mercury Communications. The initial decision was to license only one competing network because Mercury was seen as an experiment (and needed infant industry protection) and because the politicians of the day were worried that Mercury might wreck the economies of scale of the established network of BT which would then make it difficult for BT to finance service in rural areas, etc.

At about the same time, cellular technology was developed and opened the way to the expansion of mobile telephony. The first national cellular radio network licences were granted to Cellnet and Vodafone in May 1983, although they did not launch their analogue services until 1985, thus creating another duopoly. However, competition in mobile telephony was extended by introducing a service provider or retailer concept. The mobile operators were not allowed to sell services or apparatus directly to end users but were required to deal through retailers.

In addition to the creation of BT, the 1981 Act gave the Treasury the power to dispose of its interest in Cable & Wireless (s. 79).

It was soon realised that the 1981 Act was not a suitable vehicle to promote competition. It had no provision for the licensing of telecommunication services. It allowed BT to retain its exclusive privilege. The Act did not give operators like Mercury powers to dig up the streets or to erect telegraph poles. It included licensing provisions which were seriously flawed. For example, BT was to be consulted about all licences and could find out about competitors' plans. The Act had no provisions to force BT to connect Mercury's network, something which BT refused to agree to do, proposing that Mercury should build an overlay network with every customer having two phone points and phone lines, one BT and one Mercury. Overall the issues had not been thought through from the perspective of a competitor.

3.9 TELECOMMUNICATIONS ACT 1984 AND INTRODUCTION OF A SPECIAL REGULATOR

3.9.1 Telecommunications Act 1984

By the early 1980s, BT needed to modernise the public telecommunications network and required finance for this. Huge sums of money were necessary, and this conflicted with the Government's policy which demanded that a nationalised industry should cease borrowing from Government and should where possible pay money to the Government. Privatisation of BT was seen as the solution. The Telecommunications Act 1984 paved the way. It required the creation of a public limited company (plc) and the transfer to it of the assets and liabilities of the statutory corporation.

Around this time a number of utilities had made the transition from the public to the private sector and lessons had been learnt from their experience.

A common factor was that these public sector utilities had commanded a monopoly position. In moving to the private sector it was important to ensure that this did not continue. In the case of telecommunications, among other measures, Mercury was given powers which strengthened its ability to act as an effective competitor, while different techniques were employed in the other sectors such as the separation of the operation and infrastructure, as was done in the railway industry.

In addition, the 1984 Act had the aims of:

(a)   bringing about a complete liberalisation of customer apparatus to crack BT's dominance and to remove BT's control over the connection, running and maintenance of customer premises apparatus (i.e., to repair the defects in these respects of the 1981 Act);

(b)   giving Mercury a better licence than was possible under the 1981 Act;

(c)   improving the licences for cellular and local cable networks where the 1981 licensing regime had proved inadequate in detailed respects;

(d)   empowering Mercury and cable operators to dig up streets, etc., which meant modernising and generalising the Telegraphy Acts;

(e)   authorising branch systems and removing them from BT's control;

(f)   ending BT's exclusive privilege and subjecting BT to licensing controls;

(g)   controlling BT's charges to prevent monopoly profits; and

(h)   introducing controls on anti-competitive practices by BT, including in particular the ending of BT's ability to prevent interconnect.

In order to facilitate BT's privatisation, the Government made a duopoly statement to the effect that it did not intend to license operators other than BT and Mercury. Although there existed a duopoly in the fixed telecommunications market, the fledgling mobile operators were in a position to offer an alternative.

The 1981 Act had not granted the rights required to construct infrastructure, thus preventing effective competition. The Code powers contained in the Telecommunications Act 1984, s. 10 and Sch. 2 allowed operators to install apparatus under or over the street, to dig up the street and open sewers (Sch. 2, para. 9) among other works.[8] It was imperative for cable companies, as well as public telecommunications operators (PTOs), to be granted such code powers in order that they could operate and later compete in the telecoms marketplace.

To implement and monitor the changes, the 1984 Act also introduced an independent regulator known as the Office of Telecommunications (OFTEL). The Director-General of Telecommunications (DGT) was to

---

[8] Where apparatus is constructed to a height of three metres or more, a landowner may object to the installation where it affects his enjoyment of the land. This matter can be dealt with in a number of ways: compensation can be paid to the landowner; the apparatus can be required to be modified; or the court can declare that the landowner's agreement can be dispensed with. Some 40 fixed network public telephone operators licences now carry Code powers, thereby ensuring that they possess the requisite powers to install the infrastructure.

occupy an independent position analogous to that of a High Court judge. The DGT was to be appointed for a fixed but renewable term of office and could be removed only as provided for in his or her contract; and was to head a non-ministerial Government department, subject to Treasury control so far as expenditure was concerned and accountable to Parliament like any other Government department.

3.9.2 Duties of the DGT

In carrying out all his duties, the DGT should have regard to promoting the interests of consumers and effective competition. The Telecommunications Act 1984 gave him two kinds of duties. First, the duty to carry out specific functions. These are expressed so that the DGT 'shall' do these things. OFTEL's main job is to enforce observance of conditions included in licences granted to telecommunications operators. This can be done by the making of orders under ss. 16 to 18 of the 1984 Act. In practice, in the early days the sections were rarely used, as the threat of enforcement seemed to have the desired affect. However, the problem is that the non-exercise of s. 16 powers deprives the parties of certain remedies which are available under s. 18.[9]

Perhaps the next most important function is to give directions and determinations in relation to matters reserved for the DGT's decision under licences granted to telecommunications companies (or 'telcos'). This power, derived under s. 7(5) and (6) of the 1984 Act, was used extensively in relation to interconnect. In 1985, Mercury sought OFTEL's intervention in establishing an interconnection regime. In determining the terms of the interconnection agreement, the DGT had to balance a number of interests, including promoting competition and allowing BT to recover the cost of providing interconnection to Mercury.

The DGT also has the power to modify the conditions included in a telecommunication licence. There are two mechanisms for achieving this. The first is through a voluntary agreement by licensees under s. 12. The second is through a compulsory modification against the wishes of the licensee under s. 15 following a Mergers and Monopolies Commission (MMC) investigation (now the Competition Authority). Section 12 has now been revised because it involved individual licensees agreeing to license changes, which had proved difficult because of the number of licences now in operation in the UK (Part III, Electronic Communications Act 2000).

The DGT now exercises all powers in relation to the approval of apparatus. The Secretary of State appears to be removed from the process. This is in contrast to the awarding of licences, where the power is still retained by the Department of Trade and Industry.

In addition to these functions, the Director has a duty to consider complaints under s. 49 and the power to make monopoly and competition references to the Competition Authority (see Electronic Communications Act 2000).

---

[9] More orders were made in the 1990s – see OFTEL's Competition Bulletin.

Secondly, the DGT has general duties under s. 3 of the 1984 Act. These are as follows:

> (1)   . . . to exercise the functions assigned or transferred to him . . . in a manner which he considers is best calculated—
>   (a)   to secure that they are provided throughout the United Kingdom, save in so far as the provision thereof is impracticable or not reasonably impracticable, such telecommunication services as satisfy all reasonable demands for them including, in particular, emergency services, public call box services, directory information services, maritime services and services in rural areas; and
>   (b)   without prejudice to the generality of paragraph (a) above, to secure that any person by whom it falls to be provided is able to finance the provision of those services.

Section 3(1)(a) is designed to preserve the universal service obligation.
The DGT has a set of secondary duties under s. 3(2), as follows:

> (2)   Subject to section (1) above . . . to exercise the functions assigned or transferred to him . . . in a manner which he considers is best calculated—
>   (a)   to promote the interest of consumers, purchasers and other users in respect of the prices charged for, and the quality and variety of, telecommunication services provided and telecommunications apparatus supplied;
>   (b)   to maintain and promote effective competition between persons engaged in commercial activities connected with telecommunications in the United Kingdom;
>   (c)   to promote efficiency and economy on the part of such persons;
>   (d)   to promote research into and the development and use of new techniques by such persons.

He also has other duties designed to encourage investment, promote international transit services and enable providers of telecommunication services and producers of the telecommunication apparatus to compete overseas.

These duties govern the way in which the DGT exercises his functions and provide a basis for challenging decisions which are manifestly wrong. The Director operates within the framework of British administrative law, and it is very difficult to challenge any decision where it can be argued that the DGT has exercised judgment under s. 3 in a manner which he considers is best calculated to undertake his duties. There have been some challenges to the DGT's decisions, but the courts generally allow him wide discretion so that successful claims are rare. *R v Director General of Telecommunications, ex parte Cellcom Ltd and others, Independent,* 3 December 1998; *The Times,* 7 December 1998, is a prime example of an unsuccessful attempt (by Cellcom) to seek judicial review of the DGT's decision to modify licence terms. Nevertheless, such challenges are likely to become more commonplace following the Telecommunications (Appeals) Regulations 1999 (SI 1999 No. 3180), which amend the 1984 Act and allow a decision to be challenged on a broad range of grounds.

3.10 THE DUOPOLY REVIEW AND AFTER

The first major policy change since the introduction of the Telecommunications Act 1984 was the duopoly review. The Government, in its 1983 statement, which introduced the duopoly policy, dictated the timing and substance of this review. The seven-year delay until 1990 was excessive, but its length was necessitated by the need to finance Mercury and to reduce uncertainty at the time of BT's privatisation. The Green Paper was circulated in late 1990, leading up to the White Paper 'Competition and Choice; Telecommunications Policy for the 1990s' (Cm 1461) published in March 1991. This decision announced the ending of the duopoly policy. This meant that anyone who could show a need for a licence, and with the necessary financial resources, could become a public telecommunications operator with code powers to provide telephony with only limited restrictions. These restrictions included cable programme/local delivery services, which were not authorised in order to give cable operators time to complete their systems. Mobile services were also not authorised because of radio frequency limitations. Simple international resale was not allowed (see Chapter 4).

Many previous restrictions had been removed. Cable operators were allowed to provide unrestricted voice telephony. Restrictions on mobile operators providing fixed circuits were lifted. Individual companies were given wide scope to provide services.

The restrictions which prevented BT conveying cable programme services under its main licence continued. However, BT was free to apply for licences in individual areas and was authorised, as it always had been, to convey video on demand. The access deficit contribution (ADC; see 2.11) system was set up to facilitate payments by certain operators to fund universal service. In 1994 OFTEL took over the UK numbering scheme from BT and was given power through licensing modifications to introduce number portability and to change the then price-control formula of from RPI − 4.5% to RPI − 6.25% with international prices added to the basket and cut by 10 per cent.

This duopoly review in 1991 resulted in the UK having for the first time a truly liberalised telecommunications regime well ahead of most of its European partners. The OFTEL Draft Work Programme for 1999 stated that 'The UK now has over 200 licensed operators which include 5 national carriers, 4 mobile operators and over 60 companies licensed to operate international facilities'. This goes some way towards proving the success of the liberalisation measures, considering that only 20 years ago a complete monopoly existed.

In 1993, a new DGT was appointed who introduced a much more consultative, open and transparent regime of regulation. Almost immediately OFTEL published a consultative document on interconnection and accounting separation, setting out proposals on how BT's businesses should be divided for regulatory accounting purposes.

The following year OFTEL published a consultative document, *A Framework for Effective Competition*, which took a wide-ranging look at how the regulatory regime needed to evolve. A major policy statement was published in July 1995 (*Effective Competition: Framework for Action*) which considered the path regulation should take towards the goal of a competitive marketplace, recommending, *inter alia*, that

(a)   the RPI + 2% constraint on on-line rental price increases would be lifted, encouraging BT to introduce a more flexible range of service and tariff offerings to meet the needs of different groups of customers;

(b)   OFTEL would improve its handling of investigations into complaints of anti-competitive behaviour;

(c)   new arrangements for universal service provision and funding would be introduced;

(d)   changes to the service provider regime would be made;

(e)   there would be a move to incremental costs as the basis for interconnection charges.

Since then extensive use of consultation has been made to deal with changes and the implementation of EU Directives.

In the mobile telephony market, two licences were granted in 1993 to Orange and Mercury One-2-One, allowing these companies to operate digital mobile networks. To enable the mobile operators to compete on an equal basis, Vodafone and Cellnet were granted reissued licences, which were modified so that they could provide their services via digital networks, allowing the transmission of data as well as voice. As stated at 3.8 above, Vodafone and Cellnet were obliged under their licence conditions to sell their services through retailers, and this condition was retained in their modified licences to prevent them from taking unfair advantage of their market positions.

3.11   MAIN ISSUES FOR THE DGT IN THE 1990s

In addition to providing a competitive framework, the DGT had to face a number of regulatory issues which were addressed to various extents during the 1990s. Some are the subject of the other chapters in this book (such as international accounting rates, data protection and privacy, convergence, rules on ownership and global alliances, and the Internet and telephony); others are briefly outlined below.

3.11.1   Universal service

The rationale behind universal service 'is to ensure that those telecommunications services which are used by the majority and which are essential to full social and economic inclusion are made available to everybody upon reasonable request in an appropriate fashion and at an affordable price'.[10] This

---

[10] *Universal Telecommunication Services: A Consultative Document issued by the Director-General of Telecommunications* (London, OFTEL, July 1999).

obligation was included in the licences of BT and Kingston Communications in the Hull area, and could be viewed as a creature of policy.

BT and Kingston Communications were obliged under their respective licences to provide a basic level of service at geographically averaged prices. In addition, they had to provide a network of public telephone boxes and schemes for low-income households. For the consumer, this meant that they were guaranteed a basic voice service at a set price from, for example, BT. On the other hand, BT prices were slightly higher as it had to subsidise those areas that were not as profitable.

The scheme has been successful in achieving 96 per cent penetration,[11] and the current question is whether the level of universal service should now be increased. At present, basic voice telephony is provided, but as technology has advanced it has become clear that to ensure full social and economic inclusion, higher bandwidth services may need to be provided. Thus the debate is whether it is time to extend the scope of universal service, or whether this is not as yet required.

BT's licence states that:

> The Licensee shall provide to every person who requests the provision of such services at any place in the Licensed Area: voice telephony services and other telecommunication services consisting in the conveyance of messages, by means of the Applicable Systems except to the extent that the Director is satisfied that any reasonable demand is or is to be met by other means and that accordingly it would not be reasonable in the circumstances to require the licensee to provide the services requested; and the Licensee shall ensure that Applicable Systems are installed, kept installed and run for those purposes. (Condition 1)

BT therefore is obliged to ensure both that people are connected and that the infrastructure is maintained. This is in contrast to Mercury and other operators, whose licences do not require them to provide a universal service. It can be seen, however, that the obligation is subject to the opinion of the DGT, who first had to interpret the meaning of 'reasonable demand' in the PanAmSat dispute (22 March 1988). The DGT ruled that 'reasonable demand is primarily demonstrated in the market: reasonable demand exists if one or more customers will pay a fair price for the service', suggesting that the DGT has extensive powers in respect of BT's licence.

Subsequent conditions place further obligations on BT. Condition 2, for example, requires that the company provides services in rural areas, a responsibility inherited from the Post Office. Condition 11 specifies that call box services must be provided in all BT's public telephone boxes.[12] There is an obligation on all public telecommunication operators to provide access to the public emergency call service by dialling 999 or 112 (Telecommunications (Single Emergency Call Number) Regulations 1992 (SI 1992 No. 2875)).

---

[11] See OFTEL, *Communications Regulation in the UK* (London, OFTEL, 2000).
[12] Condition 11.2 lists the instances in which BT may cease to provide the services, such as when continued provision is impracticable or revenue falls below a stated minimum figure.

Thus, having established 96 per cent penetration through universal service, the question for the 1990s was whether the obligation should be extended to include the provision of broadband services. This relates to the notion that information is the new resource to which all people should have access at a reasonable price. The European Commission wish to prevent what they term a 'two-tier-society',[13] whereby some people have access to the new broadband information services while others are excluded. In 1999, OFTEL concluded that although the concept of universal service should not be extended at the present time, the matter should remain under review. It was its opinion that when the majority of the population were taking advantage of higher broadband services and they were 'essential for full economic and social inclusion'[14] the universal service obligation might be extended.[15]

The other issue relating to universal service is funding.[16] At present, BT and Kingston Communications bear the cost of their USO, and it is felt that they obtain more benefit from providing the service, in the form of positive brand image and the fact that uneconomic customers are likely to remain with BT when they become 'economic customers'. European law does allow a fund under which all the operators share the cost of the USO, but this can be established only where an unfair burden is placed on BT and Kingston. OFTEL calculates that the net benefit for BT is £8 million and the net cost is £12 million, and currently concludes that there is not an unfair burden on BT.

OFTEL did propose two alternative forms of funding:[17] an actual fund and a virtual fund. OFTEL proposed that an independent company administer the actual fund to which all operators would contribute. The virtual fund, preferred by OFTEL, requires OFTEL to collect information regarding contribution levels. This information would be passed to the public network operators, who would make their contributions directly to the universal service operators thereby eliminating the need for a central fund. The essential characteristic which each fund possesses is that it allows funding on a transparent and proportional basis.

Other options discussed include the competitive tendering of the provision of basic telecom services to uneconomic areas and the concept of 'pay or play'. The latter allows operators to provide services to low-income customers, and in so doing the operators become eligible for universal service funding.

For the time being OFTEL would appear to have rejected all these funding alternatives.[18]

---

[13] *Communication to the European Parliament, the Council, the Economic and Social Committee and the Committee of the Regions: Universal Service for Telecommunications in the Perspective of a Fully Liberalised Environment* (1996).

[14] OFTEL, *op. cit.* n. 10.

[15] See OFTEL, *Review of Universal Telecommunications Services: A Consultative Document* (London, OFTEL, 2000).

[16] *Ibid.*

[17] See footnote 10 – Proposed arrangements for Universal Service in the UK from 1997.

[18] OFTEL, *op. cit.* n. 15, chap. 4.

3.11.2 Interconnection

Competition is of paramount importance, as without it the larger operators would be at a distinct advantage due to the large customer base of their fully developed networks. In a market where numerous companies provide customers with telecommunication services, it is important that a customer on one system can communicate with customers using separate providers, and this is where interconnection comes into play. Without interconnection agreements, parties on different networks would be unable to communicate with one another. Thus provisions have been implemented to ensure that calls originating on one network are able to pass across other networks to their final destination.

Condition 13 of BT's PTO licence could be considered one of the most important provisions, as liberalisation may not have been realised without it. This concerns the ability of operators to enter into an agreement for interconnection with the BT network. Without such a condition, companies would have found it impossible to compete with BT as they would have had no access to the established national network. In 1991 Condition 13B was attached, allowing interconnection to be guaranteed by interfaces to be specified by the DGT. The notion of equal access to the existing network allows BT to impose a charge upon other operators to connect to its network, but this must be the same for all operators. BT was also required under its licence to use the proceeds to defray the cost of fulfilling its universal service obligation.

The licence therefore grants operators the right to obtain interconnection agreements, but such a right would be of no value if the underlying technology were not compatible. In this regard operators must ensure that their equipment and networks can be interconnected with those of other operators. To ensure that this is the case, operators are obliged to publish the technical specifications of their commonly used interfaces.[19] This enables new entrants to check the specifications prior to developing their own systems.

The outcome of interconnection is that operators have the ability to serve a larger customer base than those connected to their own network. This results in the ability to compete without having a nationwide infrastructure already in place.

The DGT plays an important role in stipulating conditions in interconnection agreements and has the power to intervene at the request of either party. Under the Telecommunications (Interconnection) Regulations 1997 (SI 1997 No. 2931), reg. 6 he may stipulate that either party must obey a specific condition. Under reg. 7(3), the DGT must ensure that any condition is objective, proportionate and non-discriminatory. Under reg. 6(6), in the

---

[19] Parliament and Council Directive 98/10/EC on the application of open network provision to voice telephony and on universal service for telecommunications in a competitive environment (revised voice telephony), (1998) OJ L101 at Art. 11.2. This condition requires that details of technical interface specifications for network access be provided to national regulatory bodies. In addition, where new technology is to be incorporated, the specifications should be communicated prior to implementation.

event of a dispute the DGT must attempt to bring about a resolution within six months of the parties seeking help. It should be noted that any decision made by the DGT relating to an interconnection dispute can be the subject of judicial review (see *Mercury Communications Ltd* v *Director-General of Telecommunications* [1996] 1 All ER 575). In arriving at a decision the DGT must act fairly and have regard to the market (reg. 6(8)).

3.11.3　Numbering schemes, portability and carrier pre-selection

Originally, BT administered the numbering scheme, but this was viewed as a barrier to other telecommunication providers. As stated at 3.10 above, since 1994 OFTEL has managed the national numbering scheme, under which it allocates numbers to other operators.

In a liberalised environment consumers have the ability to choose which provider they want, but market conditions failed to ensure that the transition was an easy one. Changing operator meant having to change telephone number, and this in turn resulted in extra cost for the consumer with regard to notifying people of the number change. Consequently, although the market was liberalised, barriers still existed to prevent consumers from taking advantage of the competitive prices. This situation has been remedied by number portability, which allows customers who change their service provider to retain their number on the fixed public telephone network. Consumers benefit from number portability as it enables them to exercise real choice and take advantage of the telecommunications market.

The MMC inquiry[20] on portability held that the DGT had the power to determine the charges for providing the service. The referral was made by the DGT when BT refused to accept a modification to its licence which had the effect of granting to the DGT the power of determining the cost of portability. The MMC found that the DGT did have the power to alter BT's licence and stipulate what BT was entitled to charge. BT argued that the cost of providing number portability should be borne by the operator requesting the service. Other operators, specifically Videotron, argued that operators should bear their own costs. The MMC concluded that the costs should be allocated between the parties, with BT bearing the greater proportion.

Number portability is to be distinguished from number mobility. The latter allows consumers to retain the geographic number when they change address. Number portability only covers the situation where consumers change their network operator but retain their geographic address. From 1 January 2000, companies have had to allow new customers to retain their existing telephone number[21] under the number portability rules, but have no obligation to allow them to retain their number when they also change address.

Another mechanism that allows new operators to compete is carrier pre-selection. This allows users to select another carrier for particular

---

[20] Inquiry by the Monopolies and Mergers Commission into Telephone Number Portability: Explanatory Statement from the Director General of Telecommunications (27 April 1995).
[21] OFTEL Numbering Directive: Number Portability Requirements (October 1999 and January 2000).

services, e.g., calls to the US, even though they subscribe to a specific operator. Previously, carrier pre-selection involved the consumer dialling an access code prior to each call in order that the other operator could carry the particular call. This had disadvantages, in that BT would automatically carry the call where the code was not dialled. The EC Numbering Directive[22] requires that after an initial selection the chosen carrier will automatically carry all calls, thereby eliminating the need to dial the access code every time. The system allows various options so that national and international calls can be carried by different operators. By dialling the access code under the new regime the main operator (generally BT) would carry the call.

The technology for carrier pre-selection was required to be implemented by those companies with significant market power by 1 January 2000. BT successfully sought a deferral on technical grounds, despite the fact that companies such as Deutsche Telekom and France Télécom were technically ready for carrier pre-selection. Carrier pre-selection is viewed by the EU as a means of facilitating more competition, largely through service providers. OFTEL has reluctantly accepted this approach, favouring infrastructure development as the main means of competition, which is perhaps why the regulator agreed to BT's deferral.

3.11.4 Directory information

As with all areas of telecommunications, it is the competition aspect here that is important. The party in possession of directory information obtains a competitive advantage and a barrier to other entrants is created. BT therefore is obliged to make directory information available to organisations that wish to provide a directory information service.[23]

3.11.5 Mobile telephony

Mobile telephony became increasingly significant during the 1990s. In contrast to other forms of telephony, there were only four operators by the end of 2000, the main reason for which was spectrum scarcity. Spectrum is a finite resource, and demand for bandwidths suitable for mobile communications has been increasing. Spectrum congestion and shortage have been hindering growth in this field, although technological advances have meant that higher frequencies can now be used. These factors combined to result in a situation which necessitated efficient management. The Government decided that for the third generation mobile networks, the most efficient use of spectrum would be to sell licences through an auction system.

The Radiocommunications Agency has the responsibility of managing the civil radio spectrum. The Agency grants licences on behalf of the Secretary of State under the Wireless Telegraphy Act 1949 and allocates specific frequencies. Telecommunication services require two licences to operate: one

---

[22] Directive 98/61/EC, amending Directive 97/33/EC with regard to operator number portability and carrier pre-selection (1998) OJ L268.
[23] See *Statement on Responses to the OFTEL Statement on the Provision of Directory Information Services and Products* (London, OFTEL, 1998).

under the Wireless Telegraphy Act 1949; one under the Telecommunications Act 1984. The importance of the Wireless Telegraphy Act 1998 was that it allowed licence fees to reflect the market value of the spectrum, rather than it being associated with the administrative costs of spectrum management by the Radiocommunications Agency.[24] This meant that spectrum pricing would reflect market demand and even out areas of disproportion, as those companies possessing smaller amounts of spectrum would pay less.

Prior to the new pricing structure much of the spectrum was badly managed, and such failure to make efficient use of this finite resource resulted in reduced international competitiveness. There existed little incentive for users to relinquish their unused spectrum, or to develop technology to ensure that all spectrum was used to its full potential. The system positively encouraged hoarding.

In contrast, it was argued that auctioning allowed possession of spectrum for third generation mobile communication to be determined by those who valued the spectrum most as the cost was set by the market. The auction process resulted in five third generation licences being granted in 2000, with one to the new entrant TIW UMTS (UK) Ltd. The process raised over £22 billion, with each licence costing approximately £4 billion. Those who bid successfully are required to provide a third generation network that covers at least 80 per cent of the UK population by 2007.

The auctioning of third generation spectrum[25] allowed new network operators to enter the market, but upon gaining entry such operators could still face disadvantages. Second generation operators who achieved third generation licences have the ability to use their second generation networks to provide their services. New entrants, however, will be forced to offer only a limited service while they develop their networks, thus producing a competitive disparity. It is for this reason that second generation operators who succeeded in obtaining third generation spectrum were required to accept a condition obliging them to offer roaming services to the new entrants (see Wireless Telegraphy Act 1998, s. 3).

Roaming is the system used by the customer of a mobile operator of another operator's network. It allows the entrant to utilise second generation networks for voice, facsimile and short message services. This occurs where the customer is outside the range of the mobile operator's base station. As with most conditions in the telecommunications market, the reason behind this was to eliminate barriers to entry to the market. OFTEL hopes that the roaming agreement can be reached commercially without legislative intervention. However, where this is not the case, the DGT could intervene. Under the National Roaming Licence Condition (see Chapter 4), roaming need not be provided until the network of the new player covers 20 per cent of the UK population, but this should be applicable only until 31 December 2009. New entrants therefore have a suitable period to develop their networks while enjoying the technology to compete with the other operators.

---

[24] See various consultation papers on the Agency's website – www.radio.gov.uk.
[25] See www.spectrumauctions.gov.uk.

In the 1998–99 review of the mobile market OFTEL concluded that the market was not fully competitive but that competition was developing, and despite the entry barrier of obtaining spectrum, it had the potential to become effectively competitive. Despite the awarding of third generation licences, a 2000–2001 review has subsequently been announced, which will consider how competition has developed since the 1998–99 review and take a two-year forward look at the prospects for effective competition in the mobile market. Depending on the result of this review, OFTEL will set out its proposals for withdrawing, continuing with, amending or introducing new regulation for the UK mobile market.

3.12 THE TWENTY-FIRST CENTURY

In the introduction to this book we pointed to the issues which will affect the development of telecoms generally, but which equally will apply to the UK in the new millennium. The need to regulate in the 1980s to achieve a competitive environment was followed in the 1990s by the start of deregulation as the competitive playing field became more even. However, BT still has significant market power in some sectors as we enter the twenty-first century, and therefore the regulator will have to achieve a careful balance as it relaxes controls. The forces for reform, however, are no longer dictated by the UK Government or by OFTEL. On the technical side, convergence will affect the regulatory regime (see Chapter 12), and reforms from Europe (see Chapter 8) are likely to mean that OFTEL will soon no longer exist in its present state. Ultimately, the need for a special telecoms regulator could fall away and the sector will be governed by general competition controls.

CHAPTER FOUR

Operator Licences

Timothy Leeson

4.1 INTRODUCTION

4.1.1 Grant of a licence

Under the Telecommunications Act 1984, s. 7(1), a licence to run a telecommunication system may be granted either by the Secretary of State for Trade and Industry (the Secretary of State) after consultation with the Director-General of the Office of Telecommunications (DGT), or, with the consent of, or in accordance with a general authorisation given by, the Secretary of State, by the DGT. Running a telecommunications system without a licence, or providing telecommunications services which are not authorised by a licence is an offence (Telecommunications Act 1984, s. 5).

4.1.2 Licence conditions

Licences generally take a standard form. They will contain:

    (a)   conditions which appear to the Secretary of State and/or the DGT to be 'requisite or expedient' having regard to their general duties and the need to comply with relevant EU legislation (Telecommunications Act 1984, s. 7(5)(a), as amended by Telecommunications (Licensing) Regulations 1997 (SI 1997 No. 2930), reg. 3(3)(a));[1]
    (b)   conditions requiring the payment of licence fees to the Secretary of State (Telecommunications Act 1984, s. 7(5)(b));

---

[1] For the general duties of the Secretary of State and the DGT, see the Telecommunications Act 1984, s. 3. As to s. 3, see Chapter 3.

(c) in the case of class licences (see 4.1.3), conditions requiring persons who fall within that class of persons to which the licence relates to notify the Secretary of State or the DGT of their intention to run a telecommunication system under that licence (Telecommunications Act 1984, s. 7(5)(c), as substituted by the Telecommunications (Licensing) Regulations 1997 (SI 1997 No. 2930), reg. 3(3)(b)).

It was not until the implementation of the Licensing Directive[2] that the requirement existed to grant licences on the basis of conditions which must be 'objectively justified in relation to the service concerned, non-discriminatory, proportionate and transparent' (Art. 3(2)). Almost three years after the coming into effect of the enabling regulations, consequential licence amendments are still being made (see footnotes 2 and 8 below).

Since the adoption of the Services Directive,[3] there has been an acceleration in regulatory activity at the European Union level. Arguably, this activity is now also being conducted on a global basis (see 4.12 below and Chapter 11). For the United Kingdom, these issues have not always been dealt with by way of legislation, since, it is argued, many of the issues are addressed by the regime set up pursuant to the Telecommunications Act 1984. Many, however, have now formed the opinion that the regime is ready for overhaul and that amending primary legislation is required. As this chapter will show, this view is not without merit.

4.1.3 Individual and class licences

It is important to recognise that there are two principal types of licence. The class licence relates (as the name would suggest) to a class of persons rather than to an individual and is a general authorisation applying to any persons performing activities that fall within its scope. On the other hand, an individual licence must be specifically applied for and, if granted, applies to the applicant only. Authorisations are increasingly being drafted as class licences, avoiding the need for prospective licensees to apply for an individual licence.[4] The DGT must keep a register of licences granted (Telecommunications Act 1984, s. 7).[5] The principal individual licence is that relating to public telecommunications operators (see 4.1.4 below).

---

[2] Council Directive 97/13/EC on a common framework for general authorisations and individual licences in the field of telecommunications services, (1997) OJ L 117/15, as implemented by the Telecommunications (Licensing) Regulations 1997 (SI 1997 No. 2930).
[3] Directive 90/388/EEC on competition in the markets for telecommunication services, (1990) OJ L 192/10.
[4] *Fifth Report on the Implementation of the Telecommunications Regulatory Package: Communication from the Commission to the European Parliament, the Council, the Economic and Social Committee of the Regions*, COM (1999) 537 final at Annex 3 (Fifth Report), http://europa.eu.int/comm/information_society/policy/telecom/5threport/index_en.htm. See also Art. 3(2) of the Licensing Directive on the considerations which must be taken into account when issuing individual licences.
[5] The register may be inspected at the Office of Telecommunications, 50 Ludgate Hill, London EC4M 7JJ.

4.1.4 Public telecommunications operators

A public telecommunications operator (PTO) is a person authorised by a licence to run a public telecommunications system[6] and in respect of whom s. 8 of the Telecommunications Act 1984 applies (1984 Act, s. 9(3)). Section 8 provides specific conditions that PTO licences must contain. Put simply, these include obligations:

(a) to provide telecommunication services specified in the licence;

(b) to connect to any telecommunication system, or permit the connection to the PTO's telecommunication system, as specified in the licence;

(c) to 'permit the provision' of the licensed services by means of the PTO's telecommunication system;

(d) not to 'show undue preference to, or to exercise undue discrimination' against any persons (including in respect of charges and terms and conditions);

(e) to publish, in accordance with the PTO's licence, notices of charges, terms and conditions, permissions and connections as applicable from time to time.[7]

4.1.5 PTO licence – general

Following the adoption of the Licensing Directive (see 4.1.2 above), the DGT has been undertaking a detailed review of the UK licensing regime. To the extent that it related to PTO licences, this review has now largely been completed. The five statutory instruments bringing into effect the current forms of PTO licence (and ending a long consultation exercise) came into force on 27 September 1999.[8]

There are now four types of PTO licences:

---

[6] This is defined as telecommunications system designated as a public telecommunications system by the Secretary of State (Telecommunications Act 1984, s. 9). This will be set out in the relevant licence. See 4.2 below.

[7] Note that there are further obligations in s. 8(2) and s. 8(3). See also the obligations on 'public operators' in the Telecommunications (Open Network Provision) (Voice Telephony) Regulations 1998 (SI 1998 No. 1580), reg. 21(8)(b) ('Voice Telephony Regulations').

[8] The Telecommunications (Licence Modification) (Fixed Voice Telephony and International Facilities Operator Licences) Regulations 1999 (SI 1999 No. 2451); the Telecommunications (Licence Modification) (Mobile Public Telecommunication Operators) Regulations 1999 (SI 1999 No. 2452); the Telecommunications (Licence Modification) (British Telecommunications plc) Regulations 1999 (SI 1999 No. 2453); the Telecommunications (Licence Modification) (Cable and Local Delivery Operator Licences) Regulations 1999 (SI 1999 No. 2454); and the Telecommunications (Licence Modification) (Kingston Communications (Hull) plc) Regulations 1999 (SI 1999 No. 2455). The Telecommunications (Licence Modification) (Amendment) Regulations 2000 (SI 2000 No. 1713), made minor corrective amendments to some licences.

(a)   a standard PTO licence for operators of a fixed public telephone system[9] (commonly known as the standard fixed PTO licence);
(b)   a PTO licence for BT plc and one for Kingston Communications plc;
(c)   a PTO licence for operators of a fixed public telephone system provided by way of cable (commonly known as the cable PTO licence);
(d)   a standard PTO licence for operators of a mobile public telephone system (commonly known as the mobile PTO licence).[10]

However, it would not be correct to conclude that this has introduced a simplified, easily comprehensible licensing regime. Paradoxically, the size and structure of the most standard PTO licence is daunting. For example, the standard fixed PTO licence contains four Schedules and an Annex, the first Schedule being in two parts, the second part containing 64 Conditions (Condition 64 containing five pages of exceptions and limitations). 'Many new entrants view the sheer length of licences as substantially reducing their comprehensibility and transparency while increasing the regulatory burden, in particular on small operators. Operators are confused as to which licence conditions apply to whom.'[11] The PTO licence for BT is even more cumbersome.

It gets worse. In order to interpret this document, it is essential to understand a mass of (often, not entirely consistent) EU legislation and implementing secondary legislation and guidelines issued by the Secretary of State and the DGT, respectively.

The following analysis sets out the key provisions of the PTO licence, using the standard fixed PTO licence as the basis. This will be contrasted with the other principal PTO licences as appropriate. Note that all references to Conditions and Schedules in this Chapter are to the standard fixed PTO licence unless otherwise stated.

---

[9] As to fixed public telephone system, see the Voice Telephony Regulations, *supra* n. 7, at reg. 2(1). This refers to the definition 'public telephone system', which then refers to 'fixed public telephone network' which is defined in reg. 2(2) as: 'the public switched telecommunications network which supports the transfer between network termination points at fixed locations of speech and 3.1kHz bandwidth audio information, to support *inter alia*: (1) voice telephony; (2) facsimile Group III communications, in accordance with ITU-T Recommendations in the T-series; (3) voice band data transmission via modems at a rate of at least 2400 bit/s, in accordance with the ITU Recommendations in the V-series; and where access to the end-user's network termination point is via a number or numbers in the numbering plan.' Some of these definitions originate from Directive 97/33/EC (on interconnection in telecommunications with regard to ensuring universal service and interoperability through application of the principles of open network provision), which is partly the cause of this rather clumsy drafting.
[10] As to mobile public telephone systems, see the Voice Telephony Regulations, *supra* n. 7, at reg. 2(1). Again, the drafting is rather convoluted (and indeed, circular), referring to the definition of 'public telephone system', 'mobile public telephone network', 'mobile public telephone system' and 'publicly available mobile telephone services'. Put simply, this is a system where the network termination points are 'designed or adapted to be capable of being used while in motion' (see definition of 'mobile public telephone system').
[11] See *Fifth Report*, *supra* n. 4 at p. 34, Annex 3.

4.2 PTO LICENCE

4.2.1 Licence

The two-page section entitled 'Licence' at the front of the document is signed on behalf of the Secretary of State and records the fact that a licence has been granted. Subject to the revocation provisions (which are set out in Schedule 2), the licence is granted for a period of 25 years from the date of signature (PTO licence, para. 3). As licences which existed before the implementation of the Licensing Directive were revoked and substituted with the so-called 'new form' licences, the date of signature (and thereby the start of the 25-year period) is taken to be the commencement date of the pre-existing licence.[12] For example, the duration of the BT plc PTO licence is 25 years from 22 June 1984.

Paragraph 1 of the Licence is also important as this sets out the permission given by the licence. In short, the licensee is authorised to run the applicable systems, and may connect to other telecommunications systems and provide the telecommunications services detailed in Schedule 3.

4.2.2 Applicable systems, connection authorisation and service authorisation

It is essential to look carefully at the definitions of applicable systems, the service authorisation and the connection authorisation in any licence. Unfortunately, to do this, the reader has to navigate various sections of the PTO licence (particularly in respect of applicable systems).[13] The type of drafting is unnecessarily convoluted and there is a high degree of repetition between these sections and Part 2, Conditions 1–3 (as to which see 4.3.1 below). Put briefly, the definitions 'applicable systems', 'service authorisation' and 'connection authorisation' establish a framework for PTO licences generally, and Conditions 1–3 provide greater detail of specific PTO services. These should be combined in a more simplified structure.

4.2.2.1 Applicable system   Essentially, the applicable system is a telecommunication system (as such term is defined in Telecommuncations Act 1984, s. 4(1)) which conveys signals:

(a)   to or from one network termination point ('NTP') to another place which is not an NTP (which relates to an international call); and/or

---

[12] In respect of fixed public telecommunication systems, the 'new form' PTO licence replaced various pre-existing individual licences, most notably, the International Facilities Licence (commonly known as the 'IFL') and the 'old form' PTO licence. Many operators had both licences. In this case, the commencement date of the 'new form' PTO licence was set by reference to the commencement date of tne 'old form' PTO licence (irrespective of the commencement date of the IFL).

[13] Essential elements of the definition of 'applicable systems' are to be found in para. 6 of the licence and the multiplicity of definitions in Schedule 1, Part 1 and Annex A. This becomes even more difficult when the need arises to consider the defined terms.

(b) within two NTPs which, in most cases, amounts to a domestic call.[14]

In the case of fixed telecommunications systems, the NTP is up to and including so-called network connecting apparatus or network termination and testing apparatus (i.e., a connection either to approved terminating equipment, or to a telecommunications system run by another operator; see Annex A, paras 1 and 2). For mobile telecommunication systems, this point is 'the last point at which Messages are received (i.e., at a base station), or the first point at which Messages are received' on such a system (i.e., to or from the handset antenna), as applicable (see Annex A, s. 2, s. (iii)). This means that the mobile operator not only takes responsibility for transmitting the signal from its base stations in the correct form, but also takes responsibility that such signal is received in that form at the user's handset. Operators contracting on a commercial basis would not normally accept liability for the latter (or so-called 'other' liability). Whether this much-discussed point is of material significance is, however, open to doubt.

It is important to recognise that the applicable system does not include terminal apparatus 'installed in premises occupied by a person' to whom the operator provides the telecommunications services. This apparatus would form part of the customer's system which is separately licensable (Annex A, para. 1(b)).[15]

4.2.2.2 Service authorisation and connection authorisation The service authorisation (which, as the name would suggest, relates to the services which the relevant operator is authorised to provide) and the connection authorisation (that is to say, what those services may connect to) are set out in Schedule 3 to the licence. The service authorisation (para. 3) is very broad, in that it allows the operator to provide any telecommunication services subject to certain exceptions.[16] These broadly relate to the subject matter considered by other licences.[17] Paragraph 2(a) of the connection authorisation allows the operator to connect its applicable system to that provided by another operator. As most (if not all) PTOs will need to interconnect to BT plc's network infrastructure, this is an important provision.

---

[14] Note that there are also provisions relating to 'call offices' (defined in para. 2, Annex A) and includes telephone boxes and public call centres. See Annex A, para. 2.

[15] This is licensed as part of the class licence for the running of self-provided telecommunication services or the class licence to run branch systems to provide telecommunications services. See 4.18.1 and 4.18.2.

[16] The 'old form' PTO licence authorised the provision of domestic connections and services only. Where, for example, an operator provided facilities to convey overseas telecommunications services, an international facilities licence (IFL) was required. This distinction no longer exists. As to international conveyance services and publicly available telecommunications services, see Schedule 1, Part 1. Also see 4.3.1.

[17] For example, para. 3(b) refers to the conditional access class licence and para. 3(c) refers to the access control class licence. Note also that the previous restriction in para. 3(a), which prevented the conveyance of 'entertainment services' by PTOs, has now been removed pursuant to the Broadcasting (Restrictions on the Holding of Licences) (Amendment Order) 1999 (SI 1999 No. 122).

4.3 STANDARD CONDITIONS – SERVICE PROVISION OBLIGATIONS

4.3.1 Publicly available telecommunications services, international conveyance services and entertainment services

Condition 1.1 requires operators providing publicly available telephone services (defined in Schedule 1, Part 1 to mean fixed publicly available telephone services and/or mobile publicly available telephone services; see 4.1.5) to provide so-called directory services and otherwise comply with Condition 2. Condition 2 relates broadly to the making available of directories and associated information to the extent that such information is not withheld by the relevant subscriber.[18] Note also that, under Condition 4, providers of publicly available telephone services are required to provide operator assistance, directory services and emergency services (i.e., '112' and '999') at no charge.

If the operator does not provide publicly available telephone services, Condition 1.2 obliges it to comply with Condition 3.[19] Condition 3 obliges the operator to take all reasonable steps to:

(a)   provide international conveyance services to any Schedule 2 public operator (see 4.4.5 below) who requests such services to the extent necessary to satisfy all reasonable demands for such services; or[20]

(b)   provide international directory services (which relates to information concerning users located outside the UK).

International conveyance services are the sending and/or receiving of signals to and/or from the applicable system in the UK to and/or from a licensed system overseas (Schedule 1, Part 1). Cable operators are required to run their applicable systems such that they convey services licensed under Part II of the Broadcasting Act 1990 (so-called 'entertainment' services) to any person who reasonably requests them in the relevant licensable area (Condition 1.3, PTO Licence).[21]

Note also that mobile operators are required to provide certain radio-based services if required to do so by the Crown, emergency organisations and/or certain other utility providers (Condition 1.4).

---

[18] As to the rights of subscribers to withhold personal data from directories available to the public, see Council Directive 97/66/EC on the Processing of Personal Data and the Protection of Privacy in the Telecommunications Sector, (1997) OJ L 24/1, http://europa.eu.int/eur-lex/en/lif/dat/1997/en_397L0066.html ('Telecommunications Data Protection Directive'), at Art. 11.

[19] If the operator provides both publicly available telephone services and international conveyance services, presumably both Conditions 1.1 and 1.2 apply. The exclusory nature of the drafting in Condition 1 is not entirely clear on this point.

[20] This is (presumably) a drafting mistake and should read 'and' given that the qualified service obligation in Condition 1 of the IFL related to the provision of international conveyance services.

[21] Note that licences granted under the Broadcasting Act 1990 were granted on the basis of specific geographic areas. See also *Broadband Britain – a Fresh Look at the Entertainment Restrictions*, 23 April 1998 (issued by the Secretary of State and the Secretary of State of the Department of Culture, Media and Sport).

4.3.2 Publication of charges, terms and conditions

Condition 7 has been revised to take into account the requirements of the Revised Voice Telephony Directive.[22] Amongst other things, it requires the operator to publish for consumers its standard charges, terms and conditions (including any minimum contract periods and any terms for renewal). These must be accurate and clear (Condition 7.1). Condition 7.2 requires the publication of charges, terms and conditions and certain other details in respect of certain services that the operator is obliged to provide.

Note that Condition 58 also sets out obligations concerning the publication of charges, terms and conditions, but only in circumstances where it has been determined that the operator is obliged to publish such details in relation to the provision of a particular service. This is distinct from Condition 7, which applies only to Conditions 2–6, but is broadly similar in structure (e.g., there is a detailed notice and publication procedure for amendments to charges and/or terms and conditions).

4.4 STANDARD CONDITIONS – CONNECTION AND ROAMING OBLIGATIONS

4.4.1 Connection of systems and apparatus

Condition 5.1 (Condition 5.2, mobile PTO licence) sets out the basic obligation to provide connection to the applicable system at the NTP. This applies only to the extent that the connecting party's equipment is approved or compliant with the relevant connection requirements. (As to 'approved' see the Telecommunications Act 1984, s. 22 and Condition 5.2; as to 'compliant with the relevant connection requirements', see the definition of 'compliant terminal equipment' in Schedule 1, Part 1.)

4.4.2 Service provider obligation

Condition 5.1 of the mobile PTO licence sets out a key obligation relating to mobile operators, namely the requirement to provide mobile radio telecommunication services to service providers (i.e., resellers of mobile airtime). It is important to recognise that this is triggered by a market influence determination by the DGT (see 4.9 below). Such a determination has been made in respect of (and accordingly this Condition applies to) BT Cellnet and Vodafone Airtouch plc.[23] This Condition is subject to the operator's right to step in, in circumstances where the service provider ceases to provide the mobile radio telecommunication services. In doing this, the operator needs to

---

[22] Parliament and Council Directive 98/10/EC on the Application of Open Network Provision (ONP) to Voice Telephony and on Universal Service for Telecommunications in a Competitive Environment, (1998) OJ L 101/24, as implemented by the Voice Telephony Regulations, *supra* n. 7.

[23] See *Director's Statement, OFTEL's Review of the Mobile Market* (London, OFTEL, 1999), http://www.oftel.gov.uk/competition/mmrv799.htm, and *Director's Notice*, dated 24 March 2000, that recording Vodafone Airtouch plc and BT Cellnet continue to have market influence.

give notice to the DGT and provide the end-customer with a list of other service providers who can provide the services (Condition 65.1, mobile PTO licence). Note that the operator must not 'unfairly promote' its own services at the expense of those of the relevant service provider and must provide the services directly until 'immediately prior to such cessation' (Condition 65, mobile PTO licence).[24]

4.4.3 Interconnection

Interconnection is defined in Schedule 1, Part 1 as:

> [T]he physical and logical linking of telecommunications systems used by the same or a different organisation in order to allow the users of one organisation to communicate with users of the same or another organisation or to access services provided by another organisation irrespective of whether services are provided by the parties involved or other parties who have access to the systems.[25]

The ability of one operator to interconnect to another has been and will continue to be one of the key areas of consideration for any regime of telecommunications regulation. This is especially the case in circumstances where new operators require interconnection to an incumbent's system in order to originate, deliver and/or terminate calls.

4.4.4 The obligation to interconnect

Condition 9.1 requires an operator, if so requested by a Schedule 2 public operator (see further 4.4.5), to negotiate with that operator with a view to concluding an interconnection agreement (or an amendment to an existing interconnection agreement) within a reasonable period.

The extent of this obligation is not entirely clear. The text originates from the Interconnection Directive, Art. 4(1),[26] which merely states that there is an obligation to 'negotiate interconnection', and the UK implementing legislation expresses this in a similar manner.[27] However, the language 'with a view to concluding an . . . agreement' appears neither in the Directive nor in the implementing legislation, both of which merely allude to an open-ended obligation to negotiate. It is difficult to be clear about the extent of

---

[24] This rather presumes that the service provider will provide the operator with adequate notice to enable it to take over the services. Language such as 'immediately before, on or after cessation' would be more practical. Note that the Condition 65 step-in right applies whether or not the licensee has been determined by the DGT to have market influence.

[25] This definition originates from Directive 97/33/EC on interconnection in telecommunications with regard to ensuring universal service and interoperability through application of the principles of open network provision (ONP), (1997) OJ L 268/37 ('the interconnection Directive'), at Art. (2)(1)(a), as implemented by the Telecommunications (Interconnection) Regulations 1997 (SI 1997 No. 2931) ('the Interconnection Regulations').

[26] This has been implemented by the Interconnection Regulations, *ibid.*, at reg. 3(1).

[27] *Ibid.* Note that Art. 4(1) of the Interconnection Directive deals with rights to negotiate in addition to obligations to negotiate interconnection.

either of these obligations. If this falls short of an obligation to conclude agreements, it is difficult to reconcile with the right of either the operator or a Schedule 2 public operator to request that the DGT specify what must be covered in the agreements and any time limits and conditions as appropriate (Condition 9.2).

Note that the obligations on operators with significant market power are more onerous and are dealt with at 4.8 below. Subject to any directions the DGT may give, operators without significant market power may discriminate as to the terms and conditions they negotiate with other operators, provided such discrimination is not undue (Condition 8) or otherwise in breach of the fair trading condition (Condition 31) or the Competition Act 1998 (see 4.7.2 below).

4.4.5 Schedule 2 public operator[28]

Unfortunately, the category of persons who may qualify as a Schedule 2 public operator is somewhat unclear. This term is the legacy of Art. 4(1) of the Interconnection Directive, which relates to organisations authorised to provide public telecommunications networks and/or publicly available telephone services as set out in Annex II of the Directive. Accordingly, such operators are commonly referred to as 'Annex II operators'. The text of Annex II sets out four categories of operators, each of which must be organisations which provide switched and unswitched 'bearer' capabilities. Unfortunately these 'capabilities' are neither defined nor detailed further in the Interconnection Directive.

The difficulties increase when this is set in the context of the UK regulatory regime. Much of the Interconnection Directive concentrates on authorisations to provide telecommunications services. While this may be relevant elsewhere in the EU, the UK regime is based upon running telecommunication systems and regulates the provision of services only to the extent that they must be provided over licensed systems (see the Telecommunications Act 1984, ss. 5–7, particularly s. 5(2)(b)). Moreover, where the Directive makes reference to infrastructure, this is orientated towards 'networks'[29] rather than 'systems', the latter term being considerably wider in scope. Interpretation of the Interconnection Directive in the UK context is, therefore, far from straightforward.

The equivalent regime in the UK prior to the implementation of the Licensing Directive (as reflected in Condition 13 of the 'old form' PTO licence) ascribed rights to operators wishing to interconnect only if they had relevant connectable system (RCS) status. This was also far from ideal and required such operators to have a licensed telecommunications system (which

---

[28] 'Schedule 2' refers here to Schedule 2 of the Interconnection Regulations, *supra* n. 25. This Schedule corresponds to Annex II of the Interconnection Directive. Thus, Schedule 2 operators would generally be those referred to in Annex II. As to Schedule 2 public operators, see PTO licence, Schedule 1, Part 1. The requirements for such operators are set out in the Interconnection Regulations, *supra* n. 25 at Sch. 2.

[29] For example, Art. 1(b) ('public telecommunications network') and Art. 1(c) ('telecommunications network').

did not include systems operating under a class licence) and that such system be provided 'for reward to the general public'. As the DGT had discretion to exclude certain systems, operators were far from certain as to whether RCS and, thereby, interconnection rights would be granted or not. It is difficult to argue that this approach satisfied the objectivity and transparency requirements of the Licensing Directive, Art. 3(2).[30]

Whilst it is clear that a Schedule 2 public operator includes individual licence holders and the operators of the type detailed in subparas (AA)–(EE) of Schedule 1, Part 1, what is not clear is the extent to which the general requirement of 'switched and unswitched bearer capabilities' goes beyond this and, moreover, what type of infrastructure (if any) is required to satisfy this criterion.[31]

The control as to who qualifies as a Schedule 2 public operator in respect of UK operators appears to be that the UK must have notified the European Commission that the relevant organisation is covered by Annex II of the interconnection Directive. To this effect, the prospective Schedule 2 public operator completes an application form (obtainable from OFTEL) to apply for Annex II status.

4.4.6 National roaming condition

Roaming is the use by one operator's subscribers of another operator's network to make or receive calls.[32] As this does not necessarily entail the logical and physical linking of telecommunications networks, the European Commission has determined that it falls outside the scope of the Interconnection Directive.[33] This is despite the fact that roaming enables users of one organisation to communicate with users of another organisation.

This becomes important when considering the recent allocation by auction of radio spectrum for third generation mobile services licences (under the Wireless Telegraphy Act 1998; see 3.11.5). Licence A, one of the five licences to be granted, was reserved for an operator not holding a second generation licence.[34] The other four licences (Licences B–E) were, following the auction,

---

[30] See also *Director's Statement entitled Promoting Competition in Services over Telecommunications Networks* (London, OFTEL, 1997), http://www.oftel.gov.uk/publications/1999/competition/promote/intro.htm.

[31] In *Director's Consultation Document, Rights and Obligations to Interconnect under the EU Interconnection Directive* (London, OFTEL, 1998), Appendix 3, http://www.oftel.gov.uk/publications/1995_98/competition/icd398.htm, there is an explanatory note as to the meaning of 'bearer capabilities'. This seems to suggest that this relates to 'connection services', but this does not specifically address what constitutes 'unswitched bearer capabilities'. At best, it can be concluded that there is little certainty in the understanding of this term.

[32] Usually the subscriber is out of range of his own operator's base stations. See *Director's Consultative Document: Access to Second Generation Mobile Networks for New Entrant Third Generation Mobile Operators* (London, OFTEL, 1999).

[33] See *Information Memorandum: The Next Generation of Mobile Communications* (London, DTI, Radiocommunications Agency, 1999), http://www.radio.gov.uk/rahome.htm. As to the logical and physical linking of telecommunications networks, see 4.4.4.

[34] Those using 'spectrum within the 880–915 Mhz, 925–960 Mhz, 1710–1785 Mhz or 1805–1880 Mhz bands'. Para. 9, national roaming condition.

granted to the existing second generation licensees. Such operators, when launching third generation[35] services, could also offer subscribers access to their second generation systems. Clearly, a new entrant would, without rights of access to other operators' second generation systems, be able to offer services only in areas where its own third generation systems had been developed and would, therefore, suffer a significant competitive disadvantage.

These rights of access would be required irrespective of the market power (whether dominant, significant or influential) of the second generation systems provider and, therefore, could not, it is argued, be made dependent on the application of competition-based triggers[36] or the need to show that any undue discrimination had occurred (as to undue discrimination, dominance, significant market power and market influence, see 4.8–4.9). Specific *ex ante* regulation would be required.

As the new entrant third generation operator cannot be treated as a Schedule 2 public operator (owing to the narrow definition of 'interconnection'), this situation cannot be remedied by way of the obligation to provide connection services pursuant to Condition 9. This is unfortunate.

Unsurprisingly, the language of the national roaming condition is very similar to that used for the regulation of interconnection. Paragraph 1 provides that the mobile operator (the second generation systems provider) is required to negotiate an agreement with a relevant mobile operator (that is to say, the third generation new market entrant) (para. 9), or negotiate an amendment to such an agreement, as the case may be, within a reasonable period. Note that requirements from the third-generation new market entrant and the terms and conditions contained in the agreement must be reasonable, under paras 1 and 2.

In order to prevent the relevant mobile operator relying too heavily on roaming and failing to roll out third generation systems in a timely manner, there are restrictions that may be imposed on the tenure of the agreement concluded between the parties (referred to as a national roaming agreement). The second generation systems provider is not required, under para. 1, to provide the relevant services until the relevant mobile operator has rolled out its third generation network to cover an area in which 20 per cent of the UK population lives, and may cease to provide those services after 31 December 2009. Inevitably, clauses of this nature will be arbitrary, but these requirements seem to be as good as any.[37]

The DGT may, if requested by either party, make a determination in respect of the national roaming agreement concerning:

(a) issues to be covered or observed;
(b) set time limits;

---

[35] Those using 'spectrum within the 1900–1980 Mhz and 2110–2170 Mhz bands'. *Ibid.*

[36] An alternative approach (to consider the third generation new entrant as a service provider for the purposes of Condition 5.1 of the mobile PTO) was considered and rightly rejected by the DGT. Condition 5.1 is triggered by a market influence determination. For further details, see *op. cit.* n. 32. As to market influence, see Part F, fixed/mobile PTO licence. Also, see 4.9 below.

[37] For a fuller discussion of these clauses, see *Director's Statements, OFTEL Statement on National Roaming* (London, OFTEL, July 1999 and October 1999).

(c) whether certain terms are reasonable; and/or
(d) disputes.

The second generation systems provider is obliged to comply with such a determination (paras 2–6). If a dispute occurs, the determination must represent a fair balance between the legitimate interests of both parties, and the DGT is required to take into account certain factors in assessing these interests (para. 6). One of these factors relates specifically to pricing (see 'Retail Minus', national roaming condition, para. 9). Note that the DGT is not required to make determinations where other disputes are pending, or where he has previously resolved a dispute relating to a national roaming agreement involving that relevant mobile operator (national roaming condition, para. 6; note that this is only the basis that the national roaming agreement remains valid and in 'substantially the same form'). This provision reflects the DGT's stated intention not to permit the relevant mobile operator to use 'the dispute resolution procedure to play the second-generation ('2G operators off against each other'.')[38]

The DGT has produced some guidelines in respect of the national roaming condition.[39] However, other than in respect of determinations on pricing, these are not referred to in this condition and, therefore, would seem not to be binding. There are also no expressed rights of appeal.

4.4.7 Co-location and facility sharing

Condition 9.3(f) requires the operator to comply with any facility or property sharing arrangement specified by the DGT, who may 'specify facility or property sharing arrangements (including physical co-location) after an appropriate period for public consultation during which all interested parties must be given an opportunity to express their views' (Telecommunications (Interconnection) Regulations 1997 (SI 1997 No. 2931), reg. 10(3)).

4.5 CONDITIONS – INTERFACES AND ESSENTIAL STANDARD REQUIREMENTS

4.5.1 Publication of interfaces

Under Condition 15, the DGT is required to ensure that operators make available details of technical interface specifications for network access. Additionally, operators are required to give notice of any changes to existing network interface specifications (including withdrawals of commonly provided interfaces) and of the introduction of new network interface specifications.[40] The underlying principle of Condition 15 is that sufficient notice and

---

[38] See National Roaming Licence Condition Guidelines, contained in Annex B to the *Director's Statement on National Roaming* (revised) (London, OFTEL, 1999), http://www.oftel.gov.uk/competition/roam1099.htm.
[39] *Ibid.*
[40] These requirements originate from Art. 11(1) and (4) and Annex II, Part I, Revised Voice Telephony Directive (and reg. 17(2) and Sch. 2 of its implementing legislation, the Voice Telephony Regulations), *supra* n. 22.

details are given (prior to the implementation of the modification) to allow interconnecting operators time to modify their systems.

4.5.2 Essential interfaces

Under Condition 16, the DGT may deem certain interfaces to be essential for the purposes and at the point of interconnection.[41] In a similar vein to Condition 15, Condition 16 provides detail as to the procedures by which the DGT may specify an essential interface. The operator will then be obliged to ensure that this interface is made available to any Schedule 2 public operator in accordance with the relevant standard under Condition 16.4.

4.5.3 Essential requirements and essential public interests

Condition 20 goes beyond issues concerning the point of interconnection and applies to telecommunications service issues more generally. Article 13 of the Revised Voice Telephony Directive sets out a number of requirements which apply in respect of the provision of fixed publicly available telephone services, such as the obligation to take all necessary steps to maintain network security and availability, the interoperability of services, and to ensure the effective use of frequency spectrum and to protect data in accordance with the relevant legislation (see Data Protection Act 1998; Telecommunications (Data Protection and Privacy) Regulations 1999 (SI 1999 No. 2093); Telecommunications (Data Protection and Privacy) (Amendment) Regulations 2000 (SI 2000 No. 157)). These are repeated as duties on the Secretary of State and the DGT in reg. 21 of the implementing legislation (Telecommunications (Open Network Provision) (Voice Telephony) Regulations 1998 (SI 1998 No. 1580)). Condition 20 effectively places the burden of complying with these principles on the operator. Accordingly, Condition 20 does not apply to mobile operators.

4.6 STANDARD CONDITIONS – NUMBERING

4.6.1 Numbering arrangements

It is important to note that numbers are not 'owned' by operators. They are merely allocated by the DGT pursuant to Condition 26 in accordance with the Numbering Conventions, i.e., a set of principles which is published from time to time by the DGT, having consulted with interested parties beforehand. It includes specifications as to prefixes, access codes and portability arrangements, and criteria for allocating and withdrawing numbers (see Condition 26.5(b) for a full list).

The operator must then adopt a Numbering Plan, which details the method by which it allocates numbers to end users, and provide particulars

---

[41] The DGT must (according to Condition 16.2) give the licensee the opportunity to make representations and must consider any that are made before making any direction. See Telecommunications (Interconnection) Regulations 1997 (SI 1997 No. 2931), reg. 7. As to essential interfaces, see Sch. 1, Part I.

of this plan to the DGT.[42] The Numbering Plan must comply with the Numbering Conventions. Note also that Condition 29 obliges operators to provide numbering information to other PTOs in order that such PTOs can provide directory services pursuant to Condition 2 (see 4.3.1 above).

4.6.2   Number portability

Portability is a facility whereby a user who has been provided with a number can continue to use that number irrespective of the identity of the operator (see Telecommunications (Interconnection) (Number Portability, etc.) Regulations 1999 (SI 1999 No. 3449), Sch. 2, Pt I).[43] The relevant provisions are Condition 28 of the fixed PTO licence and Conditions 28 and 68 of the mobile PTO licence. As Condition 28 relates to portability in respect of a fixed public telephone system, it is redundant in the mobile PTO licence. It should, therefore be deleted.

As a result of the implementation of the Numbering Directive,[44] Condition 28 has recently been redrafted. Rather than providing portability to another operator upon request, operators are now required to provide portability on reasonable terms at the request of subscribers (see Condition 28.1; for 'subscribers', see the Number Portability Regulations, Sch. 2, Pt II). This applies to geographic portability (i.e., numbers in the 01 or 02 range) and to non-geographic portability (i.e., numbers such as 070, 080, 0845, 0870 and 090). (As to geographic portability, see the PTO licence, Schedule 1, Part I; as to non-geographic portability, see the Number Portability Regulations, Sch. 2, Pt I.) This leaves operators and service providers to make the appropriate arrangements *inter se*, such that these services can be provided. Put simply, the relevant operator, before it contracts with its customer, must ensure that the relevant facilities are in place (i.e., with the customer's existing telephone company) so that portability can be provided.

For geographic portability, this may not be too onerous, as the operators generally know the other operators operating in a particular area. For non-geographic portability, the situation is quite different, and may involve significant additional costs being borne by operators in certain markets. Whether this regime is realistic remains to be seen.[45]

Conditions 28.1 and 68.2 (of the mobile PTO licence) provide a framework for these arrangements. If requested, the operator must provide portability on 'reasonable terms' and 'in accordance with the Functional

---

[42] The licensee will also have to notify the DGT of any material changes to the Numbering Plan (Condition 26.2). As to the Numbering Plan, see Schedule 1, Part 1.

[43] Note that this is distinct from so-called number mobility, which is a service offered by some operators which enables a user to retain a geographic number when moving address.

[44] Parliament and Council Directive 98/61/EC amending Directive 97/33/EC with regard to operator number portability and carrier pre-selection (1998) OJ L 268 ('Amending Interconnection Directive', also called the 'Numbering Directive'), as implemented by the Number Portability Regulations, applies to fixed public telephone networks only.

[45] Note that these requirements are set out in the Amending Interconnection Directive (also called the 'Numbering Directive'), *ibid.*, at Art. 2(1). For further details, see *Director's Statement, Numbering Directive: Number Portability Requirements* (London, OFTEL, 2000), http://www.oftel.gov.uk/ind_info/numbering/port0100.htm.

Specification'. The Functional Specification is a document published from time to time by the DGT following consultation. Note that Condition 68.2 applies only if the requesting operator is 'able and willing' to provide the same type of service as that requested on reasonable terms. This form of mutuality is not a requirement of the recently revised Condition 28 (see definition of 'qualifying operator' in Condition 68.2).

Condition 28.2 and Condition 68.1 deal with the types of costs that are recoverable. These must in all cases be reasonable. The process of ascertaining what are reasonable terms (or charges) may be referred for determination to the DGT, who must then consult with the requesting and providing parties (Conditions 28.4, 68.5). This is provided that the subject-matter of the dispute falls within the scope of Condition 28.5 (which it almost certainly will do). Note that there is no guidance as to which matters the DGT will have regard and there are no expressed rights of appeal.

Unfortunately, much of the drafting of Condition 68 is not compatible with the revised Condition 28.[46] However, and perhaps unsurprisingly, the EU has now proposed to modify the mobile portability regime to make it consistent with that applicable to fixed systems.[47] In the short term, however, it seems that the inconsistencies will be retained.

4.6.3 Carrier pre-selection

The requirements for carrier pre-selection (Condition 50A) are set out in the Amending Interconnection Directive.[48] This Directive requires that operators with significant market power (see 4.8 below) in the market for fixed publicly available telephone services are to provide carrier pre-selection (CPS) in respect of both national and international calls.

At present, if a subscriber directly connected to the networks of either BT plc or Kingston Communications (Hull) plc wishes to choose another carrier, the subscriber is obliged to first dial a four-digit access number (known as an 'indirect access code') to ensure that the calls are routed via the other carrier unless the subscriber uses specialist dialling equipment (known as 'autodiallers'). It could be said that having the pre-select set up in this way operates as a preference for the operators with significant market power.[49] With CPS,

---

[46] For example, the definition of 'portability' now refers to a fixed public telephone system only. This term is used throughout Condition 68. Surprisingly, there is no consideration of the amendments required to Condition 68 in either the Number Portability Regulations or the Numbering Directive Statement (see *supra* n. 44).

[47] See *The results of the public consultation on the 1999 Communications Review and Orientations for the new Regulatory Framework: Communication from the Commission* ('1999 Communications Review Consultation Results'), COM (2000) 239, http://europa.eu.int/ISPO/infosoc/telecompolicy/review99/review99.htm

[48] *Supra* n. 44. See also the Telecommunications (Interconnection) (Carrier Pre-selection) Regulations 1999 (SI 1999 No. 3448).

[49] Note that this has always been the view of the DGT; see *Director's Statement, OFTEL's Policy on Indirect Access, Equal Access and Direct Connection to the Access Network* (London, OFTEL, 1997). In this Statement, the DGT concluded that 'equal access (a.k.a. carrier pre-selection) may stifle the willingness of other operators to invest in alternative telecommunications infrastructure'.

the customer can alter the pre-selected carrier and thus can use a selected carrier[50] without having to dial the four-digit indirect access code on a call-by-call basis. However, the subscriber will retain the ability to override the pre-selected operator on a call-by-call basis using an indirect access code.

The Amending Interconnection Directive requires CPS to be implemented by 1 January 2000. This raised problems for BT, as many of its switches did not contain the inherent capacity to provide CPS.[51] Major software developments were, therefore required. Pending completion of this exercise, interim measures have been considered necessary (known as 'Interim CPS'). This involves the use of autodiallers.[52] As Kingston Communications (Hull) plc has significant market power in the Hull area only, the DGT has agreed that Kingston can provide CPS by way of autodialler on a permanent basis and that it would be uneconomic to implement a software systems upgrade as is required of BT.[53]

BT agreed to implement permanent CPS for national and international calls by the end of 2000 and for all calls during 2001. This obligation is now being met by BT.

Fixed PTO operators are required to provide CPS if requested to do so by a subscriber (Condition 50A.1). CPS must be provided in accordance with a Functional Specification which is published by the DGT. This deals with the technical issues and other issues relating to the implementation and use of CPS (Schedule 1, Part 1).

The charges for providing permanent CPS are subject to the determination of the DGT and must be reasonable and, unless the Director otherwise determines, based upon long-run incremental costs (Condition 50A.4). They are recoverable as a direct charge to the operator requesting CPS (Condition 50A.5). Note that the costs of implementing the upgrades and making adjustments to support facilities will also be recoverable, but chargeable by way of separate surcharge on relevant calls (Condition 50A.6). Where Interim CPS is being provided (i.e., via autodiallers), the charging structure is largely similar and the operator may recover its costs by way of a surcharge on relevant calls. Again, the quantum of this charge is to be determined by the DGT (Conditions 50A.7 and 50A.8).[54]

Note that the DGT is under a general duty to ensure that charges are cost-orientated (see 4.8.2) and, to the extent that the charges are made

---

[50] The selected operator must be a Schedule 2 public operator (see 4.4.5). 'Pre-selected operator' is defined in Schedule 1, Part 1.

[51] For further discussion on the functionality of BT switches, see *Director's Statement, Implementation of Carrier Pre-Selection in the UK* (London, OFTEL, 1999).

[52] *Ibid.* Note that in this statement the DGT concluded that the use of autodiallers is costly and that the 'less customer friendly process of installation' of the autodiallers may dissuade customers from using the permanent solution once it becomes available.

[53] *Ibid.*

[54] Note that the DGT has made a determination that BT should bear 50 per cent of the costs relating to the provision of CPS facilities; see *Director's Amended Determination under Condition 50A.7 of the licence of British Telecommunications plc relating to Interim Carrier Pre-selection* (London, OFTEL, 2000).

directly to consumers, that they do not act as a disincentive to use CPS facilities.[55]

4.7 STANDARD CONDITIONS – COMPETITION AND FAIR TRADING ISSUES

4.7.1 Undue preference and undue discrimination

The obligation not to 'show undue preference . . . or exercise undue discrimination' is one of the specific statutory conditions which apply to all public telecommunications operators (Telecommunications Act 1984, s. 8, see 4.1.4). Confusingly, this obligation is set out in both Condition 8 and Condition 57 (Part G) of the PTO licence. The distinction is that Condition 8 applies only in respect of the provision of specific services, namely:

(a)   directory services and/or international directory services under Conditions 2 and 3;
(b)   emergency call services and operator assistance pursuant to Condition 4;
(c)   international conveyance services (if the operator is providing such services) as in Condition 3 (Condition 8.1(a));
(d)   the connection of apparatus or systems to the applicable system under Condition 5 (Condition 8.1(b));[56] and
(e)   the granting of permission to connect such apparatus or systems for the provision of telecommunications services via the applicable system under Condition 6 (Condition 8.1(c)).

Note also that in respect of the mobile PTO licence, this applies to services that a mobile operator is obliged to provide pursuant to the national roaming condition.[57]

Condition 57 is quite separate, in that the obligation not to show undue preference or to exercise undue discrimination applies generally in respect of the operator's activities only in circumstances where it has been determined that the operator is obliged to provide certain services under Parts A–F of the licence. For example, this would be relevant to universal service providers (Part A; see 4.10.1), operators with significant market power (Parts C–E; see 4.8) and operators with market influence (Part F; see 4.9).[58]

In the 'old form' PTO licence, there was no equivalent to Condition 57. The obligation, to the extent that it related to the provision by means of the applicable system of any telecommunication service in accordance with an obligation imposed by or under this licence, was combined within a provision resembling Condition 8. The current drafting is not as concise as it should be.

---

[55] Article 1(3), Amending Interconnection Directive, *supra* n. 44; see also Carrier Pre-selection Regulations, *supra* n. 48, reg. 3, and *op. cit.* n. 51.
[56] Note that in respect of the mobile PTO licence, this also includes the Condition 5.1 requirement to provide mobile radio telecommunication services to service providers.
[57] See *op. cit.* n. 37, in particular, Annex A *bis* of the later document.
[58] This is a non-exhaustive list.

However, there are also technical difficulties. The obligation to provide services by and connections to applicable systems is contained within Condition 8.1(c), but the obligation as to maintenance, adjustment, repair or replacement of any apparatus comprised within applicable systems is contained in Condition 57.1(v), which means that it will apply only if a prior determination has been made by the DGT (e.g., market influence). As these two types of activities overlap, it is not clear why they are subjected to different regulatory treatment and which condition would apply in any particular circumstance.

As to what constitutes an undue preference or undue discrimination, these are largely questions of fact to be determined by the DGT (Condition 8.3). A common example of the type of behaviour constituting undue preference is where operators make wholesale services available to their own retail divisions on different (and more advantageous) terms than those they make available to the Schedule 2 public operators who compete at the retail level.

These provisions sit rather uncomfortably with the principle of non-discrimination which is at the heart of many of the most significant EU Directives.[59] As the two tests are quite different, it would seem that there is little scope (if any at all) for the DGT to enforce Conditions 8 and 57 where the obligation not to discriminate applies. Unfortunately, it is arguable that any deletion of this type of condition would require an amendment to the Telecommunications Act 1984 (namely the deletion of s. 8(1)(b)). Perhaps, in any case, the need for amendment has somewhat diminished given the number of anti-competitive and fair trading conditions that appear elsewhere in the licence and are otherwise available at law (see 4.7.2, 4.8 and 4.9 below).

4.7.2   Fair trading condition

Until the entry into force of the Competition Act 1998, many (including the DGT) took the view that the previous legislative regime (principally, the Restrictive Trade Practices Act 1976 and the Competition Act 1980; see Chapter 7) did not provide sufficient regulation of the telecommunications sector. This led to the introduction of the fair trading condition (the 'FTC', Condition 31).[60] The FTC deals with abuses of dominant operators and anti-competitive practices generally, and is based on Arts 81 and 82 (ex 85 and 86) of the EC Treaty.[61] Indeed, Condition 31.3 provides that any determinations made must be consistent with EU jurisprudence, though it is difficult to understand how this can take into account the ability to secure an individual exemption under Art. 81(3) (ex 85(3)) of the Treaty.

---

[59] See, e.g., Directive 90/387/EEC of 28 June 1990 on the establishment of the internal market for telecommunications services through the implementation of open network provision ('ONP Framework Directive'), (1990) OJ L 121/1), Art. 3(1) and Annex II; Services Directive, *supra* n. 3 at Art. 4, as amended by the Full Competition Directive, Art. 1(5); Licensing Directive, *supra* n. 24 at Art. 3(2); Interconnection Directive, *supra* n. 24 at Art. 6.

[60] The licence of BT plc was amended with effect from 1 October 1996 and other PTO licences were amended with effect from 17 December 1997. See also *R v Director-General of Telecommunications, ex parte British Telecommunications plc* (unreported), 20 December 1996 (QBD).

[61] Note that the Articles were renumbered by virtue of the Treaty of Amsterdam. For further details, see Chapter 8.

There have been (and remain) many issues with the drafting of the FTC (such as the absence of any meaningful appeal procedure against the decisions of the DGT), but, for present purposes, these no longer merit detailed analysis. This is because the FTC expressly provides that it will not apply if new legislation is enacted that contains similar provisions, is enforceable by the DGT and gives third parties rights at least equivalent to those afforded under s. 18 of the Telecommunications Act 1984 (relating to provisional and final orders) and the right to 'monetary penalties' if the prohibition is breached (Condition 31.9).

The DGT has taken the view that the Competition Act 1998[62] meets these criteria, and therefore the FTC ceases to apply where conduct breaches both the 1998 Act and the FTC.[63] As the Competition Act 1998 is also based on Arts 81 and 82 (ex 85 and 86) of the EC Treaty and the DGT has jurisdiction (concurrently with the Director-General of Fair Trading) under the Act (see s. 54 and Sch. 10), the DGT's view would seem to be fairly safe. However, this is not as straightforward as it may at first seem. The DGT's power and the relevant enforcement machinery are quite different (when pursuant to his concurrent power) under the Competition Act 1998 to those set out in the Telecommunications Act 1984.[64]

Note that in any event the FTC ceases with effect from 31 July 2001 (Condition 31.9(b)) and, presumably, its life will not be extended beyond this date. However, if the better view is (as expressed by the DGT)[65] that the FTC will no longer be applied, it should be deleted from the PTO licence with immediate effect. The DGT has now proposed to remove the FTC, but appears to have combined this with the ongoing statutory consultation on the conditions applicable to international business.[66]

4.8 STANDARD CONDITIONS – SIGNIFICANT MARKET POWER

4.8.1 Interconnection Directive

The DGT may determine operators (mobile and fixed) to have significant market power (known as 'SMP operators') in the provision of certain (mostly

---

[62] The Competition Act 1998 came into force on 1 March 2000. See Competition Act 1998 (Commencement No. 1) Order 1998 (SI 1998 No. 2750); Competition Act 1998 (Commencement No. 2) Order 1998 (SI 1998 No. 3166); Competition Act 1998 (Commencement No. 3) Order 1999 (SI 1999 No. 505); Competition Act 1998 (Commencement No. 4) Order 1999 (SI 1999 No. 2859) and Competition Act 1998 (Commencement No. 5) Order 2000 (SI 2000 No. 344). There are also many other specific Regulations covering various parts of the Competition Act 1998.

[63] See *Director's Statement, The Application of the Competition Act in the Telecommunications Sector* (London, OFT, 2000), http://www.oft.gov.uk/html/comp_act/technical_guidelines/oft417.html.

[64] For example, under the Competition Act 1998, a third party has the advantage that direct action can be taken without having to wait for an order to be made by the DGT. See also (1999) 10(3) Util LR 89–92; [1999] ECLR 247. Also see 7.7.

[65] See *op. cit.* n. 63.

[66] See *Director's Consultation Document, International Controls in PTO Licences* (London, OFTEL, 2000), http://www.oftel.gov.uk/publications/pricing/ipto0400.htm. As to international business, see 4.12.

interconnect-related) services (Condition 44). (See also Art. 4 of the Inter-connection Directive and the Interconnection Regulations, reg. 4(1).) This triggers additional obligations which are set out in Part C of the PTO licence.

There is an initial presumption that an operator will have significant market power when it has a market share of 25 per cent. The market is measured by reference to the geographical area in which the licensee operates (Art. 4(3), Interconnection Directive; the Interconnection Regulations, reg. 4). This presumption is rebuttable, and the DGT must take into account the oper-ator's ability to influence market conditions, its turnover relative to the size of the market, its control of the means of access to end-users, its access to financial resources and its experience in providing products and services in the market. The relevant markets are: (i) fixed public telephone networks/services; (ii) leased line services; and (iii) public mobile telephone networks/services (see Art. 4(2) and Annex 1, Interconnection Directive (Pts 1, 2, 3, respectively); see also Interconnection Regulations, reg. 5(1)(b) and Sch. 1). This type of specifically applied test is slightly different to that used for the measurement of market power for the purposes of Chapter II of the Competition Act 1998 and Art. 82 (ex 86) of the EC Treaty[67] where the relevant markets tend to be based on economic considerations rather than on those that are pre-set. In practice, however, it is arguable that the definitions of 'market' and 'market share' set out in the Interconnection Directive are capable of so many different interpretations that there is little difference.

As a result of the consultation initiated in November 1997, the DGT has determined that the SMP operators are BT and Kingston (both in respect of the fixed and leased line market) and Telecom Securicor Cellular Radio Ltd (known by its trading name, 'BT Cellnet') and Vodafone Airtouch plc (both in respect of the mobile market).[68]

The primary requirement for SMP operators is set out in Condition 45, namely, the obligation to meet all reasonable demands of Schedule 2 public operators for the conveyance of messages by way of the applicable system (Condition 45.1) (see also Art. 4(2), Interconnection Directive; the Intercon-nection Regulations 1997, reg. 3(3)). Importantly, these demands may be in respect of access to the applicable system at other than the network termina-tion points offered to the majority of end-users. This is more onerous than the Condition 9 obligation to interconnect (see 4.4.4), which is disapplied in respect of SMP operators (Condition 44.2).

This is predicated upon the obligation 'to negotiate interconnection' with the Schedule 2 public operator as set out in the Interconnection Directive (Art. 4(1); see also Interconnection Regulations, reg. 3(1)). In the context of Condition 9, this wording is merely vague (see 4.4.4). However, when combined with an obligation to meet all reasonable demands, it is both vague and confusing. In Condition 45.1, this has been transposed into an obligation to 'offer to enter into an agreement . . . (or offer to amend such an agreement)'.

---

[67] See also *Director's Statement, Identification of Significant Market Power for the Purposes of the EU Interconnection Directive* (London, OFTEL, 1998), http://www.oftel.gov.uk/publications/1995 _98/competition/smpi298.htm.
[68] *Ibid.*

[W]e have reverted to expressing the obligation for the non-SMP operators as being to negotiate agreements: in order to reflect more closely the language of the Interconnection Directive. For the SMP operators, on the other hand, by the very fact of their being in a position of market power, we believe that the objectives of the Interconnection Directive cannot be effectively secured unless their interconnect obligation is not only to negotiate agreements but to offer to enter into agreements.[69]

Notwithstanding the view of the DGT, it is difficult to be precise about the rights and obligations of the SMP operator *vis-à-vis* the Schedule 2 public operator when faced with such drafting. Possibly the argument is academic as, in practice, an obligation to act reasonably can be inferred from Condition 45.4 and disputes as to the reasonableness of any requirements may be referred by either party to the DGT for determination (Condition 45.2).

Either the SMP operator or the Schedule 2 public operator may request the DGT to specify issues to be covered by an interconnect agreement, conditions to be observed pursuant to that agreement and any time limits for negotiations.[70] Note that while the DGT must have regard to the considerations set out in Condition 45.8 (including any guidelines issued from time to time) when making a direction, there are no expressed rights of appeal.

SMP operators are also required to publish a reference interconnect offer (Conditions 46.1 and 46.2). This will form the basis of the agreements reached between the SMP operator and: (i) Schedule 2 public operators pursuant to Condition 45; and (ii) licensed operators other than Schedule 2 public operators, pursuant to Condition 48.[71] Put simply, this offer must include a service description, charges and a reference to the appropriate terms and conditions, and must be circulated to any person who requests it, to the DGT and must be made available for inspection to the public free of charge at the registered office of the licensee (Conditions 46.1 and 46.2).

The reference interconnect offer applies principally to standard services (Condition 46.2(a)) (but note that it also applies to the provision of interconnection services pursuant to Condition 46.2(b)). The provisions concerning standard services are poorly drafted. Essentially, these will include services requested by a Schedule 2 public operator in a market determined by the DGT either to be competitive, or likely to be competitive (Condition 47.1), or which the licensee first provides after having been determined to be an SMP operator. However, this drafting is defeated in the definition of 'standard services', which includes any other service which a Schedule 2

---

[69] *Implementation of the EC Licensing Directive: Changes to Existing Licences, Second Consultation* (London, DTI, 1999), at para. 44.

[70] A recent example of such a direction being made concerned the requirement for BT to provide certain services to support unmetered Internet access over its local network in response to a request made by MCI/WorldCom. See *Determination of a Dispute between BT and MCI/WorldCom concerning the provision of a Flat Rate Internet Access Call Origination Product (FRIACO)* (London, OFTEL, 2000).

[71] Note that Art. 4(2) of the Interconnection Directive is not confined to Schedule 2 public operators only. It is difficult to categorise precisely who these other licensed operators will be given the uncertainties surrounding the definition of Schedule 2 public operator. See 4.1.4, 4.4.5.

public operator has requested the SMP operator to offer to enter into an agreement to provide under Condition 45. This would seem to incorporate requested services irrespective of a market determination by the DGT. If this is correct, it would seem difficult for an SMP operator to comply with the *ex ante* reference interconnect offer publication requirements (Conditions 46.1 and 46.2).

Note that charges to Schedule 2 public operators are derived from costs (or more precisely, calculated on a forward-looking incremental cost basis) and the SMP operator is under a duty to demonstrate to the satisfaction of the DGT that this approach is being applied (Condition 47.1). Different terms and/or charges can be applied only where they can be 'objectively justified' (Condition 47.4). Changes in charges are subject to a notice procedure (Conditions 47.5–47.9). However, charges to other licensed operators need only be transparent and cost-orientated (but not cost-based) (Condition 48.3(a)) and the SMP operator is only obliged to provide interconnection services as may reasonably be requested by the other licensed operator (Condition 48.2).

Condition 49 requires the SMP operator to send a copy of each individual interconnection agreement (and any amendment) to the DGT. The document also needs to be published in accordance with conditions which are similar to those applicable to the reference interconnect offer (Condition 49.4). The SMP operator is further required to maintain a cost accounting system which is suitable to demonstrate that such interconnection charges have been fairly and properly accounted, and which otherwise complies with the detailed requirements of Art. 7(5) of the Interconnection Directive (Condition 50.1) (see also Interconnection Regulations 1997, reg. 5(d)–(e)). These charges are subject to detailed auditing requirements (Condition 50.5 *et seq.*). Note that for SMP operators having an annual turnover of more than 20 million euros in respect of telecommunications activities, there is duty to keep separate accounts for interconnection and related charges (Condition 50.4). All elements of cost (including an itemised breakdown of fixed assets) and the basis of the calculation of such costs need to be identified.

4.8.2   Revised Voice Telephony Directive and special network access

'Significant market power' is defined in the Revised Voice Telephony Directive by a similar methodology to that used in the Interconnection Directive,[72] save that it only applies to providers of fixed publicly available networks (see 4.1.5) and/or voice telephony services (see the Revised Voice Telephony Directive, Arts 1(2) and 2(1)(e); the Voice Telephony Regulations, reg. 2(1)). Part D of the mobile PTO licence is, therefore, redundant and should be

---

[72] See Revised Voice Telephony Directive, *supra* n. 22, Art. 2(2)(i). See also the Voice Telephony Regulations *supra* n. 7, reg. 6; *Director's Consultative Document, Identification of Operators with Significant Market Power for the purposes of the Application of Detailed Rules under purposes of the EC Voice Telephony and Universal Service Directive* (London, OFTEL, 1998), http://www.oftel.gov.uk/publications/1995_98/competition/smprv498.htm.

deleted. The DGT has determined that BT and Kingston are SMP operators for the purposes of the Revised Voice Telephony Directive.[73]

Annex III of the Revised Voice Telephony Directive sets out certain qualitative standards which apply to fixed networks. The SMP operator is obliged to keep up-to-date information concerning its network performance against these standards. Note also that the DGT can set other quality of service or performance standards. The SMP operator must comply with these standards and produce up-to-date information to record actual performance. These records are auditable (Condition 52) (Art. 12, Revised Voice Telephony Directive; Voice Telephony Regulations, reg. 19). Note, however, that in setting these additional standards, the DGT has an obligation to take into account the views of interested parties (Condition 52).

Note also that SMP operators are obliged to make available to users calling-line identification (i.e., the display of the calling party's number to the called party prior to the call being established), direct dialling-in (i.e., the ability to call users on a private system without the need of an operator to intervene and route the call) and call forwarding facilities (i.e., the ability to re-route incoming calls to another line). This is required, however, only to the extent that it is technically feasible and economically viable to provide these services (Condition 52.5) (see also Art. 15 and Annex I, Pt 2, Revised Voice Telephony Directive; Voice Telephony Regulations, reg. 24 and Sch. 1, Pt 2).

Furthermore, SMP operators have to provide 'special network access' (i.e., access to the SMP operator's system other than at network termination points) upon the reasonable request of an organisation providing telecommunications services (Condition 53) (see also Art. 16, Revised Voice Telephony Directive; Telecommunications (Open Network Provision) (Voice Telephony) Regulations 1998, reg. 26). This applies for the benefit of Schedule 2 public operators, other licensed operators and, importantly, to so-called systemless service providers (that is to say, an organisation providing publicly available telephone services, but which does not run a telecommunications system by means of which such services are provided; see Voice Telephony Regulations, reg. 2). This is therefore a potentially onerous obligation.

Although the provision of special network access is a matter for the agreement of the parties, the SMP operator may only charge on the basis of tariffs which are objective, transparent, properly published and non-discriminatory. These are known as the principles of cost orientation.[74] Note also that the DGT has considerable powers in respect of special network access (such as the ability to specify conditions to be incorporated into the relevant agreement) (see Conditions 53.4–53.8; Art. 16(4)–(9), Revised Voiced Telephony Directive; Voice Telephony Regulations, reg. 26).

There is also a obligation for SMP operators to apply principles of 'cost orientation' to their tariffs generally (provided, of course, that the tariffs are

---

[73] See Identification of SMP Operators Consultation, *ibid.*

[74] These are set out in Art. 2(8) and Annex II of the ONP Framework Directive, *supra* n. 59.

in respect of fixed publicly available telephone system and fixed publicly available telephone services; Condition 54.3). Condition 54.6 requires such tariffs to be published. The requirements of Condition 54.6 are similar to the publication requirements which apply to the 'reference interconnect offer' (Condition 49) (see 4.8.1). Note that changes to these tariffs can only occur 28 days after such changes have been properly published (Condition 54.5).

4.8.3 Amended Leased Lines Directive[75]

The measurement of significant market power in Part E is similar to that in Part D (see 4.8.2 above). The Amended Leased Lines Directive defines a leased line as: '. . . telecommunications facilities which provide for transparent transmission capacity between network termination points and which do not include on-demand switching (switching functions that the user can control as part of the leased line provision)' (Art. 2). The leased line market is measured according to this definition. This is a well-understood term in the industry, and there seems to be little dispute as to its scope.

The obligations of the SMP operator in Part E are fairly similar to those set out in Parts C and D of the licence (e.g., publication of information (Conditions 55.3–55.5), powers of the DGT (Conditions 55.13 and 55.14), cost orientation (Conditions 55.15–55.17)). Again, the SMP operators are BT (in the UK, apart from Hull) and Kingston (for Hull).[76]

Part E is not relevant to mobile operators and, therefore, it should be deleted from the mobile PTO licence.

4.8.4 Reform of significant market power

Many are not persuaded that this extra layer of regulation is required.

> Supporters of using the concept of dominance as a threshold for *ex ante* regulatory obligations argued that focusing on dominance was the only way for the new framework truly to reflect its objective of regulating only where necessary. Only where an operator was dominant could *ex ante* regulation be justified to safeguard competition. They argued that the SMP notion gave regulators too much latitude to intervene unnecessarily in competitive markets.[77]

The European Commission has now proposed to base the measurement of significant market power on the concept of dominance to ensure consistency with EU competition law.[78]

---

[75] Directive 97/51/EC amending Council Directives 90/387/EEC and 92/44/EEC for the purpose of adaptation to a competitive environment in telecommunications (1997) OJ L 295.

[76] See the Director's Consultation Document and Statement, both entitled *Identification of Significant Market Power for the purposes of the EU Leased Lines Directive* (as amended) (London, OFTEL, 1997 and 1998, respectively).

[77] See *The results of the public consultation on the 1999 Communication Review*, *supra* n. 47.

[78] See *Commission Proposal for a Directive on a common regulatory framework for electronic communications networks and services*, Doc. 500PC0393, http://europa.eu.int/eur-lex/en/com/dat/2000/en_500PC0393.html.

4.9   STANDARD CONDITIONS – MARKET INFLUENCE

Market influence is 'the ability to raise prices above the competitive level in the relevant market for a non-transitory period without losing sales to such a degree as to make this unprofitable' (Part F, Condition 56.1). It is therefore aimed at a lower tier of economic strength than significant market power and dominance. Its predecessor, the 'well-established operator' (or 'WEO') test, has now disappeared from the PTO licence. The market influence test was introduced as a general requirement in the PTO licence upon the implementation of the Licensing Directive, but it is neither a specific requirement of the Licensing Directive nor of its implementing regulations (Telecommunications (Licensing) Regulations 1997 (SI 1997 No. 2930)). However, the DGT concluded that the application of the WEO test, which varied according to the age and character of the relevant licence, was inconsistent with requirement for objectively justifiable licensing criteria (Licensing Directive, Art. 3(2); see 4.1.2, above). The Director has stated that the market influence test is to be applied, irrespective of the type of licence or the identity of the operator.[79]

Certainly, this reform and the subsequent production of detailed guidelines on the application of market influence principles give much greater clarity and understanding of the manner in which these principles will be applied.[80] However, it is tempting to conclude that this is merely more consistent application of the same rules coupled with a change of name. Both are based on the principle of market power and, therefore, many of the DGT's deliberations on the WEO principles continue to be relevant.[81]

The benefit of this type of regulation is that it applies to specific sectoral markets rather than having application only to the geographic area in which the operator operates, as is the case with the significant market power principles.[82] Nevertheless, there are serious concerns about the need to impose an extra regulatory tier for the telecommunications sector, and this approach seems to be in marked contrast to the DGT's aim, expressed in recently issued guidelines, to 'move to lighter regulation'.[83] In the same document, the DGT states that: 'As EU and UK competition law and jurisprudence develops the Director will forbear from using market influence

---

[79] *Consultation Paper: Implementation of the EC Licensing Directive: Changes to Existing Licences* (London, DTI, 1999), http://www.dti.gov.uk/cii/telecom/licences/condoc/index.html.

[80] See *Draft Guidelines on Market Influence Determinations* (London, OFTEL, 1999), and *Guidelines on Market Influence Determinations* (London, OFTEL, 2000) ('Market Influence Determination Guidelines'), http://www.oftel.gov.uk/fairtrade/mig0300.htm.

[81] See, e.g., *Director's Statement: Mercury as a Well-Established Operator* (London, OFTEL, 1997), http://www.oftel.gov.uk/licensing/merweo.htm, which sets out a review of Mercury's (now Cable & Wireless Communications plc) status in the market for international services to other operators and the market for international retail services, specifically addressing the UK/USA, UK/Canada and UK/Germany routes. Note also that the concept of market power is not in fact part of the statutory framework of the Competition Act 1998. The Office of Fair Trading has produced a guidance note entitled *Assessment of Market Power* (London OFT, 1999), http://www.oft.gov.uk/html/comp-act/technical_guidelines/oft415.html.

[82] See *Director's Statement, supra* n. 81.

[83] See *Market Influence Determination Guidelines, supra* n. 80.

determinations in favour of allowing general competition law to regulate all levels of market power in the telecommunications sector.' As EU and UK competition law is based on a dominance test, this raises substantial concerns:

> Some new entrants feel that this would give OFTEL excessive discretion to deal with operators having 'market power' falling short of competition law and SMP thresholds. It is not always clear what specific purpose this third category of asymmetric rules would serve (alongside the general prohibition of abuse of dominant position and the telecommunications-specific SMP), nor whether its perceived benefits are proportionate to the burden imposed on the companies involved.[84]

In contrast to the principles of significant market power (which can be traced back to the relevant EU Directives) and dominance (see 4.8.4 above; which is supported by a considerable amount of EU jurisprudence), there is no such authoritative legal precedent for 'market influence'.

While the DGT has produced guidelines concerning his interpretation of market influence (see above), it is notable that Condition 56 does not refer to them. This is not consistent with the approach taken in the drafting of the FTC where it is stated that the DGT must 'have regard' to the FTC guidelines when making determinations. Moreover, Condition 56 contains no expressed form of redress against potentially unreasonable and unexpected determinations.

The criteria to be taken into account when assessing the relevant telecommunications market for the purposes of market influence determinations, are set out in Condition 56. If the DGT makes such a determination, obligations (that otherwise lay dormant) are triggered (unless, of course, the operator is an SMP operator or a universal service provider; see 4.8 and 4.10, respectively). However, it is important to note that these obligations apply only to the extent that the operator's activities fall within the relevant market that is the subject of the market influence determination, or in respect of activities that the licensee is otherwise required to provide.[85]

In respect of the standard fixed PTO licence, there is a requirement to publish charges and terms and conditions (Condition 58), and undue discrimination (Condition 57) provisions also apply. The publication requirements follow a similar framework to those for a reference interconnect offer, in that prices and terms and conditions for relevant services are to be published in advance and operators may provide the relevant services only on the basis of the details published (Conditions 58.2 and 58.3). Note that there is no longer any obligation to provide specific services as was the case under the old WEO requirements.

As to the mobile PTO licence, in addition to the requirement to publish charges and terms and conditions, extra conditions apply, but these provisions are triggered by a market influence determination only (Conditions 56A

---

[84] See *Fifth Report, supra* n. 4, at p. 36, Annex 3. As to SMP, see 4.8 above.
[85] See Condition 57 (relating to universal service providers); Condition 50 (relating to SMP operators. Also see 4.8 and 4.10. Note that this is not the case with Conditions 56A and 56B of the mobile PTO licence.

and 56B). The need for these provisions stems from the fact that the DGT has concluded that spectrum scarcity represents an extra barrier to new mobile operators, and therefore specific controls are required such that operators with market power do not favour their own retail businesses to the detriment of independent service providers. This is based on the view that independent service providers have a positive impact on competition in the mobile market at a retail level.[86]

Condition 56A obliges mobile operators with market influence to provide mobile radio telecommunications services for resale (Condition 56.1; see also 4.2). This is if the relevant service provider can demonstrate to the reasonable satisfaction of the mobile operator that not less than 80 per cent of the services provided are to be resold to persons outside the service provider's group of companies. The service provider must demonstrate that this criterion has been met from its most recently published annual accounts. If it did not provide any telecommunication services[87] during that year, the accounts from the following financial year will be relevant (Condition 56A.1).[88] Note also that the mobile operator is not obliged to provide these services where it has reasonable cause to doubt that the service provider can provide services in a 'proper and efficient' manner or 'finance the provision of the services' (Condition 56A.2). Condition 56B requires mobile operators to carry out direct business[89] separately from their other businesses and to produce separate accounts of its costs. No details of profits are required (Condition 56B.5). This is to ensure that the DGT is able to assess whether the mobile operator is not discriminating unduly against independent service providers.[90]

Note that the DGT has determined that Vodafone Airtouch plc and BT Cellnet have market influence in the mobile market.[91]

4.10 STANDARD CONDITIONS – UNIVERSAL SERVICE OBLIGATIONS

4.10.1 Voice telephony

Universal service refers to a defined set of minimum services of specified quality which is available to all users, independent of their geographical location, at an affordable price. The scope of these services is now set out in

---

[86] See *Consultative Document, Competition in the Mobile Market* (London, OFTEL, 1999), http://www.oftel.gov.uk/competition/cmm0299.htm; *Market Influence Determination Guidelines* and *Draft Guidelines on Market Influence Determinations, supra* n. 81.

[87] Presumably, this is a drafting error and should relate to the services provided to the service provider by the mobile operator rather than telecommunications services generally.

[88] Note that Condition 56A is silent on the nature of the information the service provider needs to provide to satisfy this requirement and the consequences of any failure to achieve the 80 per cent criterion.

[89] See mobile PTO licence, Schedule 1, Part 1. Essentially, this definition relates to the retail supply business of the relevant mobile operator (including associated installation, maintenance, marketing and promotional activities).

[90] See *Market Influence Determination Guidelines, supra,* n. 81.

[91] See *Determinations that Vodafone and BT Cellnet have Market Influence under Condition 56 of their respective licences* (London, OFTEL, 2001), http://www.oftel.gov.uk/publications/mobile/mide0401.htm#Determinations.

the Revised Voice Telephony Directive (see Art. 2(2)(f) and Chap. II; see also the Voice Telephony Regulations, regs 2(1), 7–12).

The principal obligation of a universal service provider in Part A of the licence is to provide voice telephony services, '. . . except to the extent that the Director is satisfied that any reasonable demand for . . . [voice telephony services] . . . is or is to be met by other means and that accordingly it would not be reasonable in the circumstances to require the Licensee to provide the services requested' (Condition 38.2; see also Art. 5, Revised Voice Telephony Directive; Voice Telephony Regulations, reg. 8).

What constitutes a 'reasonable demand' is largely a question of fact and there is little guidance available on this point. Note also that Condition 64 provides a list of exceptions to the universal service obligations. For example, universal service providers do not have to comply with these conditions where there is 'no reasonable demand' for such services, or where it is 'not practicable' to comply with the relevant request (Conditions 64.2 and 64.4(a)). (Note that Condition 64.4 provides a general list of exceptions which specifically apply to the universal service obligations.)

Otherwise the services subject to the universal service obligations include directory services (i.e., the right of users to have entries in publicly available telephone directories),[92] certain provisions in respect of call boxes[93] and services for disabled users.[94] Note that the obligation to make available directory services is the only universal service obligation which is applicable to mobile operators (Revised Voice Telephony Directive, Art. 1(2)).

The Revised Voice Telephone Directive acknowledges that where universal services cannot be 'commercially provided', universal service funding schemes may be established so that funding of these obligations may be shared amongst operators (Art. 4). Operators who are obliged to provide universal services must give information to the DGT which shows the net costs of complying with these obligations (Condition 39; Interconnection Regulations, reg. 12(1)).[95] The DGT must then determine whether or not this places an unfair burden on the universal service provider, and whether or not this necessitates establishing a universal service fund (Interconnection Regulations, reg. 12(2)). He must also take into account the market benefit to the universal service provider which accrues from offering universal services, though it is unclear what weight the DGT will give to this and how he will do it.[96]

---

[92] Revised Voice Telephony Directive, Art. 6; Voice Telephony Regulations, regs 9 and 10. See Condition 4, PTO licence. See also Telecommunications Data Protection Directive, Art. 11.

[93] Revised Voice Telephony Directive, Art. 7; Voice Telephony Regulations, reg. 11. See Condition 24, PTO licence.

[94] Revised Voice Telephony Directive, Art. 8; Voice Telephony Regulations, reg. 12. See Condition 25, PTO licence. Note also that the obligation to make available operator assistance and emergency assistance services (other than via call boxes) is not a universal service obligation and applies to all PTO licensees. See Condition 4, PTO licence; Revised Voice Telephony Directive, Art. 9.

[95] See also Interconnection Directive, Art. 5.

[96] See *Director's Statement, Universal Telecommunications Services* (London, OFTEL, 1997), and the similarly entitled, *Consultation Document* dated July 1999 ('Universal Services Statement', 'Universal Services Consultation', respectively).

Unsurprisingly, the two universal service providers (since their licences were granted) are BT (but not in respect of Hull) and Kingston (in respect of Hull only). Condition 38 sets out the criteria to be applied in respect of the determination of further universal service providers, except in respect of the licences of BT and Kingston which are drafted to reflect their status as universal service providers.

In 1997, the DGT determined that the cost of providing universal services had not placed an unfair burden on either BT or Kingston, and to date no universal service fund has been set up.[97] More recently, the Director conducted a consultation exercise on universal services generally. This included what the scope of universal services and associated funding issues should be.[98] On the latter point, note that the DGT has stated that as the legal framework for the universal service obligation is set out in the Revised Voice Telephony Directive, any change to the scope of this obligation needs to be established at the EU level (and, therefore, changes may take some time).[99] Whether this view is legally correct is arguable.[100] Consistent with this view, the DGT concluded that no extension of the USO was warranted, nor was a change in the funding. (See 2.12 for a further discussion of funding the USO.)

4.10.2 Services other than voice telephony on request

Though similar in structure to Part A of the licence, Part B falls outside (or goes beyond) the narrower definition of universal services in the Revised Voice Telephony Directive (which applies to voice services only). The DGT has stated that as the universal service fund has become a concept of the Revised Voice Telephony Directive and the Interconnection Directive, it is not relevant to Part B.[101] This view is questionable, as the debate about contributions to a universal service fund has been ongoing for many years and it is not established that the language of the Revised Voice Telephony Directive and the Interconnection Directive is intended to be preclusive (as to the preclusive nature of the Interconnection Directive, see 4.8).

According to the DGT, Part B applies to services such as 'priority fault repair', 'maintenance services' and 'maritime services', which are relevant to

---

[97] *Ibid.*

[98] One of the matters considered was whether the roll-out of Asynchronous Digital Subscriber Line (known as 'ADSL') technology needs to be the subject of a universal service obligation. See *Review of Universal Telecommunications Services* (London, OFTEL, 2000).

[99] See *Director's Consultation Document, Universal Telecommunications Services* (London, OFTEL, 1997), www.oftel.gov.uk/publications/1999/consumer/uts799.htm.

[100] The Revised Voice Telephony Directive is unclear as to whether it prescribes a defined set of requirements, or whether it merely prescribes a minimum set of requirements and that it is open to the relevant Member State to impose additional requirements, as appropriate. See Art. 4.

[101] See *Implementation of the Licensing Directive: Changes to Existing Licences* ('*Licensing Directive Implementation*') (London, DTI, 1998), http://www.dti.gov.uk/regulatory/telecomms/implementationtelecommslicenses/index.htm.

specific service obligations contained in BT's and Kingston's PTO licences.[102]

4.11 STANDARD CONDITIONS – LICENCE FEES

The current licence fee regime for individual licences came into effect April 1999. The fixed fee payable upon grant of a licence is £40,000. There is also a renewal fee which is payable annually on 1 April. According to Condition 36.1(a), this renewal fee, which is pro-rated for the first year:

(a)   is set at £3,000 as of 1 April 1999, and is variable thereafter subject to changes in 'the value of money'; or
(b)   is an amount calculated pursuant to Conditions 36.1(c) and 36.2.

Condition 36.1(c) deals with a 'special fee' that becomes payable only upon the determination of the DGT. This determination was made on 1 January 2000 and each anniversary thereafter. The special fee is calculated on the basis of cost estimates relating to the administrative costs incurred (and to be incurred) by the DGT in the regulation and enforcement of licences and in the exercise of the other functions under the Telecommunications Act 1984, and the costs estimated to have been incurred by the Competition Commission following licence modification references under s. 13 of the Telecommunications Act 1984, such costs relating to the then current fiscal year. The fees payable by any operator are limited in amount by the provisions of Condition 36.2.[103]

4.12 STANDARD CONDITIONS – INTERNATIONAL BUSINESS

4.12.1 International simple voice resale and proportionate return

It is important to understand the terms international simple voice resale ('ISVR'; Part H of the PTO licence) and the principle of proportionate return

---

[102] See *Licensing Directive Implementation*, *ibid*. The DGT takes the view that this Part B is required and that this arises from the DGT's duty to ensure that all reasonable demands for telecommunications services are met (see Telecommunications Act 1984, s. 3(1)(a)). Note, however, that s. 3(1)(b) requires the DGT to consider whether service providers are able to finance such services.

[103] The details of this regime are also set out in the *Statement on the Revised Licence Fee Regime* (London, OFTEL, 1999), http://oftel.gov.uk/publications/1999/licensing/fees0899.htm. The limitations are based upon either a percentage of turnover calculation in respect of the turnover of the licensee, or the Condition 36.1(b) £3,000 amount (as it may be adjusted). Note, however, that the administrative costs to be taken into account for Condition 36.1(b) do not include those arising from the Competition Commission references. This is distinct from the wording in Condition 36.1(c). The reason for this is not clear. If this is an error then the circular drafting of the renewal fee and the special fee should have been avoided. Also, given that operators commonly do not respond to the DGT's requests for information (whether pursuant to Condition 33 or otherwise), the DGT may have some difficulty in setting the limitations on these fees in any case. Note also that this wording does not take into account administrative costs in the application and the grant of licences and, therefore, these costs and the £40,000 fee would not seem to be taken into account in respect of the DGT's calculations.

(Condition 59) in their historical context alongside the international accounting rate system through which much international traffic has been and, to a lesser extent, is now terminated. This system was developed at a time when international telecommunications services were supplied between dominant national carriers (often called 'correspondent' relationships) and 'settlement rates' were established for the termination of international calls from a notional mid-point on the route between the two respective territories. The calculation of all the settlement rates in each direction would lead to a net payment ('the accounting rate') by one operator to the other.

Clearly, this regime is favourable to carriers with a net inflow of traffic, and as a result (together with other factors) the level of accounting rates has not been cost-based. International liberalisation has had a marked effect on this regime. With the advent of increased competition in the telecommunications market on a worldwide basis,[104] a clear downward pressure on settlement rates has occurred.[105]

The high cost of settlement rates has for some time encouraged operators to use less expensive methods of terminating calls. One of these methods is ISVR. Using the language of the licence, this involves the connection by way of an international simple resale bearer circuit (more commonly known in the industry as an international private leased circuit, or IPLC) of a public switched network in the UK to a public switched network overseas (as to public switched network, see PTO licence, Schedule 1, Part 1). The ISVR's costs in providing these services are thereby comprised not of settlement rates, but mainly of local call termination charges and the periodic charge for renting an IPLC.

Condition 59 is redundant unless the DGT issues a notice that it applies (see Condition 59.2). The principle of 'proportionate return' is the process by which the Director measures the rate by which calls are made from the UK and compares this with the traffic coming into the UK. If he determines pursuant to Condition 59[106] in the interests of maintaining or promoting effective competition, that the rate of traffic to the UK is in excess of the rate of traffic out of the UK, he may specify a so-called reference ratio which the operator must not exceed. The logic behind this is that if the ISVR operator is primarily providing inbound traffic, this denies revenue via the accounting rate system and adversely affects the net payment to be made through that system. This is a particular problem for the UK and US, with comparatively liberalised marketplaces when the far end operator may still have a comparatively closed monopolistic regime. This results in outbound (UK or US) traffic being routed via the accounting rate system and a significant net payment thereby being incurred by UK or US operators.

---

[104] Directive 96/19/EC amending Directive 90/388/EEC with regard to the implementation of full competition in telecommunications markets, (1996) OJ L 074/13 ('Full Competition Directive'); Global Agreement on Trade in Basic Telecommunications Services, World Trade Organisation (known as the 'Fourth Protocol to the General Agreement on Trade in Services') (signed by 69 governments on 5 February 1998), www.wto.org.english.tratop_e/serv_e/serv_e.htm. For further details, see Chapter 10.

[105] See *Director's Consultation Document, supra* n. 66.

[106] At the date of writing, the DGT has not made any determinations under Condition 59.

However, there are serious problems with this 'proportionate return' condition. It is first important to note that it is route (rather than operator) based. This is despite the fact that there is no language (as there should be) that requires the DGT to issue the same notice on other operators using the same route.

Secondly, there are serious problems of measurement. While operators have a duty to provide the traffic statistics, many of the smaller operators simply do not do so and/or do not have the data and the systems to do so. Moreover, as networks become based on different protocols (e.g., IP — Internet Protocol), it may be that operators will not easily be able to distinguish between voice and data traffic for the purposes of these calculations. This also raises issues of enforcement. If the traffic cannot be adequately measured, how will the DGT be able to ensure that the reference ratio is not exceeded?

As the reference ratio is by its very nature discriminatory, it would be extremely difficult for the DGT to enforce this Condition with respect to traffic relating to a route to another Member State.[107] In any case, its implementation would infringe the Fourth Protocol to the General Agreement on Trade in Services if the reference ratio relates to a WTO country (i.e., a signatory to the Fourth Protocol). Each of the Member States is a WTO country.

4.12.2 International conveyance services

Condition 60 is the proportionate return requirement for operators of international conveyance services. While similar to Condition 59 in concept, Condition 60 applies unless otherwise specified by the Secretary of State or the DGT. It does not, however, apply in the European Economic Area (EEA) and the Secretary of State has disapplied it to WTO routes. Although Condition 60 refers to two ratios, the principle is similar to Condition 59 (i.e., a comparison between inbound and outbound traffic). One notable difference is that Condition 60 applies on a per operator basis rather than on a per route basis.

Given that the non-WTO countries are mainly served by the principal UK operators (who are less unwilling to provide traffic data), the traffic data are more accessible under Condition 60 than under Condition 59, though the difficulties of measurement continue to apply (see 4.12.1). Nevertheless, the DGT issues a quarterly update to the operator to ensure that the amount of inbound traffic is no greater than the outbound traffic with immediate effect upon receipt of this update. This is impractical.

The operator must notify the DGT (pursuant to Condition 61) before entering into an agreement (containing 'accounting methods, rates and divisions')[108] where such agreement concerns the provision of international conveyance services. Any changes to this information must also be notified to the DGT and any other licensees who operate on the route in question.[109]

---

[107] For example, Licensing Directive, Art. 3(2). This may also amount to the imposition of a quota for the purposes of Art. 28 (ex 30), EC Treaty.
[108] Presumably this should be 'methods, rates and/or divisions'.
[109] This is not practical as it assumes that each licensee will know which other licensees are operating on a particular route.

Note also that the Director may direct the licensee not to enter into such an agreement (or variation of it).[110] While the DGT has to consult with the licensee, there is no duty to provide a reasoned decision and no expressed rights of appeal. However, as most accounting rate agreements relate to WTO countries, the amount of data published is minimal.

4.12.3 Separate accounting records

Condition 62 requires the licensee to maintain separate accounting records relating to its international business (i.e., conveyance of traffic overseas) and includes the running of such parts of the applicable systems that are used for this purpose.[111] Presumably, this Condition is needed to monitor cross-subsidies from one section of the business to the other. It would seem unrealistic to require compliance from operators with no market power.

4.12.4 ISVR reform

Part H of the PTO licence was recently reviewed by the DGT with a number of conditions deleted or modified.[112] Although it might have been preferable had the DGT adopted the approach of the US regulator, triggering the Condition in Part H only where the foreign carrier has market power.[113] Additionally, given the practical difficulties in their implementation, Conditions 59 and 60 should have been deleted in their entirety. The DGT, however, determined to retain these. Rather, the DGT, while also retaining the ability to direct the licensee not to enter into or to vary such agreements (Condition 61.3), deleted the prior notification requirements from the licence (Conditions 61.1 and 61.2) and the separate accounting condition (Condition 62).

The review by the DGT also concerned Condition 63. This provided that the Director may make a determination where the operator or any associated person[114] restricts, distorts or prevents competition in the provision of any telecommunication service in the UK. It applied only if the operator or the associated person provides telecommunication services in a territory outside the UK. Again, there was no duty to provide a reasoned decision, no expressed right of appeal, and not even a duty to consult with the operator. As this provision seemed to be largely duplicating the powers available to the DGT under the Competition Act 1998, his conclusion that it is no longer required must be lauded.[115]

---

[110] To date, no such determinations have been made.

[111] Note that this does not apply to BT. The BT PTO licence requires separate accounting for each of its businesses (Condition 78). See 4.14.9.

[112] See *Statement of international controls in PTO licences*, (London, OFTEL, 2000).

[113] *Ibid*. See also *Report and Order on Reform of International Settlements Policy* (Washington, FCC, 1999), IB Docket 98-148.

[114] This is defined as any member of the licensee's group or in whom any member of such group has a participating interest as defined in the Companies Act 1985 (as amended), s. 260.

[115] The duplication was not wholesale. For example, it is arguable that Condition 63 did not require the effect on competition to be 'appreciable' or the agreement to be implemented in the UK, making the argument for its removal stronger.

4.13 STANDARD CONDITIONS – OTHER IMPORTANT PROVISIONS

4.13.1 Requirement to offer contracts for telephone services

Condition 10 was introduced with the implementation of Article 10 of the Revised Voice Telephony Directive, which requires the operator to offer to enter into a contract with each of its subscribers by way of a new written contract or a written extension to an existing agreement (Voice Telephony Regulations, reg. 15). Furthermore, whether by reference to publicly available terms and conditions or in the contract itself, the operator must make reference to certain basic terms (e.g., the supply time for the initial connection, service quality levels, refunds or compensation if these levels are not met, etc.).

Following a request by a user and/or an organisation representing consumer interests (or, indeed, at his own initiative), the DGT may direct that operators amend their contracts to contain these basic terms (Voice Telephony Regulations, reg. 15(4)). The operators would then be under a duty to comply with such a direction. Condition 10 does not require the DGT to consult with the relevant operator prior to making such a direction.[116] Equally, no appeal process is specified.

4.13.2 Itemised bills and non-payment

Condition 13 applies only to the fixed PTO licence and requires the operator to provide itemised billing at no extra charge. (This Condition reflects Art. 14 of the Revised Voice Telephony Directive. See also the Voice Telephony Regulations, reg. 22.) Note that the operator may levy an extra charge if the subscriber requires additional information beyond the 'basic level'. According to Condition 13.3, the itemised billing must be sufficient to allow the 'verification and control' of the charges levied. The itemisation should not detail calls which are made free of charge (i.e., to helplines), and should not be provided at all if the subscriber has so requested. The DGT may by way of a direction set down the level of detail required.

Condition 14 is a new condition (see Revised Voice Telephony Directive, Art. 21; the Voice Telephony Regulations, reg. 24) and requires the operator to specify that any measure it takes for the non-payment of bills will be published, proportionate and non-discriminatory. The operator is also obliged to give 'due' warning of any service interruption or disconnection arising from any non-payment (Condition 14.1).

4.13.3 Provision of information to the DGT

One of the difficulties from which the DGT suffers is a repeated failure of operators to respond to requests for information. This is particularly the case

---

[116] Although Art. 24, Revised Voice Telephony Directive specifies that operators are one of the organisations with whom the DGT has a general duty to consult on issues of 'scope, affordability and quality'. See also the Voice Telephony Regulations, *supra* n. 7, reg. 36.

in respect of general requests for information (rather than requests following a complaint). Many operators do not recognise that this may amount to a breach of Condition 33, which requires the operator:

> [T]o furnish to the Director, in such a manner and at such times as the Director may reasonably request, such information in the form of documents, accounts, estimates, returns . . . and such other information as he may reasonably require for the purpose of verifying that the operator is complying with these Conditions and for statistical purposes.

Condition 33 also contains further and more specific requirements in order that the DGT has the requisite information for certain other statutory requirements (for example, Condition 33.4 requires the operator to provide sufficient financial information as the Director may require pursuant to the Interconnection Regulations, Sch. 3, Pt IV). Other conditions have their own self-standing information provision requirements which operate in addition to the requirements of Condition 33 (e.g., Condition 15 (publication of interfaces); see 4.5.11).

The operator has a further obligation to give notice to the DGT if certain changes occur in the shareholding of the operator or of any parent company (Condition 34). Thirty days' notice must be given, or notice 'as soon as practicable' after the change of shareholding occurs (Condition 34.4). Such notice is also required if any parent company of the operator changes.

4.13.4 Controlled services

Controlled services include services which allow two persons simultaneously to conduct a telephone conversation with one another and without (in most circumstances) the parties knowing the identities of the other participants or the telephone numbers on which they can be called (so-called chatline services) and live telephone conversation services either between the provider of the service and the caller(s) to the service of between two or more callers (so-called live conversation message services) (see Schedule 1, Part 1). Condition 22.2 requires the operator in respect of such services (known as premium rate services) to comply with the Live Conversation Services Code of Practice. Obligations set out in this code of practice are largely consumer protection based and relate to monitoring and recording, content control, advertising and complaint procedures. (The Independent Committee for the Supervision of Standards of Telephone Information Services (ICSTIS) supervises the relevant code(s) of practice on behalf of the DGT.) As premium rate services are charged a higher tariff than the standard rate, the caller must also be notified of the applicable rates by way of an introductory message. (This must also give the name of the service provider and a warning as to any disallowable conversation content.)

As the service providers are largely unregulated, the intention behind this is that if a breach of the code occurs, the DGT may require the operator to desist in providing the network upon which the premium rate service is run.

For this reason, contracts for the provision of network by operators to service providers will provide suspension and termination rights for the operator in this circumstance.

Other premium rate services (such as pre-recorded services) are currently regulated on a voluntary basis, but there are plans to extend the definition of controlled services to encompass these in the future.

4.13.5 Exceptions and limitations to the general conditions

Condition 64 is an often forgotten condition, but can be important when considering whether a licence obligation has been breached. The exclusions and limitations are expressed in terms of detailed cross-referencing of other conditions and require close examination. Note, in particular, that nothing in the licence can oblige an operator to do anything which is 'not practicable', or which is beyond the operator's reasonable control, and the obligation to provide any service under Part A will not apply if there 'is no practical demand for that service' (Conditions 64.2, 64.3 and 64.4). However, it should be noted that Conditions 64.10 and 64.11 provide detailed exclusions, and these need to be considered carefully.[117]

4.14   SPECIAL CONDITIONS

4.14.1   General

Conditions 1–64 (Parts A–I) of the standard PTO licence appear largely unchanged in each PTO licence. However, some PTO licences (including all mobile PTO licences) have additional conditions (namely Part J) beyond those contained in the standard fixed PTO licence. Ideally,[118] and to achieve consistency, these provisions should apply only if triggered by one of the market power-based tests, rather than being applied specifically to a licensee (e.g., market influence (see 4.9), or, perhaps, more appropriately, significant market power (see 4.8)). However, this is not the case.

4.14.2   Charge control – general

BT's charges are principally controlled in two ways, by way of wholesale network charges and retail charges (see BT PTO licence, Conditions 69, 70 and 71).[119] Network charge control relates to the charges levied by BT on other operators for connection to and conveyance over its network, and retail price control is the method by which BT's local, national and international

---

[117] Additionally, note that Condition 64 in the PTO licence does not apply to Part J.

[118] Otherwise, it is questionable whether this approach complies with the requirements of Art. 3(2) of the Licensing Directive. See 4.1.2 above.

[119] Note that the control of private leased circuit prices largely follows the retail charges regime; this relates to analogue private leased circuits and digital private leased circuits of a capacity less than or equal to 64 Kbits. See Condition 73, BT PTO licence.

calls to geographic numbers (excluding payphones) and the charge for residential line rental is regulated.[120]

Both types of charge are regulated by agreement between the DGT and BT.[121] Since 1 October 1997, BT has been obliged to take all reasonable steps to ensure that its charges reduce on a yearly basis by not less than an amount calculated using the formula commonly referred to as 'RPI − x', where 'RPI' is a reference to the retail price index (which is produced by the Office for National Statistics) and 'x' is an amount agreed between BT and the DGT.[122]

For retail charges, the value of 'x' from 1 October 1997 is 4.5 (Condition 70.9, BT PTO licence). Therefore, if, for example, the annual RPI for a particular year is 2.5 per cent, BT is supposed to reduce its prices for the relevant services by at least 7 per cent. This retail agreement was recently extended to 31 July 2002 during which time OFTEL will conduct a further review.[123]

For network charges to begin in October 2001 through to July 2005, the price cap mechanism was set according to four groups of standard services: competitive, new, prospectively competitive and non-competitive. No caps apply to competitive services; OFTEL retains the power to apply a cap to new services.[124] The value of 'x' is 0 for prospectively competitive services and different values for 'x' apply to each of four baskets considered non-competitive, ranging from 7.5 to 13.[125] Note that in circumstances where BT is able to reduce its relevant charges by more than RPI − x in a particular year, the amount of such excess may be carried forward to the next year. Shortfalls may also be carried over to the next year (Condition 69.14 and Condition 70.10 of the BT PTO licence). There is also a general right that the DGT may require, where it is reasonable to do so, adjustments to charges (or require that they be left unchanged) for the relevant year of measurement or the next following year (BT PTO licence, Conditions 69.11 and 70.7).

The DGT may make adjustments as are reasonable if there is a material change in the relevant services to which the charge control provisions apply, or if there is a material change in the basis of calculation of RPI (BT PTO licence, Condition 69.17 (network charges) and Condition 70.13 (retail charges)).

4.14.3   Charge control – network charges

BT must ensure that its charging for standard services is based on costs (calculated on the basis of a forward-looking incremental cost approach) in

---

[120] See definition of 'general prices' in the BT PTO licence, Schedule 1, Part 1. Note that retail charge control regulates the average price for these services, with the average being weighted by the lowest spending 80 per cent of BT's residential customers.

[121] Note, of course, that if BT did not agree, the DGT would, if he wished to proceed, refer the matter to the Competition Commission for resolution. See Telecommunications Act 1984, s. 13, as amended by the Competition Act 1998, s. 45. See, generally, Chapter 7.

[122] For network charges, licence see Condition 69.6, BT PTO licence (applying to Category A, Category B and Category C services, see n. 127, *infra*). See also Chapter 2. For retail charges, see Condition 70.2, BT PTO licence.

[123] See *Proposals for Network Charge and Price Controls from 2001*, chap. 2 (London, OFTEL, 2001).

[124] *Ibid.* at 3.16.

[125] *Ibid.* at 3.43.

respect of certain network components and network parts.[126] For certain categories of services, the charges levied in respect of these components to other operators must be equivalent to the charges made by BT to its internal retail businesses (BT PTO licence, Condition 69.2).[127]

As to the reference interconnect offer (see 4.8.1 above), BT is obliged to set out the charges for each standard service required by the relevant other operator, the location of BT's standard term and conditions for interconnection and the amounts applied in respect of various of the constituent components of that offer (BT PTO licence, Condition 69.3; for constituent components, see BT PTO licence, Condition 69.3(c)).

There are also notice provisions with which BT must comply if it wishes to vary any charges for its standard services, such notice being given to the DGT and any operators with whom BT has entered (or offered to enter) into an interconnection agreement. Note that the variation cannot come into effect unless these provisions have been complied with.[128] This drafting is aimed at increases in charges and is not appropriate to decreases which other operators would wish to come into effect immediately. Note also that BT cannot offer any new standard service until the relevant notice period has elapsed. Presumably, this relates only to where the charges for the relevant new standard service are affected by the proposed variation in charges, though the drafting of Condition 69.4 of the BT PTO licence does not say this.

4.14.4 Charge control – retail charges

Note that any change in retail charges (to the extent that it falls within the definition of a 'general price') must be notified in writing to the DGT.[129] This notification must contain various details about the cost elements of the varied charge and, if applicable, the period of time in respect of which any special offer applies (which must be no more than three months; Condition 71.3, BT PTO licence).[130] Where the varied price is less than the aggregate of these

---

[126] These are contained in a list (dated 17 December 1996) agreed between the DGT and BT. See definitions of 'network component' and 'network part' in the BT PTO licence, Schedule 1, Part 1.

[127] The categories are known as Category A (call origination conveyance standard services, single transit conveyance standard services and local-tandem conveyance standard services), Category B (call termination conveyance standard services) and Category C (data management amendments to allow the routing of emergency calls to land mobile radio service operators, interconnection extension circuits, in span interconnection and customer sited interconnection, product management, policy and planning).

[128] Not less than 28 days for competitive standard services and prospectively competitive services, and not less than 90 days for other standard services: BT PTO licence, Condition 69.4. As to competitive standard services and prospectively competitive services, see 4.14.2; BT PTO licence, Schedule 1, Part 1.

[129] Note also that BT must send the notice to any person who may request it upon payment of a reasonable charge (BT PTO licence, Condition 71.7).

[130] Note that BT cannot avoid this provision by merely renewing the special offer, as the DGT may require a three-month period during which the special offer cannot apply, if he deems that a special offer is the same as or similar to a previous one. As to the cost elements, see Condition 71.3(c).

cost elements, this is known as a Type A general price. For Type A general prices, BT may not publish the varied charge as part of its standard terms and conditions without the DGT's consent, which will not unreasonably be withheld (Condition 71.4, BT PTO licence; the requirement to publish charges, terms and conditions is set out in Condition 7). Otherwise, BT is only required to publish the varied charge prior to its implementation.

4.14.5 Charge control – average call retention and average interconnection charge[131]

BT must take all reasonable steps to ensure that its average call retention does not exceed certain pre-set, pence-per-minute rates.[132] A retention is defined to mean the amount equivalent to the standard retail tariff less the amount payable to Vodafone Airtouch or BT Cellnet, as applicable (essentially, an origination call tariff) (see BT PTO licence, Condition 72.5(d)). The retention is calculated as the average business origination call tariffs and residential origination call tariffs, less any discounts in both cases, and weighted by the total call minutes in each respect (BT PTO licence, Condition 72.2(a)).[133] The per-minute rate is set for the first year, and thereafter calculations are based upon statistics from the preceding year.[134]

Note that, unless otherwise determined by the DGT, the retention rate must be the same for calls to BT Cellnet as to Vodafone Airtouch (BT PTO licence, Condition 72.3). The DGT may determine that BT should adjust this rate, or, other than in the final year (April 2001–March 2002), carry over an adjustment to the rate set for the next following year of measurement, if it fails to achieve the prescribed pence-per-minute rate (BT PTO licence, Condition 72.4).

There is a similar charge control regime contained in the licences of Vodafone Airtouch and BT Cellnet. Both Vodafone Airtouch and BT Cellnet must take all reasonable steps to secure that an average interconnection charge does not exceed certain pre-set, per-minute rates (Vodafone Airtouch/ BT Cellnet mobile PTO licences, Condition 70). This charge (commonly known as a 'termination charge') reflects the standard interconnect charge levied by Vodafone Airtouch or BT Cellnet, weighted according to call minutes. Otherwise, the rates apply for exactly the same periods and are calculated using the same measurement periods as for BT.[135] Note, however, that unlike Condition 72 of the BT PTO licence, no account is to be taken of discounts in calculating the average interconnection charge (Vodafone Airtouch/BT Cellnet mobile PTO licences, Condition 70.2(b)).

[131] BT PTO licence, Condition 72, mobile PTO licence, Condition 70 (in respect of Vodafone Airtouch and BT Cellnet only).

[132] The rates are set out in Condition 72.1 of the BT PTO licence and apply from 1 April of the relevant year, the last prescribed rate expiring 31 March 2002.

[133] Note that the calculation takes into account the calls interconnected to BT Cellnet and Vodafone Airtouch only. Condition 72.2(b).

[134] From 1 April 1999 to 31 March 2000, the rate was 3.4 pence. As to the method of calculation, see definition of 'base year'; BT PTO licence, Condition 72.5.

[135] The rate for the period 1 April 1999 to 31 March 2000 was 11.7 pence.

Vodafone Airtouch and BT Cellnet are also not permitted to levy an interconnection charge for:

(a)   calls which terminate on a pre-recorded announcement informing the calling party that a connection could not be made to the called party's mobile handset in circumstances where that handset is switched off, there is no network coverage or the called party does not answer;
(b)   calls which are diverted to another line before the call is answered (Condition 70.3, Vodafone Airtouch/BT Cellnet mobile PTO licences).[136]

These conditions arise from the findings of the MMC[137] reports, both dated December 1998 and investigating the charges levied by BT[138] and, separately, by Vodafone Airtouch and BT Cellnet.[139] Both reports concluded that there was clear evidence of insufficient competitive pressures on BT's origination charges and BT Cellnet's and Vodafone Airtouch's termination charges and, in both cases, that this could reasonably be expected to last until March 2000. The latter report is, however, of particular interest and raises questions about the legitimacy of the imposition of the average interconnection rate on BT Cellnet and Vodafone Airtouch.

Article 7(2) of the Interconnection Directive sets up a limited regime whereby the DGT can intervene in charges set in interconnection agreements. However, this provision is not intended to apply to mobile operators, save for on an exceptional basis,[140] i.e. where such operators have been notified by the DGT as having significant market power in respect of interconnection services. Neither Vodafone Airtouch nor BT Cellnet have been deemed by the DGT to have significant market power in this way, the calculation being made on the basis of input revenues (that is to say, revenues from service providers, subscriber rental, set up charges and call charges). These charges relate to the mobile market more generally.[141] However, the MMC concluded that the Interconnection Directive (Art. 9(3)) allowed the DGT to intervene on his own initiative to specify one or more conditions to

---

[136] The Monopolies and Mergers Commission (MMC) concluded that the minimal costs incurred in providing these services could be allowed for in the pre-set interconnection pence-per-minute rates.
[137] Since 1 March 2000, the MMC has been replaced by the Competition Commission: Competition Act 1998, s. 45(3).
[138] *Reports on a reference under section 13 of the Telecommunications Act 1984 on the charges made by British Telecommunications plc for calls from its subscribers to phones connected to the networks of Cellnet and Vodafone* ('MMC BT Report') (London, MMC, 1998).
[139] *Reports on references under section 13 of the Telecommunications Act 1984 on the charges made by Cellnet and Vodafone for terminating calls from fixed line networks* ('MMC Cellnet and Vodafone Report') (London, MMC, 1998).
[140] Article 7 applies only to operators of a fixed public telephone network and providers of leased line services. See Interconnection Directive, *supra* n. 25, Art. 7(1) and Annex I, Pts 1 and 2.
[141] See *Director's Consultative Document, Identification of Significant Market Power for the Purposes of the EU Interconnection Directive* (London, OFTEL, 1999). Note that this analysis shows that both BT Cellnet and Vodafone Airtouch fell significantly short of the 25 per cent significant market power presumption and thus the DGT did not make (and has not subsequently made) any determination in respect of interconnection services.

be observed in respect of an interconnection agreement. To conclude that an operator without significant market power in respect of interconnection services can have a pricing regime imposed relating to those services seems to be an odd conclusion.[142] It is also difficult to reconcile this with the language of Art. 7(2) of the Interconnection Directive. This also raises the question as to the precise limits on the scope of the DGT to modify operator licences (in respect of interconnection services) without first having to secure the agreement of the relevant operator pursuant to Telecommunciations Act 1984, s. 14. See also Chapter 5.

As a result of the significant increase in mobile phone use since 1998 (including the growth of text messaging), termination charges are the subject of regulatory review with a current consultation.

4.14.6 Charge control – Kingston

As to Kingston, the DGT has concluded that the Interconnection Directive's Art. 4 obligations on an operator with significant market power (i.e., obligations to maintain separate accounts, interconnection charges to be cost-orientated and the requirement to supply services on non-discriminatory terms) act as a sufficient (presumably, downward) pressure on Kingston's charges.[143] As a result, there are currently no retail charge control or network charge control provisions in the Kingston PTO licence.

4.14.7 Unbundling of the local loop

The means by which Schedule 2 public operators may lease local access lines from BT is known as local loop unbundling. The DGT recently determined to include such a condition in BT's licence (BT PTO licence, Condition 83).[144] This would oblige BT to provide certain facilities (essentially copper lines) from the subscriber's premises to the local BT main distribution frame (known as the 'MDF site' and, more commonly, as local exchanges, of which there are approximately 6,500 in the UK) (BT PTO licence, Conditions 83.1 and 83.2). This includes services allowing the Schedule 2 public operator to use the local access circuit connecting to the user (referred to as a 'metallic path facility') and any and all circuits (both inside and outside the MDF Site) connecting the local circuit to the telecommunications system of the Schedule 2 public operator (referred to as an 'internal tie circuit' and 'external tie circuit'). BT must also provide sufficient co-location facilities or access via 'distant co-location facilities' (i.e., where Schedule 2 public operators' equipment is actually located at a site near the MDF site) in order that such

---

[142] See MMC Cellnet and Vodafone Report, *supra* n. 139, and in particular, the letter from the Commission at Appendix 2.1.

[143] See *Director's Statement, The review of the Telecommunications Act Licences of Kingston Communications (Hull) plc and Kingston Upon Hull City Council* (London, OFTEL, 1998).

[144] *Director's Determination under Condition 83.27 of Schedule 1 of PTL granted to British Telecommunications plc Concerning the Entry into Force of the Condition Requirement to Provide Access Network Facilities* (London, OFTEL, 2000).

facilities can be used and to permit the connection of the Schedule 2 public operator's systems to those of BT. These services are referred to as access network facilities and allow Schedule 2 public operators to upgrade BT's local loop by placing digital subscriber line ('DSL') technology in the local exchange and at the MDF Site. With this technology, Schedule 2 public operators can offer services such as 'always on' high speed Internet access directly to their customers.

Note that there are certain circumstances when access network facilities do not have to be provided by BT. This includes where it is not reasonably practicable or technically and commercially viable to provide such facilities. There is also scope for the DGT to disapply these provisions (Condition 83.6, BT PTO licence). BT is also not required to provide access network facilities in circumstances where the Schedule 2 public operator connects equipment to BT's systems that does not comply with the relevant standards (Condition 83.12, BT PTO licence). These standards are set out in the Access Network Frequency Plan (which is a document either published or approved by the DGT).[145]

Charges are cost-orientated and determined annually by the DGT (Condition 83.19, BT PTO licence).[146] The agreement to provide access network facilities must only contain terms that are reasonable (Condition 83.19, BT PTO licence) and, more generally, BT may not show an undue preference or exercise undue discrimination in respect of any particular class of Schedule 2 public operators (Condition 83.24, BT PTO licence). Disputes as to reasonableness may be referred to the DGT for resolution (Conditions 83.20–83.22, BT PTO licence). Note that the DGT in making this decision must have regard to guidelines issued by him from time to time (Condition 83.22(d), BT PTO licence).[147] There are no expressed rights of appeal.

Note that this condition does not apply to Kingston. This is on the basis that there has been no significant demand for access to Kingston's local loops.[148] BT began to accept orders for co-location in BT's exchanges on 12 September 2000.[149] Full launch is currently anticipated on 1 July 2001 at the latest, though whether this will be achieved is open to doubt.[150]

---

[145] This document was published by the Director on 8 June 2000. See *Director's Consultation Document, Access to Bandwidth: Proposed Solution for the Access Network Frequency Plan (ANFP) for BT's Metallic Access Network* ('Access to Bandwidth Consultation') (London, OFTEL, 2000), http://www.oftel.gov.uk/publications/local_loop/anfp1000.htm.
[146] As to co-location and facility sharing, see Condition 9.3(f) and Condition 45.5(f); Telecommunications (Interconnection) Regulations 1997 (SI 1997 No. 2931), reg. 10.
[147] See *Director's Determination, supra* n. 144.
[148] See *Director's Statement, Access to Bandwidth: Delivering Competition for the Information Age* (London, OFTEL, 1999), http://www.oftel.gov.uk/publications/competition/a2b1199.htm.
[149] See *Director's Determination, supra* n. 144.
[150] See Access to Bandwidth Consultation, *supra* n. 145. Note that this timetable is somewhat behind that in existence elsewhere in the EU; on this point, see the Director's general comments, *Proposed Commission Recommendation on Unbundled Access to the Local Loop: a Response from OFTEL to Directorate General Information Society* (London, OFTEL, 2000), http://www. oftel.gov.uk/publications/gov_depts/uall0400.htm.

4.14.8   Prohibition on cross-subsidies and associated separate accounts[151]

For the purposes of these Conditions, it is important to understand the regulatory subdivision of BT's UK businesses (including that of its wholly owned subsidiaries). Note also that there is a similar provision in Kingston's PTO licence. These subdivisions are:

(a)   apparatus supply business (the supply, installation, maintenance, removal, etc. of telecommunications apparatus);[152]

(b)   systems business (the running of applicable systems, the installation, maintenance, removal, etc. of any apparatus which is part of the applicable systems, the commissioning of any apparatus connected to the applicable system and the provision of network services);[153] and

(c)   supplemental services business (activities relating to value added services; see Schedule 1, Part 1 for a full list).

Put simply, 'network services' is a basic service allowing end-users to transmit messages to another. As the name would suggest, a value added service is a network-based service but with additional functionalities.[154]

The DGT is empowered to direct BT (or Kingston) to take steps to remedy any situation where it appears to the DGT that BT (or Kingston) is unfairly subsidising or cross-subsidising the apparatus supply business or the supplemental services business (BT PTO licence, Condition 75.1; Kingston PTO licence, Condition 65.1).[155] Inevitably, this determination will be based on fact (and note that the action to be taken by BT or Kingston is not confined to reasonableness). BT/Kingston are obliged to record in their accounting records the full cost of any material transfers to these businesses (BT PTO licence, Condition 75.2; Kingston PTO licence, Condition 65.2).

Condition 76 of the BT PTO licence and Condition 67 of the Kingston PTO licence are pertinent to the monitoring and enforcement of the cross-subsidy prohibition.[156] These require accounting and reporting arrangements

---

[151]   BT PTO licence, Conditions 75 and 76; Kingston PTO licence, Conditions 65 and 67.

[152]   See Schedule 1, Part 1 for a full list of activities. Note that this definition applies only where such activities are not being conducted as part of the systems business or the supplemental services business.

[153]   See Schedule 1, Part 1 for a full list of activities. Note that installation, maintenance, etc. of any apparatus forming part of the applicable systems applies only where such activities are not being conducted as part of the supplemental services business. See also definition 'network services' in Schedule 1, Part 1.

[154]   The definitions in Schedule 1, Part 1 are poorly drafted in this regard. Note also that paragraph (c) of the definition allows the DGT and BT to agree additional network services. BT PTO licence, Condition 75.3 requires BT to maintain and publish a list of such services. See also Kingston PTO licence, Condition 65.3. Given the uncertainty of paragraphs (a) and (b), it would be preferable if the list included BT's network services generally.

[155]   Note that this provision also relates to land mobile radio services in the BT licence (e.g., paging) and mobile radio tail services in the Kingston PTO licence (which is undefined, but presumably has similar effect).

[156]   See *Licensing Directive Implementation, supra* n. 101 at para. 62.

to be in place, such that each operator's finances in respect of the apparatus supply systems business and the supplemental services business (and, additionally, in the case of BT, its systems business) are assessable and reported on separately from each other and from the rest of BT's or Kingston's other activities (BT PTO licence, Condition 76.1; Kingston PTO licence, Condition 67.1).[157] These reports are to be audited and sent to the DGT (BT PTO licence, Condition 76.2(c), (d); Kingston PTO licence, Condition 67.1(c), (d)). They do not need to record profits (BT PTO licence, Condition 76.5; Kingston PTO licence, Condition 67.4(b)). Note that there are further provisions concerning the publication of accounts in Condition 77 which apply to the revenue and financial position of the systems business and the BT group of companies as a whole. Oddly, there is no equivalent to Condition 77 in the Kingston PTO licence.

As to the mobile PTO licence, there is an equivalent control on unfair (cross-) subsidising activities, save that it applies to two additional businesses, namely the apparatus production business and the direct business (Condition 66).[158] Note, however, that there is no associated requirement to produce separate accounts. The DGT has taken the view that the requirements set out in Condition 56B would suffice.[159] This is largely borne out in the drafting, save that, of course, Condition 56B applies only to those operators with market influence (which means that it binds Vodafone Airtouch and BT Cellnet only).

4.14.9 Separate accounts – general

The requirement to produce separate accounts set out in Condition 78 of the BT PTO licence has more general application and applies to BT only. While it will apply in the context of unfair (cross-) subsidies, it also is specifically aimed at assessing whether an undue preference has occurred and investigating any issues of interconnection (i.e., that they are cost-based).

In short, BT is obliged to provide annual financial statements (see BT PTO licence, Condition 78.5) for each business, which must identify each of the activities and associated costs, revenues and assets. The scope and identity of each business is to be agreed between BT and the DGT, but each must include revenues, costs and assets derived from interconnection activities (see BT PTO licence, Conditions 78.2 and 78.4). Condition 78 provides considerable detail on the manner in which the financial statements are to be prepared and the content and the accounting principles to be used (BT PTO

---

[157] Note that these obligations are additional to those relevant to BT and Kingston as operators with significant market power contained in Condition 50 (relating to interconnection charges).
[158] As to the apparatus production business and direct business, see the mobile PTO licence, Schedule 1, Part 1. Apparatus production is fairly self-evident, *viz.* production of handsets, etc. See 'direct business', *supra* n. 89. As to Condition 56B and market influence, see 4.9. See also *Director's Draft Direction under Condition 66* (London, OFTEL, 2000) (in which the DGT concluded that BT Cellnet, on the basis of quarterly statistics for the period January to March 2000, had been unfairly cross-subsidising its direct business in the form of its associated company BT Mobile).
[159] *Licensing Directive Implementation, supra* n. 101, at para. 66.

licence, Condition 78.4 *et seq.*). Note also that such statements need to be audited and published (BT PTO licence, Conditions 78.7 and 78.8).

Importantly, the DGT, on the basis of the information supplied to him, may determine that a subsidy or a cross-subsidy has occurred[160] or is occurring in respect of the business agreed between BT and the DGT and BT must take such steps as the DGT may direct (BT PTO licence, Condition 78.12). Note also that there is a similar provision relating to undue preference or undue discrimination (BT PTO licence, Condition 78.14). Essentially, this is a rather convoluted manner of ensuring that Condition 57 (prohibition on undue preference and undue discrimination), which only applies to Parts A–F of the BT PTO licence, also applies to Part J.

4.14.10 Confidentiality[161]

This is a simple obligation ensuring that information acquired in the course of the systems business is not disclosed to the supplemental business and *vice versa*. One practical example of how this would apply is to prevent employees in the supplemental business acquiring commercially sensitive information about organisations contracting with the systems business for network services where such organisations are also competitors of the supplemental business. As to mobile PTO operators, the condition would apply between employees in the direct business and those in organisations working with service providers. Oddly, this provision does not appear in the Kingston PTO licence.

4.14.11 Supply of directories and databases

Note that BT is obliged to make available to other PTOs on request directories, databases it uses to compile the directories and on-line access to the database which BT uses to provide Condition 2 directory information services (BT PTO licence, Condition 81.1). This condition lapses if the DGT determines the market for providing these items is competitive (BT PTO licence, Condition 81.2). BT is required to provide the information in a fair, cost-orientated and not unduly discriminatory manner. If a person other than a PTO makes the request, Condition 82 applies. In this circumstance, BT is not obliged to provide the directories it compiles to comply with Condition 2.3 (BT PTO licence, Condition 82),[162] but is obliged to provide the databases and online access to those databases. The Kingston PTO licence contains a similar provision to Condition 81 (Kingston PTO licence, Condition 68) but, oddly, does not contain an equivalent to Condition 82.

---

[160] Note that the DGT may consider events over a period of up to six years, provided that that unfair subsidy or cross-subsidy is likely to repeated at any time in the future. See BT PTO licence, Condition 78.12(a).

[161] BT PTO licence, Condition 79; mobile PTO licence, Condition 69.

[162] Otherwise, the provisions of Condition 82 are similar to those of Condition 81.

4.14.12 Quality of service

Under the Interconnection Directive, operators with significant market power are obliged to provide the same quality of service (in respect of interconnection) to other organisations as to their own internal retail businesses (Art. 6(1)(a)). This requirement is addressed in Part C of the PTO licence. Condition 69 goes further than this and requires BT to agree to a quality schedule with the DGT which sets out (*inter alia*) certain performance parameters (see Schedule 1, Part 1). These are relevant in respect of standard services and private leased circuits.[163] BT is obliged to publish its performance against these set targets (BT PTO licence, Condition 65.1). Any operator may request that such targets be included, as a minimum, in a contract for standard services or for private leased circuits, and BT must use its reasonable endeavours to meet these targets (BT PTO licence, Condition 65.4).

There are powers for the DGT to intervene if BT has shown an undue preference in respect of these quality standards, and he may direct amendments to the quality schedule. The powers to direct amendments must reasonably relate to the undue preference (BT PTO licence, Condition 65.7). However, there is no duty to consult with BT or any expressed right of appeal. There is no equivalent condition in the Kingston PTO licence.

4.15 REVOCATION

There are certain procedures in the Telecommunications Act 1984, s. 7(13)(a), which deal with the process by which the Secretary of State may revoke a licence. Schedule 2 of the licence sets out the grounds upon which the licence can be revoked. Other than with the mutual agreement of the operator, the principal circumstances in which the Secretary of State may revoke the licence are if:

(a) any change in the ownership of certain companies within the operator's group occurs (as set out in Condition 34) and either–
(i) the change is against the interests of national security or 'relations' with any non-UK territory, or
(ii) the operator has not complied with the Condition 34 notification requirements (Condition 1(b));
(b) the operator has failed to comply with a final order (Telecommunications Act 1984, s. 16; Condition 1(d));
(c) the operator is insolvent, in administration, etc. (Conditions 1(e), (f), (g), (h) and (i));
(d) there has been a failure to pay outstanding licence fees (Condition 1(j)).

---

[163] Put simply, a private leased circuit is a telecommunications link which transmits signals between established termination points.

4.16 CONNECTION AUTHORISATION AND SERVICE AUTHORISATION

4.16.1 Connection authorisation

The operator is authorised under Schedule 3 of the PTO licence to connect to any other licensed system in the UK, any system run by the Crown (which does not need a licence) and any telecommunication system outside the UK,[164] and to any telecommunication apparatus within those systems. The old-form PTO licence only concerned domestic matters and a separate, so-called international facilities licence ('IFL') was required for international connectivity.

4.16.2 Service authorisation

The service authorisation is also very broad in that the operator is authorised to provide any telecommunications services by way of the applicable systems, except where another licence is required to do so.[165]

4.17 EXCEPTIONS AND CONDITIONS RELATING TO THE TELECOMMUNICATIONS CODE

4.17.1 Code powers

The Telecommunications Code ('the Code') applies only if the licence contains Schedule 4 (Telecommunications Act 1984, s. 10(1), Sch. 2). If applied, the Code – which allows rights to access public and private land for the purpose of creating and maintaining telecommunications systems – operates subject to the conditions set out in Schedule 4 (1984 Act, s. 10(3)). Further details about the Code are set out in Chapter 3 (see 3.9.1). The current chapter addresses the principal issues in Schedule 4 (commonly referred to in the industry as 'Code powers'). Code powers are essential for operators seeking to establish or maintain their own telecommunications systems.

Over recent years, as the number of operators installing infrastructure has increased, the environmental obligations in Schedule 4 have become increasingly significant. One example of this is the special treatment reserved for Conservation Areas according to Condition 3. Another is the obligations in respect of service lines (that is to say, lines providing the final link to user premises) and whether such lines should be installed underground or by way of overhead wires (which still prevail in many areas).

---

[164] The Secretary of State may notify the licensee at any time that connections to certain applicable systems must not be made or ceased.
[165] For example, Condition 3(a) (where a licence under s. 70, Broadcasting Act 1990 is required); Condition 3(b) (which falls within the remit of the conditional access services class licence); Condition 3(c) (which falls within the remit of the access control class licence). As to conditional access services and access control, see 4.18.4 *et seq.*

4.17.2 Service lines and other lines

Condition 1 is drafted so that overhead service lines can be flown from poles in a locality where overhead service lines are already in place. In all other areas, where practicable and taking into account the need to provide telecommunications services at the 'lowest reasonable cost', service lines should be placed underground (Condition 1.1; note also that this applies to new and replacement service lines). This is rather an inappropriate test since, if this provision is designed to take into account environmental concerns, it would seem more appropriate to measure the line installation costs rather than the costs of providing the services (which may be affected by matters other than the mere costs of implementation).

All other lines must be placed underground, irrespective of the location of existing lines. However, this again is subject to considerations of practicality and the need to provide telecommunications services at the 'lowest reasonable cost'. There is a special provision which allows telecommunications apparatus (which includes lines) to be installed on electricity pylons, which would be for the benefit of companies such as Energis plc (Condition 1.7; the electricity must be of nominal voltage of at least 6,000 volts).

4.17.3 Installation of telecommunications apparatus other than lines

If an operator wishes to install telecommunications apparatus other than lines, this requires 28 days' notice (with appropriate written details) to be given to the relevant planning authority[166] before installation works above the ground begin. This includes the erection of radio masts (Condition 2.2), but does not include cabinets, boxes, etc., provided they do not exceed certain dimensions (Condition 2.4).[167] It is likely that Condition 2 will be amended to give the relevant planning authority a more direct role in approving works, irrespective of the relevant dimensions of such installations. This is due to the intense media coverage and the increased need for such masts (estimated at a further 30,000) in connection with the future rollout of third generation mobile telephone networks. Other than in the case of emergency works,[168] there are also obligations (mostly, notification) and restrictions on the operator's ability to install contained in Condition 3 (Conservation Areas), Condition 4 (Listed Buildings and Ancient Monuments), Condition 5 (National Parks, Areas of Outstanding National Beauty, etc.) and Condition 6 (National Trust and National Trust for Scotland).

---

[166] This will be: for England and Wales, the local planning authority for the area in question within the meaning of s. 1, Town and Country Planning Act 1990; for Scotland, a planning authority for the area in question within the meaning of s. 1, Town and Country Planning (Scotland) Act 1990; and for Northern Ireland, the Department of Environment for Northern Ireland.

[167] Though if the dimensions are exceeded, the relevant local planning authority is required to approve these structures (Condition 2.5).

[168] '[E]mergency works' has the meaning ascribed to it: for England and Wales, in the New Roads and Street Works Act 1991, s. 52; for Scotland, the 1991 Act, s. 111; and for Northern Ireland, the Street Works (Northern Ireland) Order 1995, Art. 6.

4.17.4 Matters to consider when performing street works

Condition 10 contains a list of requirements relating to the quality of the work to be performed. Of course, these apply without prejudice to other statutory obligations, e.g., health and safety. Such requirements include an obligation when installing new ducts to ensure that there is 'sufficient spare capacity' to meet reasonably foreseeable requirements, thereby avoiding the need for repeated works (Condition 10.1(b)). Also, the possibility of using existing duct space must be considered (Condition 10.1(g)). Many of the other obligations in Condition 10 relate to the need to liaise with appropriate (planning, street or highway) authorities or other utilities to avoid any disruption in the services provided by those persons (Conditions 10.1(a), (c), (d), (e), (f), (n) and (o)).

Note also that according to Condition 11, the operator is obliged to keep an accurate record of underground works undertaken, and is obliged to make certain of this information available free of charge to other persons undertaking works in the vicinity of the installed apparatus (Condition 11.3).

4.17.5 Meeting liabilities

Condition 16 requires the operator to have adequate arrangements (which are subject to the review of the DGT) in place to fund any liabilities, costs and expenses related to street works if for any reason its licence is revoked. If the DGT is not satisfied that such arrangements are adequate, he may direct the operator to ensure that sufficient funds are available (Condition 16.3).

4.18 PRINCIPAL CLASS LICENCES

4.18.1 General

At the date of writing there are 23 types of class licence. Many of these are specific to a particular service or network and do not commonly appear in the spotlight of practitioners.[169] Of these, there are seven main class licences. Only two, however, have common application: (i) the class licence for the running of self-provided telecommunication services (commonly known as the 'self-provision licence' or 'SPL'); and (ii) the class licence to run branch systems to provide telecommunications services (commonly known as the 'telecommunication services licence' or 'TSL').

4.18.2 Self-provision licence[170]

4.18.2.1 Application　By far, the most important aspect of the SPL to be borne in mind is the service authorisation, which can be found in para. 3 of

---

[169] The DGT has stated that it is his intention to phase out some of the class licences and incorporate them into a more generic class licence such as the TSL. See 4.18.3. See also *Fifth Report, supra* n. 4, at Annex 3, p. 35.

[170] Self provision licence (SPL) dated 27 September 1999. Note that as of 9 April 2001, a revised SPL has been issued. For a summary of the changes see *Revocation and Reissue of TSL and SPL* (London, DTI, 2001) at http://www.dti.gov.uk/cii/regulatory/telecomms/revised.shtml.

Schedule 3, which authorises the provision of telecommunications services, other than those that are within the scope of other class licences,[171] provided that:

> [E]ach Message . . . is initially sent or is ultimately received, or both, by the operator or a member of the operator's group and neither the operator nor any member of the operator's group receives from any person other than the operator or any member of the operator's group any financial advantage or advantage in respect of the provision of the telecommunications services . . .

Thus, 'self-provide' is the key term. This licence applies generally to persons using a telephone (whether mobile or fixed), and, in this case, the telephone (and the connecting line into the socket) will constitute the operator's applicable system. This licence also encapsulates companies' internal telephone systems, where the applicable system will incorporate the switchboard and internal routing apparatus. Many large companies run their networks under the SPL.

4.18.2.2 SPL conditions   On this basis, it is perhaps not surprising that the licence conditions are not significant in number and not particularly onerous. For example, Conditions 1, 2 and 3 deal with the simple issues of using approved equipment and of the connection having to be made via appropriate connection points. As this licence binds the general public to the extent that they are telecommunications users, it is perhaps strange that it is not drafted in more easily comprehensible language.

The use of automatic calling equipment is controlled by Condition 5.[172] This provides that this equipment may be used only where the called party has consented in writing to receive such messages. The operator must keep a record of these consents.

Condition 7 (privacy of messages) has been the subject of much regulatory and judicial attention. The principal requirement of this condition is that 'every reasonable effort' is made to inform all parties to a telephone conversation that it may be recorded, monitored or intruded upon before the relevant call has begun (Condition 7.3). Although the condition does not specify how this is to be done, it is quite common for adverts to the general public (which invite calls to be made to a particular number) to carry a message to the effect that calls may be recorded or monitored. However, this

---

[171] For example, the conditional access service class licence or the access control class licence. See 4.18.4 *et seq.*

[172] An automatic calling system is a machine that can initiate calls to destinations in accordance with instructions loaded on to such machines (i.e., without human intervention). Condition 5 includes where such machines are capable of transmitting (a) sounds which are not live speech (otherwise this would include a redial button on a telephone) fax messages and (b). Condition 5 also reflects Art. 12, Telecommunications Data Protection Directive, *supra* n. 18, as implemented by the Telecommunications (Data Protection and Privacy) (Direct Marketing) Regulations 1998 (SI 1998 No. 3170), reg. 6.

condition is now to be considered against guidelines[173] issued by the DGT prior to the July 2000 enactment of the Regulation of Investigatory Powers Act 2000, the Act itself, and the Telecommunication (Lawful Business Practice) (Interception) Regulations 2000 (SI 2000/2699) promulgated under s. 4(2) of the Act.

Essentially, the guidelines set forth the DGT's pre-legislative determination of what the Art. 8 right to privacy under the European Convention on Human Rights requires (Convention for the Protection of Human Rights and Fundamental Freedoms (as amended) (ETS No. 5) Rome, 4 November 1950). They elaborate on how this applies to recording telephone calls in the workplace. In short, companies who routinely record telephone calls must ensure that their employees are able to make unrecorded calls using the same telecommunications system. One suggestion in the guidelines would be to provide a separate telephone, where private calls can be made and received without being recorded.[174] Moreover, the DGT advised that companies should restrict recording and monitoring activities to situations that are 'necessary' and 'proportionate'. For example, a misuse of company phones may require itemised telephone records (rather than a more invasive form of investigation).

The guidelines, however, go further than the decision in *Halford* v *United Kingdom* (1997) 24 EHRR 253 (where no attempt at all was made to warn Ms Halford that her calls might be recorded or monitored) as well as the 2000 Act and its ensuing regulations that were enacted to address the *Halford* judgment. There, the European Court of Human Rights found that since the interception by a public entity of calls made on its own private system was not regulated by the UK law governing interception of calls on the public telecommunications system, the interception was not pursuant to law and, thus, was in violation of Art. 8.

The Regulation of Investigatory Powers Act 2000 also made it unlawful to intercept, without consent, communications made on private systems connected to the public telecommunications system.[175] Section 4(2) of the Act creates an exception to this requirement for businesses intercepting communications for specified business purposes. These are detailed in the Lawful Business Practice Regulations 2000 issued by the Secretary of State, as permitted by s. 4(2), with effect from 24 October 2000.

The Regulations permit a fairly broad range of interceptions by commercial, charitable and other non-commercial entities without consent by the parties to the communication.[176] This includes the ability to monitor or record for the following purposes all communications sent over their systems:

---

[173] *Recording Telephone Conversations on Private Networks* (London, OFTEL, 1999). Note that the guidelines are strictly a recommendation and do not amount to change to Condition 7.

[174] In some industries, such as financial services, recording calls can be necessary in order that regulatory requirements are met (e.g., the need to keep an adequate record of business transactions).

[175] The 2000 Act repeals the Interception of Communications Act 1994 and now makes it an offence to intercept unlawfully communications both on the public telecommunications system and private systems connected to it. The Act also creates a tort of unlawful interception on a private system by the operator of the system.

[176] See The Telecommunications (Lawful Business Practice) (Interception of Communications) Regulations 2000, SI 2000/2699.

(a) establishing the existence of facts (e.g., those communications whereby business transactions are entered into);

(b) ascertaining regulatory or self-regulatory compliance;

(c) ascertaining standards achieved by users of the system (e.g., quality control);

(d) preventing or detecting crime;

(e) detecting unauthorised use of the entity's telecoms system (i.e., whether the employee's use of the system is outside that permitted by the employer);

(f) ensuring the system's effective operation (e.g., monitoring for viruses).

Further, businesses may monitor, but not record, communications to:

(g) check whether the communications relate to the business (e.g., checking employee's voice mail and e-mail in their absence to determine whether there are communications of a business nature);

(h) monitor calls to confidential counselling helplines run free of charge (e.g., to ascertain whether their employees require assistance).

While the Regulations state that they require businesses 'to make all reasonable efforts' to advise people using the system that interceptions may take place, the Secretary of State appears to require only that businesses inform staff, and not outside parties to communications, of possible interceptions.[177] Further, in contrast to the DGT's workplace guidelines, the Regulations create no positive duty on the employer to provide for (or even negotiate) employees' privacy.[178] Rather, the obligation under the Regulations is merely to inform staff of authorised uses of the system and those communications that may be monitored or recorded. It is to be questioned, therefore, whether the guidelines have continuing impact.

4.18.3 Telecommunication services licence[179]

As with the SPL, the TSL service authorisation can be found in para. 3 of Schedule 3, which authorises the provision of telecommunications services

---

[177] See Lawful Business Practice Regulations Response to Consultation (London, DTI, 2000), at Annex C, s. 4.

[178] *Ibid.*, at Annex C. The Consultation notes, however, that the Data Protection Commissioner is preparing a draft Code of Practice on the Use of Personal Data in Employer/Employee Relationships that also addresses the monitoring of employees' e-mail, telephone calls and Internet access. As both the Lawful Business Practice Regulations and the draft Code would be implementing the Telecommunications Data Protection Directive's incorporation of the Article 8 right to privacy, the intersect of these requirements will be important to business. See Draft Employment Code of Practice: Use of personal data in employer/employee relationships (Wilmslow, DPC, 2000).

[179] Telecommunications services licence (TSL), dated 22 May 2000. Note that as of 9 April 2001, a revised TSL has been issued. For a summary of the changes see *Revocation and Reissue of TSL and SPL* (London, DTI, 2001) at http://www.dti.gov.uk/cii/regulatory/telecomms/revised. shtml.

other than those that fall under other licences.[180] The licence lasts for 25 years from 22 May 2000 (TSL, para. 3).

The key point of the TSL is the definition of 'applicable system', which includes 'all of the Apparatus comprised in [the][181] system . . . situated within not more than twenty single sets of premises together with any Apparatus run exclusively for the purpose of enabling Messages to be conveyed between those premises'. ('Apparatus' means telecommunications apparatus within the definition in Sch. 2, Telecommunications Act 1984.) If the apparatus contained in each system is situated in more than 20 sets of premises, one of the more major licences will be required (e.g., a PTO licence).[182] Note that any set of premises must be within a single contiguous boundary under a common management regime, where no two points on the boundary of those premises are more than five kilometres in lateral distance from each other (para. 2, Annex A).

Perhaps unsurprisingly, as the TSL is effectively a restricted PTO licence, the licence conditions reflect many of those contained in the PTO licence (and some of those contained in the SPL). It is anticipated that some of the more obscure class licences may soon disappear and be incorporated into this general authorisation. Note that the latest version of this document has had the broadcasting restriction removed from the service authorisation (Sch. 3, para. 3(b); see 4.2.2.2 above).[183]

4.18.4 ISVR licence[184]

Although previously an individual licence,[185] the DTI recently converted it to a class licence. Article 3(2) of the Licensing Directive requires that Member States:

[E]nsure that telecommunications services and/or telecommunications networks can be provided either without authorisation or on the basis of general authorisations, . . . Member States may issue an individual licence only where the beneficiary is given access to scarce physical and or other

---

[180] In the case of the TSL, this also excludes services covered by the ISVR licence. Note that international simple data resale ('ISDR') services may be provided under the TSL.

[181] This is poorly drafted. If a licensee operates twenty-one switches from separate premises, which are not interconnected by circuits operated by the licensee, then the better interpretation is that the licensee will be operating each switch under the TSL and would not require a superior licence. This narrow definition of 'system' is not clear from this wording.

[182] Note that para. 2(b) of the licence provides that the PTO will be mutually exclusive from the TSL and, therefore, if a PTO licence is required, the operator will be running the entire telecommunications system pursuant to the PTO licence.

[183] Note that this restriction is not specifically set out in the amending statutory instrument (which applies only to PTOs). However, Art. 3(2) of the Licensing Directive requires licence conditions in general authorisations to be 'proportionate'. Accordingly, it would seem disproportionate if the TSL were not to be amended in line with the PTO licence.

[184] Class licence to run branch systems to provide international simple voice resale services dated 1 November 2000.

[185] According to para. 4 of the licence, the ISVR licence runs for 25 years from 1 November 2000.

resources or is subject to particular obligations or enjoys particular rights
. . .

Nevertheless, the DTI, as previously made known, created a hybrid form of
class licence, which requires the prospective operator to complete an application form before being able to operate lawfully under the licence. Given
that the ability of the DGT to enforce a proportionate return requirement
(ISVR licence, Condition 30; for 'proportionate return', see 4.12.1) is
considerably limited, the registration requirement seems somewhat odd. This
also begs the questions as to whether it is 'objectively justified' that data
(ISDR) are treated in a dissimilar manner to voice (ISVR).[186] Otherwise, the
licence is similar to the TSL (see 4.18.3 above).[187]

4.18.5 Conditional access and access control class licences[188]

Conditional access and access control relate to the provision of digital
television and associated interactive services.[189] It is important to note that
conditional access services are not supplied directly to end-users but to
broadcasters who wish to supply digital television services to end-users.
Access control services are a hybrid regime to regulate the supply of digital
services other than digital television services to end-users. As is commonly the
case when services are defined in the negative, there is inherent uncertainty
as to the precise scope of access control services. This is despite some very
useful guidance produced by the DGT in this area.[190]

As with the TSL and the SPL, the key points of these licences are in respect
of their scope.

4.18.5.1 Conditional access services Paragraph 4(b) of the licence defines
'conditional access' as 'telecommunications services . . . by means of which

---

[186] According to Art. 3(2) of the Licensing Directive, general authorisations need to contain
conditions which are 'objectively justified in relation to the service concerned, non-discriminatory, proportionate and transparent'. See also 4.12.1 generally.

[187] Note that 'broadcasting restriction' has not yet been removed from the ISVR licence:
Schedule 3, para. 3(a). See *supra* n. 183.

[188] Class licence for the running of telecommunications systems for the provision of conditional
access services (7 January 1997); class licence for the running of telecommunications systems for
the provision of access control services (31 August 1999).

[189] See Advanced Television Regulations 1996 (SI 1996 No. 3197), Pt IV, implementing EC
Directive 95/47/EC, dated 24 October 1995 (known as the 'Advanced Television Standards
Directive'). See also *Director's Guidelines: The Regulation of Conditional Access for Digital Television
Services* ('Conditional Access Guidelines') (London, OFTEL, 1997), http://www.oftel.gov.uk/
ind_info/broadcasting/conacc.htm.

[190] See *Guidelines on Regulated Supplier Determinations* (London, OFTEL, 2000), http:oftel.
gov.uk/publications/ind_guidelines/guideline.htm; *Statement: Digital Television and Interactive Services and the Pricing of Conditional Access and Access Control Services* (London, OFTEL, 1999),
http://www.oftel.gov.uk/publications/1999/broadcasting/dtv0599. See also definition 'access control services', access control class licence, Schedule 1, Part 1 (4.18.4.3).

access to Digital Television Services[191] may be controlled so that only those viewers who are authorised to receive such services do so'. It includes the encryption and scrambling of digital television broadcasts (see para. 4(b)(1) for 'encryption services'), the actuation and control of decoders for message transmission (including where this is done remotely) (see para. 4(b)2 for 'subscriber authorisation') and the receipt and processing of pay-per-view messages *vis-à-vis* the viewer and, importantly, the regulation of electronic program guides (see para. 4(b)(3) for 'subscriber management services').

4.18.5.2 Conditional access class licence – licence conditions The principal requirement of this licence is Condition 1, which requires the operator to provide any of these services in respect of its decoders to a broadcaster on a 'fair, reasonable and non-discriminatory basis', and also to cooperate with the broadcaster where it is necessary and reasonable to ensure the interconnection and interoperability of systems (Advanced Television Services Regulations 1996, reg. 11).[192]

Condition 2 requires the operator, if the broadcaster's digital television services are being provided by a cable operator, to ensure that effective transfer of control ('transcontrol') of the services occurs at the cable headends, and to provide all reasonable cooperation, assistance and information in respect thereto (Regulations 1996, reg. 10). The operator is also obliged to keep separate financial accounts in respect of its activity as a conditional access service provider (Conditional access services class licence, Condition 10; see also Advanced Television Regulations 1996, reg. 11).

The conditional access service provider is obliged (unless the DGT otherwise consents) to publish terms and conditions relating to any of the conditional access services, and is required to provide those services on the basis of the published terms and conditions (Conditional access services class licence, Condition 7). Importantly, Condition 7 does not require the licensee to publish a single set of charges but merely charging principles.

Note also that the licence contains the FTC (see 4.7.2 above) and the prohibitions on linked sales and undue preference or discrimination (Conditions 3, 4 and 6 respectively).[193] The licence remains in force until 31 July 2001 (para. 3).

4.18.5.3 Access control Schedule 1, Part 1 of the access control class licence contains examples of activities comprised within the definition of 'access control services'. These include:

(a) 'message processing services', such as encryption, scrambling or other processing of digital services prior to transmission to a set-top box;

---

[191] This term has the meaning ascribed to it in the Advanced Television Standards Directive, though note that the Directive leaves 'television services' undefined.
[192] See also Conditional Access Guidelines, *supra* n. 189, for the interpretation of 'fair, reasonable and non-discriminatory'.
[193] Arguably, these conditions are superfluous given the scope of Condition 1.

(b) 'authentication services', i.e., such as services which identify an end-user or a set-top box in order to permit or deny the access of that end-user or set-top box to a digital service;

(c) 'access device management services', i.e., the actuation, control, operation, or remote actuation, control or operation of set-top boxes;

(d) 'selection services', i.e., operation of an electronic programme guide through which the end-user selects digital services;

(e) 'subscriber management services', such as the preparation of smart cards or online updating of entitlements.

The definition does not include network services (essentially services consisting solely of functions enabling users to send messages to each other; Schedule 1, Part 1, para. 1(y)).[194] This definition seems to cover activities necessary to transmit the relevant signal to the set-top box (such as 'signing services'[195]) as well as signals transmitted from the set-top box (e.g., 'authentication services').

4.18.5.4 Access control class licence – licence conditions The Conditions in Part 2 of this licence apply to all providers of access control services. However, the principal part of the licence, Part A, applies only to operators who have been determined by the DGT to be regulated suppliers.[196]

It is open to the DGT to make a regulated supplier determination in one of two ways. First, a determination may be made pursuant to Condition 9.2 if the supplier has market influence in relation to any market for access control services. There are certain requirements that need to apply before such a determination is made. For example, the regulated supplier must have received a reasonable request for the provision of the access control services (Condition 9.2(c)) and must have the ability to raise prices above the competitive level for a non-transitory period without losing sales to such a degree as to make doing this impossible (Condition 92(d); for market influence, see also 4.9). It is important to recognise that only Conditions 14 and 15 of Part A apply to this type of regulated supplier (Condition 9.4; Condition 14 (prohibition on undue preference and undue discrimination); Condition 15 (publication of charges, terms and conditions)).

Secondly, the DGT may make a regulated supplier determination if the supplier is in a dominant position within the meaning of Art. 82 (ex 86) of the EC Treaty and certain other requirements are met (Condition 9.5). One of these requirements is that the supplier must be in a position of economic strength which enables it to prevent effective competition being maintained in the relevant market by affording it the power to behave to an appreciable extent independently of its competitor, customers and ultimately consumers (Condition 9.5(b)). It may be that this latter requirement forms part of the

---

[194] This also forms the basis of the definition of the 'applicable system' for the purposes of Annex A.

[195] These would seem to be contained within message processing services and access device (i.e., set-top box) management services.

[196] The process by which such a determination is reached is set out in access control class licence Part 1, para. 6, and Condition 9.

consideration of dominance, but the wording of this condition requires that it be considered separately. Note that the DGT is required to have regard to both EU and UK jurisprudence when making such a determination (Condition 9.10). Importantly, a dominant regulated supplier is obliged to comply with all of the conditions in Part A of the access control class licence.

The most significant condition in Part A is Condition 10. This requires the regulated supplier to provide access control services to third parties (mostly, broadcasters) 'on fair and reasonable terms' and to do 'whatever is necessary and reasonable' for the purposes of achieving interoperability of systems such that access control services can be provided.

Many other of the Part A conditions are similar to those in the conditional access class licence (Condition 12 (requirement to keep separate financial accounts); Condition 14 (undue preference and undue discrimination); and Condition 15 (publication of charges, terms and conditions)). However, note that to the extent that the FTC remains relevant, it appears in Part 1 of the licence. Therefore, a complainant may not need to rely on a regulated supplier determination triggering the Part A conditions in respect of activities of an operator the complainant regards as being anti-competitive or abusive (if the operator is dominant). At the very least, this is rather odd drafting.

The principal provider of access control services in the UK is currently Sky Subscribers Services Limited ('SSSL'), a member of the Sky Television group of companies. Accordingly, SSSL has been determined by the DGT to be a regulated supplier and dominant in the market of digital interactive TV services in the UK.[197] No further determinations have been made to date.

4.18.6 Private mobile radio class licence[198]

The private mobile radio (PMR) class licence permits a narrow range of mobile services, including the provision of automatic vehicle location systems, running PMR systems from a single base station (e.g., taxi firms, fleet operators, couriers, mining projects and CBS users) and small paging systems. The licence may permit the running of up to five base stations for larger networks. These type of systems are referred to in the licence as private mobile radio systems, radiopaging systems and automatic locations systems.[199]

As with all apparatus under licences of this kind, the apparatus must be approved (see Telecommunications Act 1984, s. 22) if it is to be connected to an outside telecommunications service. Furthermore, since the apparatus involves a telecommunication system which uses radio, users are required to obtain an additional licence under the Wireless Telegraphy Act 1949. There

---

[197] See *Decision as to the Status of Sky Subscribers Services Limited as a Regulated Supplier in the Market for Access Control Services for Digital Interactive TV Services* (dated 20 June 2000); see also Decision of 15 September 1999 relating to a proceeding under Art. 81 of EC Treaty (Case IV/36.359, *British Interactive Broadcasting/Open*) (1999/781/EC).
[198] Class licence to run mobile radio systems to provide telecommunications services to third parties (PMR), dated 22 May 2000.
[199] Annex A 'the applicable system'. Note that a PMR licence cannot include CT2 Apparatus or DECT Apparatus.

are severe constraints on the availability of spectrum in some frequency bands. Applicants seeking to use radio in their systems should therefore approach the Radiocommunications Agency about the availability of suitable frequencies at an early stage in the formulation of their plans. Note that the effective range of a base station is largely governed by the height of its antenna, but the Radiocommunications Agency may place limits upon the antenna location and height to avoid excessive interference.

The licence lasts for 25 years from 22 May 2000 (para. 3). It does not cover PTOs and local authorities and other public bodies (para. 2).[200]

4.18.7 Satellite services class licence

The satellite services class licence allows the running of satellite transmit and/or receive terminals (whether fixed, mobile or transportable[201]), provided that these terminals are not connected directly or indirectly (such as via a private leased circuit) to the public network.

The licence authorises the provision of a wide range of satellite services[202] and is available to all operators with the exception of the British Broadcasting Corporation.[203] It has a duration of 25 years from 22 May 2000.

Various conditions attach to this licence and restrict the extent to which an operator may operate under its provisions. The most important restriction can be found in Schedule 3 (para. 3(a)(i), (ii), the 'service authorisation') which prohibits the transmission of messages from fixed earth stations to a public network by means of satellite orbiting apparatus. The same restriction applies when messages transmitted from a fixed earth station are received by a downlink outside of the UK and then passed on to a public network. The reasoning behind this condition is simply that transmissions to and from a public network require the authorisation of a PTO licence. The only exceptions to this condition are where the connection to the public network is by means of a mobile or transportable earth station, or when transmissions to a public network are run under an approved licence authorising the connection.

4.18.8 Cordless class licence[204]

The cordless class licence permits the running of cordless mobile services. As the licence conditions are broadly similar to those of the TSL (see 4.18.3), it

---

[200] The public groups are covered by a largely similar class licence entitled class licence to run mobile radio systems by public sector organisations (dated 22 May 2000).

[201] The 'applicable system' in Annex A describes the types of telecommunication system covered by the licence. The majority of fixed terminals are receive only, as in the case of a standard satellite dish.

[202] The services allowed by the licence are one-way or two-way, point to point or point to multipoint, including voice, data, vision or any other kind of message, for reception within the UK or in any overseas country.

[203] This does not entitle operators such as BT or Mercury to use the licence in order to avoid obligations imposed upon them by any individual licence which they hold and which they should be using to operate the systems in question.

[204] Class licence to run branch systems to provide cordless telecommunications services (dated 30 May 1997). Note this class licence was due to be re-issued in May 2000. However, the new version was not available at the date of writing.

is the definition of 'applicable systems' and the service authorisation which are of importance (Annex A; Schedule 3, para. 3, respectively). The DGT has also produced a helpful explanatory guide which assists in the interpretation of these definitions.[205]

Note that the cordless class licence is technology specific (viz. CT2 or DECT) (Annex A, para. 1(a); see also Annex A, paras 3(b), 3(c)). If the applicable system does not include CT2 or DECT base stations, it is likely that the system will fall within the scope of the TSL. All of the apparatus in the applicable system must be situated in a single set of premises or, if not, in different sets of premises (together with any apparatus run exclusively to enable messages to be conveyed between these premises) provided none of those sets of premises is more than 200 metres in lateral distance from any other (Annex A, para. 1(b)).

Annex A, para. 1(b) specifies that none of the apparatus comprising the applicable systems can be used for the purpose of conveying messages to residential premises where such premises are for the principal purpose of providing residential accommodation to individuals in permanent residence. Examples of premises excluded would be residential houses and self-contained flats (even if the flats were in buildings where non-residential premises were located). Examples of premises allowed under the licence would be hotels, hostels, marinas and caravan parks (for mobile, but not static, residential caravans).

The cordless class licence allows operators to run cordless technology for business customers, provided all recipients are within a 200 metre area (Schedule 3, para. 3, the services authorisation).[206] This licence, which runs for 25 years from 30 May 1997 (Schedule 3, para. 3), is of limited use in the UK.

4.18.9   Broadcasters' satellite downlink class licence[207]

The 200 metre premises rule (see 4.18.7) also applies to this class licence (Annex A, para. 1(b)). The broadcasters' satellite downlink class licence applies only to equipment used to receive messages from earth orbiting apparatus (Annex A, para. 1(a)). This allows broadcasters to convey signals to another telecommunications system for retransmission for general reception or onward conveyance to a studio (Schedule 3, para. 3). The licence lasts for 25 years from 22 May 2000 (licence, para. 3).

---

[205] *Explanatory Guide to the Class Licence to run Branch Systems to provide Cordless Telecommunication Services* (London, OFTEL, 1997).

[206] The '200 metre rule' formed part of the TSL until it was replaced by the 'twenty sets of premises' restriction under the April 2001 revised licence. See *supra* n. 179. As to the TSL, see 4.18.3.

[207] Class licence to run telecommunication systems by broadcasters to receive messages from earth orbiting apparatus (dated 22 May 2000).

4.19   CONCLUDING REMARKS

It is important to note that this chapter generally reflects the status of the significant class licences as of 3 July 2000.[208] Given the sweeping changes currently being undertaken at EU and domestic level, it is anticipated that further changes will occur. This assessment, therefore, represents somewhat of a moving target.

Writing this conclusion some three months later, we now know that the Directives arising from the Commission's 1999 Communications Review have been issued (see 4.8.4). A full review of these is set out in Chapter 8. The principal PTO licences have all been re-issued pursuant to a new statutory instrument which came into force on 21 July 2000 (the Telecommunications (Licence Modifications) (Amendment) Regulations 2000. (See 4.1.5) Para. 1.5). The changes are, however, not significant. Also now in force is the Regulation of Investigatory Powers Act 2000 and, pursuant to this, the Telecommunications (Lawful Business Practice) (Interception of Communications) Regulations 2000 (SI 2000/2699), which deal with privacy issues. As to local loop unbundling, note also that Condition 83 of the BT PTO licence came into force on 8 August 2000.[209] We have also seen heavy criticism of the DGT in respect of his role concerning the perceived delays in the method and allocation of collocation space at BT's local exchanges (by way of the so-called 'Bow Wave' selection process').[210]

Necessary though these changes may be, these points do not address the key difficulty with the current UK licensing regime. This relates to the breadth and diversity of material that operators are required to digest to understand the environment in which they operate. This is not a simple exercise, and has become so onerous that few outside a small group of dedicated practitioners wholly understand the entirety of the relevant issues.

While in an era of hard-wired telecommunications and monopolistic source of supply, the Telecommunications Act 1984 ploughed a furrow for subsequent EU (and relevant Member State) regulation, 16 years on, in a radically different environment, the same regime is markedly less relevant. It is no longer sufficient to continue to apply multiple layers of amending statutory instruments to increasingly inappropriate legislation. Amending primary legislation is urgently required.

Although it is accepted that departures from EU Directives are often difficult to achieve as a matter of law, much too frequently, implementing secondary legislation repeats *verbatim* the inherently pan-European drafting of those Directives. However, the current difficulties cannot solely be ascribed to the absence of sufficient Parliamentary scrutiny. The drafting of the licences (particularly the PTO licence) must soon be re-addressed. All too often, the language is inconsistent and circular. Conditions remain in licences for the purposes of standardisation rather than because they apply to the

---

[208] However, updates have been made or changes noted during the editing and proofing process to material considered no longer accurate.

[209] See Director's Determination under Condition 83.27, *supra* n. 144.

[210] See also *Consultation on Local Loop Unbundling 'Bow Wave Process'* (London, OFTEL, 2000).

particular licensee. This is particularly prominent in the mobile PTO licence, which includes conditions originating from the Revised Voice Telephony Directive (which largely applies to the fixed PTO licence only). Moreover, finding the source material to give guidance on these matters can be chaotic and not fruitful.

Whether this represents a transparent licensing regime is open to doubt. If it is not, it may be said that the UK is not complying with the requirements of Art. 3(2) of the Licensing Directive.

CHAPTER FIVE

Interconnection, Access and Peering: Law and Precedent

Rohan Kariyawasam

No man is an island, entire of itself; every man is a piece of the continent, a part of the main.

John Donne, *Devotions Upon Emergent Occasions* (1624)

5.1 INTRODUCTION

Interconnect is the modern solution to the ancient problem described by Donne. Interconnection is effectively the means for ensuring cohesion in a society of many parts, a way to link disparate communication islands and, at the highest level, a means of transforming humanity's natural tendency to compete into a force for cooperation.

On a more mundane level, interconnection is the physical joining together of two separate telecommunication networks to allow customers connected to one network to communicate with customers connected to the other. The terms on which the network operators agree to connect their networks together form what is known as an interconnection agreement.

The *technical* side of the agreement specifies where the two networks will be connected (points of interconnection), how they will be connected, how calls will be transferred from one network to the other, and how end-to-end quality of service will be maintained.

The *commercial* side of the agreement specifies how much one operator will charge the other for handling its calls, how the charges will then be recorded, and how customers will be authenticated and billed.

This chapter examines the necessary arrangements for interconnection, both of the networks and of the services provided by them. The aim of the chapter is to introduce the reader to the basic principles underlying interconnection and the important elements that constitute an interconnect agreement. Section 5.2 looks at the basic principles of interconnection, and 5.3 at the negotiation and structure of a fixed-line circuit-switched (voice) interconnect agreement. Although European law on telecommunications is discussed elsewhere in this book (see Chapter 8), 5.4 below examines the application of competition law (*ex-post*) and sector-specific (*ex-ante*) legislation as it applies specifically to the area of interconnection.

In recent years, we have also seen an exponential growth in the use of data and Internet protocol (IP) networks. The interconnection of IP networks is a specialised area and is covered in 5.5 below. That section also includes an analysis of the regulatory framework beginning to emerge for Internet interconnection and concludes with a table summarising some of the key differences between traffic flows on the conventional public switched telephone network (PSTN) and the Internet, differences that regulators need to understand to be able to put in place effective regulation for the Internet.

5.2 THE BASIC PRINCIPLES OF INTERCONNECTION

Interconnection in telecommunications is based on the fundamental principle of 'any to any connectivity'. The voice telecommunications network is founded on the principle of universal connectivity – the integration of networks to enable a customer connected to one carrier's network to call a customer connected to another carrier's network. A handset, a subscription, and a number is understood to mean that the customer can reach all other numbers and can itself also be reached. No one network can stand in isolation. To give customers value for money, a network operator is compelled to interconnect with others so as to increase the overall reach of its services.

The right to interconnection is necessary in a deregulated telecommunications market. Indeed, interconnection can be described as the *key fundamental* to the viability of competition in telecommunications.[1] However, the principle of 'any to any connectivity' is not the only concept as regards the regulation of interconnect. Two others also play an important role:

(a) *equal access*, which denotes the ability of the customer directly connected to the incumbent network to access retail services of the new entrant on a seamless and equivalent basis to that on which the customer accesses the same retail services of the incumbent; and

(b) *non-discrimination*, which denotes the ability of the new entrant to be provided with interconnection services on no less favourable terms than the incumbent provides to itself.

---

[1] See, e.g., Long, C. (ed.), *Telecommunications Law and Practice* (2nd edn) (London, Sweet & Maxwell, 1998).

Other forms of regulation also assist in the governance of interconnect, such as guidelines on pricing and on the way negotiations should be structured. In Europe, for example, the European Commission has issued an Interconnection Directive (see 5.4.4 below)[2] to help national regulatory authorities (NRAs) in the various EC Member States deal with regulating interconnect.

Most countries which have opened up their telecommunications markets to competition have also established general principles which must be followed by the incumbent in order to provide interconnection (one notable exception is New Zealand; see 5.2.1 below). Furthermore, at least 72 Member States, representing 93 per cent of worldwide telecoms turnover, have taken out *specific commitments* known as the *Fourth Protocol* or *Basic Telecoms Agreement*, which came into force on 5 February 1998.[3] Part of the Basic Telecoms Agreement includes a Reference Paper which details, as part of a legal framework for liberalisation, specific rules on interconnection. Section 2.2 of the Reference Paper sets out obligations on major suppliers[4] for interconnection. Under Section 2.2, interconnection must be provided:

(a)   at any technically feasible point in the network;
(b)   on non-discriminatory terms, rates and of a quality no less favourable than for the incumbent's own supply;
(c)   in a timely fashion and on terms that are transparent and reasonable;
(d)   at cost-orientated rates; and
(e)   on an unbundled basis so that a buyer does not pay for unnecessary services.

Again, the principle of non-discrimination emerges (see also the Interconnection Directive, Art. 6, at 5.4.4 below). However, this should not be surprising considering that the WTO provisions apply globally across 72 Member States. But in effect, each country will have its own framework and principles of interconnect.[5] The structure of an interconnect agreement itself will be closely linked to and depend on the regulatory framework within which that agreement sits.

---

[2] Parliament and Council Directive 97/33/EC on Interconnection in Telecommunications with regard to ensuring universal service and interoperability through application of the principles of Open Network Provision (1997) OJ L 199/32, 26 July 1997.

[3] See Council Decision (97/838/EC) of 28 November 1997 concerning the conclusion on behalf of the European Community, as regards matters within its competence, of the results of the WTO negotiations on basic telecommunications services ((1997) OJ L 347/45, 18 December 1997). See generally Chapter 10, at 10.4.

[4] A 'major supplier' is defined in the Reference Paper as one who has market power because of: (a) its control over an essential facility; or (b) its position in the market. The important doctrine of 'essential facilities' is discussed at 5.4.2 below.

[5] Although WTO law does not usually have direct effect, under European law (Cases 267–269/81 *Amministrazione delle Finanze dello Stat v SPI* and *SAMI* [1983] ECR 801) measures converting WTO obligations into European law have to be interpreted in accordance with WTO law (*Nakajima All Precision Co. Ltd v Council of the European Communities* (Case 69/89) [1991] ECR 2069). It can be implied therefore that EU Member States should directly or indirectly apply WTO and therefore General Agreement on Trade in Services (GATS) law. See Chapter 10, at 10.4.4.

Furthermore, most jurisdictions require interconnect agreements to be lodged with the NRA. The NRA will then have the ability to review the agreement and determine if it fits with the NRA's or the government's guidelines on interconnect in that jurisdiction. Inevitably this leads to a degree of *transparency* which new entrants view as essential to help consolidate future investment plans. This transparency of terms is important if the new entrant is to have an idea of the costs and terms for interconnect with the incumbent, or the market for interconnect rates, if a competitive market exists. Often the NRA's oversight of the negotiating process plays a critical role in levelling out the playing field between a powerful incumbent and new entrants keen on interconnecting at either an infrastructure or a service level.

Inevitably, the reviewing power of the regulator will depend on how well the regulatory authorities are staffed and the technical competence of their personnel. If an NRA is respected and the regulators (whether they be in the form of a Commission, as in the US or headed by a Director-General, as in the UK[6]) are seen as fair, reasonable and beyond 'influence', the NRA's reviewing power will be generally welcomed by new entrants. The process of the review itself can act as a catalyst for both incumbent and new entrant to negotiate terms that are fair and reasonable rather than getting drawn into lengthy disputes that end up with the parties having to resort to a formal regulatory adjudication. Dispute resolution is discussed in greater detail at 5.3.4 below.

5.2.1 Policy issues on interconnection agreements and regulatory intervention

Different governments around the world have adopted varying approaches on how efficient and fair terms for interconnection should be agreed. Certain regulators in particular jurisdictions believe that the dominance of incumbent public telecommunication operators requires a regime that supports market entry by providing for regulatory intervention when terms cannot be agreed, often between new entrant and incumbent. Others believe that commercial agreements between operators should be freely negotiated without interference by the regulator. Lastly, there is an increasing worldwide recognition that competition law should apply to the incumbent to ensure that its negotiating stance does not in any way represent collusion with other similarly powerful operators or abuse of a dominant market position.

In a worldwide survey of regulatory regimes completed by the International Telecommunications Union (ITU) and published in a 1999 report,[7] the ITU found that four basic types of regulatory intervention apply:

---

[6] A draft Utilities Bill, published on 21 January 2000, proposed transferring the functions of the Director-General of Telecommunications to a new Telecommunications Authority and setting up a new Telecommunications Council, in effect abolishing OFTEL. Apparently resistance to this caused the Government to remove the provisions on telecommunications. The Utilities Act 2000 was enacted with respect only to gas and electric utilities.

[7] *Trends in Telecommunications Reform 1999: Convergence and Regulation* (ITU, 1999), chap. 6.

(a) *Commercial negotiation.* With this approach, the issues are left entirely for commercial negotiation between the parties. If they fail to agree, they may appeal to general competition and antitrust law.

(b) *Commercial negotiation but subject to regulatory intervention.* The issues are again left entirely to commercial negotiation, but are subject to regulatory intervention if the parties fail to agree.

(c) *Commercial negotiation but the NRA sets the framework.* This approach also involves leaving the issues entirely to commercial negotiation, but the NRA sets the framework for negotiations and has to approve the agreement or intervene if the parties fail to agree.

(d) *Set regime.* The last approach involves specific issues being prescribed from the outset by the NRA, leaving the parties to negotiate over the remaining issues.

Approaches (a) and (b) rely on market forces rather than regulation. New Zealand has taken this stance, letting market forces drive the interconnection agreements. Unfortunately, this resulted in almost two years of conflict through the courts before the first interconnection agreement was signed between the incumbent Telecom New Zealand and the new entrant, Clear Communications (*Telecom Corporation of NZ Ltd* v *Clear Communications Ltd* [1995] 1 NZLR 385). This laissez-faire policy is now under review. According to the ITU, the majority of African countries also let the parties negotiate most of the fundamental issues of interconnection. The main drawback of this approach is that without a regulatory framework in place, the new entrant is often left in a weaker position when negotiating with the more powerful and established incumbent.

The Americas rely more on approaches (c) and (d). In this region, increased liberalisation has led to a proliferation of interconnection agreements with the need for an external referee, such as an NRA or the sector ministry, intervening in the event of a dispute.

Europe is also adopting approaches closer to (c) and (d), allowing the NRAs to set the framework in advance of negotiations with powers to supervise the process of negotiation. Most of western Europe is also tied together through membership of an economic area customs agreement, the EC Treaty and the presence of a powerful supranational regulator, the European Commission, which plays a crucial role in the regulation of interconnection across its Member States.[8] Eastern Europe, by contrast, is in the process of developing competition with a series of privatisations of national incumbents in recent years, such as the 1999 sales of 51 per cent of BTC in Bulgaria to OTE and KPN, and 35 per cent of the Romanian operator (RomTelecom) to OTE. The accession of various Central and South East European (CSEE) countries to the EU is also proving to be a powerful catalyst for change, with various international organisations (including the WTO, EC, and the European Bank for Reconstruction and Development (EBRD)) all active in regional projects to raise standards to EU levels.

---

[8] For further details on European integration see Frankel, Jeffrey A., 'Regional Trading Blocs in the World Economic System' (IIE), 1997.

As with the CSEE region, Asia is also characterised by very different regulatory regimes. Singapore, Hong Kong and Japan all have detailed interconnection regimes. India and China are developing policies, while Sri Lanka leads the way in the Indian subcontinent in having the regulator take a more active role in negotiations.

In most jurisdictions in practice, the carriers will settle on a detailed access agreement that sets out the rights and obligations of each party. In countries such as Australia, for example, where the new entrant is required to establish the reasonableness of its interconnection request before the incumbent is required to interconnect, the new entrant will want to set out clearly in the agreement the terms on which a request is considered reasonable. Through this process, the new entrant will be able to determine its interconnection rights with the incumbent's network.

As noted, most jurisdictions require interconnect agreements to be lodged with the NRA. It is also common for the same NRA to have a reviewing power which is generally favoured, as this has the result of encouraging the parties to negotiate a fair and competitively neutral agreement from the start rather than resorting to formal regulatory adjudication, which can be expensive and time-consuming.

5.2.2 The growth in agreements

Each country needs interconnection arrangements which encourage economically efficient behaviour by the competing operators. For example, to set interconnection charges too high will restrict competition; but to set them too low will encourage entry by operators which are less efficient than the incumbent. As markets liberalise and new entrants demand interconnection, the number of agreements the incumbent will need to administer can grow to become onerous. Table 5.1 illustrates how the number of possible interconnection agreements grows with a corresponding increase in operators.

In practice, however, the number of interconnect agreements will be less than the theoretical maximum. The reason for this will be down to the market itself. In any one particular jurisdiction, or interconnection market, there may be a number of legal and strategic reasons why some parties will agree to

Table 5.1 Operators v interconnection agreements[9]

Number of operators	Number of possible interconnection agreements
2	1
5	9
10	45
20	190

[9] *Source*: Ovum Report on Interconnection (1994).

interconnect with each other and some will not. For example, it is a standard case that the mobile subsidiaries of parent fixed-line networks will want to interconnect and pass traffic across their parents' networks rather than interconnecting with a new entrant that has infrastructure of its own.[10] Similarly, new entrants may seek interconnect deals with the incumbent, but may avoid interconnecting with other new entrants.

5.2.3 Interconnection schematics

Although modern networks have given rise to a plethora of different types of interconnect agreement, from mobile networks to fixed-line networks, satellite to cable, in reality the range of possible interconnect agreements can be summarised into four basic forms: simple; transit; by-pass; and transit by-pass. All four types of arrangement are shown at Figure 5.1 and Figure 5.2.

Figure 5.1 indicates the schematic for simple interconnect. Simple interconnection involves two networks, where one operator delivers calls originated by another operator's customer. Simple interconnect agreements are often complementary, the first operator (A) needing the second (B) to deliver its customers' calls, and *vice versa*. Almost all international interconnect agreements have as their basis the simple interconnect agreement. They also form the basis of agreements between mobile operators, and between

Figure 5.1   Simple and transit interconnect

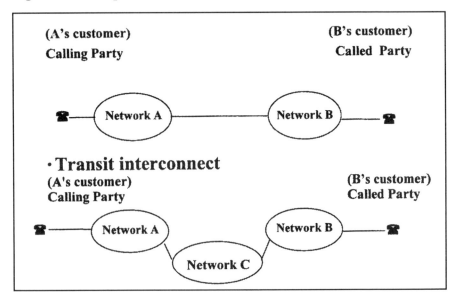

---

[10] This will generally be the case unless the customer has a choice over the mobile access link to the fixed network or the fixed network itself through a form of carrier pre-selection.

Figure 5.2   By-pass and transit by-pass interconnect

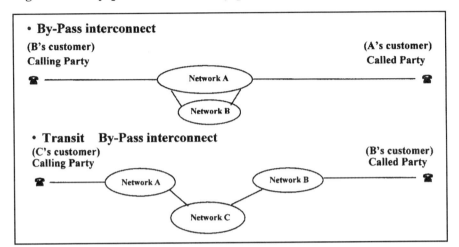

mobile operators and fixed-network operators. As each operator has something to gain from such agreements, they are often relatively easy to negotiate.

The lower part of Figure 5.1 illustrates *transit* interconnect. Here each network is connected to a third network at separate points of interconnect, and the third network is used to relay calls from one network to the other. Transit interconnect agreements are most common in the United States, or in any country where a government has decided to restrict competition at *both* a national and a state level, with constraints on the same operator being able to provide services both *inter-* and *intra*-state. In the US, transit interconnect forms the basis of agreements between most regional local network operators (e.g., a Regional Bell Operating Company, or RBOC) and long-distance operators, such as AT&T or Sprint for example.

Figure 5.2 shows *by-pass* interconnect. This involves two operators, where one operator originates calls on behalf of another operator's customers as well as delivering them. With by-pass, a call is conveyed from the calling party over the first operator's network to a switch, where the point of interconnection (POI) with the second operator's network is located and then handed over to the second operator's network (the by-pass element) to another POI, and then back to the first operator's network to the called party. Usually, but not always, by-pass interconnect agreements are regarded as competitive, i.e. operator A is competing with operator B to deliver the calls. By-pass interconnect agreements often form the basis of agreements between incumbent integrated telephone companies such as BT and new market entrants, e.g., Mercury, Energis or Colt Telecommunications in the UK.

The lower section of Figure 5.2 shows *transit by-pass* interconnect. Transit by-pass involves three different networks, where one operator originates calls on behalf of another operator's customers and a third operator delivers the calls. Like simple interconnect, transit by-pass can also describe international interconnect arrangements. But there is a very real danger with transit by-pass that the arrangement could lead to anti-competitive effects, at least from the perspective of A and C. This happens where operators A and C (shown in Figure 5.2) are competing in a jurisdiction where telecoms service and infrastructure provision is regarded as being *competitive*. Operator B, by contrast, could be the dominant incumbent in a jurisdiction where liberalisation of infrastructure and services is yet to take place, therefore leaving B with a monopoly on the market for call termination in its jurisdiction. In transit by-pass, B is then able to play A and C against each other to obtain the best call termination rate possible. This is a process called *whipsawing*, and without government intervention, for example by way of the dispute resolution process through the WTO,[11] or threatening to cut off international accounting rate payments to the government of B, operator B will continue to exact monopoly rates from both A and C.

All the interconnection models described above use either *call collection* or *call delivery* agreements, or a combination of both. For example, simple and transit interconnect use only call delivery agreements. Parties to a call delivery agreement agree only to *terminate* each other's traffic. Because each party gains from the agreement, call delivery agreements tend to be straightforward and quick to negotiate. In by-pass and transit by-pass, however, the parties use both call delivery *and* call origination agreements. Call origination agreements involve one of the parties having to hand over confidential information on its own customers to the other side. Without this information, the interconnecting operator will not be able to process billing information or determine whether particular customers are *bona fide* customers of the originating operator. Both examples in Figure 5.2 show one operator *originating* a call on behalf of the other's customer. As a consequence, call origination agreements take longer to negotiate and are more complicated as they involve confidentiality and non-solicitation provisions that need to be negotiated. The negotiation and structure of an interconnection agreement is covered in more detail at 5.3 below.

5.3   CIRCUIT-SWITCHED INTERCONNECTION: NEGOTIATION AND STRUCTURE OF A BASIC FIXED-LINE INTERCONNECTION AGREEMENT

Interconnect determines if, when and which services can be launched. It has been estimated that 40 per cent of costs for second operators go towards interconnection payments,[12] yet within a company, the complexities of the

---

[11] The complaint will be at intergovernmental level and will be to the dispute settlement body (DSB) of the WTO in Geneva. However, prior to referring the dispute to the DSB in Geneva, the trade offices of the governments concerned will try at first to achieve a diplomatic solution. They will do this in accordance with a timetable set out under the dispute resolution provisions of the GATS. See Chapter 10, at 10.4.5.

[12] Commission Recommendation on Interconnection in a Liberalised Telecommunications Market, (98/195/EC, (1998) OJ L 73/41, 12 March 1998), Pt 1 'Interconnection Pricing, at 3.1.

issues involved in interconnect may often be underestimated. In many instances the in-house legal team may consider it as just another agreement, the marketers as only a target date when they require interconnection to be available, and the network managers may simply ask for the network to be interconnected with other networks.

Not surprisingly, the management of interconnect may not always be focused. Resources are often determined by departmental budgets rather than an internal interconnection policy and responsibility is scattered amongst regulatory affairs, marketing, IT and other disciplines. Interconnection is (or should be) running one step ahead of the business planning process. Those involved with negotiating interconnect need to be proactive. The network may only be in the initial build phase, and although the marketing approach may still be unclear, at this early and critical stage, the marketers and sales representatives need to ask themselves what services need to be provided and to whom.

Successful interconnection calls for a multi-disciplinary approach. The flowchart shown in Figure 5.3 demonstrates the relationship between a company's interconnection activities and the breakdown of how an interconnection negotiation can be approached. This example demonstrates only *one* approach, and there are many more depending on the nature of the interconnect agreement to be negotiated. In Figure 5.3, the author is looking at a sophisticated interconnect agreement involving the rollout of a new network nationally and the interconnection of that network with the incumbent's at a number of POIs. The agreement involves both infrastructure leasing and services provision by the incumbent.

Figure 5.3   Flowchart of interconnection activities

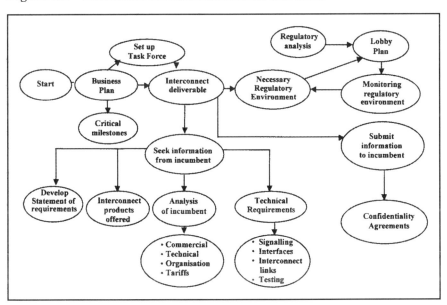

Figure 5.3 highlights the activities required to be examined by a new entrant wanting to rollout a substantial network. We see a flowchart of activities beginning with the need to set up an appropriate task force, which will consist of appointing network managers, lawyers and the commercial team. We also see the principal areas of the interconnection process that the new entrant will need to master in order to ensure that negotiations are well prepared for. Often the critical area is the scope and powers of the NRA and the regulatory framework in place at the time. A discussion of the regulatory framework in Europe and the UK is included at 5.4 below.

Interconnection agreements often comprise a main body of legal terms and conditions, and a series of schedules and specifications, all of which need to be put in order of precedence for defining the relationship between the parties. Whereas the legal terms and conditions may run to only four or five pages, the whole agreement can consist of 100 or even 200 pages including all the schedules! The detail is often left to the schedules. However, most service providers or switch-based resellers may need to negotiate interconnect agreements that run to only two or three pages in total. Annexed to the back of these simple agreements will be the tariff schedules for the services involved.

5.3.1 Practicalities

There are a number of practical considerations which should be focused upon prior to the commencement of negotiations. As indicated above, an operator must be prepared to invest adequate efforts and financial resources into negotiations for interconnect, and resource the negotiations with personnel from within the operator company who are appropriately qualified to deal with the issues.

The operator should be aware of and understand the objectives and powers of the regulator. This is extremely important. A new entrant must consider the implications of the regulatory arena prior to setting a market entry strategy, as there are many examples of new entrants failing to enter a market simply due to underestimating the legislative framework in place at the time, or even failing to anticipate changes in the framework that could affect their business.

Besides regulatory problems, the operator should also try to anticipate and understand the *objectives* of the operator from whom they want interconnection. As mentioned above, good preparation in advance of interconnect negotiations is essential.

Confidentiality is also a critical issue in negotiations. Detailed confidentiality agreements should be drawn up and signed by both parties prior to entry into discussions. Each party should state clearly in these confidentiality agreements the limited purpose for which information received from the other side can be disclosed, and a 'quarantine' should be placed upon it so that information is not 'leaked' to other parts of the company, such as marketing and new service development groups. Wording in the agreement should make it clear that information should be disclosed on a strictly 'need to know' basis and only for the purposes of negotiating the interconnect arrangements. In an ideal world, confidentiality of information should cover:

(a) provisions restricting use of customer information received from other carriers;
(b) information in relation to customer bad debts;
(c) denial of information if appropriate security procedures have not been put in place;
(d) disclosure to employees, directors and advisers; and
(e) disclosure to shareholders, privacy and data protection issues.

5.3.2 Understanding the other side

Understanding the other side is critical to the negotiating process. To help to evaluate the position of the other side, it is often useful to consider answers to a checklist of questions to focus the content of the agreement itself and where the parties should spend most of their time negotiating.

Paragraph 5.2.3 above introduced the four basic types of interconnect. If we take the first (*simple interconnect*) as an example where operator A originates a call from customer A and operator B terminates it to reach customer B, the checklist of basic questions in Table 5.2 below can be considered.

Table 5.2   Checklist of questions

Object	*Question*
Termination	What should operator B charge operator A for terminating the call?
Defining the size of the network and its hierarchy	Where should the POIs be located and how many will be required? Who is responsible for maintaining these POIs?
Call routing	Is there any choice as to how the call is routed through the other's network?
Defining the network interfaces	What form of interface should be used at the point of interconnect?
Defining the services	What services of operator B should be available to customer A, and at what charge?
Defining the network access	What form of access is to be used by operator A to B's network; direct or indirect access?

Object	*Question*
Charges	How are the interconnect charges between operators A and B recorded, how are they checked, and what conditions of payment apply?

Each of the parties to the agreement will need to ask itself how the answers to these questions will change over time. Further, and importantly, four additional questions arise in a network where *by-pass* interconnect is used. By-pass is illustrated in Figure 5.2 and has both customers A and B connected to the same network (operator A), but with the long-distance element of the call passing over operator B's network. Such a configuration involves further questions, as follows:

(a)   Which of the two operators, A or B, bills customer A for the long-distance element of the call carried over operator B's network?

(b)   If operator B does the billing, B will need to gain access to customer A's billing name and address and check that customer A is an authorised user. How will it do this?

(c)   Again, if operator B does the billing, how much does operator A charge for delivering calls to the POI between networks A and B? Will this charge include separate elements for subscriber-line and switching charges?[13]

(d)   For long-distance services, how does customer A select between operators A and B?

The other two forms of interconnect, transit and transit by-pass, involve a combination of these issues. Paragraph 5.3.3 below examines some of the terms discussed here in more detail, as they often form the most crucial areas in an interconnection agreement and are the areas most likely to lead to protracted negotiations.

5.3.3   Selected terms

As mentioned at 5.1 above, the interconnection agreement can often be divided into two basic sections, technical and commercial. The *technical* side of the agreement specifies where the two networks will be connected (POIs), how they will be connected, how calls will be transferred from one network to the other, and how end-to-end quality of service will be maintained. The *commercial* side of the agreement specifies how much one operator will charge the other for handling its calls, how the charges will then be recorded, how customers will be authenticated and billed, and provisions made for bad debt.

---

[13] For example, in the US, the Access Charge Reform Order reformed the inter-state access charge system. Access charges were to be paid by long-distance companies (such as MCI, Sprint) for access to the local facilities of the Local Exchange Carriers (e.g., BellSouth). Subscriber-line and switching charges were to become more cost-orientated, and non-traffic related costs were to be recovered through a flat-rate charge.

Often the legal terms and conditions that govern the whole agreement on liability, indemnity, warranties on performance, etc., are split away from the more complex technical and commercial schedules. The detail of the agreement is often to be found in the schedules, which can run to many hundreds of pages. In general, the detail of the schedules will be focused along the lines of the following headings, which will always be present in a standard form (circuit-switched) interconnect agreement:

(a) network configuration;
(b) access and POIs;
(c) co-location;
(d) proposed interface;
(e) capacity requirements;
(f) traffic forecasts;
(g) traffic types;
(h) proposed implementation schedule;
(i) definition of interconnection services; and
(j) charges.

5.3.3.1 Network configuration The interconnect agreement will define both operators' networks, by identifying their network termination points. The network termination points will be identified by numbers from the National Numbering Plan in the jurisdiction concerned. Often the responsibility for the allocation of numbers would have been transferred by the government to an independent body, such as an NRA. But in some jurisdictions the national incumbent may have the responsibility for the allocation of numbers, which can obviously influence the negotiating balance between incumbent and new entrant. The interconnection agreement will also need to define responsibility for network management and quality of service by reference to these network termination points.

5.3.3.2 Access and POIs Both operators will need to consider the desired locations of their POIs, bearing in mind that these should be located at the *lowest* possible level in the network architecture of the other operator so as to minimise the use made of the other operator's network (see below). In the example of a new entrant interconnecting with an incumbent, if the incumbent has already given details of the proposed location of POIs to the new entrant B,[14] B should carefully examine these locations for suitability. If necessary, it should draw up an alternative list that is more suitable. Again, without a confidentiality agreement being in place, B should not release details of its proposed POIs to the incumbent, as the latter may target these geographical locations for new business development.

Regarding access to facilities, each operator should start from the premise that it should be afforded access to the other's network at any point at which

---

[14] Which it is very unlikely to do without a confidentiality agreement first being in place. The list of network termination points will give the new entrant the information it needs to locate where (geographically) it should target its customers.

connection is technically feasible.[15] The new entrant will need to be aware that a dominant incumbent may attempt to restrict potential points of connection because of strategic and commercial sensitivity. There is no hard-and-fast rule on access. Direct access will involve the new entrant having to build out its own network infrastructure and directly connect it with the incumbent at one or more POIs. With direct access, the carrier to whose network the customer is directly connected will generally provide the basic telephone services of that customer including local, national or international. Indirect access, by contrast, makes use of a common link across a local network controlled by the incumbent. With indirect access, the customer can choose his or her service provider by dialling an access code. Alternatively the customer can opt to pre-select (or pre-subscribe in the US) different carriers for different services, e.g., local, national or international. New entrants prefer indirect access due to the lower up-front costs of infrastructure.

Often the incumbent will not want to grant access to its customer base, because new entrants will be in a better position to offer its customers a competitive service. Long-distance operators prefer equal access (call-by-call or pre-selection) because it gives them better access to the incumbent customer base than easy access (call-by-call or pre-programmed).

In terms of physical infrastructure, a POI will consist of an E1 leased line with a transmission capacity in Europe of 2 Mbps or higher (as opposed to a T1 link in the US operating at 1.54 Mbps) and will connect ports on the new entrant's switch to ports on the incumbent's switch. Where the switches adhere to different standards, the POI will also include equipment to translate between these standards.

A POI may also include equipment for calculating and recording interconnect charges. This will normally be a computer attached to one of the operators' switches. A POI may also include monitoring equipment to ensure that the quality of a call is maintained over the POI.

As mentioned above, from an economic perspective, the new entrant will want to interconnect with the incumbent's network at the *lowest possible point* in the incumbent's network. The reason for this is that a call signal will then not have to travel very far along the incumbent's network to be terminated at the incumbent's customer's network termination point. As the distance travelled along the incumbent's network is shorter, the incumbent will charge a correspondingly lower economic cost of the call to the new entrant. However, there is also a downside to this argument.

By wanting to interconnect at the lowest point in the network hierarchy of the incumbent, the new entrant will be forced to build out its own network infrastructure to at least the local exchange level. This will be extremely expensive for the new entrant whose business plan may not include national network rollout. The business plan may only be to target certain niche metropolitan areas to rollout network, or to target certain services markets in which to compete with the incumbent. Consequently there is a balance to

---

[15] This is the case in Europe under the Interconnection Directive, *supra* n. 2. The Interconnection Directive also provides for points of interconnection not otherwise available to the majority of end-users or special network access (SNA). See 5.4.8.1 below for further details of SNA.

reach between the number of POIs that the new entrant wishes to choose and *where* in the incumbent's network these POIs should be located. Where more POIs are specified, the cost of connecting the networks rises, but the cost of collecting and delivering calls falls. For any given volume of calls, therefore, there is an optimum number (and location) of POIs such that the overall cost is minimised. For most new entrants, this will probably result in the new entrant interconnecting with the incumbent at exchanges higher up in the incumbent's network hierarchy, such as at the tandem or double tandem exchange.[16]

As the new entrant's business grows, however, and the volume of traffic the new entrant sends to the incumbent increases, the balance will change. The new entrant may find that it needs more POIs, and will position these POIs lower down in the incumbent's network to reduce costs. Therefore an interconnect agreement needs to be *dynamic*, not static. The agreement has to be flexible enough to meet the new entrant's demands in the future as well as meeting present demand.

5.3.3.3 Co-location Co-location is vital for operators wishing to minimise their network costs as it involves a certain element of facilities sharing, where both interconnecting parties may share the costs of having to house their individual switches. Quite often the incumbent is in a dominant position and will through its period of past monopoly have built a series of *telehuts* or switching-facilities where it will house its own switches. The new entrant will want to reduce its costs and will seek access to the incumbent's switch facilities through the interconnection agreement. To do this, it will make a request for co-location. There are three basic options:

(a) *Remote co-location.* Here, the POI is made at the new entrant's switch, or at some mid-point between the incumbent's and new entrant's switch. The new entrant provides a dedicated line between one of its switches and the POI. The cost of the dedicated line is generally borne by the new entrant. In the UK, BT allows an 'in-span interconnect', which merely allows the interconnecting operator to site a footway box just outside the BT trunk exchange, which is then connected to the exchange itself by a transmission link known as an interconnect link. Obviously this will cause the interconnecting operator to incur additional expense in establishing and maintaining interconnect links. In some cases, for example broadband interconnect, such expenses can be prohibitive due to the high cost of laying the fibre for the interconnect link.

The ability of the new entrant to share the incumbent's facilities will help to reduce the overall costs incurred by the new entrant. The following two options are better than remote co-location.

(b) *Virtual co-location.* The POI is made at the incumbent's premises used to house its switch, but is kept physically separated (usually in a terminating

[16] Tandem and double tandem exchanges describe the larger telephone exchanges found in dense metropolitan areas, which serve a wider number of smaller branch or local exchanges. Sometimes, the exchanges where new entrants interconnect are known as Digital Main Switching Units (DMSUs), which is the usual point of handover for geographic and voice and data traffic.

unit on the outside wall of the premises). There is a line between the terminating unit and the incumbent's switch, but the distance involved is very small and the costs of the line are negligible.

(c) *Physical co-location.* The POI is made at the incumbent's premises used to house its switch, but is kept physically separated (usually at a terminating unit in an adjoining room within the premises). A short line will run from the line terminating unit between the two rooms to the incumbent's switch and the costs involved will be small. The new entrant often prefers physical co-location as signal strength is improved, but there is also a downside. In order to gain access to its own equipment, the new entrant will need to seek permission from the incumbent for access to the incumbent's telehut. The terms for access will need to be carefully drafted in the interconnect agreement, as without this right the incumbent may refuse access. The incumbent may choose to do this not only for entirely appropriate reasons (such as the new entrant's engineer failing to provide appropriate identification on demand), but also for anti-competitive reasons. As a consequence of the latter, the European Commission has included in the Interconnection Directive, Art. 11, a requirement for co-location and facilities sharing. This provision can be criticised, though, for being too weak as it only *encourages* the sharing of facilities and makes co-location a matter for commercial negotiation only and not a right. Article 11 also gives powers to the NRA to impose a facilities-sharing agreement on the parties, but only after a period of public consultation. The Interconnection Directive is discussed further at 5.4.4 below.

5.3.3.4 Proposed interface Lists setting out electrical and physical standards, signalling standards, transmission standards and general interface standards will need to be prepared in order to address compatibility of networks.

5.3.3.5 Capacity requirements At each exchange to which the new entrant is seeking access, the new entrant will need to prepare a list of initial and future capacity requirements at that exchange. This will include making the list detailed enough to determine the capacity requirements for *each* specific product that will be used at the exchange (e.g., data circuits, voice telephony, ISDN, etc.).

Alternatives should also be prepared in order that each operator can bear in mind its 'bottom line' position in negotiations. Once the lists are drawn up, the new entrant will need some form of confirmation from the incumbent that its capacity requirements can be met. If not, the new entrant will need to ensure that the incumbent provides a lead-in time for provision of this capacity.

5.3.3.6 Traffic forecasts Each party will need to prepare traffic forecasts. The new entrant will want to avoid forecasting penalties, whereas the service provider will want to impose them. The new entrant will want to ensure that there are no penalties if its actual requirements change after the preparation of the forecast.

5.3.3.7 Traffic types Each party should prepare a list of the types of traffic which it expects will be sent over the other operator's network (for example, voice telephony, data, etc.). Routing principles should also be drawn up.

5.3.3.8 Proposed implementation schedule The new entrant should prepare a list of critical physical, technical, and operational milestones that must be met in order that services can be launched by the planned deadline.

The new entrant, through its marketing and business development departments, may have already entered into contracts in advance with some of its larger customers and have guaranteed a 'ready for service' date. If the new entrant has not built these contractual deadlines into the interconnect agreement with the incumbent, the new entrant may find itself in breach of the service level agreements incorporated into its own customer contracts. This could be both damaging for the new entrant's goodwill and expensive in terms of having to grant service level credits as compensation to the aggrieved customer.

5.3.3.9 Definition of interconnection services This is obviously an important part of the agreement. To compete effectively with the incumbent, the new entrant will need to be able to market a basket of services that is at least equal to or better than the incumbent's own basket. As part of the negotiations, the new entrant should prepare a list of services required from the other side, together with quality of service provisions.

The most common service covered by an interconnect agreement will be the basic telephone (voice) service. However, interconnect agreements can also cover switched digital services (ISDN), permanent circuits (also known as leased lines), freephone, local and national rated calls, and premium rated calls. Most new entrants also want to include the provision of value added services such as emergency call handling, directory assistance and operator assistance in interconnect agreements.

Some new entrants also want to include the provision of access to underground ducts, overhead poles or radio transmitters. Such provisions may not necessarily form part of the main interconnect agreement, but they may be included in a wider commercial agreement, part of which is the interconnect agreement.

The interconnect agreement may also make provision for certain advanced services. Advanced services can be either enhanced basic services, or broadband services. Enhanced basic services are provided using intelligence built into local exchanges or into the network. Examples of enhanced basic services are call-handling services, such as calling line identification and virtual private network services. Broadband services consist of the provision of switched and non-switched circuits with a capacity equal to or in excess of 2 Mbps (1.54 Mbps in the US). Examples of broadband services are broadband ISDN, broadband leased lines, and switched multi-megabit data services.

Quite often, when negotiating the services schedule of an interconnect agreement, new entrants will prefer a *function by function* approach. With function by function, access is granted to the incumbent's network for a particular *wholesale* function that can support a number of retail services. Interconnecting a new retail service that can be supported by the incumbent's wholesale function will not, therefore, require permission to interconnect.[17] Alternatively, negotiating *service by service* involves the new entrant always having to request permission from the incumbent for interconnection of a new retail service.[18]

5.3.3.10 Charges The charging structure for interconnect services is a science in its own right, and a full discussion is beyond the scope of this chapter (see further Chapter 2). In summary, however, the interconnecting party should prepare a statement of its position on interconnection charges.

Interconnection charges can be linked either to the *tariffs*, or to the *costs* of the party providing the interconnection service. Tariffs, however, often bear little relationship to the actual costs incurred by the service provider and cost-based tariffs are preferred, although these are far more complex to calculate and raise a number of important further issues, including:

(a)   Should the basis of charge be time usage or the capacity made available?
(b)   Should marginal costs only be considered, or should other common direct or indirect costs be included?
(c)   How should costs be calculated, on a historic or forward-looking basis?

The answers to these questions will very much depend on the circumstances of the party requesting interconnect. Europe is fast moving to a basis of forward-looking costs or Long Run Incremental Costs (LRIC) and not historic costs. A move to forward-looking costs also applies in the US and Japan.

In general, the interconnect charge may consist of four basic elements, i.e. a charge:

(a)   for connecting the call;
(b)   for the duration of the call;
(c)   to meet some of the costs of providing customers' telephone lines below cost (sometimes known as an *access deficit*);[19]
(d)   to meet some of the costs of universal service obligations.

---

[17] It is important to note that for advanced services, new negotiations for a separate service schedule to the interconnect agreement may be required because the essential functionality provided by a special service may be performed remotely from the networks of the carriers themselves. This is because interconnection of special services often involves the interconnection of specialised databases with those of the carriers' networks. Third-party information suppliers who are under contract with one or even both of the network operators may operate the databases.

[18] This may be the case even if the current interconnection and access agreement with the incumbent can technically provide for the new retail service.

[19] The decision whether or not to include an access deficit charge within the interconnection charge varies by jurisdiction.

Another system of charging is to consider unbundled or element-based charges. With this system of charging, the party requesting interconnect pays only for the service required and not for a basket of bundled services that the service provider may wish to impose. The requirement for unbundled charges by new entrants has been gaining momentum in Europe with the increased pressure on large incumbents to unbundle their local loop networks. Developments in technology, particularly packet switched technology using the Transmission Control Protocol/Internet Protocol (TCP/IP), have an important bearing on the market access strategy that new entrants adopt in targeting new markets. Already we are beginning to see increased competition in the local loop in the liberalised markets of the US, Germany, Finland, Denmark, The Netherlands, and Austria.[20] The UK is planning for the unbundling of BT's local loop by July 2001.[21] Italy should follow shortly and, at the time of writing, France,[22] Ireland and Sweden were consulting on the issue. Outside Europe, unbundled access is available in the US, Australia, Hong Kong and Singapore. SMEs (Small and Medium Enterprise) and other groups inside and outside the metropolitan centres in these markets are unlikely to be willing to pay for dedicated, leased-line access to the Internet or other backbone networks and will in practice rely on the incumbent's local network until alternatives become available (due mainly to the high cost of dedicated leased-line access). Some of these alternatives are already in place, such as wireless local loop technology and the licensing of new UMTS systems. Before fast wireless access systems become widely available, however, many new entrants are looking to interim technologies, such as Asymmetric Digital Subscriber Line (ADSL) and Very Fast DSL Services (VDSL) over the local loop, to deliver fast Internet access to the home or to the SME market.

Lastly there is the concept of end-user pricing. With end-user pricing the regulator allows the incumbent to vary its charges to other operators according to the *use* to which the incumbent's network components are put. Some economists argue that end-user pricing leads to greater efficiency and that it allows new services (such as fast Internet access with ADSL across the incumbent's local loop) to be offered more profitably.[23] The main drawback is the potential for anti-competitive behaviour.

Interest in end-user pricing has grown because of the explosion in the use of data services, such as Internet-related services. Presently, a high percentage of connections to the Internet make use of the local access PSTN. Large corporates using bursty data networks might connect to their Internet service providers over Frame Relay or ATM connections, as these connections are

---

[20] See '1999 Communications Review' (November 1999), at 4.2.3, where the Commission states that the availability of unbundled access to the local loop increases competition and that it could, in addition, speed up the introduction of high-speed Internet access services. See also the Commission's position on unbundled access as set out in its decision on the Telia/Telenor merger M.1439, 13 October 1999.

[21] OFTEL spent many months consulting with industry and BT for a new BT draft licence condition (Condition 83) that would require BT to unbundle its local loop. See n. 27, *infra*.

[22] See the news article in *Telecom Markets* (20 April 2000): 'France Télécom lays down interconnect offer for rivals'.

[23] See the OFTEL Operator Policy Forum paper, *End-user Pricing*, 20 April 1999.

better for handling variable traffic flow. Some Internet services, mostly voice over IP, may substitute for services provided by the traditional telephony operators.

In an ATM/IP environment, the incumbent might find it difficult to allocate accurately costs between video, voice and data or between media and services, as they will all be just 'ones and zeroes' travelling down the same pipe within cells. Similarly, end-user pricing for voice over IP will require that internet telephony traffic be distinguished from other Internet uses. In conclusion, end-user charging is better suited to developed markets where costing information for individual elements of the incumbent's network is available, rather than to markets where such pricing information is not yet known to the regulator.

Whichever method of charging is eventually chosen, the incumbent will quite often want to set high interconnect charges to generate as much offsetting revenue as possible, and also to reduce the flexibility of new entrants to engage in price competition. The new entrant, in contrast, will want low interconnect charges to reduce its own costs and increase its flexibility to engage in price competition.

Due to the fact that each party will generally be at different ends of the spectrum, the regulator often imposes the level of charges that is eventually agreed (but this will of course depend on the powers and influence of the regulator). Further, the incumbent has to be particularly careful in justifying its tariffs, as excessive tariffs may result in a demand by the regulator to examine the cost structure of the incumbent, something that an inefficient incumbent will want to avoid.

New entrants also want *flexibility* with their rates. They would like rates to be reviewed each year to reflect the actual and current costs of the incumbent. Incumbents, however, want rates that are *fixed* over several years. This allows them to prepare their own traffic forecasts and better design network infrastructure. But rates that remain fixed over a number of years allow incumbents to benefit from their own lower costs as they become more efficient, and they may not necessarily share these benefits with new entrants. In the past, interconnect agreements between new entrants and incumbents tended to have little flexibility built into them for the review of rates. This was certainly the case in the UK and Australia, with early interconnect agreements involving BT and Mercury, and Telstra and Optus, respectively. At that time, competition was relatively new and the nature of these agreements reflected the negotiating strength of the incumbent. Now, however, interconnect agreements are much more common and the need for a more frequent review of such agreements has become standard.

There is no doubt that the new entrant/incumbent relationship is on the increase as telecommunication markets liberalise worldwide. It is also this type of relationship that often throws up the most interesting contractual tensions, due largely to the very different bargaining positions of the parties involved, leading inevitably to a need for dispute resolution, the subject of 5.3.4 below.

5.3.4   Dispute resolution

When negotiating the interconnect agreement it is important to keep in mind dispute resolution. Disputes tend to arise over many of the issues discussed above, including charging; customer access; timeliness of negotiations; indirect/direct access; services; and bundled or unbundled services/network components.

To deal with this variety of disputes a number of dispute resolution techniques have evolved, including conciliation; arbitration; urgent interim relief; governing law and submission to jurisdiction; and resolution of technical and commercial issues – expert arbitration. Where in the overall process of negotiation should dispute resolution feature? Figure 5.4 illustrates this more clearly.

Figure 5.4 introduces a new term, a 'Statement of Requirements' (Statement). The Statement establishes the overriding relationship between the new entrant and the incumbent in setting a framework for negotiations for the interconnection agreement. The Statement will specify:

(a)   general principles for negotiation;
(b)   a detailed implementation schedule/critical milestone timetable; and
(c)   reiteration of the existence of the confidentiality agreements.

Some interconnection agreements can run to many hundred of pages, and it is often easier for the purposes of negotiation to split the commercial and technical schedules apart and to negotiate them in parallel in accordance with the timetable set out in the Statement, leaving the option open for dispute resolution if each of the negotiating teams encounters difficulties. Parallel negotiation of the schedules can be seen in Figure 5.4.

In considering the choice of any dispute resolution mechanism, both parties will need to ask themselves how dispute resolution should be imple-

Figure 5.4   Dispute resolution as part of the overall negotiating framework

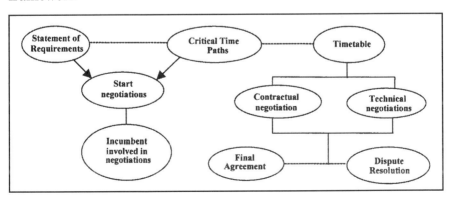

mented in the interconnect agreement. It will also be essential to set out conditions for when it will become appropriate to go to the regulator. The situation may be further complicated in *cross-border* interconnection or access agreements, and particularly within Europe.[24]

The parties will also need to consider carefully how new services are to be implemented in the agreement. We saw at 5.3.3.9 above, that new entrants often prefer a function-by-function approach to the implementation of new services, as they do not need to seek the express permission of the incumbent each time they wish to add a new service. Incumbents, however, prefer a service-by-service approach, and naturally the differences in the two approaches can often lead to disputes. The interconnect agreement therefore will need to cover this important area. And lastly, the parties will need to take account of how the agreement should cover *regulatory changes.*

Dispute resolution mechanisms will, to an extent, shape the way in which interconnection in a country is implemented. As discussed at 5.2.1 above, the ITU has found that dispute resolution mechanisms vary from region to region. In some jurisdictions, exclusive arbitration powers are vested in the regulator and the parties will resort to these powers after attempting to resolve the dispute bilaterally. This standard form of dispute resolution might, however, disadvantage the new entrant if the incumbent is very strong and has a close relationship with the regulator. Sometimes, the parties may wish to avoid going to the regulator altogether, particularly if the regulator is understaffed or does not have the technical competence to deal with the dispute. In this instance, the parties may prefer an independent committee or a number of experts to arbitrate on issues such as technical or billing disputes. In other jurisdictions, the parties will adopt standard alternative dispute resolution procedures similar to those used in other commercial agreements, or may decide not to use them or have them available in any form, and will resort to court action, as demonstrated in New Zealand, between Telecom New Zealand and new entrant, Clear Communications. Generally, in most jurisdictions, regulated arbitration, or the threat of regulated arbitration, has tended to focus the minds of the parties involved and enabled interconnection eventually to be implemented. But there can be no doubt that the way in which parties address disputes will ultimately be a strategic one, and much will depend on the regulatory environment within which the interconnect agreement sits.

5.4 THE LEGISLATIVE ENVIRONMENT FOR INTERCONNECTION

5.4.1 Regulatory framework: European law

In Europe, there are two basic aspects of law governing the regulation of interconnection. The first is *ex-post* regulation or competition law, which

---

[24] There are governing provisions in European law such as Arts 9 and 17 of the Interconnection Directive, *supra* n. 2, and Art. 26 of the ONP Voice Telephony Directive on dispute resolution in interconnection and special network access agreements. The Interconnection Directive is discussed in detail at 5.4.4.

hinges on the application of Arts 81 and 82 (ex 85 and 86) of the EC Treaty. The main facets of competition law important to interconnection are the doctrine of essential facilities and the Access Notice, the Commission's 1998 notification of how it intends to apply competition law to the liberalised telecommunications sector.[25] The second is *ex-ante*, or sector-specific, regulation, in the form of the Interconnection Directive and related legislation. Each will be discussed in turn below.

5.4.2 Doctrine of essential facilities

When discussing an essential facility in terms of 'competition issues', one is really considering the issue of access. The expression 'essential facility' is used to describe a facility or infrastructure which is essential for reaching customers and which is not economic to duplicate.

In telecommunications, access to facilities has been central in a number of alliance and merger cases, such as: *Atlas and Global One* (Case IV/35.337) (1996) OJ L 239/23, *Unisource* (Case IV/35.738 (Uniworld) & Case IV/35.830 (Unisource)) (1997) OJ L 318/1, *BT/MCI* (Case IV/34.857 (BT-MCI)) (1994) OJ L 223/36, and *BT/AT&T* (Case IV/JV.15), 30 March 1999. In most of these cases, the European Commission was able to make use of the commercial interests of the merger participants to force through important conditions on interconnection.[26] It can be argued, however, that in these alliances the merger participants were willing to pay a heavy price for obtaining clearance of their alliances, and that the Commission would probably not find such an accommodating environment for imposing conditions on access and interconnection in more litigious cases where straightforward refusals of access are involved. In such cases the Commission may look to the doctrine of essential facilities ('the doctrine') or the Access Notice to improve conditions for interconnection.

There was a long debate over whether or not there was such a thing as a 'doctrine'. This asks whether a company which controls a facility essential for reaching customers and/or enabling competitors to carry on their business, and which cannot be replicated by any reasonable means (including that it costs too much to do so), must allow others access to that facility (see, e.g., para. 68 of the Access Notice).

Another way of looking at it is to ask whether, once the new entrant has built a duplicate circuit and the incumbent has lowered its prices, the new entrant can still recoup its investment. If it cannot, the incumbent has an essential facility.

In the case of *Oscar Bronner GmbH & Co. KG v Mediaprint Zeitungs-und Zeitschriftenver-lag GmbH & Co. KG* (Case C-7/97) [1998] ECR 1-771 in the European Court of Justice, it was argued that an abuse of an essential facility

---

[25] Commission Notice on the Application of the Competition Rules to Access Agreements in the Telecommunications Sector (1998) OJ C 265/2, 22 August 1998.

[26] For example, in the *Unisource* case, conditions imposed included non-discrimination in the provision of services, accounting requirements for the provision of leased lines, publication of draft interconnection agreements, including being able to interconnect at a reasonable range of termination points, restrictions on tied sales and cross-subsidisation, amongst others.

occurs when a company, having a dominant position in the provision of facilities which are essential for the supply of goods or services in another market, refuses access to those facilities without objective justification. In other words, the owner of an essential facility that uses its power in one market in order to protect or strengthen its position in another related market, and refuses access to its competitors, infringes Art. 82 of the EC Treaty.

We have seen that an essential facility is one that it is not *economic* to duplicate. The local loop of BT, for example, can be considered an essential facility, for the costs to a new entrant in having to duplicate the local loop and provide access via telephone lines to each customer site, would be prohibitive.

Competition in the local loop is important. The European Commission itself has made the issue a priority. If the government of any one jurisdiction concerned takes a proactive approach in increasing competition in the local loop, it will need to ensure that new entrants are given non-discriminatory opportunities to interconnect with the facilities of incumbents in that local loop. Access to the local loop, for example, has already been given in The Netherlands, Finland, Denmark, Austria and in Germany, and also the US. In the UK, the national regulator, OFTEL, has consulted widely on local loop access and has finally accepted to introduce unbundling by July 2001.[27] In the UK's case, however, OFTEL's decision has less to do with the legal application of the doctrine and more to do with the need to meet the demand for potential high-speed interactive services in the near future. The plan by BT to use ADSL technology over its local loop gives it as the UK incumbent a massive advantage since, almost overnight, it is able to transform a legacy narrowband telephone network into a high-speed broadband network. It can be argued, therefore, that the unbundling of BT's network is essential in preventing BT from establishing dominance in the broadband communications market. A discussion of the doctrine is more relevant, though, for cases decided under Art. 82 (ex 86; abuse of a dominant position) EC Treaty, and particularly on the issue of a refusal to supply.

The doctrine, which can be argued to have originated in the US, has not been formally recognised in European law, although there has been a series of cases decided by the Commission under Art. 82 (ex 86) that move more clearly towards the concept of an essential facility. In particular, the Commission made use of the doctrine in *Sea Containers* v *Stena Sealink* (1994) OJ L 15/8 [1995] 4 CMLR 84, and there are a number of cases, particularly *Magill* (Joined Cases C-241/91 and C-242/91P) [1995] ECR I-743), that some would argue indicate the Commission's acceptance of the doctrine.

---

[27] See Consultation Paper, *Access to Bandwidth: delivering competition for the information age* (London, OFTEL, 1999). On 8 August 2000, Condition 83 of BT's licence came into effect. See *Access Network Facilities: Guidelines on Condition 83 of BT's Licence* (London, OFTEL, 2000) at 11.1. Condition 83 requires BT to allow other operators to place DSL (Digital Subscriber Line) technology equipment in the local exchange to upgrade the local loop for the provision of high-speed Internet services to customers. BT started taking orders from operators for co-location as of 12 September 2000, with the first connection to unbundled local loops occurring early in 2001.

The *Sea Containers* case concerned a dispute between two companies, Sea Containers and Sealink, regarding the access to be given by Sealink to Sea Containers to the port of Holyhead for the operation of high-speed ferries. The problem was that Sealink was both a ferry operator *and* the port authority at Holyhead, and Sea Containers a competitive rival wanting access to the port at Holyhead. Sealink refused access and the case went eventually to the European Commission. The Commission decided that in refusing Sea Containers access to the port of Holyhead, Sealink had abused its dominant position in the market for port services.

The *ratio* in the *Sea Containers* case is an important one in the context of interconnection because, applying some lateral thinking, it is not difficult to see that a dominant telecommunications operator refusing to interconnect could use its position in the market for access and interconnection to distort or even eliminate competition in related markets. Without access to and interconnection with the network of the incumbent, new entrants will not be able to provide services in an economic manner.

However, doubts over the applicability of the doctrine in European law surfaced in the case of *Oscar Bronner* v *Mediaprint* (above). In *Bronner*, the European Court of Justice rejected an argument that a newspaper home delivery service was an essential facility. In this case, Mr Bronner, who owned a newspaper publishing house, wanted to gain access to another newspaper publisher's (Mediaprint's) home delivery distribution system. To some the conclusion was obvious, as Mr Bronner had a number of alternative, less convenient means of delivery available to him. On the facts in *Bronner*, the Court found no abuse of a dominant position, and held that by withholding access to its home delivery distribution system, Mediaprint was not acting abusively even if it had a dominant position. The Court set out a three-part test under which refusal to grant access would constitute an abuse:

(a)   the refusal to provide access to the facility would be likely to eliminate all competition from the undertaking requesting access;

(b)   access is indispensable for the competitor to carry on its business in that there is no actual or potential substitute to the facility in existence; and

(c)   the refusal is incapable of being objectively justified.

The decision by the European Court of Justice in *Bronner* therefore sets a high threshold to be met before a court will mandate access to facilities regarded as essential where refusal to grant access is by a dominant undertaking. As applied to telecommunications, given the alternative access technologies now emerging in the local loop (viz. digital satellites, digital cable, ADSL/xDSL, wireless local loop and third generation mobile or UMTS platforms), *Bronner* suggests a more cautious approach to the application of *ex-post* remedies to the issue of access to a dominant operator's network.

As with any true test of effective competition, it is also important to be able to determine the *market* in which the alleged abuse is said to be occurring. For example, in both its Consultation Papers on the 1999 Communications

Review,[28] the European Commission stresses the need to establish the relevant market before introducing any form of *ex-post* or *ex-ante* legislation to regulate that market. In its discussion of dominant positions and significant market power for example, the Commission suggests that for the telecommunications market, determinations of the relevant markets, and of the positions of market players on the markets, would be carried out by the NRAs on a regular basis.[29]

This need to define the market in question has been critical in a number of refusal-to-supply cases. In both *Sea Containers* and *Hugin* v *Commission* (Case 22/78) [1979] ECR 1869, the Commission applied a very *narrow* market definition to find an abuse. For example, in *Sea Containers,* the Commission found that the relevant market was the central corridor of ferry routes between Great Britain and Ireland, within which market Holyhead was the only available port. In *Hugin,* a case involving a refusal to supply spare parts, the Commission decided that the relevant market was the market for Hugin spare parts.

In *MCI/WorldCom* (Case IV/M.1069) (1999) OJ L 116/1, the market definition used by the Commission was crucial.[30] The Commission had to decide whether the merger of the two parties' Internet businesses would create or strengthen a dominant position, the result of which could lead to effective competition in the Internal Market being weakened. The Commission decided that the market structure was hierarchical or pyramidal, with different characteristics at different levels, and that the relevant geographic market was the global market for backbone connectivity. (The MCI/WorldCom merger is discussed in more detail at 5.5 below.)

As a result of the debate over essential facilities, the Competition Directorate-General of the EC began in the mid-1990s to accept the important role that Arts 81 and 82 (ex 85 and 86) of the EC Treaty had in regulating the market behaviour of companies. The Competition Directorate-General considered a series of cases,[31] most of which never gave rise to any formal decisions. But

---

[28] Commission Communication, 'Toward a new framework for electronic communications, infrastructure and associated services: The 1999 Communications Review' (although this Communication is commonly itself called 'the 1999 Communications Review', it will hereafter be referred to as the 'November Communication', being one of two important documents of the Commission's review process begun in 1999), COM (1999) 539, 10 November 1999. Commission Communication, 'The results of the public consultation on the 1999 Communications Review and Orientation for the new Regulatory Framework' (hereafter the 'April Communication', the second of the consultation documents part of the referenced Review), COM 2000/239 Final.

[29] See DG (Directorate General) Information Society Working Document, 'Access to, and interconnection of, electronic communications networks and associated facilities' (INFSOC A/1), 27 April 2000.

[30] *Application of WorldCom, Inc. and MCI Communications Corporation for Transfer of Control of MCI Communications Corporation to WorldCom, Inc.* CC Docket No. 97–211.

[31] A complaint against Deutsche Telekom in January 1996 over its tariff scheme (Commission Press Release IP/96/543, 25 June 1996); complaints against Belgacom for its reluctance to supply subscriber data on reasonable terms to competitors (Reuter EU briefing: 'EU to probe Belgacom price rises', 17 July 1996; and potential anti-competitive practices regarding the use of web browsers and search engines on the Internet ('Commission regulators probe Internet monopoly abuse', EuroInfotech, 10 April 1997).

importantly, these early deliberations did germinate the seeds that would eventually grow into the Access Notice.

Where the doctrine is important, as regards telecommunications and the regulation of interconnection, may be in its application *in* the Access Notice itself, and particularly in the Commission's analysis of a refusal to supply and abuse of dominant position under Arts 83–87 of the Access Notice.[32] The Access Notice is discussed at 5.4.3 below.

5.4.3 Access Notice

Given the Commission's move more towards the application of *ex-post* principles in the telecommunications industry, the Access Notice is becoming an increasingly important document. The Access Notice is also relevant where, for example, existing sector-specific legislation on the regulation of interconnection under the Interconnection Directive or the proposed Access and Interconnection Directive is found to be lacking.[33] The Notice is not a legislative text, however, and therefore does not bind the Commission. It is more a series of guidelines, one purpose of which is to explain how EU competition rules will be applied across the converging sectors involved in the provision of new multimedia services.

While it gives some guidance on how the Commission will apply Arts 81 and 82 (ex 85 and 86) of the EC Treaty, in practice the Access Notice does not take existing case law much further than now. Its most interesting feature is its attempt to define and clarify the relationship between competition law and sector-specific legislation, both at Community and at national level.

The Access Notice does build on existing case law in the application of Art. 82 (ex 86). The most likely abuse in the telecommunications sector will be a refusal by an incumbent dominant operator to grant access to an essential facility (such as a local loop) and/or the application of discriminatory terms. A refusal to grant access will be abusive only if it affects competition. The Commission recognises that a refusal to grant access in the services market is likely to affect competition (Access Notice, para. 83).

Under the Access Notice, there are three basic scenarios that the Commission will regard as demonstrating abusive behaviour and that are important from an interconnection perspective (Access Notice, paras 83–87). The first is a refusal to grant access where another operator has already been given access (discriminatory); the second is a refusal to grant access which no other operator enjoys; and the third is the withdrawal of access from an existing customer (withdrawal of supply).

The first and third scenarios are relatively straightforward as they are well covered by existing competition case law. The first involves *discriminatory* treatment by the dominant operator. The dominant operator is under a duty to provide access in such a way that any services offered to downstream

---

[32] Section headed 'Refusal to grant access to facilities and application of unfavourable terms'.

[33] The EC in its 1999 Communications Review set out some proposals for a review of the current Interconnection Directive (97/33) which will result in a new Access and Interconnection Directive. The Interconnection Directive and the Commission's proposals for its reform are discussed below at 5.4.4 and 5.4.5.

operators are available on the same terms as to its own downstream operations. The third scenario is covered by classical competition law cases such as *United Brands* v *Commission* (Case 27/76) [1978] ECR 207, and *Commercial Solvents* v *Commission* (Joined Cases 6/73 and 7/73) [1974] ECR 223, which deal with the cutting off of supplies to existing customers. The real problem arises with the second scenario, as it is here that the doctrine of essential facilities (see 5.4.2 above) arises and has significance.

The second scenario involves a refusal to grant access which no other operator enjoys. This scenario could be more problematic and may require a case-by-case analysis. This is particularly so where there are no capacity constraints justifying the refusal, or where the dominant telecommunications operator has not provided access to any of its own downstream operations. In other words, there appears to be no *objective reason* for the dominant operator's refusal to grant access. In this scenario, the starting-point for the European Commission's analysis of the case will be to ask a series of questions to help determine the relevant market (see Access Notice, para. 91):

- Is access to the facility essential for companies to compete in the related market?
- Is there sufficient capacity available to provide access?
- Is the facility owner failing to satisfy demand on an existing service or product market, or blocking a new service?
- Is the company seeking access willing to pay reasonable and non-discriminatory rates?
- Is there any objective justification for refusing to provide access?

There is no doubt that dominant operators have a duty to deal with requests for access efficiently. The Commission will compare the response to a request for access with the usual time frames and conditions where the dominant operator grants access to its own subsidiaries. Excessive pricing for access may also count as a refusal.

In summary, the Access Notice has clear application in markets where full liberalisation in telecommunications may have been effected from a legal perspective but where that market is still characterised by the presence of a dominant incumbent telecommunications operator. The Notice does provide some comfort to new entrants in negotiating rights for access and interconnection to the networks of incumbent telecommunication operators, and these rights are a crucial requirement for any new entrant investing in a particular telecommunications market.

Recourse to the competition rules under the Access Notice may (in the future) be the principal way forward for new entrants in gaining access to the networks of significant market power (SMP) operators, where the latter are developing emerging digital services for customers that new entrants want but to which they are prevented from gaining access and where they are not helped by existing *ex-ante* (sector-specific) legislation.[34] However, we also

---

[34] See 5.4.5 below for access. See also *op. cit.* n. 28.

need to take note of the fact that the *Bronner* decision (see 5.4.2 above) suggests a more cautious approach to the application of *ex-post* remedies to the issue of access to a dominant operator's network.

For now, most cases on access litigated under existing competition law will fall under the headings of (i) refusal to supply, (ii) monopoly leveraging and (iii) discrimination. However, in situations where the dominant operator does *not* use its 'essential facility' in its own downstream operations, the doctrine of essential facilities, and its application under the Access Notice, may be of some help.

5.4.4 The Interconnection Directive

The Interconnection Directive (97/33/EC)[35] requires adequate and efficient interconnection of principal networks and imposes obligations on public fixed and mobile operators, suppliers of leased lines and providers of international facilities to negotiate interconnection. The Directive is one of those essential to operators wishing to enter/sustain their position in the market in telecom network and service provision. It is part of the open network provision (ONP) 'family' of Directives (see Chapter 8).

The Interconnection Directive sets out a harmonised framework of regulation by NRAs of interconnection of telecommunication networks and services. The aim of the Directive is to ensure 'any-to-any' connectivity, and it attempts to guarantee the rights of market players to obtain interconnection with other networks where this is 'reasonably justified'.

Importantly, the Directive attempts to categorise operators by listing them in two basic Annexes. Those operators falling into Annex I are SMP operators (generally recognised as having 25 per cent of their geographic market), who *must* offer interconnection in accordance with a standard reference interconnect offer.[36] By contrast, those operators falling into Annex II also have an obligation to provide interconnect but can *negotiate* the terms freely on a commercial basis.

5.4.4.1 Member States' obligations Under Art. 3 of the Interconnection Directive, Member States have to take all necessary measures to remove any restrictions preventing authorised organisations from providing publicly available telecommunication networks and services. Nothing in the laws of Member States must continue to support barriers to market entry by organisations which have been authorised to provide services.

Member States also have a responsibility to ensure that the organisations listed in Annex I of the Directive can interconnect and interoperate with and between each other. This includes all those operating public fixed mobile networks and those providing leased line services. If Member States have not implemented such steps, an operator may need to take legal action to ensure the implementation of the Directive.

---

[35] *Supra* n. 2.
[36] In 1998, the ONP Committee published an indicative reference interconnection offer, listing the minimum content of such offers. See the EC document 'Indicative Reference Interconnection Offer ONPCOM 98-11'.

5.4.4.2 Obligations of organisations with SMP Operators with SMP have more onerous obligations to interconnect with other organisations than those who do not have SMP. Such obligations include the following:

(a) SMP operators must meet all reasonable requests for access to their network, including access to points other than the network termination points offered to the majority of end-users (Art. 4(2)).

(b) Where they exist, charges relating to the sharing of the cost of USOs shall be unbundled and identified separately (Art. 5).

(c) SMP operators must stick to the principle of non-discrimination in their interconnection offerings to other organisations (Art. 6).

(d) They must give information and specifications to prospective inter-connecting operators, including changes planned for implementation within six months, unless otherwise agreed by the NRA (Art. 6).

(e) They must communicate interconnection agreements to the NRA and make them available to interested parties (unless they cover commercial strategy) (Art. 6).

(f) Interconnection charges must be transparent and cost-orientated (in line with ONP principles) (Art. 7(2)).[37]

(g) Reference interconnection offers have to be published by the NRA and broken down into components according to market needs (including tariffs) (Art. 7(3)).

(h) Charges must be unbundled (Art. 7(4)).

5.4.4.3 Obligations of organisations not having SMP status Unlike SMP organisations which have obligations to interconnect, the Directive provides that non-SMP organisations are only obliged to *negotiate* interconnect agreements. The NRA is also entitled to limit the obligation on non-SMPs to interconnect on the grounds that commercially viable alternatives exist (Art. 4(1)).[38]

Operators with non-SMP status and falling under Annex II are organisations which provide publicly available telecommunications networks/services and control the means of access to network termination points (NTPs) identified by numbers from the National Numbering Plan (Annex II, Art. 1).[39] This definition will include most organisations licensed to provide services in the UK, and the EU if also licensed to provide services in the UK and therefore authorised to have a direct numbering allocation from the NRA. Organisations coming under Annex II of the Directive will fall into the following three broad categories:

---

[37] The cost-orientation provisions of the ICD have been given 'teeth' with the publication of various Recommendations by the Commission on Interconnection Pricing: 'Part 1 — Intercon-nection Pricing' (1998) OJ L 228/30; and 'Part 2 — Accounting Separation and Cost Accounting' (1998) OJ L 141/6. See also Commission Communication on Interconnection Pricing in a Liberalised Telecommunications Market (1998) OJ C 84/3.

[38] Any such limitation is to be made public by the NRA under Art. 14(2).

[39] The footnote to Annex II provides further explanation of the term 'control to the means of access', being the ability of an operator to 'control the telecommunications services available to the end-user at the network termination point and/or the ability to deny other service providers access'.

(a) organisations providing leased lines to users' premises;
(b) those with exclusive or special rights to provide international telecommunication circuits;
(c) those permitted to interconnect in accordance with relative national licensing or authorisation schemes.

There was considerable debate as to whether the definition above could apply to Internet service providers (ISPs) as it was thought that Internet domain names[40] are not numbers from the National Numbering Plan.

One of the principal advantages of falling into Annex II is that an operator is entitled to negotiate cost-orientated interconnection rates with SMP operators and interconnection with other Annex II operators (Art. 4(1), Interconnection Directive). For certain ISPs who are infrastructure owners (and some that are not), the ability to get cheaper wholesale (and not retail) interconnection rates is important given that almost 40 per cent of a new entrant's costs are interconnection costs. A number of ISPs have argued, therefore, that although domain names are *not* numbers from the National Numbering Plan, they *are* allocated IP addresses which have been assigned to them from a global system of IP addressing.[41] Because no two ISPs can hold the same IP address (theoretically), the ISPs who do hold blocks of IP addresses argue that domain name allocation *does* give them the means to control access to their individual customers. Due partly to this persuasive argument,[42] the UK regulator OFTEL now considers certain ISPs as falling into Sch. 2 of the Telecommunications (Interconnection) Regulations 1997 (SI 1997 No. 2931), as transposed from Annex II of the Interconnection Directive, and therefore entitled to cost-orientated rates of interconnection. The Interconnection Regulations are discussed at 5.5.6.1 below.

5.4.4.4 Criticisms of the Interconnection Directive The Directive has been in force now in Europe for more than three years. Although its remarkable achievement has been to introduce harmonising legislation on interconnection throughout the Member States, it can be criticised for leaving *too* much discretion to the same individual Member States. For example, while NRAs may set time limits within which negotiations on interconnection are to be completed, they are not bound to do so and no time period is suggested. Further, NRAs are only required to 'encourage' co-location of facilities, Annex V allows NRAs discretion in relation to the particular cost accounting systems to be adopted by operators with SMP, and Annex VII allows considerable discretion over the type of conditions an NRA may include in interconnection agreements.

---

[40] The unique name that identifies an Internet site. For example, a given computer server may have more than one domain name, but a given domain name points to only one computer server.
[41] In most respects, an IP address is equivalent to a domain name, except that a domain name is easier to remember and understand. A domain name consists mainly of alphanumeric letters and not a series of numbers.
[42] It also depends on the type of dial-up arrangements that the ISP uses in allowing its customers access to its network, a discussion of which is beyond the scope of this chapter.

Possibly because of these shortfalls, and the obvious restriction that the Directive applies mainly to narrowband voice and data networks[43] (and not so much to broadband networks that are becoming increasingly relevant), and also because the Commission's wish to move to a more *ex-post* regime of regulation involving less rigid market dominance triggers (such as SMP), the need to review the Interconnection Directive has gained increased importance.

5.5 THE 1999 COMMUNICATIONS REVIEW

In 1999, the European Commission entered a review process of the overall regulatory framework. Precipitated by the review clauses of the 1998 harmonisation Directives, this process included a number of studies on specific issues.[44] One of these was the overall review of the Interconnection Directive by the Ovum Consultancy. Its recommendations, published in its October 1999 report, formed part of the Commission's overall strategy for a new framework for communications regulation and infrastructure as set forth in its November Communication and ensuing documents. The interconnection aspects of this follow.

In May 2000, the European Commission held a public hearing in Brussels to discuss a new regulatory framework for electronic communications networks and services. In readiness for that hearing, the Commission published five important Working Papers that summarised its thinking on reform.[45] Two of those Papers, the 'Access' and 'Framework' Papers, formed the basis for new draft Directives: 'on access to, and interconnection of, electronic communications networks and associated facilities' (the Draft Access Directive),[46] and 'on a common regulatory framework for electronic communications networks and services' (the Draft Framework Directive),[47] both published by the Commission in July 2000.

The Draft Access and Framework Directives contain proposals for access and interconnection that will affect, in a strategic way, the regulation of SMP dominant operators under present *ex-ante* legislation, such as the Interconnection Directive, or *ex-post* competition law, as set out in Community case law, respectively.

Here we discuss:

---

[43] See Pt 1 (Annex I), Interconnection Directive, which sets out bandwidth limitations for public networks at only 3.1KHz and data rates of at least 2.4Kbps.

[44] *The 1999 Communications Review* (London, OFTEL, 14 August 2000), http://www. oftel.gov.uk/internat/99rev.htm

[45] The papers include: (a) A common regulatory framework for electronic communications networks and services ('Framework Paper'); (b) The authorisation of electronic communications and networks and services; (c) Universal service and users' rights relating to electronic communications networks and services; (d) Access to, and interconnection of, electronic communications networks and associated facilities ('Access Paper'); and (e) The processing of personal data and the protection of privacy in the electronic communications sector. See http://europa.eu.int/ISPO/infosoc/telecompolicy/en/comm-en.htm#misc for further details.

[46] COM (2000) 384.

[47] COM (2000) 393.

(a)   the proposals set out by the Commission in its November Communication;[48]

(b)   the Commission's reforms in this area following publication of the results of its public consultation on the 1999 Review in April 2000 (the 'April 2000 Communication');[49]

(c)   the consequent Working Papers; and

(d)   the Draft Access and Framework Directives that arose from the Working Papers.

5.5.1   November Communication

5.5.1.1   Access and interconnection   With the publication of its November Communication, the European Commission proposed a substantial review of interconnection legislation which involved merging three existing European Directives – the Interconnection Directive, the Television Standards Directive (95/47), and the ONP Leased Lines Directive (92/44) – into one overall Access and Interconnection Directive. This thinking reflected the very real differences beginning to emerge between the concept of *access* to a network and the *interconnection* of existing networks, and was in part spurred by the exponential growth of data networks and the need for more efficient and faster access to the Internet.

In its November Communication, the Commission argued that interconnection covered situations where an operator requested interconnect for call termination and where there was *no* commercial relationship between the operator requesting interconnect and the called customer. Access, however, described a scenario where a supplier requested access to a network or facility in order to establish *directly* a commercial relationship with the customer of the access provider (see 4.2.1 and 4.2.2, November Communication). An example of the latter was that of an ISP seeking access to the broadband transmission capabilities of a cable TV operator in order to provide high-speed Internet access to customers of the cable TV network, generating direct revenue from those cable customers.

The Commission stressed the importance of access, saying that there could be a clear conflict of interest between infrastructure owners and organisations seeking access, especially when these firms compete in the same downstream markets. Examples of disputes on access included:

(a)   access by new entrants to the local loops of incumbents;

(b)   access to mobile network infrastructures;

(c)   access to intelligent network functionality of fixed and mobile networks;

(d)   access to broadband, submarine, and satellite networks and systems;

(e)   access for content providers (broadcasters) to cable TV networks or satellite systems;

---

[48] *Supra* n. 28.
[49] *Ibid.*

(f)　　access by ISPs to cable TV networks;

(g)　　access to set-top box facilities, notably conditional access systems, application program interfaces (APIs), and API-dependent systems like electronic programme guides (EPGs); and

(h)　　access to broadcasters' networks for interactive applications.

The Commission's thinking on access and interconnect seemed very straightforward, and one would think, following publication of its November Communication, that the Commission was planning to introduce new legislation that would improve the rights of network and service providers in gaining access to the networks of SMP operators. But this was not so. In fact, the wording contained in the access and interconnection sections of the November Communication suggested proposals that would further restrict access to SMP networks by new entrants.

5.5.1.2　Access to content　As to the rights for access to content, the November Communication was mostly silent.[50] Access to content is a crucial area, as, increasingly, the value of content is rising as the number of distribution vehicles and platforms for delivery of that content also rises (viz. digital satellites, digital cable, ADSL, wireless local loop and third generation mobile or UMTS platforms). For example, in the interconnection of Internet networks, often those ISPs hosting websites and sourcing popular content are in a powerful position when it comes to negotiating interconnection with operators much larger than themselves in terms of national presence and numbers of customers. Consequently, any rules on access to content will be of high importance to SMPs and new entrants alike.

However, following publication of the Commission's Working Papers on a new regulatory framework in April 2000, the situation on content did not change. In the recitals to the Framework Paper for example, the Commission stated that the new regulatory framework would not cover services such as broadcast content or electronic commerce services. Section 2 of the Framework Paper set out the definition of an 'electronic communication service':

'Electronic communications service' means services provided for remuneration which consist wholly or mainly in the transmission and routing of signals on electronic communications networks; it covers *inter alia* telecommunications services and transmission services in networks used for broadcasting. It does not cover services such as the content of broadcasting transmissions, delivered using electronic communications networks and services.

The vague drafting of this most important term was surprising as it was so crucial to the Commission's approach to the regulation of electronic networks and services. For example, the DTI argued in its Response to the Commission's Working Papers that it was not clear from the Commission's definition

---

[50] However, in footnote 41 to the November Communication, the Commission did say that issues associated with access to content would be dealt with in a separate Communication.

whether it covered the provision of television programmes, video on demand and/or e-commerce services.[51]

Perhaps as a result of these criticisms, the Commission's drafting of the definition of 'electronic services' has now been amended. In the Draft Framework Directive, under Art. 2, the definition now excludes 'services providing, or exercising editorial content over, content transmitted using electronic communications networks and services'. In other words, it would appear that any service that would possibly require a broadcasting licence (under UK law anyway) are to be excluded.

5.5.1.3 New pricing and dominance In the November Communication, the Commission also proposed strategic changes to the pricing for interconnection and access services. In 1998, the Commission published soft legislation on the pricing for call termination services in the form of its Recommendation on Interconnection Pricing.[52] The Recommendation put forward a basis of long-run average incremental costs (LRAIC) for cost-based pricing and introduced a range of benchmark interconnect prices to which Member States' interconnect tariffs should fall (see Chapter 2). Each month the Commission would review its benchmark rates and publish them on the Internet. Since its launch, the Recommendation has been remarkably successful in bringing down call termination charges to within benchmark levels across the EU, which in a way demonstrates the power of transparency. In the November Communication, the Commission went further in proposing fundamental changes to the type of operator having to provide cost-orientated rates, by introducing new pricing guidelines on charges for those seeking access to a network and reforming existing guidelines on interconnection for call termination services.

Under the present Interconnection Directive, SMP operators must provide cost-orientated rates for interconnection (Art. 7(2)). However, under the proposals set out by the Commission in its November Communication, this obligation was to fall away, with SMP operators only having to negotiate, on a commercial basis, access and interconnection charges. Dominant operators, however, had to offer cost-orientated rates (see 5.4.4 above).

5.5.2 The results of the 1999 Review: April Communication

In its April 2000 Communication,[53] the European Commission outlined the approach it intended to take for proposals for Directives that would form the

---

[51] *An initial response from the United Kingdom from the Department of Trade and Industry, the Department of Culture Media and Sport, the Office of Telecommunications, and the Radiocommunications Agency* (May 2000).

[52] The cost-orientation provisions of the Interconnection Directive have been given 'teeth' with the publication of various Recommendations by the Commission on Interconnection Pricing: Part 1 Interconnection Pricing (1998) OJ L 228/30 (adopted 29 July 1998); Part 2 Accounting Separation and Cost Accounting (1998) OJ L 141/6 (adopted 8 April 1998); and Commission Communication on Interconnection Pricing in a Liberalised Telecommunications Market (1998) OJ C 84/3.

[53] *Supra* n. 28.

basis for its new regulatory framework. The Commission also set out the objections that it received to its plans to introduce two thresholds for regulation, both from industry and from regulatory authorities. Network operators were unsurprisingly in favour of the higher threshold of dominance, whereas service providers (and most regulatory authorities) wanted to continue with the current use of the SMP threshold for the imposition of *ex-ante* obligations.

There was also criticism of the Commission's proposals to impose on SMP operators an obligation only to negotiate access (effectively diluting the provision of Art. 4(2) of the Interconnection Directive as discussed at 5.4.4.2 above). New entrants feared that with such a provision, SMP operators would not take their requests for access seriously. SMP operators (including cable operators) countered by saying that the obligation to *negotiate* access would in practice have the same effect as an obligation to *provide* access, since service providers would not negotiate seriously but wait for the regulator to impose a price (April Communication, at 2.3.1).

New entrants also feared that where regulatory obligations such as cost-orientation were only *imposed* on operators with dominance (as defined under competition law), they would face real difficulties in competing with incumbents. Several commentators also raised concerns about the measurement of market share, arguing that where it was measured by *value*, incumbent operators' market share would be far lower than when measured by *volume*.

5.5.3   The Commission's Working Papers

5.5.3.1   Threshold test of SMP   In response to criticisms of its proposals in the November Communication, the Commission decided to scrap its plans to introduce two thresholds for *ex-ante* regulation (SMP and dominance). Under the Framework Paper, the Commission decided to impose *ex-ante* obligations only on those operators judged as having SMP. The current definition of SMP as set out in Art. 4(3) of the Interconnection Directive was to be replaced with a market threshold trigger more in accordance with EC competition law. The current SMP trigger sets the market share threshold at 25 per cent.[54] Under the Commission's Framework Paper, NRAs would designate undertakings as having SMP where:

(a)   the undertaking has financed infrastructure partly or wholly on the basis of special or exclusive rights which have been abolished, and there are major legal technical or economic barriers to market entry, in particular construction of network infrastructure; and/or

(b)   the undertaking concerned is a vertically-integrated entity and its competitors necessarily require access to some of its facilities to compete with it in a downstream market.

---

[54] See Art. 4(3), Interconnection Directive, which states that 'An organisation shall be presumed to have significant market power when it has a share of more than 25% of a particular telecommunications market in the geographical area in a Member State within which it is authorised to operate.'

The Commission added that both of these provisions were to apply where both national and EU competition law remedies could not ensure effective competition and choice in the market concerned.[55]

NRAs were also required to draw up a list of organisations with SMP for the purposes of implementing *ex-ante* obligations and to notify this list to the Commission (Access Paper, s. 8(5)). Further, the type of markets that would attract *ex-ante* obligations would be set out by the Commission in a special Notice on relevant product and service markets (Framework Paper, s. 14(2)).[56] The Commission stressed in s. 14 of its Framework Paper that the markets identified in the Notice would be the *only* markets where NRAs could impose *ex-ante* regulation without the *prior* agreement of the Commission.

Not surprisingly, these and other provisions came under detailed criticism by the UK's DTI. In its Response to the Commission's proposals,[57] the DTI argued that the 'Commission seeks to rely on competition law to a degree that is not yet appropriate'. The new SMP test in particular was subjected to minute examination, with the DTI setting out four main objections:

(a)   The proposals amounted to raising the level of dominance to a new height of 'super-dominance'. In this way, operators who had SMP status under the present regime would not be caught by the Commission's new proposal for SMP and would therefore be able to obstruct market entry by new entrants. The DTI argued that this could be particularly dangerous for new entrants intent on capturing first-mover advantages and that 'A dominant operator which does not pass the Commission's proposed SMP test is also capable of such obstruction'.

(b)   Current Community case law was not sufficient to help justify a regulatory approach based on the concept of joint dominance.[58]

(c)   In the absence of a dominant position by an operator, there could still be failure of effective competition. Using competition law to regulate some markets was simply not enough and specific *ex-ante* legislation would still be required to combat a failure in effective competition.

(d)   The drafting of the wording in the Framework Paper led to the unexpected result that those operators currently classed as having SMP would not attract obligations under the new SMP test to put in place local

---

[55] The full definition is given at s. 13, Framework Paper. The Commission included at s. 13(2) a reference to joint dominance, by stating that 'an undertaking shall be deemed to have significant market power if, either individually or jointly with others as a result of economic interdependence between them, it enjoys a position of economic strength affording it the power to behave to an appreciable extent independently of competitors, customers, and ultimately consumers'.

[56] Also, Annex II of the Access Paper identifies a list of wholesale markets to be considered for inclusion in the Notice. The Notice may also include specific retail markets.

[57] See *supra* n. 51.

[58] The Commission proposed that the new form of dominance ('SMP') would embrace single company dominance, joint dominance and the leverage of a dominant position onto an associated market. See s. 13(2), Framework Paper. In fact, the Commission has decided to retain this provision under Art. 13(2), Draft Framework Directive.

loop unbundling, mobile carrier selection, the supply of conditional access services and retail tariff regulation, obligations that had already been sanctioned by the Commission under the old (in fact current) SMP test under the Interconnection Directive.

However, the DTI's main objection to the Commission's proposals lay with s. 14 of the Framework Paper, which defined the procedure on market analysis. It included a process of consultation between a new body, the High Level Communications Group,[59] and the Commission, to come up with the above special Notice, and also a need for NRAs to complete a market analysis on the product and service markets identified in the Notice at least two months after publication of the Notice by the Commission (Framework Paper, s. 14(2), (3)). The DTI argued that s. 14 could lead to excessive centralisation, contrary to the principle of regulating close to the market. This, it argued, could slow down the whole process of regulation, which was ironic, as this was the very issue the Commission wanted to avoid. The DTI said that: 'The Commission is not in a position to reach conclusions as to whether a particular market in a particular Member State is one where a competition problem arises. Rather NRAs have the appropriate expertise and local knowledge to take on this task.'

The sheer range of references in the Access and Framework Papers to such terms as 'market', 'market and/or economic analysis', also led to much confusion. For example, there was doubt whether the market analysis required for the determination by an NRA of SMP status (ss. 13 and 14, Framework Paper) was the same as that required under the procedure for review of (*ex-ante*) obligations for access and interconnection (s. 7, Access Paper).

5.5.3.2   Changes to SMP under the Draft Access and Framework Directives   To some extent, the Commission, having taken note of criticisms made of its Access and Framework Papers, has now revised the wording in both. For example, the definition of undertakings with SMP has now been amended, to a more 'streamlined' version, the Commission stripping out awkward references to 'legal, economic and technical barriers to market entry' and a vague reference to a possible essential facilities concept. The provisions on joint dominance and leverage of dominance in related markets remains similar to the wording found in the Access and Framework Papers, but the main 'economic strength' test has now been revised as follows:

2.   An undertaking shall be deemed to have significant market power if, either individually or jointly with others, it enjoys a position of economic strength affording it the power to behave to an appreciable extent independently of competitors, customers and ultimately consumers. (Art. 13(2), Draft Framework Directive)

---

[59] Under s. 23, Framework Paper, this group is to consist of representatives of the Member State NRAs and a representative from the Commission.

The market analysis procedure has also changed. Now, instead of issuing a 'Notice' that sets out the relevant markets that could attract *ex-ante* conditions by Member State NRAs, the Commission is to publish a 'Decision' (Art. 14(1), Draft Framework Directive). Furthermore, the Commission includes a new provision for including in the Decision those markets that it believes are 'transnational'. For transnational markets, NRAs are now jointly to conduct market analysis for the imposition of *ex-ante* obligations (Art. 14(1), Draft Framework Directive). This perhaps reflects the increasing trend towards pan-European networking and intra-EU telecommunications trade.

The Commission would also appear to have gone some way towards taking note of the DTI's criticisms (discussed at 5.5.3.1 above). For example, the DTI's concern that the Commission was in fact raising the level of dominance as defined in current competition law to a new level of 'super dominance', would now no longer seem relevant as the new provisions on SMP in the Draft Framework Directive have been streamlined to be more in accordance with the current view on dominance under Community competition law. In this way, those operators caught by SMP obligations on local loop unbundling, carrier pre-selection, supply of conditional access services, etc., will still be caught under the Framework Directive. However, the Commission has retained the wording in the Framework Paper in the Framework Directive on its regulatory approach to the concept of joint dominance (see Art. 13(2), Draft Framework Directive), although the DTI argues that current Community case law is not sufficient to justify an approach based on joint dominance.

The Commission has also tidied up s. 7 of the Access Paper, removing the confusion on the need to complete market analysis to inform the NRA's decision on whether or not to impose, maintain and remove *ex-ante* obligations on operators. Under Art. 7 of the Draft Access Directive, the Commission now makes it clear that the relevant markets for the *imposition* of obligations are to be published in a Decision, whereas the NRA's role in either *maintaining or removing* those obligations is to be informed by periodic market analysis.[60]

5.5.3.3 Interconnection and access   Unlike the Interconnection Directive, the application of which is restricted to narrowband networks, the recitals to the Framework Paper made clear that the new regulatory framework was to apply to a range of broadband communications networks, including the PSTN, IP networks, cable TV, mobile and terrestrial broadcast networks. This position has not changed under the Draft Access and Framework Directives. Also, the recitals to the Draft Access Directive make clear that the Directive covers access and interconnection arrangements between service suppliers; it does not, however, apply to networks used for the provision of services available only to a specific end-user or to a closed-user group, neither does it deal with

---

[60] The market analysis to be done in accordance with the procedure set out in Art. 14, Framework Directive.

access for end-users or others who are not supplying publicly available services (see Recital 1, Draft Access Directive).

For the regulation of public electronic networks and services, the Commission also found widespread support for *ex-ante* sector-specific rules on interconnection and access continuing alongside competition rules, until such time that there was full and effective competition in all segments of the market. There was also widespread support for the Commission's view that call origination, transit and termination be regarded as separate markets, with differing levels of competition in each. In its Access Paper, under s. 4, the Commission stated that every operator would have to abide by the *primary interconnection* rule, that:

> All undertakings authorised to operate electronic communications networks for the provision of publicly available communications services shall have a right and, when requested by other undertakings so authorised, an obligation to negotiate interconnection with each other for the purpose of providing the services in question, in order to ensure provision of services throughout the Community. In the absence of agreement, the national regulatory authority shall have the power to intervene at its own initiative or at the request of either of the parties involved, in order to secure the objectives set out in Section 3(3).

Section 3(3) imposed an obligation on NRAs to ensure that they encouraged and secured 'adequate network access and interconnection'. Section 4 of the Access Paper revealed an interesting point, which was not lost on the UK's DTI, which was that the obligation to interconnect appeared to cover access *as well*. Further, the NRA could be required to intervene in *any* dispute between operators, regardless of whether or not one of the operators had SMP. There was, therefore, a substantial difference in the approach taken by the Commission in its Access Paper compared with that of the current Interconnection Directive.

Under the current Interconnection Directive the obligation to negotiate interconnection is covered by Art. 4(1), and the obligation to provide access (by SMP operators) by Art. 4(2). The interconnection provision attracts the right for the parties to call the NRA to help resolve disputes, but the access provision does not appear to confer a similar right. The proposals put forward by the Commission under the Access Paper appeared to allow the parties to call on the NRA in *both* access and interconnection disputes. The DTI was unhappy with these provisions, fearing that they could lead to a higher administrative burden falling on the UK's NRA, OFTEL, and therefore asked the Commission to dilute the burden by effectively giving the NRA the power to forbear from hearing disputes where one of the operators did not have SMP. However, the DTI's request also had problems. With a higher threshold to reach SMP under the Commission's Framework Paper, in effect putting in place a new status of 'super dominance', the DTI's suggestion could, in itself, have led to further difficulties for new entrants in gaining the ear of the regulator when dealing with 'awkward' incumbents.

Perhaps as a result of these arguments, the primary interconnection rule has now been modified. Article 4(1) of the Draft Access Directive no longer makes any reference to the intervention of the NRA in interconnection disputes, and therefore the confusion as to whether or not an NRA should get involved in disputes on access *and* interconnection now falls away. Interestingly, however, Art. 17 of the Draft Framework Directive does set out the procedure on dispute resolution by the NRA between undertakings, without carving out any exemption from hearing disputes on access or complaints brought by an operator without SMP. Furthermore, Art. 5 of the Draft Access Directive also makes clear that NRAs should intervene in disputes on access and interconnection, when called upon by one of the parties to do so, or even on its own initiative.

The Commission also introduced vague wording in s. 3(4) of the Access Paper, which could have been interpreted as having the effect of scrapping Annex II of the current Interconnection Directive. As mentioned at 5.4.4 above, Annex II categorises certain operators as qualifying for cost-orientated interconnection rates from SMP operators. In s. 3(4) of the Access Paper, the Commission stated that: '. . . member states shall not maintain legal measures whereby network operators grant network access or interconnection under terms and conditions that differ according to factors that are not related to the actual services provided'. This was woolly wording, interpreted possibly as treating service providers in exactly the same way as infrastructure providers in obtaining cost-orientated rates. Unsurprisingly, this provision has now been dropped in the Draft Access Directive.

As regards access to cable networks, the Commission suggested in its November Communication that SMP operators would be obliged to negotiate access to their networks, whereas dominant operators would have to grant access.[61] Under the Access and Framework Papers, the Commission dropped the 'forced access' argument, saying that 'there would be no specific regulatory obligations in community legislation to impose e.g. access for service providers to cable TV networks, or to mobile networks'. The Commission suggested instead that 'imposing such access obligations on infrastructure owners would be made in the light of prevailing market conditions, the effectiveness of competition, and the extent of customer choice'.[62] It appeared, therefore, that the cable operators had successfully resisted to some extent any 'forced access' obligation. The mobile network operators too had evaded the 'mandatory or forced access' obligation.

Despite complaints cited by the Commission in its April 2000 Communication, by users who wanted mandated access to mobile networks in certain circumstances, and who argued that the current market structure was nationally focused, with inflated roaming charges and mobile operators refusing to conclude virtual private network deals with business customers (again forcing them to pay high roaming fees), the Commission's position on 'forced access' to mobile and cable networks has not changed under the Draft

---

[61] November Communication, *supra* n. 28, at 4.2.1.
[62] April Communication, *supra* n. 28, at p. 24.

Access and Framework Directives. This will not please new entrants or end-users. It would appear, therefore, that any complaints such user groups will continue to have with the mobile operators under the new Access and Framework Directives will probably need to be brought under *ex-post* provisions and not through sector-specific *ex-ante* measures.

5.5.3.4 Obligation for cost-orientation   Under s. 13 of the Access Paper, the Commission introduced a provision which would allow NRAs to impose obligations for cost-orientation of prices for interconnection and/or access in situations where lack of effective competition could lead to an operator sustaining prices at an excessively high level. In practice, therefore, the obligation to provide cost-orientated rates would not automatically fall on the shoulders of an operator with SMP but could do so, and again, following a market analysis. This position has been maintained by the Commission under Art. 13(1) of the Draft Access Directive.

Section 8(3) of the Access Paper (modification of obligations) allowed an NRA to impose one or more obligations (including that of providing cost-orientated rates) on operators that had SMP. Under the Commission's proposals in its November Communication, the Commission suggested that the cost-orientated obligation would fall away for SMP operators (SMP as currently defined under the Interconnection Directive) but would remain for operators with dominance (as defined under competition law). The proposals under the Access Paper, however, allowed NRAs much greater flexibility in choosing *when* to impose the cost-orientation obligation on an operator, regardless of whether or not that operator had SMP (defined as an operator with dominance under competition law). Under Art. 8 of the Draft Access Directive (imposition, amendment or withdrawal of obligations), this flexibility to impose cost-orientated rates whether or not the operator has SMP still remains.

However, many aspects of s. 8 of the Access Paper have been substantially revised. Under Art. 8 of the Draft Access Directive, the NRA can now impose obligations that would normally fall on an SMP operator on any other operator only in order to comply with *international commitments on interconnection.*[63] The original wording under s. 8 of the Access Paper allowed for a much wider power to impose obligations, and not just for interconnection alone. This power to impose SMP obligations on 'any other operator' has, therefore, been restricted. However, under Art. 8 of the Draft Access Directive, NRAs are now able to impose obligations on SMPs that go beyond those envisaged by Arts 9–13 of the Access Directive. This can be done without the prior agreement of the Commission. This is, therefore, a broader

---

[63] For example, specific commitments given by the EU in the WTO's Fourth Protocol and the regulatory Reference Paper. The international commitments envisaged under Art. 8, Draft Access Directive could have important implications for incumbent operators with dominance in the local access network with the potential to leverage that dominance into their IP transit and long-distance networks. For example, such incumbents could be caught by the interconnection conditions set out in the WTO regulatory Reference Paper.

power than originally envisaged in the Access Paper, which did require the prior agreement of the Commission.

5.5.3.5 Conclusion In reality, the Commission is planning to dilute the current SMP operators' obligations, most likely in a bid to protect investment in newly emerging services being developed by these operators. To compete with the new digital services of the larger SMP operators, new entrants will have to offer at least the same or a more developed set, and at competitive prices to win market share. If *ex-ante* legislation proves to be inadequate, new entrants will inevitably turn to *ex-post* legislation or competition law to gain access to an SMP's network in the face of its refusal to grant access.[64] Of course, this increased reliance on competition law is what the Commission wants.

In effect, the Commission is proposing to make the European Union an even more attractive marketplace for SMPs, by:

(a) allowing the regulator to forbear from imposing the more onerous *ex-ante* obligations (obligations to supply unbundled, cost-orientated interconnection services); and

(b) imposing obligations to negotiate access and interconnection only, and to observe the need for transparency.

Cable and mobile operators, too, have escaped the 'forced access' provision suggested by the Commission in its November Communication.

However, SMPs will not immediately be able to take advantage of these new proposals. The transitional arrangements set out at s. 7 of the Draft Access Directive (review of former obligations for access and interconnection) will mean that the current obligations on SMPs imposed under the Interconnection Directive (non-discrimination, transparency, cost-orientated and unbundled rates) will continue to apply until entry into force of the new regulatory framework, and following a market analysis by the NRA (at least two months thereafter).[65]

Bearing in mind that most regulators outside of Europe still require their operators with market power to observe requirements for cost-orientated interconnection charges along LRIC (long run incremental costs) principles, the Commission's thinking is far-reaching, in putting in place a more flexible

---

[64] This may be through a notification to the Commission for abuse of a dominant position in not granting access to an 'essential facility' as defined in the Access Notice. See particularly para. 68, which defines an 'essential facility' and paras 81–82 on the abuse of a dominant position. There will of course be other remedies, such as through any *ex-post* provisions in national law, for example in the UK by way of the Competition Act 1998.

[65] Under Art. 7(1), Draft Access Directive, Member States will maintain all obligations set out under Arts 4, 6, 7, 8, 11, 12, and 14, Interconnection Directive; Art. 16, Directive 98/10 (Amended Voice Telephony Directive); Arts 7 and 8, Directive 92/44/EC (Leased Lines Directive); and Art. 3 of Regulation on unbundled access to the local loop COM (2000) 394. When the new Draft Directives come into force, the Commission states that existing Directives, such as the Interconnection and Voice Telephony Directives, for example, will be repealed. See the Explanatory Memorandum to the Draft Framework Directive for further details.

regime for introducing *ex-ante* obligations. But its effect on new entrants seeking access to the customers connected to incumbent networks for the provision of advanced TCP/IP services, for example, will need to be carefully monitored. Otherwise these new entrants will turn to competition law under the new framework for help with abuse of market position, only to find possibly that the horse has already 'bolted'.

5.5.4 Regulatory framework: UK law

One of the most important points to grasp in UK telecommunications law, is that operators are regulated *simultaneously* by the conditions in their licences and the telecommunications laws and regulations in force at the time. So, for example, under their licences, BT and Kingston Communications are required to meet a universal service obligation. These two companies are required to make a public telephone service available to everyone in their licensed area – BT everywhere in the UK, except for the municipal area of Kingston upon Hull, where Kingston Communications is the incumbent operator. Other companies may have service coverage obligations in their licences. The obligations may also be linked to specific dates. At the same time, operators must conform to the large body of telecommunications legislation that has been transposed into UK law from European Directives.

The main body of legislation governing the conditions in operators' licences at European level is the Licensing Directive,[66] which has been implemented into UK law by the Telecommunications (Licensing) Regulations 1997 (SI 1997 No. 2930). As regards interconnection, we have seen that the main body of law governing the regulation of interconnection at a European level is the Interconnection Directive, which was implemented into UK law by the Telecommunications (Interconnection) Regulations 1997 (SI 1997 No. 2931). Therefore, the two principal legislative 'pillars' affecting operators as regards interconnection are the Interconnection Regulations and the operator's licence conditions. Each will be discussed briefly in turn.

5.5.4.1 Interconnection Regulations The Interconnection Regulations form the basis for the *ex-ante* (sector-specific) regulatory regime for interconnection in the UK. They follow the format of the Interconnection Directive and govern the terms on which the organisations offering public telecommunications networks/services have rights and obligations to interconnect.

Until interconnection provisions in all licences were changed as a result of the Regulations, only those organisations with relevant connectable system ('RCS') status were entitled to interconnect at wholesale prices and at the non-network termination points of other PTOs.

Under the Interconnection Regulations, operators now entitled to interconnect at wholesale prices are those falling under Sch. 2 to the Regulations. To determine whether an operator falls within Sch. 2, the following questions need to be asked:

---

[66] Directive 97/13 on a common framework for general authorisations and individual licences in the field of telecommunications services (1997) OJ L 117/15, adopted 10 April 1997.

(a)   Is the public operator someone authorised to provide switched and unswitched bearer capabilities to users upon which other telecommunication services depend?[67]

(b)   Is the public operator someone who:

(i)   provides public fixed telecommunications networks, or publicly available telecommunication services or a combination of both, and thereby controls the means of access to one or more network termination points identified by one or more unique numbers in the national numbering plan;

(ii)   provides leased lines to users' premises (usually this person will fall within the above category anyway);

(iii)   is someone with special exclusive rights to provide international telecommunication circuits between the EU and third countries (now abolished in the UK);

(iv)   provides the services described in the first category above and who is authorised to connect its systems to other public operators and who is required by the terms of its licence to provide interconnection (this describes the old RCS (Relevant Connectable System) system in the UK)?

As mentioned above, the Interconnection Regulations follow the format of the Interconnection Directive discussed at 5.4.4. There is no need to repeat some of those provisions here, other than to mention Sch. 4 to the Interconnection Regulations, which is quite important. Schedule 4 establishes a basic framework for negotiating interconnect agreements. It specifies areas where sector-specific regulation may be set, for example, in dispute resolution, equal access, facilities sharing and co-location. Furthermore, it sets out some of the basic areas that one would expect to find in an interconnect agreement, such as terms of payment, technical standards for interconnection, intellectual property rights and maintenance.

5.5.4.2   Licence conditions   The UK has obligations to ensure that the Telecommunications Act 1984 is in conformity with the Licensing Directive. Article 22.1 of the Licensing Directive requires Member States to make all necessary efforts to bring authorisations in force at the date of entry of this Directive into line with its provisions before 1 January 1999. In fact, the UK Government was able to defer this date to 30 June 1999.

The main thrust of the Licensing Directive is to introduce a system of general authorisations, with specific authorisations being reserved for scarce resources such as spectrum and number resources, for example.

---

[67] Neither the Regulations nor the Interconnection Directive define what is meant by 'switched' and the question of whether an IP-based network offering functionality equivalent to switching involves the provision of switched bearer capabilities for this purpose remains to be explored. Note, however, that in the UK, OFTEL has now accepted certain ISPs with particular dial-up access arrangements as falling under Sch. 2 of the Regulations. See OFTEL Consultation Paper, *Rights and obligations to interconnect under the Interconnection Directive* (London, OFTEL, 1998), at http://www.oftel.gov.uk.

5.5.4.3　Changes brought about by the Licensing Directive　As mentioned at 5.5.4, the Licensing Directive has now been implemented into UK law with the coming into force of the Telecommunications (Licensing) Regulations 1997. After introducing the Licensing Regulations into UK law, the DTI launched a series of Consultation Papers[68] touching on proposals to change existing UK licences. After the period of consultation was over, the UK Government introduced new and, some would argue, controversial[69] legislation in the form of the Telecommunication (Licence Modification) (Standard Schedules) Regulations 1999 (SI 1999 No. 2450) and the Telecommunications (Licence Modification) (Mobile Public Telecommunication Operators) Regulations 1999 (SI 1999 No. 2452), each coming into force on 27 September 1999.

Under this mass of new legislation, new template licences for fixed and mobile PTOs were published by the DTI on 15 September 1999. These new templates contain important conditions on interconnection.

5.5.4.4　Interconnection conditions　Due to the changes brought about by the Licensing Directive, there now exists a range of conditions to be found in the new fixed and mobile PTO licences that govern interconnection.[70] These new conditions are:

(a)　*Condition 9.* Requirement to provide connection services including co-location and facility sharing.[71] Condition 9 sets out the requirements for Schedule 2 public operators to interconnect with each other. It reflects the requirements set out in Art. 4 of the Interconnection Directive, as transposed into reg. 6(3) and (4) of the Interconnection Regulations. In effect, under this condition such operators have both *rights and obligations* to interconnect with each other. There are also important provisions relating to co-location and facilities sharing set out in Condition 9.3(e) and 9.3(f).

(b)　*Condition 44.* Operators with SMP for the purposes of the Interconnection Directive. This condition sets out the requirements for an operator being determined to have SMP. Condition 44, together with the conditions that follow (Conditions 45–50), sets out the obligations for SMP operators as found in the Interconnection Directive. Some of these obligations were mentioned in 5.4.4 above.

---

[68] DTI Consultation Paper, *Implementation of the EC Licensing Directive: Changes to existing licences*, First Consultation (November 1998), Second Consultation (April 1999).

[69] The reason why these statutory instruments may be regarded as controversial is that some commentators argue that they seek to impose licence conditions on operators, particularly mobile PTOs, in a way that bypasses the statutory consultation provisions set out under ss. 12–15, Telecommunications Act 1984. A full discussion is beyond the scope of this chapter.

[70] See also Chapter 3. OFTEL has also published a series of guidelines on interconnection and interoperability (July 1999) that will work in conjunction with the operator's licence conditions. The guidelines explain how OFTEL will approach enforcement of rules on interoperability of services between separate networks and between customer premises equipment and networks. The rules cover requirements to (a) make services available for interconnection; (b) consult with interested parties concerning new or changed interfaces; and (c) publish technical interface specifications. The guidelines are not legally binding on the DGT.

[71] This condition also features as Condition 9 in new cable licences.

Condition 45 sets out the obligations on an SMP operator when interconnecting with a Schedule 2 public operator, and Condition 45.5(e) and (f) set out the requirements for co-location and facilities sharing. When interconnecting with Schedule 2 operators, Condition 47.1 sets out the requirement that any charges for interconnection services by the SMP operator must be reasonably derived from the costs of providing the service on a forward-looking incremental costs approach. By contrast, when the SMP operator is only providing access to its network (discussed earlier), as governed by Condition 48, the requirement is only that SMP charges be transparent and cost-orientated.

Other important licence conditions relating to interconnection include:

(a) *Condition 8* (prohibition on undue preference and undue discrimination);

(b) *Condition 15* (publication of interfaces (Condition 16 in BT's and Kingston's licences)); and

(c) *Condition 16* (essential interfaces (Condition 17 in BT's and Kingston's licences)).

5.5.5 Access control services

In 5.4.1 to 5.5.4 above, the concepts of access and interconnection are examined both under competition law provisions and under sector-specific legislation, particularly in the context of the Interconnection Directive and the Commission's new proposals for a regulatory framework for electronic communication networks and services. In these earlier paragraphs, access is looked at from the point of view of access to network infrastructure for telecommunication and Internet services. However, the issue of access also applies to digital broadcasting, as there is concern that a small number of digital TV broadcasters could end up controlling the interactive services which pass to end-users through a gateway, such as a cable TV network or a multiplex system.[72] Therefore, as part of an overall discussion of access and interconnection, particularly in the light of recent mergers and joint ventures between telecommunication operators and broadcasters,[73] it is also useful to look briefly at access control services under UK law (see also Chapter 12).

5.5.5.1 Access control regime The access control regime in effect goes further than the existing regulatory regime that applies to conditional access systems. Conditional access is another term for decryption. It is the technology that allows providers of encrypted programme services, including analogue or digital over cable, satellite or terrestrial means, to allow their subscribers the key to decrypt the signals to view their services. Conditional access technology can come embedded in three main forms:

---

[72] A multiplex system is used in digital transmission broadcasts over existing TV terrestrial networks. It is used in conjunction with a conditional access system such as a set-top box, which controls the end-user's access to certain digital TV channels and services.

[73] See, for example, AT&T's purchase of MediaOne and AOL's merger with Time Warner.

(a)   a new TV set which integrates the decoder without the need for a separate box;
(b)   in a proprietary set-top box; or
(c)   in a detachable conditional access module which can be inserted into a common interface socket in a set-top box.[74]

The access control regime is intended to apply to new interactive services, such as digital download and text-based information, home shopping and interactive games, which cannot strictly be classed as television services. Television services are covered under the conditional access regime[75] and the Broadcasting Acts 1990 and 1996.

On 31 August 1999, OFTEL issued the access control class licence, which authorises all persons to provide access control services but imposes certain, more onerous obligations on those determined by OFTEL to be regulated suppliers with market influence or dominance. In November 1999, OFTEL issued a draft determination that Sky Subscribers Services Limited (SSSL) was a regulated supplier and therefore had market power for access control services amounting to dominance. SSSL supplies access control services to digital broadcasters, Open and BSkyB.

OFTEL came to its determination after conducting a competition law analysis of the market for access control services in the UK. It decided that SSSL would continue to have dominance in the market given that existing competition from operators such as Ondigital, CWC (now merged with ntl) and BT was still not enough to influence SSSL's market share.

In a final decision published on 21 June 2000,[76] OFTEL confirmed that it would require SSSL to allow other companies to have access to its encryption services to provide interactive services over digital TV sets. This will now mean that competing companies can use the technical services embedded in BSkyB's set-top boxes to provide interactive services.

Although OFTEL's decision on access control has been criticised for being too interventionist, particularly in the development of a new market, the SSSL decision provides useful guidance on how far a national regulator is willing to go to ensure that access for new entrants is secured in emerging markets. The point is an interesting one, as OFTEL's approach would appear to contrast with that of the Commission in its proposals to lighten the regulatory burden on SMP operators, as discussed at 5.5.3 above. This slightly diverging view on access from that of the Commission can also be

---

[74] For more information on conditional access, see the report by Intermedia, 'Digital Terrestrial TV, descrambling the issues' (April 1997, Vol. 25, No. 2). On the regulation of conditional access, see Cave, M. and Cowie, C., *Regulating Conditional Access in European Pay Broadcasting*, Telecommunications Policy Research Conference, 1996.

[75] See Directive 95/47 (use of standards for the transmission of television signals) and Directive 98/44 (the legal protection of services based on, or consisting of, conditional access); and, in the UK, the Advanced Television Services Regulations 1996 (SI 1996 No. 3151), amending s. 4 of the Telecommunications Act 1984 to extend the definition of a telecommunications system.

[76] See *Decision as to the status of Sky Subscriber Services Limited as a Regulated Supplier in the market for access control services for Digital Interactive TV Services* (London, OFTEL, 2000).

seen in OFTEL's recent consultation on whether cable operators should be required to offer open access for the delivery of services over their networks.[77]

OFTEL has also published Guidelines on special network access (July 2000). Both the Revised Voice Telephony Directive (Directive 98/10, replacing Directive 95/62) and the Interconnection Directive provide for access to networks at points *other* than the network termination points offered to the majority of end-users. This is special network access (SNA). The meaning of the term continues to be the subject of discussion by EU NRAs, and is also under consideration by the European Commission, as indicated in its Access Paper.[78]

OFTEL's Guidelines on SNA set out how organisations should seek SNA from network operators, what role OFTEL expects to play and what criteria OFTEL will apply when it is asked to judge the reasonableness of any disputed request for SNA. The Guidelines are important in that they state that, unlike the regime which applies to interconnection of networks by Annex II operators, there are *no* special prior qualifications for seeking SNA. Operators with Annex II status may request SNA under Condition 45 of the new PTO licences, whereas organisations without Annex II may request SNA under Condition 48. SNA may also be requested from fixed SMP operators under Condition 53 by *any* organisation providing telecommunications services. No doubt these Guidelines on access will continue to be increasingly important as more new entrants enter the digital market.

5.6 PACKET-SWITCHED INTERCONNECTION: NEGOTIATION AND STRUCTURE OF PEERING AND TRANSIT AGREEMENTS

Here we examine packet-switched networks using the transmission control protocol/Internet protocol (TCP/IP) and the interconnection of such networks through peering (see 5.6.3 below).

5.6.1 Introduction

The Internet is the interconnection of a whole range of packet-switched networks, some of which are virtual, most of which are in the public domain, and some of which are private. There are three basic classes of participant in the Internet:

(a) end-users;[79]

---

[77] See Consultation Document, *Open Access to Communications Networks: Ensuring competition in the provision of services* (London, OFTEL, 2000) and the subsequent Statement, *Open Access: Delivering effective competition in communications markets* (London, OFTEL, 2001).

[78] See s. 12, Access Paper, where it states that 'NRAs shall be able to impose obligations on operators to grant access to, and use of, special facilities and/or associated services, in order to correct or prevent a distortion of competition . . .'.

[79] This category will include residential and small business end-users (SMEs) and the large corporate end-user, all of whom will be contracting with the ISP on a retail basis.

(b) ISPs, Internet portal companies (IPCs), and Internet commerce companies (ICCs);

(c) transit service providers (TSPs) and Internet backbone providers (IBPs).[80]

End-users send and receive information; ISPs allow end-users to access TSPs and backbone networks; IBPs route traffic between ISPs and TSPs, and interconnect with other IBPs.

IPCs, by contrast, are providers of content, often not charging subscription fees, and either functioning as search engines for ISPs and/or providing a 'click through' service on their websites to other search engines. Examples include Lycos, Yahoo, and Alta Vista. IPCs derive much of their revenue from contracts with advertisers or other content providers, guaranteeing a certain number of image impressions or 'hits' on the website of the advertiser's banner. Closely connected with IPCs are the ICCs, which are companies that conduct business solely through the Internet (e.g., Amazon.com). IPCs also include the increasingly successful business-to-business (B2B) companies and B2B Internet exchanges, such as Covisint, a consortium formed by General Motors, Ford and Daimler Chrysler to connect the world's top automakers and their suppliers. In recent months, B2B exchanges have come under the closer scrutiny of the antitrust authorities.[81]

The role of the TSP is more difficult to define. The use of the backbone network to aggregate the traffic of smaller, geographically-remote networks introduced the concept of transit. Transit across one or more networks is necessary when a user on a smaller ISP wishes to send an e-mail or a file to a user on a remote network. If the two networks do not have a direct connection, communication can occur only through a third (or more) network(s). In this sense transit networks perform a wholesale function, and, at some point, a transit network will be indistinguishable from a backbone network. Generally what will separate a TSP from an IBP is that the latter will have invested a great deal in international infrastructure either in the form of leasing international private leased circuits (IPLCs), or having ownership of capacity of submarine cables through an indefeasible right of use (IRU) or on satellite links.

Many IBPs are vertically integrated and, thus, are also TSPs and ISPs. For example, prior to the divestiture of its Internet business to C&W, MCI acted both as an IBP and an ISP. Examples of ISPs include: AOL and MSN (national on-line services), PSI Net, WholeEarth Networks (regional access ISPs[82]), UUNet, Demon, and BT Internet (national service providers). ISPs providing free Internet access include the revolutionary Freeserve, floated on the UK stock market in 1999.

---

[80] This category will include the carriage service providers and the equipment vendors.

[81] For example, Covisint has been the subject of an investigation by the Federal Trade Commission in the US, and MyAircraft.com by the European Commission.

[82] Which will also include wide area network (WAN)/local area network (LAN) operators, large businesses and universities.

Other players have now entered the UK Internet market with free access, including retail stores (such as Tesco) and clearing banks (such as Barclays). Due in part to the success of the free, dial-up ISPs, the market in the UK has been forced to move towards a flat-rate system of charging. For example, BT has recently launched its Surftime product, which allows unmetered Internet access.[83]

In Asia, ISPs include Net Asia, Asia-Online, HiNet, Pacific Internet, and Dispro. By contrast, examples of IBPs (numbering a smaller group) include C&W, BT, WorldCom/MCI, GTEI,[84] Asia Internet Holding (AIH), Sprint, AT&T WorldNet and Netcom. No doubt due to the rapidly changing nature of the Internet industry, this list will probably be out of date by the time this chapter goes to print.

In early 2000, WorldCom/MCI submitted a merger filing application to the US Federal Communications Commission (FCC) for a merger between itself and Sprint, estimated to be worth some US 115 billion. It had been estimated that post-merger, the combined company could become the fourth largest carrier in the world. Naturally, critics were concerned, as they were with the MCI WorldCom merger a few years earlier,[85] that WorldCom/Sprint could emerge to dominate the market for backbone services.[86] The WorldCom/Sprint merger was subsequently blocked by both the Department of Justice in the US, and the European Commission.[87]

5.6.2 Internet architecture

Before going on to consider Internet interconnection in greater detail, it would be useful to understand how backbones, ISPs, and end-users interact with each other visually (see Figure 5.5).

---

[83] See *Communications Week International*, 7 December 1999, 'New tariffs allow unmetered Internet in the UK'.

[84] Bell-Atlantic in its merger with GTE Corp required GTE to spin off its nationwide Internet business arm into a separate public corporation (now called Genuity). See action by the Federal Communications Commission, 16 June 2000, by Memorandum and Order (FCC 00-221), and CC Docket No. 98-184.

[85] *Application of WorldCom, Inc. and MCI Communications Corporation for Transfer of Control of MCI Communications Corporation to WorldCom, Inc.* CC Docket No. 97-211. See also the European Commission's decision in WorldCom and MCI (Case IV/M.1069) (1999) OJ L 116/1.

[86] See the US Senate Committee on the Judiciary hearing on the proposed MCI WorldCom/Sprint merger at http://www.senate.gov/~judiciary/11499jfr.htm (4 November 1999). On 11 January 2000, the European Commission decided to initiate proceedings after finding that the MCI WorldCom/Sprint merger notification raised doubts as to its compatibility with the common market. The initiation of proceedings opened a second phase investigation (Case COMP/M.1741). On 27 June 2000, the US Department of Justice (DoJ) blocked the merger. A day later, the European Commission followed suit. The MCI/WorldCom merger is discussed later in this chapter at 5.6.7.

[87] See the DoJ's press release of 27 June 2000, where it refers to a suit filed in the US District Court in Washington DC, seeking a permanent injunction to prohibit the merger between WorldCom and Sprint. The press release can be seen at http://www.usdoj.gov. One day later, on 28 June, the European Commission announced a formal decision to block the proposed merger: IP/00/668 of 28 June 2000.

Figure 5.5   Internet network architecture

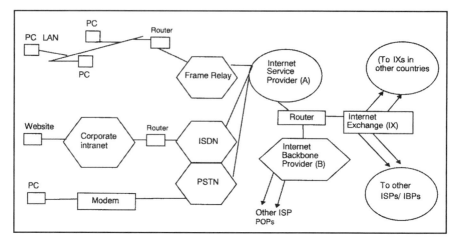

The top part of Figure 5.5 illustrates a corporate network linking a number of personal computers (PCs) by way of a local area network (LAN). The LAN is connected by way of a router[88] and frame relay connection to the ISP. Corporate data networks tend to generate a lot of bursty traffic. Frame relay is often considered here for connecting to the ISP, as frame relay cells are of variable size and can handle such variable traffic flow.[89] But frame relay is not good for time-sensitive applications, such as voice and video.

The middle section of Figure 5.5 illustrates another corporate network, but utilising an *intranet*. An intranet is a private network that uses the Internet protocols (TCP/IP) and net applications such as e-mail, file transfer, and the web. Connection to the ISP may be by dedicated E1 lines.

An intranet is often a combination of private facilities and public presence. Although an intranet is a network of private-leased circuits, it can also be built using the Internet (a public network) as its connectivity. Because of this, intranets must have authentication, security and encryption. *Extranets*, by contrast, are virtual networks formed by the *partial* interconnection of several different companies' intranets. Again security is required in the form of *firewalls*.[90] The bottom part of Figure 5.5 shows the dial-up user accessing the Internet by way of a modem and the PSTN.

To the right of the figure, we see the various interconnects between the ISP and backbone networks (or even transit networks) at the *network* interface. What is not shown in the figure (for reasons of simplicity) is the internal structure of the ISP itself. The ISP's internal structure will consist of three

---

[88] A router is a device, which connects two separate LANs using the same protocols.

[89] The superior (and more expensive) option is to use a technology called asynchronous transfer mode (ATM).

[90] A firewall will use hardware, but more often than not software, to protect a networked system from damage by outsiders (hackers) while maintaining connectivity. The firewall will generally sit between the LAN of the customer and the telecommunications link to the Internet server of the ISP.

principal sections: the *access server*; the *application servers*; and the *internal network*. The ISP's access server will consist of a *customer* interface, effectively a modem pool for dial-up users and for permanently connected customers (such as the large corporates), and an access router, which at a minimum could have eight ports supporting 30 ISDN (integrated services digital networks) channels.

The application server will consist of a series of partitioned servers or separate servers dedicated to each application being offered by the ISP, such as e-mail, web hosting, newsfeeds, interactive relay chat and games. Some ISPs also offer a managed access service for corporate clients, also known as 'virtual hosting'.[91] The ISP's internal network will depend on the number of Points of Presence (PoPs) it has. Customers like to connect to a PoP in a local call zone so that timed charges for long-distance tariffs can be avoided. For this reason, to offer a uniform service quality and to take advantage of economies of scale, the ISP may need to have a number of PoPs, each permanently connected by a permanent virtual circuit (PVC) leased from carriers.[92]

The interconnect arrangements on the *network* side of the ISP will generally be at a wholesale level[93] and interconnect may be by way of private bilateral or multilateral peering or transit agreements, or by peering at public network access points, such as the London Internet Exchange (LINX) situated at London Telehouse in the UK, or MAEWEST and MAEAST in the US for example.

The essential service provided by IBPs is a transmission of information between all users of the Internet. Although IBPs compete with one another for ISP customers, they must also cooperate with one another, by interconnecting, to offer their end-users access to the full range of content and to other end-users that are connected to the Internet. As a result of this interconnection among IBP networks, the Internet is often described as a 'network of networks'.

5.6.3 Introducing peering and transit

Service providers interconnect with one another through what is called a 'peering' agreement. 'Peering' is defined as:

> An interconnection of two public networks that provide connectivity to hosts whose routes are advertised on the global internet, on a settlement free basis that allows customers of one network to exchange traffic to customers directly on the second ISP's network.[94]

---

[91] This service involves setting up a router and leased line to the customer's premises and management of the firewall between the customer and the Internet.

[92] In the UK, the need for an ISP to have a series of PoPs is minimised through use of BT as an originating carrier and the purchase of Number Translation Services (NTS) to route the customer's call to the relevant ISP.

[93] As opposed to interconnection at a retail level, which would describe the access by the corporate or dial-up customer to the ISP's modem pool.

[94] See OECD Report, *Internet Traffic Exchange: Developments and Policy* (DSTI/ICCP/TISP(98)1/FINAL), 1998. See also Cukier, K.N., 'Peering and Fearing: ISP interconnection and regulatory issues' at http:ksgwww.harvard.edu/iip/iicompol/papers/cukier.html.

Figure 5.6   Peering

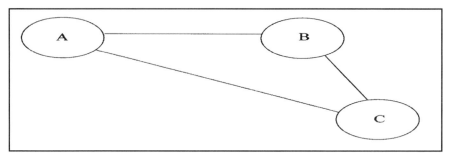

In a peering arrangement, two service providers agree to exchange traffic that originates from an end-user connected to one provider and terminates with an end-user connected to another. The Australian Competition and Consumer Commission's (ACCC) Consultation Paper on Internet interconnection defines peering more simply, as 'the establishment of a connection between computers and/or networks'.[95] It leaves out the basis of peering as being 'settlement free'.

The ACCC, in its detailed examination of the Australian Internet industry, believes that peering has moved on from a straightforward settlement-free basis, and considers that the financial and other administrative arrangements governing peering should be referred to separately as 'settlement arrangements'.[96] This is probably the correct approach, although in this chapter, and for the sake of simplicity, peering is described as an arrangement that has two main characteristics:

(a)   in general, peering is 'settlement free' i.e. the service providers do not charge each other for terminating traffic. This will normally be the case where the two networks are of roughly the same size, size being defined by the number of customers that each provider has on its respective network, backbone capacity, and traffic volume;

(b)   one peer will not allow traffic from another peer to transit its network to a third IBP.

Figure 5.6 illustrates peering between three ISPs, A, B, and C. If A only has a *peering* arrangement with B, and B with C, then B will *not* allow customers of A to send traffic to or receive traffic from customers of C by way of B's network. In order to provide access to the customers of C, A must either peer with C or enter into a paying *transit agreement* with either B or C if C refuses to peer directly with A. C may refuse to peer with A if A does not generate enough traffic across its network to warrant peering on a settlement-free basis.

---

[95] ACCC, *Internet Interconnection: Factors affecting commercial arrangements between network operators in Australia* (Sydney, ACCC, 2000), http://www.accc.gov.au/media/mediar.htm.
[96] *Ibid.*, at p. 33.

5.6.3.1 Paying transit The alternative to peering is a 'paying transit' relationship. A transit arrangement differs from peering in two respects:

(a) In contrast to peering, in which service providers generally exchange traffic without charge, in a transit arrangement one provider pays the other to carry its traffic. The amount of this charge generally depends upon the capacity of the connection, or the volume of traffic flowing across the POI.

(b) In contrast to peering, in which service providers terminate each other's traffic only, in a transit arrangement a provider agrees to deliver *all* Internet traffic that originates or terminates on the paying provider regardless of the destination or source of that traffic.[97] Therefore, in Figure 5.6, if A becomes a paying transit customer of B then, as a paying customer of B, A will be able to send traffic to and receive traffic from C via B's network, regardless of the source or destination of that traffic.

Negotiations for peering do not just occur horizontally between ISPs but also vertically between 'small local ISPs' and 'large national IBPs'. In the latter case, the large national IBPs have a stronger bargaining position because they not only provide access to their customer and content base, but also act as a gateway to the rest of the Internet

Peering and transit agreements allow smaller ISPs to extend their reach into regions where they would otherwise lack infrastructure, and to keep traffic on Internet protocol (IP) networks longer before it reaches a gateway to the pricey PSTN/PSN network, where the call is completed. Such interconnections are vital for smaller ISPs, since only by interconnecting can the IP traffic travel furthest and the cost benefit of using the net be maximised.[98]

However, ISP interconnection may increasingly require complex settlement mechanisms to compensate both parties for transporting traffic. Many ISPs are now offering a wide range of high-speed digital applications, such as IP telephony, on-line video games and web hosting.[99] Further, ISPs who are also infrastructure providers and backbone operators may offer switched co-location for internet access, private line services (dedicated telephony and voice), virtual private networks (VPNs) and non-switched IP telephony. If peering and transit agreements are to include more sophisticated payment formulas, such agreements will increasingly come to include the complex service schedules found in current interconnection agreements for circuit-switched interconnect.

---

[97] It is important to appreciate that with packet-switched networks, traffic could be coming on to A's network from anywhere in the world (regardless of source). Likewise, traffic could be leaving C's network for onward transmission to any point (regardless of destination).

[98] Note that peering agreements may not be necessary if carriage and other value added Internet services are acquired from an international private leased circuit provider or another ISP (acting as a reseller). General peering agreements are likely to be in standardised form, and are relatively informal when compared to circuit-switched interconnect agreements in the telecoms sense.

[99] There are already a number of operators who have moved to a usage-based system for payment.

5.6.3.2 Settlement mechanisms Settlements for circuit-switched interconnect are commonplace, and through the years many forms of interconnect pricing have emerged with most of the developed world settling on a form of long-run incremental cost as the basis for pricing interconnect payments. Interconnect pricing for voice (circuit-switched) networks is covered in more detail in 5.3.3.10 above. Settlements between circuit-switched networks are determined mainly on the basis of the volume of traffic flowing across the POI, with the traffic being measured through the use of servers at the POI and the basis of billing dependent on the processing of call detail records (CDRs). Customers are identified for billing purposes through the exchange of calling line identification (CLI) numbers and provisions are agreed for bad debt.

In the packet-switched world there are no similar arrangements, although some commentators have argued for some form of standardised record of usage similar to the call detail records to help with Internet interconnection payments and as a reference model for billing systems, as TCP/IP networks and the applications that run over them proliferate.[100]

Settlements for specialised or general internet traffic would radically alter the Net's current economic model; at present it is generally settlement-free between backbone networks, which generally sell connectivity based on leased-line capacity rather than actual usage, although other models for payment also exist. Variations on forms of settlement include:

- supplier-customer model;
- sender keeps all;
- bilateral settlement;
- multilateral settlement; and
- discounted settlement.

A detailed discussion of settlements is outside the scope of this chapter. For this, the reader is directed to the ACCC Paper on Internet interconnection, which sets out a comparative analysis of the different forms of settlement mechanism in common use in the industry today.[101] A brief examination of each form is, however, included below.

In the ACCC Paper, the supplier-customer model is described as a unilateral charging model based on traffic delivered to downstream networks (inbound traffic). For this type of settlement, traffic is measured in megabytes and the receiver is billed in accordance with the volume of inbound traffic. This arrangement is effectively the same as the paying transit scheme described at 5.6.3.1 above. Advantages of this arrangement include encouraging downstream ISPs to manage their network resources more efficiently, and also encouraging the development of local content rather than downloading content from the upstream TSP's or IBP's network, where the original source of the content may often have come from overseas, probably the US.

---

[100] See Lucas, M., 'IP Detail Record Initiative', *Billing World*, July/August 1999, at 30–32.
[101] *Op. cit. supra* n. 95, at 45.

Sourcing US content continues to keep IBP prices high, as the IBP often has to pay for the full cost of the international circuit to the US.[102] The IBP will then seek to pass these costs on to the TSP or domestic ISP. This latter point demonstrates one of the disadvantages of the supplier-client model, in that it tends to allow the supplier to free-ride on the local domestic ISP's network by passing costs down to the ISP. In turn, the domestic ISP will try (although it may find it very difficult in an increasingly competitive market) to pass these costs on to the end-user. In effect, the supplier-client model often ends up with the IBP or TSP setting the price floor faced by the end-user.

With the 'Sender keeps all' approach, the interconnecting parties agree that traffic volumes are nearly balanced and it is more cost-efficient to exchange traffic on a settlement-free basis.[103] Such arrangements tend to work more efficiently where the interconnecting parties have networks that are roughly the same size, interconnect using similar capacity links, and exchange similar volumes of traffic. This type of arrangement describes the conventional view of peering on a settlement-free basis, described above.

With bilateral settlement, the interconnecting parties agree on a price for exchanging traffic, measure the difference in the bi-directional flow of traffic, and then reimburse the operator suffering the *net* inflow. This form of settlement is very similar to the international accounting rate settlement mechanism used for international accounting settlements between operators. By contrast, multilateral settlement involves the joint funding of a network access point (NAP), with each of the operators paying for linking to the NAP. At the NAP, the operators will exchange traffic on a 'sender keeps all' or settlement-based arrangement.

Lastly, there is discounted settlement. This form of settlement is a variation of the supplier-customer relationship described above, except that as the local ISP continues to download increased volumes of traffic from the upstream TSP or IBP, the local ISP will attract larger discounts. The advantages of discounted pricing are that cost savings are passed on to the ISP with increased traffic volumes, and these savings can in turn be passed on to end-users. In effect, as with the supplier-customer model, discounted settlements influence the retail price floor set by the domestic ISP, although in a more positive way.

There is no doubt that, in time to come, the larger TSPs and IBPs will increasingly want to interconnect at private peering points rather than continue to peer at the public NAPs on a settlement-free basis with other service providers, particularly the smaller ISPs and TSPs. This is due to the increased flow of traffic over TCP/IP networks as PC Internet penetration increases worldwide and the increased revenues that the larger TSPs and

---

[102] Note, however, that in a press release by APEC (30 May 2000), APEC and the United States seem to have reached an agreement on the payment for international charging arrangements for international services. The Agreement notes that international charging arrangements should reflect: (a) the contribution of each network to the communication; (b) the use by each party of the interconnected network resources; and (c) the end-to-end costs of international transport link capacity.

[103] *Op. cit. supra* n. 95, at 46.

IBPs can earn from increasingly sophisticated settlement mechanisms at private peering points. The move to a system of private networks is also due to a desire by the IBPs and larger TSPs to guarantee some form of control and end-to-end service level quality to their larger business and corporate customers, increasingly dependent on revenues generated through e-commerce.

Inevitably, the costs for Internet interconnection agreements will rise with the greater need for both commercial and legal input. The regulation of peering and transit agreements, and their similarity with circuit-switched interconnect agreements, is looked at in greater detail at 5.6.5 below.

5.6.3.3 ISP connections For the moment, most ISPs will maintain both peering and transit agreements with local ISPs via the various public Internet exchanges, as well as peering/transit with one or more service providers or clearing houses in the US through IPLCs or IRUs in submarine cables.[104] An ISP rolling out a service will therefore need to consider what network architecture it wishes to adopt and to what extent interconnection with these various exchanges will be sufficient to provide a narrowband service initially. The ISP will also need to consider whether it should be party to various multilateral peering arrangements at public Internet exchanges, or whether it should make its own bilateral arrangements with other ISPs at private peering points. The latter often has the advantage of coming with guaranteed levels of service through a service level agreement with the TSP or IBP. More often than not, the ISP will connect up to these peering points through leased lines bundled with other Internet services provided by another ISP, or in the UK acquired from BT or C&W, or any other operator licensed to provide them. In such a case, the form of these contracts will be determined by the tariff service offered by BT *et al.*

Leased lines may be required for large subscribers or content providers requiring direct access to the ISP's network (and on a 'permanently-on' basis). In some jurisdictions, regulatory controls may restrict the flexibility of PTOs to amend tariffs on leased circuits, and this is to be welcomed. For example, for many years, Europe has been well behind the US in the provision of competitive tariffs for leased-line circuits. As leased lines provide the basic infrastructure for most ISPs (and in some cases IBPs), the lack of competitive rates has restricted the growth of IP networks, resulting in inflated end-user prices for access.

In some parts of Europe the situation has become so extreme that the market research consultancy Ovum, in its recommendation for a review of the Interconnection Directive, suggests that leased-line tariffs should form part of the reference interconnection offers of all operators with SMP.[105] In response to such concerns, the European Commission adopted a Recommendation on

---

[104] An IRU is effectively a long-term lease of capacity on a submarine cable, typically for 15 years. In certain circumstances, the grant of an IRU can confer ownership rights in the cable itself, unlike an IPLC.

[105] See Lewin, D. and Rogerson, D., *A review of the Interconnect Directive, initial proposals for discussion*, Ovum Consultation Paper, June 1999.

Figure 5.7 Bargaining power: the different roles

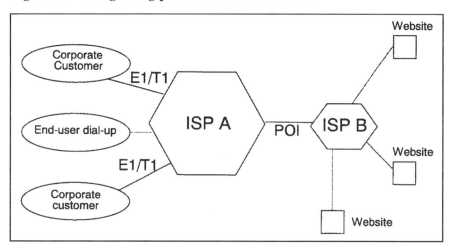

leased-line interconnection pricing, specifically addressing 'price ceilings for short distance leased line part circuits (i.e. the circuit between the customer premises and the point of interconnection').[106]

In practice, the ISP will have a combination of both private and public peering agreements. At the public peering points, such as the LINX or MAEWEST or MAEAST, the ISP will have to comply with a code of conduct set by the public Internet exchange; or, where peering at private points, with the acceptable use policy (AUP) of the other peering partner (see 5.6.4 below).

5.6.3.4 Bargaining positions What follows is a typical negotiating scenario between two ISPs. Figure 5.7 shows two ISPs (which both have facilities), where A is larger in terms of national presence in customers than B, but receives a traffic *imbalance* when peering with B who sends more traffic to A.

It is important to remember that the nature of the negotiation will be influenced by the category of the service providers seeking interconnection, whether an IBP, a TSP, or an ISP, etc. How negotiations are structured will depend on where in the network hierarchy the operator requesting interconnect falls. For example, the ACCC's Paper on Internet interconnection distinguishes clearly between single node[107] ISPs, having only one interconnection with an upstream TSP or IBP, and multinode ISPs, where the ISP has a number of nodes interconnecting with a range of other ISPs, TSPs and IBPs.[108] In the former case, the bargaining position of the ISP is weak, and

---

[106] C (1999) 3863, 24.1.1999.
[107] A node being different from a PoP. A PoP describes the location of the ISPs customer access and network application servers whereas a *node* may describe only a point of interconnection between two networks at either a public or private peering point.
[108] *Op. cit. supra* n. 95, at 91.

the upstream IBP or TSP may impose a supplier-customer arrangement with the ISP; whereas in the latter case, the ISP has more options for negotiating a better service level agreement, or pricing the service it receives from the upstream operator by reference to the service being accessed and the cost of that service.

To complicate matters further, the negotiating position of the parties concerned is not influenced only by *where* in the network hierarchy the operator falls, but also by whether or not that service provider has been able to attract important content providers on to its network. This latter point is explained more clearly in the negotiating scenario described at Figure 5.7.

In the scenario, B specialises in web hosting[109] as an Internet value added service, which it considers to be highly profitable. There are three basic types of website that B can host for its customers, who mainly feature corporates and small- to medium-sized enterprises (SMEs):

(a)   *content* sites, which consist of colourful pages to entertain the visitor;
(b)   *transaction* sites, which use on-line transactions to sell goods, conduct business or provide customer services; and
(c)   *promotional* sites, which currently form the majority of sites found on the World Wide Web (WWW) and are mainly used to advertise brands and are marketing-based.

How A and B come together to negotiate peering will depend entirely on their bargaining positions. In the scenario shown at Figure 5.7, the ability of B to host web content puts it in a strategic bargaining position. This is because there is an inherent traffic imbalance between networks that *host* content and are therefore net *exporters* of data, and those networks with many subscribers that *request* the data and are net *importers* of data.

Often a smaller network is forced to become the customer of a dominant network or another upstream provider and to connect its customers with the customers of the dominant network. Frequently the dominant IBP or larger ISP will query the number of customers that the smaller ISP has on specific peering routes, to verify whether peering is justified on that route. This is done by asking for the 'AS' reference numbers of the peering routes used by the smaller ISP. AS references are discussed further below at 5.6.4.

But the scenario shown in Figure 5.7 is different. Here, A's customers make electronic requests for B's hosted web pages, and B responds by sending a great deal of traffic to A across the POI. Consequently, A has to invest in adequate network resources to ensure that it has the necessary bandwidth to carry B's traffic to its own (A's) customers. As A considers B to be a far smaller operator, in terms of numbers of customers, it makes the decision to force a paying transit agreement on B, rather than continue peering

---

[109] A service whereby the operator maintains and monitors the websites on behalf of individual customers for a fee. The operator will do this by way of servers and associated software. The website may be anything from a collection of visually interesting documents to an interactive site performing more active tasks for its viewers such as taking orders, registering product interest, etc. Servers are often individual computers dedicated to a particular task, e.g., name servers, file servers, and linked together.

on a settlement-free basis in a bid to recoup some of its costs. It calculates that B will have to accept this condition as A (the much larger network) will threaten to cut off peering with B, and therefore access by B to A's larger customer base.

But in this scenario A has miscalculated. B is hosting valuable content to which A's customers want access. By cutting the interconnection with B, A will be denying its own customers a proven popular service. In fact B can counteract by demanding a payment from A in order to cover the costs incurred by B in maintaining a high bandwidth connection with A who is at the POI. The approach by B clearly demonstrates how demanded content can give the operator providing that content a greater bargaining position in peering negotiations.[110] Although A, the larger network, would deny more customers to B than B to A, terminating the interconnection would prove very unproductive for both sides. Both ISPs will lose out.

So who makes the payment? For the moment there is no set industry approach. Generally what happens in the marketplace is that a single IBP or ISP acts like A in some situations and like B in others. Without effective transparency in peering and transit brought about by the publication of such agreements,[111] this continues and all IBPs or ISPs seek to gain a competitive advantage.[112]

The range of terms that will be included in a peering (packet-switched interconnect) agreement differs from some of the terms that would normally be found in a circuit-switched (voice) agreement (see 5.3.2.1). The reason for this lies in the fundamental differences between circuit-switched and packet-switched networks. For example, on TCP/IP networks, users stay on-line for longer than the average three- to five-minute voice call, putting demands on the network, and in particular on the switches beyond those foreseen for voice purposes.

The PSTN is a circuit-switched network, a design that has not changed for a century. Circuit-switched technology dedicates a fixed amount of capacity for the duration of a call, thereby tying up an entire circuit or portion of the network for its duration. IP-based packet-switching technologies split the information into bits, send them across the network using the most cost-effective route ('least-cost routing') and far cheaper routers,[113] and reassemble them at the other end. Consequently, the cost of moving information through an IP network is much lower than through a traditional circuit-switched network because IP technology makes much more efficient use of the transmission link. IP networks can transport large volumes of traffic more efficiently and at a much lower cost than traditional networks.

For this reason, interconnection agreements involving packet-switched or IP networks tend to be cheaper to negotiate and are often less complex than

---

[110] Often the ISP will examine the routes used by the other ISP in a bid to evaluate how much traffic is flowing across such routes. As mentioned, it does this by referring to AS reference numbers for each route. It will then use this information in negotiations with the other party.
[111] Either by the players themselves, or possibly through an NRA to whom peering/transit agreements are sent for inspection. In the circuit-switched voice industry, transparency is covered by regulation under Art. 6, Interconnection Directive, *supra* n. 2. See also 5.4 above.
[112] For a more detailed discussion of this negotiating scenario, see Cukier, *op. cit. supra* n. 94.
[113] Which are simply computers. This is to be contrasted with Public Branch Exchanges (PBXs), which are more expensive and are used to switch voice calls.

their circuit-switched counterparts. No doubt as the range of services over IP networks becomes increasingly sophisticated, so too will the payment mechanisms and the agreements themselves. Some of the more important contractual terms for Internet interconnection are considered at 5.6.4 below.

5.6.4   Selected terms and conditions for Internet interconnection

Terms that both parties will need to look at carefully before signing a peering and/or transit agreement will include the following:

(a)   *Provisions prohibiting transit traffic.* Definitions of transit traffic (sometimes called third-party traffic) vary by agreement, but generally transit traffic is defined as traffic between destinations, where neither of the destinations is a subscriber (or the customer of a subscriber) of the other party. Limiting transit traffic is important, as excessive traffic will lead to congestion on the network, which in turn will affect the quality of service to existing customers. The only way of limiting transit traffic is to define carefully the *class* of end-users and customers belonging to each of the negotiating parties to the agreement.

(b)   *Third-party routing.* Both parties will want to put in place restrictions on connectivity to ensure that other multi-user networks do not gain unauthorised access to the other party's network through:

(i)   the placement of third-party routers that are not agreed;

(ii)   the placement of any computer in the network path that is capable of IP routing, thereby diverting third-party traffic to the other party's facility;

(iii)   proxying, i.e. the use of a proxy server to redirect unauthorised traffic. A proxy server is a form of a computer that is assigned the specific task of administering a network's internal IP addresses. It can also act as an efficient copier of web pages and as a firewall to the World Wide Web.

(c)   *Any term establishing a peer as a last resort.* A route of last resort is often a *default* route. Usually a party to a peering agreement will want to restrict the other party from establishing a default route directed at the other party's Internet network by rewriting nexthops (a hop being a specific route taken across public and/or private interconnection points) or modifying third-party routing information. Generally both parties will agree to a list of specific routers that will be annexed in a schedule to the peering agreement itself. Any traffic then exchanged under the peering agreement will be accepted only from the routers listed in the schedule. Breaching an agreement on restricting default routes will often allow the innocent party to impose filtering techniques on third-party traffic, such as route filtering, packet filtering, rate limiting and other measures to limit traffic exchange.

(d)   *Provisions dealing with operational matters (maintenance, network upgrades, bandwidth requests, etc.).* Sometimes at private peering points, the more powerful IBP can degrade the quality of interconnection at the POI by implementing slow-roll increases in capacity, only agreeing to interconnect at congested NAPs, or being very slow in installing the interconnect link in the first place. The smaller ISP will guard against such anti-competitive behaviour by seeking specific provisions on operational matters.

(e) *Restrictions on monitoring or capturing customer data.* Both parties will want to put in place restrictions on the other being able to monitor customer data, except for control data required for operational use. Normally each party will be able to monitor and use IP headers (addressing information in a packet), transport headers, and packet characteristics for its own operational needs.

(f) *Liability for content of information passing across the POIs.* Content liability clauses and the warranties and indemnities that go with them are a standard feature of any peering agreement. US law is far more advanced than most other regimes as regards the liability of ISPs and carriers. Potential losses (for damages) in the US relate mainly to copyright,[114] trademark infringement, defamation,[115] pornography, and dissemination of viruses and international torts.

In Europe, the E-Commerce Directive[116] covers the liability of ISPs. Again, ISPs can be classed as mere conduits of information and not subject to liability for the content of information transmitted so long as they conform to specific conditions on initiation of the transmission, selection of the receiver of the transmission, and modification of the content of the transmission (Art. 12). Article 13 exempts liability for caching, and Art. 14 liability for hosting, again on grounds that specific conditions are met. Under Art. 15, there is no general obligation on the ISP to monitor the information which the ISP transmits or stores.[117]

---

[114] Under the Digital Millennium Copyright Act (DMCA) 17 USC §512, an ISP is afforded a safe harbour from liability for copyright infringement committed by users of the ISP if the ISP takes certain steps set out in the statute to bring itself within the safe harbour. This is particularly the case if the ISP has no knowledge of the infringing material and receives no financial benefit and, once put on notice, responds expeditiously to a request to remove. Prior to the enactment of the DMCA, there were a number of high-profile copyright infringement cases: *Sega Enterprises* v *Maphia*, 857 F. Supp. 679 (ND Cal 1994), *Religious Technology Center* v *Netcom On-Line Communications Services Inc.* 907 F. Supp. 1361 (ND Cal 1995), and *Playboy Enterprises Inc.* v *Frena*, 839 F. Supp. 1552 (MD Fla 1993). The DMCA does not, however, cover direct copyright infringement by an ISP. For cases of direct infringement, a specific indemnity will be required.

[115] Before the enactment of the US Telecommunications Act 1996, there was uncertainty as to the liability of an ISP for defamatory comments made by users of its service. However, under s. 230 of the Act, ISPs are classed as mere distributors of information provided by others and cannot be held liable for defamatory content. A series of US cases (*Doe* v *America Online* 718 So. 2d 385 (Fla App. 1998), *Kenneth M. Zeran* v *America Online, Inc.* 958 F. Supp. 1124 (ED Va. 1997), and *Sidney Blumenthal et al.* v *Matt Drudge and American Online, Inc.* 992 F. Supp. 44 (DDC 1998)) has confirmed this view. By contrast, in the UK, following the recent case of *Godfrey* v *Demon Internet Ltd* [1999] 4 All ER 342, any defence available under s. 1, Defamation Act 1996 could be damaged if the ISP is put on notice of potentially defamatory material but does nothing expeditiously to remove it.

[116] Directive 2000/31/EC of the European Parliament and of the Council on certain legal aspects of information society services, in particular electronic commerce, in the Internal Market (2000) OJ L 178/1.

[117] However, ISPs should be wary of two recitals in the E-Commerce Directive that appear to contradict the wording of Art. 15. For example, Recital 47 says that Member States are prevented from imposing a monitoring obligation on service providers of a general nature, but monitoring obligations may apply in specific cases. Also, Recital 48 could allow Member States to require ISPs to apply a duty of care (that may be specified in national law) to detect and prevent certain types of illegal activity.

As far as the contracts are concerned, often in financially valueless peering agreements both parties will attempt to restrict their liability to zero; but in other agreements (where a great deal of traffic is at stake and the carriers may be both infrastructure providers and ISPs) the situation is different and the risks are greater. A discussion of liability in the context of peering may be better explained by referring back to Figure 5.5 on Internet network architecture (see 5.6.2 above).

In Figure 5.5, if the backbone provider B were to sell a wholesale Internet access service to the ISP, A, the service schedule in the agreement might stipulate that this will allow A's customers (and *their* customers) to originate Internet traffic across A's network and which will pass across the POI (peering point) on to B's network for onward transmission to anywhere in the world.[118] Looking at Figure 5.5, it is possible to see that the data from A can come from anywhere: for example, data networks in Germany, corporate web-sites in France, and dial-up users in the UK. The content of data that will cross the POI can include: files, news group postings, on-line contracts, e-mails, confidential information, software, websites, intellectual property rights, obscene material, pornography and defamatory content – quite a nasty cocktail. The situation is even worse when B peers with its peering partners around the world. Depending on the contractual provisions it has in place with these other peering partners, B may have to accept liability for *any* damage caused by A's content.

To limit its liability, B may seek an unlimited liability indemnity from A that will cover all of B's losses in connection with any content supplied by A across the POI. The seeking of unlimited liability indemnities is becoming increasingly common in the Internet industry, and particularly in the US, where the party seeking the indemnity is likely to be a larger player, such as an IBP. Whether A will accept such an onerous condition will depend entirely on the commercial value of the agreement to A and the bargaining positions of the parties concerned.

Also because of the potential hazards, to further minimise liability to B, B's peering agreement with A may require A to include certain terms in A's agreements with its own customers (A's ISP and business customers, whether or not they resell A's services). The terms may relate to content responsibility, warranty and liability limitations, the exclusion of liability for consequential loss, the obligations of customers to comply with local laws (particularly export laws if there are restrictions on the export of software, as in the US), and the obligation for customers to relinquish IP addresses on termination of services. If A should fail to include such terms in its agreements with its own customers, any loss suffered by B as a result of such breach could result in a claim for damages against A.

A in turn will try to limit its liability to B by:

(i)   reviewing its own (wholesale) peering and transit agreements;

(ii)   ensuring that its own (retail) customer agreements can be terminated or suspended at short notice. This will allow A to isolate damaging

---

[118] This will be as a consequence of B's peering relationships with other backbone carriers and ISPs.

content quickly once A is put on notice about the material, and therefore (in the UK at least) avoid the result in *Godfrey* v *Demon*;

(iii) making sure that on termination any IP addresses originally assigned to the customer are immediately relinquished;

(iv) reviewing regularly the credit of customers with a view to future litigation (there is no point in suing an insolvent customer);

(v) reviewing insurance arrangements. In the US, insurance houses are increasingly providing more favourable terms for insuring ISPs;

(vi) reviewing the corporate structure of the company. Company laws, of course, vary by jurisdiction, but in the UK (with the availability of limited liability vehicles) it may be more convenient for A to turn its Internet division into a limited liability company, or to place a limited liability company between the parent A and its subsidiary Internet company.

(g) *Acceptable use policy (AUP)*. Another term frequently seen in peering agreements is a reference incorporating each of the parties' AUPs into the agreement. In the example cited at Figure 5.5 (see 5.6.2), to minimise B's liability for carrying A's content further, B may ask A to comply with any AUP in force by A, or to comply with B's own AUP. Besides covering the guidelines on the transmission of content, the AUP will also contain provisions on damaging material, such as viruses, e-mail forging, usernet spamming, and creating congestion on networks through the use of chain letters. Alternatively, if the parties are peering at public peering points, such as the London Internet Exchange (LINX) in the UK or MAEWEST and MAEAST in the US, both parties will need to conform to the Acceptable Codes of Practice of the public Internet exchanges.

(h) *The AS reference numbers for the peering routes sought.* Each ISP network advertising its routes is assigned an Autonomous System (AS) number. The AS number is included in all IP packet headers, and so is relatively easy to track. IP headers also contain source and destination addresses, allowing tracking of which domains are sending/receiving traffic. For example ASxxxx might refer to the European link of A's network between London and Paris. If A suggests that it intends to peer on this route on a settlement-free basis with B, B may check the traffic patterns on this route and determine that the traffic flowing across the route is so negligible that it does not warrant peering on a settlement-free basis. In this case, B may demand to peer on the *complete* A network, including all of A's more profitable routes and not just the ASxxxx route that A had originally selected. Therefore A must have a good idea of the traffic flowing across its different peering routes (sometimes called 'strings') before entering into negotiations with B, and decide on a bottom-line position on peering routes sought and offered.

(i) *Packet loss.* This should be defined carefully, as some peering partners like to impose a penalty if (say) their networks sustain a packet loss of 5 per cent over a period of one to three months. The penalty might be to purchase transit from the peering partner instead of peering on a settlement-free basis. Therefore, if the use of A's network leads to packet losses of 5 per cent or more, the injured party (B) may demand that A purchases transit. A, however, may prefer to terminate the agreement, or to seek a transit agreement with a provider of its own choice.

(j) *Performance standards.*   Each of the parties will need to define terms on latency (time for a packet to reach a destination), redundancy, network downtime, etc.

(k) *Any terms restricting caching.*   Web caching allows ISPs to store frequently requested web pages on to their own servers (often closer to the customer requesting the pages) to speed users' connection times. In effect, caching reduces load on transit networks because a web page is stored much closer to the requesting user. The server is often located at the terminating ISP's premises and can be programmed to download the original page only when it has been updated, or at periodic intervals. A proxy server performs the same role, while mirror sites are copies of entire sites that may be updated overnight. The ACCC's Consultation Paper on internet interconnection cites industry estimates indicating that a cache can reduce international traffic to the point where the cache accounts for up to 40 per cent of total traffic.[119] This represents major savings in time for a web page to be returned from a remote host. The process of caching had been the subject of controversy in Europe, with draft Directives on the protection of copyright and electronic commerce being at odds with each other over the right to cache. The point of contention was whether copyright in the web pages was being breached by the ISPs in temporarily storing the pages. The ISP industry believed that caching was simply a way of preventing traffic congestion on the Net, whereas the anti-caching lobby, particularly the music industry, felt that caching involved the copying and the making of infringing copies of web pages.[120] Caching is often used by ISPs and smaller IBPs to reduce traffic volumes from the US and the attendant payments to US and domestic backbones.

Some peering agreements can run to many tens of pages, whereas other, financially valueless agreements, in which both partners may restrict their liability to zero, may run to only two or three pages at the most. However, in all peering negotiations it is important to appreciate that the larger backbone players control two vast resources – not just the transit of traffic, but also the accessibility of other networks to the end customers on their network. It is for these two reasons that much attention has fallen on recent or planned mergers in the Internet industry, particularly between the backbone players. For example, some commentators argued that the (now failed) merger between MCI/WorldCom and Sprint could create a combined carrier that would exert dominance in the market for backbone services.[121] This was also

---

[119] *Supra* n. 95.
[120] E-Commerce Directive, *supra* n. 116, at Art. 13.
[121] See the US Senate Committee on the Judiciary hearing on the proposed MCI WorldCom/Sprint merger at http://www.senate.gov/~judiciary/11499jfr.htm (4 November 1999). On 11 January 2000, the European Commission decided to initiate proceedings after finding that the MCI WorldCom/Sprint merger notification raised doubts as to its compatibility with the common market. The initiation of proceedings opened a second phase investigation (Case COMP/M.1741). The Commission invited interested third parties to submit their observations. On 28 June 2000, following the US Department of Justice's decision to block the merger the day before, the European Commission also rejected the proposed merger: IP/00/668.

the case when MCI/WorldCom announced their merger (discussed at 5.6.5.2 below). In that instance, the regulators on both sides of the Atlantic moved to readdress the perceived imbalance. The regulation of Internet interconnection agreements is discussed above.

5.6.5 The regulation of Internet interconnection

5.6.5.1 Introduction Before discussing the regulation of peering and transit in any depth, it is important to recognise some of the fundamental trends that have been occurring in the Internet industry over the last two years and that have brought about calls for regulating peering (see 5.6.3–5.6.4 above). These trends may be summarised as follows:

(a) numbers of IBPs are shrinking due to consolidation (i.e., the BT/AT&T, GTE/Bell Atlantic, MCI/WorldCom, and failed WorldCom/Sprint mergers);

(b) the differences between IBPs and ISPs are growing wider;

(c) there is a trend by IBPs to peer less with smaller ISPs;

(d) often the terms for peering by IBPs are kept private; and when ISPs do peer with IBPs, they are often forced to sign non-disclosure agreements;

(e) the termination of a peering agreement by IBPs can require very little notice in advance;

(f) the technical dialogue that takes place between IBPs and between IBPs and larger telecommunication networks can be regular and private, often to the exclusion of smaller ISPs.

5.6.5.2 Abuse of market position The larger the market share of the IBP or TSP, the more important it is for the ISP to interconnect with the IBP/TSP to reach its customers. Gerald Brock, in *Telecommunications Policy for the Information Age*,[122] states that:

> If one company had a large enough market share so that no other company could provide a useful service without interconnection with the first company, then the first company could use its dominant position to either take over the market or extract payments from the smaller companies.

The fear is, therefore, that a large IBP or a number of IBPs could eventually emerge to dominate the market for backbone services. The smaller ISPs argue that the industry is fast moving to an environment in which smaller ISPs are becoming paying customers of the larger backbones and transit operators. They argue that there is an increased need for greater transparency and guidelines on interconnection in the industry. This is primarily because of the potential for monopolistic pricing and anti-competitive behaviour, i.e. the ability of one competitor to raise the costs of others for a service element needed by all competitors and supplied by one or few operators.

---

[122] Brock, Gerald W. (Cambridge, Mass, Harvard University Press, 1994).

In a report commissioned by the APEC Telecommunications Working Group,[123] a number of possible anti-competitive practices that IBPs could apply were identified,[124] such as a 'refusal to deal', which is an attempt to drive a competitor out of business or to raise the costs of doing business with the impact of reducing its marketplace attractiveness. Another would be to apply a price squeeze, i.e. an attempt to raise competitors' costs and lower their marketplace attractiveness by increasing the cost of an essential facility, bottleneck or service element needed by the smaller ISP to provide a complete end-to-end service.[125] Anti-competitive behaviour could also include predatory pricing and/or using deliberate below cost rates. The IBP could also leverage its market power in more specific ways by:

(a) extracting from smaller ISPs agreements not to compete in certain service or geographical markets;
(b) setting a price floor on the service offered by the smaller ISP;
(c) linking the smaller ISP's access to a desired service, e.g., long-haul backbone trunks; or
(d) forcing a commitment to buy or lease less desirable and/or less competitively provisioned services.

So what are the regulators doing about regulating for access? Should there be some form of transparency and non-discrimination in Internet interconnection arrangements, as currently available with the regulation of circuit-switched (voice) agreements under the Interconnection Directive, for example?[126] Regulation is discussed at 5.6.6 below.

5.6.6 Regulating for access

5.6.6.1 Europe Several commentators on the Green Paper on Convergence[127] did focus on the need for competition rules to be applied against discriminatory behaviour by existing network operators, with concerns focusing on:

(a) the risk of discrimination;

---

[123] *A study of compatible and sustainable international charging arrangements for Internet services* (1999), referred to here as the 'ICAIS report'.
[124] Although the research of interconnection practice in Asia that the report covered seemed to indicate that IBPs were not practising these kinds of anti-competitive techniques.
[125] A margin squeeze was a concern of the UK regulator OFTEL in its recent determination of an Internet interconnection dispute between BT and WorldCom discussed later in this chapter under *National Treatment*.
[126] Article 6 of the Directive sets out broad conditions for transparency and non-discrimination for interconnecting operators. For example, the requirement on operators with SMP to publish their interconnection charges gives a greater degree of certainty to new entrants' investment plans and helps with the 'build or buy' decision.
[127] Green Paper on *The Convergence of the Telecommunications, Media and Information Technology Sectors, and the Implications for Regulation* (COM(97)623), and the subsequent Commission Communication, *Results of the Public Consultation* (COM(99)108).

(b) unfair cross-subsidisation;
(c) funding of access and services; and
(d) the overall approach to the charges paid by ISPs for interconnection and other telecommunication services.

The European Commission has yet to make law its proposals for interconnection and access as set out in its April 2000 Communication[128] and in the series of Working Papers that the Commission published in readiness for its public hearing in Brussels on a new regulatory framework for electronic networks and services in May 2000. Early in 1999, there was talk in Brussels that the subject of access to Internet infrastructure was to be covered by an inquiry into competition and infrastructure issues regarding the Internet in the last quarter of 1999.[129] However, when the Commission published its November Communication,[130] it did not raise the issue of a specific inquiry.

In its November Communication, the Commission did make clear that it planned to merge the ONP leased-line, TV Standards and Interconnection Directives into one overall Access and Interconnection Directive. The document stated vaguely that ISPs would be covered under this generic Directive, with ISPs looking for fair and non-discriminatory interconnection from other ISPs and operators, and looking to the NRA to enforce these provisions (November Communication, at 4.2.2). However, the November Communication did not lay out any specific principles for interconnection *between* ISPs. For example, the Commission envisaged commercial negotiation of interconnection requests for operators with SMP, and cost-orientation obligations to interconnect from dominant operators.[131] But how do we determine the market dominance of an ISP? By the number of peering relationships it has? By the volume of traffic across its POIs? Or by the number of servers and routers it owns?

Nevertheless, in the Draft Access Directive and Draft Framework Directive (see 5.5 above), the Commission sets out a more detailed treatment for the interconnection of TCP/IP networks. Unlike the Interconnection Directive, the application of which is restricted to narrowband networks, the recitals to the Framework Directive make clear that the new regulatory framework is to apply to a range of broadband communications networks, including the PSTN, TCP/IP networks, cable TV, mobile and terrestrial broadcast networks.

For the regulation of *all* these types of networks, the Commission found widespread support for *ex-ante* sector-specific rules on interconnection and

---

[128] See *supra*, n. 28.

[129] IIR Conference speech by Herbert Ungerer (DGIV) ('Brussels, February 1999, Competition Law in Telecoms').

[130] See *supra* n. 28.

[131] Following publication of the April 2000 Communication (*supra* n. 28), the Commission has now abandoned plans for a 'two-tier' test for market power. Instead the Commission is to impose *ex-ante* obligations only on those operators who are judged as having SMP, which could be confusing as this new test of SMP does not accord with the old test as set out in Art. 4(3) of the Interconnection Directive (i.e. 25 per cent of the relevant market) but with a new test of what the DTI calls 'super-dominance'.

access continuing alongside competition rules, until such time as there was full and effective competition in all segments of the market. There was also widespread support for the Commission's view that call origination, transit and termination should be regarded as separate markets, with differing levels of competition in each. Under Art. 4 of the Draft Access Directive, *every* operator will have to abide by the *primary interconnection* rule, which states that:

All undertakings authorised to operate electronic communications net-works for the provision of publicly available communications services shall have a right and, when requested by other undertakings so authorised, an obligation to negotiate interconnection with each other for the purpose of providing the services in question in order to ensure provision and interoperability of services throughout the Community.[132]

The Commission's new proposals have the potential to change in a crucial way the treatment of Internet interconnection agreements. Whereas in the past, the larger IBPs could get away with imposing virtually any terms that made commercial sense, often requiring as a condition of interconnect that smaller ISPs sign non-disclosure agreements, under the Commission's new proposals on access and interconnect, Internet interconnection agreements negotiated between ISPs (who are authorised to operate electronic communi-cations networks) could fall under the jurisdiction of the NRA in the region where interconnection takes place. This in turn could mean that the larger IBPs and TSPs could be required to submit their Internet interconnection (peering and transit) agreements to the NRAs for inspection as a commitment to transparency and verification that the principle of non-discrimination continues to apply. As with conventional circuit-switched (voice) intercon-nect agreements, Internet interconnection agreements could then be made available for public inspection (albeit with the commercial schedules blacked out).

If the Commission's proposals are adopted Europe could find itself ahead of the US in its treatment of Internet interconnection. This would be ironic, given that an American executive, David Holub, President of Whole Earth Networks, argued that Internet interconnection regulation was analogous to telecommunications carrier interconnection in the US in 1997.[133]

Around the time that UUnet was stepping back from accepting new peering requests in May 1997, it was suggested that a possible solution was for State Public Utility Commissions (PUCs) in the US to regulate peering agreements. State Commissions are allowed to regulate interconnection agreements among inter-exchange carriers and local exchange carriers

---

[132] Article 3(3) imposes an obligation on NRAs to ensure that they encourage and secure 'adequate network access and interconnection'.
[133] See Cukier, *op. cit. supra* n. 94.

(LECs) under §251 of the US. Telecommunications Act 1996.[134] Under the current policy of the FCC, however, ISPs are *not* classified as common carriers under the Telecommunications Act 1996 when they provide Internet services using the packet transmission service of a common carrier affiliate. Instead, such services are classed as information services, and therefore do not attract the rights and obligations normally associated with common carriers.[135]

By contrast, the current European Union regulatory framework allows Member States to impose proportionate obligations which, in the case of operators offering either a public telecommunications network or a publicly available voice telephony service (whether by IP or PSTN), can be more onerous than for operators offering other services, such as ISPs.[136] Although there are advantages for an ISP in being classed as a public telecoms network operator or as a provider of public voice services, e.g., the ability to gain interconnection rights, there are also obligations. These obligations can involve having to incur additional costs, such as a requirement for an individual licence under the Licensing Directive, Art. 7(2) or a requirement to contribute to the costs of universal service under the Interconnection Directive, Art. 5(1). As such, some ISPs, who (for example) offer voice over the Internet protocol (VoIP) services, may want to obtain the status of a voice telephony operator and get access to cost-orientated interconnection rights, but they will also have to meet the obligations.[137]

Other ISPs will not want these obligations, preferring instead to offer data services, thus avoiding the obligations that a voice telephony operator would attract. The European position on whether or not a VoIP service can be classed as a voice service is encapsulated by a Commission Notice[138] published in 1998, setting out the status of voice on the Internet under the Full Competition Directive.

Under the Voice Telephony Notice, the Commission considered that voice over the Internet would not be a voice telephony service, and therefore not subject to standard voice telephony regulation, until certain conditions were met, including that:

(a) the service has to be provided to the public;
(b) it involves direct transport and switching of speech in real time;

---

[134] See §251(d)(3) Part II (Development of competitive markets), Telecommunications Act 1996. Although under this section the FCC will not preclude the enforcement of any regulation or order by a State Commission on LEC obligations for access and interconnection, the FCC has also reserved a power for itself to act under §251(g) of the Act. See also Jew, B. and Nicholls, R., *Internet Connectivity: Open Competition In The Face of Commercial Expansion*, presented at the Pacific Telecommunications Conference (Honolulu, 16 April 1999), http://www.gtlaw.com.au/pubs/opencompetition.html.

[135] See §B(5), *AT&T v City of Portland*, 216 F. 3d 871 (9th Cir. 2000), rev'g, 43 F. Supp. 2d 1146 (D.Or. 1999). See also 5.6.7.2 below.

[136] See the Licensing Directive (97/13/EC) and Directive 90/388/EEC ('the Full Competition Directive', as amended by Directive 96/19).

[137] This is the case in Germany, where several VoIP providers have applied for a 'Klasse 4 Licence' (voice telephony).

[138] Commission Notice, 'Status of voice communications on Internet under Community law and, in particular, under Directive 90/338/EEC', (1998) OJ C 6/4 ('Voice Telephony Notice').

(c)   communications are the subject of a commercial offer; and

(d)   the service is provided between NTPs on the public network.[139]

It must be remembered that there is a clear difference between VoIP and voice over the Internet. Whereas the former is a generic name for the transport of voice traffic over an IP stream, the latter is a specific application of VoIP which uses the public Internet as the communications medium for the IP stream. Generally speaking, VoIP is most common over private networks where operators are able to guarantee some form of quality of service standard, whereas voice over the Internet many involve the IP stream moving across a number of public network access points or 'hops', where quality cannot be guaranteed, although this is fast improving.

Since the publication of the Voice Telephony Notice in 1998, technology and the Internet industry have rapidly moved on. In June 2000, the Commission launched a public consultation on the Voice Telephony Notice that sought to review the position of voice over the Internet (and presumably VoIP, although the distinction with voice over the Internet is not made clear from the Commission's Consultation Paper) in the light of recent technological improvements that could allow the four conditions set out above to be met.[140] One of the main problems with VoIP in the past has been the standard of quality of service that customers could expect, but technical and operational improvements now enable VoIP operators to offer differential quality of service through packet and flow labelling, routing improvements, migration from version 4 to version 6 of the IP, all of which could lead to real-time services. Furthermore, certain national incumbents have started to offer VoIP over their data backbone networks, which could lead to problems as to whether or not certain obligations, such as a requirement for cost-orientation and the provision of special network access as set out under the Revised Voice Telephony Directive 98/10,[141] should apply to the data network elements of the incumbents' networks (see s. 2.2(iii), Voice Telephony Review).

The Commission, however, is not seeking to change the regulatory status of voice over the Internet/VoIP overnight. It makes it quite clear in s. 3 of the Voice Telephony Review, that, following the consultation period, it intends to confirm that:

> [I]nternet telephony still continues to fall outside the definition of voice telephony . . . and generally speaking, that Member States should continue to allow Internet access providers to offer voice over the Internet protocol under data transmission general authorisations, and that specific licensing conditions are not justified.

---

[139] This last point is interesting, in that if access to the Internet is by way of a leased line then any VoIP services offered over that line could *not* be considered as voice telephony.

[140] *Consultative communication on a review of the 1998 notice by the Commission on the status of voice over the Internet under Community law, and in particular, under Directive 90/388/EEC*, 2000/C 177/03 (27 June 2000) ('Voice Telephony Review'). The result of the review was published as a Supplement to the 1998 Notice, (2000) OJ C 369/3.

[141] Directive 98/10 replacing Directive 95/62 on the application of Open Network Provision (ONP) to voice telephony and on universal service for telecommunications in a competitive environment, (1998) OJ L 101/24.

In summary, the European Commission's position on the status of ISPs, as regards whether or not they attract the rights and obligations that would normally fall to a licensed voice telephony operator, would appear to be a little further developed than the position taken by the FCC in the US on ISPs as common carriers.

In specific Member States, such as the UK, certain ISPs are already classed as voice telephony providers and have access to cost-orientated interconnection rights (and the corresponding obligations). The UK position is discussed at 5.6.7 below.

5.6.6.2 Internet interconnection and the WTO A question arises with the interconnection model under the Fourth Protocol's Reference Paper and its relevance to the Internet. What effect would a move to include VoIP as either a voice or a packet-switched data service have on the EU's specific commitments to the WTO?[142] As part of a legal framework for liberalisation, the Reference Paper details additional commitments on regulatory principles, including specific rules on interconnection. Section 2.2 sets out obligations on major suppliers for interconnection.[143]

The point of interest in this discussion on Internet interconnection is that for the supply of voice or packet-switched data transmission services, for *all* modes of supply covered under the EU's specific commitments (i.e., (i) cross-border supply; (ii) consumption abroad; (iii) commercial presence; and (iv) presence of natural persons), the EU has placed *no* restrictions on market access or national treatment.[144] This would mean that if VoIP were classed as either a voice or a packet-switched data service, the interconnection obligations that the EU has decided to accept as an additional commitment under the EU's Schedule of Specific Commitments (i.e., the Reference Paper) would apply to all major suppliers of such services in the EU. This in turn would place an obligation on the major suppliers to interconnect with ISPs in accordance with WTO guidelines in the following way:

(a) at any technically feasible point in the network;

(b) on non-discriminatory terms, rates and of a quality no less favourable than for the incumbent's own supply;

(c) in a timely fashion and on terms that are transparent and reasonable;

(d) at cost-orientated rates; and

(e) on an unbundled basis so that a buyer does not pay for unnecessary services.

This obligation to interconnect by a major supplier would benefit *any* ISP providing public telecommunications transport networks or services. How-

---

[142] In a statement by the Director of the WTO's trade in services division, David Hartridge highlights the urgent need for WTO Member States to clarify their existing WTO agreements, making it clear which sections apply to e-commerce (and the Internet). See Total Telecom 'WTO Director slams dangerous e-commerce ideas' (14 July 2000).

[143] A 'major supplier' is defined in the Reference Paper as one who has market power because of: (a) its control over an essential facility; or (b) its position in the market.

[144] With certain exceptions, however, reserved for Luxembourg, Greece, Spain, Ireland and Portugal. See the WTO's Trade in Services Paper, GATS/SC/31/Suppl.3, 11 April 1997.

ever, even if ISPs did not fall into the category of being a supplier of public networks or services (possibly because some ISPs do not necessarily advertise all their peering routes and tables at public Internet exchanges, such as MAEWEST/MAEAST in the US or the LINX in the UK, preferring instead to interconnect at private peering points (in effect running private networks)), such ISPs could instead be argued to be running closed user groups (CUGs). The interesting point is that the EU's additional commitment representing its offer on the Reference Paper also includes an obligation on major suppliers to interconnect with suppliers of CUGs.

This obligation arises as a consequence of a footnote inserted by the European Union in its additional commitment.[145] Following the wording of this footnote, it would appear that major suppliers still have an obligation to interconnect with suppliers of CUGs on terms, conditions and rates which are non-discriminatory, transparent and cost-orientated. It would appear, therefore, that the significance of this obligation for transparency, when applied to negotiations between large IBPs and ISPs, where the larger IBP is found to be a major supplier, would be to undermine the current industry practice of the IBP requiring negotiations be governed by a non-disclosure agreement. In other words, IBPs who are classed as major suppliers could be required to 'come clean' with their terms on peering. In addition, an ISP with third-country stakeholders could threaten to complain to the WTO if the IBP refuses to structure its peering arrangements on non-discriminatory terms with all its downstream customers, regardless of whether or not those customers are the IBP's own affiliates. The upshot of this would be that an IBP would no longer be able to give preferential terms for peering to its own downstream affiliates.

Certainly, in the telcoms industry in general, there has been more wide-spread take-up of potential referrals to the WTO's Dispute Settlement Body (DSB) throughout the latter part of 2000 and early 2001.[146] A decision to go to the WTO's DSB will depend to a large extent on the value of the Internet

---

[145] Footnote 6, Additional Commitment by the European Communities and their Member States (GATS/SC/31/suppl.3). Footnote 6 states that 'Suppliers of services or networks not generally available to the public, such as closed user groups, have guaranteed rights to connect with the public telecommunications transport network or services on terms, conditions and rates which are non-discriminatory, transparent and cost-orientated. Such terms, conditions and rates may, however, vary from the terms, conditions and rates applicable to interconnection between public telecommunications networks or services.'

[146] See generally Chapter 10, at 10.4.5. Also see the entries in Total Telecom at http://www.totaltele.com/results.asp: 'US slams BT over DSL access' (17 April 2000); 'US threatens to take Mexico to WTO' (4 April 2000); 'US threatens South Africa's Telekom with WTO complaint' (3 April 2000); 'US threatens Japan with WTO action' (30 March 2000). Issues at local access level have even proved worthy enough for potential referral to the WTO. For example, in the UK, due to the delay by BT in accepting Condition 83, which would require BT to unbundle its local loop, US operator Covad Communictions complained to the US Office of Trade (USTR) of breach of the UK's specific commitments under the WTO's Fourth Protocol, citing delay and discrimination on the part of BT in implementing local loop unbundling. See the news article in *Communications Week International* (17 April 2000) for further details.

interconnection agreements in dispute, which is likely to increase rapidly.[147] Another important factor would be the willingness of the DSB to involve itself in areas that, some would argue, might be better handled by national NRAs.

It may be, however, that the ISP (or a third country stakeholder in that ISP) need not go as far as complaining to the WTO to ensure that the principles of transparency and non-discrimination as set out in the Reference Paper are enforced. In Europe, under the new regulatory package of measures proposed by the Commission, particularly the Draft Access and Framework Directives, the ISP may only need to turn to the NRA in the jurisdiction which has authorised the incumbent to have the WTO obligations on interconnection enforced. This remedy arises out of Art. 8 of the Draft Access Directive. Under Art. 8(2), an NRA may:

> [I]mpose on undertakings, including undertakings other than those with significant market power, the obligation set out in Articles 9–13 of this Directive, in relation to interconnection, in order to comply with international commitments, and exceptionally, with the prior agreement of the Commission.

The obligations set out in Arts 9–13 include obligations on transparency, non-discrimination, unbundling and cost-orientation. The wording of Art. 8(2) proves interesting reading, as although the term 'international commitments' is not defined anywhere in the Access Directive, it would be difficult to deny that such a term would not apply to the EU's commitments under the GATS and, particularly, the EU's Schedule of Commitments under the Fourth Protocol. Article 8 in its present form could therefore require an NRA to ensure that a major supplier structures its peering agreements in such a way that they were non-discriminatory to third parties. Also, at some point in the future, when regulators may deem it necessary, it could also require incumbents to publish their terms of peering and/or transit as part of a reference interconnect offer, or to submit peering/transit agreements to the NRA for inspection as a requirement for transparency.[148]

This obligation to interconnect on non-discriminatory and transparent terms would appear to cover major suppliers only under the Reference Paper. The term 'major supplier' is of course defined in the Reference Paper as one who has control of an essential facility and is able to use its position in the market to influence competition and price. This definition follows competition law principles, but there is an important difference from the term 'dominance' proposed by the Commission that forms its new threshold for SMP under the Draft Framework Directive. Under Art. 13(2) of that Directive, 'significant market power' is defined as follows:

---

[147] Market researchers from IDC predicted ten million users of VoIP by 2001. The Internet hardware provider, Networks, estimates that more than 25 per cent of the worldwide voice traffic will be VoIP by 2010. See Kraatz, Klaus-Jurgen, 'Voice over IP – a Challenge to Regulation', *International Business Lawyer* (May 2000).

[148] In accordance with s. 2.4, WTO's Reference Paper.

An undertaking shall be deemed to have significant market power if, either individually or jointly with others, it enjoys a position of economic strength affording it the power to behave to an appreciable extent independently of its competitors and ultimately consumers.

We can see quite clearly that the WTO's 'major supplier' term refers to the concept of ownership of an essential facility, which would seem to cover only those operators who were 'super-dominant';[149] whereas the term 'dominance' used by the Commission in the Draft Framework Directive is based on an economic analysis test,[150] where dominance could include any operator who could consistently keep prices high independently of competitors, regardless of whether or not that operator owned an essential facility.[151] Also, the WTO's definition of major supplier refers to an operator's 'position on the market'. This is fairly vague wording and it is not entirely clear whether such a definition would in competition law terms fall squarely within the definition for SMP (dominance) as proposed by the Commission. If the Draft Access and Framework Directives are adopted with their current wording intact, it may be that this distinction between 'major supplier' under the WTO Reference Paper and 'dominance' under the new EU Directives will become crucially important as regulators become more experienced with anti-competitive practices arising in the new TCI/IP markets.

5.6.7 National treatment

There are signs in Europe that national regulators are taking a more active role in regulating interconnection between ISPs. For example, in France, the French regulator ART has allowed France Télécom to launch a new Internet calling plan using flat-rate access tariffs, but on condition that France Télécom provides access to *all* ISPs and indirect interconnection for other backbone providers. In the UK, OFTEL has already published guidelines on new Category 4 operators. Category 4 is a subdivision of those operators classed as falling into Sch. 2 to the Interconnection Regulations. A consultation document on Annex II of the Interconnection Directive came out in March 1998; and in April 1999, OFTEL published a statement suggesting that some ISPs could fall into Category 4.[152]

---

[149] This would be particularly relevant given the high threshold test for the interpretation of an 'essential facility' given by the European Court of Justice in the case of *Oscar Bronner* v *Mediaprint* (Case C-7/97) [1998] ECR I-7791).

[150] The definition of dominance under Community case law was originally seen in *United Brands* v *Commission* (Case 27/76) [1978] ECR 207.

[151] However, in the earlier version of the Draft Framework Directive, the Working Paper on a new regulatory framework, published by the Commission in April 2000, the term 'dominance' included a reference to an essential facility. Following criticisms that the Commission was trying to create a new level of 'super-dominance' that would catch only those operators who would have enjoyed special or exclusive rights before the 1998 liberalisation watershed, this reference was dropped.

[152] See Consultation Paper, *Rights and obligations to interconnect under the EC Interconnection Directive* (London, OFTEL, April 1999).

OFTEL's position on interconnection between ISPs provides a useful pointer as to how other NRAs throughout Europe could move in the treatment of peering and transit. At para. 1.32 of the April 1999 Consultation Paper, OFTEL states clearly that ISPs falling under Sch. 2 to the Interconnection Regulations will be entitled to cost-orientated rates from BT,[153] and, further, that peering arrangements between ISPs in Annex 2 (transposed into Sch. 2 to the Regulations in the UK) will be treated as interconnection agreements. This latter point is crucial as, for the first time, OFTEL is extending its jurisdiction into regulating agreements between ISPs (since, under Art. 9(4) of the Interconnection Directive, OFTEL has the power to call for and inspect any agreement classed as an 'interconnection' agreement). Given that OFTEL's position on peering is an important extension by a regulator, to extend its jurisdiction into regulating aspects of the Internet, the Internet industry (particularly the dominant IBPs) has been surprisingly silent as to its implications.[154]

5.6.7.1 Australia Other regulators, such as the ACCC in Australia, have increased their attention to Internet interconnection as national incumbents enter the market. In 1998, the ACCC issued a competition notice on the Australian national incumbent (Telstra) for pricing arrangements that Telstra had put in place for charging downstream ISPs and TSPs for traffic volumes.[155] The ACCC has also issued a very useful Consultation Paper on Internet interconnection, which has already been referred to at 5.6.3 above. The ACCC's Paper examines varying approaches to the problem of Internet settlements and poses questions on how best the industry should distribute the costs for peering between end-users, ISPs, TSPs and IBPs. The Paper is probably one of the most comprehensive discussion documents yet released by a national regulator on the issue of peering. It suggests a number of options for a model for Internet interconnection that could be applied to negotiations and the attendant settlement arrangements. Options include building an interconnection model on the principles set out in the WTO's Reference Paper and the APEC Framework for Interconnection.[156]

5.6.7.2 United States Three significant cases with potential impact on peering and access have arisen in the US.

---

[153] However at para. 1.34 of the 1999 Consultation Paper, OFTEL also states that for ISPs to benefit from BT's standard interconnection charges, ISPs will need to invest in infrastructure in the form of C7-based terminating equipment. C7 equipment are effectively switches that can translate the signalling CCS7 protocol used by conventional PSTN switches. Services that would attract cost-orientated rates would include number translation, termination of international simple resale traffic, and IP interconnect with BT's IP services operated from its systems business (e.g., BT Net).

[154] It is important to appreciate, however, that OFTEL's requirement to inspect the peering agreements of ISPs, should it deem it necessary, has only appeared in a Consultation Paper and is not set out as a specific provision in the Interconnection Regulations.

[155] ACCC competition notice issued pursuant to s. 151AL, Trade Practices Act 1974, 17 June 1998, available from the ACCC public register.

[156] APEC Framework for Interconnection, at http://www.apii.or.kr/telwg/interTG/principl.html.

(a)   MCI/WorldCom   The MCI/WorldCom merger[157] generated a great deal of press attention. There was strong opposition in the industry, and commentators on the MCI filing argued that the merged entity, taking advantage of its increased size, would increase the costs of interconnection, either by charging for peering, or by eliminating peering altogether and converting peers into transit customers, which would ultimately increase end-user prices. In addition, commentators claimed that MCI would degrade the quality of interconnection with rivals in order to induce their rivals' customers to migrate to the MCI/WorldCom network. Lastly, they suggested that MCI/WorldCom could exploit their ISP customers without fear of reprisal because of the difficulty of changing IBPs.

Perhaps one of the most interesting aspects of the case was the way in which regulators on both sides of the Atlantic worked together. The European Commission has in practice avoided disputes on jurisdiction where American undertakings are concerned, by making use of the cooperation agreements between the EC and the US on the application of their respective competition laws.[158] As a condition of the merger, MCI agreed to sell its entire Internet business (both retail and wholesale) to the British telecommunications operator Cable & Wireless. Both the US Department of Justice and the European Commission approved the merger.[159]

In *MCI/WorldCom*, the market definition used by the Commission was crucial. The Commission had to decide whether the merger of the two parties' Internet businesses would create or strengthen a dominant position, which could lead to effective competition in the Internal Market being weakened. The Commission decided that the market structure was hierarchical or pyramidal, with different characteristics at different levels. At the lower levels there was generally a range of suppliers and a few barriers to entry; whereas at the top of the pyramid, the industry was much more concentrated, with only four dominant suppliers of backbone connectivity – Sprint, GTE, WorldCom and MCI (the 'Big 4').

Applying the market influence test of whether a small but significant and non-transitory increase in price in a particular product would cause users to switch to another product,[160] the Commission distinguished between backbone networks and other lower level networks by defining a market for the provision of top-level Internet connectivity. The Commission argued that the

---

[157] *Application of WorldCom, Inc. and MCI Communications Corporation for Transfer of Control of MCI Communications Corporation to WorldCom, Inc.* FCC Docket No. 97-211. See also the European Commission's decision in WorldCom and MCI (Case IV/M.1069) (1999) OJ L 116/1.
[158] Agreement between the Government of the United States of America and the Commission of the European Communities regarding the application of their competition laws (1995) OJ L 95/47. See also the Agreement between the European Communities and the Government of the United States of America on the application of positive comity principles in the enforcement of their competition laws (1998) OJ L 173/28.
[159] *WorldCom/MCI* (Case IV/M.1069), (1999) OJ L 116/1. The divestment ordered by the Commission was at the time the largest divestment ever to result from antitrust action, quoted in Vajda, C. and Gahnström, 'EC Competition Law and the Internet' [2000] ECLR 94, at n. 19.
[160] See Commission Notice on the definition of a relevant markets for the purposes of Community competition law (1997) OJ C 372/5.

relevant geographic market was the global market for backbone connectivity. After several other methods of estimating market share had failed,[161] on an assumption of market size and shares based on revenue and a model designed to calculate market share by reference to traffic flow, the Commission estimated that the combined MCI/WorldCom would hold over 50 per cent of the relevant backbone market. Further, the Commission concluded that the big four were the only networks able to provide transit to all parts of the Internet, and that a rise in prices for access to the top-level networks would therefore affect consumers worldwide.

Commentators argue that much of the European Commission's decision dealing with the impact of the proposed concentration on competition is assertion with very little factual evidence to support it.[162] That in essence, the analysis in *WorldCom/MCI* was somewhat *a priori*. They also argue that, following *Bronner* (decided after *MCI/WorldCom*), the existence of a comprehensive network (a home delivery network) does not of itself create an essential facility.[163]

The US Federal Communications Commission (FCC) also examined the case to determine whether the sale would raise any further issues regarding the Internet. It found that the merger would not have any anti-competitive effects on condition that the divestiture was carried out. The important thing to note, however, is that the FCC did hold back on imposing any further conditions on the merger by *not* requiring MCI/WorldCom to adopt non-discriminatory peering criteria.

The FCC did note the difficulties new entrants were having in interconnecting with IBPs, and noted that peering was likely to remain an issue that warranted further monitoring. But the FCC also said: 'the MCI/WorldCom merger proceeding is not the appropriate forum to address these concerns'.

Some would argue that this was a lost golden opportunity, as the ruling left a great deal of uncertainty over the whole issue of transparency in peering and transit.

(b) Sprint/WorldCom Perhaps following on from the mixed success of the MCI/WorldCom merger, the US Department of Justice has now blocked the WorldCom/Sprint merger. In a press release issued on 27 June 2000, the Department briefly set out its position, arguing that if 'WorldCom were allowed to acquire Sprint large and small businesses and millions of individual consumers would have to pay higher prices and accept lower service quality and less innovation'. This seems a bit steep, but in its press release, the Department of Justice summarised the key markets where the proposed merger could give rise to antitrust concerns. The markets of key interest to this chapter's discussion of Internet interconnection include:

(a) *Internet backbone services* providing top-level connectivity throughout the US. Here the Department argued that WorldCom operated the largest

---

[161] For example, aggregate capacity in interconnecting links, bandwidth, numbers of IP addresses reachable, and the number of PoPs.
[162] See *supra* n. 159.
[163] *Ibid.*

Internet backbone network, which carries approximately 37 per cent of all Internet traffic. Sprint operated the second largest network, with 16 per cent of Internet traffic.

(b) *International private line services* between the US and more than 60 foreign countries. The Department of Justice argued that in each of these markets, the combined share of WorldCom and Sprint is at least 37 per cent, and a combined share including AT&T (making up the 'Big 3') is at least 82 per cent.

(c) *Data network services* to large business customers in the US. This market includes inter-LATA[164] data services for large businesses over private lines, X.25, asynchronous transfer mode (ATM), and frame relay data networks. The Department of Justice argued that each of these markets, and the market for data network services combined, is again dominated by the 'Big 3'.

The Department also covered other markets of concern, including custom network services, long-distance services to residential customers in the US, and international long-distance services.

A day after the Department of Justice issued its press release, the European Commission followed suit and acted swiftly to end the hopes of WorldCom and Sprint merging. In a decision published on 28 June 2000, the Commission issued a press release setting out its objections to the merger.[165] The Commission identified three specific markets in which the merged entity could exert a dominant position and behave independently, both of its competitors and customers:

(a)   the market for top-level universal Internet connectivity (the backbone Internet market);

(b)   the market for the provision of global telecommunications services to multinational companies; and

(c)   the market for international voice telephony in the US retail and wholesale long-distance markets.

Following the Commission's objections to the merger, the parties offered to divest Sprint's Internet business from Sprint's other activities. However, the proposal failed on the grounds that Sprint's Internet business was too closely intertwined with its traditional telecoms activities for the divestiture to have any real effect. The Commission was also concerned that together with BT's Concert and BT's alliance with AT&T, the merged entity and BT/AT&T would control the majority of the market for global telecommunications services to multinational companies. As to the market for international voice telephony effecting US retail and wholesale long-distance, the Commission felt that dominance in that market was more of an issue for the US

---

[164] The term 'inter-LATA' means telecommunications services that originate in one and terminate in another Local Access and Transport Area (LATA). Each LATA typically includes no more than one metropolitan area.
[165] IP/00/668, 28 June 2000.

Department of Justice than for the European Commission. WorldCom has appealed against the Commission's judgment in the European Court of First Instance; and although WorldCom's chances seem slim, public perception is that the appeal is intended more to create a favourable precedent for future Internet deals rather than to achieve success in having the Commission's judgment overturned.[166] Only time will tell.

(c) AT&T/Portland case Another US case that concerns the access rights of ISPs to infrastructure is *AT&T* v *City of Portland* 43 F. Supp. 2d 1146 (D.Or. 1999), rev'd, 216 F. 3d 871 (9th Cir. 2000). Whereas the *MCI/WorldCom* and *Sprint/WorldCom* cases involve competition issues with regard to access to Internet backbone infrastructure, the *AT&T* case is about access to *cable* infrastructure. Nevertheless, the case does provide useful pointers to how US courts view access to infrastructure for Internet services. In the *AT&T* case, AT&T appealed a decision by the US District Court of Oregon upholding the City of Portland's condition for the transfer of TCI's cable licence to AT&T, that AT&T must open up its cable network in Oregon to other ISPs, i.e. that AT&T grant non-discriminatory access to its cable modem platform.

The District Court's decision would have allowed other operators, such as US West and GTE, to have their ISPs connect *directly* to AT&T's cable modem platform, thus bypassing @Home, AT&T's proprietary cable ISP. AT&T successfully appealed, the District Court's holding being reversed by the US 9th Circuit Court of Appeal (see *AT&T* v *City of Portland*, 216 F. 3d (9th Cir. 2000), *rev'g*, 43 F. Supp. 2d 1146 (D.Or. 1999)).

The *AT&T* case is important from a policy context because it describes a conflict between a new breed of ISP, @Home, and the more typical ISPs that connect with the Internet via leased lines, which subscribers access through dial-up connections over ordinary telephone lines. @Home, by contrast, operates *both* a broadband cable infrastructure (which it owns) and a proprietary national backbone that connects with other backbone networks at multiple network access points.

@Home's ability to restrict its subscribers from purchasing alternative cable broadband access separately from unaffiliated ISPs was something that local competitors, such as common carrier US West and other ISPs, thought worth litigating over. In the ruling of the US District Court, Judge Thomas cites some of the arguments presented by US West and other ISPs at the various public hearings that formed part of the case material:

> US West and the Oregon Internet Service Providers Association called for open access to TCI's cable broadband network, citing – in addition to consumer welfare – the need for 'a level playing field' with US West's common carrier obligations and a very real potential that consumer (internet) access businesses could go out of business.

---

[166] See Total Telecom: 'EU confident over WorldCom appeal 16th September 2000', http://www.totaltele.com.

In the end, the US Circuit Court of Appeals rejected this plea and AT&T won.[167] However, following the Circuit Court ruling, the then FCC Chairman, William E. Kennard, issued a press release proposing that 'the FCC begin a formal proceeding on the issue of multiple Internet service providers gaining access to a cable company's platform,[168] noting that the decision from the Circuit Court confirmed the FCC's role in establishing a national broadband policy for the country. The Chairman also agreed with the City of Portland on the goal of an open cable platform, saying that 'there are powerful marketplace incentives that will move the cable platform to an open platform', but questioned how that goal should be achieved, whether by government intervention or market forces.

The important points, therefore, to take away from *AT&T* v *City of Portland* are that:

(a)   cable broadband access, under current US law, is not a cable service;

(b)   ISPs which *own* their own cable broadband infrastructure and run proprietary content over that infrastructure offer both information (unregulated) and telecommunication (regulated) services;[169]

(c)   cable broadband operators, however, are not yet classed as common carriers subject to obligations to interconnect under US law (even though they may offer telecommunication services, and even though DSL operators, competitors to cable broadband operators, *are* subject to common carrier obligations[170]); and

(d)   the *AT&T* v *City of Portland* case (for now) sets a precedent that lets cable broadband operators off the hook as regards 'forced access'.

So, if the US courts have stepped back from imposing a forced access condition on cable operators, and the FCC is yet to decide on the point (which would have direct relevance to any policy on Internet interconnection), what is the position on forced access to networks in Europe?

5.6.7.3   Europe   With the publication of its November Communication,[171] the European Commission appeared to be preparing itself for some far-reaching proposals on forced access. The Commission argued that cable operators with SMP should be obliged to negotiate access to their networks,

---

[167] However, in a bizarre twist to the tale, AT&T has announced that it will be willing to open up its cable lines to other ISPs as part of an experimental test in Colorado. AT&T is still operating under an exclusive ISP agreement with Excite that is expected to expire in 2002. See 'Cable Biz agrees to open access' (3 July 2000), at http://www.wired.com/news.

[168] See FCC press release (30 June 2000) 'FCC Chairman to launch proceeding on "cable access"', at http://www.fcc.gov/Bureaus/Cable/News_Releases.

[169] However, the FCC has not yet determined whether high-speed Internet access over cable is a 'telecommunications' service, which the US 9th Circuit Court's decision seems to imply. See the FCC press release, *supra* n. 168.

[170] See GTE Operating Companies Tariff No.1, 13 F.C.C.R. 22466 (1998).

[171] *Supra* n. 28.

whereas dominant operators would have to grant access.[172] This requirement, which fell just short of 'forced access', would then have been at odds with US Federal law on granting access to cable networks.

However, in various responses to the November Communication, commentators argued that a requirement for forced access would have a serious impact on investment in infrastructure, possibly diminishing the incentive for investment in developing digital services. Rather than imposing *ex-ante* conditions for mandatory or forced access on new players with networks (particularly the cable operators), the new regulatory framework should provide for *ex-post* remedies to deal with specific abuses of power.

With the publication of its April 2000 Communication,[173] the Commission dropped the forced access argument, saying that 'there would be no specific regulatory obligations in community legislation to impose e.g. access for service providers to cable TV networks, or to mobile networks'. The Commission suggested, instead, that 'imposing such access obligations on infrastructure owners would be made in the light of prevailing market conditions, the effectiveness of competition, and the extent of customer choice' (April Communication, at 3.3). This position remains very much the same under the Draft Access and Framework Directives published by the Commission in July 2000. As such, the European position is now not so different from that of the US, albeit that the European Commission has still left the door open to regulate at some stage in the future if a competition analysis of the market so dictates.

In the UK, OFTEL has recently concluded that cable operators should not be required to provide access to their networks, since they do not possess market power in the relevant markets.[174] In addition, OFTEL's guidelines on SNA[175] are important, in that they state that, unlike the regime which applies to interconnection of networks by Annex II operators, there are no special prior qualifications for seeking SNA. Operators with Annex II status may request SNA under Condition 45 of the new PTO licences, whereas organisations without Annex II status may request SNA under Condition 48. SNA may also be requested from *fixed* SMP operators under Condition 53 by *any* organisation providing telecommunications services.

At a European level, the meaning of the term 'special network access' continues to be the subject of debate. Both the Revised Voice Telephony

---

[172] See November Communication, at 4.2.4, on access to cable and must carry rules. Also, and separately on the issue of dominance, in the market research consultancy Ovum's view, dominance will mean 'being able to behave independently of customers or rivals to an appreciable extent in the supply of an interconnection service'. Practically, this could mean 50 per cent of market share, which will be defined by an EU-wide test on (a) number of competitors, (b) market share, (c) control of an essential facility, which is effectively a facility that cannot be replicated and is essential for reaching customers (see 5.4.2, above). SMP means at least 25 per cent of a geographical market and the ability to extract excessive profits in the supply of an interconnection service. See Art. 4(3), Interconnection Directive, *supra* n. 2.

[173] *Supra*, n. 28.

[174] OFTEL Statement, *Open Access: Delivering effective competition in communications markets*, (London, OFTEL, 2001).

[175] *Guidelines on Special Network Access* (London, OFTEL, 2000).

Directive[176] and the Interconnection Directive provide for access to networks at points other than the network termination points offered to the majority of end-users, which is commonly known as SNA. SNA was also under consideration by the European Commission as part of its 1999 Review.[177]

OFTEL's more relaxed position on opening up access to networks has also been extended to the interactive digital TV market. In a decision published on 21 June 2000,[178] OFTEL required Sky Subscribers Services Ltd to allow other companies to have access to its encryption services to provide interactive services over digital TV sets. This means that competing broadcasters should now be able to use the technical services embedded in BSkyB's set-top boxes to provide interactive services.

5.6.8 Future solutions?

Although models for Internet interconnection are beginning to appear, mainly in Australia and the UK, there are no clear models that would have universal appeal across a number of jurisdictions, such as the WTO's guidelines for circuit-switched (voice) interconnect as set out in its Reference Paper. Therefore, should there be some generalised form of interconnection agreement precedent for peering and transit? Further, would disclosure of such an agreement to NRAs lead to fair terms and equal bargaining power, or just to uniform terms and a lack of innovation?

These are difficult questions to answer, but regulators could follow the lead taken by OFTEL in the UK by placing a *potential* obligation on backbone providers to disclose their peering and transit agreements, bringing a certain degree of transparency into the industry. Also, with the publication of the Commission's Draft Access and Framework Directives in July 2000, the reforms to *ex-ante* legislation proposed by these Directives may be sufficient to allow NRAs the power to determine whether an ISP is dominant and ask it to submit its peering and transit agreements for inspection, again offering some form of transparency and resolution mechanism in the event of a dispute. In future, it is not inconceivable that we may end up with dominant ISPs/IBPs under the new regime, having to publish reference interconnection offers setting out all their terms and conditions for TCP/IP access, just as incumbents publish terms for interconnection as currently required by the Interconnection Directive.[179]

---

[176] *Supra* n. 141.

[177] See the EC's Working Paper, *Access to, and interconnection of, electronic communications networks and associated facilities*, at http://www.ispo.cec.be/infosoc/telecompolicy/review99/pres10-11e)/index.htm published 27 April 2000). The Access Paper includes a definition of the term 'access' and states that NRAs shall be able to impose obligations on operators to grant access to, and use of, special facilities and/or associated services, in order to correct or prevent a distortion of competition. See s. 12, Access Paper.

[178] See Decision as to the status of sky subscriber Services Limited as a Regulated Supplier in the market for access control services for Digital Interactive TV Services (London, OFTEL, 2000). Access control is also discussed at 5.4.7 above.

[179] See *supra* n. 2. Under Arts 7(3), 14(1) of the Interconnection Directive, operators with SMP are required to publish a reference interconnection offer. The ONP Committee published an indicative reference interconnection offer, listing the minimum content of such offers, in 1998. See the EC document 'Indicative Reference Interconnection Offer ONPCOM 98-11'.

If the *ex-ante* reforms fail to have the desired effect, there may be other solutions, such as imposing obligations through *ex-post* means, as in the MCI/*WorldCom* and *AT&T* v *City of Portland* cases. But use of *ex-post* remedies is increasingly reliant on an effective understanding of regulatory economics, which can be particularly difficult when dealing with a rapidly developing area such as the Internet. In a report commissioned by the APEC Telecommunications Working Group,[180] bridging the division between tele-communications economics and Internet economics was identified as one of the key challenges. The report suggests that on the telecommunications side there are economic issues of bandwidth pricing, access arrangements and the perceived circumvention of telecommunications pricing models. On the Internet side, the core issues involve the value of content, the expansion of Internet infrastructure and access to it, and the relegation of carriage to a subsidiary role. A further disadvantage with the *ex-post* approach is that the harm may already have been done before the regulator or competition authority has had the time to act to remedy the abuse, possibly up to six months after the 'event'.

Alternatively, ISPs could make better use of technology. The technology for TCP/IP network access is improving all the time, yielding greater capacity and better routers, and thereby alleviating the strain on backbone providers constantly to upgrade networks (thus reducing their costs). Better routers will reduce the number of 'hops' between peering points, leading to better quality of service for customers. As the strain on backbone providers reduces, so will the need to convert peering partners to downstream paying transit customers, as the smaller ISPs will be better able to handle increased traffic flow across their networks. This, in turn, will reduce the reliance on detailed intercon-nection agreements, where backbone players often have the stronger negoti-ating position.

Connected with this is the very important need for policy makers to understand better how traffic exchange occurs on the Internet.[181] There needs to be an increase in the momentum of infrastructure competition. It is ironic that efforts to restrict the opening of certain national markets has actually increased IP traffic, including purely domestic traffic, being hubbed in foreign countries with the most competitive communication markets.[182]

Lastly, we could adopt a market position. Following the publication of its April 2000 Communication, this is something that the European Commis-sion is increasingly pushing. We could let the market drive itself towards a self-regulated approach. As smaller ISPs improve on value added Internet services – such as web hosting, audio and video streaming applications, for example – their ability to generate demanded content will give them greater bargaining power. The golden rule of the Internet is that 90 per cent of all requests are for just 10 per cent of the available content. In the end, those

---

[180] *Supra* n. 123.

[181] See OECD Report, *supra* n. 91.

[182] Lack of effective infrastructure competition has been a particular problem in Asia, with much content being sourced from North America. However, this is now rapidly changing, as detailed in the ICAIS Report, referred to *supra* notes 123 and 180.

ISPs who succeed in controlling that 10 per cent will have all the negotiating clout required in dealing with the larger backbones players, or so it is argued.

There is no doubt that to guard against potential anti-competitive behaviour, regulators will need to be fully aware of the fundamental differences in the structure of and traffic flows of TCP/IP networks and of conventional circuit-switched voice networks, differences that need to be understood to help shape the future regulation of competition and infrastructure issues regarding the Internet. Points to reflect on include the comparisons made in Table 5.4.

Table 5.4 Comparison of Internet and PSTN traffic

Public Internet	*PSTN*
More than 90% of Internet traffic passes through the USA.	Around 30% of all international traffic is routed through the USA.
To link to the US Internet backbone, a foreign operator must pay the leased-line costs for the full circuit.	Generally a half circuit regime with a notional POI midway and shared revenues and costs.
Numbering and domain name policy effectively set in the USA.	Numbering policy established nationally following international recommendations.
Traffic flows are multilateral: a single session may poll many countries.	Traffic flows are bilateral.
Web-browsing is a dominant form of traffic: traffic flow is dominantly towards the user who initiates the call. Consequently, web traffic is highly asymmetric.	
Newer forms of Internet traffic (IP telephony, push media, streaming videos, etc.) reverse the traffic flow to be from the customer who initiates the call.	
Peering arrangements are usually simple and based on capacity or volume of traffic exchanged.	Interconnection agreements are complex and based on a range of pricing and capacity indicators.
No end-to-end international settlement payments.	International accounting rate and settlements system applies.[183]

---

[183] Note, however, the recent FCC Order (FCC International Docket Phase II 90-337) in the US imposing benchmarks for international accounting rate settlements and, across the Atlantic, the move by the European Commission to move towards cost-based interconnection rates (Commission's Recommendation on Interconnection Pricing (1998) OJ C 84/3).

Public Internet	PSTN
Regulation of peering agreements only beginning to emerge.[184]	Domestically regulated interconnect regimes under *ex-post* and *ex-ante* legislation.
No transparency at present.	Some transparency. Requirement in Europe that interconnect agreements are approved by the regulator and made available for public inspection.[185]

Source: International Telecommunications Union

---

[184] See the comments made about OFTEL's position on peering in the UK at 5.6.5.2 above.
[185] Under the Interconnection Directive. Except certain schedules, which may be classed as commercially sensitive. Interconnect rates are published, however. See 5.5.4 above for further details.

CHAPTER SIX

Telecommunications Contracts: Outsourcing

Dr Michael Sinclair

6.1 INTRODUCTION

6.1.1 What is outsourcing?

6.1.1.1 General Outsourcing has recently come to mean sourcing externally anything that would otherwise have to be provided internally in order to support business operations. However, the traditional conception of an outsourcing is somewhat narrower than this contemporary meaning. It connotes two elements:

(a) the transfer out of the business of some kind of infrastructure into the new outsourced service provider; and
(b) the provision by the new outsourced service provider of some kind of service back to the business.

6.1.1.2 Transfer of infrastructure The infrastructure to be transferred may be made up of a combination of one or more of employees, land and buildings, other physical assets, the benefit of contracts, licences (including for software and intellectual property rights), other intangible assets (such as intellectual property rights), documentation, and other information and data. The infrastructure transferred usually consists of everything owned or used by the customer in order to provide the service itself prior to the outsourcing.

The transfer is usually effected by a transfer agreement under which the customer transfers ownership of all assets owned by it and assigns the benefit (or novates) contracts and licences to the outsourced service provider. The transfer agreement is usually entered into for a nominal consideration and often resembles a sale of business agreement. The outsourced service provider may push for the inclusion of warranties in relation to the condition of assets included in the infrastructure. Such warranties are very often resisted by a customer on the basis that the infrastructure is required merely for use by the outsourced service provider for a temporary period before the infrastructure is supplemented or entirely replaced (by a new and improved infrastructure in order to achieve enhanced service provision).

In the most basic kinds of outsourcing there may be little or no transfer of infrastructure. This may be because no infrastructure is required in order to provide the service, the supplier intends to use its own infrastructure to provide the service, or because the infrastructure will be entirely replaced by a new and improved infrastructure. Where no infrastructure is transferred or used in the provision of the service, the boundary between outsourcing and a mere services agreement is difficult to draw, and the blurring of this distinction explains the contemporary use of the word 'outsourcing' to cover services agreements as well as the more traditional infrastructure/service back outsourcings. In this chapter 'outsourcing' refers to the traditional meaning of that word.

6.1.1.3 Coupled with service back Once the infrastructure has been transferred to the outsourced service provider, it uses that infrastructure to provide a 'service back' to the customer. The service will fall somewhere in the continuum between a 'process outsourcing' and what can (for want of a better expression) be called a 'functionality outsourcing'.

A functionality outsourcing, in simple terms, means the provision of a function formerly provided in-house by the business to itself. A classic example might be the provision of IT and IT support. Process outsourcings, in contrast, do not involve the provision of a discrete function used in the operation of the business, but rather involve the outsourced service provider performing a business process or range of processes formerly performed by the business itself. An example is accounting and related business processes, human resources, payroll and supply chain management. Process outsourcings depend upon mapping the processes used to achieve the result required. Functionality outsourcings, on the other hand, rely on providing the function itself.

6.1.2 Rationale for outsourcing

6.1.2.1 Concentrating on core business The decision to outsource as a business strategy gained considerable support from economic arguments underlying national privatisation policies implemented by various governments, both in the UK and abroad. Underlying these policies is the idea that governments should concentrate on their core activities and divest themselves of functions and processes which are not truly governmental in character.[1]

---

[1] See Sinclair, M., *Common Law Constraints in Public and Private Law Over the Exercise of Privatised Functions* (Ph.D dissertation held in the Cambridge University Library, 1994).

Similarly, the economic rationale for outsourcing is that it allows a business to concentrate on its core activities, leaving functions and processes in respect of which it is not an expert to be performed by an expert (the outsourced service provider).

The outsourced service provider, in supplying similar services to numerous customers, achieves economies of scale and is able to pass the resulting savings back to the customer in the form of reduced costs for the provision of the service.

6.1.2.2   Application to telecoms arena[2]   The core business of most companies is not, of course, telecoms, but telecommunications networks are at the core of many of their daily operations. Because telecoms services are inherently technology-dependent, a business's telecoms infrastructure may quickly become outdated. This is one reason why outsourcing is attractive, because the outsourced service provider, through benefits obtained from economies of scale, may be able to implement regular technology refreshes.

The growth in the dependence on computers in business has also led to the convergence of computer and telecoms technology in the areas of data transfer and data networks that (in the case of a large business) may be national or global in scale. Because of the difficulties in maintaining the integrity of a national or global network, businesses increasingly look to outsource the provision and maintenance of such networks.

In a traditional outsourcing the customer is concerned only with the service or the outcome, and not with the method by which it is achieved. However, telecoms services present challenges for this traditional model because a business wanting an outsourced telecoms solution, while caring about the standard of service it receives, may also care about the technology platform upon which that service is delivered. It is for this reason that a telecoms outsourcing tends to raise more technology-related issues than other types of outsourcings.

6.1.3   Issues applying to all outsourcings

6.1.3.1   Improved service   Outsourcings often involve the transfer of functions and processes that, to the business, have been problematic in terms of service delivery and that have led to dissatisfaction with that service. The business will frequently look to the outsourced service provider to improve upon that service. This finds its most basic expression in the fact that many outsourcings involve a gradual (or even immediate) replacement of existing infrastructure with an improved infrastructure designed to enhance service delivery.

There may be a migration period during which the service provider is given grace before improving service levels, but it is almost always the case that the

---

[2] See, generally, Sinclair, M. and Durie, R., 'Telecommunications Outsourcing', in *Outsourcing Practice Manual* (London, Sweet & Maxwell, 1998, chap. I); Sinclair, M., 'IT and Telecoms Outsourcing In Europe and the Law', in *The Strategic Guide to Outsource IT and Telecoms* (London, World Trade Magazines, 1999), at 42.

customer will expect improved service levels over time. This is certainly true of telecoms outsourcings, where the customer will expect existing telecoms infrastructure (such as handsets, switches, routers, leased lines and cabling) to be replaced very quickly after service commencement. Service levels (for example, successful call connections, repair of defective equipment, network down time) will also be expected to improve.

6.1.3.2 Decreased involvement of management All outsourcings are characterised by decreased involvement of a business's management in the daily operations of the outsourced service. Indeed, the relevant management personnel may themselves be transferred to the outsourced service provider as part of the infrastructure transfer.

6.1.3.3 Reserving strategy/policy decision-making function A business outsourcing services to an outsourced service provider will generally wish to reserve certain high-level policy or strategic decision-making powers to itself. In the context of telecoms, this might include decisions about matters as simple as the required functionality for handsets, up to sophisticated policy decisions about the extent to which the service provider ought to be required to use certain types of network technology. Reserving policy decision-making may also extend to technology refresh and replacing technology infrastructure over time. A customer certainly would not wish to be locked into a type of technology that quickly became outdated, or that made it difficult for the customer to bring the service back in-house at the end of the outsourcing agreement.

6.1.3.4 Transfer of assets As mentioned at 6.1.1.2 above, most outsourcings involve the transfer of some form of infrastructure. At its most sophisticated, this will be by way of a transfer agreement resembling a sale of business agreement. At its most simplistic, it could be by way of one or two clauses in the outsourcing agreement that transfer ownership of assets referred to in a schedule. The question of consideration should always be dealt with, as the transfer of assets may involve stamp duty or other tax implications. In the context of telecoms, the transfer of assets may also involve obtaining certain consents in relation to software or other licensed rights used in relation to the assets transferred. This issue is discussed in detail at 6.4 below.

6.1.3.5 Transitional arrangements and migration to new service Most outsourcings involve a grace period during which the supplier prepares to migrate to the new service levels. This is normally by way of a migration plan, which is essentially a time line with stepped service levels. Very often transitional arrangements will be required during which there is a handover of the infrastructure from the customer to the supplier as and when consents for the transfer of certain assets or licences are obtained. The outsourcing agreement will have to provide for the allocation of responsibility during such transitional arrangements.

The received wisdom is that customers should not enter into outsourcing agreements without having final service levels and the date at which they are to apply. This is because, once the outsourced service provider has had transferred to it the infrastructure, it in effect holds the customer as a 'captive audience' because the customer will not easily (without considerable cost and effort) be able to take the service back in-house. Accordingly, unless the customer has agreed the final service levels prior to the outsourcing taking effect, it will have little bargaining power to push for final service levels that are acceptable to it after that time.

6.1.3.6 Acquired Rights Directive – allocating liability Outsourcings frequently involve the transfer of personnel from the customer to the outsourced service provider along with the accompanying infrastructure. At the end of the outsourcing those personnel, if used primarily for the provision of services to the customer, may find that the supplier no longer requires their services. In the interim the personnel may have changed over time, as the supplier may have taken on additional personnel to meet the new service levels required.

The provision of the service may be transferred back in-house into the customer, or it may be sourced from a new service provider. In either case, the personnel used by the incumbent service provider may make claims for redundancy or unjustified dismissal against the incumbent service provider, the customer or successor service provider under regulations implementing the Acquired Rights Directive (77/187/EC). In the UK these regulations are the Transfer of Undertakings (Protection of Employment) Regulations 1981 (SI 1981 No. 1794).

The Acquired Rights Directive and the implementing regulations are intended to provide protection to employees who, because of an outsourcing (or at the end of it), find their terms and conditions of employment have changed to their disadvantage, or who find that they are now without employment as a result of an outsourcing (or at the end of it). For example, a telecoms expert retained by a business that subsequently outsources its telecommunications infrastructure to a telecoms service provider may find that, if the parties have not agreed that the service provider will employ the telecoms expert, he or she is without employment. In these circumstances the employee may claim that the telecommunications 'undertaking' has transferred to the new service provider and that the 1981 Regulations therefore deem the new service provider to be his or her employer. Because the new service provider has disclaimed responsibility for employing that telecoms expert, the telecoms expert has a claim against the new service provider.

The Acquired Rights Directive and the implementing Regulations have the effect, by automatic operation of law, of deeming an employee to be employed by one or other of the parties. Because the parties are unable to avoid this effect by agreeing contractual provisions to the contrary, it is usually the case that they will agree to allocate liability by way of indemnities under the outsourcing agreement. For example, a customer might agree to indemnify the supplier for all claims made against the supplier by employees arising prior to the date of transfer, and the supplier may agree to give a similar indemnity for all post-transfer liabilities.[3]

6.1.3.7 Technology refresh Many outsourcings are to a greater or lesser extent technology-dependent. Where the technology is key to the provision of an adequate service, it will be important for the customer to negotiate obligations on the part of the outsourced service provider to update the technology from time to time. If the customer does not do this there will be no incentive for the service provider to update the technology over time, as this will be a cost that it cannot recoup.

Technology refresh is particularly important in telecoms and IT outsourcings, where the rapid pace of technological change means that systems and networks quickly become outdated. Telecoms service providers will frequently argue that it should not matter to the customer what form of technology platform is used to deliver the service as all the customer should be concerned about is the standard of service received. However, as mentioned at 6.7 below, frequently customers will have certain minimum technology platform requirements to which they require outsourced service providers to adhere.

6.1.3.8 Network security (IT security and data security) If the outsourced service provider provides or has access to the customer's networks and systems, and has access to or stores or processes the customer's data, the outsourcing agreement should provide for IT and data security. Generally, there should be a provision which requires the outsourced service provider to take all steps in accordance with best industry practice to prevent the introduction of viruses into the customer's systems and networks and to prevent corruption of the customer's data; and provision for an indemnity if it fails to take such steps and the customer suffers damage as a result.

If the outsourced service provider is storing or processing the customer's data then, if those data are commercially sensitive or otherwise confidential in nature, the outsourced service provider should be required to store them logically and physically separate from the data it holds in relation to its other customers. Protections such as these become very important in the case of telecoms outsourcings, because telecoms networks may be used to transfer data which, if corrupted, may cause business losses to the customer and the customer will wish to ensure that its voice and other networks are not being hacked. For this reason, it may be necessary to require the outsourced service provider to implement monitoring systems against breaches of security and promptly to inform the customer if it becomes aware of any breaches of security.

6.1.3.9 Exit management and successor supplier Early outsourcing agreements very often did not provide for what would happen at the end of the outsourcing relationship. The outsourcings they implemented were

---

[3] On the Acquired Rights Directive, see generally Sargeant, M., 'Employment' in *Outsourcing Practice Manual* (London, Sweet & Maxwell, 1998, chap. D).

characterised by a protracted negotiation towards the end of the relationship during which the customer would sometimes be 'held to ransom' by the existing supplier who, because it knew that it would be losing the contract, wished to extract maximum revenues for any hand-over or termination services it had to provide.

The infrastructure and existing know-how very quickly come to reside with the existing outsourced service provider. Accordingly, unless the outsourcing agreement provides for obligations on the outsourced service provider to provide hand-over services, the customer will be in a weak position to negotiate for such services at the end of the relationship. For this reason an outsourcing agreement should provide for a detailed exit management plan which the existing supplier must implement and follow during the final stages of the relationship. This could include (in the case of a telecoms outsourcing) requiring the outsourced service provider to:

    (a)   undertake an audit or inventory of all existing handsets, switches and other equipment used by it to provide the services;

    (b)   provide a list of all leased lines and other contracts used by it in providing the services;

    (c)   provide details as to the numbering plan used for the customer's networks;

    (d)   provide a database of the configurations and a database of helpline call resolutions; and

    (e)   provide all other documentation and process maps used by it in providing the services.

The outsourced service provider should be required to provide all cooperation and assistance reasonably requested by the customer to achieve a smooth transition from the existing outsourced service provider to the customer or a successor supplier as the new supplier of the services. Although it might be reasonable for the existing outsourced service provider to charge for such services, generally these rates should be agreed in advance, or they should be at no more than the outsourced service provider's existing consultancy rates. The outsourced service provider should also be required to assist the customer in porting the existing telephone numbers to any new supplier (this is discussed in detail at 6.5.3 below).

As the customer may wish to buy back certain infrastructure, or to send it on to a successor supplier, the pricing principles and obligation to sell such equipment should be prescribed in the outsourcing agreement. Generally, outsourced service providers are only too willing to sell existing infrastructure back to customers because, of course, second-hand IT and telecoms infrastructure is not particularly valuable. It is also a way of recouping certain costs which would otherwise be sunk costs not able to be recovered by the outsourced service provider.

The exit provisions in the outsourcing agreement might also need to provide for the grant of any intellectual property rights or software licences owned or used by the outsourced service provider in providing the services.

6.2 TYPES OF TELECOMS OUTSOURCINGS

6.2.1 Voice

Voice is the most common type of telecoms outsourcing and involves the outsourcing of standard telephony infrastructure to the outsourced telecoms service provider. This may include transferring handsets to the outsourced telecoms service provider which it will subsequently update. The outsourced telecoms service provider then provides standard voice lines at agreed PSTN tariffs.

6.2.2 Data

It is also very common to outsource the carriage of data traffic. Data telecoms outsourcings are distinguished from voice outsourcings by virtue of the increased need for bandwidth capacity.

There is, of course, no sharp distinction between voice and data outsourcings, because increasingly voice data packets are sent across the data network. Similarly, facsimiles sent via the voice network blur the distinction between the two. The distinction has blurred further by the sending of voice packets or data across the Internet (and then into telecoms connections linked to the Internet).

6.2.3 Mobile data – WAP applications

Very recently, customers in telecoms outsourcings have been asking their outsourced service provider to provide an option for the customer to request mobile data functionality. This involves the use of a wireless application protocol (WAP) which is the radio frequency spectrum equivalent to protocols used for the Internet.

WAP does not increase the bandwidth or data carrying capacity of a mobile network but allows that network to carry information otherwise carried through wires in accessing the Internet. WAP is of limited use until the launch of third generation mobile telephony (discussed at 6.2.5 below) because of the limitations in bandwidth capacity.

6.2.4 Networks

The outsourcing of the carriage of voice and data traffic invariably involves outsourcing of the accompanying networks. This can include switches, routers, leased lines, other dedicated lines, cabling infrastructure and associated software. Networks can include local area networks (LANs) and wide area networks (WANs) (discussed below).

6.2.4.1 LANs At it most simple, a LAN consists of a local network of computers linked to central servers. The most common type of LAN is a computer network used within a single building.

6.2.4.2   WANs   A WAN consists of the telecommunications links linking LANs. It may link buildings, local offices in an entire country, or be global in nature. A WAN can cover both voice and data, but it is normally used for data.

6.2.4.3   Virtual private networks   A virtual private network (VPN) is a software-emulated dedicated telecommunications network designed to act as if it were dedicated to the particular customer (even though at any time lines used by a VPN may carry the traffic of more than one customer). A VPN is private in the sense that it is intended to guarantee the provision of bandwidth capacity required by the customer at any time, allowing the customer to 'burst' above its usual capacity requirements and have the network meet such requirements. It is a 'virtual' network in the sense that the software driving it does not depend upon a dedicated route for the data.

6.2.5   Mobile telephony

A mobile telephony outsourcing in many respects looks just like a mobile telecommunications services agreement, except that existing handsets and user contracts in relation to those handsets may need to be transferred to the outsourced service provider.

Mobile telephony outsourcings will become more important with the advent of 'third-generation' mobile telephony, bringing with it the ability of mobile telephony to provide increased bandwidth capacity (allowing faster and greater access to the Internet in conjunction with WAP). Third-generation mobile telephony licences have been available in the United Kingdom from April 2000 and it is anticipated that the first third-generation mobile functionality will become available commercially on the market sometime in 2001.

6.2.6   Video conferencing

Video conferencing is really a species of data network outsourcing. Because this technology depends on high bandwidth capacity, it is anticipated that it will be in more demand with more bandwidth becoming available and enhanced video conferencing technologies being released on to the market.

6.2.7   Call centres

Although not strictly telecoms outsourcings as such, call centre outsourcings tend to involve numerous telecoms-related issues. This is because call centre outsourcings may often involve the outsourced service provider taking over telecoms infrastructure to provide call centre services.

6.2.8   Maintenance

In a full telecoms outsourcing, the provision of network maintenance will be part of the service. For example, the outsourced service provider will be required to fix network down time and call failures within time frames specified in the service level agreement. However, a customer might wish to maintain ownership and operation of, say, its data network, but outsource the maintenance of that network to an outsourced service provider. Here the service levels will relate to fix times.

6.2.9 E-commerce-related infrastructure

With increased use and reliance by business on the Internet as an accepted basis for conducting business, Internet and e-commerce-related infrastructures are being outsourced. These very often involve telecoms infrastructures. Some examples are set out below.

6.2.9.1 Dedicated trading information exchanges Dedicated trading information exchanges can take various forms over the Internet. A common example is where a service provider provides a customer and its suppliers with access to a dedicated server containing information posted there by the customer and its suppliers. In this way the customer and suppliers can exchange information on a secure basis over the Internet without the need to use more complicated electronic data interchange (EDI) arrangements which had, until the advent of the Internet, been the general way of exchanging supply chain information electronically in a secure fashion.

The information exchange is 'dedicated' in the sense that passwords are given out by the customer to its suppliers and no one else may (in the absence of hacking) access information held on the server without such passwords. The customer may also seek additional security comfort by requiring the service provider to provide the data in encrypted form when they are released from the server.

6.2.9.2 IP tunnelling IP tunnelling uses encryption technology for the creation of what are, in effect, dedicated lines of communication maintained through telecommunications networks into and across the Internet and out into the telecommunications network on the other side between nodes of a WAN. The most common example is a business wishing to exchange information internally to other offices across the globe through the use of the Internet. IP tunnelling can be used for both voice and data, and the technology both overlaps and relies upon encryption software.

6.2.9.3 Encryption Because technology in the telecoms and Internet arenas is converging, telecoms service providers providing data traffic carriage across telecommunications lines into the Internet are often being asked to provide a 'one stop shop' through secure encryption of the data transferred. This can apply also to voice transmissions.

6.2.9.4 Application Service Provider (ASP) applications 'ASP' is commonly referred to as 'renting software' or 'bureau use' of software over the Internet. Put simply, it means that a customer does not itself need to be licensed to use software in order to have its data processed by that software, but instead pays a subscription fee to a service provider who provides or 'rents' access to the software over the Internet. The use of ASP applications generally involves large bandwidth capacity, and it is for this reason that telecommunications service providers are particularly interested in this kind of technology.

6.2.10   Cabling and related infrastructure

The outsourcing agreement will need to define the boundary (if any) between the network and services provided by the outsourced service provider and any retained network held by the customer. For example, the customer might wish to outsource everything from the exit terminal from its private automatic branch exchange (PABX) to the outsourced service provider. This would mean that it would retain responsibility and ownership of the PABX, cabling and related physical infrastructure, including handsets, within its building. However, the more common type of outsourcing involves the outright transfer of the entire infrastructure, including cabling and handsets.

The Telecommunications Act 1984, Sch. 2, para. 27(4) (the 'Telecoms Code') provides that, as between the owner of land and the telecoms service provider, the service provider owns the cabling installed on, under or attached to land or any building. This overcomes the outcome that would result from the law of fixtures. Under the Telecoms Code, a telecoms service provider is required to remove cabling when it ceases to provide the service and there is no prospect of the cabling being used by it (clause 22 of the Telecoms Code). Therefore, if, at the end of an outsourcing, a customer wishes to retain cabling, etc. installed by the outsourced service provider (this will be important where the customer wishes to take the service back in-house, and to achieve a smooth transition to a new service provider), the outsourcing agreement should provide that the outsourced service provider shall not have the right to remove any cabling installed by it and that it shall permit the customer or its successor supplier to use it to provide the services.

6.3   REGULATORY ISSUES SPECIFIC TO TELECOMS OUTSOURCINGS

6.3.1   Licence to operate as a telecommunications service provider

An outsourced telecommunications service provider running a telecommunications system (other than a purely domestic network not connected to another network) requires a licence in order to do so. The licensing provisions in the UK are subject to the implementation in the UK of the EU Licensing Directive (97/13/EC).

A telecommunications licence authorises the running of one or more telecommunications system. A telecommunications system may, however, be only one link in a much larger network. When, for example, a caller makes a call from one building to another building (both of which are occupied by the same business) there may be three systems involved (the first being the PABX and internal extensions, the second being the public network, and the third being the PABX and internal extensions at the other end). As far as the outsourced service provider is concerned, the relevant licence is its licence to operate these various systems.[4]

6.3.2 Other issues

Because telecommunications service providers operate in a relatively detailed regulatory framework, many aspects of their operations are subject to licence conditions or supervision by the regulator. This includes, in the UK, price regulation, number portability, data protection, carrier pre-selection, the provision of a universal service, the availability of certain information (including technical interface specifications for network access) and the provision of leased lines with specific capacity and transparent pricing. This regulatory framework is discussed in detail in Chapter 4 and is beyond the scope of this chapter.

6.4 TRANSFERRING THE INFRASTRUCTURE

6.4.1 Transferring physical assets

Physical assets include PABXs, switches, routers, cabling and handsets. If owned by the customer, they are usually listed in a schedule to the transfer agreement and transferred by way of sale to the outsourced service provider (usually for a nominal consideration).

It is important to agree a consideration for these assets, as there may be stamp duty implications. There are also VAT concessions available if physical assets, together with all other assets comprised in the undertaking, are transferred in a way that enables the transfer to be viewed as the transfer of a business as a going concern. Article 5 of the Value Added Tax (Special Provisions) Order 1995 has the effect that, if the transfer is not a supply of goods or services but a sale of a business as a going concern, it is not subject to VAT.

As assets transferred may include embedded software, it is important to check any documentation under which such assets were originally supplied for restrictions against on-sale or for obtaining consent for on-sale.

6.4.2 Novating existing service contracts

Where a business conducts its business operations at a range of sites in one country or in more than one country, it may well be the case that it has existing service contracts with suppliers on a regional basis which cannot be terminated before the implementation of the new outsourcing arrangement. Where that is the case, unless these overlapping contracts can be terminated

---

[4] For further discussion of the requirements in relation to telecommunications licences, see Sinclair, *op cit. supra* n. 2.

with the agreement of the existing supplier, the customer will be left paying twice for the service after the outsourcing. In such circumstances the new outsourced service provider should be required, either before or as part of the migration process, to enter into negotiations with existing suppliers for the novation of existing suppliers' service contracts to the new outsourced service provider. These contractual provisions can appear either in the outsourcing agreement or in the accompanying transfer agreement. They normally provide for the allocation of costs, responsibilities and for pre- and post-transfer indemnities for existing service contracts novated.

Where existing service contracts cannot be novated the customer may wish to oblige the outsourced service provider to take on the role of contracts manager (this is discussed at 6.4.8 below).

6.4.3   Novating leased-line contracts

Just as with other types of existing service contracts, where the customer uses leased lines in providing itself a telecommunications network prior to the outsourcing, it will be necessary to have these terminated or transferred to the outsourced service provider. There are very often fixed costs associated with terminating leased lines so that, if necessary, the existing arrangements can merely be terminated and the existing supplier paid out.

6.4.4   Novating managed switches

The customer may, prior to the outsourcing, have already outsourced the provision and maintenance of switches to one or more service providers. In an entirely 'managed service' outsourcing the customer will wish to relinquish responsibility for managing these relationships and will wish the outsourced service provider to take over the switches themselves (or to supply replacement switches). Accordingly, the provisions dealing with novation of existing contracts should also cover managed switches.

6.4.5   Novating network software licences

In a very limited number of circumstances the customer may be using free-standing diagnostic or other network software in the operation of its network (an example is Novell software). If the existing infrastructure is to be used for a time after the outsourcing is to take effect, the licence for the use of the software will need to be novated to the outsourced service provider or it will need to obtain its own licence to use this software. The principle is the same as the novation of other existing service contracts.

6.4.6   Obtaining consent

The contractual provisions in the outsourcing agreement or the transfer agreement need to allocate various responsibilities to the customer and the outsourced service provider for obtaining consent to the assignment or novation of the various contracts and licences referred to above.

If the customer is in a particularly strong bargaining position it may be able to get the outsourced service provider to assume sole responsibility for obtaining such consent (and for implementing replacement systems and services at its own cost if such consent is not obtained). The circumstances in which a customer might achieve this position are relatively rare.

It is more usual that the obligation to obtain consent is a shared responsibility, and the real issue becomes who should bear the cost of procuring replacement systems if consent is not obtained. This is something which should be specifically provided for in the contractual provisions.

6.4.7 Procedure if consent is not obtained

The contractual provisions relating to consent should say that if consent is first refused, the relevant party should continue to attempt to procure such consent for a period (to be specified) and the other party should provide reasonable assistance in procuring such consent. The provisions should be clear about whether efforts to obtain such consent and to provide such assistance include the payment of money.

If consent is not obtained after a certain period of time, the contracts or licences at issue should fall into the class known as 'managed contracts'. Sometimes the parties agree from the outset that certain contracts will not be novated but will be managed (as 'managed contracts') on an ongoing basis by the outsourced service provider.

6.4.8 Managing suppliers not novated

Where contracts and licences cannot be novated, or it is agreed that they will not be novated, the customer should require the outsourced service provider to assume the role of managing agent in relation to those contracts. This will mean that the outsourced service provider, and not the customer, will be responsible for their day-to-day administration and for liaising with the existing suppliers in relation to the customer's requirements. This will enable the customer to receive a seamless service (called a 'managed service') and a one-stop shop from the outsourced service provider.

6.4.9 Allocation of liability – novated and managed contracts

As mentioned at 6.4.2 above, the contractual provisions should provide for a pre- and post-transfer indemnity in relation to existing contracts and licences which are novated to the outsourced service provider. For example, claims relating to a contract novated which relate to the period prior to the novation should generally be borne by the customer, and it should indemnify the outsourced service provider if such claims are made against the outsourced service provider.

Similarly, where the outsourced service provider manages existing contracts and licences which are not novated, the customer should ask for an indemnity for claims made against it arising out of the outsourced service provider's activities beyond the scope of its authority to manage those contracts.

6.5   CONTRACTUAL ISSUES SPECIFIC TO TELECOMS OUTSOURCINGS

6.5.1   Restrictions on network use

The outsourced service provider will generally require the customer to agree in the outsourcing agreement that the customer shall not use the services for the transmission of any material which is defamatory, offensive or abusive, or of an obscene or menacing character, or in a manner which constitutes an infringement of the intellectual property rights of any person.

6.5.2   Unauthorised access to network

The customer will want comfort in the outsourcing agreement that it will not have to pay any service charges arising out of hacking of the network by unauthorised third parties. Accordingly, the outsourcing agreement should provide that, where there is such unauthorised use of the network, the customer shall not be liable to pay service charges unless such authorised use results from:

(a)   the negligence, fraud or failure by the customer to keep equipment physically secure from unauthorised use; or
(b)   the disclosure by the customer of passwords supplied to it by the outsourced service provider for accessing the network.

6.5.3   Number portability

As explained in detail in Chapter 4, in the UK and within the European Union the provisions of the Numbering Directive (98/61/EC) (implemented in the UK as the Telecommunications (Interconnection) (Number Portability, etc.) Regulations 1999 (SI 1999 No. 3449)) require that service providers provide number portability in relation to fixed telecommunications services (but not for mobile telephony).

In the case of mobile telephony, specific number portability provisions should be provided for in the outsourcing agreement. However, even in the case of fixed telephony, it is advisable to include certain obligations in relation to number portability (because the obligations that apply under the Numbering Directive and its domestic implementations are relatively limited as far as the customer is concerned). Accordingly, the outsourcing agreement might provide for the following in relation to number portability:

(a)   That the outsourced service provider shall, in accordance with a migration plan, at its own cost take all reasonable steps to enable the customer to port the then current telephone numbers supplied through existing suppliers so that the customer can continue to use them as part of the outsourced services.
(b)   That the customer shall have the right to apply for registration and to register telephone numbers allocated to it under the agreement as trade or

service marks, whether on their own, or in conjunction with some other words or trading style or device, or represented as words. See 800-Flowers Trade Mark [2000] FSR 697, where Phonenames Limited owned a number of telephone numbers (such as the phone number 0800 356 9377 corresponding to the UK freephone number 0800 Flowers) and opposed an attempted registration by 1-800 Flowers Inc. of the trademark '800-Flowers' in the UK in relation to flower services. Jacob J held that '0800 Flowers' (and 0800+ word numbers in general) did not have any inherent capacity to distinguish the goods and services of any one business and so was not registrable as a trademark. Although this case may not be the last of its type, it means that, at least so far as the law exists at the moment, a customer wishing to reserve a specific right to apply for the alpha-numeric representation of a phone number as a trademark may face considerable difficulties in obtaining such a registration.

(c)   That the supplier shall not be entitled to withdraw or change any telephone number, or code or groups of codes designated for the customer once such numbers have been allocated to it, except in order to comply with any provision of a licence or any applicable numbering scheme, or if required by law or the relevant regulatory authority. Where such change is required, the outsourced service provider should be required to give the customer the maximum period of notice practicable and indemnify the customer if it fails to do so. This is important because, for large business organisations, costs involved in publicising and changing telephone numbers can be extremely high.

(d)   That on termination or expiry of the outsourcing agreement, the outsourced service provider shall at its own cost take all reasonable steps to enable the customer to port the then current telephone numbers allocated to it so that it can continue to use them with a successor supplier.

(e)   That the outsourced service provider shall comply with the provisions of the Numbering Directive and relevant domestic implementations of the same.

6.5.4   Ownership of intellectual property in network software

If the outsourced service provider is, as part of the service, to develop software for use in operating the network, and such software would be required by the customer or a successor supplier in order to operate the infrastructure at the end of the outsourcing, the outsourcing agreement should provide for a perpetual royalty-free licence to use such software at the end of the agreement (and an obligation on the outsourced service provider to deliver a copy of the software to the customer).

In the relatively rare circumstances in which software is developed specifically for an infrastructure and part of the service charges includes the development of that software, the customer might wish to own the intellectual property rights in it rather than merely be licensed to use it on termination. Here the outsourcing agreement should provide for obligations in relation to assigning the intellectual property rights in the software to the customer.

6.5.5 Business continuity plans – network down

Because telecommunications and data infrastructures are business critical to the operation of most (if not all) businesses, it is essential that any outsourcing agreement in relation to telecoms includes provisions for business continuity and disaster recovery. This should include:

(a) requiring the outsourced service provider to have in place at all times a business continuity plan approved by the customer;

(b) requiring the outsourced service provider to comply with such plan;

(c) requiring the outsourced service provider to provide alternative networks and infrastructure if the network is down for a specified period of time;

(d) allowing the customer to terminate the agreement if such business continuity plans are not complied with and a replacement service is not quickly implemented.

Sometimes business continuity plans include requiring the outsourced service provider to have contractual arrangements in place with a disaster recovery network service provider for the implementation of business continuity network services on short notice. This of course has cost implications which are inevitably borne by the customer.

6.6   GUARANTEEING SERVICE LEVELS

6.6.1 Service level agreement

6.6.1.1 General Although called a service level 'agreement', the service level agreement is actually just a definition of the service and the performance levels required in relation to that service – it is not a contract separate from the outsourcing agreement.

The service level agreement should include a detailed description of the service to be supplied together with the service levels applicable to that service. The service description should include a description of the carriage part of the service, the managed component of the service (i.e., for full managed services, it should prescribe the obligations in relation to the hardware and equipment estate) and all other services to be provided. Outlined at 6.6.1.2 to 6.6.1.7 below are some telecoms-specific issues which should be dealt with in a telecoms outsourcing service level agreement.

6.6.1.2 Network availability Obviously the customer will wish the network to be available for use 24 hours a day, seven days a week. However, recognising that there may need to be a very limited latitude for down-time, many customers for outsourced telecoms solutions are prepared to agree that the service level for network availability shall be something less than 100 per cent. Normally it is something like 98.5 or 99.5 per cent availability. This will, of course, differ according to the nature of the customer's business.

6.6.1.3 Platform fix The service level agreement should also provide for fix times for errors or faults in the technology platform – for example, for fixing a defective switch or router. These are generally specified in terms of hours for critical faults, and possibly hours or even days for non-critical faults.

6.6.1.4 Logical and physical moves Logical moves are software-implemented moves relating to the configuration and ability of a switch to recognise a call as a numerical extension number and route it to the appropriate physical extension. A physical move, on the other hand, relates to the physical relocation of handsets connected to the PABX.

Most telecoms outsourcing agreements which cover handset and extension infrastructure permit the customer to request a certain number of logical and physical moves for free, allowing the customer to relocate offices and personnel as part of its daily business operations. Beyond certain limits the customer will be charged. Because the customer will have requirements to have logical and physical moves implemented quickly, service levels for the implementation of them should be specified. These should be expressed as a number of hours or days from the date and time of the request.

6.6.1.5 Hotdesking and virtual extensions Hotdesking and virtual extensions refer to flexible call routing (often required by businesses whose personnel operate from an unfixed location or from out of the office from time to time).

In the most simple PABX configuration, a virtual extension requires a notional extension number which is allocated to a specific user. This is sometimes referred to as an analogue or digital '0' extension number. This does not include the supply of a handset, but may include PABX features and facilities, calls within the same site, on net calls and PSTN access to the outsourced telecommunications service provider's network. The analogue or digital 0 extension service can be used alone, or in conjunction with voicemail or hotdesking services.

Hotdesking, on the other hand, includes the supply of the analogue or digital 0 extension number, but, unlike a virtual extension, to work hotdesking requires the allocation of a DDI (Direct Dialling Inward; or 'DID': Direct Inward Dialling) number. Hotdesking therefore consists of the analogue or digital 0 number with an accompanying DDI number.

The service level agreement should provide for the response times for implementing hotdesking and virtual extensions when requested by a user.

6.6.1.6 Call failure rates The service level agreement should provide for the customer's requirements in relation to successful calls and call failure rates. It will provide something like: 'The service provider shall provide a grade of service of 1:100 from the handset to any PSTN number between the required maintenance cover times for all category A sites across the countries [or sites] covered by the agreement'. The service level '1:100' means that in the busy hours not more than one call in 100 is not available. It is sometimes described as 'PO1'. Therefore, PO2 would mean two out of 100 calls are not available in busy hours.

6.6.1.7 Data integrity The service level agreement should also provide for the procedures and processes that the outsourced service provider should follow in order to maintain integrity of voice and data carried across the network. This should include maintaining operational surveillance of the network and undertaking appropriate diagnostic and analytical software scans.

6.6.2 Best industry practice and total quality management

The outsourcing agreement should provide that, in providing the services, the outsourced service provider must comply with best industry practice. Sometimes a service provider will even agree to comply with world best practice in relation to telecommunications.

A customer may also require the outsourced service provider to comply with certified total quality management (TQM) procedures in the provision of the service or in managing the service.

6.6.3 BS standards

A customer may also require the outsourced service provider to comply with certain BS standards in relation to such matters as caller resolution and other processes. A typical example is requiring the outsourced service provider to comply with BS 7799 security protocols.

6.6.4 User satisfaction surveys

Apart from cost savings, the main factor in judging the success of a telecoms outsourcing is user satisfaction. Accordingly, it is increasingly the case that customers wishing to embark on telecoms outsourcings require their outsourced service providers to undertake periodic user satisfaction surveys based on criteria prescribed in the outsourcing agreement.

The outcome of such surveys can be measured according to objective criteria which may be linked to rewards or performance incentive bonuses payable to the outsourced service provider.

A customer with strong bargaining power may also reserve to itself the right to terminate the agreement if user satisfaction surveys fall below certain measurable thresholds of satisfaction.

6.6.5 Helpline – caller triage and call resolution

Certain kinds of telecoms-related outsourcings require the outsourced service provider to implement and follow certain mapped processes in providing services. A classic example is call centre services, where caller resolution is process mapped as part of the development of the service level agreement. Similarly, time frames to achieve call resolution can themselves be measured and be made subject to service levels.

6.6.6 Service level and network audit rights

In order to monitor the outsourced service provider's compliance with the service level agreement, a customer may reserve to itself in the outsourcing agreement a right to send in technical auditors to audit compliance with the service level agreement and to examine the integrity of the network. Such rights are invariably resisted by network service providers, but provided they are limited by reasonable notice periods and obligations to respect confidentiality, they are sometimes agreed to.

6.6.7 Remedies for breach of service levels

6.6.7.1 Service credits and non-exclusive remedies There are several contractual routes a customer might choose to use in order to motivate an outsourced service provider to comply with the service level agreement. The most commonly used is the right to receive service credits if the outsourced service provider fails to comply. The service credits regime is usually coupled with key performance indicators and a formula for calculating the quantum of service credits according to the magnitude of the breach.

There is always a risk, of course, that service credits could constitute a penalty, and therefore that they may not be enforceable. However, from a customer's perspective, it should not allow the outsourced service provider to use service credits as a *de facto* cap on the service provider's liability. If, for example, a breach of the service level agreement resulted in a total quantifiable loss to the customer of £100,000 (only £50,000 of which was attributable to sourcing a replacement service, with the remainder constituting other direct losses), there should be no reason why the customer cannot recover the remaining £50,000 as damages (assuming it has recovered the first £50,000 as service credits).

In order to reserve such a right, the outsourcing agreement should provide that service credits are in addition to, and not in replacement for, any rights or remedies available to the customer under the agreement or at common law or equity, including the right to claim damages.

6.6.7.2 Breach constituting a persistent breach or material breach Most services agreements provide that the customer has the right to terminate for 'material' breach of the agreement. Just what constitutes a material breach may depend on the circumstances, and it is certainly not free from doubt that a breach of the service level agreement will always constitute a material breach.

It is therefore best (from the customer's perspective) to provide in the outsourcing agreement that, for the avoidance of doubt, a breach of the service level agreement constitutes a material breach. This, of course, will be of little comfort to the customer if the breach can be remedied in time by the outsourced service provider (generally rights of termination in relation to material breach are coupled with a right on the part of the supplier to remedy the breach if it is able to do so). Accordingly, the customer should also negotiate for the inclusion of the right to terminate if there is a *persistent* breach. The agreement should prescribe what constitutes a persistent breach. For example, it may constitute all of the following:

(a)   a single non-compliance with the service level agreement continuing over, say, two months; or
(b)   more than, say, three unrelated non-compliances with the service level agreement occurring in one month (obviously the range of options here is considerable).

6.6.7.3 Termination rights If the outsourcing agreement covers more than one site or country, the customer should consider reserving to itself the right to terminate the agreement in so far as it relates to that site or country, but to keep the remainder of the agreement in full force. In this way if the customer suffers from poor service at one site or country, it can remove that site or country from the scope of the agreement without having to terminate the whole agreement. Generally termination of the whole agreement would relate to very serious breaches, and non-compliance in one country or site may not be enough to persuade the customer to exercise such right.

The outsourced service provider will wish to reserve to itself the right to terminate the agreement if for any reason its licence to operate a telecommunications system is revoked and a substantially similar licence cannot be obtained.

6.7 TECHNOLOGY PLATFORM

6.7.1 Generic requirements – equipment and network

Earlier in this chapter it was mentioned that it is best practice in telecoms outsourcings to impose certain minimum requirements on the outsourced service provider in relation to the technical performance of the technology platform (including equipment and the network). This is because, although an outsourcing is mostly service-based, the equipment and network used in the outsourcing impact upon the quality of service delivery. Therefore it is not unusual for a customer to ask for an obligation on the outsourced service provider to ensure that the equipment and the network (and anything else used as part of the technology platform) comply with agreed technical specifications (which would consist of certain minimum technical specifications set out in a schedule to the agreement). These might include such things as the type of operating platform, switches, routers and switching protocols used.

6.7.2 Heritage/legacy platform

Where the service provider inherits (as part of the infrastructure transferred) heritage or legacy technology platform, it will normally argue that it should not be required to make the heritage or legacy platform comply with any minimum specifications or other requirements. From a customer's perspective this may be acceptable if there is a short migration period to a new technology platform. However, where it is envisaged that the existing platform will be used for some time, the customer may well argue for certain minimum safeguards. These might include requiring the outsourced service provider to meet the same specifications or other performance criteria as existed prior to the outsourcing.

6.7.3 Resilience of the technology platform

A major issue in telecoms outsourcings is the resilience of the technology platform used. This relates to the ability of the system to carry traffic uninterrupted and without corruption over sustained periods.

With voice traffic it is immediately apparent when resilience has not been achieved, but this can be less obvious in the case of data traffic. Accordingly, the obligation on the outsourced service provider to ensure that the technology platform meets certain minimum requirements should include requirements in relation to resilience.

6.7.4 Compatibility with in-house systems

One of the difficulties with telecoms outsourcings (as with all outsourcings involving a transfer of infrastructure) is that the customer may be faced with difficulties in bringing the system back in-house at the end of the outsourcing relationship. This problem will be particularly acute if the systems used by the outsourced service provider are incompatible with any residual systems retained by the customer. For this reason a customer may wish to specify in the technology platform specification (in relation to both equipment and the network) that the systems and network used by the outsourced service provider must remain compatible with the customer's remaining systems.

6.7.5 Restriction on changing the technology platform

For the same reason, the outsourcing agreement may need to provide that the outsourced service provider may not make changes to the technology platform without the consent of the customer (the customer may agree that such consent shall not be unreasonably withheld). Sometimes outsourced service providers see such an obligation as unduly restrictive on their power to supply the services by whatever means they choose, and therefore this issue often turns on the respective bargaining strengths of the parties.

6.7.6 Testing the technology platform

The customer may require the outsourced service provider to test components of the technology platform before rolling it out to the customer. Such testing should generally be coupled with a report mechanism allowing the customer to see the results of the tests and allowing it to observe such tests if requested.

6.7.7   Technology refresh

The efficacy and benefits of telecoms outsourcings can be quickly eroded through advances in technology if those advantages are not quickly made available to the customer. From the outsourced service provider's perspective, however, there is little incentive to make new technology available to a customer once an outsourcing has started, as this will represent a further sunk cost that the outsourced service provider cannot then recoup. Accordingly, a customer wishing to 'future proof' itself in relation to advances in technology has two options:

(a)   to insist that the agreement be of a relatively short duration. This will inevitably have adverse pricing consequences for the customer;
(b)   to agree a procedure by which the customer can insist upon technology refresh, if necessary by shouldering additional costs itself.

Technology refresh can include anything from replacement of existing handsets and PABXs up to increasing bandwidth and the technology used for transmitting data packets across the network.

Generally the customer should require the outsourced service provider to report to it, say, on a three-monthly basis about any technological advances available in the marketplace in relation to the services provided by the outsourced service provider.

6.8   ENSURING CHARGES REMAIN COMPETITIVE

6.8.1   Basis of charging determines method of monitoring costs

If pricing is transparent then the customer will want to be able to monitor the basis for calculating charges. Although numerous charging models are available, some of the more common for telecoms outsourcings are set out below.

6.8.2   'Cost plus'

'Cost plus' is a transparent pricing basis under which the outsourced service provider provides the service at the raw cost of providing the service, plus a percentage reward on such raw costs for its management of the service.

6.8.3   'Per seat'

'Per seat' pricing is generally non-transparent and is set according to the number of users receiving the service.

6.8.4   'Open book'

'Open book' pricing may or may not be on the basis of cost plus, and involves complete transparency of all costs incurred by the outsourced service provider in providing the service. It is generally coupled with rights of financial audit.

6.8.5 Benchmarking PSTN tariffs

There are numerous ways in which to benchmark pricing for outsourced telecoms services. Benchmarking can range from an obligation to pass savings back to the customer to sophisticated arrangements involving an external indicator (by which to adjust the pricing).

For mobile telephony, benchmarking tends to focus on the most cost-effective tariff on a per user basis. This is because user/caller patterns in the case of mobile telephony can more easily be linked to an individual tariff than those in relation to fixed voice or data services.

For fixed voice or data telephony services, benchmarking may occur once or twice yearly, and the purpose of such benchmarking is to provide a mechanism to review the PSTN tariff rate element of usage charges. It will involve comparing the PSTN tariff rates as a whole with PSTN tariff rates offered by similar suppliers in the marketplace.

Although the types of benchmarking may range from informal to formal, the strongest kind from the customer's perspective is to use a benchmarking agency to undertake the comparison. The criteria used by the agency should be agreed in advance (to make sure that there is a comparison of like with like). The procedure should prescribe whether the benchmarking can result in increases, or merely in decreases in the PSTN tariff rates. Obviously, current market trends indicate that generally benchmarking should result only in decreases.

6.9 PAN-EUROPEAN AND INTERNATIONAL CONSIDERATIONS

6.9.1 Scope of coverage

If the outsourcing agreement provides for service in more than one country, the outsourced service provider may need to use other service providers in countries where it itself does not have an operating presence. This will have consequences in terms of the service it can provide, and some of the issues relevant to international coverage are as set out below.

6.9.2 Direct and indirect models of supply

Where the indirect model of supply is used (subcontracting), the outsourced service provider should not be excused from supplying the service in accordance with the service levels merely because it subcontracts the provision of the service. Moreover, reporting obligations in relation to compliance with service levels should be on a per country basis in order to detect non-compliance on a per country basis. Service credits and rights of termination should similarly be linked on a per country basis.

6.9.3 Liability allocation on a per country basis

If the outsourced service provider is subcontracting in various countries, it may be appropriate to divide liability upon country lines so that there is a separate cap on liability for claims arising in each country. This will mean that if the customer suffers variable service in one country, but consistent service in another, the outsourced service provider's total liability cap will not be 'used up' in relation to other countries because of exceptionally poor performance in one particular country.

6.9.4 Varying service levels internationally

Where the outsourced service provider is using other suppliers in various countries in order to provide a global solution, it may well push for service levels which vary between countries. Although from a supplier's perspective this might seem reasonable, it may not be acceptable to a customer wishing to implement a globally consistent service.[5]

6.10 FUTURE TRENDS IN TELECOMS OUTSOURCINGS

The technologies associated with telecoms outsourcings have been characterised by convergence with those used in relation to the Internet, broadcasting (particularly radio) and cable. This is particularly so in the case of data traffic (which could equally be carried through the Internet or on cable infrastructures).

Convergent technologies have resulted in regulators having to coordinate a consistent response to the technologies, because one of the most important principles accepted by the European Union is that regulation in this area should be technology-neutral. We are therefore now witnessing a convergence in the regulatory framework. This point was made particularly clear in a Communication from the European Commission to the European Parliament, the Counsel, the Economic and Social Committee and the Committee of the Regions.[6] In that Communication the European Commission set out a framework for communications regulation on a technology-neutral basis covering liberalisation, licensing and authorisations, access to interconnection, universal service and telecoms data protection (see Chapter 5, at 5.5 for full details).

It is clear from the Communication that inconsistencies in the regulatory frameworks are to be removed if in substance the technologies are similar. This will have interesting implications for outsourcings in relation to telecoms, particularly those that include the use of the Internet as a method of traffic carriage.

The rollout of WAP and third generation mobile telephony constitutes a stark example of convergence which will require a coordinated regulatory response. This will apply as much in telecoms outsourcings as in other areas of telecoms regulation.

---

[5] In relation to varying service levels internationally, see Sinclair, M., 'IT and Telecoms Outsourcing in Europe and the Law', *op. cit. supra* n. 2, at 42.
[6] The 1999 Communications Review, 1999.

CHAPTER SEVEN

Competition Law in Telecommunications

Edward Pitt

7.1 BEHAVIOURAL CONTROLS: REGULATION THROUGH COMPETITION LAW

It is a mantra of UK Government telecommunications policy that the regulation of the telecommunications industry should, wherever possible, be achieved by applying general competition law rather than specific regulation for telecommunications. Detailed, telecoms-specific regulation should be withdrawn in stages. A past Director-General of OFTEL was described as making a 'bonfire of regulation' in pursuit of this policy.

In this chapter we will try to unpick that analysis: competition law (and its enforcement procedures) can provide a framework for effective regulation in the telecommunications sector, but competition law has, and always will have, considerable limitations as the only source of telecoms regulation. Regulations specifically designed for the telecommunications sector will still be needed, even after the special rules put in place to stimulate market entry at the expense of the incumbent monopolist (in the UK, BT) have been repealed.

The telecommunications market makes for an interesting competition law analysis: both in the UK and in most European countries (and in a different way, in the US), it is not a market which developed 'naturally' in the beginning and its development is still not 'natural' now. For over 70 years (from the time that the local telephone companies were put together under the General Post Office in 1912) the UK has had a centrally planned and managed telecommunication system (see Chapter 3). Certain elements were key: network integrity and compatibility throughout the UK; a universal service, available to all who needed it or wanted it, on reasonable terms; and a robust system with high technical levels of service. Against that background the decision to privatise the telecommunications industry – both the domestic telephone business, run by the General Post Office (now BT), and the UK Government's overseas telephone business, run by Cable & Wireless – was not simply a government decision to sell it off and walk away. The Telecommunications Act 1984 and the instruments to privatise BT and Cable & Wireless ensured that the Government, while it sold the ownership of the systems, retained a close and tight control over the way in which they were developed once in the private sector. For example, the number of network licensees was at first limited to two; licences are now freely available. Since privatisation there have been other attempts to redesign and manage the market, through evolving policies on issues such as entitlement to interconnection terms, number portability, indirect access and local loop unbundling.

It is against that background that we will assess the competition rules, as they apply to telecommunications. This management of the competitive process will be analysed under six headings: experiments in market design; manipulation of the designed structure; control of behaviour through mainstream competition rules; special competition rules for telecommunications; market failure of competition – sector-specific rules; and procedures for enforcement of the competition rules. We will then show how these principles have been applied, both by the EU Commission and by the UK Government, when approving structural changes – mergers and joint ventures – in the telecommunications sector.

7.2   EXPERIMENTS IN MARKET DESIGN

In order to understand how competition law is applied today in the telecommunications sector, it is necessary to go back to 1984, the moment of privatisation in the UK, when the ground rules for current telecommunications policy were laid. There were two premises underlying the Telecommunications Act 1984:

(a)   the private sector (stimulated by the demands of shareholders) would be more efficient in the allocation and management of resources than the public owner; and

(b)   to deliver real efficiency gains there needed to be competition in the provision of physical telecommunication networks, not just competition between providers of services over one network.

As to the former, BT has greatly improved efficiency – the cost of calls to both business and residential customers has consistently come down, so that it is now 50 per cent of what it was, in real terms, in 1984.[1] BT has made very considerable savings in costs, achieved partly through a great reduction in staffing and partly through technological advances. That process continues.

As to the latter, the building of, and provision of services over, competing physical networks has developed more haphazardly. At the time of privatisa-

---

[1] OFTEL, Market Research Report, February 1999.

tion the idea was that one competitor to BT in the provision of a fixed network would be enough to stimulate competition. Mercury, a subsidiary of Cable & Wireless, the UK's overseas telephone operator (operating in particular in many Commonwealth countries), would provide competition to all BT's services. In practice, Mercury focused on certain sectors, in particular the business market. In 1991, the Government published the outcome of the so-called Duopoly Review as a White Paper.[2] It concluded that competing networks to provide mass consumer services were not being built. Further steps should be taken to encourage the building of cable networks to provide telephony services to the mass consumer market. Cable companies had already started to be franchised to build networks of fibre-optic and coaxial cable. For an exclusive period (typically 15 years) they alone were entitled to broadcast screened entertainment (television programmes, feature films, etc.) to consumers in those franchised areas. After the Duopoly Review, cable franchisees would be able to offer both telephony and broadcast services and, therefore, have two sources of revenue. BT was banned from broadcasting until at least 2005 (since brought back to 2001 – see 7.3.6 below). The years 1989 to 1995 saw the award of some 130 franchise licences to some 70 different companies, who were granted exclusive franchises to broadcast in defined areas. In those areas they were now also free to provide telephony services. Investment in these franchises was funded by investors, particularly from the United States. However, by 1995 BT still had close on 95 per cent of all residential connections and 92 per cent of telephony revenues from domestic customers. It appeared that small cable companies would never have the commercial and financial muscle (or incentive) to be able to invest in national advertising campaigns and to invest in large networks using rapidly developing technology. Accordingly, after 1995 there was a fairly rapid period of consolidation between cable franchisees, with Government encouragement. In the UK today we now have just two groups providing mass-market combined broadcast and telephony services, Telewest and ntl, the latter incorporating Cable & Wireless's consumer cable businesses.

The mass consumer market for fixed telephony access services is a concentrated market, i.e. there are just three main providers of fixed network services on a national basis – BT, ntl/CWC and Telewest. There are very high barriers to entry, i.e. it is very expensive for a new entrant to enter the market by building its own network. Further, all operators, including those providing fixed network services to the business market or 'backbone' services to other operators (the 'Carrier's Carrier'), are interdependent on each other for delivery of each other's calls. These two factors have implications for the way in which competition law is applied and adapted in the telecommunications sector. It also means that there are special additional obligations in the nature of competition rules, imposed on the members of the oligopoly having significant market power (SMP; see Chapter 4), which are of a type that would not be imposed in other markets.

---

[2] *Competition and Choice: Telecommunications Policy for the 1990s* (London, DTI, 1991). See Chapter 3.

Mobile telephony is, at present, seen by OFTEL as a separate product market from telephony services over fixed networks. The mobile market has been designed by the Government with the same considerations as for the fixed telephony market, i.e. competition is most effective if there are the greatest possible number of providers of services who each build, own and control their own networks. The first two analogue mobile licences were granted in 1985; when digital technology became viable, allowing for more efficient use of the available spectrum, two further licences were issued, in 1993, to Orange and to One-2-One. The auction of so-called 'third generation' mobile telephony licences was constructed to ensure that a fifth mobile network operator would be introduced to the market to further stimulate network competition between mobile operators. This has now happened, with the TIW consortium being awarded the main licence in the third generation auction.

Notwithstanding a policy of encouraging the building of competing networks, both the fixed and mobile networks are (at least as respects the mass consumer market) in the hands of a very limited number of operators – true 'oligopolists'. Accordingly, to deal with those oligopolistic market structures special steps have been taken to micromanage the structure further. These are analysed at 7.3 below.

7.3   MANIPULATION OF THE DESIGNED STRUCTURE

The policy that two or three networks serving the mass consumer market would inject sufficient competition into the system was overoptimistic. The failure of Ionica to build a wireless fixed access network further dampened the optimism. Because of the unusual structure of the fixed and the mobile markets, i.e. a very few operators all interdependent on each other (and a dominant incumbent operator in the UK, BT, with an entrenched position providing services over its fixed network), various steps have been taken to stimulate competition and assist market entry – or to recast the rather overused analogy, to make sure that the playing field was not level and that the ex-monopolist, BT, should be playing rugby uphill, into the wind and rain. These special rules to manipulate the designed market structure include:

(a)   special rules for interconnection;
(b)   mandatory indirect access (IA) over BT lines (and now carrier pre-selection (CPS));
(c)   a special regime for mobile service providers;
(d)   BT's calls and access tariffs;
and, most recently:
(e)   the proposals for local loop unbundling (LLU).

7.3.1   Special rules on interconnection

Under normal competition rules only a dominant operator is obliged to supply services to another undertaking. In telecommunications, all licensees satisfying the tests for so-called 'Annex II' interconnection status must interconnect with all other licensees having that status (Telecommunications (Interconnection) Regulations 1997 (SI 1997 No. 2931)). The main purpose of the interconnection rules is to foster interdependence, to ensure that all licensed operators, who are interdependent on each other, are able to deliver each of the calls, originating from their customers both nationally and overseas, over systems run by other operators. There is a secondary purpose in the way the interconnection rules have been set up and BT's interconnection prices (which act as a benchmark for the industry) are set. An interconnecting operator with 'Annex II' status pays lower prices to transmit or terminate calls originating on its network than would be paid even by a business customer with a high volume of calls and a discount for this volume. The purpose of this privilege is to offer an economic incentive to those companies which are prepared to make some contribution to building out further infrastructure, or offer some other genuine value-added service, to do so. Even since the revision of the UK interconnection rules, in order to comply with the EU Interconnection Directive (97/33/EC), in practice interconnection rates are mainly available to those companies which are prepared to build additional infrastructure, even if investment in infrastructure is limited to acquiring an international private leased circuit (IPLC) and installing a large switch. The interconnection rules have been manipulated so as to encourage the building of further infrastructure, with the aim of stimulating competition.

Once a licensee has Annex II status (whether as an ISVR licensee, or as the holder of a fixed mainline PTO network licence – see further Chapter 4), an arbitrage opportunity arises. The licensee having Annex II status can in effect buy call minutes at wholesale rates from BT (or any other operator) and can then resell those minutes at retail rates to its customers who may access their service, for example, via an IA code. The effect of small operators taking advantage of this arbitrage opportunity has been to force other network operators, in particular BT, to reduce their prices (which, for example, have come down significantly on very profitable overseas routes).

7.3.2 Indirect access

Indirect access is the facility which enables the customer of a fixed network operator or service provider to make calls by dialling a four- or five-digit access code. The BT line provides the access, but the call is managed and billed to the customer by the IA operator. The calls pass over BT's fixed network and then, normally via the IA operator's switch, to its terminating destination. The IA operator pays BT, as the network operator, for the carriage of the originating call at interconnection rates. It then charges its customers a retail rate and it makes money on the 'turn'.

Indirect access was introduced as a means of forcing BT to reduce its prices; it allows a BT customer to have a choice as to which operator should carry each call, the choice being made on a call-by-call basis.

7.3.3 Carrier pre-selection

Carrier pre-selection is a variant of IA. Again, as with IA, only BT is obliged to allow its customers the freedom to use CPS if they wish. Other network operators do not have to offer it. Its introduction has a similar economic purpose. A customer will be able to use a fixed operator for access (i.e., for the right to use the line against payment of a monthly or quarterly rental fee), but his or her telephone is pre-programmed to use another carrier for carrying all outgoing calls. (It is not necessary to dial the four- or five-digit prefix as with IA.) The pre-selected carrier makes its money in the same way as an IA operator, i.e. it carries the traffic over BT's and other networks at their wholesale interconnection rates and charges its customer a retail price.

Carrier pre-selection is designed to give customers a greater choice over which operator carries their calls, thus further stimulating competition between operators (Telecommunications (Interconnection) (Carrier Pre-Selection Regulations) 1999 (SI 1999 No. 3448)).

7.3.4 Mobile service provision

When the first analogue licences were granted to Vodaphone and Cellnet to provide mobile telephony services, the Government saw that with just two network operators there might be little incentive for them to keep prices low. It thought that one way to force network operators to reduce prices would be to oblige them to sell airtime, again at wholesale rates, to mobile service providers. They would resell the call minutes to their customers under their own brand and under their own price packages. The thinking was that if independent distributors or dealers (the mobile service providers) competed with each other to sell airtime to their customers, that competition would in turn force them to make their suppliers (the network operators) reduce the wholesale airtime costs to service providers. Accordingly, Vodafone and Cellnet are obliged by their licences to provide airtime at wholesale rates to mobile service providers or resellers. It is not obvious that the policy has been wholly successful. OFTEL has therefore tried to change and relax the rules. However, Vodafone and Cellnet remain under obligations to sell airtime at wholesale rates and to sell it at a price which allows sufficient headroom or margin for independent mobile service providers to make a profit. The effect is that those two operators (but not Orange and One-2-One) are obliged to supply airtime at wholesale rates, when under normal competition rules they would not be so obliged.

Vodafone and Cellnet also have their own wholly owned subsidiaries which act as mobile service providers, and which therefore compete head-on with independent service providers. The obligation to provide airtime to independent service providers on reasonable terms, which leaves the service provider a margin to cover its reselling costs and to make a profit, is in fact a variant of the prohibition on undue discrimination placed on any operator having

SMP. Undue discrimination includes unfairly favouring a downstream business, such as a wholly owned mobile service provider.[3]

7.3.5 Calls and access tariffs

BT's 'Calls and Access' tariffs result from the obligation imposed on BT by its licence to supply capacity and access to its network to third parties at a price which excludes BT's retail costs. In effect, the tariffs enable third parties to sell a message conveyance service under their own brand, and providing their own billing, using BT's underlying services. It is a very similar concept to the obligation placed on mobile operators with SMP to supply airtime to service providers who re-sell it under their own brand. Again, the purpose is to offer choice and increase competition.

7.3.6 Local loop unbundling

Local loop unbundling is the jargon term for forcing BT to allow other operators to take over and run the copper pair 'local loop' connection between the BT local exchange and the end customer. Unbundling refers to the fact that the wires are physically transferred from BT's main frame at the exchange and reconnected to another operator's switch. The new operator then pays BT a set fee for each line, for the use and management, for its own benefit, of the line.

For a long time the UK Government was opposed to mandatory LLU, because it would mean that other operators would have no incentive to build competing infrastructure to reach mass consumers and to connect each home. Other European countries (notably France and Germany) favoured it as a 'quick fix' to introduce competition at the local level. The UK Government has now changed its policy, in part because of the implications for broadcasting. BT is now itself able to broadcast. The cable network operators (now consolidated into two groups) already provide a combined telephony and broadcast transmission service. In order to stimulate competition, other providers of telephony and broadcast services will be able to have access to BT's 'local loop' – the last line connection from the local exchange to the end customer. Developments in DSL, and in particular ADSL (asynchronous digital subscriber line), technology now mean that it is possible to send not only high-speed data down a traditional local line made of copper pairs, but also broadcast material. ADSL will allow BT and others to provide a comparable broadcast, high-speed data and voice service to that provided by ntl or Telewest over their coaxial and fibre optic cable networks.

LLU forces competition in the local loop, by enabling customers to switch between operators for a combined telephony and broadcast service. Normal competition rules did not oblige BT to do this.[4]

---

[3] The obligation to supply airtime at the wholesale rates and the DGT's ability to change the licence conditions in this respect was covered extensively in *R v Director-General of Telecommunications, ex parte Cellcom Ltd and others* [1999] ECC 314.

[4] A full analysis of how LLU will work can be found in *Access to Bandwidth: Proposals for Action* (London, OFTEL, 1999) and *Access to Bandwidth: Indicative Pricing and Principles* (London, OFTEL, 2000).

Each of the above measures is an obligation to supply imposed on BT, which it would not have been obliged to do under normal competition rules.

7.4 CONTROL OF BEHAVIOUR THROUGH MAINSTREAM COMPETITION RULES

In July 1995, OFTEL carried out a major review of the effectiveness of the rules contained in BT's licence and the conditions attached to it.[5] The licence conditions, especially those dealing with pricing, retail price control, network charge control and interconnection, were extremely detailed. This involved continuous intervention by OFTEL in relatively minor issues. Consideration was therefore given to whether a broadly written competition rule could be used to substitute for the many detailed licence conditions. After a long battle between OFTEL and BT (and, behind closed doors, between OFTEL and the DTI), BT eventually accepted the incorporation into its licence of the so-called 'fair trading condition' (FTC), which was a look-alike of the competition rules in the EC Treaty.[6] A similar condition was then incorporated in all other important licences granted under the Telecommunications Act 1984. The FTC has now been duplicated and hence replaced by the Competition Act 1998, Chapter I and Chapter II of which contain prohibitions in more or less identical terms to Arts 81 and 82 (ex 85 and 86), EC Treaty.

A full analysis of Arts 81 and 82 (ex 85 and 86) of the EC Treaty, and of the Chapter I and Chapter II prohibitions, is outside the scope of this work. We will focus here, therefore, on the special issues which arise when applying competition law to the telecommunication sector. For further guidance on how the competition rules apply to the particular circumstances of telecommunications, reference can be made to two sets of guidelines issued by the European Commission,[7] and also to the guidelines on the application of Chapter I and Chapter II prohibitions published by OFTEL.[8]

7.4.1 Mainstream competition rules: prohibition of anti-competitive agreements

EC and UK competition law prohibit agreements which have the object or effect of preventing, restricting or distorting competition. The prohibition covers not only written contracts, but also decisions by trade associations and 'concerted practices' (a gentlemen's agreement, or a mere exchange of

---

[5] *Effective Competition: Framework for Action* (London, OFTEL, 1995).
[6] BT appealed by way of judicial review against the licence modification: *R v Director-General of Telecommunications, ex parte BT* (unreported) Trans Ref CO 5596/96 20 December 1996 (QBD).
[7] See 'Guidelines on the Application of EC Competition Rules in the Telecommunications Sector' (1991) OJ C 233/02 and on the Notice Application of the Competition Rules to Access Agreements in the Telecommunications Sector: Framework, Relevant Markets and Principles' (1998) OJ C 265/02.
[8] *Application of the Competition Act in the Telecommunications Sector* (London, OFTEL, 2000).

confidential commercial information). The anti-competitive nature of an agreement is judged according to its actual or intended effects on competition; its legal form is irrelevant. The rules are mandatory and apply regardless of what particular law applies to a contract.

7.4.1.1 Agreements between undertakings which compete with each other ('horizontal agreements') Agreements between competitors which are likely to infringe the prohibition include (amongst others) those which:

(a)   directly or indirectly fix purchase or selling prices, or any other trading conditions, such as agreements between network operators as to prices, or discount levels offered to business or domestic customers;

(b)   limit or control production, markets, technical development or investment, such as an agreement to refuse to supply a particular type of service provider, or only to supply them at particular rates;

(c)   share markets or sources of supply, such as agreements to allocate customers or types of customer between competitors, or between distributors, dealers or service providers;

(d)   collude with competitors when tendering for big contracts;

(e)   exchange otherwise commercially confidential information, e.g., as to prices or imminent price rises, or as to volumes of business done with particular customers, and even exchange of information as to costs;

(f)   form joint ventures to develop or produce products which the undertakings could have offered separately.

There have so far not been traditional 'cartel' type cases relating to the pricing of telecommunication services, i.e. price information exchange or price collusion between network operators. The European Commission is, however, believed to be examining such allegations.

Horizontal agreements between competitors or potential competitors have been considered by the European Commission in the field of joint ventures to develop new products.

One type of joint venture agreement where competition issues do arise is in consortium arrangements to build long-distance cables or networks, such as for large-capacity conveyance internally within the UK, or for international routes, whether to other Member States or internationally, outside the EU, for example to the United States. Here, the following basic principles apply:

(a)   Normally, each participant in the joint venture, if it has an interest in a share of the capacity of the cable (for example, in the form of an IRU), should be free to use its share capacity as it wishes, including subleasing it to any customer it wishes to supply on terms that participant alone sets.

(b)   It should also be free to assign all or part of the benefit of the capacity – there should be no undue restrictions on a participant disposing of its share in capacity either outright, or by way of lease of capacity, subject to appropriate guarantees as respects on-going liabilities, e.g., for maintenance.

7.4.1.2 Agreements between suppliers and customers ('vertical agreements')
Agreements between suppliers and customers will also be caught by the prohibition where they unduly exclude market entry by competitors, or make this more difficult for them.

Restrictions in many so-called vertical agreements, between a supplier and its customer, are normally exempted (see the UK block exemption for vertical agreements: Competition Act 1998 (Land and Vertical Agreements) Exclusion Order 2000 (SI 2000 No. 310)). This is subject to two major exceptions, however:

(a)   However small an undertaking's market share, a restriction by the supplier on its commercial customer (such as a dealer) as to the price at which it resells the products (including services) will never be allowable.

(b)   A restriction as to the export of products (including services) will also always be prohibited.

A practical example of this principle would be a restriction by a network operator on the price at which an IA operator should sell its own services; this would be prohibited. Similarly, a restriction by a mobile network operator on the price at which a mobile service provider re-sells its airtime, or the format in which it packages airtime, would also be prohibited.

Where a restrictive vertical agreement does or may affect trade between EU Member States, Art. 81(1) (ex 85(1)) EC Treaty will also apply. This will be so particularly if an agreement, or a network of similar agreements, impedes entry to the UK market. The EC Block Exemption for distribution-type agreements applies only where the supplier has a market share below 30 per cent.[9]

Where either the supplier or the customer has a market share above 30 per cent tougher rules apply, for example, as respects exclusivity requirements, non-compete or 'most favoured customer' clauses. Thus, for example, a requirement by BT that its commercial customer should buy all its telephony requirements from BT, or locking in that customer for a unduly long period (say, over two to three years) may be prohibited.

Under the UK Exclusion Order, the Office of Fair Trading (OFT or OFTEL, in the telecommunications sector) is able to withdraw an exemption in individual cases. It is reasonable to assume that the OFT/OFTEL is likely to do so in cases where an operator's market share exceeds 25–30 per cent and the relevant restrictions significantly impede market entry.

7.4.1.3 Exemptions   Some agreements which do restrict competition may have wider benefits to economic efficiency or for consumers which more than offset their anti-competitive effect. These agreements are capable of exemption. The restrictions in them must be essential, however, to make the agreement work.

---

[9] EC Commission Regulation (EC) 2790/1999, 'Applying Art. 81(3) to certain categories of vertical agreements and concerted practices', (1999) OJ L 336/29/12/1999.

Exemption can be obtained in one of two ways:

(a)   the parties can apply to the Director General of Fair Trading (DGFT) or to the European Commission for an individual exemption; or
(b)   the parties can ensure that their agreements fit within the terms of an EC or UK block exemption. In essence, a block exemption sets out lists of terms of standard types of agreement which are acceptable, even though they are restrictive of competition.

The main EU block exemptions at present in force cover: exclusive dealership agreements and purchasing agreements; patent and other technology licensing agreements; agreements for joint research and development; and franchising agreements.

Undertakings unsure as to whether their agreement infringes the prohibitions can notify the agreement to the DGFT or to the European Commission with a view to obtaining a declaration of non-infringement (negative clearance), or for an individual exemption if no block exemption applies.

7.4.2   Mainstream competition rules: prohibition of abuse of dominant position

Both the EC Treaty and UK domestic competition law have special rules to stop anti-competitive behaviour which is an abuse by an undertaking of its dominant position. An undertaking (i.e. a corporate group taken as a whole) is likely to be dominant if it has a market share of a relevant product market of more than 40 per cent. In some circumstances an undertaking with an even lower market share can be dominant.

Markets are geographic (say, just one EU Member State, or an area within the United Kingdom) and by product. A product market exists where one product directly substitutes for another. It is often narrowly defined. For example, the European Court of Justice has held that bananas are a separate product market from other fruits such as apples or pears (*United Brands* v *Commission* (*'Chiquita'*) (Case 27/76) [1978] ECR 207); and vitamins A, B and C are each separate product markets (*Hoffmann-La Roche* v *Commission* (*'Vitamins'*) (Case 85/76) [1979] ECR 461). In telephony, the mobile market is separate from the market for services over fixed networks; the wholesale interconnection market is separate from the retail market; local leased lines are a separate product market from long-distance leased lines; there are distinct markets for wholesale services over particular international routes, e.g., London to the north-east coast of the United States; the business market is distinct from the mass consumer retail market; London is different from the rest of the United Kingdom; access (line rental) is a separate market from call conveyance.

Tougher standards apply to an undertaking which is dominant in any of these markets; its conduct may be an abuse, where the same conduct of a non-dominant undertaking would be lawful.

Typical examples of an abuse include, amongst others:

(a) predatory pricing – selling at below the marginal cost of production with the effect (even if not intended) of driving a competitor from the market, or severely damaging it;

(b) discriminatory pricing – charging customers in comparable positions different prices, where the costs of supply do not differ;

(c) purchase of a patent which 'teaches' the only practical alternative to the product made under the patent of the dominant supplier;

(d) any conduct to exclude a competitor from a market;

(e) excessive pricing – pricing which bears little or no relationship to the costs of supply; and

(f) refusal to supply a product or service.

Some of the tests used to work out if behaviour is an abuse have been refined for telecommunications. For example, price predation normally occurs where sales are made at below-average variable cost; they are presumed to be predatory if made at below marginal cost (the costs of direct labour, power and raw material, with no attribution for overhead). The marginal cost of conveying a telephone call is often very close to zero. Accordingly, average variable cost is replaced by long-run average incremented costs (LRAIC). Broadly, this involves linking the cost of an additional service to the additional cost of providing a further unit of capacity.

In practice in the United Kingdom, it is most often BT which is dominant in certain market segments. BT has internal systems in place designed to ensure that it does not breach EC and UK competition rules. In a few cases, abuse of a dominant position has been alleged against BT. The *BT Chargecard* (see Report of the Advisory Body on Fair Trading in Telecommunications, Telecommunications Act 1984 Draft Final Determination under Condition 18A of BT's Licence 1996) case is interesting, because although there appeared to be a clear 'margin squeeze' on other operators competing with BT in the downstream market, OFTEL had difficulty in applying the FTC (the licence condition now replaced by the Competition Act 1998) because of difficulties in isolating the relevant market. A BT customer can access BT's services by using a chargecard. Calls overseas using the card were very profitable for BT; domestic calls were supplied at a loss. Other suppliers of chargecard-based telephony services competed by buying in the underlying local conveyance element of the call (e.g., from a phone box) from BT. The price they had to pay BT for this connection was hardly less than BT's charge for the call to its retail chargecard customer. It left no margin to cover their costs. However, it appeared that the 'relevant market' in which BT's prices would have been predatory was not the market for national calls using a chargecard, but the market for both national and overseas calls together. Taken as a whole, BT's overseas service was profitable. The matter was settled by OFTEL using other powers under the licence.

Much academic comment has focused on an enhanced form of dominance – the concept of an 'essential facility', i.e. the ownership of a so-called bottleneck, through which all other operators must pass. The essence of the European Commission's position is that an 'essential facility' is more than mere dominance, but covers a close or total monopoly over a particular part of the network. Where an operator enjoys ownership or control it is obliged to supply all who request passage through it – whether an existing 'dependent' customer or a newcomer. Refusal to supply will be an abuse. The concept has never been properly tested. In practice obligations to supply are imposed by other rules specific to telecommunications. Thus the obligation to offer interconnection arises under the Interconnection Directive; the obligation to supply conditional access and related services flows from the Conditional Access Directive and regulations made under it. The concept of an 'essential facility' (and the related concept of an absolute obligation to supply on reasonable terms) has been severely curtailed by the European Court in *Oscar Bronner GmbH & Co.* v *Mediaprint Zeitungs und Zeitschriftverlag GmbH & Co. KG, and others* (Case C-7/97) [1998] ECR 1-7791.

7.5 SPECIAL COMPETITION RULES FOR TELECOMMUNICATIONS

The telecommunications sector has two features which distinguish it from many other markets: (i) it has an entrenched incumbent with a very high share of the residential market; and (ii) the barriers to market entry to build a national fixed (or mobile) network are very high. This means that the fixed and mobile network markets are supplied by a very few operators. Accordingly:

(a)   special competition rules have been put into BT's licence (as the ex-monopolist incumbent) to assist market entrants;

(b)   any operator which has significant market power (SMP), even if it is not 'dominant' using the normal tests under competition law, is subject to additional obligations not to discriminate in its dealings with other operators.

7.5.1   Special competition rules to assist market entry

There are two conditions in BT's licence which go beyond 'normal' competition rules. Both are designed to assist market entry. These are: (i) the prohibition on undue discrimination (and the related obligation to publish tariffs); and (ii) the rules to control cross-subsidy.

7.5.1.1   Prohibition on undue discrimination   Condition 57 of BT's licence provides that BT shall not 'show undue preference to, or exercise undue discrimination against, particular persons or persons of any class or description' as respects the provision of certain of its key services. Undue preference or discrimination extends to BT unfairly favouring any other business which it carries on.

The prohibition of undue discrimination not only covers the extremely low ('predatory') price offered on a selective basis, but also prevents BT from offering prices which discriminate more generally according to, for example, the size of customer or the geographical location of the customer, even if sales are made at a profit and cover BT's costs. Not every instance of price discrimination, even when exercised by a dominant operator, is inevitably an 'abuse' of its dominant position; it is too simplistic to say that once an operator is dominant it must justify all price differences on the basis of differences in the costs of supply. For example, even a dominant operator is able to, and frequently does, without committing an abuse, respond to price competition with a price which is still above fully allocated cost, but it will not necessarily be the same price charged to other customers in the same position. In practice, the prohibition of undue discrimination in BT's licence is a harsh rule. In effect it means that if BT faces price competition in just one segment (say, business lines to large customers), it has to reduce its tariff across the board, so that there is still some cost relationship between services supplied to different classes of customer. This has a 'knock-on' effect on the way BT has to comply with the retail price control imposed on it. Even if the price for a particular service is not subject to price control, if BT drops the price for that service, other (controlled) prices should fall in line with it.

Since the condition covers any discrimination, not just price discrimination, it is also a very flexible tool: between 1996 and 1999, some 12 orders for enforcement of the condition in BT's licence prohibiting undue discrimination were made against BT. An analysis of those orders shows that not all covered behaviour which was 'abusive' in an Art. 82 sense. For example, mere inefficiency by BT in connecting up a new entrant's pay phones (when BT had an installed base of 80,000 pay phones) was determined to be discriminatory against the new entrant; it probably was not 'abusive' applying Art. 82 (ex 86) tests.[10]

Whether discrimination is 'undue' is a very broad rule. For example, it would include the case where the incumbent operator is obliged to sell certain services at a published, non-discriminatory tariff, but as part of a 'deal' with a major customer it offers certain other services (e.g., advice on how to set up a private network) at a low cost. Although a broad rule, whether discrimination is 'undue' is normally decided according to one of two tests:

(a)   is the difference in treatment between two customers in a comparable position just too great; or, more normally

(b)   does the discrimination have a significantly adverse effect on competition.[11]

The licence condition prohibits not only undue discrimination against or between third parties, but also undue preference by the licensee in favour of its own downstream business. Thus, where BT supplies an essential input (e.g., local leased lines) to its own downstream, corporate network-management business, it must do so on terms identical to the terms on which it supplies those lines to third-party competitors. Further, it must not price the downstream business too low; it must allow a reasonably efficient competitor in the downstream market enough 'headroom' to make a living.

---

[10] See Director-General's Determination on 15 April 1997 as respects MainTel.
[11] See, e.g., Director-General's Provisional Order of 22 October 1996 as respects a marketing agreement between BT and BSkyB.

The obligation not to discriminate is backed up by a price publication rule (Condition 58 of BT's licence). Broadly, BT has to publish all its retail (residential and business) tariffs. The purpose of this rule is so that customers can check that they have the same tariff as is applied to others in the same or comparable position – that there has been no discrimination.

7.5.1.2 Unfair cross-subsidy Another area of behaviour where special rules are required (i.e., Art. 82 or its 'lookalike' in Chapter II of the Competition Act 1998 is not enough) is unfair cross-subsidy of a downstream operation, in which latter market BT may not be dominant.

Condition 78.12 of BT's licence gives the DGT a wide power to issue directions where:

(a)   BT has been, or is, unfairly subsidising or cross-subsidising all or any part of its businesses (as defined); and

(b)   the DGT is satisfied that the unfair subsidy or cross-subsidy has or could have a material effect on competition.

Condition 78.12 is not a prohibition on such subsidy but a power for the DGT to investigate and make a direction if he thinks fit on a case-by-case basis. Two examples of the exercise of this power show how it works.

In 1994, the DGT received complaints that BT was selling terminal equipment (faxes, etc.) at such low prices that independent suppliers of such equipment could not sell at a profit. The allegation was that BT was selling the equipment at a very low price so as to retain customers for its network services. The DGT made a direction that BT raise its prices of equipment to a level at which it made a reasonable profit (the current DGT has since withdrawn the direction, as the equipment market is now deemed fully competitive).[12]

In 1996, the DGT issued a similar direction that BT raise its prices for certain managed network services (sold through its BTMNS division). These were value-added services where BT put together systems for large corporate users for the transmission of data. These systems used BT lines and leased circuits. The allegation, in essence, was that BT agreed to put together systems for large users at a very low price, to ensure that such customers went on using BT's other underlying network services. Service providers who added value by putting together such systems, but who relied on BT's network to do it, were left no 'headroom' to make a profit.[13]

OFTEL's experience is that the conditions in BT's licence controlling cross-subsidy are notoriously difficult to operate. Examination of the accounts of a downstream part of, for example, BT's business is very labour-intensive and involves some difficult questions of cost allocation.

---

[12] Director-General's Direction of 22 September 1995 (amended 27 March 1997 and now revoked), 'Telephone Equipment Direction'.

[13] Director-General's Direction as respects BTMNS of 7 February 1996.

7.5.2 Special competition rules for operators with signficant market power (SMP)

The prohibition on undue discrimination is also imposed on all licensees who have SMP, or are what are termed 'well established operators' (a similar concept). The policy purpose is to impose stricter obligations on operators who, while not dominant in Art. 82/Chapter II terms, nevertheless enjoy market power because they are members of an oligopoly. The principle has now been taken up in the Interconnection Directive. Thus those operators designated by an NRA as having SMP must:

(a)   offer 'cost orientated' interconnection prices;
(b)   not discriminate as to the terms and conditions of interconnection which they offer;
(c)   offer to supply services to all who request them, unless there is a good reason not to.

BT and Kingston have been designated as being SMPs in the fixed market; and Vodafone and Cellnet have been so designated in the mobile market, but not in the wholesale market for interconnection.

Under a related concept, Cable & Wireless is still considered to have market power on a few international routes and cannot unduly discriminate as respects its prices for services to those destinations.

The special rules imposed on those operators having SMP is a recognition of the fact that, unlike other economic sectors, the provision of networks infrastructure (which is very expensive to build) may be in the hands of only 2 or 3 operators, no one of whom is dominant. Article 82, EC Treaty and the Competition Act will not catch any abusive behaviour on their part.

7.6   MARKET FAILURE OF COMPETITION – SECTOR-SPECIFIC RULES

In addition to competition rules which tilt the playing field against the incumbent, or which deal with SMP to assist or protect the new entrant, there are other special rules which are needed in the telecommunications sector to ensure that the competitive process works properly.

7.6.1   The limitations of general competition rules as instruments of regulation: some general points

The obligation for one operator to interconnect with, and deliver the calls of, another operator cannot be 'shoe-horned' into the framework of Arts 81 and 82 (ex 85 and 86) and, now, the Chapter I and Chapter II prohibitions of the Competition Act 1998. Some attempts have been made to suggest that ownership of a part of the network, and control by an operator of access to its own customers, is in some sense an 'essential facility', or bottleneck, to which the operator must allow others access; to refuse to do so would be an abuse of that operator's 'dominant' position in the 'market' made by the bottleneck. An often-cited example is the need for an operator to be able to deliver calls to a customer of another network operator. It is, however, very artificial to say that every operator (not just BT) which owns and controls the 'local loop' to its own customer is 'dominant', in competition law terms, in a 'market' which is access to each of its customers. Hence, the specific rules to require interconnection and delivery of calls will always be needed.

Price control is also outside the scope of normal competition rules. There has never been a case under Art. 82 (ex 86) of the EC Treaty, involving simple excessive pricing, i.e. overcharging because there is no competition. The EC cases on excessive pricing (which in themselves are few and far between) have all involved some form of exclusionary and/or discriminatory behaviour (see, e.g., *United Brands* v *Commission* ('*Chiquita*') (Case 27/76) [1978] ECR 207 and *General Motors Continental NV* v *EC Commission* (Case 26/75) [1975] EC 1367, [1976] 1 CMLR 95). The Commission's proceedings in 1997 against Deutsche Telekom in respect of its leased-line prices show that Art. 82 (ex 86) is an inadequate instrument of price control.[14] It is therefore reasonable to assume that it will rarely be possible to use the Chapter II prohibition in the Competition Act 1998 to control simple excessive pricing, without evidence of exclusionary behaviour or some form of price discrimination which has no objective justification and an adverse effect on competition.

Article 82 (ex 86) (and now the Chapter II prohibition) also has its limits in the context of controlling misuse of market power by a small group of companies, no one of which is dominant, but which together control the market – so-called joint dominance. It has been suggested that in certain situations two telecoms operators might have joint dominance. For example, BT and one cable operator might be the only two operators offering a service to residential customers in a particular area. We suggest that the idea that those two might be 'jointly' dominant is an artificial construct; if there are elements of behaviour, e.g., pricing, which need to be dealt with, they should be dealt with under the Fair Trading Act 1973, which has deliberately been left in place to deal with complex monopoly behaviour.

Lastly, conditional access must be considered. Conditional access is the technical means of access to a particular service – the 'set-top box' which enables you to unscramble a television signal or a digital message. The Conditional Access Directive[15] lays down detailed rules as to the terms on which other broadcasters can reach their customers through the set-top box and on which manufacturers can require a licence to make the boxes. It is not at all clear whether general competition law (in particular Art. 82 (ex 86), EC Treaty) could have been used to achieve the same result.

7.6.2 Limitations on general competition rules as instruments of regulation: some examples

Given the particular features of the telecommunications market, in particular the lack of effective competition in certain sectors, some additional rules have

---

[14] See European Commission Competition Report for 1998.
[15] Directive 95/47/EC on the use of standards for the transmission of television signals (1995) OJ L 281/51.

been put in place to deal with market failure, i.e. where market forces and competition do not provide a solution. We highlight below, in particular, rules relating to: number portability; retail price control for residential customers; network charge control; interconnection obligations; and price control over mobile termination rates.

7.6.2.1 Number portability Number portability is the right of a customer, when moving to a new operator, to retain his or her existing number, and not to have a new number allocated by the new operator. As a result of a detailed report by the then MMC in 1995, BT is now obliged to offer this facility. The costs of providing it are shared between BT and the operator taking over the customer. The purpose of mandating number portability is to make it easier for customers to switch supplier, hence sharpening competition between network operators for customers.

7.6.2.2 Retail price control The controls on BT's retail and network charges expire in July and September 2001. (See 4.14.2 for discussion of control updates.)

For the five years to 2001, retail price control covers line rental and the price for local, national and international calls. Controls are linked to the expenditure of the lowest spending 80 per cent of residential customers. The current cap for those customers is set at RPI − 4.5 per cent, over the five-year period of the control. There are special controls for small businesses and private leased circuits below 64 Kbits capacity. The basic principle is that price controls are only needed in markets which are not yet fully competitive.

The important point, from the perspective of the competition rules, is that those rules, and in particular the prohibition on BT exercising undue discrimination between one category of customer and another, impact on how BT is able to implement price changes as respects services still subject to price control. Thus, while, on the face of it, BT has flexibility in how it prices its services to the highest spending 20 per cent of its customers (which are outside the price cap), in practice BT cannot drop prices for one category of retail customers without dropping them for all.

Retail price control at present preserves a distorting feature of the UK retail price structure – the unbalanced tariff, where call prices are set, in relation to their cost, too high, and the cost of access (the monthly or quarterly rental) is set too low. This discourages people making calls. It remains to be seen what happens under the next retail price control.

7.6.2.3 Network charge control Under the network charge control, which applies to the charges which BT makes to other operators for interconnection, a cap of RPI − 8 per cent is applied for three baskets of non-competitive services and a safeguard cap of RPI + 0 per cent for services which are deemed to be prospectively competitive.

The same approach applies as with the retail price control (see 7.6.2.2 above), i.e. no control is applied in segments which are judged to be fully competitive; again BT is constrained, however, in relation to markets which are fully competitive by the obligation not to discriminate between one category of wholesale customer and another (an obligation reinforced by the terms of the Interconnection Directive (see Chapter 5)).

7.6.2.4 Interconnection obligations   Suffice it to say here that OFTEL has put forward the view that each operator has a monopoly, and is hence 'dominant', in a market which is comprised by the access which that operator has to each and every one of its customers for incoming calls. If that hypothesis stood up to close analysis, OFTEL and the NRAs could rely on the competition rules to force each operator to allow other operators to deliver calls to the terminating operator's customers and on reasonable terms, since a refusal by the latter to do so would be an abuse of each operator's dominant position in the 'market' for terminating calls on its own network.

This adventurous thinking has never been tested; the obligation to connect and deliver calls does not arise under the competition rules but under the interconnection rules. Once an operator has Annex II interconnection status to allow it to deliver its own customers' outgoing calls over other networks, it must deliver the incoming calls to those customers.

7.6.2.5 Mobile termination rates   The Chapter I and Chapter II prohibitions in the Competition Act 1998 (on restrictive agreements and abuse of a dominant position) were thought by some to be sufficient as a complete set of national domestic competition rules, because they parrot Arts 81 and 82, of the EC Treaty. The reality is that the EC competition rules are not a perfect template for national competition legislation. There still needs to be a mechanism to be able to look at unexpected anti-competitive behaviour, which is not automatically prohibited under the Art. 81/82 (ex 85/86) type-rules, and be able to order remedial action on a case-by-case basis. The price of calls to mobiles was just such a case.

Following a reference by the DGT to the then MMC, the MMC concluded that the market for delivering calls on to mobile networks was not fully competitive, if only because the terminating mobile operator's immediate customer (the fixed network operator, which had a call to deliver) was not actually paying the bill – it merely passed it on to its own customer. Accordingly, conditions have been put in the relevant licences so that the prices which the mobile network operators can charge for delivering each call to their network customers are controlled. Similarly BT's 'retention', i.e. the bit of money which it keeps as respects calls which start on its network, has been forcibly reduced.[16]

7.6.2.6 Co-location   In order to run interconnecting networked systems, it is often necessary for competing operators physically to place equipment or

---

[16] Cellnet and Vodaphone: Reports on references under s. 13 of the Telecommunications Act 1984 on the charges made by Cellnet and Vodafone for terminating calls from fixed-line networks: [House of Commons/Command Number 011 5154590] published 21 January 1999; British Telecommunications plc: A report on a reference under s. 13 of the Telecommunications Act 1984 on the changes made by BT plc for calls from its subscribers to phones connected to networks of Cellnet and Vodafone [House of Commons/Command Number 011 5154504] published 21 January 1999.

lines on the same premises, i.e. to 'co-locate' them. Some thought has been given as to whether the ex-monopoly national incumbent, which is dominant, by owning sites for equipment (line boxes, local exchanges, etc.) controls access to an 'essential facility'. In order to avoid being in breach of Art. 82 (ex 86) of the EC Treaty, or the Chapter II prohibition, it must (so the argument goes) share these sites with other operators, i.e. allow co-location.

This view has not been tested. In the UK, in practice, if there is an obligation on an operator (not just BT) to allow another to co-locate on its premises, this results not from Art. 82 (ex 86)/Chapter II,[17] but from its interconnection obligations, or under the rules requiring BT to unbundle its local loops (under Condition 83 of BT's licence and under EC Regulation 2887/2000).

7.7 PROCEDURES FOR ENFORCEMENT OF THE COMPETITION RULES

In the United Kingdom, supervision of the telecommunications market, as respects both the general competition rules contained in the Competition Act 1998 and the competition rules specific to telecommunications contained in the licences granted to run telecommunications systems, is in the hands of the DGT. The European Commission has jurisdiction to enforce the EC competition rules where the arrangements or conduct in question have a real effect on trade between EU Member States.

Both the EC and UK general competition rules are self-executing, i.e. affected third parties can enforce them by proceedings before the courts, by way of action for damages or for injunction (see *Garden Cottage Foods* v *Milk Marketing Board* [1984] AC 130, [1983] 3 CMLR 43). Competition rules specific to telecommunications, on the other hand, contained in licence conditions, can only be enforced by the DGT. Under the Competition Act 1998, the DGT has jurisdiction to enforce the Chapter I and Chapter II prohibitions (and investigate alleged breaches of them) where the conduct in question 'relates to commercial activities connected with telecommunications'. In practice the DGT has two distinct sets of powers to deal with allegations of anti-competitive behaviour in the telecommunications sector: (i) powers under the Competition Act 1998; or (ii) powers to enforce licence conditions (in particular the condition which prohibits undue discrimination, which is very broad in its scope).

7.7.1 Competition Act enforcement powers

Under the Competition Act 1998, the DGT has the same powers of investigation and enforcement in the field of telecommunications as the DGT has across the economy as a whole. Thus the DGT has power:

(a) to require any person (an individual or a company) to produce any document or information which he thinks relevant (s. 26(1), Competition Act 1998);

---

[17] See, e.g., *Access to Bandwidth: Delivering Competition in the Information Age* (London, OFTEL, 1999), para. 7.7.

(b)   to enter a company's premises on notice and require the production of documents and an explanation of what is in them (s. 27(5), Competition Act 1998);

(c)   to enter a company's premises forcibly, with a warrant issued by a judge, to search for such documents (s. 28(2), Competition Act 1998).

Where there is sufficient evidence of an infringement of the Chapter I or II prohibitions in the 1998 Act, the DGT has powers:

(a)   to give directions to bring the infringements to an end (ss. 32 and 33, Competition Act 1998);

(b)   to order interim measures to protect the position of affected parties or to preserve the position pending completion of the investigation (s. 35, Competition Act 1998);

(c)   to fine a company up to 10 per cent of its group's UK turnover where it has intentionally or negligently infringed either of the prohibitions.

These are severe powers.

7.7.2   Licence condition enforcement powers

Where there is an alleged breach of a competition rule in a licence the DGT's powers of both investigation and enforcement are weaker. Thus, the DGT can only order the disclosure of documents or information (s. 53, Telecommunications Act 1984) and has no power to enter a licensee's premises to search for evidence of a breach of licence condition. Similarly, the DGT's powers to enforce licence conditions are not as strong as under the Competition Act 1998:

(a)   Where a licensee is contravening, or has contravened, any conditions of its licence, and is likely to do so again, the DGT may make a provisional order (in effect an interim measure) (s. 16(2), Telecommunications Act 1984).

(b)   Where the DGT is satisfied of a past or ongoing breach, the DGT may make a final order (s. 16(1), Telecommunications Act 1984).

(c)   The DGT has no power to fine for past breach of a licence condition,[18] but once a licensee breaches his order the DGT may obtain a court order, breach of which would be in contempt of court. Third parties harmed by breach of an order of the DGT can enforce it themselves by actions in the courts for injunction or damages (s. 18(5), Telecommunications Act 1984).

There is no real indication, yet, of how the DGT will use his powers under the Competition Act 1998. Experience of the way in which the European Commission enforces the EC competition rules suggests that a great many

---

[18] Now that telecoms has been dropped from the Utilities Act 2000, we will have to wait for the Communications Bill in the next Parliament to cover this.

complaints will be settled informally. Certainly the majority of complaints to OFTEL alleging breaches by a licensee of a licence condition (about 80 per cent of which have at least, in the past, been levelled against BT) have been settled. Nevertheless, since 1995 the DGT has made some 16 orders for enforcement (again, mostly against BT), using powers under the Telecommunications Act 1984.

The practice of settling cases is supposed to free up OFTEL's resources to handle more serious infringements. The practice may have the reverse effect – 'soft' enforcement takes up more administrative time than a 'short, sharp shock'. It remains to be seen how much injured parties will seek to enforce their rights under the Competition Act 1998 directly, by action before the courts. However inefficient the process, it is most likely that the least expensive (and most effective) course will remain, as before, a complaint to OFTEL in the first instance. Another technique available to the complaining party is to generate adverse publicity for the undertaking against which a complaint is made.

OFTEL may make claims to be a competition authority, with special expertise in telecommunications. In reality it is much more than that; it is a regulatory agency with powers to manage the market going way beyond those of a normal competition body.

7.8 STRUCTURAL CONTROLS: REGULATION THROUGH COMPETITION LAW

7.8.1 EU policy: main themes

7.8.1.1 Introduction   The formal legal position of the European Commission is that mergers (which fall to be dealt with under Council Regulation 4069/89 ('the Merger Regulation')) and joint ventures (where they need clearance, either under the Merger Regulation or under Art. 81(3) (ex 85(3)) of the EC Treaty) are assessed according to whether they will give rise to a dominant position or the potential exercise of undue market power and hence have an adverse effect on competition. In practice, the Commission's approach to mergers is considerably more nuanced. The following are the key features of the European Commission's current approach to mergers in telecommunications and related sectors:

(a)   The EU has a policy of encouraging network infrastructure competition wherever possible, as does the UK Government, i.e. to generate competition, competing physical networks should be built; however, the Commission places a greater emphasis than the UK Government on stimulating competition between service providers.

(b)   The Commission is particularly vigilant to ensure that the national incumbent ex-monopolist in each Member State does not use a merger as a means further to restrict entry into its national market.

(c)   Perhaps of greatest concern to the Commission is the fact that vertical integration between a telecommunications network operator and an operator in another sector (e.g., a broadcaster) can be as great a threat to competition as consolidation between network operators.

(d) US investment into the European Community raises particular issues, including the related issue of EU operators' access to US markets.

Each of these key features is discussed in more detail below.

7.8.1.2 EC jurisdiction over structural concentrations A detailed explanation of the scope of the EC Merger Regulation and its procedures is outside the scope of this work. For the purposes of the analysis which follows, it is sufficient to bear in mind these key features of the European regime:

(a) The EC Merger Regulation applies to mergers where the combined turnover, in their last financial year, of all the parties involved in the concentration exceeds 5 billion Euro. In such cases Member States cannot apply their own national merger controls. The Regulation does not apply, however, where the combined turnover of the parties within the Community (disregarding turnover elsewhere in the world) arises as to at least two-thirds in one and the same Member State; in that case the merger control procedures of that Member State apply.

(b) The EC Merger Regulation will also apply where the turnover in at least three Member States of at least two of the undertakings concerned in the concentration is above certain thresholds, and the combined worldwide turnover of all the undertakings concerned exceeds 2.5 billion Euro; in such a case the national rules of any Member State will also not apply.

(c) Under Art. 21(3) of the EC Merger Regulation, although Member States may not apply their national *competition* rules to a merger falling under the Regulation, they may take measures to protect their 'legitimate interests'. These include 'public security', 'plurality of the media' and 'prudential rules'. The second criterion is particularly important for Member States wishing to ensure a wide variety of choice in broadcasting and newspapers; this exception to the clear division of responsibility between Brussels and the Member States has a direct impact on the approach to mergers in the telecommunications sector.

(d) So-called 'concentrative joint ventures' (where the parties give up independent activity in the field of the joint venture) are normally dealt with under the EC Merger Regulation; where the parties both remain as independent suppliers in this field, or related fields, clearance is dealt with under Art. 81(3) (ex 85(3)) EC Treaty. (See, e.g., Commission Decision 96/546/EC (1996) OJ L 239/23 (*Atlas Decision*, Case No. IV/35.337); and Commission Decision 96/547/EC (1996) OJ L 239/57 (*Phoenix/Global One Decision*, Case No. IV/35.617), the joint ventures between France Télécom, Deutsche Telekom and Spring.)

7.8.2 EC merger and joint venture clearances

7.8.2.1 Encouragement of network and service competition Generally, the European Commission has adopted a positive approach to structural mergers and joint ventures which lead to the building of significant new infrastructure.

In 1999, the Commission cleared (under Art. 81 (ex 85), EC Treaty, rather than under the Merger Regulation) a joint venture to build a long-distance backbone network, partly along the French railways. The joint venture was set up by SNCF, which has control of the French rail network, and Cegetal, itself a joint venture owned by Mannesmam, Vivendi (originally the French water utility), BT and SBC International. The main benefit of the joint venture would be to provide a second wholesale network operator in France, to compete with France Télécom. The joint venture was therefore cleared without any conditions being attached.

7.8.2.2 National incumbent and ease of entry to national markets Several EU mergers and joint ventures have involved link ups between one or more national, ex-monopolist, incumbent network operations. Where these have occurred, particular concerns have been as follows:

(a)   Where a national incumbent seeks to enter a downstream market on a joint venture basis with another national incumbent, it must make available its own network facilities on equal terms to competitors in that downstream market.

(b)   National incumbents must not link arms to impede market entry in other ways.

Both the Infonet case (*Infonet* (1992) OJ C7/03) and the Atlas ((1995) OJ C 337) and Phoenix ((1996) OJ L 239) joint ventures between France Télécom and Deutsche Telekom (which latter have now ended in tears) show these points.

Infonet is a company that provides value-added services – managed networks for large corporate users, primarily for data transmission. To do this it uses leased lines to build private or virtual private networks for its customers, based on the X25 packet switch. In 1987, 25 per cent of the company was owned by Computer Sciences Corporation of the United States, and the remaining 75 per cent was held in varying proportions by 12 national telephone companies – including, in the Community, France Télécom, Deutsche Telekom, and the Dutch PTT. As its 'price' for exemption, under what is now Art. 81(3) (ex 85(3)), EC Treaty, the Commission required that:

(a)   the telecommunications operator shareholders in Infonet established in the Community had to make available leased lines to third parties on the same terms and conditions as they were made available to Infonet;

(b)   where the national incumbent telecommunications operator shareholder in Infonet acted as the Infonet distributor in its national territory, the European-based national telecommunications operator shareholders in Infonet must not cross-subsidise that business.

The terms of the undertakings given by the national telecommunications operators based in Community Member States were very loosely drafted. The

Commission learned, not for the first time, how difficult it is in practice to impose, monitor and properly enforce behavioural undertakings, as distinct from requiring structural change as a condition for clearance.

Phoenix/GlobalOne, the joint venture of the respective overseas businesses of France Télécom and Deutsche Telekom, raised the same policy issues as Infonet, but written much larger.

Atlas was a joint venture set upon a 50:50 basis by France Télécom and Deutsche Telekom to provide corporate value-added services in Europe. Phoenix/GlobalOne was set up by Atlas, with a participation by Sprint, to provide corporate telecommunications services, and traveller and carrier services for other operators on both a regional and a global basis. Exemption of both joint ventures was conditional:

(a)   Deutsche Telekom and France Télécom could not offer leased-line or PSTN/ISDN services to Sprint or any joint venture entity on more favourable terms than those offered to third parties.

(b)   Telecommunications services must also be offered on non-discriminatory terms.

(c)   There should be no discrimination between the joint ventures and third parties as to the timing or manner of introduction of new network interfaces.

Many of the principles developed and applied to the joint venture partners in these cases are now applied generally to all operators designated as having SMP. (See further Chapter 4.)

7.8.2.3   The threats posed by vertically integrated telecommunications operators   This book is about telecommunications; it is not about broadcasting. However, in order to understand EU (and UK) policy towards structural change in the telecommunications sector, it should be remembered that telecommunications businesses will always look for the opportunity for a second revenue stream from their networks, for example, by providing broadcast material as well as just transmitting it.

Telecommunications is about conveying messages; a telecommunications operator makes its money from conveying millions of messages. In the UK, the cable companies have a dual source of revenue from conveying both telephone messages and broadcast material (feature films, news programmes and other screened entertainment). Significant extra revenue can also be earned by providing the message itself. Network operators may look for additional revenue through providing their own programme material.

Several telecommunication operators have sought to maximise revenue by integrating backwards into providing the message itself and integrating downstream to provide various types of value added services. The European Commission has had to consider several such cases.

British Interactive Broadcasting ('OPEN') (BIB) was a joint venture set up by BT, BSkyB (owned as to 39 per cent by NewsCorporation), HSBC (Midland Bank) and Matsushita. Its purpose was to provide digital interactive television services, so that banks, travel agents and supermarkets can interact directly with customers. The services would be integrated with other services such as broadcast programmes (which could also be interactive, such as voting in quiz shows) and Internet services, such as e-mail, downloading music or games, or Internet access.

The primary concern, in competition policy terms, was that these services had to be accessed through the set-top box, for which BSkyB, or related companies, own the intellectual property rights. BT, through using other technology, was at least a potential competitor to BSkyB to provide interactive digital services. The joint venture therefore at least restricted potential, rather than actual present, competition between them.

The Commission imposed a series of detailed conditions to the exemption it granted to the BIB joint venture for seven years. The main conditions imposed were as follows:

(a)   Retailers of the set-top boxes could not require a customer also to take BSkyB's Pay TV services when he or she buys a set-top box.

(b)   Measures to protect the position of distributors of programme channels who use other platforms.

(c)   BT had to dispose of its interests in its cable franchises (which would compete with the service).

(d)   Measures to control the cross-subsidy of the sale price of the set-top box.

(e)   Measures to make set-top box interface information available to third parties in a timely manner.

These conditions highlight the Commission's concern not to allow excess market power to those who control bottlenecks in the delivery of programme material.

Bertelsmann/Kirch/Premiere (Case IV/M.799) (1999) OJ L 53/1 and *Deutsche Telekom/Beta Research* (Decision 1999/54) (1999) OJ L 53/31 brought into sharp focus the Commission's understandable objections to excessive market power in the telecommunications sector through vertical integration. The proposals would have brought together a variety of interests to provide a package of digital Pay TV services: set-top box technology, broadcasting facilities (Bertelsmann), access to cable and/or satellite networks (Bertelsmann and Deutsche Telekom), and programming content (Kirch). The Commission blocked both proposals. The contribution of technologies would, the Commission held, lead to bottlenecks in the provision of Pay TV and similar programme services. The mergers would have further strengthened, to an unacceptable extent, Kirch's dominant position in the provision of Pay TV services.

7.8.2.4 Transatlantic market entry   In BT/MCI (Case No. IV/M.856, BT/MCI Commission Decision 97/815 (1997) OJ L 336/1) (lapsed), the proposed merger between BT and MCI in the event did not go ahead (MCI merged with WorldCom instead – see below). Nevertheless, the proposed merger raised some interesting issues of transatlantic trade policy where there would have been a link up between a major European and a major American telco. MCI's position in the UK market (and in other EU Member States) was weak. In the UK there was no overlap between BT's and MCI's respective businesses in the residential market; there was little overlap in the business market. Nevertheless, BT and MCI would have had a powerful joint position in a distinct market, namely, the provision of wholesale capacity on transatlantic routes. Accordingly, as the price for letting this merger go through, the European Commission would have imposed requirements as to access to that capacity, and in particular required BT and MCI to dispose (by outright sale or grant of IRUs) of overlapping capacity in the eastern end of the transatlantic routes, which the Commission saw might be a bottleneck. There were two other interesting features in this proposal:

(a)   The fact that the merger needed approval under the EC Merger Regulation did not stop the UK DGT seeking to place additional controls on BT on non-competition grounds (which Art. 21(3) of the EC Merger Regulation, referred to at 7.8.1.2 above, allows a Member State to do) to protect the legitimate interest of consumers in the United Kingdom. In this case the DGT (had the merger gone ahead) would have placed a 'ring fence' around BT's UK business, so that it would not have been unduly exposed to improvident overseas investment by BT, to the detriment of the UK consumers. (See *Domestic Obligations in a Global Market*, OFTEL, 1997.)

(b)   Some other US operators appear to have used the EC merger clearance process to seek to secure other concessions from BT. Thus it appears that they sought to lean on the US regulatory agencies to approve the merger under US merger control rules only provided the UK Government were to change its then policy on local loop unbundling (see 7.3.6 above), thereby hoping to gain greater access to the UK market for US operators.

The Vodafone/Airtouch merger (*Vodafone/Airtouch*, Case IV/M.1430 (1995) OJ C 295/2) led to the creation of the largest worldwide mobile network operator, supplying service in many EU Member States and in the United States. Since there was no overlap between the two groups' geographic coverage (EU and US respectively), the merger was cleared without the European Commission imposing any conditions.

MCI/WorldCom was the first case where the Commission looked specifically at the position of operators in the provision of Internet, as distinct from conventional switched voice telephony (see Case IV/M.1069 *WorldCom/MCI* Commission Decisions (1999) OJ L 116/1). The Commission made, over several months, an in-depth investigation of the various submarkets of the Internet. It concluded that the merger would result in a dominant position in the provisions of top level or universal Internet connectivity. As a condition of the merger, MCI was forced to dispose of various parts of its Internet-related businesses.

The BT/AT&T (Case IV/JV.15-*BT/AT&T*) joint venture has been set up to provide global telecommunications services to multinational companies and international carrier services to other telecommunication network operators. The European Commission, in a Phase II investigation lasting four months, looked closely at these markets and the distinct markets for traffic on the UK/US routes and international voice telephony markets in the UK. On the main markets it found that, although the parties had a high share of the relevant markets (between 30 per cent and 50 per cent), they had a much lower, combined share of capacity, which was causing prices to fall. The joint venture, as originally structured, would nevertheless have adversely affected some specific UK markets. As a condition, some UK businesses were disposed of and OFTEL imposed some additional conditions in BT's licence.

The common thread in each of these cases is that where operators are based on both sides of the Atlantic, the European Commission will not raise substantive objections to mergers designed to give the combined entity global coverage.

7.8.3   UK policy towards mergers and joint ventures

At paragraphs 7.2 and 7.3 above, we discussed how the UK Government has sought to 'design' the structure of the UK telecommunications market and how it has adapted that design over time in the light of experience. The legal instruments to control mergers have been also used to support this policy of market manipulation.

7.8.3.1   Fair Trading Act 1973   Where a merger falls under the EC Merger Regulation, the UK Government has no jurisdiction to block the merger, or to impose conditions under the Fair Trading Act 1973. The UK merger control provisions will, however, cover mergers below the thresholds at which the EC Merger Regulation would apply. Mergers fall within the Fair Trading Act 1973 either where the gross assets of the undertaking to be acquired exceed £70 million, *or* where both parties are in the same product market (which can be narrowly defined) and the merger will bring their combined market share in the United Kingdom to, or increase it above, 25 per cent.

7.8.3.2   UK policy themes   Vertical integration has been of particular concern to the OFT and the DTI in looking at mergers which needed approval under the Fair Trading Act 1973.

Another concern of the UK Government has been to ensure that UK-based companies are able to compete effectively in overseas markets, to take advantage of the head start which they had as a result of privatisation occurring earlier in the UK than elsewhere.

As stated in Chapter 3, the basic thrust of UK Government policy since the White Paper on Duopoly Review in 1991 (and indeed before that) has been to encourage the building of competing physical networks. Although obvious, it should be stated: BT, as the incumbent ex-monopolist in the UK, has never been allowed to buy further capacity by acquiring a competitor. There has, however, been no restriction on BT building further capacity. By the same token, after 1995 there was no restriction on the merger of franchised cable licensees, where the franchisees did not compete in the same exclusively franchised areas.

7.8.4 UK treatment of mergers and joint ventures in the telecommunications sector

7.8.4.1 Consolidation of cable operators In the late 1980s, about 130 exclusive regional franchises were granted to some 70 different companies. By 1998, a process of consolidation had reduced the number of cable franchise operators to three – Telewest, CWC (Cable & Wireless) and ntl. This happened with Government encouragement. Ntl has now acquired CWC's cable business.

Ntl's acquisition of CWC was the first acquisition by one cable company of another to be referred to the Competition Commission. The reasons for the referral to the Competition Commission were not because of the combined market power of ntl and CWC in the retail fixed network telecommunications market, but because of the merger's potential effect on the wholesale market for Pay TV content. In the event the merger of ntl and CWC cable franchise businesses was cleared without conditions, partly because the Competition Commission felt that OFTEL and the ITC together had sufficient regulatory powers to handle any misuse of market power in the broadcasting markets.

7.8.4.2 Vertical integration with a telco Vivendi, the French water, utility and communications conglomerate, which also has a 49 per cent in Canal Plus, bought 24.9 per cent in BSkyB, the leading UK supplier of Pay TV services. The merger was referred to the Competition Commission because of concerns as to (i) the acquisition of broadcasting rights for sports and films, and (ii) the supply of conditional access technology.

The Competition Commission concluded that BSkyB's position as the acquirer of national sports rights was a strong one, but the merger would not materially enhance it. It also concluded that the respective interests of BSkyB and Vivendi in the NDS and SECA set-top box technology would not materially restrict the availability of such technology to third parties.

7.9 OUTSTANDING POLICY ISSUES

The shape of telecommunications markets is changing very quickly, but a few comments on the approach to merger control policy can be made:

(a) It is extremely difficult for merger control agencies (in the UK or the European Commission) to predict or plan market structure, even a few years ahead. Just as politicians are charged with being slaves to the outdated theories of dead economists, so merger control agencies need to be very wary of focusing too heavily on the problems of last year (cross-subsidy by the ex-monopolist of one service by another, market access, price control, etc.).

(b) At the other extreme, many say that the Internet has developed free of regulation and therefore telecommunications regulation can move in the same direction. This view is certainly misguided. As the Internet increases in reach and becomes a mass consumer service, various issues come sharply into focus: universal service obligations, pricing of bottlenecks, interoperability of systems and networks. All of these are real, practical consumer issues which merger control agencies will always need to control carefully in order to be seen to be protecting the public interest.

CHAPTER EIGHT

European Union Telecommunications Law

Ian Walden

8.1 INTRODUCTION

The past decade has seen an extraordinary level of regulatory activity in the telecommunications sector within the European Union (EU). Well over 100 different directives, decisions, regulations, recommendations and resolutions, relating to every aspect of the industry, have been adopted since 1984.[1] Such activity brings into sharp relief a point raised in Chapter 1 of this book: that market liberalisation must not be confused with concepts of market deregulation. From a UK perspective, European regulatory intervention in the telecommunications sector has seldom touched the wider public consciousness, largely due to the developments that had already been put in place under the Telecommunications Act 1984. However, some Member States have experienced significant domestic political consequences following on from European Commission initiatives in the area, such as public sector industrial action.

The basis for Commission involvement in the telecommunications market has primarily been founded on two different strands of European Treaty law: competition law (Arts 81–86 (ex 85–90)) and the establishment of the 'Internal Market' (Art. 95 (ex 100a)). The former Articles have been used to open up national markets to competition, while the latter has addressed competition issues between national markets, through harmonisation measures. Initiatives within each area have been the responsibility of different

---

[1] Council Recommendation 84/549/EEC concerning the implementation of harmonisation in the field of telecommunications (1984) OJ L 298/49.

departments of the European Commission – harmonisation measures originating within the Information Society Directorate-General and liberalisation issues residing primarily with the Competition Directorate-General.[2]

The development of EU telecommunications policy and legislation can be broadly distinguished into three phases. In the first phase, between 1987 and 1993, the objective was the liberalisation of telecommunications equipment and certain service sectors, while preserving for the incumbent the provision of network infrastructure, seen by many as a natural monopoly. In order to protect the network, it was believed that it was necessary to safeguard the revenues of the incumbent. As the provision of voice telephony services constituted the incumbent's main source of income, such services were categorised as a 'reserved service', not subject to the process of liberalisation. The Commission outlined its initial position on the role of telecommunications in the creation of the Single Market in a Green Paper of 1987.[3] This Paper set out three basic principles upon which the regulatory framework would be established:

(a)   liberalisation of areas currently under a monopoly provider;
(b)   opening access to telecommunication networks and services, through harmonisation and the development of minimum standards;
(c)   full application of the competition rules.

In the second phase, from 1993 to date, full market liberalisation became politically acceptable as concerns about the impact of liberalisation failed to materialise. In parallel, and somewhat in contrast to the liberalisation strand, telecommunications has also become an aspect of the policy to promote Trans-European Networks (TENs), established under the Treaty on European Union. Under TENs, the concept of harmonisation was extended beyond the negative integration of national markets, to a more positive objective of 'promoting the interconnection and interoperability of national networks as well as access to such networks' (Art. 154 (ex 129b)).[4]

The key commitment on liberalisation came on 22 December 1994, when the Council of Ministers committed themselves to the target date of 1 January 1998 for full liberalisation of the voice telephony monopoly and telecommunications infrastructure in the majority of Member States.[5] The fact that such a fundamental change in the legal framework governing a market was undertaken and substantially achieved in a relatively short period of time illustrates the considerable degree of consensus between Member States, the Community institutions and industry itself. However, the reality of a fully

---

[2] Formerly known as DG-XIII and DG-IV respectively.
[3] Commission Communication on the Development of the Common Market for Telecommunications Services and Equipment, COM (87) 290 final of 30 June 1987. See also Commission Communication on the Way to a Competitive Community-Wide Telecommunications Market in the Year 1992, COM (88) 48 final of 9 February 1988.
[4] See generally Sauter, W., *Competition Law and Industrial Policy in the EU* (Oxford, Clarendon Press, 1997), chap. 5.
[5] Council Resolution of 22 December 1994 on the principles and timetable for the liberalisation of telecommunications infrastructures, (1994) OJ C 379/4.

competitive market is likely to take considerably longer, as the divergent interests involved emerge and are fully expressed during the process of implementation.

A third phase of EU telecommunications policy can be seen emerging from the Commission's 1999 Communication Review.[6] The most distinctive feature of this developing landscape is the issue of convergence, which is occurring between previously distinct industries, particularly the telecommunications, broadcasting and information technology sectors. As a result of the review, the Commission published a package of six legislative measures aimed at broadening the scope of the regulatory framework, to embrace all forms of 'electronic communications networks and services'. The proposals are also intended to simplify the legal framework by moving towards greater reliance on the application of general European competition rules (see 8.5 below, and Chapter 5).

The growth of the Internet and related services has also been the subject of considerable regulatory attention within the EU over recent years. Inevitably, aspects of the resultant legislative framework impact on the telecommunications sector, such as ISPs. Under the E-Commerce Directive, for example, the mere transmission of information or provision of access to a communications network is granted immunity from liability arising from the nature of the information being communicated.[7] However, such content-based regulations are beyond the scope of this chapter.

This chapter is broadly divided into two parts: the first part reviews the development and key components of the EU regulatory framework; the second part examines particular issues addressed within the framework. It is not the objective of this chapter to provide a detailed analysis of every European legal instrument in the field, in part because many are examined in detail in other chapters of the book. It is designed to place this mass of laws, decisions and regulations into a comprehensible framework.[8]

8.2 LIBERALISATION OF THE EU TELECOMMUNICATIONS MARKET

The role of the European Commission's Competition Directorate-General in the development of EU policy in the telecommunications sector has been very considerable. Indeed, the manner in which EU competition law has been applied to the telecommunications sector provides an important case study of the significance of competition law within the *acquis communautaire*. In

---

[6] See Commission Communication, 'Towards a new framework for electronic communications infrastructure and associated services: The 1999 Communications Review', COM (1999) 539, 10 November 1999, at p. vi.
[7] Directive 2000/31/EC of the European Parliament and of the Council on certain legal aspects of information society services, in particular electronic commerce, in the Internal Market, (2000) OJ L 178/1, at Art. 12. See also a similar limitation of liability provision in the Common Position of the Draft Directive on the harmonisation of certain aspects of copyright and related rights in the Information Society (14 September 2000), at Art. 5(1).
[8] See also Commission Staff Document, 'Europe's Liberalised Telecommunications Market – A Guide to the Rules of the Game', October 2000.

particular, Art. 86 (ex 90) of the Treaty establishing the European Community bestows a supervisory function upon the Commission, supported by special law-making powers. Therefore, in addition to the more traditional forms of regulatory intervention by a competition authority against undertakings engaged in anti-competitive practices, the Commission could require Member States fundamentally to alter the terms of entry into a particular market.

The first indications of the potential impact of European competition law arose from a Commission decision against the UK incumbent, British Telecommunications (BT), for an 'abuse of dominant position' under Art. 82 (ex 86) of the Treaty of Rome. The decision concerned a 'scheme' adopted by BT prohibiting private message-forwarding agencies in the UK from relaying telex messages received from and intended for relay to another country (see Decision 82/861, (1982) OJ L 360/36). The Commission's decision was appealed by the Italian Government to the European Court of Justice, while the British Government intervened in support of the Commission (*Re British Telecommunications: Italy v Commission* (Case 41/83) [1985] 2 CMLR 368).

One issue for the Court to decide was whether BT, as a public body, was subject to the competition rules of the Treaty of Rome. The Court found that despite its public sector status, BT was operating as an 'undertaking' for the purposes of Art. 82 (ex 86). It noted that any regulatory powers that had been given to BT were strictly limited and, therefore, the particular scheme in question 'must be regarded as forming an integral part of BT's activities as an undertaking' (para. 20). In a subsequent decision, the Court confirmed that Art. 82 (ex 86) was applicable to 'undertakings' holding a dominant position even where that position arose through law rather than the activities of the undertaking itself (*Centre Belge d'Etudes de Marché-Télé-Marketing v Compagnie Luxembourgeoise de Télédiffusion SA and Information Publicite Benelux SA* (Case 311/84) [1986] 2 CMLR 558).

The Italian Government also argued that BT was exempt from the competition rules by virtue of being entrusted with the provision of services of 'general economic interest', under Art. 86(2) (ex 90), which could be threatened by the loss of revenue resulting from the provision of private message-forwarding services. The Court held that it was for the Commission, under Art. 86(3), to ensure the application of this provision and there was no evidence that such activities would be detrimental to the tasks assigned to BT (paras 28–33). The Court also noted that BT's statutory monopoly extended only to the provision and operation of telecommunication networks, not to the supply of services over such networks (para. 22).

The *British Telecom* case was a landmark decision in the development of EU policy in the telecommunications sector and led to further investigations by the competition authorities into the activities of European incumbent operators. In 1988, the Commission took the almost unprecedented step of issuing a Directive under Art. 86(3) (ex 90) of the EC Treaty, on competition in the market for telecommunications terminal equipment (the Equipment Directive). A further Directive followed on telecommunication services in

1990 (the Services Directive). The scope of such 'Commission' Directives was viewed by a number of Member States as an illegal exercise of the Commission's competence. Both Directives were challenged before the European Court of Justice, but were decisively upheld (see 8.2.1 below).

The Commission has therefore applied European competition law to the activities of telecommunications operators through behavioural and structural controls. The former have been pursued both in detailed legislative instruments, in respect of telecommunications equipment and services (see 8.2.3 and 8.2.4 below), and through the imposition of behavioural undertakings as conditions for the approval of certain commercial agreements. Structural controls have been imposed primarily through investigations and decisions relating to agreements, joint ventures and merger activities in every aspect of the sector. Such regulatory intervention has extended to alliances and mergers between national incumbents (e.g., *France Télécom and Deutsche Telekom* (Case No. IV/35.337 – Atlas) (1996) OJ L 239/23; *Telia and Telenor* (Case Comp/M.1439) (2001) OJ L 40/1), in the mobile sector (e.g., *Vodafone Airtouch and Mannesmann* (Case No. Comp/M.1795, 12/4/00), concerning the Internet infrastructure (e.g., *WorldCom and MCI* (Case IV/M.1069) (1999) OJ L 116/1), and with providers of content (e.g., *AOL and Time Warner* (IP/00/1145: 11/10/00); see further Chapters 5 and 7). The Commission has been concerned to protect the interests of European consumers and industry against the inevitable commercial pressures created by the developing global economy.

The Commission has also issued guidelines on the applicability of competition law to the telecommunication sector.[9] Such 'soft law' is designed to provide operators with legal certainty, although it has no formal legal basis. The promotion of competition has also led to the adoption of measures concerning the procurement practices of telecommunication operators operating under special or exclusive rights, primarily national incumbent operators.[10]

The process of telecommunications liberalisation in Europe has been underpinned by certain legal concepts, specifically those of 'special or exclusive rights' and 'essential requirements'.

8.2.1 'Special or exclusive rights'

As discussed at 8.2 above, Art. 86(1) (ex 90) of the EC Treaty concerns 'public undertakings or undertakings to which Member States grant special or exclusive rights'. The primary mechanism by which the Commission decided to liberalise national telecommunications markets, under the Equip-

---

[9] See Guidelines on the Application of EEC Competition Rules in the Telecommunications Sector (1991) OJ C 233/2; and Commission Notice on the application of the competition rules to access agreements in the telecommunications sector – framework, relevant markets and principles (1998) OJ C 265, p. 2.

[10] For example, Directive 93/38/EEC coordinating the procurement procedures of entities operating in the water, energy, transport and telecommunication sectors (1993) OJ L 199/84, as amended by Directive 98/4/EC (1998) OJ L 101/1.

ment and Services Directives, was by requiring Member States to withdraw the grant of any such 'special or exclusive rights' in respect of such activities. Rather than simply addressing the *exercise* of such rights, the Commission went further and challenged the continued *existence* of such rights. Their existence was seen as distorting competition within the markets at Community level; while their abolition would not 'obstruct, in law or in fact, the performance' of any service of 'general economic interest' (Art. 86(2)), such as universal service, which had been entrusted to undertakings granted such 'special or exclusive rights'.

Member States challenged both Directives before the European Court of Justice (*French Republic (with Italy, Belgium, Germany & Greece) v Commission of the European Communities* (Case C-202/88) [1991] ECR I-1223; and *Kingdom of Spain and others (France, Belgium, Italy) v Commission of the European Communities* (joined cases C-271/90, C-281/90, C-289/90) [1992] ECR I-5833). The Court found in the Commission's favour in respect of the withdrawal of exclusive rights, but upheld the claims of the Member States in respect of the limitation imposed on the granting of special rights. The Court held that neither the Directives' provisions nor the recitals specified what constituted 'special rights' or the reasons that such rights were contrary to the provisions of the Treaty, therefore such provisions were void.

As a consequence, the Commission amended the Services Directive to clarify the distinction between 'exclusive rights' and 'special rights':

– 'exclusive rights' means the rights that are granted by a Member State to one undertaking through any legislative, regulatory or administrative instrument, reserving it the right to provide a telecommunication service or undertake an activity within a given geographical area . . .

– 'special rights' means rights that are granted by a Member State to a limited number of undertakings, through any legislative, regulatory or administrative instrument, which, within a given geographical area,

   – limits to two or more the number of such undertakings, otherwise than according to objective, proportional and non-discriminatory criteria, or

   – designates, otherwise than according to such criteria, several competing undertakings as being authorised to provide a service or undertake an activity, or

   – confers on any undertaking or undertakings, otherwise than according to such criteria, legal or regulatory advantages which substantially affect the ability of any other undertaking to provide the same telecommunications service or to undertake the same activity in the same geographical area under substantially equivalent conditions. . .[11]

Examples of 'special rights' include powers of compulsory purchase and derogations from laws on town and country planning.[12] The Court of Justice

---

[11] See Art. 2(1) of Commission Directive 94/46/EC of 13 October 1994 amending Directive 88/301/EEC and Directive 90/388/EEC in particular with regard to satellite communications, (1994) OJ L 268/15.
[12] *Ibid.*, at Recital 11.

subsequently approved this formulation in *R* v *Secretary of State for Trade and Industry, ex parte British Telecommunications plc* (Case C-302/94) [1996] ECR I-6417, at para. 34).

Despite full market liberalisation, Art. 86(3) (ex 90) may continue to be relevant to the European telecommunications market. First, in a number of Member States the incumbent operator continues to be a 'public undertaking', through full or partial state ownership, and as such could be subject to state measures which infringe EU competition law. Secondly, where an operator has been granted 'special or exclusive' rights in a different sector of activity, such as broadcasting or water supply, the exercise or existence of such rights might be perceived as distorting the competitive provision of telecommunications services. (For the application of Art. 86 (ex 90) to the broadcasting sector, see *Elliniki Radiophonia Tileorassi* (Case C-260/89) [1991] ECR I-2925). To address this second concern, the European Commission has proposed that operators in this position should maintain separate accounts for the provision of services in the telecommunications market, 'to the extent that would be required if these activities were carried out by legally independent companies' and ensure structural separation from the activity pursued under the 'special or exclusive rights'.[13]

8.2.2   Essential requirements

A key element in the Commission's liberalisation Directives was reference to the concept of 'essential requirements'. The free movement of goods (i.e., telecommunications equipment) and the freedom to provide services was achieved by restricting the ability of a Member State to prohibit the supply of equipment and services except for 'non-economic reasons in the general public interest', otherwise referred to as the 'essential requirements'. Such reasons reflect the derogations expressly provided for in the EC Treaty, i.e. 'on grounds of public policy, public security or public health' (Art. 46 (ex 56)) and Court of Justice case law, e.g.:

> . . . Member States retain . . . the power to examine whether the said equipment is fit to be connected to the network in order to satisfy the imperative requirements regarding the protection of users as consumers of services and the protection of the public network and its proper functioning. (*Régie des Télégraphes et des Téléphones* v *GB-Inno-BM SA* (Case C-18/88) [1991] ECR I-5941)

The 'essential requirements' obviously differ between telecommunications equipment and services, and have been amended over time to reflect evolving public policy concerns and market conditions (see Table 8.1 below). Over recent years public policy concerns have broadened to encompass the protection of personal data (see further Chapter 11) and environmental

---

[13] Proposal for a Decision of the European Parliament and of the Council on a regulatory framework for radio spectrum policy in the European Community, COM (2000) 407 final, 12 July 2000, at Art. 12(1)(a).

Table 8.1   Essential requirements for equipment and services

Telecommunications Equipment[14]	Telecommunications Services[15]
1. Health and safety of user and any other person	1. Security of network operations
2. Electromagnetic compatibility requirements	2. Maintenance of network integrity
3. Effective use of radio frequency spectrum	3. Interoperability of services★
4. Interworking of apparatus via the network	4. Data protection★
5. Protection of the network from harm or misuse of network resources	5. Effective use of radio frequency spectrum★
6. Features protecting the privacy of subscribers and users†	6. Avoidance of harmful interference★
7. Features ensuring avoidance of fraud†	7. Protection of the environment★
8. Features ensuring access to emergency services†	8. Town and country planning objectives★
9. Features facilitating use by users with disabilities†	

† Where proposed by the Commission with the approval of a committee of Member State representatives.
★ Conditions imposed under such reasons are permissible only 'in justified cases'.

issues, impacting on the building of network infrastructure, such as mobile transmitters and digging up streets to lay cable.

In the first stages of liberalisation, much concern was directed towards the impact on the 'national' (i.e., incumbent) network of new operators connecting 'unregulated' telecommunications equipment and generating substantial volumes of additional traffic. The network, as a strategic component of Member State economies, was viewed as being vulnerable in a competitive environment. Over time such concerns for the 'national' network have generally proven to be greatly overstated. Incumbent operators have, however, continued to rely on one or more of the 'essential requirements' as the basis for imposing restrictive conditions on new entrants, e.g.:

- In Germany, Deutsche Telekom imposes an obligation upon other operators to provide additional interconnection points once they exceed a certain traffic capacity over an existing interconnection point on to Deutsche Telekom's network. Such a 'build' obligation has been approved

[14] As defined by Art. 3 of Directive 1999/5/EC on radio equipment and telecommunications terminal equipment and the mutual recognition of their conformity, (1999) OJ L 91/10.
[15] As defined by Art. 1(1) of Directive 90/388 (as amended by Directive 96/19/EC) and Art. 2(6) of Directive 90/387.

by the national regulator as being necessary to protect the integrity of Deutsche Telekom's network.[16]

- In the UK, BT has used concerns about 'network security' as the justification for requiring separate co-location rooms for operators implementing ASDL at BT's local exchanges, which impacts on an operator's time scales and costs for the introduction of competing services.

Such restrictions must be 'applied without discrimination and in proportion to the objective' and should be notified to the Commission to enable an assessment of proportionality (Directive 90/388/EC, Recital 8). However, new entrants have expressed concern that national regulatory authorities have not always examined the evidence for some of these 'essential requirement' claims.[17] Under the recently adopted European Regulation on unbundled access to the local loop, refusal to provide access is permitted only 'on the basis of objective criteria, relating to technical feasibility or the need to maintain network integrity'.[18] This would seem to indicate a need for *a priori* evidence, as well as a narrowing of the grounds on which a restriction can be imposed.

8.2.3 Telecommunications equipment

At the outset, liberalisation of the telecommunications terminal equipment market primarily focused on the application of the principle of the free movement of goods under Arts 28–31 (ex 30–37) of the EC Treaty. For example, in 1985, the Commission intervened on the basis of Art. 37 against Germany in respect of a proposed regulation extending the Bundespost's monopoly over telecommunications equipment to cordless telephones (*Re Cordless Telephones in Germany* [1985] 2 CMLR 397).[19] As with other product areas, mutual recognition was the initial vehicle for the achievement of a 'Single Market'.

The first legislative initiative was a Council Directive in 1986 that called upon Member States to implement mutual recognition in respect of conformity tests carried out on mass-produced terminal equipment.[20] However, a more comprehensive and controversial measure was taken by the Commission in 1988, when it adopted a Directive, under Art. 86(3) (ex 90) of the EC Treaty, calling upon Member States to withdraw any 'special or exclusive'

---

[16] See 'Fifth Report on the Implementation of the Telecommunications Regulatory Package', COM (1999) 537, 10 November 1999, at Annex 3, p. 41.

[17] See Commission Communication, 'Sixth Report on the Implementation of the Telecommunications Regulatory Package', COM (2000) 814, 7 December 2000, at p. 16 *et seq.*

[18] Regulation of the European Parliament and of the Council on unbundled access to the local loop, 2000/0185 (COD), 5 December 2000, at Art. 3(2).

[19] See also *Régie des Télégraphes et des Téléphones v GB-Inno-BM SA* (Case C-18/88) [1991] ECR I-5941, where it was held that Art. 30 (now 28) of the Treaty precludes an undertaking from having the power to approve telephone equipment for connection to the public network without being susceptible to legal challenge.

[20] Council Directive 86/361/EEC on the initial stage of the mutual recognition of type approval for telecommunications terminal equipment, (1986) OJ L 217/21.

rights that may have been granted to undertakings relating to telecommunications terminal equipment.[21] While the first 'mutual recognition' measure can be viewed as ensuring competition between Member State undertakings, the 1988 Directive addressed the issue of competition within national markets.

The Directive stated that the only grounds upon which a Member State could restrict or regulate economic operators importing, marketing, operating and maintaining terminal equipment were either where such equipment could be shown to have failed to satisfy the 'essential requirements' (see 8.2.2 above), or where the economic operator failed to possess the necessary technical qualifications in relation to the equipment (Art. 3).

The mutual recognition process, first established under the 1986 Directive and extended under a series of measures addressing terminal equipment,[22] has comprised a number of inter-linked principles and procedures:

(a)   the notification and publication by Member States of technical specifications relating to the terminal equipment, commonly referred to as 'type approval specifications';

(b)   equipment meeting relevant harmonised standards (published in the *Official Journal*) is presumed to be compliant with the 'essential requirements';

(c)   the establishment of independent 'notified bodies' (designated by Member States[23]) to carry out an *a priori* examination and assessment of conformity of a specimen of the proposed equipment with the 'essential requirements', and the issuance of an 'EC-type examination certificate' in relation to the particular piece of equipment;

(d)   declaration obligations imposed upon manufacturers that–
   (i)   all equipment produced is in compliance with the certificate, and
   (ii)   such equipment was produced under a quality assured system; and

(e)   the adoption of a 'CE conformity marking' scheme to enable identification of terminal equipment that is suitable for connection to the public telecommunications network.

These procedures have been further simplified under a consolidated regime adopted in April 2000, intended better to reflect the 'pace of technology and market development' by making it easier for manufacturers to place products on the market.[24] This is achieved primarily by removing the requirement for equipment to be tested by 'notified bodies' prior to its manufacture. Instead,

---

[21] Commission Directive 88/301/EEC on competition in the markets of telecommunications terminal equipment, (1988) OJ L 131/73, at Art. 2.

[22] For example, Council Directive 91/263/EC on the approximation of the laws of the Member States concerning telecommunications terminal equipment including the mutual recognition of their conformity, (1991) OJ L 128/1 (repealing Directive 86/361); and Directive 98/13/EC relating to telecommunications terminal and satellite earth station equipment, including mutual conformity recognition, (1998) OJ L 74/1 (repealing Directive 91/263).

[23] In the UK, there are 11 such bodies, including the British Approval Board for Telecommunications and BSI Product Services.

[24] Directive 1999/5/EC, at Recital 7. The Directive has been implemented into UK law by the Radio Equipment and Telecommunications Terminal Equipment Regulations 2000 (SI 2000 No. 730).

greater emphasis is to be placed upon manufacturers documenting their compliance with 'Conformity Assessment Procedures' relevant to the particular type of equipment.

8.2.4 Telecommunications services

Historically, the European Commission's approach to liberalisation has been focused on the competitive provision of services, rather than on network infrastructure over which such services are carried. This stance can be contrasted with the position adopted in the UK, particularly by the DGT, where there has been concern to promote competition at the network level as much as at the services level.

The Commission's 1990 Services Directive (Directive 90/388/EEC) was limited only to liberalisation of the provision of non-voice telephony services, and did not include 'telex, mobile radiotelephony, paging and satellites services'. However, the Services Directive addresses for the first time the need for objective, transparent and non-discriminatory licensing and declaration procedures for operators wishing to enter the market, which was subsequently comprehensively applied to the telecommunications sector under the Licensing Directive (see 8.4.1 below; on its implementation in the UK, see Chapter 4).

In order to be able to enter the market for the provision of telecommunications services, new entrants need to have access to leased transmission circuits from the providers of network infrastructure, traditionally the incumbent operator. The Services Directive therefore requires Member States to ensure that requests for leased circuits are met within a reasonable period of time and that any increase in charges is justified, partly through a reporting obligation on Member States to inform the Commission of the factors responsible for any increase (Art. 4). The use of any leased circuits should not be restricted, although prohibitions on offering simple re-sale to the public were permissible until 31 December 1992 (Art. 3), in order to protect the incumbent's rights in respect of the provision of voice telephony.

Following the European Court's decision in *Kingdom of Spain and others (France, Belgium, Italy)* v *Commission of the European Communities* (Case-289/90) [1992] ECR I-5833, upholding the Commission's right to liberalise the services market under Art. 86(3) (ex 90) of the EC Treaty, the Commission adopted a series of Directives amending the Services Directive to encompass a broader range of telecommunications services, i.e.:

(a)   satellite services;[25]
(b)   the use of cable TV networks;[26] and

---

[25] Commission Directive 94/46/EC amending Directive 88/301/EEC and Directive 90/388/EEC in particular with regard to satellite communications, (1994) OJ L 268/15. This was the first liberalisation Directive to result in a Court of Justice ruling for non-compliance: *Commission* v *Luxembourg* (Case 59/98).
[26] Commission Directive 95/51/EC amending Commission Directive 90/388/EEC with regard to the abolition of the restrictions on the use of cable television networks for the provision of already liberalised telecommunication services, (1995) OJ L 256/49.

(c)   mobile and personal communications.[27]

It also adopted the Full Competition Directive.[28]

The Full Competition Directive required Member States to withdraw all 'exclusive rights for the provision of telecommunications services, including the establishment and the provision of telecommunications networks required for the provision of such services' (Art. 1(2)). This removed the 'reserved service' exception that had been granted over the provision of voice telephony services because it was viewed as an integral component in the provision of network infrastructure (Recital 4).

The Full Competition Directive committed the Member States to the deadline of 1 January 1998. This timetable corresponded with the international liberalisation process achieved under the Fourth Protocol to the WTO's General Agreement on Trade in Services, to which the Community and Member States were party.[29] Transitional periods were granted to countries considered as having less developed or very small networks, i.e. Ireland, Spain, Portugal, Greece and Luxembourg. Greece was the final EU Member State to liberalise its market fully on 1 January 2001.

Concurrent with the regulatory acceptance of voice telephony as a fully competitive service, the emergence of voice telephony as a service capable of being offered over the Internet presented the Commission with an interesting definitional issue: Do such Internet-based services fall within the regulatory definition?

> . . . 'voice telephony' means the commercial provision for the public of the direct transport and switching of speech in real-time between public switched network termination points, enabling any user to use equipment connected to such a network termination point in order to communicate with another termination point. (Directive 90/388/EEC, Art. 1(1))

If the answer were 'Yes', two consequences would flow. First, the provision of a voice telephony service over the Internet would be in breach of any exclusive rights granted to an operator by a Member State in those countries subject to transitional periods. Secondly, the providers of such services would be subject to the regulatory requirements imposed on providers of voice telephony services, such as contributing towards the provision of universal service. In a 1998 Notice, the Commission held that the then technology and market for Internet-based voice telephony did not constitute voice telephony, because such services were not generally the subject of distinct commercial provision; rather, they were user enabled utilising an Internet access service.

---

[27] Commission Directive 96/2/EC amending Directive 90/388/EEC with regard to mobile and personal communications, (1996) OJ L 20/59.
[28] Commission Directive 96/19/EC amending Commission Directive 90/388/EEC regarding the implementation of full competition in telecommunications services, (1996) OJ L74/13.
[29] Council Decision 97/838/EC of 28 November 1997 concerning the conclusion on behalf of the European Community, as regards matters within its competence, of the results of the WTO negotiations on basic telecommunications services, (1997) OJ L 347/45. See further Chapter 10, at 10.4.3.

However, the Commission noted that at some point in the future, Internet-based telephony was likely to become a form of 'voice telephony'.[30]

Since 1998, a further Commission Directive on the liberalisation of the telecommunications services market was an amendment to the measure concerning cable TV networks. Under the original Directive, Member States were required to ensure accounting transparency and separation where an operator provided both telecommunications network infrastructure and cable TV network infrastructure (Art. 2), to prevent anti-competitive utilisation of the two networks. The effectiveness of such behavioural measures was subsequently reassessed and the Commission concluded that the continued existence of joint ownership would delay the introduction of integrated broadband communications networks.[31] The Commission therefore decided to introduce controls requiring any operator to establish separate legal entities for the operation of each network where such an operator:

(a)   is controlled by that Member State or benefits from special rights;

(b)   is dominant in a substantial part of the common market in the provision of public telecommunications networks and public voice telephony services; and

(c)   operates a cable TV network established under special or exclusive rights in the same geographic area.[32]

With the implementation of the Full Competition Directive by Greece at the end of 2000, the market for telecommunication services in the EU is now fully liberalised at a regulatory level. In July 2000, the Commission issued a proposed Directive consolidating the legal framework and repealing the Services Directive and the subsequent Directives.[33] Even with the progressive enlargement of the EU, we are unlikely to see further Commission Directives in the area, since the liberalisation framework is clearly set out for future Member States. However, Art. 86 (ex 90) Directives may continue to have a role to play in the liberalisation of the European broadcasting market, which through convergence may impact on the telecommunications market.

8.3   HARMONISATION OF THE EU TELECOMMUNICATIONS MARKET

While the liberalisation initiatives aimed at opening up national markets to competition through the withdrawal of 'special or exclusive rights', har-

---

[30] Commission Notice, 'Status of voice communications on Internet under Community law and, in particular, under Directive 90/388/EEC', (1998) OJ C 6/4. See also the Supplement to the Communication by the Commission, (2000) OJ C 369/3.

[31] Commission Communication concerning the review under competition rules of the joint provision of telecommunications and cable TV networks by a single operator and the abolition of restrictions on the provision of cable TV capacity over telecommunications, (1998) OJ C 71/4.

[32] Commission Directive 1999/64/EC amending Directive 90/388/EEC in order to ensure that telecommunications networks and cable TV networks owned by a single operator are separate legal entities, (1999) OJ L 175/39.

[33] Draft Commission Directive on competition in the markets for electronic communications services, (2001) OJ C 96/2.

monisation measures were required to address competition across national markets through the 'establishment of a Community-wide market for telecommunications services'. The European Commission has pursued harmonisation across a broad range of issues, from technical standards to the applicable tax regime.

The need for common standards is clearly a critical aspect in the development of an Internal Market in telecommunications.[34] At an institutional level, the European Commission encouraged the establishment of the European Telecommunications Standards Institute (ETSI), by the Conference on Postal and Telecommunications Administrations, in 1988. In the mobile sector the development of European-wide services has been pursued through the adoption of a series of legislative measures reserving common frequency bands within Member States, most importantly in respect of second generation GSM digital mobile services and third generation universal mobile telecommunication systems (UMTS).[35]

In parallel with the Commission's Services Directive in 1990, the Council adopted a Directive, under Art. 95 (ex 100a) of the EC Treaty, establishing the concept of 'open network provision' (ONP). The so-called 'ONP framework' programme was conceived to provide the regulatory basis for imposing harmonisation:

> This Directive concerns the harmonisation of conditions for open and efficient access to and use of public telecommunications networks and, where applicable, public telecommunications services.[36]

Reflecting the liberalisation process, the scope of the ONP programme was initially limited to issues of access to the network infrastructure and 'reserved services' provided by the incumbent operator. As such, the harmonisation framework envisaged the drafting of proposals on ONP conditions across a range of issues of concern to providers of non-reserved services:

(a)   the need for appropriate technical interfaces between open network termination points;

(b)   the identification of additional service features;

(c)   harmonised supply and usage conditions, such as maximum periods for provision and conditions on the re-sale of capacity; and

(d)   tariff principles, such as the unbundling of individual service elements (Annex II).

---

[34] For example, Council Resolution of 27 April 1989 on standardization in the field of information technology and telecommunications (1989) OJ C 117/1.

[35] I.e. Council Directive 87/372/EEC on the frequency bands to be reserved for the coordinated introduction of public pan-European cellular digital land-based mobile communications in the Community (1987) OJ L 196/85; and Council Decision 128/1999/EC of the European Parliament and of the Council on the coordinated introduction of a third generation mobile and wireless communications system (UMTS) in the Community (1999) OJ L 17/1.

[36] Directive 90/387/EEC on the establishment of the internal market for telecommunications services through the implementation of open network provision (1990) OJ L 192/1.

Such conditions are subject to basic principles concerning the use of objective criteria, transparency and non-discrimination, while any restrictions placed on access must be limited to reasons based on the 'essential requirements' (Art. 6).

Subsequent ONP measures have been adopted in a number of areas: the provision of leased lines; packet-switched data services;[37] integrated services digital networks (ISDN);[38] voice telephony, interconnection[39] and universal service.

The Leased Lines Directive[40] supplements the general supply obligations under the Services Directive (90/388/EC, Art. 4) by defining a 'minimum set of leased lines with harmonized technical characteristics' that must be made available to service providers upon request. In addition, conditions relating to the supply, termination, access and usage of the 'minimum set' are also addressed. The applicable tariffs are required to follow principles of 'cost orientation and transparency' in accordance with an accounting system that distinguishes between direct costs and allocated common costs (Art. 10). The implementation of the Directive is the responsibility of the NRA, although a non-binding conciliation procedure is provided for, which would enable a dispute to be resolved at Community level by a group established under the auspices of the ONP Committee (Art. 12).

With the extension of the liberalisation process to infrastructure as well as services, the Leased Lines Directive was amended to reflect the new environment, introducing *ex-ante* regulations for certain telecommunications operators.[41] In particular, Member States were required to designate operators who were required to provide the 'minimum set', usually comprising 'organisations with significant market power':

. . . an organisation shall be presumed to have significant market power when its share of the relevant leased-lines market in a Member State is 25% or more. The relevant leased-lines market shall be assessed on the basis of the type(s) of leased line offered in a particular geographical area. The geographical area may cover the whole or part of the territory of a Member State. (Art. 2(3))

---

[37] Recommendation 92/382/EEC on the harmonised provision of a minimum set of packet-switched data services (PSDS) in accordance with open network provision (ONP) principles (1992) OJ L 200/1.

[38] Recommendation 92/383/EEC on the provision of harmonised integrated services digital network (ISDN) access arrangements and a minimum set of ISDN offerings in accordance with open network provision (ONP) principles (1992) OJ L 200/10.

[39] Directive 97/33/EC of the European Parliament and of the Council on Interconnection in Telecommunications with regard to ensuring Universal Service and Interoperability through Application of the Principles of Open Network Provision (1997) OJ L 199/32. See further Chapter 5.

[40] Directive 92/44/EEC of 5 June 1992 on the application of open network provision to leased lines, (1992) OJ L 165/27, at Art. 1.

[41] Directive 97/51/EC of the European Parliament and of the Council of 6 October 1997 amending Council Directives 90/387/EEC and 92/44/EEC for the purpose of adaptation to a competitive environment in Telecommunications, (1997) OJ L 295/23.

NRAs are required to notify the Commission that organisations have been so designated (Art. 11(1a)) and have the discretion to determine that an organisation on either side of the 25 per cent figure falls outside the presumption (Art. 2(3)), based on factors such as the operator's access to financial resources and its experience in the market.

The concept of the so-called 'SMP operator' has subsequently been applied in the ONP measures on interconnection and voice telephony, imposing *ex-ante* obligations on certain participants in each national market, particularly the incumbent. The 25 per cent market share trigger represents a lower threshold than the traditional competition law concept of 'dominance', which has generally been considered to exist somewhere over 40 per cent of market share, although market share is not usually the sole factor in determining market power for competition purposes. The potential discrepancy between the 25 per cent SMP regulatory trigger and the concept of dominance has been the subject of criticism, and indeed the German Government has refused to use the 25 per cent trigger for the application of the SMP obligations, arguing:

> . . . if the definitions used in the Directive resulted in a treatment of companies concerned, that is not in line with EC competition law, the question arises whether such a sector-specific special provision is legally admissible.[42]

Justifying the lower threshold, the Commission has argued that traditional competition law principles are not adequate to deal with some of the unique features of the telecommunications market, while the trigger also reduces the burden upon NRAs to assess 'dominance' on a case-by-case basis.[43] However, in the Commission's recent proposals revising the existing regulatory framework, while the term 'significant market power' is retained, the 25 per cent trigger has been replaced:

> An undertaking shall be deemed to have significant market power if, either individually or jointly with others, it enjoys a position of economic strength affording it the power to behave to an appreciable extent independently of competitors, customers and ultimately consumers.[44]

As well as addressing concerns about the legitimacy of the 25 per cent trigger, the change is also designed to reflect the European Union's commitments under the WTO Reference Paper, which are applicable against 'major suppliers'.[45]

The principle of 'non-discrimination' in the Leased Lines Directive was also amended, from a requirement to treat all other service providers equally

---

[42] Letter from Dr Sidel, German Economic Ministry, to Mr Cockborne, DG-XIII, dated 13 July 1998; quoted in Tarrant, A., 'Significant market power and dominance in the regulation of telecommunications markets' (2000) 7 ECLR 320.
[43] *Ibid.*
[44] Proposed Framework Directive, *supra* n. 13, at Art. 13(2).
[45] See Chapter 10, at 10.4.3.1.

to an obligation to treat other service providers in the same manner as such services are provided to the operator itself or its subsidiaries or partners (Art. 8(2)). Under the original Directive, Member States were required to encourage the establishment of 'one-stop' procedures for the ordering and billing of leased lines throughout Europe (Art. 9), as part of the drive towards establishing the Internal Market. However, little progress was made in this area and the provision was deleted from the amended version.

In 1995, the ONP framework was applied to voice telephony.[46] Under this measure, the NRAs were given a broad range of obligations to ensure that the provision of 'fixed' voice telephony to users, which included residential customers as well as competing service providers, was under harmonised conditions. Such conditions included the connection of terminal equipment; targets for supply time and quality of service; service termination; user contracts and the provision of advanced facilities, such as calling-line identification and call forwarding. Issues usually considered to fall within the concept of 'universal service', such as the provision of low-usage schemes, directory services and public-pay telephones, were also addressed (see 8.4.3 below).

Further market liberalisation led to the replacement of the Voice Telephony Directive in 1998. The Revised Voice Telephony Directive[47] introduced further *ex-ante* regulations for 'organisations with significant market power', including the provision of 'special network access' (Art. 16) and compliance with the principles of cost orientation for tariffs and the operation of cost accounting systems (Arts 17 and 18). The new measure also extended certain provisions to mobile voice telephony, such as the provision of operator assistance services (Art. 9), although it was made clear that Member States could extend all the provisions to mobile networks and/or services.

The increasingly global nature of the telecommunications market has also required EU harmonisation in respect of the applicable tax regime for telecommunication services. In the mid-1990s, EU-based operators were finding themselves at a competitive disadvantage in the provision of telecommunication services to EU-based customers *vis-à-vis* operators outside the EU, since the existing VAT regime operated on the basis of the place of establishment of the service provider. So, for example, an EU-based ISP would be required to charge VAT on its subscription services, while a US-based operator (e.g., CompuServe) could provide the same services free of VAT. It was therefore necessary to amend existing EU law to enable Member States to make foreign service providers subject to the same VAT obligations as EU operators.[48]

Harmonisation between Member State markets has inevitably involved greater complexity and detailed regulatory intervention than that required for

---

[46] Directive 95/62/EC on the application of open network provision to voice telephony, (1995) OJ L 321/6.
[47] Directive 98/10/EC on the application of open network provision (ONP) to voice telephony and on universal service for telecommunications in a competitive environment, (1998) OJ L 101/24.
[48] Council Directive 1999/59/EC amending Directive 77/388/EEC as regards the value added tax arrangements applicable to telecommunications services (1999) OJ L 162/63.

the liberalisation of national markets. Such detail arises both from the scope of the issues addressed (e.g., supply and usage conditions and related cost and tariff provisions) and from the imposition of asymmetric obligations on market participants. One feature of the harmonisation process is the key role played by the NRAs in implementing and complying with the principles contained in the harmonisation measures. Such reliance on national regulators has, in some cases, generated new areas of divergence between market conditions and practices in the Member States.[49] This is reflected, in part, by the fact that the Commission is currently pursuing 51 infringement proceedings against Member States in respect of the harmonisation Directives, as compared with 16 under the liberalisation Directives.[50]

8.4 ISSUES IN EU TELECOMMUNICATIONS LAW

The previous sections have outlined the two primary sources of European telecommunications law: market liberalisation and harmonisation. While they may be viewed as distinct policy objectives, it is also clear that they contain significant areas of overlap, constructing a regulatory framework that defines the rights and obligations of the providers of telecommunications networks and services. This section reviews some of the main regulatory issues that have developed in European telecommunications law since the 1987 Green Paper.

8.4.1 Authorisation

In contrast to other commercial sectors, such as information technology, the right to provide telecommunications networks and services has been subject to national licensing or authorisation regimes. Prior to competition, the right of state-owned incumbent operators to operate was generally provided for under primary legislation. However, with the entrance of the first competitor, governments were required to clarify the nature of the legal authority under which such activities were carried out. This often involved the drafting of licences for the incumbent as well as the new entrant. The manner in which such licences were granted has been a critical factor in the introduction of competition into national markets and has, therefore, been the subject of increasingly detailed attention within the European regulatory framework.

The Services Directive required Member States to ensure:

. . . that the conditions for the grant of licences are objective, non-discriminatory and transparent, that reasons are given for any refusal, and that there is a procedure for appealing against any such refusal. (Art. 2)

It also required that a body independent of the incumbent operator carried out 'the grant of operating licences' (Art. 7, see 8.4.2 below). However, such

---

[49] See generally the Sixth Implementation Report, *supra* n. 17.
[50] *Ibid.*, at p. 5.

provisions left Member States with substantial discretion in the operation of any regime. In a Council resolution of 1994 it was recognised that one element of the regulatory framework required for liberalisation was the establishment of common principles for 'the setting up of licensing procedures and conditions'.[51] Similar sentiments calling for more harmonised licensing regimes were expressed in subsequent communications and resolutions. In 1997, a common framework was finally adopted, the Licensing Directive.[52]

The Licensing Directive distinguishes between two forms of authorisations – 'general authorisations' and 'individual licences':

'general authorisation' means an authorisation, regardless of whether it is regulated by a 'class licence' or under general law and whether such regulation requires registration, which does not require the undertaking concerned to obtain an explicit decision by the national regulatory authority before exercising the rights stemming from the authorisation,

'individual licence' means an authorisation which is granted by a national regulatory authority and which gives an undertaking specific rights or which subjects that undertaking's operations to specific obligations supplementing the general authorisation where applicable, where the undertaking is not entitled to exercise the rights concerned until it has received the decision by the national regulatory authority . . . (Art. 2(1))

However, the Directive gives clear priority to the former type of authorisation. Member States are able to impose individual licences only for a limited range of purposes: to obtain access to radio frequencies or numbers; to give the licensee rights to access public or private land; to impose obligations requiring the provision of networks or services, including universal service; and to impose conditions upon operators with SMP (Art. 7). Provision is also made for the establishment by the Commission of a 'one-stop-shopping procedure', whereby operators can apply for multiple jurisdiction authorisations through a single location (Art. 13), although little progress has been made in this area to date.

The Licensing Directive details the types of conditions that may be imposed on operators, such as protecting the rights of users and subscribers in respect of 'detailed and accurate billing' (Annex), as well as the procedures to be followed when granting such authorisations, e.g., requiring decisions within a time limit of six weeks. In addition, the applicable fees that may be levied on operators for authorisation may only cover 'the issue, management, control and enforcement' of the licence (Arts 6 and 11). An important exemption to this licence fee limitation is provided for the allocation of 'scarce resources', where charges may 'reflect the need to ensure the optimal

---

[51] Council Resolution of 22 December 1994 on the principles and timetable for the liberalisation of telecommunications infrastructure, (1994) OJ C 379/4.
[52] Directive 97/13/EC of the European Parliament and of the Council of 10 April 1997 on a common framework for general authorisations and individual licences in the field of telecommunications services, (1997) OJ L 117/15. For its implementation in UK law, see Chapter 4.

use of these resources' (Art. 11(2)). This has enabled Member States to implement auctions for the allocation of radio spectrum, particularly UMTS.[53]

Despite such detailed harmonised provisions, the European Commission has continued to find significant divergences between Member States in the implementation of the Licensing Directive, including varying numbers of service categorisation and information requirements.[54] Therefore, in July 2000, the Commission published a new proposal to replace the Licensing Directive.[55] Under the proposal, the current arrangements will be amended in a number of ways:

(a)   only general authorisations will be applicable to the provision of all electronic communication services and networks, with specific rights being granted in respect of the assignment of radio frequencies and numbers only;

(b)   the categories of licence conditions have been clarified further;

(c)   licensing procedures have been further simplified, e.g., the provision of information evidencing compliance with the conditions may not be required prior to market entry; and

(d)   the level of administrative fees and charges should be further lowered through ongoing transparency obligations, coupled with requirements to make adjustments where charges exceed costs within any year.[56]

The proposal also grants undertakings, operating under a general authorisation, specific rights to establish 'electronic communications networks' and provide 'electronic communication services'. This reflects the Commission's desire to rationalise national authorisation schemes in the face of increasing convergence at the level of communications infrastructure.

8.4.2   Regulatory authorities

As discussed at 8.1 above, two different Commission Directorate-Generals (Competition and Information Society) have pursued EU telecommunications policy. The former has treaty-based authority, under Art. 85 (ex 89) EC Treaty, to impose behavioural and structural controls on the activities of telecommunications operators, subject to the jurisdictional requirement that the anti-competitive practice 'may affect trade between Member States'. Otherwise, such anti-competitive practices will have to be addressed by the competent authorities within the Member States, whether a specific telecommunications regulator, a general competition authority or both.[57]

---

[53] In the UK, BT and One 2 One have commenced legal proceedings against the Government in respect of the operation of the recent UMTS auction, alleging, amongst other things, breach of the Licensing Directive.

[54] See Fifth Implementation Report, *supra* n. 16, at p. 12.

[55] Proposal for a Directive of the European Parliament and the Council on the authorisation of electronic communications networks and services, COM (2000) 386, 12 July 2000.

[56] The exception for the optimal use of radio frequencies has been extended to numbers and rights of way.

[57] In the UK, the DGT has concurrent powers with the general competition authority, the DGFT: see further Chapters 3 and 7.

The *ex-ante* controls detailed in the ONP measures (see 8.3 above) and drafted by the Information Society Directorate-General, are implemented by the Member States, usually through secondary legislation. The Member States either have an obligation to designate operators to whom certain obligations apply (e.g., the Leased Lines Directive), or the discretion to so designate (e.g., Revised Voice Telephony Directive). The Commission currently exercises a monitoring role only, based on information supplied by the NRAs through notification and reporting obligations. As such, key aspects of EU telecommunications policy are dependent on being appropriately implemented by the NRAs.

One of the central features present in the Member States prior to liberalisation of the telecommunications market was the fact that the institution responsible for regulating the market, e.g., the Ministry of Communications, was usually also responsible for controlling the commercial activities of the incumbent operator. It was recognised that such merged functions would not be appropriate in a competitive market.[58] Under the Equipment Directive, the Commission required the obligations imposed by the Directive to be 'entrusted to a body independent of public or private undertakings offering goods and/or services in the telecommunications sector'.[59] The interpretation of this provision has been the subject of a significant amount of European Court of Justice case law, primarily because those bodies entrusted with the responsibilities under the Directive did not have the necessary technical expertise to carry out the required examinations and tests on terminal equipment. Regulators tended, therefore, to be dependent on the incumbent to carry out such activities on their behalf, which gave rise to plenty of scope for abuse. Most recently, the Court held that Art. 6:

> . . . must be interpreted as precluding the application of national rules which prohibit economic agents from, and penalize them for, manufacturing, importing, stocking for sale . . . terminal equipment without furnishing proof, in the form of a type-approval or another document regarded as equivalent, that such equipment conforms to certain essential requirements . . . where there is no guarantee that a test laboratory responsible for technically monitoring the conformity of the equipment with the technical specifications is independent from economic agents offering goods and services in the telecommunications sector. (*Thierry Tranchant and Téléphone Store SARL* (Case C-91/94) [1995] ECR I-3911)[60]

The Services Directive reiterated the need for Member States to ensure that 'a body independent of the telecommunications organisations' carried out the

---

[58] See generally the Green Paper of 1987, *supra* n. 3.
[59] Commission Directive 88/301/EEC of 16 May 1988 on competition in the markets of telecommunications terminal equipment (1998) OJ L 131/73, at Art. 6. This position had previously been taken by the Court of Justice in *GB-Inno-BM*, *supra* n. 19.
[60] See also *Procureur du Roi* v *Lagauche & others*, *Evrard* (Cases C-46/90 and C-93/91) [1993] ECR I-5267; *Ministère Public* v *Decoster* (Case C-69/91) [1993] ECR I-5335; *Ministère Public* v *Taillandier-Neny* (Case C-92/91) [1993] ECR I-5383.

regulatory functions (Art. 7). What this formulation does not adequately address is the issue of regulatory independence from the Government as owner, in part or whole, of the incumbent operator.

Where a government is concerned to maintain the value of its stake in the incumbent, with an eye to some form of future asset divestiture, it has a natural incentive to inhibit the emergence of competition in the market. Phased divestiture of the government shareholding, as has occurred in most Member States, extends this dependency relationship over a longer period of time. Privatisation will generally have a direct impact on government borrowing which, in an era of monetary union, may be of critical importance to a government. Even post-divestiture, particularly in the short term, a government may show continued concern as regards the performance of the 'national champion's' share price, as new shareholders among the general public represent future electorate.

The issue of independence from government, as owner of the incumbent, was first addressed within the context of the ONP initiative. Initially, indirect reference was made to the need to conform to the 'principle of separation of regulatory and operational functions'.[61] Direct reference was subsequently made to the establishment of a 'national regulatory authority' (NRA) 'legally distinct and functionally independent of the telecommunications organisations'.[62] However, it was not until 1997 that the issue of independence from government became the subject of a specific legislative provision:

> In order to guarantee the independence of national regulatory authorities:
> – national regulatory authorities shall be legally distinct from and functionally independent of all organisations providing telecommunications networks, equipment or services,
> – Member States that retain ownership or a significant degree of control of organisations providing telecommunications networks and/ or services shall ensure effective structural separation of the regulatory function from activities associated with ownership or control.[63]

In addition, the decisions of a NRA must be capable of being appealed by any affected party to 'a body independent of the parties involved' (Art. 5a(3)). The European Commission, in a recent proposed Directive, has extended the regulatory requirement for independence through structural separation to include local authorities that retain 'ownership or control' over operators and are involved in the granting of rights of way (proposed Directive Art. 10(2)). In the UK, such a provision would be applicable to the City of Kingston upon

---

[61] Council Directive 92/44/EEC of 5 June 1992 on the application of open network provision to leased lines, (1992) OJ L 165/27, at Recital 14.

[62] See Council Directive 95/62/EC, of 13 December 1995, on the application of open network provision to voice telephony, (1995) OJ L 321/6, at Art. 2(2).

[63] Directive 97/51/EC of the European Parliament and of the Council of 6 October 1997 amending Council Directives 90/387/EEC and 92/44/EEC for the purpose of adaptation to a competitive environment in telecommunications, (1997) OJ L 295/23, at Art. 1(6), inserting Art. 5a into Directive 90/387/EEC.

Hull, which has a controlling shareholding in Kingston Communications (Hull) plc.

Another aspect of the position of any regulatory authority is that such a body must be given the resources to carry out its assigned tasks. The effectiveness of a regulator depends to a considerable degree on the resources made available to it. This issue is indirectly addressed through the recitals of some of the ONP measures. Initially reference was made to an authority having 'the necessary means to carry out these tasks fully' (see Council Directive 95/62/EC, at Recital 10). Such tasks include passing information to the European Commission to enable it to monitor implementation of EU regulatory measures and the process of liberalisation in each Member State (Art. 26). This sentiment was subsequently strengthened:

> . . . whereas the national regulatory authorities should be in possession of all the resources necessary, in terms of staffing, expertise, and financial means, for the performance of their functions . . . (Directive 97/51/EC, at Recital 9)

To meet this objective, the NRA must either look to government, or to the regulated industry for the necessary resources. In an era of public sector spending restraint, sufficient resources from government must always appear doubtful. In terms of the providers of telecommunications networks, equipment or services, one source of income is through the operation of the licensing regime. However, under the Licensing Directive, NRAs are only permitted to charge fees that cover the 'costs incurred in the issue, management, control and enforcement' of the licensing regime (Directive 97/13/EC, Arts 6 and 11), which clearly emphasises the need to minimise the costs of regulation.

In the Commission's review of Member State implementation of the package of telecommunications legislation, issues of NRAs' 'independence' and 'structural separation', as well as adequacy of resources, are all examined.[64] Member States have adopted a diversity of models in establishing regulatory institutions, such as the 'Autorite de Regulation des Télécommunications' (ART) in France, which comprises an independent official within the Ministry. In some countries, such as Italy and Austria, the powers under the regulatory regime are dispersed between a number of separate regulatory authorities, which is seen as significantly weakening the exercise of such powers against the incumbent. Regulatory dependency on the incumbent for the provision of information as well as expertise continues to be perceived as a problem by some new entrants in a number of jurisdictions (e.g., in the UK and Sweden). In terms of resources, the main reported problem is the retention of staff in such a fast-moving, well-remunerated employment market, which leads to over-reliance on seconded personnel from operators including the incumbent.

In the Commission's 1999 review of the regulatory framework (see Chapter 5 and 8.1 above), it continued to express concern in respect of a number of areas of NRA activity:

---

[64] See Sixth Implementation Report, *supra* n. 17, at p. 12 *et seq.*

(i) strengthening the independence of NRAs, (ii) ensuring that the allocation of responsibilities between institutions at national level does not lead to delays and duplications of decision making, (iii) improving cooperation between sector specific and general competition authorities, and (iv) requiring transparency of decision making procedures at a national level. (at 4.8.3)

To address these concerns, the Commission has published a proposal that consolidates existing provisions on regulatory independence, and sets out in some detail the obligations of NRAs in the regulation of the provision of electronic communications networks and services. Member States will be required to publish procedures for consultation and cooperation between different NRAs, particularly competition and consumer law authorities. The proposed Directive requires that 'there is no overlap between the tasks of those authorities' (Art. 3(4)), which would not seem to be the current position in the UK where the DGT exercises certain functions concurrently with the DGFT (i.e., Telecommunications Act 1984, s. 50(3), as amended by the Competition Act 1998). It is also a requirement that any NRA decision be capable of appeal to an independent body. Such an appeal must extend not only to procedural issues (i.e., judicial review), but also to considerations of 'the facts of the case' (Art. 4(1)). In the UK, the Telecommunications Act 1984 has already been amended to enable decisions to be appealed on one or more of the following grounds: (i) a material error as to the facts; (ii) a material procedural error; (iii) an error of law or some other material illegality (s. 46B, inserted by the Telecommunications (Appeals Regulations 1999 (SI 1999 No. 3180); see also *British Telecommunications plc v Director-General of Telecommunications* (2000) LawTel 12.10.2000).

Under existing European law, NRAs have various obligations to notify the Commission in respect of specific decisions made in compliance with particular measures (e.g., Revised Voice Telephony Directive, Art. 25). Under the new framework proposal, NRAs would be obliged to consult with the Commission and the NRAs of other Member States prior to the adoption of measures on certain issues, such as the management of radio spectrum. The consulting NRA would then be obliged to take into account any comments received from the other NRAs, but could be required by the Commission 'to amend or withdraw the draft measure' (Art. 6(4)). This provision represents a significant enhancement of the Commission's authority, enabling *ex-ante* intervention in national implementation of the Directives. It is therefore likely to meet substantial opposition from Member State governments.

In the exercise of their regulatory functions, the NRAs must take 'all reasonable measures' to ensure that certain fundamental principles and objectives are 'exclusively' met:

(a) '. . . the need for regulation to be technologically neutral; i.e. that it neither imposes nor discriminates in favour of the use of a particular type of technology';

(b) promotion of an open and competitive market, e.g., by encouraging 'efficient investment in infrastructure';

(c)   contribution to the development of the Internal Market, e.g., by ensuring non-discrimination; and

(d)   promotion of the interests of European citizens, e.g., through ensuring 'affordable access to a universal service' (Art. 7).

Inevitably, these principles may, in particular situations, be in conflict or require different courses of action from which the NRA will be obliged to choose. (See *R* v *Director-General of Telecommunications (Respondent), ex parte Cellcom* [1999] ECC 314, with respect to reconciling the principles contained in s. 3(2) of the Telecommunications Act 1984.)

Under existing legislative measures, NRAs may be required to make decisions in respect of disputes between undertakings, such as in interconnection arrangements. However, the speed of NRA decision-making has been reported to the European Commission as a potential barrier to entry in some jurisdictions.[65] Inexperience, insufficient powers and appeal procedures can introduce significant delays, which usually disadvantage the market entrant. The Commission has therefore proposed that NRAs be required to reach a binding decision within two months (Art. 17), a significant advance on its initial proposal of six months.[66]

One proposal to address issues of NRA independence and harmonisation of decision-making between Member States has been the establishment of a European regulatory authority.[67] Currently, the Commission has advisory committees composed of Member State government representatives, the 'ONP Committee' and the 'Licensing Committee' (established under Directive 90/387, Art. 9 and Directive 97/13, Art. 14, respectively), and an *ad hoc* group composed of the regulatory authorities in the Member States (established by the Commission under Council Resolution of 17 December 1992 on the assessment of the situation in the Community telecommunications sector). The Commission's recently published proposed Directive aims to consolidate and formalise these institutional arrangements by creating two new advisory bodies:

(a)   a 'Communications Committee', 'composed of representatives of the Member States'; and

(b)   a 'High Level Communications Group', 'composed of representatives designated by the national regulatory authorities' (Arts 19 and 21).[68]

However, in a parallel proposal, the Commission also intends to increase the number of advisory bodies through the establishment of an advisory body to assist it in 'the strategic planning and harmonisation of the use of radio

---

[65] See Fifth Implementation Report, *supra* n. 16, at Annex 3.
[66] See DG Information Society Working Document, 'A common regulatory framework electronic communications networks and services', 27 April 2000.
[67] See a Commission-funded report by NERA and Denton Hall, *Issues Associated with the Creation of a European Regulatory Authority for Telecommunications* (March 1997). See also Worthy, J. and Kariyawasam, R., 'A pan-European telecommunications regulator?' (1998) 22 *Telecommunications Policy* 1.
[68] See also the 1999 Communications Review, *supra* n. 6, at 4.8.1.

spectrum in the Community'.[69] The body would comprise representatives from the Member States.

After further examination, the Commission has decided that there is currently no need for a European telecommunications authority.[70] There will therefore continue to be institutional asymmetry in the regulation of the telecommunication sector, in contrast to the existence of Member State and European Union competition authorities.

8.4.3 Universal service

One key area of on-going concern to Member States regarding the policy of market liberalisation has been the ability to preserve and pursue the potentially conflicting public policy objective of 'universal service' – the provision of access to telecommunications services for all the state's citizens. In many jurisdictions, the belief that the telecommunications market was one of natural monopoly was closely allied with this need to ensure 'universal service'.

The Treaty establishing the European Community, at Art. 86(2) (ex 90), recognises that undertakings may be entrusted 'with the operation of services of general economic interest' and that the competition rules may be not be applicable to such undertakings where they 'obstruct the performance, in law or in fact, of the particular tasks assigned to them' (the so-called 'public service defence').[71]

The initial liberalisation process envisaged under the 1987 Green Paper was not seen as greatly disturbing the policy of universal service, since the provision of voice telephony (as a 'reserved service') and network infrastructure remained with the national incumbent operator. However, the issue came to the forefront of EU telecommunications policy with the Commission's 1992 telecommunication review, which proposed extending the liberalisation process from services to network infrastructure.[72] The endorsement of this policy by the Council and the European Parliament was qualified by the need to protect universal service, e.g.: '. . . the process of liberalization has to be accompanied by maximum protection of the universal service . . . especially that of weaker consumers and that of peripheral and disadvantaged countries and regions'.[73]

In response, the Commission adopted a Communication addressing the importance of protecting universal service in a liberalised environment, and outlined some of the key issues that comprise a policy on universal service.[74]

---

[69] Proposal for a Decision of the European Parliament and of the Council on a regulatory framework for radio spectrum policy in the European Community, COM (2000) 407 final, 12 July 2000, at Art. 3.

[70] *Ibid.*, at section 2.5. See also Report on the value added of an independent European Regulatory Authority for telecommunications (September 1999).

[71] See Taylor, S.M., 'Article 90 and telecommunications monopolies', (1994) 15 ECLR 332.

[72] Commission Communication to the Council and European Parliament, '1992 Review of the situation in the telecommunications services sector', SEC (92) 1048, 21 October 1992.

[73] European Parliament Resolution of 20 April 1993 on the Commission's 1992 review of the situation in the telecommunications services sector, (1993) OJ C 150/39.

[74] Commission Communication to the Council and the Council and European Parliament, 'Developing universal service for telecommunications in a competitive environment' COM (93) 543, 15 November 1993.

The legislative framework for the European Union's policy on universal service was initially set out in the ONP Voice Telephony Directive (95/62/EC), which detailed the various tiers that comprise the policy. First, a basic voice telephony service must be offered and provided on request without discrimination to all users. Secondly, this service must be supplied under certain harmonised conditions, including the quality of service, provision of information to consumers and billing procedures. Thirdly, certain advanced voice telephony facilities, such as calling-line identification, should be made available (Art. 9 and Annex III).

To ensure transparency of any policy on universal service there is a need to define the scope of universal service:

> . . . a defined minimum set of services of specified quality which is available to all users independent of their geographical location and, in the light of specific national conditions, at an affordable price. (Revised Voice Telephony Directive, Art. 2(2)(f))

Under the principle of subsidiarity, each Member State is able to detail the range of specific services that fall within the 'set', although certain minimum services are required to be made available:

(a)   connection to the fixed public telephone network and access to fixed telephone services at a fixed location;
(b)   the connection to enable the making and receipt of national and international calls, supporting speech, facsimile and data communications;
(c)   directory services;
(d)   public-pay telephones;
(e)   specific measures for disabled users and users with special needs (Revised Voice Telephony Directive, Chapter II).

Even this 'minimum list' represented a process of upward harmonisation for some countries within the Union.

It is also recognised that the definition of 'universal service' will need to evolve over time to reflect the pace of technological and market development. Under the 1999 Communications Review, consideration was given to extending the concept of 'universal service' to include the provision of broadband services, although it was dismissed as premature (section 4.4.1). However, the Commission has proposed that the obligation to provide a connection to support data communications should be further refined to require that the connection be 'at data rates that are sufficient to permit Internet access'.[75] As well as encompassing new service elements, any review may also result in other elements being re-designated as mandatory service components imposed on operators without compensation.[76] The Commission has proposed

---

[75] See Proposal for a Directive of the European Parliament and of the Council on universal service and users' rights relating to electronic communications networks and services, COM (2000) 392, 12 July 2000, at Art. 4(2).
[76] *Ibid.*, at Chapter IV.

a process for a periodic review of the scope of 'universal service', taking into account factors such as whether the majority of consumers use the specific service.[77]

Once defined, the regulatory framework will designate which operators are required to ensure provision of the 'set' of services. While in most Member States the obligation will primarily lie with the incumbent operator, as markets become fully competitive, a USO may be imposed on a number of operators. Alternatively, the provision of different service elements within the 'set' may be placed with different operators.[78]

Defining the scope of universal service also enables regulators to determine the costs associated with its provision and, therefore, mechanisms for ensuring that adequate financing is present within a competitive market. The Full Competition Directive is the first to address the issue of the cost of universal service and related funding mechanisms. In particular, the burden should be placed only upon undertakings providing 'public telecommunications networks', i.e. transmission infrastructure, rather than upon all telecommunication service providers.[79] This contrasts with the position adopted in the United States, where '[e]very telecommunications carrier that provides interstate telecommunications services' is required to contribute.[80]

The Full Competition Directive also addresses the need for incumbent operators to rebalance their tariffs in order to reduce the burden of universal service. Within the broader debate on universal service, the issue of rebalancing has been one of the most politically sensitive for Member State governments to tackle. Historically, incumbent operators have cross-subsidised the cost of installation (i.e., line rental) from future call revenues, particularly long-distance and international. This approach was partly justified on the grounds of ensuring universal service. Indeed, European Court of Justice jurisprudence has recognised that the performance of such tasks of 'general economic interest' (under Art. 86(2) (ex 90), EC Treaty) may involve cross-subsidisation between service elements and could justify the restriction of competition in the profitable market sectors (see *Corbeau* (Case C-320/91) [1993] ECR I-2533, at para. 17 *et seq*). However, with market liberalisation the incumbent is required to remove such cross-subsidies as potential barriers to entry, and to move towards cost-based tariffs. The consequence for customers is that they will often experience significant price rises in line rental and local call charges, while the cost of international and long-distance calls falls.[81] However, the price rises may impact on government policies, particularly inflation targets, as well as being unpopular with the electorate. Therefore, to counter any potential reticence at Member State level, the Directive mandates that:

---

[77] *Ibid.*, at Art. 15 and Annex V.
[78] *Ibid.*, at Art. 8.
[79] Directive 96/19/EC, Art. 6, inserting Art. 4c into Directive 90/388/EC (the Services Directive).
[80] 47 USC §254(d). EU companies have complained that this approach effectively means that EU operators are subsidising US operators.
[81] See Sixth Implementation Report, *supra* n. 17, at p. 27.

Member States shall allow their telecommunications organisations to rebalance tariffs taking account of specific market conditions and of the need to ensure the affordability of a universal service. (Full Competition Directive, Art. 6)

European law also recognises that the move towards cost-based tariffs may require 'progressive adjustment', through the continued use of price caps and geographic averaging, to ensure continuing affordability for certain geographical areas and vulnerable members of society. In particular, Member States must enable operators to offer 'special or targeted tariff schemes' (Revised Voice Telephony Directive, Art. 3).

The term 'universal service' is supposed to have been originally coined by Theodore Vail, Chairman of AT&T, in 1907,[82] although the concept he was promoting was that of universal interconnection, rather than universal access. However, there is an important relationship between network interconnection and the promotion of universal service. If an operator is providing elements of a universal service policy, such as full national network coverage, and also has an obligation to interconnect to any new entrant operator, the former operator may be placed in a disadvantageous competitive position. In the absence of a regulatory obligation to provide such services, the operator would inevitably withdraw from the provision of any uneconomic universal service elements. This connection was recognised by the Council in its 1994 Resolution on universal service, and was given explicit recognition in the Interconnection Directive.[83]

Under the terms of the Interconnection Directive, where a Member State determines that meeting any USOs represents an unfair burden upon an operator, the Member State may:

> . . . establish a mechanism for sharing the net cost of the universal service obligations with other organisations operating public telecommunications networks and/or publicly available voice telephony services. (Art. 5(1))

Such a mechanism may be in the form of a separately administered scheme, such as a universal service fund, or a supplementary charge added to the interconnection charge (Art. 5(2)). Currently nine Member States have established a universal service funding mechanism, although only two, France and Italy, have actually implemented their schemes.[84]

As with many aspects of telecommunications regulation, a key issue is the determination of 'net costs' involved in meeting the USOs, i.e. the additional costs attributable to the obligations.[85] The Interconnection Directive details

---

[82] Stated by Garnham, N., 'Universal Service', in *Telecom Reform* (ed. Melody) (Technical University of Denmark, 1997), at 207.

[83] *Supra* n. 39.

[84] Fifth Implementation Report, *supra* n. 16, at p. 17. The Commission has commenced legal proceedings against France on the basis that its current scheme does not calculate costs in a 'transparent, objective or proportional way' (*Financial Times*, 28 April 2000).

[85] See Chapter 2. See also Commission Communication, 'On assessment criteria for national schemes for the costing and financing of universal service in telecommunications and guidelines for the Member States on operation of such schemes', COM (96) 608, 27 November 1996.

the means by which such cost should be calculated, specifically through the identification of those services provided, or categories of persons served, 'at a loss or under cost conditions falling outside normal commercial standards' (Annex III). Any revenues accruing from the service should be incorporated into the calculation of net cost on a 'forward-looking' basis, since revenues from line rentals, call charges, interconnection and international transit charges may, over the lifetime of the customer, render a service economic. In addition, the NRAs may take into account any market benefits that are perceived to accrue from the provision of universal service, such as the perception of ubiquity in the marketplace (Art. 5(4)).

An alternative proposed mechanism for determining the net cost of 'universal service' is through the operation of public tenders or auctions.[86] Under such an approach operators would be asked to bid for the level of public subsidy that they would require in order to meet the 'universal service' obligation or specific elements of it. The bidder requesting the lowest subsidy would then be 'awarded' the obligation.

To date, Member State experience would not appear to reflect the historic concern shown regarding the threat posed by a competitive market to the provision of universal service. As noted by the Commission:

The availability in the market of a full range of voice and data services at competitive prices, including low-use fixed and mobile tariffs, mobile SMS services and free Internet access or reduced Internet connection, *has removed any concerns which may have been expressed at the outset of liberalisation concerning the availability of a comprehensive service for the entire population* [emphasis added].[87]

Conversely, significant concerns have been raised by new entrants that the potential cost of the USO operates as a barrier to market entry, benefiting the incumbent. Calls have been made for the cost of universal service, as a social policy objective, to be borne by governments, through general taxation, rather than imposed on operators. Responding to such concerns, the Commission has proposed that governments be able to choose between a mechanism for compensation 'from the general government budget', or for the sharing of the cost.[88] It will be surprising if governments are enthusiastic about the former option!

8.4.4   Consumer protection and quality of service

Closely linked to the issue of universal service, European telecommunications law also addresses the quality of services being provided to users and related consumer protection issues. In contrast to universal service, the introduction of competition is generally seen as being of benefit to users in terms of choice, cost and quality. The concern in respect of quality of service issues would

---

[86] Proposal on universal service, *supra* n. 74, at Arts 8(3) and 12(1)(b).
[87] Sixth Implementation Report, *supra* n. 17, at p. 21.
[88] See Commission proposal on universal service, *supra* n. 74, at Art. 13(1).

seem to be primarily in relation to the period of liberalisation, before a market is fully competitive and operators with SMP are the norm.

Part of the liberalisation process commenced under the Equipment Directive and Services Directive (see 8.2 above) addressed provisions regarding customer contracts. From the European's Commission's perspective, such provisions were necessary to facilitate the opening up of the markets by granting customers of telecommunications operators a right to terminate long-term contracts, subject to minimum notification periods.[89] However, the Court of Justice annulled these provisions on the basis that such private contractual arrangements were not 'State measures' to which Art. 90 (now 86), EC Treaty was applicable. Any legal measures against such agreements would need to be the subject of case-by-case decisions made under Arts 85 and 86 (now 81 and 82). Subsequently, provisions governing subscriber contracts and quality of service issues were introduced under the ONP framework.

In pursuance of ensuring quality of service, significant powers of intervention have been granted to NRAs. Under the ONP Voice Telephony Directive, for example, NRAs were given a broad right 'to require alteration of the conditions of contracts' (Art. 7(3)), although this right has subsequently been narrowed to particular types of condition, such as supply time for initial connection (Revised Voice Telephony Directive, Art. 10). The issue of compensation provisions for failing to meet quality of service levels was the subject of a disagreement between the Council and the European Parliament, with the Parliament inserting a general rule in favour of compensation arrangements into the Council's Common Position (i.e., the ONP Voice Telephony Directive, Art. 7(1)).

It would seem questionable whether such powers of intervention should continue to be available in a competitive market. In its 1999 Review, the Commission recognised this point, noting that 'good quality services are more likely to be provided as a result of competition between suppliers rather than from regulation, and consumers may demand services of different quality at different prices' (at 4.5.5). However, the Commission concluded:

> . . . it is considered prudent to maintain some reserve powers for NRAs to take action in the event of market failure, particularly to deal with issues of end-to-end quality in a multi-network environment where no single operator has overall control.

The latter reference is clearly applicable to the growth of the Internet as a communications environment. In addition, a recent report on Member State implementation of the European regulatory package identified a lack of compliance monitoring on consumer issues by NRAs in most Member States, the existence of considerable differences 'in the quality of essential elements of the fixed telephony service' between Member States, and a general rise in the number of consumer complaints.[90]

---

[89] Respectively, Art. 7 of Directive 88/301 (minimum notice one year) and Art. 8 of Directive 90/388 (minimum notice six months).
[90] See Sixth Implementation Report, *supra* n. 17, at p. 22 *et seq.*

Other consumer protection issues addressed in European law are those concerned with data protection, dispute resolution and the transparency of information relating to the provision of the services (e.g., tariffs). The use of personal data is the subject of a separate set of regulatory initiatives, addressing privacy concerns arising between subscribers and their service providers, subscribers and users and the caller and called (see Chapter 11). With respect to the latter issues, it is debatable whether such matters are more appropriately addressed through horizontal measures, such as rules governing distance sales and electronic commerce,[91] rather than sector-specific regulation.

8.4.5 Numbering

In a monopoly environment, one task historically carried out by the incumbent operator is the allocation of telephone numbers. In a liberalised environment, control over such a critical and potentially scarce resource can obviously result in anti-competitive behaviour. Indeed, under the Licensing Directive, the issuance of individual licences may be justified for the purpose of granting access to numbers (Art. 7(1)). As such, numbering is an activity which forms part of the liberalisation process and which, under European Union law, must be 'carried out by a body independent of the telecommunications organisations' (Services Directive, Art. 7). In addition, numbering is seen as a critical access mechanism for European business and citizens, and therefore a key enabler in the development of a competitive market.[92]

To date, European numbering policy has encompassed several different perspectives:

(a)   the introduction of a Europe-wide numbering system;
(b)   the allocation of numbers; and
(c)   number portability and carrier selection.

The Commission has also broadened its attention to encompass 'naming and addressing' schemes that are utilised in packet-switched and Internet environments. In contrast to voice telephony numbering, the governance of IP addresses is carried out by the Internet Corporation for Assigned Names and Numbers (ICANN) (see their website at www.icann.org). ICANN coordinates the operation and allocation of the IP address space and domain name system, especially in relation to top-level domains. However, the actual distribution of addresses is delegated to 'Registries', private entities granted exclusive rights to manage a particular domain. To date, the Commission's ability to intervene in the regulation of the domain name system has therefore been limited to coordinating Member States' positions in the appropriate international organisations and forums.[93] Recently, the Commission has

---

[91] For example, Directive 97/7/EC of the European Parliament and of the Council of 20 May 1997 on the protection of consumers in respect of distance contracts.
[92] Green Paper on a Numbering Policy for Telecommunications Services in Europe, 'Toward a European Numbering Environment', COM (96) 590 final, 20 November 1996.
[93] 1999 Review, *supra* n. 6, at 4.6.1. Proposed Framework Directive, *supra* n. 13, at Art. 9(6).

proposed the creation of a new top-level domain, .eu,[94] and a registry to administer the domain,[95] as part of its effort to promote Trans-European Networks.

8.4.5.1 Europe-wide numbers The introduction of Europe-wide numbers, within a so-called 'European Telephony Numbering Space' (ETNS), has been viewed as an important harmonisation measure towards the achievement of a Single Internal Market.[96] In particular, Europe-wide numbers would enable companies to utilise non-geographic European codes for the provision of pan-European services, such as the provision of mobile services.

In 1991, a common emergency call number (112) was adopted, and in the following year a common international access code (00).[97] However, further progress on the issue has been hindered by the need to obtain an appropriate allocation from the ITU.

8.4.5.2 Number allocation The Services Directive imposes a general obligation upon Member States to ensure that 'adequate numbers are available for all telecommunications services' and that they are allocated in an 'objective, non-discriminatory, proportionate and transparent manner' (Art. 3b, as incorporated by Commission Directive 96/19/EC, Art. 1(3)). The ONP Voice Telephony Directive provided that to ensure fair competition, national telephone numbering plans should be controlled by the NRAs.[98] A consolidated set of principles governing numbering was introduced under the Interconnection Directive, Art. 12. Further consolidation is proposed under a new Directive establishing a common regulatory framework for the electronic communications networks and services.[99]

8.4.5.3 Number portability and carrier selection A critical element in the establishment of a competitive market is the need to lower the barriers to entry faced by potential new entrants. In the telecommunications sector, one such barrier to entry is the need for customers to change telephone numbers when moving to a new service provider. Changing telephone numbers is recognised as being an expensive and time-consuming process which will dissuade many customers from moving between operators.[100] In order to overcome such a potential barrier, the Interconnection Directive called upon the NRAs to encourage the introduction of 'number portability'.

---

[94] See Communication from the Commission, 'Internet Domain Name System – Creating the EU Top Level Domain', COM (2000) 421, 5 July 2000.

[95] Press Release, IP/00/1444, 12 December 2000.

[96] Council Resolution of 19 November 1992 on the promotion of Europe-wide cooperation on numbering of telecommunications services (1992) OJ C 318/2.

[97] Council Decision 91/396/EEC of 29 July 1991 on the introduction of a single European emergency call number, (1991) OJ L 217/31; Council Decision 92/264/EEC of 11 May 1992 on the introduction of a standard international telephone access code in the Community, (1992) OJ L 137/21.

[98] Directive 95/62/EC, Art. 21(1). However, Directive 98/10/EC, at Art. 1(3), replaced Directive 95/62, but contains no similar provision due to the Interconnection Directive, *supra* n. 39.

[99] Proposed Framework Directive, *supra* n. 13, at Art. 9.

[100] See Council Resolution 1992, Recital 5.

Number portability enables customers to retain their telephone numbers for a particular type of service irrespective of the operator providing the service. Under the Interconnection Directive, this concept was introduced in respect of the 'fixed public telephone network' (Art. 12(5)). The time-scales for the achievement of this objective were modest, with a target date for major centres of population of 1 January 2003. However, the Commission soon recognised the critical importance of this initiative for the promotion of liberalisation within Europe and, in 1998, amended the Interconnection Directive.[101]

Under the amended Directive, NRAs were obliged to ensure that number portability was introduced for both fixed line and ISDN services by 1 January 2000.[102] In addition, the amendment introduced the concept of carrier pre-selection. Carrier pre-selection allows a subscriber to access any interconnected provider of service through the use of a particular number. This feature was also seen as a critical facility to enable customers to move between competing operators with minimum effort. The concept is sometimes referred to as 'equal access' and contrasts with the concept of 'easy access'. Under 'easy access' procedures, if a customer chooses to subscribe to a competing operator from that to whom he or she is connected, he or she is able to access that operator through the use of additional numbers prior to the dialling of the called-party's number, e.g., a four-digit number, which identifies to the incumbent's network that calls should be routed to the interconnected operator. However, even this relatively straightforward procedure is seen as a factor that is likely to dissuade customers from changing operators, due to the need for additional numbers. 'Equal access' means that when the customer chooses an operator, the number he or she is allocated comprises the same number of digits irrespective of the operator to whom he or she has subscribed. In addition, the subscriber is required to be given the facility to override this pre-selection on a call-by-call basis through the use of a short prefix, i.e. the methodology of 'equal access' (Number Portability Directive at Art. 1(3), incorporating Art. 12(7) into the Interconnection Directive).

8.5 FUTURE DIRECTIONS

In November 1999, the Commission published the '1999 Communications Review'. This document was intended to set the direction of European Union regulatory policy for the next decade, in a similar fashion to the 1987 Green Paper. The title itself gives an indication of the way in which the market is perceived to be developing, moving from a narrow concept of telecommunications to the broader term 'communications'.

The 1999 Review echoes many of the drivers present in the 1987 Green Paper, including the crucial role that telecommunications plays in enabling

---

[101] Directive 98/61/EC of the European Parliament and of the Council of 24 September 1998 amending Directive 97/33/EC with regard to operator number portability and carrier pre-selection, (1998) OJ L 268/37.

[102] *Ibid.*, at Art. 1(2), replacing Art. 12(5) of the Interconnection Directive. Extended periods were granted to those Member States which had been granted additional transitions periods under the Full Competition Directive, *op. cit. supra* n. 28.

the EU industry to compete in the global information economy, as well as helping to integrate the Member States and reduce regional disparities. However, attention is focused on the ways in which the environment has changed over the past 13 years. In particular, the global liberalisation of the telecommunications market under the WTO agreements; the dramatic impact that mobile telephony and the Internet have had on the delivery of services to users; and the convergence between historically distinct industries, specifically broadcasting and telecommunications.

The Commission has proposed two fundamental shifts in the current regulatory framework. First, there will be a comprehensive reduction in the number of specific legislative instruments regulating the market, from 20 to six, and moving to greater reliance on general principles of competition law. This reflects a belief that the European market has substantially completed the process of transition to a competitive marketplace. The majority of respondents to the consultation process stressed, however, the need to retain much of the *ex-ante* regulatory regime for the time being, due to the continued dominance of the incumbent.[103]

Secondly, a single regulatory structure will be established whereby all forms of electronic communications infrastructure and associated services will be governed in a similar fashion:

'electronic communications network' means transmission systems and, where applicable, switching or routing equipment and other resources which permit the conveyance of signals by wire, by radio, by optical or by other electromagnetic means, including satellite networks, fixed (circuit- and packet-switched, including Internet) and mobile terrestrial networks, networks used for radio and television broadcasting, and cable TV networks, irrespective of the type of information conveyed . . .[104]

All issues relating to the provision of services over such infrastructure will fall outside the regime.

In July 2000, the Commission published six draft Directives, as well as a Regulation on local loop unbundling which has already been adopted.[105] The Directives are intended to comprise the new proposed regulatory framework, and are likely to be implemented in national law by 2003 at the latest.

---

[103] See Commission Communication, 'The results of the public consultation on the 1999 Communications Review and Orientations for the new Regulatory Framework', COM (2000) 239, 26 April 2000.
[104] See generally the Proposal for a Directive of the European Parliament and of the Council on a common regulatory framework for electronic communications networks and services, COM (2000) 393, 12 July 2000.
[105] *Supra* n. 18.

CHAPTER NINE

Overview of US Telecommunications Law

Karen Lee & Jamison Prime

9.1 INTRODUCTION

The US telecommunications market is a dynamic sector that is responding to the commercial changes brought about by the Internet and other new technology. As in Europe, the convergence of fixed, mobile and other media is forcing the bodies who regulate telecommunications to rethink how they approach regulation of this rapidly changing market. Also as in Europe, there is a strong emphasis on rigorous competition along with consumer protection measures, an absence of regulation in new sectors and de-regulation of existing telecommunications infrastructure, with obligations on dominant operators tailored to address market failures and bottlenecks, such as the local loop.

This chapter focuses on the regulation of the provision of telecommunication services and the operation of telecommunication networks in the US, principally in the fixed and cable sectors, but mobile regulation is briefly touched upon. The chapter begins by giving a brief history of US telecommunications regulation of fixed and cable systems, and provides an overview of the numerous regulatory bodies involved in the US telecommunications market. It summarises the licensing requirements under the Communications Act 1934, as well as briefly explaining the US approach to certain key regulatory issues in the EU: spectrum auctioning, local loop unbundling, universal service and interconnection. It concludes with future regulatory reform of the Federal Communications Commission.

9.2 SUMMARY OF US TELECOMMUNICATIONS HISTORY AND KEY REGULATORY DEVELOPMENTS

9.2.1 Terrestrial networks

As in the European Union, the introduction of full competition in the fixed market has occurred via incremental changes. Competition in the local market was mandated following passage of the Telecommunications Act of 1996, which was at the time praised by lawyers, politicians and regulators, but the implementation of which has been delayed following extensive litigation. The Act is, however, the final step in the process towards a competitive market that began in the late 1960s with the introduction of competition in the long-distance markets.

9.2.2 Pre-Communications Act 1934

9.2.2.1 Initial federal regulation Early federal regulation of the telegraph and, later, the telephone helped to establish the basic framework of common carrier regulation for terrestrial networks. In 1866, Congress allowed telegraph operators rights of way along post roads and public lands. In return, the operators agreed to the basic tenet of common carrier regulation – that they would provide service to any customer without discrimination. By the time the telegraph and telephone were formally subjected to federal regulation in 1910, both courts and lawmakers had long regarded the telegraph and telephone to be common carriers akin to railroads and ferry boats. The First Amendment and its restrictions on government regulation of speech played no part in the development of these policies. Instead, regulation of the telephone flowed from regulation of the telegraph, the growth of which coincided with the growth and regulation of America's railroad networks.

9.2.2.2 Evolution of the Bell network With Alexander Graham Bell's development of the telephone, the Bell Company ('Bell') – now better known as AT&T – benefited from its 1876 patent monopoly. The growth of Bell's systems was accelerated by a Supreme Court ruling interpreting the patent broadly, and an agreement whereby Bell would not enter the telegraph business in exchange for Western Union dropping pending patent disputes and litigation. After the Bell patents expired, however, competition flourished, beginning in the mid-1890s. Although independent companies eventually provided up to half of the telephone stations, they were unable to form a nationwide network and service remained primarily local in nature. In addition, many local systems were not interconnected, and it was not unusual for businesses to subscribe to two or more local telephone networks utilising separate lines and equipment. Bell, meanwhile, successfully reorganised its local phone systems into a vertically integrated company and began to acquire the independent phone companies at a rapid pace. By the 1910s, the first era of telephone competition was in decline.

9.2.2.3   The Kingsbury Commitment and universal service   In 1913, AT&T responded to the threat of federal antitrust litigation by agreeing to the Kingsbury Commitment. Under this agreement, AT&T agreed to interconnect with the independent phone companies and to obtain approval before it acquired any competing companies. Although the agreement aided in the development of a nationwide interconnected telephone network, it did little to prevent Bell's growth. Exploiting loopholes in the agreement, Bell continued to acquire local phone systems and eliminate competition. In addition to its local and long-distance telephone infrastructure, Bell also dominated equipment manufacture through its Western Electric unit and communications research via Bell Telephone Laboratories. By the time of the adoption of the Communications Act of 1934, regulators had concluded that the telephone was a natural monopoly that was best served by a single firm. The Bell company, with its local operating companies and long-distance lines, appeared to be that firm.

9.2.3   Communications Act 1934

The Communications Act of 1934 (1934 Act) is significant in that it established the Federal Communications Commission (FCC) as the primary US communications regulatory body and, thus, is the basis for modern federal communications regulation. The text of the 1934 Act, however, generally replicated and consolidated existing legislation. Telecommunications carriers are regulated by Title II of the Act, which was patterned after the 1910 Mann-Elkins Act.[1] The Mann-Elkins Act, in turn, was based on the Interstate Commerce Commission Act of 1877,[2] which set forth common carrier regulation for railroads. Title III of the 1934 Act, which pertains to regulation of radio stations, replaced the Radio Act of 1927[3] which governed the assignment of radio frequencies and radio interference. The Act confers to the FCC broad authority to act on the basis of 'public convenience, interest, or necessity', which serves as the foundation of FCC action and is a basic principle of US telecommunications regulation. Today, most US telecommunications companies own facilities that are subject to both Title II and Title III of the 1934 Act, although Title II continues to serve as the basis for common carrier regulation.

9.2.4   The evolution of competition: 1950–1996

Under the 1934 Act, the FCC's primary duty was to secure universal service. For several decades, the FCC allowed AT&T to retain its monopoly on telecommunications; in turn, AT&T subsidised the cost of line rentals and free local calls by charging heavy mark-ups on national and international calls. Over time, the FCC challenged the view that the provision of telecom-

---

[1]   Mann-Elkins Act (18 June 1910, ch. 309, 36 Stat. 539).
[2]   Interstate Commerce Act (4 February 1887, ch. 104, 24 Stat. 379) (codified in various sections of 49 USC).
[3]   Radio Act of 1927 (23 February 1927, ch. 169, 44 Stat. 116).

munications services was a natural monopoly and gradually sought to introduce increasing levels of competition in long-distance and other markets. This evolution can be broken down into roughly three stages: (i) the introduction of competition into the long-distance market; (ii) the divestiture of the Bell Operating Companies from AT&T; and (iii) the introduction of competition into the local exchange markets.

9.2.4.1 Long-distance competition In 1969, the FCC granted a licence to Microwave Communications, Inc. (MCI) to install and operate microwave facilities that would enable limited inter-office communications to subscribers. The grant of such a licence put MCI in competition with AT&T services, and a myriad applications for similar licences was then filed. In 1971, the FCC in its *Specialized Common Carrier* decision (*Decision in MCI Telecommunication Corp.*, 60 FCC 2d 25 (13 July 1976)) determined that point-to-point communications by private line services (which would effectively allow MCI and others to compete for long-distance business customers) were in the 'public interest'.

The FCC argued that demand for all types of telecommunications services, specifically data transmission, was increasing. Data users required special services that were not adequately being provided by the existing carriers. Users required more diverse and flexible means of communications. Moreover, established carriers would retain the volume of communications they provided, although there might be a relative loss of market share. Thus, the FCC concluded that the introduction of competition in this sector was 'reasonably feasible' and was expected to have 'some beneficial effect'.

Despite permitting competition in private line services, the FCC staunchly opposed the entry of additional common carriers in the public voice telephony market. This ended, however, in 1977, when the United States Court of Appeals for the District of Columbia (the DC Circuit Court) overturned the FCC's order requiring MCI to cease operation of its Execunet division, which essentially provided interstate long-distance service to the public (*MCI Telecommunications Corp. v FCC*, 561 F. 2d 365 (DC Cir. 1977)).

9.2.4.2 Interconnect access and charges Having won the right to provide publicly available long-distance services, MCI and other operators also needed the right to interconnect to AT&T's long-distance and local access facilities. In *Specialized Common Carrier* (see 9.2.4.1), the FCC had ruled that carriers such as AT&T had to provide interconnection services on reasonable terms and conditions to new entrants. Reluctant to enable the new entrants to compete for its customers, AT&T permitted access to residential customers but resisted providing access to its lucrative business customers. MCI and other carriers challenged AT&T, and the FCC ruled in their favour, arguing that new entrants were entitled to similar interconnection services as those enjoyed by AT&T, provided they were technically feasible. The FCC subsequently overturned its own order, but the DC Circuit Court in *Execunet II* later ruled that new entrants were legally entitled to interconnection (*MCI Telecommunications Corp. v FCC*, 580 F. 2d 590 (DC Cir. 1978)).

In parallel with these rulings, the FCC also reviewed the charges interstate common carriers paid to local exchange operators to terminate long-distance calls, which were at the time determined by a complicated settlement rate system. The FCC endorsed the industry's attempt to reach a settlement, but in the early 1980s it was forced to review the issue in its entirety. The results of the FCC review are too detailed to summarise here; however, its exercise focused on AT&T's need to re-balance tariffs in line with costs in order to remove the market distortions and artificial arbitrage opportunities which arose as a result of the funding of universal service.

9.2.4.3 Divestiture of AT&T and the Modification of Final Judgment In 1974, the US Department of Justice brought a suit against AT&T, Western Electric, and Bell Telephone Laboratories, Inc. alleging that the monopoly held by the defendants in several telecommunications service areas and equipment manufacturing violated the Sherman Antitrust Act. The case was pending for eight years until Judge Harold Greene of the DC Circuit Court entered the Modification of Final Judgment (MFJ), which slightly modified divestiture provisions voluntarily agreed to by the parties (*US v AT&T Corp.*, 552 F. Supp. 131 (DC Cir 1982), *aff'd sub nom Maryland* v *US*, 460 U.S. 1001 (1983)). The MFJ ordered AT&T to divest itself of its 22 Regional Bell Operating Companies (RBOCs), which resulted in the separation of local and interexchange (long-distance) markets, and established procedures for the implementation of divestiture.

Under the provisions of the MFJ, the 22 RBOCs, which were eventually reorganised into seven main holding companies (which, by 2001, had been consolidated into four) would provide communication in 'exchange areas' (also known as local access and transport areas (LATAs)). Exchange areas referred in part to a geographic area that encompassed one or more contiguous local exchange areas serving common social, economic and other purposes, even where such configuration transcended municipal or other local governmental boundaries (*US v AT&T Corp*, at 229). Within these exchange areas, RBOCs could originate and terminate calls, while AT&T and other long-distance providers, such as MCI, would carry calls between exchange areas.

In exchange for retaining their monopolies within these exchange areas, RBOCs were prohibited from providing some types of communications services. RBOCs and any affiliated enterprises could provide neither interexchange telecommunication services nor information services. The original settlement provisions sought to restrict the manufacture and provision of customer premises equipment. The MFJ did allow RBOCs to market equipment once they divested from AT&T. However, they could not 'provide any other product or service . . . that is not a natural monopoly service actually regulated by tariff'. These three stipulations limited RBOCs to the provision of toll, private line and 'intercity' services.

The MFJ also sought to ensure that all interexchange service providers (e.g. MCI and Sprint) obtained equal access to RBOC services. The judgment imposed a duty on local exchange carriers to provide service on an 'unbundled, tariffed basis' that was equal in quality, type and cost to that provided to AT&T and its affiliates. In addition, RBOCs were prohibited from discriminating against other service providers in favour of AT&T in the following areas: procurement, establishment and dissemination of technical information, interconnection standards, interconnection and provision of new services and facilities.

Although the RBOCs retained monopolies in local exchange services under the MFJ, they did remain subject to state regulators who did, in some cases, attempt to introduce competition in the local exchange market. In certain jurisdictions, GTE and rural telcos competed with RBOCs for the provision of local exchange services. However, it was not until the passage of the Telecommunications Act of 1996 that the United States formally adopted, at a national level, an aggressive competition policy in local-exchange services.

9.2.5 Competitive carrier rulemaking

With the growing emphasis on market competition in the late 1980s, the FCC initiated a series of proceedings examining how best to adapt the regulatory framework to promote competition among common carriers. Prior to the FCC's investigation, new entrants were subject to the same regulatory obligations under § 214 of the 1934 Act as was AT&T. For example, new entrants were required to (among other things) obtain prior FCC approval for all new tariffs and construction of facilities and file all interconnection agreements. These obligations made market entry less desirable. The FCC therefore sought to minimise the regulatory burden on new entrants while imposing requirements designed to facilitate pricing transparency and curb anti-competitive behaviour by entrenched market players, such as AT&T.

In a series of rulings which mirror OFTEL's distinction between operators with and without so-called 'Market Influence' and 'Significant Market Power', the FCC distinguished between common carriers with market power ('dominant' carriers) and common carriers without market power ('non-dominant' carriers). Dominant carriers were subject to all of the requirements of Title II of the 1934 Act, including the need to provide 90 days' notice for new tariffs and to notify decisions to roll-out network infrastructure. Such restrictions on non-dominant carriers, on the other hand, were removed, as the FCC elected to 'forbear', whereby it did not enforce all of the common carrier requirements of the 1934 Act. However, non-dominant carriers had to ensure that their service charges were not 'unjust or unreasonable'.

To determine whether a common carrier had market power, the FCC defined certain relevant markets, utilising traditional antitrust analysis. These markets were the provision of all interstate, domestic and interexchange services in the US, including Hawaii, Alaska and the US territories. Unsurprisingly, it declared AT&T and local exchange operators, such as GTE, dominant, citing their control of local access facilities and their share of the residential market. Resellers and other companies, such as MCI, were deemed non-dominant.

In subsequent proceedings in the early 1990s, the FCC again examined AT&T's position in the long-distance market. It found that the business long-distance market was 'substantially competitive' and it removed the regulatory requirements on this aspect of AT&T's business but retained the regulatory obligations (including price caps) on AT&T's residential long-distance services. In a controversial order made in 1995, the FCC reclassified AT&T as a non-dominant carrier in all service markets. (Motion of AT&T to be Re-classified as a Non-dominant Carrier, 11 FCC Rcd 327 (1995).

9.2.6 Value-added services

In addition to promoting fixed network competition in the 1970s, the FCC also advocated competition in the value-added or 'enhanced' services area. In *Computer Inquiry I* (Regulatory Pricing Problems Presented by the Interdependence of Computer and Communication Facilities, Final Decision and Order, 28 FCC 2d 267 (1971)), the FCC considered the need to regulate common carriers who were beginning to provide data-processing services over traditional telephony lines and, more broadly, the need to regulate the data-processing industry as a whole. The FCC declined to regulate data-processing by drawing artificial distinctions between 'hybrid communications' which were regulated and 'hybrid data processing' which was not. The FCC did, however, mandate that any common carrier whose turnover exceeded US $1 million and who wished to offer data-processing services, had to do so by a separate corporate entity. In practice, the requirement affected only AT&T and the large RBOCs that were originally part of AT&T, and was imposed to minimise their ability to use telephony revenue to cross-subsidise their data-processing businesses to the detriment of their fixed telecommunication subscribers.

In *Computer Inquiry II* (Amendment of § 64.702 of the Commission's Rules and Regulations, Second Computer Inquiry, 77 FCC 2d 384), the FCC revisited the issue of value-added services following the inevitable confusion that arose as a result of *Computer Inquiry I*. The FCC distinguished between so-called 'basic' and 'enhanced' services. Regulated 'basic' services consisted of providing transmission capacity, whereas unregulated 'enhanced' services were basic transmission services coupled with computer processing applications. *Computer Inquiry II* is also significant as the FCC removed the structural separation requirements from all carriers with the exception of AT&T and the RBOCs.

Following the implementation of the MFJ, during which it strongly advocated structural separation, the FCC issued *Computer Inquiry III* (Amendment of § 64,702 of the Commission's Rules and Regulations, Third Computer Inquiry, Report and Order, 104 FCC 2d 958 (1986)), which permitted the RBOCs to integrate their basic and enhanced services. The FCC remained concerned, however, about the ability of the RBOCs to leverage their dominance in network access markets, but argued that cost-allocation methods and targeted regulations were sufficient to prevent RBOCs from abusing their market power to the detriment of enhanced service providers. Because of procedural errors, the FCC's decision was overturned on appeal (*People of the State of California* v *FCC*, 905 F.2d 1217

(9th Cir. 1990), but the FCC eventually adopted cost-allocation methods and targeted regulations (see *Computer III*, Further Remand Proceedings: Bell Operating Company Provision of Enhanced Services, 10 FCC Rcd 8760 (1995)). The FCC continues to require incumbent, local-exchange carriers to provide commercial mobile services through affiliates.

9.2.7 Local-exchange competition and the Telecommunications Act of 1996

The Telecommunications Act of 1996[4] (the 1996 Act) marks the first time Congress has established policy objectives for the telecommunications sector since the adoption of the 1934 Act. The 1996 Act is significant in that it declares invalid all state regulation that prohibits or restricts the entry of competitors into intrastate telecommunications services. The 1996 Act over-turned the MFJ provisions which allowed the RBOCs to retain monopolies in the lucrative local market. In addition, the 1996 Act removed the MFJ's restrictions on the provision of interstate telephony services by local exchange owners, provided, however, they comply with a 'competitive' checklist.

Section 251 of the 1996 Act imposes a general duty on all telecommunication carriers to interconnect 'directly or indirectly' with the facilities of other carriers. It goes on to require the following of incumbent local exchange carriers and new entrants to the market:[5]

(a)   to permit re-sale on reasonable and non-discriminatory terms;
(b)   to provide number portability;
(c)   to provide dialling parity and access to telephone numbers, directory assistance and operator services;
(d)   to afford access to poles, conduits and rights-of-way; and
(e)   to establish reciprocal compensation arrangements for the transport and termination of telecommunications.

The 1996 Act, however, imposes additional obligations on incumbent local exchange carriers which are outlined below. An incumbent must:

(a)   allow interconnection to any technically feasible point within its network. Rates charged by the incumbent for interconnection also must be fair and non-discriminatory. The service provided must be equal in quality to service supplied to itself or any affiliate;
(b)   provide 'non-discriminatory access to network elements on an unbundled basis at any technically feasible point on rates, terms and conditions that are just, reasonable and non-discriminatory';

---

[4] Pub. L. 104–104, 110 Stat. 56 (8 February 1996) (codified at 47 USC §§251–261, 271–276, 336, 363, 571–573, 549, 613, 160–161, 560–561, 230, 232, 614, and at 15 USC §79z–5c).
[5] However, the 1996 Act does exempt from the local exchange provisions rural telephone carriers and local exchange carriers with less than 2 per cent of the US's subscriber lines, provided the Public Utility Commission determines it is in the public interest and has no adverse effect on consumers. 47 USC §251(f)(1)–(2).

(c)   offer for re-sale on a wholesale basis any retail telecommunications services that it provides. The terms of re-sale also must be reasonable and non-discriminatory;

(d)   provide any information that affects the interoperability of facilities and networks;

(e)   furnish physical co-location of equipment necessary for interconnection or unbundled network elements, again on just, reasonable and non-discriminatory rates, terms and conditions (47 USC § 251).

Under § 251(d) of the 1996 Act, the FCC was charged with the task of establishing regulations implementing the requirements for local competition, and in particular, the three ways in which service providers can enter the local telephony market: full facilities-based entry, the purchase of unbundled network elements, and the re-sale of an incumbent's existing retail services.

The implementation of the 1996 Act has proved difficult for the FCC and its benefits have not been as rapidly seen as the lawmakers had hoped. Recently progress has been made, although certain difficulties continue.

9.3   CABLE

Since its inception in the 1950s, cable television has evolved from a video transmission service to a likely competitor for advanced voice and data services. As one would expect, government attitudes toward and regulation of the medium have likewise evolved.

9.3.1   History and development

Cable systems are primarily local in nature, due to their design and regulation. Typically, a cable 'head end' facility receives over-the-air broadcast and satellite signals via a series of antennae and dishes. These signals are then transmitted via wire throughout the community the cable company serves, usually on telephone poles or along streets and other public rights of way, and an individual cable line runs to each subscriber. Because a cable signal weakens the further it is from the head end, there is a technological limit to the scope of an individual cable system. Also, due to their use of local rights of way, cable systems are subject to local regulation and must obtain and periodically renew a local franchise licence in order to operate.

The first cable systems served as community antenna television (CATV) systems, and allowed households in mountainous regions to view local television stations whose signals would otherwise be unavailable. Later, cable service expanded into metropolitan areas that could receive over-the-air broadcasts. In the late 1970s and throughout the 1980s, cable began to provide programming unavailable through over-the-air broadcast stations. These services included specialised channels, such as CNN and MTV, and 'pay cable' services, such as HBO and 'pay-per-view' sporting events and movies, for which the subscriber pays a premium above the normal monthly cable fee. In part due to cable's potential to provide non-video programming, many cable systems began upgrading their systems in the 1990s with the promise of hundreds of channels of specialised programming and advanced voice and data services. At the same time, the industry began to consolidate – first within the cable industry and, more recently, between cable companies and other communications providers.

9.3.2   Regulation of cable

Initially, the FCC declined to regulate cable. However, as cable evolved beyond simple community antenna systems, the FCC and state regulators became concerned that cable's carriage of free-to-air broadcast signals could fragment audiences and harm local broadcasters' revenue bases. Concern also arose that cable was profiting from the free retransmission of copyrighted programming paid for by the local broadcasters. In the 1960s, without specific statutory authority to do so, the FCC began its regulation of cable by adopting policies designed to protect free-to-air broadcasters. Despite the FCC's initial hostility toward cable, the medium continued to grow. By 1980, the FCC had relaxed many of its initial cable regulations and Congress passed the first laws specifically addressing the medium.

The Cable Communications Act of 1984[6] (the 1984 Cable Act) served a dual purpose: while it furthered efforts to deregulate cable, it set forth the first statutory framework for cable regulation. The 1984 Cable Act gave the FCC explicit authority to regulate cable, but it removed issues such as subscriber rates and program carriage from its jurisdiction. Similarly, the 1984 Cable Act limited state and local regulation, which at that time was viewed as an impediment to the growth of cable. Cable rates rose rapidly after de-regulation, and both the FCC and Congress soon faced public pressure to do something about the situation. Congress acted by passing the Cable Television Consumer Protection and Competition Act of 1992,[7] which repealed many provisions of the 1984 Cable Act. Congress greatly expanded the FCC's role in cable regulation. This legislation was a departure from the previous approach, which emphasised less regulation and greater competition, particularly in rate regulation.

Only a few years later, as part of its broad review of communications law and policy in the Telecommunications Act of 1996, Congress again modified cable regulation. The 1996 Act repealed certain cable-specific regulation, and adopted policies designed to encourage the broad provision of telecommunications services. To that end, the 1996 Act removed restrictions that had limited telephone companies from providing cable services, while concurrently, over a three-year period, phasing out many of the cable rate regulations adopted in 1992. The 1996 Act further limited local and state regulation of cable, although municipalities continue to play a role in granting and renewing local cable franchises.

The role of the FCC's Cable Services Bureau, established in 1993 to implement and enforce the 1992 Cable Consumer Act, has nevertheless

---

[6] Cable Communications Policy Act of 1984, Pub. L. 98–549, 98 Stat. 2779 (30 October 1984).
[7] Pub. L. 102–385, 106 Stat. 1460 (5 October 1992).

expanded despite passage of the Telecommunications Act of 1996. Today, the Cable Services Bureau monitors and acts to promote competition in the broadly defined multichannel video programming marketplace, and monitors pricing and the state of competition. It enforces several mandates, including television broadcast signal carriage, commercial leased access and program access. It also regulates 'open video systems' and other competitors to traditional, incumbent cable operators.

Throughout the evolution of cable, the courts have generally upheld efforts to regulate the medium. In 1968, the Supreme Court acknowledged the FCC's right to regulate cable, concluding that it was 'interstate commerce by wire or radio' subject to the FCC's authority under the broad provisions of the Communications Act of 1934 (*United States* v *Southwestern Cable Co.*, 392 U.S. 157 (1968)). Although cable providers are akin to broadcasters and newspapers, in that they select programming for distribution, they are also similar to common carriers in that they mostly transmit, unaltered, content originated by third parties. Courts have been deferential to cable regulation, and have been unwilling to afford the types of First Amendment protection from regulation offered to newspapers and, to a lesser extent, to broadcasters.

9.3.3   The future of cable

Because cable is physically wired into each subscriber's home or office, it offers an enviable conduit for the delivery of broadband services beyond basic video programming. Cable providers have explored the possibility of cable-delivered telephony, and many have begun offering cable-delivered Internet services. In conjunction with this development, many Internet service providers (ISPs) have begun to lobby for 'open access' to cable networks, in which third parties could obtain access to existing cable infrastructure at reasonable rates. In September 2000, the FCC issued a Notice of Inquiry seeking to develop a record in this area. In addition, the FCC adopted certain conditions in approving the AOL and Time Warner Merger in January 2001 that were viewed favourably by proponents of open access. The ultimate resolution of this issue, however, remains uncertain.

Although individual cable systems remain local in nature, the industry as a whole has undergone a rapid consolidation and evolution since passage of the Telecommunications Act of 1996. First, within the industry, small and regional cable companies have been bought out by cable conglomerates. The end of the 1990s saw the first large-scale convergence between cable entities and other telecommunications providers, as AT&T acquired cable giant TCI, and Internet provider America Online (AOL) merged with cable and content giant Time Warner. At the same time, realistic competitors have emerged for cable's traditional video delivery. Direct broadcast satellite (DBS) systems, which allow consumers to receive video via pizza box-size dish antennae, the 'overbuilding' of separate cable infrastructures to compete with incumbent cable operators, and radio-delivered video programming, all offer additional means for households to receive video programming. One selling point for these competing video providers – and a possible detriment to cable's entry into advanced services – is the cable industry's reputation for spotty service quality and the perception of price gouging that lingers from the Cable Communications Act of 1984. However, the trend toward cross-service consolidation may allow cable to side-step these public perception problems as cable companies merge with telecommunications providers that have more favourable reputations.

9.4 OVERVIEW OF KEY US REGULATORY BODIES AND PROCEDURAL PRINCIPLES

Telecommunications regulation occurs at both state and federal levels in the United States, and the number and different types of regulatory bodies reflect the diversity of the 50 states and the federal government, as well as the involvement of the executive and legislative branches of government in this area.

At the federal level, the FCC, principally responsible for all interstate and foreign telecommunications issues and (following the passage of the Telecommunications Act 1996) certain intrastate issues, is the most well-known regulatory body. Its jurisdiction covers numerous sectors, including fixed, mobile, satellite and broadcasting, as well as licensing and enforcement. This is unlike the UK where different regulatory bodies are responsible for licensing, enforcement and various sectors, although the recent Communications White Paper proposes that the UK adopt an Office of Communications, similar in size and scope to the FCC. The work of the FCC is complemented by that of the National Telecommunications and Information Administration, the Department of Justice and the Federal Trade Commission.

At the state level, each of the 50 states and the District of Columbia has a public utility or public commission responsible for all telecommunications issues, including policy, licensing and enforcement, arising within its jurisdiction. Having said that, state jurisdiction has in certain areas been reduced by the Telecommunications Act 1996 and the use of the federal pre-emption doctrine (see 9.8). The work of the state regulators is also coordinated by the National Association of Regulatory Utility Commissioners.

The FCC is unique in that it wields a significant amount of policy-making authority. It has expansive jurisdiction over telecommunications issues, despite certain statutory limitations contained in the Communications Act 1934. It exercises its authority via its rule-making and order functions, but like all federal governmental agencies, remains subject to certain restrictions and key procedural principles contained in the Administrative Procedure Act.

9.5 FEDERAL BODIES

9.5.1 The Federal Communications Commission

9.5.1.1 Role and jurisdiction The FCC has full jurisdiction over all issues surrounding interstate (or interLATA) and foreign communications which originate and/or are received in the US, including all aspects of fixed, mobile, cable, satellite, broadcasting and commercial radio spectrum and, in particular, tariffs, mergers and acquisitions. The FCC's jurisdiction covers both service providers and facilities-based operators, unlike in the UK where the scope of primary legislation is currently limited to the so-called 'running' of telecommunications systems. Within its jurisdiction, the FCC has broad authority to ensure compliance with federal telecommunications law, subject to the requirement that any action taken is 'consistent with the public interest, convenience and necessity', and is specifically granted the power to 'perform any and all acts, make such rules and regulations, and issue such orders . . . as may be necessary in the execution of its functions'. It is important to note that the regulatory power is conferred to the FCC as a whole rather than to an individual as in the UK and certain other European countries.

9.5.1.2 Commissioners The FCC currently consists of five Commissioners (it originally had seven), each of whom is appointed by the President. The US Senate must, however, confirm the President's selections, and potential candidates are usually subject to a public confirmation hearing. Commissioners serve five-year terms, although a Commissioner may be re-appointed. All Commissioners must be US citizens, and a maximum of three Commissioners may have the same political party affiliation. On a practical level, the Commissioners are responsible for formulating key policy initiatives, implementing new legislation and adopting agency rules and regulations. However, the Commissioners delegate the day-to-day running of the FCC to its bureaux and offices.

One of the five Commissioners is designated by the President to serve as chairman, whose general duty is to coordinate the 'prompt and efficient disposition of all matters within the jurisdiction of the Commission'. The Chairman presents the views of the FCC as a whole and benefits from the ability to set the agency's agenda. Each Commissioner, including the Chairman, has the discretion to present his own non-binding views on any particular issue.

9.5.1.3 Bureaux and offices The 1934 Act confers on the FCC the general power to organise its staff into integrated bureaux and/or other divisional organisations as it deems necessary. It may also (in the interests of efficiency and cost-effectiveness) delegate its powers to its employees. The FCC may not delegate certain functions, such as evaluating the lawfulness of tariffs and the resolution of complaints, but, effectively, the bureaux share with the Commissioners the duties of the day-to-day running of the FCC. The FCC is staffed by a staff of approximately 2,000 employees, the vast majority of whom work in the FCC's Washington, DC headquarters. The FCC also operates a technical laboratory in Maryland, a licensing office in Pennsylvania, and has a small network of enforcement field offices throughout the United States.

Following a recent restructuring, the FCC now has seven operating bureaux, which handle the FCC's workload. In 2001, the FCC continued to be structured by the types of services the FCC regulates. For example, the Common Carrier Bureau is concerned primarily with 'traditional' fixed and radio common carriers, or public telecommunications operators as they are known in the UK. It is responsible for the licensing of these entities, including the disconnection and reduction of services, and mandating the minimum accounting standards and reporting methodologies. It also evaluates merger applications. Other major offices include: the International Bureau, which is responsible for the FCC's international telecommunications and satellite programs, implements international treaties concerning telecommunications, and licenses cable landings as well as satellite and earth stations; the Mass Media Bureau, which is charged with regulating AM and FM radio stations and television broadcast stations; and the Wireless Telecommunications Bureau, which regulates all aspects of mobile communications, including cellular services, personal communications services, paging, public safety radio frequencies, amateur and other personal radio services, specialised mobile and microwave radio services. The FCC is supported by 11 offices which, among other things, represent its legal interests, provide technology and economic advice, and offer general administrative support.

9.5.1.4 Enforcement powers Unlike the limited enforcement powers conferred on the UK's DGT under the Telecommunications Act 1934, the FCC enjoys broad and powerful enforcement mechanisms. The FCC may enforce the provisions of the Communications Act 1934 directly, or request the United States federal district courts to initiate enforcement proceedings. Breach of the 1934 Act's provisions may result in monetary fines, revocation of the underlying authorisation or obligations to take the necessary steps to remedy the breach. The FCC and the district courts may also require authorised carriers to produce documentation relevant to the investigation upon request.

9.5.2 National Telecommunications and Information Administration

The National Telecommunications and Information Administration (NTIA) was created by executive order in 1978 and by statute in 1993 (Executive Order 12046 and statute codified at 47 USC §901 *et seq.*). It is an agency of the Department of Commerce. Whereas the FCC manages 'public' spectrum, the NTIA administers spectrum for exclusive government use, such as those radio frequencies used by the armed services. In addition, the NTIA advises the President on telecommunications policy. For example the NTIA has been involved in recent efforts to identify suitable spectrum for 3G wireless applications in the US. The NTIA also negotiates for greater market access in foreign countries for US companies and administers granted programs related to telecommunications. Although it has no official power over non-governmental interests, the NTIA's actions can affect the interests of private entities, and industry leaders have criticised the NTIA for its lack of openness. However, the agency has initiated programs that seek to include participation by the private sector.

9.5.3 Competition authorities

Federal antitrust law has played a key role in the regulation of telephony and to a lesser extent in other areas such as broadcasting and television. The primary US antitrust laws are the Federal Trade Commission Act,[8] Clayton Act[9] and the Sherman Anti-trust Act.[10] All of the legislation is enforced by the Federal Trade Commission's Bureau of Competition and the Antitrust division of the Department of Justice (DoJ). Technically the jurisdiction of these two bodies overlaps, but the agencies in practice agree which one will initiate an investigation into alleged anti-competitive conduct. Both the DoJ and the Federal Trade Commission have also been heavily involved in assessing the competitive effect of several key industry mergers, including the AT&T and BT joint venture, SBC's acquisition of Pacific Bell and MCI WorldCom's attempted purchase of Sprint (which faltered due to antitrust concerns in the US and in Brussels). The antitrust division of the DoJ also advises the FCC on applications by RBOCs to provide competitive long-distance service.

9.5.4 Courts

The passage and implementation of the Telecommunications Act 1996 has triggered a flurry of legal challenges to the federal courts (and the DC Circuit Court in particular), resulting in several key decisions by the Supreme Court regarding federal pre-emption and, most recently, unbundled network elements. Judicial intervention is not new in the telecommunications area and, where judicial authority has been exercised in the past, the courts have tended to adopt a more pro-competitive approach than the FCC. For example, it was Judge Greene of the DC Circuit Court who entered and monitored the implementation of the MFJ, which resulted in the divestiture of AT&T (see 9.2.4.3 above).

9.5.5 Congress and the President

The FCC is an 'independent' agency established by Congress under the Communications Act 1934. However, both Congress and the President exercise considerable influence over the agency.

The Congress consists of the Senate and the House of Representatives. The Senate is composed of 100 members two are elected from each of the 50 states. Each member ('senator') serves a term of six years. The House of Representatives, on the other hand, is composed of 435 representatives from all of the 50 states. The number of representatives for each state is determined by the population that resides there. Each state is entitled to at least

---

[8] Federal Trade Commission Act, ch. 311, 38 Stat. 717 (26 September 1914) (codified at 15 USC §41–58).
[9] Clayton Act, ch. 323, 38 Stat. 730 (15 October 1914) (codified at 15 USC §12–278 and 29 USC §§52, 53).
[10] Sherman Anti-trust Act, ch. 647, 26 Stat. 209 (2 July 1980) (codified at 15 USC §1–7).

one representative, who serves a term of two years. Broadly speaking, any proposed legislation must be approved by a majority of representatives in both the Senate and the House of Representative before it is passed to the President, who will decide whether to sign the proposed legislation into law.[11]

The FCC's budget, which in 2001 exceeded US$300 million, is authorised by Congress, although a large portion of this amount comes directly from regulatory fees and other FCC-collected funds. The FCC must account for its annual spending and file an annual report to Congress containing information to facilitate Congressional review of its performance. Congress can also pass legislation directing the FCC to implement specific policy objectives, such as to auction a designated frequency block by a set date. In recent years, Congress has tended to enact legislation which somewhat constrains the FCC's traditional freedom to establish telecommunications policy within a broad legislative framework. In addition, Commissioners are frequently called to testify before Congressional committees. Given its degree of influence over the FCC, it is not surprising that Congress is heavily lobbied by industry participants and consumer advocate groups. Members of Congress are not hesitant to criticise the FCC's actions publicly, particularly when they believe the FCC is implementing laws in ways that are inconsistent with Congressional intent.

The President (and his Administration) also play a role via the appointment of FCC Commissioners, including the Chairman, the majority of whom may represent his political party. However, these appointments are subject to approval by the Senate.

9.6 STATE BODIES

9.6.1 Public Utility Commissions

The 1934 Act conferred extensive interstate jurisdiction on the FCC, while at the same time explicitly reserving jurisdiction over intrastate communication services to the 50 states as well as the District of Columbia. The state Public Utility Commissions (PUCs) are responsible for telecommunications regulation at this level. State jurisdiction over telecommunications has, in some areas, been reduced by the Telecommunications Act of 1996 and the use of the federal pre-emption doctrine by the FCC (see 9.8). The PUCs approve tariffs and interconnection rates for intrastate telephony, handle customer complaints and issue intrastate licences.

In addition to regulating telecommunications, PUCs oversee all other public utility functions. The structure and size of the PUCs and each of their telecommunications policies differ (significantly in some cases) from state to state, but generally all PUCs are state-created agencies with a division specialising in telecommunications regulation. Historically, some PUCs, in states such as Illinois, New York and California, embraced competition in the local exchange markets; others have thwarted competitive efforts by the FCC.

---

[11] For further information, see, for example, www.lc.web.loc.gov.global/legislative/about.html.

Although the Telecommunications Act of 1996 extends the FCC's authority to cover local competition, state regulators retain some jurisdiction over telephony issues. Their jurisdiction is limited, however, in many cases to ensuring compliance with federal regulations rather than developing policy. State regulators have the right to prohibit market entry of service providers if necessary to advance or preserve universal service, public safety and telecommunications services. However, any regulation imposed by the states must be done so on a 'competitively neutral basis' and be consistent with the universal service obligations (USOs) set forth in § 254 of the 1934 Act.

9.6.2 National Association of Regulatory Utility Commissioners

In addition to the PUCs, the National Association of Regulatory Utility Commissioners (NARUC) also plays a role in the development of US telecommunications. The Association is comprised of federal and state utility regulators and strives to coordinate action by state regulators and to develop cooperation between federal and state regulators. Despite these aims, in practice the Association represents the interests of state regulators and becomes publicly involved with issues only when consensus already exists among the PUCs. It has six standing committees, including one for communications.

9.7 PROCEDURAL PRINCIPLES AND MECHANISMS: THE ADMINISTRATIVE PROCEDURE ACT

9.7.1 Administrative law principles

Because the FCC is neither a judicial nor a legislative body, it operates under the general principles of administrative law. Administrative agencies such as the FCC are considered to have regulatory expertise in discrete subject areas, and Congress usually passes laws containing general guidelines as opposed to specific regulations (but see the discussion at 9.9.5). Under a theory of delegation, agencies exercise broad discretion to interpret and apply those laws and will use their legislative authority to enact their own specific rules and regulations. For example, § 303(a) of the 1934 Act gives the FCC broad authority to classify radio stations. The FCC has used this authority to establish rules for and to license specific radio services, such as the 39 GHz Microwave Service or Low Power FM Radio. Each agency's rules are compiled in the Code of Federal Regulations (CFR). The FCC's rules are contained in Volume 47.

9.7.2 Administrative Procedure Act – rulemaking

Although administrative agencies such as the FCC have broad discretion to interpret and apply laws, they must act within established procedural guidelines. The Administrative Procedure Act[12] sets forth the basic 'notice and comment' framework that the FCC uses in promulgating rules, and ensures both publication of proposed rules and the opportunity for the public to comment before a rule is adopted. Either on its own motion, or in response to a 'Petition for Rulemaking', the FCC typically issues a 'Notice of Proposed Rulemaking' that announces proposed rules, describes the legislative authority on which the rules are based, and provides the public with an opportunity to file comments addressing the proposal. The FCC may first issue a 'Notice of Inquiry' that contains no proposals in order to generate a public record in a subject area, although this is rarely done. After considering the record developed by the Notice of Proposed Rulemaking, the FCC will issue a 'Report and Order' adopting final rules. These rules typically take effect 60 days after publication in the Federal Register, which is the US government's daily compilation of actions taken by the FCC and other agencies. In a typical proceeding, however, the FCC may issue a document adopting rules while simultaneously proposing additional rules. Thus, it is common for the docket in a proceeding to remain 'open' for years. Although a majority of Commissioners' votes are needed to adopt an item, it is typical for individual Commissioners to attach statements explaining their decisions.

9.7.3 Issuance of orders – adjudicatory action

Much of the FCC's day-to-day work involves the issuance of adjudicatory orders addressing individual applications and petitions brought under the existing rules. Although these orders generally relate to a discrete matter, they are significant in that they provide insight as to how the FCC interprets its own rules and may be cited as precedent in subsequent actions before the FCC. Many of these orders are issued under delegated authority, either by a bureau chief or deputy, or by a division chief, although some orders are adopted by the FCC as a whole. FCC staff may also resolve matters by issuing a non-published letter, although this option is often used for routine processing matters, such as the dismissal of a defective application.

9.7.4 Review of FCC action

Review of FCC action is generally accomplished by the filing of a 'Petition for Reconsideration', or, if the action was taken under delegated authority, by an 'Application for Review'. A party must file its application or petition within a set time period (generally 30 days) to preserve its right for review.

---

[12] The Administrative Procedure Act, ch. 324, 60 Stat. 237 (11 June 1946) (codified at 5 USC §§551–559, 701–701, 1305, 3344, 4301, 5335, 5372, 7521) generally refers to specific sections of Chaps 5 and 7 of Pt 1 'The Agencies Generally' of Title 5, 'Government Organization and Employees', US Code. Chapter 5 'Administative Procedure' governs procedures for various agency decision-taking as permitted by the agency's underlying statute (although this chapter also includes, *inter alia*, The Freedom of Information Act, 5 USC §552 and the Privacy Act, 5 USC §552a). Chapter 7 'Judicial Review' addresses the review of such decision by the federal courts.

In addition, the FCC may set aside an action on its own motion within 30 days. Although both the Administrative Procedure Act and the FCC's rules contain provisions for formal hearings once the FCC has addressed these petitions and applications, these procedures have become uncommon. Instead, parties typically bypass formal hearings and appeal directly to federal courts, in particular the DC Circuit Court.

When reviewing an FCC decision, a court will consider whether the FCC acted within its powers, both within the broad powers of the Communications Act 1934 and under the specific legislation upon which the FCC based its rules or action. In addition, a court may, under the Administrative Procedure Act, set aside the FCC's decision if it is arbitrary, capricious, an abuse of discretion, or unsupported by evidence in the record. Courts often invoke the Administrative Procedure Act to set aside or remand an action when the FCC has not explained the basis for its decision in the written order it adopted.

9.8 THE PRE-EMPTION DOCTRINE AND FCC JURISDICTION

The 1934 Act created a two-tier system of regulators: (i) the FCC, which is responsible for regulating interstate and foreign commerce in wire and radio communications; and (ii) state PUCs, with implicitly reserved powers to regulate intrastate communications. However, under the Tenth Amendment of the US Constitution, all powers not expressly given to the Federal Government are reserved to the states. The creation of dual regulators reflected this need to balance the interests of state and federal governments in the US federal system, and, in theory, states retain complete control over common carriers providing telecommunication services within their borders.

The actual power states have to regulate intrastate commerce, however, has been reduced as a result of expansive interpretations of Commerce Clause[13] powers by the Supreme Court and the use of the pre-emption doctrine based on the Supremacy Clause. Broadly speaking, the Supremacy Clause explicitly enables Congress and federal agencies, acting within the scope of their statutory authority, to pre-empt state law when, for example, state law frustrates the federal purpose of legislation. In the telecommunications sector, the Supreme Court has found that many seemingly *intrastate* activities directly and/or indirectly affect *interstate* commerce and, thus, fall within the ambit of the FCC.

The FCC's need to rely on the pre-emption doctrine did not arise until the 1960s, when it sought to stimulate competition in the intrastate telephony market and tension between state regulators arose over the funding of universal service.[14] *North Carolina Utilities Commission* v *FCC* 537 F. 2d 787, (4th Cir.), *cert. denied*, 429 US 1027 (1976) (*NCUC I*) was the first in a series of cases that enlarged the jurisdiction of the FCC to include some power over intrastate communications via reliance on the pre-emption doctrine. *NCUC*

---

[13] The Commerce Clause of the US Constitution gives the Federal Government the power to regulate commerce 'among the several states' and with foreign nations.
[14] 'Universal service' is described more fully in 9.12.

I arose because several state regulators imposed conditions on the interconnection of non-AT&T telephone hardware to the local system in an effort to limit the scope of the FCC's *Carterfone* decision (*In re the Use of the Carterfone Device in Message Toll Service* v *AT&T*, 13 FCC 2d 420 (1968), which permitted apparatus conforming to AT&T's system specifications to connect to the phone network. The Fourth Circuit reasoned that because the same handsets were used by customers to place interstate and intrastate calls, the state and federal regulations were incompatible with each other and that state regulation had to give way to federal law.

The case is significant as it attempted to define the ambiguous terms – 'interstate' and 'intrastate' – found in the 1934 Act. The court held that § 2(b) of the 1934 Act only limits the FCC from regulating matters that 'in their nature and effect are separable from and do not substantially affect the conduct or development of interstate communications' (*NCUCI* at 793). Under this two-prong test, state regulators retain jurisdiction over issues that are separable from interstate communications and that have no impact on interstate telecommunications. If separation of interstate and intrastate communications is impossible, the FCC has or acquires jurisdiction.

The Supreme Court modified the *NCUC I* test in *Louisiana Pub. Serv. Commission* v *FCC* 476 U.S. 355 in 1986. In *Louisiana*, the Court held that the FCC has jurisdiction only if the FCC can demonstrate that interstate and intrastate issues are inseparable and that the exercise of jurisdiction by the state frustrates the statutory authority of the FCC.

The Telecommunications Act of 1996 further augmented the scope of the FCC's jurisdiction. Under § 251(d), the FCC is now required to introduce competition into the local loop. Sections 251(d)(3)(A)–(C) expressly enable the FCC to pre-empt any state legislation that contravenes the purposes of local competition. In addition, the FCC may pre-empt any state regulation that may 'prohibit or have the effect of prohibiting the ability of any entity to provide interstate and intrastate telecommunications service'.

Attempts by the FCC to implement measures to introduce local competition have, however, been challenged by incumbent local exchange carriers (ILECs) and PUCs on the grounds that the FCC lacks the requisite authority to promulgate rules on such issues as pricing of local services and dialling parity. The Supreme Court in *AT&T Corporation* v *Iowa Utilities Board*, 525 U.S. 366 (1999), however, affirmed that the FCC has general jurisdiction to implement the provisions of the 1996 Act, notwithstanding the provisions of the 1934 Act which reserve jurisdiction over intrastate matters to the states.

9.9 THE LICENSING OF COMMON CARRIERS

As in the UK, the FCC issues individual and class authorisations. The jurisdiction of the FCC is, however, broader than that of its UK counterpart. In the US, authorisations are required to operate telecommunication systems and to provide telecommunications services. Thus resellers or 'systemless service providers' who provide interstate or international communication services fall within the ambit of the FCC. The thrust of US regulation,

however, centres on providers of publicly available services, or so-called
'common carriers'. Depending on the nature and the means of the service,
common carriers must obtain the relevant § 214 authorisation, pursuant to
which they must comply with certain tariff and non-discriminatory obligations. If carriers also wish to provide intrastate services, they must also apply
for the requisite authorisations in each relevant state. Carriers that wish to
use radio broadcasting, such as microwave links, as part of that service must
also obtain authorisations from the FCC to use that portion of the radio
spectrum.

9.9.1 Common carriers defined

The 1934 Act unhelpfully defines a 'common carrier' as 'any person engaged
as a common carrier for hire, in interstate or foreign communication by wire
or radio or in interstate or foreign radio transmission of energy'. However,
under common law the term means any carrier who holds itself out to the
public for hire on general terms. Examples of authorised common carriers
include AT&T, MCI WorldCom and Sprint.

9.9.2 General obligations

Following its competitive carrier rulemaking (see 9.2.5 above), the FCC
elected not to apply the general obligations of the 1934 Act to non-dominant
carriers. As part of its biennial regulatory review required under the 1996 Act,
the FCC has attempted further to simplify the tariff filing regime. Dominant
common carriers, such as the ILECs (with the exception of Bell Atlantic, now
Verizon), must now submit to the FCC all new tariffs and changes to existing
tariffs 30 days prior to their implementation. Carriers must provide an
explanatory cover letter, FCC Form 159 (a fee-remittance schedule), the
appropriate fee and underlying cost justification. ILECs subject to price cap
regulation must also submit annual price cap filings, detailing the costs of
services falling within defined 'regulatory baskets'. Dominant common carriers may elect to file the tariffs electronically.

9.9.3 Application process generally

The type of service the applicant wishes to provide determines the requisite
licence and the information and fee that the FCC will require to process the
application. Applications for new licences are reviewed by FCC staff, who
may require additional information to process the application. If the FCC
decides to grant the application for a common carrier licence, it must issue a
public notice and give no less than 30 days for the public to comment.
Interested parties may petition, arguing that the grant is inconsistent with the
public interest.

9.9.4 Common carrier authorisation for provision of domestic fixed services

Persons wishing to provide domestic or intrastate communications services, or to construct facilities, must apply to the FCC for a domestic § 214 authorisation. There is no specific form to complete. Applicants must submit certain information listed in § 63 of the FCC's Rules in the form of a pleading. To receive the authorisation, the applicant must demonstrate that its grant will serve the public interest, convenience and necessity. Details should include the state of incorporation, a company tree showing all parties who directly or indirectly own at least 10 per cent of the applicant, and a description of the service to be provided. The applicant may also need to apply for the necessary authorisations to use the relevant radio frequencies, as the FCC also requires licences for all radio broadcasting, with the exception of certain unlicensed devices (such as television remote controls), and certain personal radio services that are licensed by rule (such as CB radios).

9.9.5 Common carrier authorisation for provision of international services

As a result of its 1998 biennial regulatory review, the FCC has streamlined the application process for grant of a § 214 authorisation for the provision of international services. Provided an applicant is not (i) affiliated with a foreign carrier who possesses market power in the destination market, (ii) affiliated with a dominant US carrier, or (iii) requesting authorisation to provide services over private lines to a country the FCC has not previously authorised, the FCC may grant the authorisation 14 days after providing public notice. The applicant may provide services 15 days after the FCC's publication of a notice to the public. It takes up to 90 days for the FCC to process a filing made by an applicant caught by one of the above conditions.

Applicants must electronically file the same information as domestic common carrier applicants (see 9.9.4 above). In addition, they must certify any affiliation with a foreign carrier, the countries to which services will be provided and the absence of any special concessions. Pursuant to this authorisation, the applicant must file copies of all interconnection agreements with terminating foreign operators.

9.9.6 Common carrier mobile and personal communications services (PCS) authorisations

As is the growing trend in Europe, the FCC awards licences for mobile authorisations, including PCS, by auction. The spectrum is typically allocated to the highest bidder, although successful applicants must also be able to demonstrate their technical, financial and legal ability to provide the underlying service. Unlike the UK, where mobile operators must obtain two licences (a Telecommunications Act 1984 licence and a Wireless Telegraphy

Act 1949 licence), a successful applicant in the US requires only one licence. Spectrum licences are usually of a ten-year duration with an expectation of renewal, so long as build out or service thresholds are met. Most services are licensed on a geographic basis – either nationwide, or in defined service areas. Licensees are permitted to partition (geographically split) their licence and/or disaggregate (divest a portion of the spectrum within their licensed area). Roll-out obligations vary, with nationwide licences typically requiring construction of base stations to cover between one-third to 40 per cent of the US population within five years and two-thirds to 75 per cent of the US population within ten years, or that the carrier provides 'substantial' service upon renewal, which takes into account the nature and scope of communication services that have developed in the radio band. The FCC attempts to prevent companies from obtaining market dominance through a variety of means, including mandating spectrum caps, setting auction rules that exclude bidding by licensees of like services, and allocating multiple frequency channels within a given market.

9.9.7 Section 271 applications for the provision of interLATA services

A key provision of the Telecommunications Act 1996 was the right of RBOCs to provide interstate telephony services, provided they comply with a 15-point 'competitive checklist'. The RBOCs must, however, file a § 271 application with the FCC (copied to the DoJ and relevant PUC) before providing inter-local access and transport area (interLATA) services. In December 1999, the FCC awarded its first § 271 authorisation to Bell Atlantic (now Verizon), conditional on meeting certain conditions in the State of New York. Several other RBOCs have subsequently received similar approval within other states.

The application consists of a legal brief setting out the substantive arguments and supporting documentation. In previous § 271 proceedings, applications have exceeded several thousand pages, and the FCC has recently imposed maximum page requirements.

The FCC must issue a public notice, following which interested third parties have 20 days to make objections. The FCC has 90 days to determine whether to grant an application, which it must issue if the RBOC has satisfied the competitive checklist and the 'public interest, convenience and necessity' test.

9.9.8 Local entry licences

In addition to the above licensing requirements, facilities-based operators and resellers who wish to provide publicly available intra- and interLATA services must also apply for the requisite licences in each of the 50 states. The application forms and specific requirements differ for each state and are too detailed to summarise here. Broadly speaking, however, each PUC requires basic information about the applicant (name and contact details), as well as information about the technical, administrative and financial ability of the applicant to provide the service.

9.9.9 Foreign ownership requirements

Until recently, the FCC had a long-standing policy of protecting its domestic markets as well as US carriers abroad under the guise of promoting effective competition. For example, it required all foreign carrier applicants to satisfy the 'effective competitive opportunities' (ECO) test when applying for international § 214 licences, indirect ownership in a radio licensee in excess of the 25 per cent maximum in § 310(b)(4) of the 1934 Act or a cable landing licence. This test required a showing that there were no legal or practical restrictions on US carriers' entry into the foreign carrier's domestic market.

On 15 February 1997, the US and 68 other countries adopted the WTO Basic Telecommunications Agreement in addition to specific market entry commitments contained in the telecommunications 'Reference Paper' (see Chapter 10 at 10.4.3.1). In light of the requirements of the Basic Telecommunications Agreement, the US has substituted the ECO test with an 'open entry' standard for applicants from WTO countries. The FCC will now presume that a licence should be granted to a foreign carrier unless it is shown that the foreign carrier poses a high risk to competition in the US. The FCC's recent decision to approve the transfer of radio licences from Voice Stream to Deutsche Telekom, demonstrates a further shift in its foreign ownership policy (*In re* Applications of Voice Stream Wireless Corporation, Powertel, Inc and Deutsche Telekom, *Memorandum Opinion and Order*, 27 April 2001). In its decision, the FCC found that foreign control of radio licences was in the public interest. It held that sections 310(a) and (b)(4) of the 1934 Act do not prohibit foreign governments from having indirect ownership of FCC radio licences in excess of 25 per cent unless the FCC finds that the public interest is otherwise served by the denial in a particular case. Notwithstanding the recent decision, applicants from non-WTO signatories must continue to satisfy the ECO test.

9.10 SPECTRUM AUCTIONS

As in Europe, the need to decide how to allocate scarce spectrum resources was one of the primary reasons for federal regulation of communications, and regulators and policy-makers continue to struggle with this issue.

In the 1980s, the traditional means of awarding scarce resources – the competitive hearing (or 'beauty parades' as they are known in the UK), in which the FCC used an exhaustive administrative hearing to determine which applicant was best qualified to hold the licence under the FCC's broad public interest standard – came under attack as inefficient and poorly suited to the rapidly evolving telecommunications market. The first alternative to competitive hearings – lotteries – quickly proved equally problematic. With little or no cost to apply for a licence, applicants often had neither the means nor the desire to build out systems. Instead, winners would 'flip' (or trade) their licences to entities that truly wished to hold a licence, and would reap considerable profits in the transaction. Those who were not selected often used administrative procedures, such as the filing of petitions to deny, that undermined one of the primary goals of lotteries – the quick issuance of licences. The FCC, in turn, was overwhelmed by the number of applicants. It is noteworthy that lotteries, authorised in 1991, lasted only two years before Congress granted the FCC authority to auction spectrum.

Section 309(j) of the Communications Act of 1934, added in 1993, gave the FCC the ability to use competitive bidding (or auctions) as a means to allocate licences for mobile telecommunications services where there are 'mutually exclusive' applications (i.e., more than one entity is seeking a single licence). Although the billions of dollars in public revenue raised by spectrum auctions have attracted considerable attention, the 1934 Act (as amended) requires the FCC to consider efficient spectrum use – and not the expectation of revenues – as the dominant factor in designing and implementing auctions. An auction winner does not acquire a property right in the underlying spectrum, but can expect to hold and renew the licence without having to participate in subsequent auctions. However, auction winners are subject to all FCC rules, including fines and the possibility that the licence may be revoked for good cause. The FCC is also mandated to ensure that licences are disseminated among a 'wide variety of licensees', including small businesses, rural telephone companies, and women- and minority-owned businesses. The FCC has addressed this requirement by establishing bidding credits for certain 'designated entities', and, in the case of PCS, setting aside a block of spectrum exclusively for these entities.

The current auction process promotes both efficiency and participation by serious applicants. Prior to an auction, each bidder must file a Form 175 'short form' application detailing its qualifications and submit an upfront deposit in relation to the licences it wishes to bid on. The auction is conducted remotely via computer software, and consists of multiple rounds in which bids may be increased only by a set increment. Once bidding activity drops below a set level, the auction closes. Shortly thereafter, winning bidders must file a 'long form' application and submit payments. Bid withdrawal and default penalties are designed to ensure that only serious bidders participate. In addition, the FCC has adopted rules designed to prevent bidding collusion.

The spectrum auction policy is considered to be a success, as the 1994 Broadband PCS auction proved. Auctions can quickly allocate licences and promote the rapid deployment of service. In addition, the FCC has developed considerable expertise in designing and conducting auctions that has served as a model for other countries (as in the UK's auction for third generation mobile licences) considering their own spectrum auctions, and the FCC is currently examining more complex auction models. The policy has not been without problems, however. The FCC has faced the greatest difficulties in implementing its designated entity procedures. Constitutional challenges undermined the FCC's women and minority bidding preference programs, and some designated entities have either defaulted on instalment payments or declared bankruptcy. In addition to hindering the rapid deployment of service, these developments have pitted the FCC against federal bankruptcy courts and have left the status of several licences in question. Policy-makers have also struggled with the question of what is appropriate to auction. Broadcasters, who traditionally are considered to 'pay' for their spectrum through public interest requirements, were not initially subject to auctions; public safety entities have also been exempt. However, Congress has endorsed auctions by expanding the FCC's authority and mandating the use of auctions in additional circumstances. For example, some private radio spectrum may now be subject to auction, even though spectrum auctions were originally authorised only for commercial subscription services. Despite these unsolved public policy and legal issues, spectrum auctions have become a frequent and routine part of the FCC's business.

9.11 LOCAL LOOP UNBUNDLING AND BROADBAND ACCESS

With the adoption of Regulation (EC) No. 2887/2000 of the European Parliament and the Council of 18 December 2000 on unbundled access to the local loop and OFTEL's well-published difficulties requiring BT to unbundle its loops, it is worthwhile considering the US position. While the Telecommunications Act 1996 required the FCC to adopt within six months regulations imposing unbundled access on ILECs, the sweeping changes the 1996 Act promised have not yet materialised. This is in part due to the lengthy judicial review actions brought by the incumbents, differing applications by the PUCs of the FCC's rulemakings and an absence of market demand by LECs. The UK has focused on the rapid roll out of broadband services, in the US the requirement to unbundle the local loop in the US was initially driven by the need to promote local competition, although increasingly its focus has also been to facilitate broadband services.

Section 251 of the Telecommunications Act 1996 imposes a broad duty on ILECs to provide any requesting telecommunications carrier 'non-discriminatory access to network elements on an unbundled basis at any technically feasible point on rates, terms and conditions that are just, reasonable and non-discriminatory'. ILECs must also provide such unbundled network elements (UNEs) so that requesting carriers are able then to combine the UNEs to provide telecommunications services. Typically, this involves access to the ILECs' copper loops.

The principle of UNEs is similar to the European Commission's concept of special network access, although it is much narrower in its application. It applies only to fixed ILECs. Mobile and cable common carriers do not fall within the scope of § 251 of the 1996 Act. It is also important to note that in the US all carriers (including resellers and facilities-based) are entitled to UNEs, whereas in the UK OFTEL has stipulated that to be eligible for BT local loops, operators must run a system and have sufficiently invested in infrastructure to qualify for Annex II status.

The concept of UNEs is woolly, but the 1996 Act lists two factors the FCC must consider in determining which network elements must be unbundled:

(a)   if proprietary network elements are involved, is access 'necessary'; and
(b)   if non-proprietary network elements are involved, would failure by the ILEC to provide the network element 'impair' the ability of the telecommunications carrier seeking access to provide the services it seeks to offer?

The 1996 Act provides no guidance on the terms 'necessary' and 'impair', and the FCC has had difficulty in developing a legal standard that passes Supreme Court muster.

In its Local Competition First Report and Order (*In re* Implementation of the Local Competition Provisions in the Telecommunications Act 1996, First Report and Order, 11 FCC Rcd 15499 (1996)), the FCC defined 'necessary' to mean 'an element that is a prerequisite for competition', and 'impair' to mean 'to make or cause to become worse; diminish in value'. It also established a minimum level of national unbundling requirements, which included seven elements (principally local loops and related equipment). The FCC adopted a national standard to ensure a level playing field for new entrants leaving state PUCs able to impose additional requirements, subject to compliance with the pro-competitive principles of the 1996 Act. To further ensure a level playing field, the FCC also required PUCs to adopt forward long-run incremental pricing of UNEs. These provisions were immediately challenged, and appealed to the Supreme Court.

In *FCC* v *Iowa Utilities Bd.*, 525 U.S. 1133 (1999), the Court implicitly accepted that the FCC had the authority to establish a minimum level of national requirements and the associated costing methodologies. However, it rejected the FCC's definitions of the 'necessary' and 'impair' standards stipulated in the 1996 Act, citing the overbreadth of the FCC's definitions and the FCC's failure to impose a limiting standard on the ability of new entrants to access network elements. In particular, the FCC did not sufficiently take into account the availability of elements outside the incumbent's network and wrongly assumed that any increase in cost (or decrease in quality) rendered access to an element necessary and impaired the ability of the new entrant to provide services. This price sensitivity criterion set a subjective standard whereby new entrants rather than the FCC would determine the network elements to be unbundled. The Court remanded the case back to the FCC for further consideration.

Shortly afterwards, the FCC issued its Third Report and Order and Fourth Notice of Proposed Rulemaking (*In re* Implementation of the Local Competition Provision of the Telecommunications Act of 1996, Third Report and Order and Fourth Further Notice of Proposed Rulemaking, 15 September 1999), in which it again tried to define the various standards as they apply to proprietary and non-proprietary systems, taking into account the Court's concerns. For the purposes of the 1996 Act, the FCC has now ruled that a proprietary network element is 'necessary', and so must be unbundled, if, taking into consideration the availability of elements outside the incumbent's network (e.g., self-provisioning and alternative suppliers), access to that element would as a practical, economic and operational matter preclude the requesting carrier from providing the services it intends to offer. In certain limited cases, the FCC may also require unbundling of proprietary network elements, subject to the requirements of the impair standard, where, for example, an ILEC cannot demonstrate that the service is not proprietary (see 47 CFR § 51.307 *et seq.*).

The definition of the 'impair' standard adopted by the FCC is similar. Refusal to unbundle a non-proprietary network element will now impair a competitor's ability to provide service if, taking into consideration the availability of alternative elements outside the incumbent's network, lack of access materially diminishes the new entrant's provision of service. Again the FCC will look at all circumstances, including the cost, timeliness, quality, ubiquity and operational issues of the alternative. In addition, the FCC will consider several other factors, including: the ability of a UNE to bring rapid introduction of competition in local markets; the extent to which a UNE will promote facilities-based competition, investment and innovation; the need to reduce regulation and create regulatory certainty; and administrative practicality.

To the delight of ILECs, the two new standards adopted by the FCC as a result of *AT&T* v *Iowa Utilities Bd.*, establish a much higher test for UNEs than had originally been anticipated. The standards now used, with their emphasis on alternative suppliers and ability to self-provision, implicitly adopt an 'essential- facilities'-type focus, which ILECs advocated during the rulemaking proceedings. Arguably, the new standards may make it more difficult for the FCC and state PUCs to mandate certain UNEs, although the FCC has required the unbundling of local loops, sub-loops, network interface devices, circuit switching, signalling and call-related databases, operations support systems and interoffice transmission facilities. It has also required ILECs to line share with DSL providers.

The FCC's decision requiring ILECs to line share demonstrates the increasing political pressure on the FCC to promote faster Internet access. As in Europe, attention has turned to the possibility of imposing open access on cable operators, such as TCI and certain ISPs, such as AOL,[15] who have started to deploy broadband cable modems in their networks. The FCC dealt with this issue directly during its review of the AT&T–TCI merger, but refrained from imposing conditions with respect to open access. Consistently with its growing emphasis on de-regulation, it argued that the public interest would be better served by allowing the market to evolve and by AT&T–TCI's commitment to the FCC to allow other ISPs to serve TCI customers via its cable network (see 9.3.3 above).

An issue closely related to UNE is co-location, which has proved to be highly contentious, as in the UK. Under § 251(6) of the 1996 Act, ILECs are required to provide physical co-location at their local exchange, subject to technical and space limitations, in which case they must provide virtual co-location. The FCC's Local Competition First Report and Order imposes additional obligations. ILECs must permit the co-location of all equipment

---

[15] America Online has been a strong proponent of open access, although following its merger with Time Warner, it appears to be re-evaluating its position.

used for interconnection and/or use with UNEs. Space within an exchange is allotted on a first-come, first-served basis, and ILECs are not obliged to construct or lease additional space to facilitate co-location, but must take into account projected demand for co-location of equipment when planning construction work.[16] Notwithstanding these obligations, ILECs have been able to exploit the statutory dispute resolution procedures to cause delays for new entrants.

9.12   UNIVERSAL SERVICE OBLIGATIONS (USOs)

The concept of universal service arose in the early 1900s. Bell first conceived the term to promote a public policy whereby a telephone company would provide all who wanted service in an area in return for continued regulation as the sole service provider in a given area. Later, as universal service came to represent the policy that all Americans should have basic telephone access at a reasonable rate, the primary issues related to the subsidy of high-cost users (such as rural and residential customers) by low-cost users (such as urban and business customers).

Some 80 years after the concept was first adopted, § 254 of the Telecommunications Act 1996 finally wrote the principle of universal service into law. However, the 1996 Act declined specifically to define universal service, instead recognising it as an 'evolving level of telecommunications services' that is based on seven broad principles, such as quality service at reasonable rates and access to telecommunications services in rural and high-cost areas. The 1996 Act further directed the FCC and a Federal-State Joint Board established under the 1996 Act to adopt mechanisms to fund and support a universal service policy based on these seven principles. The FCC took an expansive view of USOs in its orders implementing the 1996 Act.

Although universal service continues to represent the idea that all Americans should have access to a basic level of communications services, and continues to be, at heart, a cost-shifting mechanism, it has changed in two significant ways since the 1996 Act. First, in light of the new competitive opportunities established by the 1996 Act, the FCC required substantially more telecommunications providers to contribute to universal service funding. Secondly, the 1996 Act expanded the concept of universal service to include the principle that schools, libraries and health care providers should have access to advanced telecommunications services. The 'e-rate' program, which furthers the latter's goal, provides 20 to 90 per cent discounts on telecommunications services, Internet access and internal connections to schools and libraries. Critics have attacked the implementation of the program, and consumers have complained about the higher fees they have to pay to support the expanded universal service mandates. The FCC, however, has described the program as a success and, in 1999, announced that the e-rate had connected more than one million classrooms to the Internet.

---

[16] ILECs who reject co-location applications citing space constraints must permit applicants to 'walk through' the relevant local exchange so they can confirm that no space is in fact available.

9.13   INTERCONNECTION

The 1996 Act required the FCC to introduce a number of network access measures under the rubric of interconnection on local exchange carriers (LECs) and incumbent local exchange carriers (ILECs) alike to facilitate network interoperability. Some of the key obligations are briefly summarised below.

9.13.1   Re-sale

All LECs must make all of their telecommunications services available for re-sale on reasonable and non-discriminatory terms and of an equal quality. Incumbent LECs must provide the re-sale service on a 'retail-minus' basis that subtracts avoided retail costs, as determined by a reference to cost study prepared by the relevant state PUC. Cost rules differ depending on the state PUC's definition of geographic areas designed to reflect cost differences.

9.13.2   Dialling parity

LECs and ILECs are required to provide 'dialling parity' (or carrier pre-selection, as it known in Europe) for all originating telecommunications services. LECs must not cause unreasonable dialling delay and must provide customers with the option of using different carriers for local calls as well as inter- and intraLATA service. Implementation plans must be filed with and be approved by the relevant PUC. The FCC has also introduced 'anti-slamming' measures prohibiting carriers from changing a customer's designated carrier(s).

9.14   RECIPROCAL COMPENSATION

Under the 1996 Act, all LECs must establish reciprocal compensation arrangements, defined as arrangements between two carriers in which an operator receives financial compensation for local calls which originated on another carrier's local exchange. In the UK, these services encompass transit and network termination services, and the compensation BT retains for providing BT network termination services (NTS) is determined, in part, by the NTS formula set by OFTEL; all other terminating operators are now able to set the rates they charge for call termination.

In the US, the rates for all carriers (including competitive LECs) were until recently heavily regulated and determined by the state PUCs with reference to FCC orders. Rates for incumbent LECs were determined on a long-run incremental cost (LRIC) basis, and in the event that a PUC lacked access to adequate cost information, a default rate was used. PUCs could also select a 'bill and keep' arrangement, whereby neither operator charges the other for termination services, provided a roughly equal amount of traffic is exchanged between the two carriers. As a result of the requirement of 'symmetrical' reciprocal compensation, competitive LECs had to charge ILECs an amount equal to the rates ILECs levied on them.

With the increasing number of local calls to ISPs to access the Internet in the late 1990s, reciprocal compensation arrangements had a significant impact on LEC revenue. In 1999, the FCC was forced to issue a Declaratory Ruling in which it concluded that calls made to ISPs were interstate calls and hence fell outside the scope of the reciprocal compensation arrangements. However, it ruled that LECs should be bound by their existing interconnection agreements as interpreted by the state PUCs, which in the absence of a federal rule on inter-carrier compensation for ISP traffic, has to assess whether the parties intended for such traffic to be covered by the reciprocal arrangements.

Bell Atlantic (now Verizon) later challenged the FCC's Declaratory Ruling and in *Bell Atlantic Telephone Companies* v *FCC*, 206 F. 3d 1 (2000), the Court of Appeal vacated certain provisions of the FCC's ruling. The FCC has since expressly held that telephony traffic delivered to ISPs is interstate access traffic and is not subject to the reciprocal compensation rules (*In re* Implementation of the Local Competition Provisions of the Telecommunications Act 1996, Intercarrier Compensation for ISP Bound Traffic, *Order on Remand and Report and Order* FCC 01-131, 18 April 2001). In addition, the FCC has recognised that reciprocal compensation gave rise to regulatory arbitrage and distorted market incentives and it has stated that it will phase out the existing arrangements over a three-year period. On 19 April 2001 the FCC issued a Notice of Proposed Rulemaking which marks the FCC's re-examination of regulated forms of intercarrier compensation (see *In re* Developing a Unified Intercarrier Compensation Regime, *Notice of Proposed Rulemaking*, FCC 01-132).

9.15 REGULATORY REFORM

Despite the criticism that the Telecommunications Act of 1996 has not delivered competition to the US telecommunications marketplace as quickly as planned, it has led to significant changes in US policy and is already having far-reaching effects. To that end, it represents the most significant telecommunications legislation since the original Communications Act of 1934 and the establishment of the FCC. Although competition in the local market has lagged behind expectations, other segments of the field have benefited from increased investment, lower rates and new entrants – which can, in part, be attributed to the 1996 Act. Moreover, it is unlikely that US policy-makers will substantially revisit US telecommunications policy soon. Instead, Congress is likely to make minor modifications to the 1996 Act that are designed to spur competition within particular segments of the telecommunications market. Whether these laws are likely to limit the regulatory power of the FCC or the states is unclear. The FCC, for its own part, has announced plans to reorganise itself to support three main functions: the provision of universal service, consumer protection and information; enforcement and promotion of pro-competition goals; and spectrum management activities. To support these goals, the FCC may replace its current structure, which is based on bureaus that regulate discrete communications services (such as cable or wireless services), with a functional structure organised into such activities as enforcement, licensing and policy-making. Nevertheless, given the rapid pace of evolution within the telecommunications industry, and the belief that implementation of the 1996 Act has not promoted competition as rapidly as was expected, it is likely that lawmakers, telecommunications providers and the public will keep the FCC and other regulators under close scrutiny for the foreseeable future.

CHAPTER TEN
The International Regulatory Regime

Ian Walden

10.1 INTRODUCTION

Telecommunications is an inherently transnational technology. As such, the development of telecommunications has always required substantial cooperation and agreement between nation states. Cooperation can be seen at a number of different levels, including the need for adherence to certain standards, both technical and operational. Historically, the need for on-going cooperation between States has meant the establishment of intergovernmental organisations, of which the International Telecommunication Union (ITU) lays claim to the oldest pedigree. These intergovernmental institutions have been responsible for laying down much of the framework that comprises international telecommunications law and regulation.

In addition, the nature of the industry demands the construction of communications links across jurisdictions subject to both domestic and international law. Consequently, the telecommunications industry has been subject to treaties and conventions established under public international law for the treatment and use of common natural resources, specifically, the sea and outer space.

Over recent years, the sources of international telecommunications law have diversified as the industry and national markets have undergone fundamental change. At a technical level, the need for internationally agreed standards has expanded exponentially with the growth of data communications and the increasing range of services available over communication networks. The rate of technological change has required more flexible and dynamic decision-making procedures and institutions. Historically, standards-making bodies comprised monopolistic operators that were part of a national public administration. With market liberalisation, the numbers of participants in the standards-making process have risen dramatically, while the effective role of governments has diminished significantly. As a consequence, we are witnessing a period of change in those international institutions toward which the attention of telecommunications lawyers has traditionally been focused. International industry associations have emerged to challenge the primacy of intergovernmental organisations. At the same time, governments, particularly of developed nations, are increasingly looking to scale-down their involvement in the governance of the telecommunications sector. This is driven both by a desire to reduce demands on public finance, as well as by a recognition that they are not necessarily best placed to make appropriate decisions in such a rapidly evolving environment.

International telecommunications organisations such as the ITU are also experiencing institutional competition from other intergovernmental bodies. In particular, the World Trade Organisation (WTO) and the associated multinational trade agreements have focused on telecommunications as a distinct economic activity, a tradable service, rather than simply as a medium or conduit for conducting trade. As the industry undergoes fundamental structural shifts, with operators merging to become global entities as well as pondering the consequences of convergence, attention has shifted to issues of market access as the primary concern in international telecommunications law. The ITU has experienced a loss of status in the face of such new priorities, and is therefore engaged in a re-examination of its role in the changing environment.

Despite the global trend towards market liberalisation, there continues to be an inevitable divergence of views between developed and developing nations toward the telecommunications sector. While all nations recognise the critical role of telecommunications in a nation's economic infrastructure and development, many countries continue to see telecommunications as a public resource, and even a natural monopoly, in which governments have a right and obligation to intervene. Developing countries are experiencing considerable pressure to embrace the credo of market liberalisation from a number of directions. First, the need to attract foreign investment into the telecommunications sector. Second, developments in technology, particularly Internet-related, increasingly erode the ability of States to exercise effective regulatory control over the sector. Third, developmental organisations, such as the World Bank and the European Bank for Reconstruction and Development, have imposed liberalisation conditions as part of their loan programmes for infrastructure investment projects in telecommunications.

This chapter broadly examines three substantive aspects of international telecommunications law:

    (a)   the construction of international telecommunications network infrastructure, both satellites and submarine cables;

    (b)   the standards and operating rules established under the framework of the ITU;

    (c)   the impact of the WTO and associated trade agreements on national telecommunication markets and legal regimes.

10.2   INTERNATIONAL NETWORK INFRASTRUCTURE

As at a national level, the physical construction of telecommunications networks is subject to a particular regulatory framework not applicable to the provision of services over such networks. For example, issues concerning rights of way across public and private property are a central element in the licensing of a public telecommunications operator (see Chapter 4). At an international level, similar issues arise concerning the rights and obligations of those wanting to construct either wireless (e.g., satellite) or wireline (i.e., cable) networks across and between sovereign jurisdictions. This section reviews the law governing the launch and operation of communication satellites and the laying of submarine cables. (Issues relating to the assignment of frequency spectrum and orbital slots are discussed at 10.3.2 below.)

10.2.1   Satellite regulation

The launch of TELSTAR I in 1962 marked the beginning of satellite technology for use in telecommunications and broadcasting. Satellite systems can be classified as geostationary or non-geostationary systems. A geostationary system is based above the equator (around 36,000 kms) and revolves at the same speed as the Earth, thereby appearing to be stationary (i.e., a synchronous orbit). An advantage of a geostationary system is its ability to provide continuous and relatively comprehensive coverage of the Earth with only three satellites.[1] Disadvantages include the fact that the equator can only accommodate a limited number of systems, and the quality of communications is diminished somewhat by the transmission delay caused by the substantial distance travelled by signals to and from such satellites, particularly for voice telephony.

Recent developments in the satellite market have been in the proliferation of non-geostationary systems operating in medium Earth orbit (MEO) and low Earth orbits (LEOs), such as ICO and Globalstar. Such systems require a considerably greater number of satellites to ensure continuous coverage.[2]

The launch and operation of satellites are subject to international space law. Historically, satellite systems were developed under international conventions between States, such as Intelsat, Inmarsat and Eutelsat. However, current non-geostationary systems are multinational private consortia operating under private agreement and subject to national legal regimes.

10.2.1.1   International space law   International space law comprises a set of agreed principles embodied in a series of treaties and conventions. These principles encompass the launch and operation of satellites, particularly in respect of liability for any damage caused by the satellite or any other space object.

---

[1] Except regions above latitudes 75° north or south. The angle of elevation in northern Europe does significantly limit reception.
[2] For example, ICO, operating in MEO (10,390 km above sea level), uses 10 satellites, while Globalstar uses 48 satellites.

In 1963, the UN General Assembly adopted a Declaration comprising nine fundamental legal principles governing the use to be made of 'outer space'.[3] This formed the basis of the 'Outer Space' Treaty agreed in 1967.[4] This Treaty continues to be of primary international legal instrument governing the launch and operation of telecommunications satellites.

In terms of economic exploitation, the Treaty declares that outer space and celestial bodies may not be subject to national appropriation (Art. II). States are also responsible under international law for their activities in outer space, whether carried out by governmental or non-governmental authorities, the latter requiring authorisation and on-going supervision (Art. VI). Liability for damage caused by any object placed in space would rest jointly with the State that launches, or procures the launch of, the object and the State 'from whose territory or facility an object is launched' (Art. VII). Jurisdiction and control over any object in outer space remains with the State that registers the object, while ownership is unaffected by the presence of the object in space or its return to Earth outside of the registering State (Art. VIII). To facilitate international cooperation in the use of outer space, States are required to provide information to the United Nations regarding their activities in, and use of, outer space (Art. XI).

The 1972 Convention on International Liability for Damage Caused by Space Objects further elaborated the liability provisions of the Outer Space Treaty.[5] The Convention defined the concept of 'damage' in the following terms: 'loss of life, personal injury or other impairment of health; or loss of or damage to property of States or of persons, natural or juridical, or property of international intergovernmental organisations' (Art. I(a)). Consequential losses, such as future traffic revenues, apparently are not encompassed within this definition.[6] Reflecting the terms of the 1967 Treaty, liability lies with the 'launching State', which encompasses both the State that launches or procures the launch of the space object and the State from where it was launched (Art. I; launching includes any attempts). Where a launch involves two or more States, liability is joint and severable (Art. V).

Under the Convention, liability is *absolute* where the damage is caused on the Earth or to an aircraft (Art. II), unless it can be shown that the damage is the result of 'gross negligence or an act or omission done with intent to cause damage' by the claimant State (Art. VI). The only formal claim that

---

[3] Resolution 1962 (XVIII), adopted at UN General Assembly, 13 December 1963 (GAOR Annexes (XVIII) 28, p. 27). The physical boundaries of outer space are somewhat unclear, although 100 km above sea level, representing the boundary between the lower and outer atmosphere, is a generally accepted figure. See Cheng, C., 'The legal regime of airspace and outer space: the boundary problem', in *Studies in International Space Law* (Oxford, Clarendon Press, 1997), at 425–56.

[4] Treaty on Principles Governing the Activities of States in the Exploration and Use of Outer Space, including the Moon and Other Celestial Bodies (London, Moscow and Washington, 27 January 1967; TS 10 (1968); Cmnd. 3519).

[5] London, Moscow and Washington, 29 March 1972; TS 16 (1974); Cmnd. 5551. The Treaty entered into force for the United Kingdom on 9 October 1973.

[6] See generally Beer, T., 'The specific risks associated with collisions in outer space and the return to Earth of space objects – the legal perspective' (2000) XXV *Air and Space Law* 42.

has been submitted under Art. II was by Canada in 1979, claiming $6 million from the Soviet Union for damage caused by the radioactive debris from the re-entry of Cosmos 954 in January 1978. The claim was settled for $3 million, without liability being acknowledged.[7] Fault-based liability applies where the damage is to the space object of another launching State caused elsewhere than on the Earth (Art. III). A State may claim damages on behalf of itself, its natural or legal persons (i.e., the State of nationality), or those sustaining damage while in its territory (Art. VIII). Claims for compensation are subject to certain time limits and, where diplomatic settlement is not achieved, may be decided upon by a Claims Commission established at the request of either party (Arts XIV–XX).

Underpinning the 1962 Declaration and the Outer Space Treaty was the concept that each State would maintain a register detailing the space objects for which the State claimed jurisdiction and control. The 1975 Convention on the Registration of Objects Launched into Outer Space formalised such registration procedures.[8] Under the Convention, the launching State accepted an obligation to maintain a register (Art. II), although its contents and conditions of use could be determined by the 'State of registry'. However, certain information is required to be furnished to the Secretary-General of the United Nations for general publication (Arts III and IV).[9] This information should be distinguished from that maintained under the auspices of the ITU in respect of the allocation of frequency spectrum and orbital slots (see 10.3.2 below).

Aspects of the treaties comprising international space law have been implemented in UK law by the Outer Space Act 1986. The Act applies to the 'launching or procuring the launch of a space object', 'operating a space object', or 'any activity in outer space' (s. 1) – all licensable activities.[10] Under the terms of any such licence, a licensee is subject to a number of obligations, including supplying certain information for inclusion in a register to be maintained by the Secretary of State and avoiding 'interference with the activities of others' (s. 5). In terms of liability, the licensee is obliged to obtain third-party liability insurance for any loss or damage arising from the authorised activities (s. 5(2)(f)), as well as indemnifying the Government against any claims (s. 10).

In terms of jurisdiction, a satellite system can be distinguished into two components: the 'Earth segment' and the 'space segment'. The 'Earth segment' comprises those stations that send ('uplinks') and receive ('downlinks') transmissions from the satellite and which are subject to the laws of the jurisdiction in which they are physically located. (The geographical

---

[7] *Ibid.*, at 48.

[8] New York, 14 January 1975; TS 70 (1978); Cmnd. 7271. The Convention entered into force for the United Kingdom on 30 May 1978.

[9] The information to be supplied is: the name of the launching State or States; an appropriate designator or registration number for the space object; the date, territory or location of launch; basic orbital parameters and the general function of the space object. See generally www.oosa.unvienna.org.

[10] Such licences are separate from those required under the Telecommunications Act 1984; see generally Chapter 4.

coverage of a satellite's transmissions is known as its 'footprint'.) The 'space segment' has been defined as: '. . . the telecommunications satellites, and the tracking, telemetry, command, control, monitoring and related facilities and equipment required to support the operation of these satellites' (Intelsat Agreement, Art. 1(h)). Jurisdictional responsibility for the 'space segment' can be subdivided between the state that launched the satellite and the State from where the satellite is controlled. If control is distributed among a series of sites in multiple jurisdictions, it is the jurisdiction where the controlling operator has its principal place of business.

10.2.1.2 International satellite organisations With the successful launch of Sputnik I in 1957, the operation of satellite systems was initially a highly charged political arena with important military (and therefore 'Cold War') implications. However, the 1962 UN Resolution represented an important acceptance by the international community that space should be treated as a common resource of 'all mankind'. In addition, the industry then consisted of national, generally state-owned, monopoly operators. With these factors in mind, it was therefore perhaps inevitable that the first satellite systems were the subject of international treaty, rather than private endeavour.

The first international satellite organisation was established in 1964 under 'Interim Arrangements for a Global Commercial Communications Satellite System'[11] and, subsequently, the Agreement Relating to the International Telecommunications Satellite Organisation ('Intelsat').[12] Intelsat has legal personality (Art. IV) and operates in accordance with the intergovernmental Agreement and an 'Operating Agreement'. Member countries are required to grant Intelsat, and certain of its officers and employees, legal and taxation privileges and immunities (Art. XVII). Intelsat's stated prime objective is: '. . . the provision, on a commercial basis, of the space segment required for international public telecommunications services of high quality and reliability to be available on a non-discriminatory basis to all areas of the World' (Art. III).

Intelsat currently comprises 143 member countries and signatories, as well as over 200 'investing entities'. In the UK, BT is the designated signatory to Intelsat, reflecting the governmental origins of the organisation, although more than 20 other UK-based operators are currently designated as 'investing entities'. Intelsat operates some 19 geostationary satellites. In 1998, it established an independent and competing operating entity, New Skies Satellites NV, as part of an on-going policy to commercialise fully its operations. New Skies operates five satellites transferred from the Intelsat fleet.

The International Mobile Satellite Organisation ('Inmarsat') was established in 1979 as an intergovernmental organisation providing satellite services for the maritime and aeronautical sectors, particularly communications in

---

[11] Washington, 20 August 1964 to 20 February 1965; TS 12 (1966); Cmnd. 2940.
[12] See Agreement relating to the International Telecommunications Satellite Organisation (INTELSAT) (with Operating Agreement) (Washington, 20 August 1971; TS 80 (1973); Cmnd. 5416).

situations of distress and safety.[13] In 1994, it established a separate private company, I-CO Global Communications Ltd, to build and provide a non-geostationary mobile satellite-based telecommunications system.[14] Until 1999, Inmarsat's organisational structure was very similar to Intelsat's. The vast majority of its operations were privatised in 1999, and it has declared an intention to float an issue on the public stock markets at some point in the future.

A third international satellite organisation to which the UK is a member signatory is the European Telecommunications Satellite Organisation (Eutelsat), which comprises 48 member countries.[15] While the Convention and Operating Agreement are modelled closely on the Intelsat texts, in contrast to Intelsat only one operator per member is a shareholder, which for the UK is British Telecommunications plc. The prime objective of Eutelsat is 'the provision of the space segment required for international public telecommunication services in Europe' (Art. III(a)). As with Intelsat and Inmarsat, Eutelsat is committed to a process of privatisation. It is thus providing services through a private company, Eutelsat SA, while the intergovernmental organisation is continuing to operate in order to 'ensure that basic principles of pan-European coverage, universal service, non-discrimination and fair competition are observed by the company'.[16]

With market liberalisation, concerns arose that incumbent operators could utilise the treaty-based satellite systems to restrict access to space-segment capacity and satellite services. In particular, a service provider wanting to purchase satellite capacity was generally required to procure the capacity via its local signatory, i.e. the incumbent operator. Not only did this generate revenue for the signatory, but also associated 'coordination procedures' required details of the proposed service to be widely disclosed, e.g.:

> To the extent that any Party or Signatory or person within the jurisdiction of a Party intends individually or jointly to establish, acquire or utilize space segment facilities separate from the INTELSAT . . . such Party or Signatory, prior to the establishment, acquisition or utilization of such facilities, shall furnish all relevant information to and shall consult with the Assembly of Parties . . . to ensure technical compatibility . . . and to avoid significant economic harm to the global system of INTELSAT. (Art. XIV (d))

Such procedures could obviously be abused to restrict competition either directly, e.g., by blocking the provision of a service, or indirectly, e.g., by the incumbent operator commencing a competing service.

---

[13] See Convention on the International Maritime Satellite Organisation (INMARSAT) (with the Operating Agreement), London, 3 September 1976; TS 94 (1979); Cmnd. 7722. It changed its name in 1994.

[14] See generally Inmarsat-P Case No. IV/35.296 (1995) OJ C 304/6.

[15] See Convention establishing the European Telecommunications Satellite Organisation (EUTELSAT) (Paris, 15 July 1982; TS 15 (1990); Cmnd. 956, as amended by a Protocol of 15 December 1983, Cmnd. 9154). The United Kingdom instrument of ratification of the Convention was deposited on 21 February 1985 and the Convention, Operating Agreement and Protocol entered into force on 1 September 1985.

[16] See www.eutelsat.com: 'Introduction to Eutelsat'.

As part of the EU's liberalisation programme, Member States party to any of the international satellite organisations, i.e., Intelsat, Inmarsat, Eutelsat and Intersputnik, are required to notify the European Commission of any measures which could breach European competition law.[17] In addition, a 1994 Council Resolution called for the rules of the international satellite organisations to be adjusted to ensure strict separation between regulatory and operational aspects, as well as separation or flexibility between ownership of investment shares and usage of the systems.[18]

To minimise the potentially anti-competitive operation of the satellite organisations, the European Commission believed it was necessary to ensure that 'users obtain direct access to space segment capacity, while providers of this space segment should obtain the right to market space capacity directly to users'.[19] Such direct access has subsequently been implemented in most Member States, although through separate ancillary agreements rather than amendments to the provisions of the international agreements.[20] However, the Commission does not consider such developments to be sufficient to ensure a fully liberalised market in the provision of satellite-based services. It therefore recently proposed strengthening the obligation placed upon Member States, such that they will be obliged to 'take all appropriate steps to eliminate' incompatibilities between the international conventions and the EC Treaty.[21]

With the progressive moves towards full commercialisation and privatisation, the treaty-based satellite systems are becoming less relevant as a feature of international telecommunications law. From a competition law perspective, however, the process of privatisation raises a number of issues. These include the need to ensure that the private operating entity does not retain any of the legal immunities granted to the international organisation, and opening up the shareholding to non-participant entities, preferably through a public offering.[22] Such operators will then be subject to the scrutiny of competition regulators in the same way as other multinational satellite ventures.[23]

---

[17] Commission Directive 94/46/EC of 13 October 1994 amending Directive 88/301/EEC in particular with regard to satellite communications (1994) OJ L 268/15, at Art. 3. See generally Chapter 8.

[18] Council Resolution on further development of the Community's satellite communications policy, especially with regard to the provision of, and access to, space segment capacity (1994) OJ C 379/5.

[19] Communication from the Commission,'Towards Europe-wide systems and services – Green Paper on a common approach in the field of Satellite Communications in the European Community', COM (90) 490 *final*, 20 November 1990. See also the 1991 Guidelines, at paras 122–128.

[20] See Communication from the Commission, 'Fifth Report on the Implementation of the Telecommunications Regulatory Package', COM (99) 537 final, 10 November 1999.

[21] Draft Commission Directive on competition in the markets for electronic communications services (2001) OJ C 96/2, at Art. 11(2).

[22] Ungerer, H., 'The transformation of the International Satellite Organisations – some aspects from a European perspective', 11 April 1999, published on the Competition Directorate-General website. See also Press Release, 'Commission gives green light to Inmarsat restructuring', IP/98/923, 22 October 1998.

[23] See, e.g., Commission competition decisions *International Private Satellite Partners* (Case IV/34.768) (1994) OJ L 354/75, and *Iridium* (Case IV/35.518) (1997) OJ L 16/87.

10.2.2 Submarine cables

Submarine cables have been a component of the international telecommunications infrastructure since 1851, when the first submarine cable for telegraphy was laid between England and France. The first commercially successful transatlantic telegraph cable was operational in 1866; the first transatlantic coaxial copper telephone cable (TAT-1) in 1956; and the first transatlantic fiber optic cable (TAT-8) in 1988.[24] The emergence of satellite technology was generally seen as signalling the demise of submarine cable as a transmission medium. However, submarine cable has continued to prosper and expand as the dominant medium for international traffic due to its superior transmission quality, reliability and security.

The expense of laying submarine cables has meant that, historically, consortia of operators from different jurisdictions carried out such projects under private agreement, often referred to as 'cable clubs'. Such 'clubs' usually comprised the monopoly operators from each jurisdiction connected to the cable. In contrast to the first satellite systems, such consortia were not the subjects of international conventions. Increasingly, the 'club' model has been replaced by single private ventures, such as Global Crossing and FLAG. Huge cable-laying projects are currently underway throughout the world, driven by the exponential growth in demand for bandwidth to carry data traffic. For example, the Africa Optical Network ('Africa ONE') will comprise a cable laid around the whole continent of Africa, a trunk and branch network covering approximately 40,000 km.[25]

In terms of regulatory issues, submarine cabling can be divided into:

(a)   the laying of the cable itself;

(b)   the provisioning of capacity in the form of IRUs and, subsequently, as IPLCs;

(c)   the operation of the cable landing station; and

(d)   the facilities required to connect the operator's domestic network to the cable landing station, commonly referred to as 'backhaul'.[26]

Cable laying raises issues of public international and national marine law, in respect of landing rights. The establishment of cable landing stations usually involves a complex array of national and/or local planning and environmental laws. The provisioning of capacity and 'backhaul' facilities, as well as access to landing stations, increasingly concerns telecommunications regulatory authorities in terms of competition.

---

[24] See generally Wagner, E., 'Submarine cables and protections provided by the law of the sea', in *Open Governance: Strategies and Approaches for the 21st Century* (ed. Mensah) (Proceedings of The Law of the Sea Institute, 28th Annual Conference, 1994), at 95–109.

[25] See Nellist, J.G. and Gilbert, E.M., *Understanding Modern Telecommunications and the Information Superhighway*, (Norwood, Artech House, 1999), chap. 5, 'The Undersea Information Superhighway'.

[26] See Hogan and Hartson, *Submarine Cable Landing Rights and Existing Practices for the Provision of Transmission Capacity on International Routes*, Report to the European Commission, August 1999.

In similar fashion to satellites, the international law of the sea governs the laying of submarine cable and associated liabilities for damage, where such cable lies outside the territory of a State. The primary international treaty governing ownership of the seas is the United Nations Convention on the Law of the Sea 1982, which came into force only in November 1994.[27] The UK instrument of accession was deposited on 25 July 1997 and the Convention came into force in the UK on 24 August 1997.[28] In March 1998, the European Community acceded to the Convention in respect of those matters for which competence has been transferred to it by those Member States that are parties to the Convention.[29]

The 1982 Convention divides the sea into five different zones, each subject to different legal regimes:

(a) *internal waters*, which are 'on the landward side of the baseline of the territorial sea' and are part of a State's sovereign territory (Art. 8);

(b) *territorial waters* extending 12 nautical miles in breadth and over which the coastal State has sovereignty (Art. 3), subject to the right of 'innocent passage' (s. 3);

(c) *the continental shelf*, comprising 'the sea-bed and subsoil of the submarine areas that extend beyond its territorial sea' up to 200 nautical miles (Art. 76), and over which the coastal State exercises 'sovereign rights for the purpose of exploring it and exploiting its natural resources' (Art. 77);

(d) *the exclusive economic zone* extending over a 200 nautical mile zone, where the State has the right to declare exclusive economic interests in the resources (Part V); and

(e) *the high seas* which are open to all States, both coastal and land-locked (Art. 87).

A coastal State is entitled to lay submarine cables in its territorial waters, provided that they do not obstruct the rights of use of others, such as innocent passage (Art. 21(c)). Any State is entitled to lay cables on the continental shelf, subject to the rights of other users already present, as well as the right of the coastal State to take reasonable measures in respect of exploitation, control of pollution and the imposition of conditions on cables entering its territory or territorial waters (Art. 79). States are also free to lay cables in the exclusive economic zone (Art. 58) and the high seas (Art. 87), subject to an obligation to respect existing cables and pipelines (Art. 112).

The need to protect submarine cables from damage caused by other uses of the sea, such as fishing, gave rise to the Convention for the Protection of Submarine Cables in 1884,[30] applicable outside of territorial waters.[31] The

---

[27] See UN General Assembly Resolution A/48/263 of 28 July 1994.
[28] Treaty Series No. 81 (1999), Cm. 4524.
[29] Council Decision of 23 March 1998 concerning the conclusion by the European Community of the United Nations Convention of 10 December 1982 on the Law of the Sea and the Agreement of 28 July 1994 relating to the implementation of Part XI thereof, (1998) OJ L 179/1, at Annex II.
[30] Paris, 14 March 1884 (75 BFSP 356; C 5910).
[31] Primarily in the continental shelf zone: Wagner, *op. cit. supra* n. 24, at 100.

1884 Convention was implemented in English law by the Submarine Telegraph Act 1885, although any contradictory provisions within the 1982
Convention supersede its provisions (Art. 311.2). Under the 1885 Act, it is
an offence unlawfully and wilfully, or by culpable negligence, to break or
damage a submarine cable under the high seas (s. 3(2)). Conversely, where
a shipowner can prove damage to his or her equipment in order to avoid
damaging a submarine cable, that shipowner may claim compensation from
the cable owner, provided that all reasonable precautionary measures were
taken (Continental Shelf Act 1964, s. 8(1); see *Agincourt Steamship Co.
Ltd* v *Eastern Extension, Australasia and China Telegraph Co. Ltd* [1907] 2 KB 305,
CA).

In similar fashion to the international satellite organisations, the
cooperative nature of the 'cable clubs' raises competition concerns. In a
liberalising environment, competing operators will want to purchase capacity
on the cable and may need access to the cable landing stations to connect
their networks physically to the international circuits. Cable owners, historically incumbent operators, may delay the provisioning of capacity on the
cable, levy excessive tariffs or make landing station access difficult, in order
to obstruct the competitor's entry into a market. Therefore, in some EU
Member States (e.g., Italy), national regulators have imposed access and
interconnection obligations upon incumbent operators.[32]

10.3   INTERNATIONAL TELECOMMUNICATIONS UNION

The ITU was founded in 1932, although its origins can be traced back to the
International Telegraph Union established in 1865. As such, the ITU is the
oldest of the intergovernmental organisations, which illustrates the inherently
international nature of the telecommunications industry. It became a
specialised agency of the United Nations system in 1947. Based in Geneva,
the ITU exists to further the development of telegraph, telephone and radio
services, to promote international cooperation for the use of telecommunications and the development of technical facilities, and to allocate radio
frequencies. The International Telecommunications Convention and Constitution, to which the United Kingdom is a party,[33] contain the basic principles
for the conduct of international telecommunication services, the basis for
membership of the ITU and its organisation and permanent organs.

The Constitution sets forth the fundamental principles of the ITU, while
the Convention details the operational procedures which may be subject to
periodic review. The 'supreme organ' within the ITU structure is the

---

[32] See Hogan and Hartson, *op. cit. supra* n. 26. Also Commission Communication, 'Sixth Report
on the Implementation of the Telecommunications Regulatory Package', COM (2000) 814,
7.12.2000.
[33] See Constitution and Convention of the ITU, Geneva, 22 December 1992 (Treaty Series No.
24, 1996, Cm 3145), as amended by the Final Acts of the Plenipotentiary Conference of the
ITU, Kyoto, 14 October 1994 (Treaty Series No. 65, 1997, Cm 3779), which entered into force
on deposit of the UK's Instrument of Ratification on 11 February 1997; and as amended by the
Final Acts of the Plenipotentiary Conference of the ITU, Minneapolis, 6 November 1998, which
entered into force on 1 January 2000. See generally http://www.itu.int/.

Plenipotentiary Conference, which comprises every Member State and meets every four years (Constitution, Art. 8). Between meetings, a Council, comprising no more than 25 per cent of the total membership, acts on behalf of the Plenipotentiary (Constitution, Art. 10(3)). The work of the Union is then subdivided into three sectors:

    (a)   the Radiocommunications Sector (ITU-R);
    (b)   the Telecommunication Standardization Sector (ITU-T); and
    (c)   the Telecommunication Development Sector (ITU-D).

The work of each sector is carried out by a series of organisational entities: world and regional conferences, boards, assemblies and numerous study groups examining particular topics. An administrative 'Bureau', within the General Secretariat, supports each sector, and the Secretary-General, currently Yashio Utsumi, heads the General Secretariat.

The ITU has two categories of membership:

    (a)   'Member States', i.e. national governments, of which there are currently 189; and

    (b)   'Sector Members', representing all the various categories of player within the telecommunications industry and numbering over 600.

Sector Members have been involved in the work of the ITU since the Rome Telegraph Conference in 1871, with the sponsorship of a Member State (Convention, Art. 19(1)(a)). In 1998, the Convention was amended to enable Sector Members to apply directly to join the ITU, although the applicant's Member State must approve such a procedure (Convention, Art. 19(4*bis*)–(4*quarter*)). Despite being eligible for membership, it was not until the Plenipotentiary in 1994 that 'other entities dealing with telecommunication matters' could formally participate in the decision-making processes of the ITU (Convention, Art. 19(9)); and it was only in 1998 that Sector Members were recognised as having formal rights of participation under the Constitution:

> In respect of their participation in activities of the Union, Sector Members shall be entitled to participate fully in the activities of the Sector of which they are members, subject to relevant provisions of this Constitution and the Convention:
>
>   (a)   they may provide chairmen and vice-chairmen of Sector assemblies and meetings and world telecommunication development conferences;
>
>   (b)   they shall be entitled, subject to the relevant provisions of the Convention and relevant decisions adopted in this regard by the Plenipotentiary Conference, to take part in the adoption of Questions and Recommendations and in decisions relating to the working methods and procedures of the Sector concerned. (Art. 3(3))

The fundamental legal instruments of the ITU – the Constitution, Convention and Administrative Regulations (see 10.3.4 below) – continue to be under the exclusive jurisdiction of the Member States.

With the liberalisation of the telecommunications industry and the proliferation of commercial operators, tension has grown over the position of industry members within the ITU structure. On the one hand, governments are wary of relinquishing their historic rights to control the organisation; on the other hand, they recognise industry's legitimate interests in the work of the Union and want industry to contribute an ever-greater proportion of the costs associated with its operations and activities. The issue of industry involvement dominated the ITU's most recent Plenipotentiary Conference (Minneapolis, October–November 1998), where a single category of industry membership was finally recognised: '*Sector Member:* An entity or organization authorized in accordance with Article 19 of the Convention to participate in the activities of a Sector' (Constitution, Annex).

In terms of financing the work of the ITU, the Member States amended the Constitution to place Sector Member contributions on an equal footing to their own (Art. 28). In addition, new 'Advisory Groups' were established for each sector, with a broad remit to review the 'priorities, programmes, operations, financial matters and strategies' of the various bodies within each sector (Convention, Arts 11A, 14A, 17A). These new bodies should increase the influence of Sector Members within the ITU as Member States and industry will participate on an equal footing.

As part of a broad review of the ITU's role and strategy for the future, an ITU Reform Advisory Panel recently made the following recommendation with respect to the balance of influence between Member States and Sector Members within the ITU: 'The decision-making functions of the ITU should reflect the modern, competitive telecommunications environment in which the private sector plays the lead role while the regulatory agencies act as an arbitrator for the wider public interest.'[34] While such a sentiment will be welcomed by the telecommunications industry, the degree to which Member States will continue to intervene in the 'public interest' may give cause for concern. Currently, there are no institutional procedures to enable Sector Members to appeal against a decision made by Member States, or for arbitration in a dispute with a Member State.

The work of the ITU can be divided into three major areas: standardisation; spectrum management and orbital slots; and development issues.

10.3.1 Standards

It was the issue of technical standards that gave rise to the establishment of the International Telegraph Union in 1865, when governments recognised the need for standards to extend the telegraph network throughout Europe. Standards represent the cornerstone of the global telecommunications indus-

---

[34] ITU Reform Advisory Panel (RAP), Observations and Recommendations for Reform, 10 March 2000.

try, and the ITU is one of the leading international institutions for *de jure* standards-making. Its remit extends not only to technical issues, but also to operational and tariff structures for international telecommunication services (see further 10.3.5).

Over recent years, the ITU's pre-eminent position in the standards-setting field has somewhat diminished in the face of regulatory competition from regional organisations,[35], industry bodies[36] and, most significantly, *de facto* standards organisations such as the Internet Engineering Task Force (IETF) which are able to develop standards much more rapidly than formal bodies such as the ITU. Recognising such developments, the ITU is examining ways to reposition itself: 'ITU-T could become a facilitator for collaboration, convening meetings among different standards bodies and industry forums, in particular on interworking between the Internet and telecommunications networks, both fixed and mobile.'[37] As such its standards-development role would be focused on those areas where it currently leads: optical transmission, voice services, numbering, signalling and network management.

10.3.2 Radio communications

The development of radio communications at the beginning of the twentieth century also gave rise to the need for international cooperation to avoid harmful interference. The International Radiotelegraph Union, established in 1906, adopted operating principles that have continued to form the basis of the ITU's regulation of radio communications. Member States were required to notify each other of any new service utilising the radio spectrum and were obliged to ensure that such services did not interfere with other uses of the frequency.[38]

The Radiocommunications Sector of the ITU, primarily operating through the Radio Regulations Board, exercises a regulatory function in respect of the use of two scarce resources: radio-frequency spectrum and the geostationary satellite orbit (Constitution, Art. 1(2)(a), (b), Chapter II (Arts 12–16); Convention, s. 5 (Arts 7–12)).[39] The ITU is responsible for the allocation of bands of the radio-frequency spectrum to Member State administrations and then registers the assignment of particular radio frequencies by an administration to a specific operator. Such procedures are designed 'to eliminate harmful interference . . . and to improve use made of the radio-frequency spectrum'.[40]

---

[35] For example, the European Telecommunications Standards Institute (ETSI): www.etsi.org.
[36] For example, the GSM Association: www.gsmworld.com. It comprises some 449 member companies from 149 countries.
[37] RAP, *supra* n. 34, at Recommendation no. 3.
[38] See Allison, A., 'Meeting the Challenges of Change: The Reform of the International Telecommunications Union' (1993) 45 *Federal Communications Law Journal* 498.
[39] The ITU's procedures cover both geostationary and non-geostationary satellite systems.
[40] 'Harmful interference' is defined as 'Interference which endangers the functioning of a radio navigation service or or of other safety services or seriously degrades, obstructs or repeatedly interrupts a radio communication service operating in accordance with the Radio Regulations.' (Constitution, para. 1003). See also Art. 45.

The ITU expects Members to bear in mind that countries have 'equitable access to [the resources], taking into account the special needs of the developing countries and the geographical position of particular countries' (Constitution Art. 44(2)). This provision was introduced in 1973 to reflect the interests of developing countries concerned about reserving a portion of the relevant resources until such time as they were in an economic position to exploit them.

However, one of the dominant issues of current concern in the Radio-communications Sector is the problem of overfiling of requests for orbital slots with associated frequencies for satellite systems. In particular, Member State administrations have been accused of filing for 'paper satellites' that have little or no real prospect of becoming operational. The filing is designed to pre-empt competing claims to what is perceived as an ever-diminishing resource in the face of multinational, private satellite consortia, such as Globalstar and ICO. The administration can then realise the value of the allocation by re-selling or leasing the slot to the highest bidder at some later date. The consequence of such practices is to lengthen substantially the procedure for genuine satellite systems to obtain the necessary allocations.

To address the problem of overfiling, the ITU proposed in 1997 that administrations be required to provide specific evidence of the proposed satellite system, referred to as administrative and financial 'due diligence', and to make regular submissions on the implementation of the system, including the contractual date of delivery, the number of satellites procured and the proposed launch date. Financial constraints would include an annual coordination and registration charge, as well as a refundable deposit. To date, only the administrative obligations have been implemented, while the need for the financial measures will be reconsidered in 2002.[41]

10.3.3   Telecommunications Development

From 1947, membership of the ITU expanded rapidly among developing nations. As their numbers grew, so did their share of the votes and ability to influence the direction and activities of the ITU. At the Nairobi Plenipotentiary Conference in 1982, such increasing influence resulted in the adoption of a new basic purpose of the ITU: 'to promote and to offer technical assistance to developing countries in the field of telecommunications, and also to promote the mobilization of the material and financial resources needed for implementation' (Constitution, Art. 1(1)(b)). Therefore, since 1982, the ITU has given equal priority to telecommunications development, standards-setting and radio communications.

The Telecommunication Development Sector operates through a Telecommunication Development Bureau, Telecommunication Development Conferences and associated Study Groups. In particular, the ITU has worked with other development agencies, such as the World Bank and the International Bank of Reconstruction and Development, to improve the flow of

---

[41] Press Release, *supra* n. 22.

technology, funds and expertise into developing countries. The Reform Advisory Panel has recently proposed that the ITU's development focus should be expanded 'from technical assistance towards helping developing countries establish pro-market regulatory frameworks',[42] which would seem to reflect the influence of the WTO in the telecommunications sector.

10.3.4   Legal instruments of the ITU

As international treaties, the Constitution and Convention of the ITU are legal instruments that bind Member States (Constitution, Art. 6(1)). While primarily detailing the rules governing the establishment and operation of the ITU, the Constitution also embodies certain fundamental legal principles governing international telecommunications (Chapter VI). Members give recognition to certain rights of users, i.e. the 'right of the public to correspond by means of the international service' (Art. 33) and 'ensuring the secrecy of international correspondence' (Art. 37). The majority of the principles, however, represent reservations that Members have the right to exercise, such as in respect of the 'stoppage of telecommunications' (Art. 34) and the 'suspension of services' (Art. 35), as well as the avoidance of any responsibilities for damage and related claims (Art. 36).

Complementing the Constitution and Convention are Administrative Regulations, subdivided into:

(a)   International Telecommunications Regulations; and
(b)   Radio Regulations.

The Administrative Regulations comprise the general principles to be observed in the provision of international telecommunication services and networks, and in the assignment and use of frequencies and orbital slots. Such Regulations 'shall be binding on all Member States' (Constitution, Arts 4 and 54). At the time of accession to the Constitution and Convention (i.e., 27 June 1994 in the case of the United Kingdom), a Member State may make reservations in respect of any of the existing Administrative Regulations (Art. 54(2)). Any subsequent partial or complete revision of those Regulations requires Member States to indicate their consent to be bound, by depositing an instrument of ratification, acceptance or approval, or by notifying the Secretary-General (Art. 54(3)A), although a Member State will be provisionally bound from the entry into force of the revision if the Member State has signed the revision (Art. 54(3)D).

Under the Constitution, Member States are also required to

take the necessary steps to impose the observance of the provisions of this Constitution, the Convention and the Administrative Regulations upon operating agencies authorized by them to establish and operate telecommunications and which engage in international services or which operate

---

[42] RAP, *supra* n. 34.

stations capable of causing harmful interference to the radio services of other countries. (Art. 6(2))

However, this blanket provision is qualified by the concept of a 'recognised operating agency' (ROA):

> Any operating agency . . . which operates a public correspondence or broadcasting service and upon which the obligations provided for in Article 6 of this Constitution are imposed by the Member State in whose territory the head office of the agency is situated, or by the Member State which has authorized this operating agency to establish and operate a telecommunication service on its territory. (Constitution, Annex)

Historically, ROAs were generally the state-owned incumbent operator. However, in liberalised markets, the categories of ROAs could potentially extend to any provider of international services, including re-sale services.

The current applicable International Telecommunications Regulations are those adopted at Melbourne in 1988 (ITR 88), comprising ten substantive Articles and a series of Appendices. Reiterating the Constitution, the Regulations are binding only on 'administrations' (i.e., Member States and ROAs). Administrations do, however, have the freedom to enter into 'special mutual arrangements' for the provision of international telecommunications networks and services (ITR 88 Art. 9). This provides considerable flexibility for countries such as the US and the EU Member States that have regulated to ensure liberalisation, e.g., the application of interconnection regulations to intra-EU international traffic. There have recently been calls for the International Telecommunications Regulations to be revised, partly due to the considerable changes in the market since 1988, but also arising from concerns that the Regulations may conflict with other international agreements, such as those administered by the WTO.[43]

In addition to the binding legal instruments, the various bodies of the ITU adopt Recommendations, Resolutions and Decisions. While the Administrative Regulations comprise the general principles to be complied with, the ITU-T and ITU-R Recommendations detail the manner in which they are to be implemented and represent the bulk of ITU rule-making (e.g., over 2,600 ITU-T Recommendations are currently in force). Such Recommendations do not have 'the same legal status as the Regulations' (ITR 88, Art. 1.4), although 'administrations' 'should comply with, to the greatest extent practicable, the relevant' Recommendations (Art. 1.6; see also the opinion of the Advocate-General in *Italy* v *Commission* [1985] 2 CMLR 368, at 373). The various sectoral 'Study Groups' prepare draft Recommendations that enter into force either through approval at the relevant assemblies or conferences, or through direct correspondence with Member State administrations (Convention, Arts 11(2) and 14(1)).

---

[43] See documents issued by the ITU Expert Group on the International Telecommunications Regulations. See also 10.4 below.

Any disputes regarding the interpretation of any of the legal instruments – Constitution, Convention or Administrative Regulations – are to be settled either through mutually agreed bilateral or multilateral arrangements, or, if not settled by such means, via an arbitration procedure (Constitution, Art. 56). The decision of the arbitrator(s) shall be 'final and binding upon the parties to the dispute' (Convention, Art. 41), although no enforcement mechanism exists in the event of non-compliance. There is a compulsory arbitration procedure under an Optional Protocol to the Convention, between Members that are party to the Protocol (Constitution, Art. 56(3)).[44]

10.3.5 International accounting rates

As discussed at 10.3 above, the International Telegraph Convention, the predecessor of the ITU, was established to extend the operation of telecommunication networks beyond national borders. As well as the need for common standards for the transmission of messages between different networks, such international traffic also raised the issue of payments to be made between national operators for the carriage of each other's traffic. The historic regime established for the making of such payments is known as the 'International Accounting Rate system' and the principles of its operation are contained in the ITU's International Telecommunications Regulations (Art. 6).

The International Accounting Rate system comprises a series of related rates that are intended to provide for an equitable payment to the terminating operator for the termination of an international call and, where relevant, to any transit operators that have handled the call (either direct transit or switched transit). The 'collection charge' (ITR 88, Art. 2.9) is the retail price levied on the originating customer by the originating operator. The 'accounting rate' is essentially a wholesale rate representing the agreed cost of transmitting each unit of traffic between the calling parties.[45] The 'settlement rate' is the payment made by the originating operator to the terminating operator and is usually 50 per cent of the accounting rate. Such payments are made on a net settlement basis between operators, since traffic generally flows in both directions; therefore the operator originating the most traffic is required to make the periodic payments.

Although the system is embodied in the International Telecommunications Regulations, elaborated in a series of Recommendations, it operates through bilateral contractual agreements between telecommunication operators in each jurisdiction: 'For each applicable service in a given relation, administrations (or recognized private operating agencies) shall by mutual agreement establish and revise accounting rates to be applied between them' (ITR 88, Art. 6.2.1).

While the essential elements of the International Accounting Rate system have remained the same over many years, the system was in fact designed to

---

[44] The United Kingdom has ratified the Optional Protocol, 27 June 1994.
[45] Usually expressed in terms of Special Drawing Rights (SDRs) under the International Monetary Fund, or the gold franc. Convention, Art. 38; ITR 88, Art. 6.3.1.

operate under certain conditions no longer present in most telecommunications markets:

(a) jurisdictional symmetry with respect to both call origination and traffic flows;
(b) collection charges higher than the accounting rate;
(c) relatively constant inflation and exchange rates; and
(d) monopoly operators in each jurisdiction providing the international service.

As these conditions have either disappeared or altered, the International Accounting Rate system has given rise to substantial payment flows between operators, representing invisible trade imbalances between countries. In 1996, for example, US operators paid around US$6 billion to operators in other jurisdictions, of which it was estimated that 70 per cent constituted 'an above-cost subsidy from US consumers to foreign carriers'.[46] Indeed, under the current regime, the co-existence of liberalised telecommunications markets with traditional monopolistic environments can actually reward the latter at the expense of the former. In particular, a practice known as 'whipsawing' has arisen, whereby monopolistic operators in one country negotiate with competing operators in other countries to achieve substantially lower accounting rates for the termination of traffic originating in the monopoly country. Alternatively, the monopoly operator may lease its own circuit in the liberalised terminating regime, therefore bypassing the accounting regime for outbound transmissions (commonly referred to as 'one-way bypass').

The payment imbalance is exacerbated by the fact that, historically, accounting rates were not based on actual cost but were often priced at a premium. For some countries, such as the US, the accounting rate system has therefore come to be seen as an unacceptable regime that positively disadvantages the introduction of competitive markets. However, countries which are net creditors under the accounting rate system, often (although not exclusively) developing countries, usually view the system as constituting an important source of foreign 'hard currency' revenue for investment into the domestic market, either in the form of network rollout or through subsidising the cost of access (e.g., line rental). Such revenues can be viewed as contributing to a universal service policy, at a global level as well as for individual countries.[47] Indeed, the ITU's Secretary-General has noted that developing countries receive more revenue from the accounting rate system in one year than they received from development banks, such as the World Bank, for telecommunications programs during the first half of the 1990s.[48]

---

[46] Federal Communications Commission, In the matter of International Settlement Rates, Report and Order, IB Docket No. 96-261, 7 August 1997 ('Benchmark Order'), para. 13.
[47] See Tyler, M., 'Transforming economic relationships in international telecommunications', Chapter 8, Briefing Report for ITU Regulatory Colloquium No. 7 (1997). Also, Stanley, K., 'International settlements in a changing global telecom market', in *Telecom Reform* (ed. Melody) (Technical University of Denmark, 1997), at 371–94.
[48] Tarjanne, P., 'Reforming the International Accounting Rate System', (1998) 2 *ITU News*.

Over recent years there has been significant pressure for the International Accounting Rate system to be reformed, from governmental concern to reduce trade deficits, as well as to benefit end-users through reductions in the cost of international telecommunications.[49] In addition, technological developments have resulted in a proliferation of alternative calling procedures designed, either directly or indirectly, to avoid the normal operation of the international accounting regime. Such procedures can be broadly divided into two categories:

(a) 're-origination' techniques, which take advantage of asymmetric rates on particular routes to minimise the cost of the accounting rates, e.g., call-back,[50] country-direct, calling cards, refile;[51]

(b) 'by-pass' techniques, which completely circumvent the international accounting regime, e.g., international simple re-sale services, VSATs,[52] Internet telephony.

These practices inevitably lead to a reduction in the revenues of the monopoly provider of international telecommunication services and, in some cases, are infringements of national law.[53] However, while re-origination techniques represent a loss in collection revenues, the concurrent increase in settlement payments from inbound traffic may significantly offset the impact for the incumbent and will encourage the maintenance of high accounting rates.[54]

The ITU is in an uneasy position in respect of such activities and has called upon Member States to take appropriate action against operators in their jurisdiction who are breaching the laws and regulations of other Member States.[55]

Proposals to change the system take two main forms. First, there have been moves within the ITU to lower accounting rates towards the actual cost of terminating international calls. Such cost-based tariffing reflects the regulatory position adopted in liberalised markets, such as that applicable to interconnection agreements (see Chapter 6). It also reflects existing obligations under the International Telecommunications Regulations 1988, where Member States are required to revise accounting rates 'taking into account

---

[49] See ITU Report of the Informal Expert Group on International Telecommunications Settlements, March 1997.

[50] Various forms of 'call-back' exist, but it essentially involves a reversal in the direction of the call, e.g., a call from a country with high originating international tariffs is manipulated to appear to come from the terminating country which has low originating international tariffs, using features of call signalling systems.

[51] 'Refile' involves routing a communication from country A to country B via a third country, C, where the sum of the tariff rates for calls between A–C and C–B are less than A–B.

[52] Very Small Aperture Terminals, used for satellite-based telecommunications direct to home.

[53] See ITU Resolution 21 of the Plenipotentiary Conference, Kyoto, 1994: 'Special Measures concerning Alternative Calling Procedures on International Telecommunication Networks' (revised at the Minneapolis Plenipotentiary, 1998) (noting that 86 Member States prohibit 'call-back' (as of October 1998)).

[54] See Secretary-General's Paper on Accounting Rate Reform, ITU-T, COM 3-2-E (November 1996).

[55] Resolution 21, *supra* n. 53.

relevant [ITU-T] Recommendations and relevant cost trends' (Art. 6.2.1). Recommendation D.140, 'Accounting rate principles for international telephone service', calls upon administrations to move accounting rates towards a cost-based approach, by identifying those operational elements considered legitimate components of the accounting rate:

(a)   international transmission facilities;
(b)   international switching facilities; and
(c)   national extension.

The direct costs of utilising these facilities, with some allocation of the associated common costs, should comprise a cost-based settlement rate. Despite Recommendation D.140 and a fall in accounting rates by 12 per cent over the past three years, many ITU members view progress towards cost-orientated rates as too slow. As a result, an Annex to D.140 was adopted at the recent World Telecommunication Standardization Assembly, containing indicative target rates and specified deadlines for each country.[56]

The second approach to address the present accounting rate system is through the adoption of a range of alternative rate systems, which are designed to reflect the different conditions present in many markets. Five alternative models have been suggested:[57]

(a)   *Call termination charges*, where a single rate is charged to terminate into a country from any other country, as is currently operated for the international telegram service. The primary advantages of such a system are transparency and non-discrimination.

(b)   *Facilities-based interconnection charges*, as already required under European Union law (Interconnection Directive; see Chapter 6) and generally in operation for mobile roaming.

(c)   '*Sender keeps all*', where no payments are made between national operators, historically the system adopted between the UK and Ireland. Such an approach also reflects the 'peering' arrangements present in the Internet (see Chapter 6). However, as with peering, it does operate on a presumption of equality in traffic flows.

(d)   *International private leased circuits*, where the charge will reflect the cost of leasing such capacity.

(e)   *Volume-based payments*, fixed per traffic unit carried, as currently used in Internet-based transit arrangements.

The ITU's developmental role has created problems when addressing the reform of the International Accounting Rate system, since the system is perceived in many Member States as contributing funds to the broader

---

[56]   Montreal, 27 September–6 October 2000.
[57]   For example, ITU-T Recommendation D.150, 'New system for accounting in international telephony' (June 1999).

development of telecommunications in their jurisdiction. Indeed, the ITU specifically recommends that accounting rate apportionment in favour of a developing country should be used for telecommunications improvements.[58]

Pressure to reform the system is also being driven, in part, by decisions made by regulatory authorities in certain jurisdictions. In particular, the FCC in the US created considerable consternation in certain countries when it issued its International Settlement Rates Order in 1997.[59] The Order represented a fundamental policy shift from the previous Uniform Settlements Policy (USP), which had been operating since 1980.[60] Under the USP approach, all US-licensed operators were required to operate under the same accounting rate with foreign correspondents, which addressed the problem of 'whipsawing', as well as obliging operators to maintain proportionate inbound and outbound traffic volumes.

However, the FCC recognised that the WTO 'basic agreement' had the potential to sharply worsen the US balance of payments deficit on international services, since incumbent operators in non-liberalised markets would be free to establish US-based operations subsidised from their monopolistic international revenues. The progress of reform within the ITU was slow, therefore the FCC decided to take unilateral steps to drive the pace of change towards cost-based settlement rates.

The Order lays down benchmark 'settlement rates that carriers subject to FCC jurisdiction may pay for termination of US-originated traffic' (para. 312). Countries were categorised into four tiers, representing different stages of economic development. The rates are to be implemented over a transition period, over one to four years, and operators were able to appeal against a rate determination (para. 74). The regime came into effect on 1 January 1998 and the first targets were to be achieved by 1 January 1999. The rates were based on a methodology known as 'tariffed components pricing' (TCP), which comprised the three elements specified in Recommendation D.140: international transmission; international exchange; and national extension. All US-licensed carriers were subject to the Order, while for foreign-affiliated operators compliance was a condition of obtaining FCC approval for the provision of long-distance services to the home jurisdiction (para. 207).

The Benchmark Order generated opposition in many countries, such as those in the Caribbean region, over the potential impact it would have on domestic operator revenues.[61] In addition, the European Commission and Japan raised concerns about the compatibility of the Benchmark Order with

---

[58] Resolution 22, 'Apportionment of revenues in providing international telecommunication services' (Kyoto, 1994).
[59] Benchmark Order, *supra* n. 46.
[60] *Uniform Settlement Rates on Parallel International Communications Routes*, 84 FCC 2d 121 (1980), applicable to international telephone services since 1986. See *Implementation and Scope of the International Settlements Policy for Parallel Routes*, CC Docket No. 85-204, Report and Order, 51 Fed. Reg. 4736 (7 February 1986).
[61] But see Petitions for Enforcement of International Settlement Rates Benchmark Rates, 4 August 2000 (seeking enforcement of 19 cents benchmark rate against Trinidad and Tobago), http://www.fcc.gov/Bureaus/International/Public_Notices/2000/da001768.doc.

the United States' commitments under the General Agreement on Trade in Services, specifically the principle of 'most-favoured-nation'.[62]

In 1998, Cable & Wireless brought an action before the US courts challenging the legality of the Benchmark Order. Over 100 other petitioners and intervenors, comprising national governments, regulators and operators, soon joined the case on both sides. The main thrust of the complaint was that the FCC had exceeded its authority through the extraterritorial nature of the Order's provisions (*Cable & Wireless et al. v FCC*, 166 F. 3d 1224 (DC Cir. 1999)).[63] The court found overwhelmingly in favour of the FCC, holding that it had the requisite powers to make decisions regulating the actions of US-licensed operators, including the contractual arrangements entered into for international settlement rates (see 47 USC §§205(a), 211(a)): 'the Commission does not exceed its authority simply because a regulatory action has extraterritorial consequences.' The court dismissed objections to the use of the TCP methodology on the grounds that the FCC had acted reasonably, and criticised the petitioners for withholding actual cost data as well as failing to propose alternative methodologies.

During the course of the proceedings, the Australian operator Telstra entered a petition against the Benchmark Order on the grounds that it did not address the issue of international Internet connections. Telstra complained that the Order was based on a circuit-switched environment, where traditionally each correspondent operator is responsible for the provision of half of the international circuit. Telstra argued, however, that in an Internet environment non-US operators were effectively forced to purchase a full circuit in order to connect to the Internet exchange points based primarily in the US (see 166 F. 3d, at 1235–36; see also Chapter 6). As a consequence, US carriers were obtaining significant financial benefits from the current arrangements for international Internet connections. The court denied Telstra's petition as constituting insufficient grounds for overturning the FCC Order, but the issue has subsequently been pursued within the ITU.

In April 2000, ITU-T Study Group 3 approved a draft Recommendation on International Internet Connection that had been proposed by Australia. Draft Recommendation D.120 was presented to the World Telecommunication Standardization Assembly (WTSA) for adoption in October 2000:

> Noting the rapid growth of the Internet and Internet based services: It is recommended that administrations negotiate and agree to bilateral commercial arrangements applying to direct international Internet connections whereby each administration will be compensated for the costs that it incurs in carrying traffic that is generated by the other administration.

For many Internet-based services, such as the World Wide Web, traffic flows are asymmetric, as an individual request for a page generates large flows of data towards the requester. Such data is generally from servers based in the

---

[62] *Ibid.*, at para. 109. See also 10.4 below.
[63] See www.fcc.gov/ogc/documents/opinions/1999/cable.html.

US and connected to the Internet by US operators. Under the draft Recommendation, such operators would have been required to pay transit and termination fees to operators in other jurisdictions to which the individual requester is connected, such as Australia, rather than the current settlement-free 'peering' system (see Chapter 5, at 5.6), with operators such as Telstra having to pay for full international circuits.

The draft Recommendation generated significant opposition from the US and Europe, but was supported by many developing nations' members. An amended version was eventually adopted at WTSA:

> [R]ecommends that administrations involved in the provision of international Internet connections negotiate and agree to bilateral commercial arrangements enabling direct international Internet connections that take into account the possible need for compensation between them for the value of elements such as traffic flow, number of routes, geographical coverage and cost of international transmission amongst others.

The shift from mandatory to voluntary compensation enabled the proposal to be adopted, although the US and Greece made reservations and stated that the Recommendation would not be applied in their jurisdictions. Despite the agreed position, it can be expected that the ITU will be required to address this issue again over the coming years, as Internet-based data communications continue to expand as a proportion of total international traffic.

The International Accounting Rate system is gradually disappearing in its current form, to be replaced by a multitude of different arrangements reflecting the state of liberalisation in Member States, technological developments and the commercial positions of the respective parties. However, political pressure to accelerate such change has shifted somewhat in recent years from the ITU to the World Trade Organisation (WTO), although a moratorium was agreed between certain Member States not to pursue a legal action before the WTO on accounting rates in the near future.[64]

10.4 WORLD TRADE ORGANISATION

The World Trade Organisation (WTO) was established in 1994 as part of the final act embodying the results of the Uruguay Round of multilateral trade negotiations.[65] The function of the WTO is to facilitate the implementation, administration and operation of certain multilateral trade agreements (Art. III(1)). Its unique feature is the establishment of a dispute settlement body to enforce the obligations accepted by Member States within the context of the agreements (see 10.4.3 below). The existence of this enforcement mechanism has been a key factor in pushing the WTO to the forefront of intergovernmental organisations.

---

[64] See WTO Report of the Group on Basic Telecommunications (S/GBT/4), 15 February 1997.
[65] See the Agreement Establishing the World Trade Organisation with Understanding on Rules and Procedures Governing the Settlement of Disputes and Trade Policy Review Mechanism (Marrakesh, 15 April 1994; TS 57 (1996) Cm 3277; (1994) 33 ILM 15; (1994) OJ L 336/1). The Treaties entered into force on 1 January 1995.

For the telecommunications industry, the accelerating process of market liberalisation coincided with the GATT Uruguay Round, which commenced in 1986. Significantly, the Uruguay Round was the first time that trade in services was included within the scope of the multilateral negotiations due to its increasing importance as a sector of trade, particularly for developed nations. Telecommunications was recognised as a critical element, both as a facilitator of trade in services and as an increasingly tradable service in its own right. Such recognition ensured that telecommunications issues moved towards the top of the agenda for countries such as the US and the UK.

The most directly relevant of the WTO-administered trade agreements for the telecommunications industry are the General Agreement on Tariffs and Trade (GATT),[66] in respect of telecommunications equipment, and the General Agreement on Trade in Services (GATS).[67] However, the Agreement on Trade-Related Aspects of Intellectual Property[68] is also of obvious importance to an industry so heavily dependent on its investments in research and development. This section will primarily focus on the GATS as establishing a framework for international telecommunications law.

10.4.1   General Agreement on Trade in Services

The GATS contains an Annex on telecommunications (see 10.4.2) and, subsequently, a Protocol establishing commitments in basic telecommunications (see 10.4.3). Taken together, these agreements have required Member signatories substantially to open up their telecommunication markets to international competition.

The GATS comprises a number of fundamental 'General Obligations and Disciplines' with which all Members were required to comply from the moment the agreement entered into force (Part II). These general obligations are then supplemented by specific commitments accepted by a Member in Schedules of Commitments appended to the GATS (Parts III and IV). Each schedule specifies:

(a)   terms, limitations and conditions on market access;
(b)   conditions and qualifications on national treatment;
(c)   undertakings relating to additional commitments;
(d)   where appropriate, the time-frame for implementation of such commitments; and
(e)   the date of entry into force of such commitments (Art. XX).

These schedules represent a baseline or codification of conditions in a specific national market upon which a foreign service provider can rely. In addition, they constitute the starting-point for future negotiations to liberalise the sector further. A Member may modify or withdraw a commitment only after three years from the date it entered into force (Art. XXI).

---

[66] GATT (1947) 55 UNTS 187, and GATT (1994) TS 56 (1996) Cm 3282; (1994) 33 ILM 28.
[67] TS 58 (1996) Cm 3276; (1994) 33 ILM 44.
[68] TS 10 (1996) Cm 3046; (1994) 33 ILM 81.

The best known general obligation upon Members is the 'most-favoured-nation treatment', that 'each Member shall accord immediately and unconditionally to services and service suppliers of any other Member treatment no less favourable than that it accords to like service and service suppliers of any other country' (Art. II). However, a Member may specify that this principle shall not be applicable to certain measures listed in an Annex on Article II Exemptions (Art. II(2)). Such exemptions are subject to review after a five-year period and should not exceed a duration of ten years (Annex on Article II Exemptions, paras 5–7).

There is some debate whether the 'most-favoured-nation' principle should operate in respect of the International Accounting Rate regime (see 10.3.5 above), since in many non-competitive markets the amount an incumbent operator charges for the termination of international calls will vary significantly between different originating jurisdictions. Member States have an obligation to ensure that any 'monopoly supplier of a service' does not act in a manner inconsistent either with the 'most-favoured-nation' principle, or with any of the specific commitments made by the Member (Art. VIII(1)). However, settlement rates are the subject of bilateral contractual agreements between operators, so that it is questionable whether such agreements fall within the jurisdiction of the GATS. The 'most-favoured-nation' principle would seem to be applicable only if accounting rate agreements were considered to be a 'measure by Members', i.e. taken by governments and authorities, or by 'non-governmental bodies in the exercise of powers delegated by central, regional or local government or authorities' (Art. I(3)(a)). Where an operator falls into the latter definition, it may then be unclear whether a bilateral agreement constitutes the exercise of a delegated power, even if in compliance with an ITU Recommendation which the Member State administration has accepted.

Article VI of the GATS addresses 'domestic regulation'. It requires Members to ensure that any authorisation procedures are handled 'within a reasonable period of time' (Art. VI(3)) and are capable of 'objective and impartial review' by a judicial or administrative body (Art. VI(2)). Such commitments are obviously applicable to licensing procedures for the provision of telecommunication services. In addition, there is an on-going commitment to develop disciplines to ensure that 'qualification requirements and procedures, technical standards and licensing requirements do not constitute unnecessary barriers to trade' (Art. VI(4)).

Competition law issues are addressed under Part II, 'General Obligations and Disciplines', in Arts VIII 'Monopolies and Exclusive Service Suppliers' and IX 'Business Practices'. Such rules may be used to prevent an abuse of dominant position or restrictive trade practices. These provisions are likely to be of particular interest to telecommunication operators trying to provide services into countries whose legal systems have historically had no legal rules addressing general competition issues (e.g., Asian countries; see further Chapter 14, at 14.4.2).

In contrast to the GATT, the principle of 'national treatment' constitutes a specific commitment applicable to particular service sectors and detailed in a Members' Schedule to the GATS, whereby: 'each Member shall accord to services and service suppliers of any other Member, in respect of all measures affecting the supply of service, treatment no less favourable than that it accords to its own like services and service suppliers' (Art. XVII) (see GATT (1947),[69] Art. III, 'National Treatment on Internal Taxation and Regulation').

The other key specific commitment under the GATS concerns 'market access' (Art. XVI), under which Members detail those service sectors into which service suppliers from other Members may enter.

10.4.2   Telecommunications Annex

At the time of the GATS, Members also adopted a supplementary Annex on Telecommunications. Its objective was to clarify the position of Members 'with respect to measures affecting *access to and use of* public telecommunications transport networks and services [emphasis added]' (para. 1). The Annex is therefore concerned with the supply of value-added telecommunication services over such public networks and services rather than any right to provide the networks and services.

The Annex imposes obligations of transparency of conditions of access and use, including tariffs, terms and conditions, and specifications of technical interfaces with the public networks and services (para. 4). The first draft of the Annex stated that access and use should be on cost-orientated terms, but this was removed in the face of opposition.[70] Access should be 'non-discriminatory', a term which embraces both the 'most-favoured-nation' and national treatment principles. Service providers should be permitted to attach terminal equipment to the public network, interconnect private circuits and utilise any operating protocols that do not interfere with the availability of the public network (para. 5(b)). In terms of restrictions, Members may only impose conditions that are necessary:

(a)   to safeguard the public service responsibilities of the suppliers of public networks, i.e. the USO;

(b)   to protect the integrity of the network; or

(c)   to comply with a Member's commitments in its schedule (para. 5(e)).

Such conditions may include restrictions on the re-sale of such services, compliance with any 'type-approval' regime (see Chapter 8, at 8.2.3), or licensing and notification obligations. In addition, a developing country may impose conditions 'necessary to strengthen its domestic telecommunications infrastructure and service capacity and to increase its participation in international trade in telecommunications services' (para. 5(g)). To assist the growth of telecommunications in developing countries, developed Members are encouraged to make available information and opportunities concerning

---

[69] *Supra* n. 66.
[70] Stated in Zutshi, B., 'GATS: Impact on developing countries and telecom services', in *Transnational Data and Communications Report* (July–August 1994), at 24.

the transfer of telecommunications technology and training to the least-developed countries.

10.4.3 Fourth Protocol

At the conclusion of the Uruguay Round, ministers adopted a decision to enter into further voluntary negotiations on the liberalisation of trade in the provision of basic telecommunication networks and services ((1994) 33 ILM 144). Pending the conclusion of these negotiations, Members were granted a 'most-favoured-nation' exemption for measures affecting the provision of such basic telecommunications (GATS, Annex on Negotiations on Basic Telecommunications). These negotiations, carried out under the auspices of the 'Group on Basic Telecommunications', were scheduled to conclude no later than 30 April 1996. However, by the deadline, there had been insufficient offers from Members to enable a conclusion to be reached; therefore negotiations continued until an agreement was finally reached on 15 February 1997.[71]

This agreement is commonly referred to as the 'Basic Agreement on Telecommunications', although the term is somewhat misleading since the agreement consists primarily of a series of 'Schedules of Specific Commitments and a List of Exemptions from Article II concerning basic telecommunications' submitted by some 69 Members.[72] These commitments supplement or modify any existing submissions made by Members and are annexed to the existing Schedules through a device referred to as a Protocol, which becomes an integral part of the GATS (Art. XX). As such, these submissions constituted the Fourth Protocol to have been entered into by certain Members of the WTO. The Fourth Protocol was intended to enter into force on 1 January 1998, but further delays meant that it became effective only on 5 February 1998.

Supplementary to the Schedules, the Chairman of the Group on Basic Telecommunications issued two explanatory notes clarifying certain issues applicable to the scheduling of commitments. First, they defined a 'basic telecom service' in the following terms:

(a)   it encompasses local, long-distance and international services for public and non-public use;

(b)   it may be provided on a facilities basis or by re-sale; and

---

[71] For a detailed history of the negotiations, see Sherman, L., '"Wildly Enthusiastic" about the first multilateral agreement on trade in telecommunications services' (1999) 51 *Federal Communications Law Journal* 61.

[72] The initial 69 Schedules have been supplemented by three, submitted by Barbados, Cyprus and Surinam. The 15 EU Member States submitted one Schedule: see Annex to Council Decision 97/838/EC of 28 November 1997, concerning the conclusion on behalf of the European Community, as regards matters within its competence, of the results of the WTO negotiations on basic telecommunications services ('Council Decision'), (1997) OJ L 347/45. The US FCC has stated that it would treat Bermuda as a WTO Member as a consequence of its being a dependent overseas territory of the UK (FCC Order File No. ITC-214-19990709-00412, released 18 February 2000).

(c) it may be provided through any means of technology (e.g., cable, wireless, satellites).[73]

Secondly, any qualifications made by Members that market access was limited due to the scarcity of spectrum/frequency were compatible with the GATS and need not be specifically noted in the Schedule of Commitments.[74]

The Basic Agreement is seen as the most significant development in the global liberalisation of the telecommunications market. It has been estimated that the Member countries represent over 90 per cent of global revenues in telecommunications.[75] Members' commitments encompassed market access, foreign direct investment and, for the majority of Members, adherence to a set of pro-competitive regulatory principles. The Protocol addressed the introduction of competition into the four biggest bottleneck markets within telecommunications: satellite services; international public voice telephony; domestic long-distance; and the provision of the local loop.

In respect of the 'most-favoured-nation' exemptions, a number of countries specified accounting rates as outside the scope of the Basic Agreement, including India, Pakistan, Sri Lanka and Turkey. The US maintained a 'most-favoured-nation' exemption for Direct-To-Home (DTH) and Direct-Broadcast-Satellite (DBS) services to enable the continuation of existing 'reciprocity' regulations.

One unique feature of the Fourth Protocol was the adoption of a Reference Paper by 59 of the 72 Member signatories as an additional commitment incorporated into the Schedules (a further six Members adopted some aspects of the Reference Paper). It comprises a set of definitions and principles on the regulatory framework governing the provision of basic telecommunications.[76] The principles address particular objectives for the establishment of a pro-competitive regulatory regime, rather than the mechanisms or processes for their achievement. As such, the Reference Paper represents an important body of international legal principles for the telecommunications sector; of considerably greater significance than the ITU constitutional principles, which merely address the rights of the State *vis-à-vis* the users of telecommunications systems (see 10.3.4 above). In addition, where a Member State has incorporated the Reference Paper into its Schedule of Commitments, the principles are enforceable before the WTO Dispute Settlement Body.

In terms of competition law, the Reference Paper first defines two key concepts – 'essential facilities' and 'major supplier':

Essential facilities mean facilities of a public telecommunications transport network or service that
(a) are exclusively or predominantly provided by a single or limited number of suppliers; and

---

[73] Note by Chairman, S/GBT/W/2/Rev. 1, 16 January 1997.
[74] Note by Chairman, S/GBT/W/3, 3 February 1997.
[75] See Spector, P.L., 'The World Trade Organisation Agreement on Telecommunications' (1998) 32 *The International Lawyer* 217.
[76] Council Decision, *supra* n. 72, at p. 52.

(b)   cannot feasibly be economically or technically substituted in order to provide a service.

A major supplier is a supplier which has the ability to materially affect the terms of participation (having regard to price and supply) in the relevant market for basic telecommunications services as a result of:
(a)   control over essential facilities; or
(b)   use of its position in the market.

The concept of 'essential facilities' originates in US antitrust law, although it has also been embraced within European Union competition law. (For US law, see *MCI Communications v AT&T*, 708 F. 2d 1081 (7th Cir. 1983), *aff'd*, 464 U.S. 891 (1983); for EU law, see *Oscar Bronner GmbH & Co. KG v Mediaprint Zeitungs-und Zeitschriftenverlag GmbH & Co. KG and others* (Case C-7/97) [1998] ECR I-7791.) The concept of 'major supplier' is similar to the EU term 'organisation with significant market power', representing a lower threshold of applicability than the concept of 'dominance' within a traditional competition analysis, including the 'essential facilities' doctrine (see Chapters 7 and 9). The perspective of the Reference Paper is the supplier's ability to affect others' access to the market, reflecting its international trade origins. By contrast, the European Commission recently proposed amending the concept of 'significant market power', from a market share trigger (i.e., 25 per cent) to the perspective of the supplier having the power 'to behave to an appreciable extent independently'.[77]

The first two substantive issues addressed in the Reference Paper concern controls to be placed upon the ability of a 'major supplier' to restrict competition. First, a supplier who, alone or with others, constitutes a 'major supplier' must be subject to 'appropriate measures' to prevent anti-competitive practices, whether current or future. Three specific anti-competitive practices are then listed:

(a)   cross-subsidisation;
(b)   the use of 'information obtained from competitors with anti-competitive results', such as the forecast traffic volumes in interconnection arrangements; and
(c)   'not making available to other services suppliers on a timely basis technical information about essential facilities and commercially relevant information which are necessary for them to provide services' (para. 1.2).

Secondly, interconnection with a major supplier should be 'ensured at any technically feasible point in the network'. Such interconnection should be on non-discriminatory terms and conditions, not less favourable than that provided for its own 'like services', echoing the 'national treatment' principle under the GATS (see 10.4.1 above). The interconnection must be achieved in a timely fashion and at 'cost-oriented rates that are transparent, reasonable,

---

[77] See the Proposal for a Directive of the European Parliament and of the Council on a common regulatory framework for electronic communications networks and services, COM (2000) 393, 12 July 2000, at Art. 13(2). See also Chapter 8, at 8.3.

having regard to economic feasibility, and sufficiently unbundled so that the supplier need not pay for network components or facilities that it does not require for the service to be provided'. Interpretation of this critical concept of 'cost-oriented' is already the subject of international dispute (see 10.4.4 below). Lastly, the request for interconnection may be in respect of points which are not offered to the majority of users, an obligation also present in the EU Interconnection Directive (Art. 4(2); see further Chapter 6).

Building on the Annex on Telecommunications, the procedures and arrangements for interconnection with a major supplier must be transparent, including publication of 'either its interconnection agreements or a reference interconnection offer'. A service supplier must have recourse to an independent domestic body to resolve any disputes that may arise in respect of interconnection.

The other four issues covered in the Reference Paper address broader aspects of a pro-competitive telecommunications market:

(a)   Defining a 'universal service obligation' will 'not be regarded as anti-competitive *per se*', provided it is addressed in a transparent and non-discriminatory manner and is necessary to achieve the universal service defined by the Member State (para. 3).

(b)   Reflecting Art. VI of the GATS, any licensing criteria must be publicly available, as must 'the terms and conditions of individual licences', and the reasons for any licence denial must be made known to the applicant (para. 4).

(c)   Although the need for, and form of, any regulator is not addressed, the Reference Paper imposes an obligation upon a Member State to ensure that any such regulators are 'separate from, and not accountable to, any supplier of basic telecommunications services' (para. 5) (see Chapter 8, at 8.4.2).

(d)   The allocation and use of scarce resources, 'including frequencies, numbers and rights of way', should be carried out in an objective, timely, transparent and non-discriminatory way (para. 6).

While the Reference Paper addresses 'ends' rather than 'means', its influence is likely to be considerable at both a national and an international level. First, as part of the Schedules of Commitments, the Reference Paper represents a Member State's commitment to which foreign service providers may refer. Secondly, over time national legislators are likely to reflect and incorporate such principles into domestic law. Thirdly, the Reference Paper represents a baseline from which any future multilateral negotiations will depart.

10.4.4   Status of WTO law

The Reference Paper (see 10.4.3 above), as a unique set of international legal principles for the telecommunications sector, is not only pro-competitive, but would also seem sufficiently detailed to constitute possible grounds upon which to instigate legal proceedings in the event that a Member State failed to comply. However, this begs the question of the status of WTO law in the legal order of those some 60 nations that have incorporated it into their Schedule of Commitments. This issue can be further divided into the following questions:

(a) Whether the WTO rules, and in particular the Reference Paper, may be used in the interpretation and application of national or regional (e.g., EU) telecommunications regulations?

(b) Whether the Reference Paper could be used as the basis for initiating proceedings before a court in the event of a conflict with existing regulations, i.e. have direct effect?

Within the European legal order, the European Court of Justice has addressed the first issue, that of interpretation, on a number of occasions. In *Commission* v *Germany (International Dairy Agreement)* [1996] ECR I-3989, it held that where the Community has entered into international agreements, the provisions of secondary Community legislation 'must, as far as possible, be interpreted in a manner that is consistent with those agreements' (para. 52). Further, in *Hermès International* v *FHT Marketing* [1998] ECR I-3603, the Court held that national courts, when interpreting a Community measure that falls within the scope of a WTO agreement, must apply national legislation 'as far as possible, in the light of the wording and purpose' of the agreement (para. 28). Therefore, a court should consider the principles contained in the Reference Paper when interpreting the application of European telecommunications laws implemented in national law.

With regard to the second issue, that of direct effect, the final recital in the Community Decision adopting the WTO agreements states: 'by its nature, the Agreement establishing the World Trade Organisation, including the Annexes thereto, is not susceptible to being directly invoked in Community or Member State courts.'[78] Despite this, the European Court of Justice has been required to consider the issue of the status of WTO agreements on a number of occasions, most recently in *Portugal* v *Council* [1999] ECR I-8395. First, the Court addressed the status of the WTO agreements in the legal order of the Member States, concluding that: 'the WTO agreements, interpreted in the light of their subject-matter and purpose, do not determine the appropriate legal means of ensuring that they are applied in good faith in the legal order of the contracting parties' (para. 41). Secondly, it examined their status within the Community legal order. The Court considered that the WTO agreements were based on the 'principle of negotiation', which distinguished them from other international agreements that were recognised as having direct effect (para. 42). The Court also noted that the EC's major trading partners did not give direct effect to the agreements, which would effectively disadvantage the Community in future negotiations. Therefore, the

---

[78] Final recital in Council Decision 94/800/EC, of 22 December 1994, concerning the conclusion on behalf of the European Community, as regards matters within its competence, of the agreements reached in the Uruguay Round multilateral negotiations (1986–1994), (1994) OJ L 336/1.

Court concluded that: 'the WTO agreements are not in principle among the rules in the light of which the Court is to review the legality of measures adopted by the Community institutions' (para. 47).

The Court's reasoning in this case has been heavily criticised for undermining the status of the WTO agreements.[79] However, the Court did confirm its previous jurisprudence that the GATT rules could have direct effect either where the adoption of the measures implementing obligations assumed within the context of the GATT is at issue, or where a Community measure refers expressly to specific provisions of the General Agreement (para. 111) (see *Germany* v *Council* (Case C-280/93) [1994] ECR I-4973, paras 103–112). In this regard, it is interesting to note that the European Commission's recent package of measures in the telecommunications sector makes explicit reference to the commitments made by the Community and its Member States in the context of the Fourth Protocol to the GATS.[80]

In terms of UK law, the general applicability of the WTO agreements is somewhat uncertain due to the lack of clarity as to which aspects of the agreements fall within the competence of the Community, as opposed to the individual Member States. The problems raised by such joint competence were examined inconclusively in a dispute brought by the United States against the Community, the UK and Ireland, in 1997, in respect of the tariff classification of LAN equipment.[81] In terms of the regulation of the provision of telecommunications services and networks, it would seem that the Community has competence in all aspects addressed in the Reference Paper.[82]

In the absence of direct effect, either under European or under national law, the only mechanism by which a party could seek enforcement against a Member State for failure to comply with its obligations in respect of the telecommunications sector is the WTO Dispute Settlement Body.

10.4.5 Dispute resolution

Another unique feature of the multinational trade negotiations concluded in 1994 was the establishment of a dispute settlement mechanism applicable to the trade agreements.[83] For the first time, disputes between Member governments about compliance with an international treaty can be submitted to an independent body, the Dispute Settlement Body (DSB), and a defaulting

---

[79] See generally Zonnekeyn, G., 'The status of WTO Law in the EC Legal Order' (2000) 34(3) *Journal of World Trade Law* 111; and Griller, S., 'Judicial Enforceability of WTO Law in the European Union: Annotation to Case C-149/96, *Portugal* v *Council*', (2000) 3(3) *Journal of International Economic Law* 441.

[80] For example, the Proposed Framework Directive, *supra* n. 77, at Recital 22. See generally Chapter 8.

[81] *Customs Classification of Certain Computer Equipment*, WTO doc. series WT/DS62, WT/DS67 and WT/DS68. See also Heliskoski, J., 'Joint Competence of the European Community and its Member States and the Dispute Settlement Practice of the World Trade Organisation', (1999) 2 *The Cambridge Yearbook of European Legal Studies* 61.

[82] See Opinion 1/94 of the Court of Justice [1994] ECR I-5267.

[83] Understanding, *supra* n. 65. See generally, Merrills, J.G., *International Dispute Settlement* (3rd edn) (Cambridge, Cambridge University Press, 1998).

party may be made subject to enforcement procedures.[84] The 'Understanding' encompasses the GATS and therefore is applicable to disputes concerning commitments made in respect of national telecommunications markets (Understanding, Appendix 1).

Under the agreed procedures, a Member government may request the establishment of a Panel by the DSB, with the following terms of reference:

> To examine, in the light of the relevant provisions in (name of the covered agreement/s cited by the parties to the dispute), the matter referred to the DSB by (name of party) in document . . . and to make such findings as will assist the DSB in making recommendations or in giving the rulings provided for in that/those agreement/s. (Art. 7.1)

However, it would not seem appropriate to characterise the DSB as a judicial body. The Panel will comprise three individuals chosen by the DSB Secretariat with the consent of the parties. In the absence of agreement, the Director-General may appoint the panellists. After an investigation, the Panel submits a report, detailing its findings and conclusions, to the DSB for consideration. The DSB will usually adopt the Panel report unless one of the parties notifies the DSB of its intention to lodge an appeal to the Appellate Body (Art. 17). The Panel or Appellate Body will decide whether a particular Member State measure is inconsistent with the terms of the relevant agreement, and may recommend ways of overcoming the issue. A Member, against whom a decision has been reached, is obliged to implement the recommendations and rulings of the DSB within a reasonable period of time (Art. 21).

In the event that a Member fails to comply, the Understanding allows for the payment of compensation or the suspension of concessions (Art. 22). The ability to suspend trade concessions granted to an infringing Member is the real stick under the WTO's dispute settlement procedure. A complaining party may be able to suspend concessions or obligations not only in the sector of dispute (e.g., telecommunications), but also, where appropriate, in other sectors under the same agreement (e.g., GATS), or even under another covered agreement. The DSB must authorise any such suspension, which should be 'equivalent to the level of the nullification or impairment' (Art. 22.4).

While the WTO dispute procedures are between governments, industry obviously plays an important role in bringing such matters to the attention of governments. Under European law, complaints may be submitted in writing to the Commission and a formal examination procedure may be invoked prior to the decision to pursue a dispute.[85] In the US, the Office of the United States Trade Representative (USTR) is annually required to solicit comments

---

[84] The dispute settlement system under GATT 1947 was essentially a conciliation procedure.
[85] See Council Regulation 3286/94/EC of 22 December 1994, laying down Community procedures in the field of the common commercial policy in order to ensure the exercise of the Community's rights under international trade rules, in particular those established under the auspices of the World Trade Organisation, (1994) OJ L 349/71.

from industry on the implementation of the 'Basic Agreement' pursuant to the Omnibus Trade and Competitiveness Act of 1988.[86]

To date, only two disputes in the telecommunications sector have gone to the dispute settlement process. The European Union has pursued formal proceedings before the DSB against both Korea and Japan in respect of preferential trade practices favouring US suppliers of telecommunications equipment, which were resolved by agreement.[87] However, in the vast majority of situations, it is the threat of WTO proceedings that is used as a stick to encourage resolution through negotiations. The United States have been particularly willing to issue such threats, most recently against the following countries:

(a)   Mexico, regarding the lack of regulatory control exercised against Telefonos de Mexico SA, the former state monopolist; the removal of a surcharge levied against US carriers on inbound international traffic; and failure to ensure timely and 'cost-oriented' criteria;[88]

(b)   Canada, regarding discriminations against US-based carriers transmitting international traffic;[89]

(c)   Germany, regarding Deutsche Telekom's failure to meet interconnection obligations and discrimination against foreign carriers for call completion;[90] and

(d)   Belgium, regarding the licensing practices and conditions imposed by Belgacom on the publishing of telephone directories.

Both the European Commission and the US have threatened to take action against Japan over its failure to introduce the long-run incremental cost methodology for interconnection rates, as current rates are not considered to meet the 'cost-orientated' principle required under the Reference Paper.[91] Such threats underpinned on-going bilateral negotiations, which reached a successful conclusion in July 2000.[92]

---

[86]   19 USC § 1377. A determination that a foreign country either is not in compliance with a telecommunications-related agreement that it has entered into with the US, or denies US companies the market opportunities provided for under the agreement, is treated as a violation of a trade agreement under the Trade Act of 1974, s. 304(a)(1)(A), 19 USC §2101.

[87]   See WTO Report, 'Overview of the State-of-Play of WTO Disputes', 10 August 2000: www.wto.org.

[88]   See USTR Press Release, 'US to request WTO consultations with Mexico regarding telecommunications trade barriers', 28 July 2000.

[89]   See 1998 Annual Report of the President of the United States on the Trade Agreements Program, at 257.

[90]   See 'US warns on German telecoms', *Financial Times*, 12 August 1999. See also 1999 Annual Report, at 293.

[91]   For a description of the methodology, see Chapter 2. See 'US uses WTO threat to challenge Japanese pricing' (20 September 1999): www.totaltele.com.

[92]   See USTR Press Release, 'United States and Japan agree on interconnection rates', 18 July 2000.

10.5 CONCLUSION

The international regulatory regime for the telecommunications industry comprises a substantial body of principles, rules and regulations. At the highest level, the international trade agreements address issues of market access and promoting competition throughout the telecommunications sector. The treaties governing the use of space and the sea determine the obligations of operators, through their respective governments, when utilising common resources in the provision of telecommunications services.

At the next level down, the ITU continues to represent the primary source of rules and regulations detailing the manner and means by which operators in different jurisdictions cooperate to achieve international telecommunications services. Industry consolidation through global mergers and joint ventures is likely to have minimal impact on the need for such rule-making. As such, the ITU is likely to continue to be one of the main international forums for the telecommunications industry.

The process of liberalisation has resulted in the decline in importance of the international satellite Conventions, which may eventually disappear as instruments of international telecommunications law, though not as operating entities. The rise of the WTO as *the* forum for telecommunications law over recent years has been very significant. However, over time its role may diminish, as open competitive markets become the international norm. A similar process can be seen within Europe, where the European Commission is currently in the process of overhauling the existing regulatory framework to reflect the end of the phase of liberalisation, enabling moves towards a less detailed, competition-based regulatory regime.

CHAPTER ELEVEN
Communications Privacy

Christopher Millard[1]

11.1 INTRODUCTION

11.1.1 Scope of this chapter

The jurisprudence of privacy has a fragmented history. Privacy, as a distinct legal concept, probably has its origins in an essay published in the *Harvard Law Review* in 1890. In 'The Right to Privacy',[2] Samuel Warren and Louis Brandeis reviewed the long history of protection under the English common law for various individual liberties and private property, and extrapolated a general 'right to privacy'. Ironically, more than a century later, the United States still does not have a privacy law with general application to the private sector. Instead, it has a patchwork of sector-specific laws and regulations covering such diverse matters as consumer video rental records (Video Privacy Protection Act of 1998, 18 USC §2710 (1994)), consumer financial services (e.g., Fair Credit Reporting Act of 1970, 18 USC §1681 (1988); the Fair Credit Billing Act of 1976, 15 USC §§1601, 1602, 1637, 1666 (1988); the Right to Financial Privacy Act of 1978, 12 USC §§3401–3422 (1994); Gramm-Leach-Bliley Financial Modernization Act of 1999, 15 USC §§6801–6810, 6821–6827), interception of electronic communications (Electronic Communications Privacy Act of 1986, §2510 *et seq.*), and the on-line privacy rights of children (Children's Online Privacy Protection Act of 1998, 15 USC §6501 *et seq.*; Children's Online Privacy Protection Rule, 16 CFR Part 312).

---

[1] Copyright Clifford Chance 2000. All rights reserved.
[2] (1890) 4 *Harvard Law Review* 193.

Even in jurisdictions that have specific privacy or data protection legislation, various other rights and obligations may exist that are analogous to privacy rights and have an impact on communications activities. For example, in the United Kingdom, telecommunications privacy is regulated primarily under the Data Protection Act 1998 ('the DPA 1998') and the Telecommunications (Data Protection and Privacy) Regulations 1999 (SI 1999 No. 2093) ('the 1999 Regulations').[3] In addition, however, various other statutes have a direct impact on telecommunications privacy, including the Wireless Telegraphy Act 1949, the Telecommunications Act 1984 and the Interception of Communications Act 1985. Moreover, the Human Rights Act 1998 and the Regulation of Investigatory Powers Act 2000 are now of significant importance in this field. More tangentially, individuals may also be able to assert unrelated common law rights, such as confidentiality, or unrelated statutory rights, such as copyright or defamation, as a means of controlling, for example, the use of recordings of telephone conversations or the dissemination of e-mail messages.

Following an overview of the international context, the focus of this chapter will be on current and proposed UK legislation that has a direct impact on communications privacy. The complex and overlapping rules in this area will be analysed by reference to specific activities, such as interception of communications and use of telecommunications services for direct marketing purposes. Common law and statutory rules affecting message content but only indirectly having an impact on privacy, such as confidentiality, copyright and defamation, are beyond the scope of this chapter.[4]

11.1.2 Jurisdictions with and without privacy laws

Eighty years after Warren and Brandeis's seminal article, popular concerns about the implications of widespread use of computers in the public and private sectors led to the adoption of data protection laws in various European jurisdictions. The first was the German state of Hessen in 1970.[5] Since then over 40 jurisdictions around the world have enacted data protection legislation intended to protect individuals' rights to privacy by restricting the manner in which information about them may be processed in the private sector.[6] A number of other jurisdictions have legislation regulating processing of personal data in the public sector (e.g., in the United States, the Privacy Act of 1974, 5 USC, §§552 *et seq.*).

---

[3] The 1999 Regulations are likely to be replaced in due course as a result of implementation of a proposed EU Directive on privacy in electronic communications – Proposal for a Directive of the European Parliament and of the Council concerning the processing of personal data and the protection of privacy in the electronic communications sector (COM (2000) 385 final) ('Proposed Electronic Communications Privacy Directive'). See discussion in 11.3–11.7, below.

[4] See generally Reed, C. and Angel, J. (eds), *Computer Law* (4th edn) (London, Blackstone Press, 2000).

[5] Hessisches Datenschutzgesetz (HDSG), 30 September 1970, Hess. GVOBL. I 1970, P. 625. The first national law was the 1973 Swedish Data Act, as amended in 1997.

[6] For details of existing data protection laws, see Millard, C. and Ford, M. (eds) *Data Protection Laws of the World* (London, Sweet & Maxwell, 1998).

Most of the existing data protection laws with general application to the private sector are in Europe. Almost all of those laws have recently been, or soon will be, replaced as the European Economic Area (EEA) Member States, and other countries with association agreements with the European Union, implement the 1995 and 1997 EU data protection directives (see 11.1.3.3 below). While the vast majority of countries in the world do not yet have data protection laws, a number of jurisdictions either have general privacy rights, sometimes entrenched in a constitution, or have sector-specific privacy rules that have an impact on communications.

11.1.3 International initiatives to harmonise data protection rules

11.1.3.1 OECD privacy guidelines The proliferation of national data protection laws has given rise to various transnational initiatives over the last three decades to limit the emergence of inconsistent national rules that might become obstacles to cross-border trade. In 1974, the Organisation for Economic Cooperation and Development (OECD) established an Expert Group, the Data Bank Panel, to study various aspects of computers and privacy.[7] A second Expert Group, established under the chairmanship of Mr Justice Kirby, chairman of the Australian Law Reform Commission, developed Guidelines on basic rules to facilitate harmonisation of national data protection laws and pre-empt unnecessary restrictions on transborder data flows. A Recommendation containing the Guidelines was adopted by the OECD Council and became applicable on 23 September 1980.[8] The Memorandum accompanying the OECD Guidelines contains a recommendation that Member countries 'take into account in their domestic legislation the principles concerning the protection of privacy and individual liberties set forth in the Guidelines . . . [and that] . . . Member countries endeavour to remove or avoid creating, in the name of privacy protection, unjustified obstacles to transborder flows of personal data'.

The OECD Guidelines represent an attempt to balance the conflicting priorities of data protection and the free flow of information. The most fundamental limitation of the Guidelines is that they have no legal force. They are not embedded in any convention. Moreover, the open-textured nature of the Guidelines means that they can serve only as a loose framework for the harmonisation of national laws.

11.1.3.2 Council of Europe Convention Unlike the OECD, which is essentially concerned with the economic development of its Member States, the Council of Europe has a broader political mandate. In 1968, the Parliamentary Assembly of the Council of Europe expressed concern over the adequacy of the European Convention on Human Rights in securing privacy protection in the context of information technology. As a response, the Committee of Ministers conducted a study and subsequently passed two Resolutions

---

[7] In 1977 the Data Bank Panel organised a symposium in Vienna, out of which came *Transborder Data Flows and the Protection of Privacy* (Paris, OECD, 1979).

[8] OECD, *Transborder Data Flows and the Protection of Privacy* (Paris, OECD, 1981).

establishing data protection principles, one for the private sector (Resolution (73) 22), the other for the public sector (Resolution (74) 29). The Committee of Experts that prepared the Resolutions called for the development of an international data protection agreement. After many drafts, the final text of the Convention for the Protection of Individuals with regard to Automatic Processing of Personal Data[9] was adopted by the Committee of Ministers and was opened for signature on 28 January 1981. The Convention came into force on 1 October 1985 after five states had ratified it. The United Kingdom ratified the Convention on 26 August 1987, with effect from 1 December 1987. At the time of writing, 20 states had ratified the Convention.[10]

The Convention deals with the automatic processing of any information relating to an identifiable individual. Ratifying states must place obligations on controllers of files to comply with various principles and to grant various rights to data subjects. In relation to transborder data flows, the Convention prohibits the imposition, on the grounds of privacy protection, of restrictions on the transfer of data from the territory of one Convention party to that of another. Two exceptions are permitted. One is where the first party gives special protection to a particular category of data and the second party does not. The other is where the data are to be re-exported to a non-Convention state.

11.1.3.3 European Union data protection initiatives In 1981, the same year that the Council of Europe's Convention was opened for signature, the European Commission recommended that the EC Member States that had not already done so should sign the Convention and seek to ratify it by the end of 1982.[11] The Commission indicated in its Recommendation that it would engage in a compulsory harmonisation programme if Member States were too dilatory in ratifying the Council of Europe Convention. In July 1990, the Commission submitted to the Council of Ministers a series of proposals, including two draft Directives intended to harmonise data protection laws. The first would deal in general terms with data protection and transborder data flows,[12] the second specifically with data protection aspects of public digital telecommunications networks.[13]

After five years of protracted debates in the European Parliament and European Council, a substantially revised version of the first proposal was finally adopted as Directive 95/46/EC of the European Parliament and of the Council of 24 October 1995 on the protection of individuals with regard to the processing of personal data and on the free movement of such data (the

---

[9] European Treaty Series No. 108.
[10] These were Austria, Belgium, Denmark, Finland, France, Germany, Greece, Hungary, Iceland, Ireland, Italy, Luxembourg, The Netherlands, Norway, Portugal, Slovenia, Spain, Sweden, Switzerland and the United Kingdom.
[11] Recommendation of the Commission 81/679/EEC, (1979) OJ L 246/31.
[12] Proposal for a Council Directive concerning the protection of individuals in relation to the processing of personal data, (1990) OJ C 277/3, s. 11.
[13] Proposal for a Council Directive concerning the protection of personal data privacy in the context of public digital telecommunications networks, in particular the Integrated Services Digital Network (ISDN) and Public Digital Mobile Networks, (1990) OJ C 277/12, s. 11.

'Data Protection Directive'). It took a further two years before the adoption of Directive 97/66/EC of the European Parliament and of the Council of 15 December 1997 concerning the processing of personal data and the protection of privacy in the telecommunications sector (the 'Telecoms Data Protection Directive'). The deadline for the 15 European Member States to implement both directives was 24 October 1998. At the time of writing, the Data Protection Directive had been implemented by all of the EU Member States except Denmark, France, Germany, Ireland, Luxembourg and The Netherlands. The Telecoms Data Protection Directive had been implemented by all of the EU Member States except Belgium,[14] France, Germany, Ireland and Luxembourg.

The provisions of the Telecoms Data Protection Directive that relate to direct marketing activities were implemented initially in the UK by means of the Telecommunications (Data Protection and Privacy) (Direct Marketing) Regulations 1998 (SI 1998 No. 3170) ('the 1998 Regulations'). The 1998 Regulations came into force on 1 May 1999, but on 1 March 2000 were revoked and superseded by the Telecommunications (Data Protection and Privacy) Regulations 1999 (see 11.1.1 above). The 1999 Regulations implemented the entire Telecoms Data Protection Directive, with the exception of Art. 5. Article 5, which deals with monitoring and interception of communications, has since been implemented in the Regulation of Investigatory Powers Act 2000 ('the RIP Act'), which came into force in October 2000. A proposed Directive of the European Parliament and of the Council concerning the processing of personal data and the protection of privacy in the electronic communications sector ('Electronic Communications Privacy Directive')[15] would replace the Telecoms Data Protection Directive with the intention of clarifying and, to some extent, widening the application of privacy rules to on-line communications.

In January 1995, the EU Council of Ministers adopted a Resolution on the lawful interception of telecommunications.[16] This Resolution addressed various technical issues in relation to interception of communications by law enforcement agencies. The privacy implications of the Resolution were discussed in detail in a May 1999 Recommendation of the EU Data Protection Working Party.[17] The Working Party expressed concern at the scope of the interception measures envisaged by the Resolution and stressed the need for the national law of the EU Member States to specify the precise circumstances and manner in which surveillance should be authorised.

The Working Party has also adopted various other recommendations and opinions on privacy issues relating to telecommunications and the Internet. These include a Recommendation on Anonymity on the Internet,[18] a Work-

---

[14] A Belgian Royal Decree of 8 July 1999 implemented some of the provisions of the Telecoms Data Protection Directive.
[15] COM (2000) 385 final Brussels, 12 July 2000.
[16] (1996) OJ C 239/1.
[17] Recommendation on the respect of privacy in the context of interception of telecommunications, 5005/99/final, WP 18, adopted on 3 May 1999. The Working Party is established under Art. 29 of the Data Protection Directive.
[18] Recommendation 3/97, XV D/5022/97/final, WP 6, adopted on 3 December 1997.

ing Document entitled *Processing of Personal Data on the Internet*,[19] a Recommendation on Invisible and Automatic Processing of Personal Data on the Internet Performed by Software and Hardware,[20] a Recommendation on the Preservation of Traffic Data by Internet Service Providers for Law Enforcement Purposes,[21] an Opinion on certain data protection aspects of electronic commerce,[22] and an Opinion concerning the general review of the telecommunications legal framework.[23]

11.2 INTERCEPTION, MONITORING AND RECORDING OF COMMUNICATIONS

11.2.1 Wireless Telegraphy Act 1949

Under s. 5(b) of the Wireless Telegraphy Act 1949, it is an offence if a person, without official authority, either:

(i)   uses any wireless telegraphy apparatus with intent to obtain information as to the contents, sender or addressee of any message (whether sent by means of wireless telegraphy or not) . . . or,

(ii)   except in the course of legal proceedings or for the purpose of any report thereof, discloses any information as to the contents, sender or address of any such message, being information which would not have come to his knowledge but for the use of wireless telegraphy apparatus by him or another person.

This provision has a very broad scope. Not only is the entire wireless sector covered, regardless of whether a communication is via a public or a private telecommunications system, but disclosure in the wake of interception may also constitute a criminal offence.

Section 65 of the Regulation of Investigatory Powers Act 2000 makes various amendments to s. 5 of the Wireless Telegraphy Act 1949 with the intention of ensuring that it is compliant with the Human Rights Act 1998.[24] The principal effects of these amendments are to establish much more detailed requirements for authorised interceptions of wireless telegraphy (see also 11.2.5 and 11.2.6).

11.2.2 Telecommunications Act 1984

In marked contrast to the broad reach of the privacy provisions in the Wireless Telegraphy Act 1949, the privacy provisions in the Telecommunications Act 1984 ('the 1984 Act') have a much narrower scope. Section 44(1)

---

[19] 5013/99/final, WP 16, adopted on 23 February 1999.
[20] 5093/99/final, WP 17, adopted on 23 February 1999.
[21] 5085/99/final, WP 25, adopted on 7 September 1999.
[22] 5007/00/final, WP 28, adopted on 3 February 2000.
[23] 5009/00/final, WP 29, adopted on 3 February 2000.
[24] See Explanatory Notes on the Regulation of Investigatory Powers Act 2000 as brought to the House of Lords from the House of Commons on 9 May 2000, paras 315–317. Available at http://www.publications.parliament.uk/pa/ld199900/ldbills/061/en/00061x–.htm.

of the 1984 Act provides that '[a] person engaged in the running of a public telecommunications system who otherwise than in the course of his duty intentionally modifies or interferes with the contents of a message sent by means of that system shall be guilty of an offence'. Similarly, under s. 45(1) of the 1984 Act, it is an offence for a person engaged in the running of a public telecommunications system (otherwise than in the course of his duty) to disclose intentionally to any person:

(a)   the contents of any message which has been intercepted in the course of transmission by means of that system; or
(b)   any information concerning the use made of the telecommunication services provided for any other person by means of that system . . .

These provisions apply only to employees of public operators and do not apply to modification, interception or disclosure of messages in the context of private telecommunications systems.[25]

11.2.3   Telecommunications services licence and self-provision licence

The monitoring and recording of phone calls on private networks are regulated by the class licences under which almost all telecommunications users run their telecommunications systems. The two main class licences covering non-public telecommunications systems are the self-provision licence (SPL) and the telecommunications services licence (TSL). These licences have been granted by the Secretary of State under powers granted to him by s. 7 of the Telecommunications Act 1984 and are subject to various conditions (see further Chapter 4). Both class licences contain a condition entitled 'Privacy of Messages'. In the SPL this is Condition 7; in the TSL it is Condition 11, but the content of the two conditions is identical.

These conditions apply in circumstances where telecommunication apparatus comprised in or connected to a telecommunication system authorised under the relevant licence is used to record, silently monitor or intrude into live speech telephone calls.[26] The licensee should make every reasonable effort to inform all parties to the call that the call may or will be recorded, silently monitored or subject to intrusion. It is also necessary to keep a record of how that obligation is complied with, and such information must be available for inspection by the DGT on request.

The DGT can consent to a licensee not complying with the requirements of the privacy of messages condition. He is required to keep a register of all

---

[25] A system is a public telecommunication system if it is designated as such by the Secretary of State: s. 9(1) of the Telecommunications Act 1984. See Chapter 3 for a discussion of the concepts of public telecommunications system and public telecommunications operator.
[26] 'Silent monitoring is the establishment of a receive-only transmission path to a third terminal, enabling a third party to hear the call. Intrusion is the establishment of a both way speech transmission to another terminal enabling a third party to hear and be heard by at least one of the other parties to the call' (OFTEL Explanatory Notes for the TSL and SPL).

the occasions when such consent has been given and must make that register available for inspection on request. The emergency services are exempt from the privacy of messages condition, and it does not apply where apparatus is being used for the purposes of law enforcement or in the interests of national security. It also does not apply where the apparatus in question is not telecommunication apparatus. This would include apparatus that has not been constructed or adapted for use in transmitting or receiving telecommunications messages. In particular, the condition will not apply to recording devices that are acoustically coupled to a telecommunication system, such as a separate tape recorder used, for example, by an investigative journalist. If a licensee fails to comply with the privacy of messages condition, the DGT may make an order to secure compliance (Telecommunications Act 1984, s. 16). Failure to comply with the terms of such an order may constitute a criminal offence, and the licensee may also be liable to persons affected by its contravention of an order (Telecommunications Act 1984, s. 18).

In practice, licensees respond in a variety of ways to the requirement to make 'every reasonable effort' to provide the requisite information to all parties to calls that are recorded or monitored. Examples include informing customers on publicity material or other written material that they receive prior to a call, using warning sounds on equipment, or making pre-recorded or scripted announcements. As there is no publicly available record of the number of calls monitored, it is not possible to assess the proportion of users who are granted an exemption by OFTEL from these conditions.

In addition to the privacy of messages condition, both the SPL and the TSL contain a condition entitled 'Privacy, confidentiality and metering systems' which, among other things, requires the licensee to

take all reasonable steps to safeguard the privacy and confidentiality of:

(a) any Message conveyed for a consideration by means of the Applicable Systems; and
(b) any information acquired by the Licensee in relation to such conveyance. (SPL Condition 9; TSL Condition 12)

11.2.4 Interception of Communications Act 1985

Section 1 of the Interception of Communications Act 1985 (now repealed) provided that '. . . a person who intentionally intercepts a communication in the course of its transmission by post or by means of a public telecommunication system shall be guilty of an offence'. This was subject to various exceptions, notably that the interception had been authorised by a warrant issued by the Secretary of State, or that the interceptor had reasonable grounds for believing that the sender or recipient of the message had consented to the interception. The only grounds for issuing a warrant were that it was '. . . necessary (a) in the interests of national security; (b) for the purpose of preventing or detecting serious crime; or (c) for the purpose of safeguarding the economic well-being of the United Kingdom (s. 2(2))'.[27] The Secretary of State was required to consider whether the information that was sought could reasonably be acquired by other means (s. 2(3)).

With regard to its scope, it became clear that the Interception of Communications Act 1985 ('the 1985 Act') had no application to an interception that took place outside a public network (see, for example, *R* v *Effick* [1994] Crim LR 832, 99; Cr App Rep 312, 158, in which the court held that interception by the police of telephone conversations on a cordless telephone was not subject to the 1985 Act). The Regulation of Investigatory Powers Act 2000 has repealed the 1985 Act and has replaced it with a much broader regime covering all types of communications via both public and private networks (see 11.2.6 below).

11.2.5 European Convention on Human Rights and Human Rights Act 1998

In *Halford* v *United Kingdom* [1997] IRLR 471, the European Court of Human Rights ruled that interception of telephone calls made on an internal telecommunications system operated by Merseyside police was an infringement of Art. 8 of the European Convention on Human Rights. Article 8(1) provides that 'Everyone has the right to respect for his private and family life, his home and his correspondence'. Article 8(2) adds that public authorities may interfere with this right only 'in accordance with the law'. The Court considered the scope of the Interception of Communications Act 1985 and concluded that, because it did not apply to interception via a private network, such interception could not be 'in accordance with the law'.[28] Partly in response to that ruling, in June 1999 the Home Office issued a Consultation Paper entitled *Interception of Communications in the United Kingdom* (Cm 4368), in which it proposed, among other things, that the regime in the Interception of Communications Act 1985 should be widened to cover all communications networks.

In August 1999, following a request from the Home Office that was also in response to the *Halford* decision, OFTEL issued new guidance on recording of telephone conversations.[29] This confirmed the validity of the privacy of messages conditions in the SPL and TSL (see 11.2.3 above), but sought to clarify the rights of employees in relation to workplace monitoring of their phone calls. In particular, the guidance states that employees have a legitimate expectation of privacy in relation to workplace communications and that merely warning them that their calls may be monitored may be insufficient to override that expectation. Accordingly, there should be some means by which employees can make or receive calls at work that will not be

---

[27] The economic well-being justification is available only in relation to 'information relating to the acts or intentions of persons outside the British Islands' (s. 2(4)).

[28] More recently, the European Court of Human Rights ruled in *Khan* v *United Kingdom*, *The Times*, 23 May 2000, that use by the police of a covert listening device breached Art. 8 of the Convention as there existed at the time no statutory system to regulate the use of such devices.

[29] http://www.oftel.gov.uk/releases/pr47_99.htm.

monitored or recorded. This might be achieved by providing adequate access to non-monitored pay-phones in the workplace. The guidance also advises that employers

> restrict recording and monitoring activities to situations where they are both absolutely necessary and proportionate to the problem to be overcome. For example, misuse of office phones could be detected by an itemised call record, which is less intrusive than recording or monitoring of the actual calls.

The Human Rights Act 1998, which received Royal Assent on 9 November 1998, incorporates the European Convention on Human Rights into United Kingdom law. Section 19 of the Act came into force on 24 November 1998, and has since then required the Government to make a written statement in relation to any proposed legislation as to whether the Bill in question is or is not compatible with the Convention (Human Rights Act 1998 (Commencement) Order 1998 (SI 1998 No. 2882)). The remaining provisions of the Act were brought into force on 2 October 2000 (Human Rights Act 1998 (Commencement No. 2) Order 2000 (SI 2000 No. 1851)).

11.2.6 Regulation of Investigatory Powers Act 2000

The RIP Act was enacted on 28 July 2000 and some of its provisions had been brought into force by 24 October 2000 (Regulation of Investigatory Powers Act 2000 (Commencement No. 1 and Transitional Provisions) Order 2000 (SI 2000 No. 2543)). The RIP Act has replaced the Interception of Communications Act 1985 (see 11.2.4 above) and, among other matters, regulates 'intrusive investigative techniques', empowering the police and other authorised persons to compel individuals or organisations to disclose information necessary to decipher encrypted messages. While these encryption-related provisions clearly have an impact on telecommunications privacy, a detailed discussion of those rules is beyond the scope of this chapter.

With regard to interception of communications, s. 1(1) of the RIP Act makes it 'an offence for a person intentionally and without lawful authority to intercept, at any place in the United Kingdom, any communication in the course of its transmission by means of (a) a public postal service; or (b) a public telecommunication system'. Section 1(2) creates a similar offence in relation to private telecommunication systems, with the exception that no offence is committed if the interception is either made by a person with the right to control that system, or is made with the consent of the system controller (s. 1(6)). The Explanatory Notes to the bill that preceded the RIP Act give examples of activities within this exception, such as the use of a second handset in a house to monitor a call and routine recording of calls by a financial institution to provide evidence of transactions. Section 5(1) permits the Secretary of State to issue a warrant authorising or requiring the interception of communications in specified circumstances.

In addition to the criminal offences created by s. 1(1) and (2), s. 1(3) has created the following new tort of unlawful interception on a private network:

(3)   Any interception of a communication which is carried out at any place in the United Kingdom by, or with the express or implied consent of, a person having the right to control the operation or the use of a private telecommunication system shall be actionable at the suit or instance of the sender or recipient, or intended recipient, of the communication if it is without lawful authority and is either–
(a)   an interception of that communication in the course of its transmission by means of that private system; or
(b)   an interception of that communication in the course of its transmission, by means of a public telecommunication system, to or from apparatus comprised in that private telecommunication system.

Thus, a system controller who is protected from criminal liability under s. 1(2) may nevertheless face civil proceedings for breach of s. 1(3). As the Explanatory Notes to the bill that preceded the RIP Act observe, 'where an employee believes that their employer has unlawfully intercepted a telephone conversation with a third party, either the employee or the third party may sue the employer' (para. 21). However, the key issue will be whether the employer has 'lawful authority' to intercept the communication. There are two main grounds on which lawful authority might be based. First, on the fact, or reasonable belief, that both the sender and the intended recipient of the communication in question have consented to its interception (s. 3(1)). This may lead to employers inserting consent clauses in employee contracts, and possibly also in customer or other individual third-party contracts. There may be many situations, though, where the consent of both parties to a communication cannot be obtained. This is likely, in particular, to be a problem in relation to senders of communications, as an employer usually cannot predict who will send communications to its employees. As a result, considerable reliance will in practice have to be placed on an alternative ground for lawful authority, as set out in the Telecommunications (Lawful Business Practice) (Interception of Communications) Regulations 2000 (SI 2000 No. 2699), issued pursuant to s. 4(2) and (3) of the RIP Act ('Lawful Business Practice Regulations').

The Lawful Business Practice Regulations 2000 authorise the interception of a communication if it is effected by or with the express or implied consent of the system controller (e.g., an employer) for specific purposes relating to monitoring or keeping a record of communications relevant to the system controller's business (reg. 3). Communications are relevant if they are transactional, otherwise relate to the business or otherwise take place in the course of carrying on the business (reg. 2(b)). Qualifying business purposes include establishing the existence of facts, ascertaining compliance with regulatory or self-regulatory practices or procedures, and ascertaining or demonstrating that standards have been achieved (e.g. quality control or training). In addition, such interception may be justified in the interests of national security, for crime prevention or detection purposes, for investigating or detecting unauthorised use and for purposes related to effective system operation (reg. 3(1)). Furthermore, the Lawful Business Practice Regulations authorise monitoring for the purpose of distinguishing business from non-business-related communications (reg. 3(1)(b)).[30] In every case, however, the system controller must have made 'all reasonable efforts' to inform every user of the system that communications may be intercepted (reg. 3(2)(c)). Rather curiously, the Lawful Business Practice Regulations state that interception for business purposes is authorised only to the extent permitted by Art. 5 of the Telecoms Data Protection Directive. This perhaps suggests that a challenge is anticipated to the pragmatic way in which the power to override the confidentiality rule in that Article has been used.

In addition to the uncertainty that the Lawful Business Practice Regulations have introduced, substantial concern and confusion has arisen from the publication by the Data Protection Commissioner of a Draft Code of Practice on the Use of Personal Data in Employer/Employee Relationships.[31] Probably the most controversial section of the Draft Code is that relating to employee monitoring in general, and monitoring of communications in particular (Draft Code, s. 6). Section 6 envisages that employers who wish to monitor the communications of their employees are constrained by various restrictions that go well beyond those established by the RIP Act and the Lawful Business Practice Regulations. For example, the Draft Code recommends that, in relation to e-mail, unless it is unavoidable, traffic records only should be monitored, not e-mail content; the 'autonomy' as well as the privacy of recipients of e-mails should be respected; and employees should be provided with a means by which they can 'effectively expunge from the system e-mails they receive or send' (Draft Code, s. 6.3.2). This latter recommendation betrays a surprising lack of understanding of technical and commercial realities. Even if it were feasible from a technical perspective, to give employees the means to remove e-mails from an employer's systems, permanently and without trace, would appear to be a fraudster's charter. At the time of writing, a public consultation exercise is under way in relation to the Draft Code and it is to be hoped that some of its more impractical provisions will be modified.

11.3 RESTRICTIONS ON USE OF TRAFFIC, BILLING AND LOCATION DATA

Part II of the Telecommunications (Data Protection and Privacy) Regulations 1999 ('the 1999 Regulations') (regs 6–10) implements Art. 6 of the Telecoms Data Protection Directive that requires regulation of traffic and billing data. Regulation 6 applies to 'personal data' processed by a telecommunications network or service provider in order to connect a call. The definitions of the Data Protection Act 1998 are applicable in the 1999 Regulations. Accordingly, 'personal data' means data relating to an identifiable living individual.

---

[30] The Regulations also permit monitoring of 'communications made to a confidential voice-telephony counselling or support service which is free of charge (other than the cost, if any, of making a telephone call) and operated in such a way that users may remain anonymous if they so choose' (reg. 3(1)(c)).

[31] See http://www.dataprotection.gov.uk/ (Guidance & other publications/Codes of Practice).

However, reg. 6 also applies to data relating to a corporate subscriber, if the data in question would constitute personal data if that subscriber were an individual. Subject to limited exceptions, upon termination of the call in question, such data must be erased or made anonymous.

Regulation 7 applies to certain types of billing data (as set out in Sch. 2) that are held by network or service providers for purposes connected to billing of subscribers and billing for interconnection charges. Such billing data may be held only for the period in which proceedings may be brought in respect of the payments due. Based on current limitation rules, this means that such data may be held for six years only, or, if proceedings have commenced within that period, until the end of those proceedings, marked by the expiry of the time to appeal or the conclusion of appeal proceedings.

Relevant billing data identified in Sch. 2 are personal data (or data that would be regarded as personal data if the subscriber were an individual), including the number (or other identification) of the subscriber's station; the subscriber's address and type of station; the total number of units of use by reference to which the sum payable in respect of an accounting period is calculated; the type, starting time and duration of calls and the volume of data transmissions in respect of which sums are payable by the subscriber and the numbers or other identification of the stations to which they were made; the date of the provision of services that do not constitute calls; and other matters concerning payments including, in particular, advance payments, payments by instalments, reminders and disconnections.

A telecommunications service provider may process billing data (again as set out in Sch. 2) for the purposes of marketing its own telecommunications services if, but only if, the consent of the subscriber has been obtained (reg. 8). More generally, reg. 9 of the 1999 Regulations restricts processing of traffic and billing data to what is necessary for the purposes of the following activities:

- management of billing or traffic;
- customer enquiries;
- the prevention or detection of fraud;
- the marketing of any telecoms services provided by the relevant provider; and
- with respect to traffic data, the erasure or anonymisation of the data.

The data categories listed in Sch. 2 seem to have been drafted with voice and fax communications in mind. The proposed Electronic Communications Privacy Directive (see 11.1.3.3 above) would dispense with Sch. 2 and simply permit any data to be processed by providers of publicly available electronic communications networks or services where such processing is necessary for the purposes of subscriber billing and interconnection payments. In addition, a service provider may use traffic data to market its publicly available electronic communications services and to provide value-added services, but only if it has obtained the subscriber's prior consent (Art. 6(3)). Lastly, the service provider will need to make the subscriber aware of the types of traffic data being processed and of the duration of such processing (Art. 6(4)).

The proposed Electronic Communications Privacy Directive stipulates that if an electronic communications network is capable of processing data other than traffic data that can be used to identify the geographic position of the terminal equipment used by a user or subscriber ('location data': Art. 2(1)(c)), all such location data must be made anonymous before processing, unless the service provider intends to process such data in order to provide a value-added service and the subscriber has given consent. In obtaining consent, the service provider must notify the user or subscriber of the type of location data collected, the purposes and duration of processing and whether the location data will be transferred to a third party in order to provide the value-added service (Art. 9(1)). The user or subscriber must have a simple means, free of charge, to prevent such processing temporarily for each connection to the network, or for each transmission of a communication (Art. 9(2)).

11.4 ITEMISED BILLS

Regulation 29 of the 1999 Regulations requires telecommunications service providers to provide non-itemised bills to a subscriber if so requested. Regulation 30 requires the Secretary of State and the DGT, in exercising their powers in relation to telecommunications licensing, to

> have regard to the need to reconcile the rights of subscribers receiving itemised bills with the rights to privacy of calling users and called sub-scribers, for example by ensuring that sufficient alternative means for the making of calls or methods of paying therefor are available to such users and subscribers.

Examples of such 'alternative means' might be public pay-phones that take either cash or anonymous prepaid cards.

11.5 CALLING AND CONNECTED LINE IDENTIFICATION

As regards outgoing calls, service providers must provide, free of charge, a 'simple means' of preventing the presentation of the identity of the calling line on the connected line, subject to the exceptions outlined below. This facility must be offered to users originating a single call (1999 Regulations, reg. 11(2)), and to subscribers to a line who should be able to bar identification with respect to all calls made from that line (1999 Regulations, reg. 11(3)). Given the wide meaning of 'user', the right to withhold calling number identity must be offered on calls from pay-phones and other telephones to which the public have access.

The corollary right from the perspective of incoming calls is that where presentation on the connected line of the identity of the calling line is available, the service provider shall ensure that the called subscriber has a 'simple means' to reject the calls in question (1999 Regulations, reg. 12(4)).

Similarly, the subscriber can also reject calls where the identity of the calling party is not revealed.

Further, as regards incoming calls on a line, where presentation of identity of the calling line on the connected line is available, the called subscriber must be provided with a 'simple means', without charge for the reasonable use of the facility, of preventing the presentation of the identity of a calling line on the connected line (1999 Regulations, reg. 12(2)). Lastly, where presentation on the calling line of the identity of the connected line is available, the relevant service provider must give the called subscriber a 'simple means' to prevent, without charge, the presentation of the identity of the connected line on any calling line (1999 Regulations, reg. 12(3)).

Exceptions to these rules exist in relation to emergency calls and malicious or nuisance calls. In order to facilitate responses to emergency calls, there is no right to withhold the identity of the calling line. Indeed, there is a prohibition on preventing such presentation with respect to calls made to the national emergency number (999) or the single European emergency call number (112) (1999 Regulations, reg. 13; see also Chapter 8, at 8.4.5.2). As regards unwanted calls, where subscribers inform a service provider that they require the tracing of malicious or nuisance calls, the service provider may override anything done to prevent the presentation of the identity of the calling line on the affected subscriber's called line, in so far as it appears to the provider necessary or expedient (1999 Regulations, reg. 14(1) and (2)). This freedom to act on the part of the service provider overrides any contractual provision to the contrary (1999 Regulations, reg. 14(3)). The service provider or a network provider may hold and make available to those with 'a legitimate interest therein' data containing the identification of a calling subscriber, if the data were obtained during the period in which it was attempted to trace malicious or nuisance calls (1999 Regulations, reg. 14(4)).

11.6 DIRECTORIES

Part IV of the 1999 Regulations applies to directories (both printed and electronic) of subscribers to publicly available telecoms services and equivalent information held by directory enquiry services (1999 Regulations, reg. 17(1)). As regards entries relating to individuals, unless a subscriber's consent has been obtained, a directory may not contain personal data except information necessary to identify the subscriber and the number allocated to him (1999 Regulations, reg. 18(2)). Furthermore, a producer of a directory must comply with a request from an individual to be excluded from the directory, a request that the entry not contain a reference to the subscriber's sex, and a request to exclude a specified part of the subscriber's address (1999 Regulations, reg. 18(3)). If a directory has already been produced before the request is made, the request applies to the next edition of the directory (1999 Regulations, reg. 17(3)). Service providers must also comply with a request to exclude from a directory a number relating to a corporate subscriber (1999 Regulations, reg. 19). Neither individuals nor corporate subscribers may be charged for the right to have their number(s) excluded from a directory.

11.7 USE OF TELECOMMUNICATIONS SERVICES FOR DIRECT MARKETING PURPOSES

11.7.1 Automated calling systems

The 1999 Regulations prohibit the use of automated calling equipment to make direct marketing calls to individuals or corporates, except where the consent of the subscriber concerned has been obtained (1999 Regulations, reg. 22). The equipment regulated is equipment that operates to make calls without human intervention. Although somewhat unclear, this is likely to apply only to a call that is initiated and completed without human intervention. An automated dialling system that sets up calls that are taken over by a live operator when answered would not appear to be covered by this rule.

11.7.2 Voice calls

The 1999 Regulations put on a statutory footing the old telecommunications preference service ('the TPS'). Under the 1999 Regulations, the TPS has become the responsibility of the DGT, although in practice its operation has been delegated to the Direct Marketing Association. It is open to any individual to put his or her telephone number on the TPS's register. Numbers appearing on the old non-statutory register were deemed to have been registered with the statutory TPS. The 1999 Regulations prohibit direct marketing calls to individuals whose numbers appear on the TPS's register, or who have previously notified the caller that they do not wish to receive such unsolicited calls for the time being (1999 Regulations, reg. 25). It is possible for an individual to object to the receipt of direct marketing calls generally, but to agree (perhaps by accepting an organisation's terms and conditions) that a particular organisation may, nevertheless, make direct marketing calls to him or her.

11.7.3 Fax

As regards the sending of unsolicited communications by fax, the 1999 Regulations established a fax preference service ('FPS') which, like the TPS (see 11.7.2 above), is the responsibility of the DGT but is in practice administered by the Direct Marketing Association. Regulation 23 prohibits the sending of unsolicited direct marketing materials by fax to corporates that have registered with the FPS, or have notified the sender that they do not wish to receive such faxes. Again, it is possible to bypass a general opt-out by a subscriber if that subscriber has notified a particular caller that he does not object to receiving direct marketing communications from that caller.

Regulation 24 prohibits the sending of unsolicited direct marketing materials to an individual subscriber by fax without obtaining the prior consent of the subscriber.

11.7.4   E-mail

The terminology used in the 1999 Regulations suggests that they were drafted with conventional voice and fax calls in mind. It is not clear whether the restrictions on direct marketing activities apply also to e-mail communications. Depending on the circumstances, e-mail can be characterised as being analogous either to conventional mail, on the one hand, or to a voice or fax call on the other. In many instances, an e-mail message will be sent to the intended recipient's ISP, where it will be stored until such time as the recipient connects to the ISP to retrieve the message. Such an arrangement is rather like a conventional mail system using post office boxes, and is certainly very different from a real-time phone or fax 'call'. On the other hand, where the recipient has a real-time connection to the Internet a message may be received almost instantaneously. Indeed, a lengthy document can be delivered via e-mail in such circumstances in a small fraction of the time it would take to deliver the same document via fax. It is possible that the sending of an e-mail message in such circumstances might be regulated as an unsolicited direct marketing call. If that were the case, reg. 22 would prohibit the sending to either business or individual recipients of unsolicited e-mails using an automated calling system. A computer that is used to distribute a mass e-mail mailing may constitute such a system as it may 'make calls without human intervention'. Even where an automated mailing system is not used, it may be a breach of reg. 25 to send a marketing e-mail to an individual subscriber who has either requested the particular sender not to send such messages, or who is listed on the TPS register. An alternative, and probably better, interpretation of these Regulations is that the references to telephone numbers and the use of concepts such as 'subscriber's line' and 'unsolicited call' indicate that the 1999 Regulations are intended to apply only to conventional voice and fax calls.

The proposed Electronic Communications Privacy Directive would make it clear that unsolicited e-mails for the purposes of direct marketing are to be treated in the same way as such communications sent via phone or fax (see Art. 13(1)).

11.8   GENERAL APPLICATION OF THE DATA PROTECTION ACT 1998 TO THE COMMUNICATIONS SECTOR

11.8.1   Jurisdictional reach

The DPA 1998 applies to 'data controllers' in respect of particular 'personal data' only if the controller either is established in the United Kingdom and the data are processed in the context of that establishment, or the controller is established outside the EEA 'but uses equipment in the United Kingdom for processing the data otherwise than for the purposes of transit through the United Kingdom' (s. 5(1)). A data controller who falls into the second category must nominate a representative in the United Kingdom in relation to its obligations under the DPA 1998.

This apparently straightforward statement of territorial scope is fraught with difficulty in the telecommunications context. For one thing, due to the breadth of the establishment concept in the DPA 1998 it is possible that, for example, a telecommunications operator or an ISP will be established in multiple states within the EEA.[32] Similarly, a commercial organisation may find that it is subject to multiple, and in certain respects inconsistent, national rules in relation to its internal cross-border Intranet. Even where a data controller is not established in multiple EEA states, it may at least use equipment in multiple states. The EU Data Protection Directive, Art. 4(1)(a) makes it clear that 'when the controller is established on the territory of several Member States, he must take the necessary measures to ensure that each of these establishments complies with the obligations laid down by the national law applicable . . .'.

The second problematic aspect of the territoriality rule is the exception for the processing of data using equipment in the United Kingdom that is merely 'for the purposes of transit through the United Kingdom' (DPA 1998, s. 5(1)(b)). What if, for example, a website on a server in the United States is 'mirrored' by a UK-based ISP on a server in the United Kingdom to facilitate access to that site by UK-based customers of the ISP? Will the ISP in the United Kingdom become a data controller in relation to any personal data contained in that website? Will the ISP in the United States be treated as established in the United Kingdom merely because an ISP in the United Kingdom has chosen to make a copy of the site (quite possibly without the site controller's knowledge)? What if a website on a server in the United States plants a 'cookie' on the PC of a UK-based visitor to the site and subsequently interrogates that cookie remotely each time the visitor returns to the site? Is the data controller in the United States using equipment in the United Kingdom (i.e., the visitor's PC) to process data about that visitor? Given that 'processing' includes 'obtaining, recording or holding . . . information or data' such a construction is possible. This would, however, be an absurd result as the website operator in the United States would presumably have to appoint the United Kingdom visitor as its representative for the purposes of compliance with the DPA 1998!

11.8.2 Notification obligations

Subject to various exemptions, under the DPA 1998 it is a strict liability offence for a data controller to process personal data without first giving a notification to the Data Protection Commissioner (ss. 17(1) and 21(1)). The DPA 1998 lists various 'registrable particulars' which must be included in a notification, including the controller's name and address, or that of any nominated representative; a description of the personal data to be processed; the purposes for which the data are to be processed; the recipient(s) to whom

---

[32] Section 5(3) of the DPA 1998 provides that, in addition to United Kingdom individuals, companies and partnerships, '. . . any person who maintains in the United Kingdom— (i) an office, branch or agency through which he carries on any activity, or (ii) a regular practice' will be treated as established in the United Kingdom.

the data may be disclosed; and details of countries outside the EEA to which the data may be transferred. In addition, a notification must specify 'a general description of measures to be taken for the purpose of complying with the seventh data protection principle' (s. 18(2); see 11.8.6 below).

11.8.3 Information provision requirements

The first data protection principle provides that '[p]ersonal data shall be processed fairly and lawfully . . .' (DPA 1998, Sch. 1, Pt I, para. 1). The interpretation provisions make it clear that personal data will not be considered to be processed 'fairly' unless certain information is provided, or made readily available, to the individual concerned (Sch. 1, Pt II, para. 2(1)). The information to be given to data subjects must include the identity of the data controller and any nominated representative, the purpose or purposes for which the data are intended to be processed, and 'any further information which is necessary, having regard to the specific circumstances in which the data are or are to be processed, to enable processing in respect of the data subject to be fair' (Sch. 1, Pt II, para. 2(3)).

11.8.4 Justification for processing data

Personal data must not be processed unless one of a number of conditions is satisfied. These are set out in Sch. 2 to the DPA 1998. In summary, processing is legitimate if the data subject has given his or her consent; or if it is necessary for the performance of a contract to which the data subject is a party or for taking steps to enter into a contract, for compliance with a legal obligation (other than contractual), or for certain public sector purposes.[33] In addition, processing is justified if it is

> necessary for the purposes of a legitimate interest pursued by the data controller or by the third party or parties to whom the data are disclosed, except where the processing is unwarranted in a particular case by reason of prejudice to the rights and freedoms or legitimate interests of the data subject.

More stringent conditions apply to processing of sensitive data. These are set out in Sch. 3 to the DPA 1998. The DPA 1998 defines 'sensitive personal data' as 'personal data consisting of information as to' a data subject's racial or ethnic origin, political opinions, religious beliefs or other beliefs of a similar nature, membership of a trade union, physical or mental health or condition, sexual life, or commission or alleged commission or proceedings in relation to any offence (s. 2).

Processing of sensitive data will be legitimate only if the data subject has given his or her 'explicit consent'; the processing is necessary in relation to

---

[33] Broadly, these are that the processing is necessary for the administration of justice, in relation to any statutory or government function or other public function exercised in the public interest.

an employment right or obligation; the processing is necessary to protect the vital interests of the data subject or another person in circumstances where consent is not obtainable; the processing is by a charitable body in relation to its members; the data subject has made the data public; the processing is necessary in relation to legal proceedings or advice; or the processing is for certain public sector purposes. In addition, processing may be legitimate in the public or private sectors where it is carried out for medical purposes by a health professional, or where it is carried out, with appropriate safeguards, for ethnic monitoring purposes to promote or maintain equality. The Data Protection (Processing of Sensitive Personal Data) Order 2000 (SI 2000 No. 417) has established various additional circumstances in which sensitive data may be processed. Of potential significance in the telecommunications context is an exemption covering certain processing activities for the purposes of preventing or detecting any unlawful act (Schedule, para. 1(1)).

11.8.5 Data subject rights

The sixth data protection principle requires data controllers to process personal data 'in accordance with the rights of data subjects under this Act' (DPA 1998, Sch. 1, Pt I, para. 6). An interpretation provision states that a person will be regarded as contravening this principle only if he fails to provide access to data as required, fails to comply with a notice from a data subject requiring him to stop processing data for certain purposes, or fails to comply with the procedures relating to automated decision-making (Sch. 1, Pt II, para. 8). This restrictive statement should, however, be read in conjunction with the general right which an individual has under s. 13 of the DPA 1998 to compensation where he or she has suffered damage as a result of contravention by a data controller of any of the requirements of the Act. The difference between these provisions is that a breach of the sixth principle may trigger the service on the data controller by the Data Protection Commissioner of an enforcement notice, whereas breach of s. 13 may form the basis for a civil claim for compensation for damage and, possibly, distress.

11.8.6 Security obligations

The seventh data protection principle provides that '[a]ppropriate technical and organisational measures shall be taken against unauthorised or unlawful processing of personal data and against accidental loss or destruction of, or damage to, personal data' (DPA 1998, Sch. 1, Pt I, para. 7). Given the degree of public concern regarding the security, or otherwise, of communications and transactions via the Internet, this principle needs to be considered carefully, notwithstanding that public concerns may be vastly overstated.

The DPA 1998 contains some interpretation of this principle from which a number of practical conclusions can be drawn. The first is that what constitutes 'appropriate' security will vary widely depending on the circumstances. Relevant factors include the nature of the data to be protected, an assessment of the harm that might result from unauthorised or unlawful processing or accidental loss, destruction or damage, the state of technological development and the cost of any security measures (Sch. 1, Pt II, para. 9). This suggests, for example, that whereas publication on a website of information that is already in the public domain might require little or no security cover, the collection via e-mail or the web of medical or other sensitive data might necessitate adoption of rigorous security measures.

Secondly, data controllers are required to 'take reasonable steps to ensure the reliability of any employees . . . who have access to the personal data' (Sch. 1, Pt II, para. 10). Again, the use of the word 'reasonable' suggests that a range of steps may be appropriate depending on the circumstances, ranging from minimal supervision to positive vetting.

Thirdly, where a data controller uses a data processor, the controller will automatically be in breach of the seventh principle unless the following criteria are satisfied:

(a)   the processor provides 'sufficient guarantees in respect of the technical and organisational security measures governing the processing to be carried out' and the controller takes 'reasonable steps to ensure compliance with those measures' (Sch. 1, Pt II, para. 11);

(b)   the processing is governed by a written contract requiring the processor to act only as instructed by the controller and to comply with security obligations equivalent to those imposed on the controller (Sch. 1, Pt II, para. 12).

This requirement to document arrangements between controllers and processors is clearly of broad significance to the telecommunications industry, characterised as it is by numerous interconnection, outsourcing and service provider relationships. Specifically in the Internet context, data controllers will need to ensure that they have appropriate, and properly documented, contractual arrangements in place with any ISPs or other third parties which process data on their behalf, for example by hosting websites.

11.8.7   Transborder data flows

The eighth data protection principle provides that '[p]ersonal data shall not be transferred to a country or territory outside the European Economic Area unless that country or territory ensures an adequate level of protection for the rights and freedoms of data subjects in relation to the processing of personal data' (Data Protection Act 1998, Sch. 1, Pt I, para. 8). The interpretation provisions add that adequacy depends on 'all the circumstances of the case', including the nature of the data, the country or territory of origin and final destination of the data, the law in force and international obligations of those jurisdictions, the purposes and duration of the intended processing, 'any relevant codes of conduct or other rules which are enforceable in that country or territory', and any security measures taken in the destination country or territory (Sch. 1, Pt II, para. 13).

The Data Protection Directive, Art. 25(6), envisages that the European Commission may find that particular countries outside the EEA provide an adequate level of protection for personal data. Following a procedure involving a Committee of Representatives of the Member States (Art. 31(2)), such countries may be added to what is, in effect, a 'white list' of approved destinations. At the time of writing, such adequacy findings had been made only in relation to Switzerland,[34] Hungary,[35] and the 'Safe Harbor Privacy Principles' issued by the US Department of Commerce.[36] The detailed arrangements relating to the Safe Harbor are complex and beyond the scope of this chapter. In general terms, however, the benefit of the Safe Harbor is available only to organisations that are regulated either by the Federal Trade Commission or by the US Department of Transportation[37] and that publicly commit to adhere to a set of principles that are broadly similar to the principles of the Data Protection Directive. Details of organisations that are within the Safe Harbor are available on a public website.[38] The Data Protection Act 1998 provides that 'Community findings', such as those relating to Switzerland, Hungary and the Safe Harbor, are conclusive for the purpose of demonstrating adequacy under the eighth data protection principle (Sch. 1, Pt II, para. 15).

Although over time the list of 'adequate' destination countries will no doubt grow, it is likely that there will remain many situations in which it cannot be demonstrated that a destination country ensures an adequate level of protection. To overcome the eighth principle's prohibition on transfer in such cases, it will be necessary to rely on one or more of the exemptions listed in Sch. 4 to the DPA 1998. There are nine exemptions, the first seven of which apply 'automatically', in the sense that no prior regulatory approval is needed. The remaining two exemptions are not automatic and require the prior approval of the Data Protection Commissioner.

Probably the most straightforward automatic exemption is that the data subject has consented to the transfer (Sch. 4, para. 1). Although the Internet is perceived by some as a threat to privacy, it may in fact prove to be a particularly effective medium for obtaining data protection consents. An individual can be provided, by e-mail or via a webpage, with the requisite information to make an informed decision about an international transfer. The consent of that individual can then be captured via a return e-mail or a 'click-through' on a website.

---

[34] Commission Decision 2000/518/EC of 26 July 2000 pursuant to Directive 95/46/EC of the European Parliament and of the Council on the adequate protection of personal data provided in Switzerland, (2000) OJ L 215/1.

[35] Commission Decision 2000/519/EC of 26 July 2000 pursuant to Directive 95/46/EC of the European Parliament and of the Council on the adequate protection of personal data provided in Hungary, (2000) OJ L 215/4.

[36] Commission Decision 2000/520/EC of 26 July 2000 pursuant to Directive 95/46/EC of the European Parliament and of the Council on the adequacy of the protection provided by the safe harbour privacy principles and related frequently asked questions issued by the US Department of Commerce, (2000) OJ L 215/7.

[37] This means, for example, that regulated financial institutions cannot enter the Safe Harbor.

[38] The Safe Harbor List can be found at http://www.ita.doc.gov/td/ecom/FRN2.htm.

The second and third automatic exceptions to the prohibition on transfer relate to contracts which a data controller might enter into with or for the benefit of a data subject, as well as preparatory steps in relation to such contracts (Sch. 4, paras 2 and 3). Again, there may be many instances in the telecommunications and Internet contexts where one of these exemptions will justify the transfer of personal data to inadequate countries. Obvious examples would be the various transfers necessary to set up and complete an electronic commerce transaction. These might include payment arrangements with credit card issuers and fulfilment arrangements with suppliers and shippers.

The remaining automatic exemptions are likely to be of much more limited relevance in the telecommunications and Internet contexts. The fourth covers transfers that are necessary for reasons of substantial public interest (Sch. 4, para. 4). The fifth applies to transfers that are necessary in connection with legal proceedings, legal advice or for establishing, exercising or defending legal rights (Sch. 4, para. 5). The sixth is available where the transfer is 'necessary to protect the vital interests of the data subject' (Sch. 4, para. 6), and the seventh covers transfers of personal data from a public register (Sch. 4, para. 7).

This leaves the two non-automatic exemptions to the prohibition on transfers. These are the only other grounds on which personal data may lawfully be transferred to a non-EEA country that fails to ensure adequate protection for data subjects. The first covers transfers that are 'made on terms of a kind approved by the Commissioner as ensuring adequate safeguards for the rights and freedoms of data subjects' (Sch. 4, para. 8). The second covers transfers that have been 'authorised by the Commissioner as being made in such a manner as to ensure adequate safeguards for the rights and freedoms of data subjects' (Sch. 4, para. 9). At the time of writing, the Commissioner had neither approved any standard contract terms nor issued any specific authorisation.[39]

Nevertheless, the Data Protection Commissioner has stated that she 'intends to take a pragmatic approach to the issue of transferring personal data to third countries.'[40] To a significant extent, however, her flexibility may be constrained by the European Commission, by the other EU national data protection regulators and, ultimately, by the EU Council of Ministers. Some important guidance has been published by the Working Party on the Protection of Individuals with Regard to the Processing of Personal Data.[41] The

---

[39] Although it may be that she is waiting for the European Commission to approve EU-wide model contract terms for transborder data flows. See 'Preliminary draft of a Commission decision under Article 26(4) of the Directive 95/46/EC on standard clauses for the transfer of personal data to third countries that do not provide an adequate level of protection for the processing of personal data', available at http://europa.eu.int/comm/internal_market/en/media/dataprot/news/callcom.htm.

[40] Note entitled: 'Data Protection Bill: Transferring Data to Third Countries', available at http://www.open.gov.uk/dpr/transfer.htm.

[41] See, in particular, the Working Party's working document entitled, *Transfers of personal data to third countries – applying Articles 25 and 25 of the EU Data Protection Directive*, adopted on 24 July 1998 (DG XV D/5025/98/final, WP 12).

views of this Working Party are strongly indicative of likely regulatory practice across the EEA, as it is comprised of the various national data protection regulators in the EEA. So far, the Working Party seems determined to adopt a strict approach to assessing both adequacy and special exceptions to the prohibition on transfer to non-adequate countries. This is consistent with the EU Data Protection Directive, in which a discussion in the preamble regarding transborder data flows concludes with the simple statement '. . . in any event, transfers to third countries may be effected only in full compliance with the provisions adopted by the Member States pursuant to this Directive' (Recital 60).

Article 26 of the EU Directive, on which these exemptions are based, provides that a Member State which grants any special authorisation must provide details to the European Commission and the other Member States. If a Member State or the Commission raises a valid objection to the authorisation, the Commission must 'take appropriate measures' and the national regulator would be required to 'take the necessary measures to comply with the Commission's decision' (Art. 26(3)).

Even that may not be the end of the story, however. Article 31 of the EU Directive has established a further committee, comprising representatives of the Member States. The European Commission is required to submit to this committee drafts of any measures to be taken in relation to special international transfer authorisations. The committee may disagree with the Commission's approach, resulting in suspension of the relevant 'measures' and referral to the EU Council of Ministers that may ultimately 'take a different decision' (Art. 31).

The transborder data flow rules in the EU Directive and the Data Protection Act 1998 seem to be based on a presumption that international data traffic always follows precise and predictable routings. This assumption is fundamentally at odds with the way in which information is in fact conveyed via digital telecommunications networks and, in particular, the Internet, for at least two reasons. First, the Internet, which is a vast and dynamically configured network of networks, has a so-called 'self-healing' architecture. Messages, or data representing information of any other kind, are split into 'packets' that are sent to their intended destination via the most efficient routing at any given instant. A technical obstacle to the transmission of particular packets will be bypassed automatically and the packets concerned will be forwarded via a different route. Transfers are thus not predictable in geographical terms.

Secondly, because Internet e-mail can be downloaded, and web pages can be viewed, anywhere on the planet where an individual or organisation has a connection to an ISP, the sender of a message or operator of a website has no effective control over where a particular message will be downloaded or web page viewed. Even where, for example, there are rigorous access controls on a particular website that enable a website operator to verify conclusively the identity of a particular visitor to that website, it is not possible currently for the website operator to be sure of the physical location of that visitor. Consequently, it must be assumed that data contained in Internet e-mail messages and web pages potentially may be transferred to any country in the world, without regard to the adequacy or otherwise of the local data protection safeguards, if any.

Moreover, the sheer volume of personal data that is conveyed via the Internet and the vast number of data transfers make it inconceivable that more than a tiny minority of transfers can be regulated in any meaningful way under the cumbersome rules established by the EU Directive and the Data Protection Act 1998.

CHAPTER TWELVE

Regulatory Convergence: the Impact of Broadcasting and Other Laws

Jonathan Kembery & John Angel

12.1 INTRODUCTION

12.1.1 What is 'convergence'?

The question that must be answered at the outset is what we mean by 'convergence'. In its straightforward context it means 'coming together'. Convergence may occur within an industry – most obviously in the case of telecommunications, where technological advances are blurring the distinction between the facilities and characteristics of a mobile network by comparison with those of a fixed network. However, more generally, it is used to describe the confluence of separately regulated types of enterprise, for example telecommunications and broadcasting – to no little extent because this type of convergence generates the most significant legal and commercial challenges.

OFTEL, in its second submission[1] to the Parliamentary Select Committee inquiry into audio-visual communications and the regulation of broadcasting described convergence as arising from the coming together of the following activities:

(a)   telecommunications (both voice and data services);
(b)   computing (both hardware and software when used in conjunction with public communications networks);

---

[1] 'Beyond the telephone, the television and the PC III' (3/98) – see www.oftel.gov.uk (publications section).

(c)   broadcast and other networked audio-visual services; and
(d)   any combinations of the above (e.g., interactive services over the Internet).

Thus 'convergence' is the expression used to describe the amalgamation of telecommunications, broadcasting, media and information technology.

12.1.2   Why is convergence happening?

It is possible to see convergence as an industry-led process. Entrepreneurial companies see the opportunity to utilise new technologies and to avail themselves of regulatory gaps in order to integrate in a vertical (or horizontal) fashion, owning or joint venturing with, and therefore capturing the profit element in, separate stages in the process of delivering content and services to customers. However, it is perhaps better understood as a technology-driven process, the key technology being the widespread application of digitisation.

Digitisation is the process by which information is converted into a form that may be processed in a computerised fashion. At the most simple level, computers may be said to perform operations in response to a series of 'switches' which may be viewed as being either on or off, the positions of these switches being represented in binary code as '0' or '1'. Virtually any type of information – be it music, text or television pictures – may be reduced to a series of binary instructions.

The representation of information in binary form (referred to as encoding) has several clear advantages. First, signals that are transmitted in digital form consist of a series of individual, simple instructions. As such they are less vulnerable to certain types of distortion or attenuation than analogue signals that vary (or 'modulate') over a range of values, meaning, for example, that a greater range of frequency channels can be used for terrestrial digital transmission than for analogue. Secondly, it is easier to correct signal deficiencies. Further, it is technologically more straightforward to carry out cryptographical processes on a stream of binary values, creating more secure techniques for the delivery of pay content such as television, but also for computer programs and other interactive content.

Perhaps most importantly in terms of the process of convergence, however, digitisation facilitates the use of compression and routing technologies that greatly increase the amount of information that may be conveyed by means of a given distribution system, be that copper wire, fibre optic cable or wireless telegraphy, during a particular period of time. Moreover, any form of content, be it still or moving picture, sound, text or data, can be stored and made available by common transmission mechanisms. As computer power has become cheaper and compression technologies more widespread and sophisticated, so the delivery of video footage by means of the Internet to a PC, a prime example of convergence, has been enabled. Similarly, the development of packet switching and digital multiplexing has enabled the delivery of different streams of information, to all intents and purposes simultaneously, by means of the same transmission mechanism.

One packet switching technology in particular, TCP/IP, the protocol that underlies the Internet, has also facilitated the transfer of messages across logically separate networks operating on different hardware platforms, and consequently has facilitated the move towards the creation of platform neutral content.

The above technological advances create the conditions for convergence, namely an environment in which almost any form of information may be digitised and transmitted by means of any digital transmission infrastructure (television, wireless, or fixed telephony or Internet) and utilised in its original form by one or many recipients.

12.1.3   What does convergence mean in the commercial world?

Convergence represents an opportunity for companies to present a combined or cross-platform offering to consumers. It has already been (and is likely to be in the future) a springboard for a series of opportunistic alliances to take advantage of the trends (or in all probability, to protect market position and share in a changing environment). The purpose of this chapter is to describe in broad terms the legal factors that will influence the nature of that opportunity and to explain the regulatory background against which innovation will occur.

It is, however, difficult at an entirely theoretical level to conceptualise what a converged alliance or company might look like, or how the process will alter the economics of the industries involved. Accordingly, before looking at the legal aspects it is worth considering in more depth what characteristics a converged organisation may have. One model amongst several that have been used to depict the possible interrelationship of companies is the Pyramid Model, set out at Figure 12.1 below.

The Pyramid Model, developed by PricewaterhouseCoopers, envisages that a convergent offering to a customer will involve three key elements:

(a)   *content*, for example pay per view movies or electronic information resources;

(b)   *transactional services* that enable payments to be processed from the customer and other revenue to be generated by advertising and/or other forms of electronic commerce bundled with content; and

(c)   *a transport layer*, namely the communications facility and information technology by which the content and other services will be transmitted to and received by the customer.

In the model a significant role is given to branding as the means by which customers will distinguish between available and competing services. The role of branding in a converged environment is discussed at the end of this chapter.

Open, the joint venture between BSkyB, Matsushita, HSBC and BT, has been held out as a prime example of a convergent alliance. Open offers services to more than 3 million viewers by means of a combination of

Figure 12.1   The Pyramid Model of Convergence

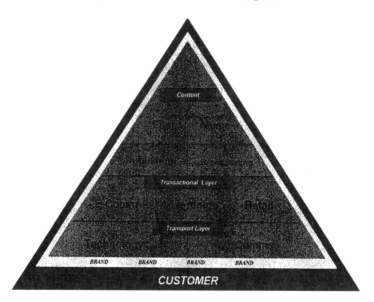

technologies. Video, sound text and still images are transmitted by means of digital satellite to viewers' set-top boxes where users may play games, receive information, shop and bank, using a modem return path facility within the set-top box to access further information on an individual request basis.

In addition, the later part of 1999 saw two key mergers that have been held out as prime examples of significant companies understanding what convergence could mean for their industries and respective competitive opportunities. In the first, AOL and Time Warner announced that they were intending to merge, with the telecommunication company taking over the media giant in a deal valued at US $350 billion. The parties spoke of a 'network world' in which households would have a 'home gateway', giving them access to a range of convergent services from telephony and e-mail through to music, shopping, games and banking. Meanwhile, in the UK, Telewest, the second largest cable TV and communications company in the country, and Flextech, the media assets business, announced that they were also intending to merge in a deal worth £10.7 billion to create (in their words) a 'new type of company for the digital age'.

Convergence is also likely to have significant impact not only upon the way in which existing information services are delivered to customers, but also on the businesses concerned and the nature of the legal processes involved. For example, as the delivery of high-quality music on-line becomes more feasible, so record companies may migrate from being manufacturers, at least one stage removed in the value chain from end-users, to become on-line distributors of content.

Technological solutions are likely to emerge to deal with the issues of digital rights management that may build upon or even replace copyright as the legal tool of choice for those whose business assets comprise intellectual property rights. In these circumstances the legal issues associated with such technologies and rights may be key in shaping the way in which a converged industry operates.

The rest of this chapter will explore the legal issues to be faced by AOL/Time Warner and its actual or future competitors, and the way in which the regulatory framework needs to, and is likely to, respond to technological change.

12.2 CONVERGENCE AS A REGULATORY ISSUE

It is important to understand why convergence represents a significant regulatory challenge, since the nature and extent of the regulatory problems are likely to determine the extent and purpose of regulation in the short to medium term.

A root cause of regulatory problems is the speed of technological advance itself. Take the telecommunications sector as an example. The process of liberalisation of telephony in the EU broadly began with two key Directives in 1990, the Services Directive (90/388) and the ONP Framework Directive (90/389) (see Chapter 8). Within a decade, at least 12 more Directives or amendments to Directives relating to the sector were adopted by the EU to harmonise the EU telecommunications markets during the process of liberalisation. This culminated in a review at the end of 1999 to assess the appropriateness and efficacy of the framework of these Directives as a cohesive package.[2] Some would say this reflects the complexities of telecommunications and the different stages of market development in the EU Member States; however, it is clear that the need for the EU to amend and ultimately review a set of legislative texts so soon after their implementation reflects a market in great flux, driven heavily by the pace of technological development.

The UK Government and regulatory bodies are faced with a similar dilemma. OFTEL, the UK telecommunications regulator, announced in its Management Plan for 2000/01[3] that it would be working with the Department of Trade and Industry and the Department for Culture Media and Sport on proposals to update and reform the Telecommunications Act 1984 and the Broadcasting Act, 'to enable the development of a competitive market for converging services with appropriate consumer protection'. The Telecommunications Act 1984 is thought of as out of date and cumbersome in the new world of communications, where the traditional distinctions between the provision of facilities and infrastructure and the provision of

---

[2] Commission Communication, 'Towards a new framework for Electronic Communications infrastructure and associated services: The 1999 Communications Review', COM (1999) 539, 10 November 1999.
[3] OFTEL's proposals for implementing OFTEL's strategy – 2000/01, Management Plan, April 2000.

services (including the content of those services) have long since broken down.

The fundamental principle underpinning the Telecommunications Act 1984 is the concept of 'running or using a telecommunication system', but the emergence of 'systemless service providers' in recent years has challenged this traditional delineation as the regulators have watched service providers drop out of the regulatory net for no better reason than a legal disparity. This is just one example of the growing legislative problems facing the UK regulators in deciding how to reform the current framework to reflect the emerging market structures. This issue is also reflected in the development of 'Internet telephony' (discussed in Chapter 13) which has presented a more immediate challenge for the regulators.

The Services Directive[4] defines 'voice telephony' as 'the commercial provision for the public of the direct transport and switching of speech in real-time between public switched network termination points, enabling any user to use equipment connected to such network termination points in order to communicate with another termination point'. Since the adoption of the Services Directive, however, technology has moved on with the introduction of IP or so-called 'Internet telephony'. Although perhaps of minor consequence at the moment, largely down to the current quality of voice telephony over the Internet, IP telephony has the potential to affect, manifestly, the economics of the industry, with some analysts predicting that IP telephony could account for up to 40 per cent of the market on key international routes within the next five years. Yet, at present, at least in the form of *ad hoc* use by ISP subscribers, it would seem that it is not caught by the above definition of 'voice telephony'. This regulatory distinction over the concept 'voice telephony' is being driven not by the service (i.e., the capacity to exchange speech in real time) but by the infrastructure carrying that service. It is very possible to envisage a time when answering a communication device at home will happen without knowing through which network (i.e., the public switched telephone network or the IP network) the voice call was delivered. But today the provision of that voice call could fall to be regulated in two completely different ways, affecting not only the level of service expected to be received, but (if the regulators are achieving one of their primary goals) also the consumer protections expected to be gained in relation to that service.

As the European Commission has pointed out in a 1998 Notice, IP telephony is rarely offered to consumers as a stand-alone service, thereby failing to meet the commercial test.[5] It is generally only available to individuals with dial-up modem access to an ISP (rather than over the PSTN) and its packet switched status means that it cannot, at present, be considered as a standard real-time voice service.

Another effect of falling outside the scope of the above Directive is that, unless additional regulation applies, Internet voice telephony provided as

---

[4] Council Directive 90/387/EC of 28 June 1990.
[5] *Commission Notice on the status of voice communications on the Internet under Community law* (OJ C 6, 10.1.1998).

above cannot be regulated by means of individual licences in Member States and no contribution from ISPs is required towards the costs of maintaining universal service for voice telephony in the relevant country. The concept of universal service maintains both standards and costs through geographic de-averaging and ensuring the provision of basic services to all. On the other hand, telecommunications operators and providers who utilise TCP/IP and Internet infrastructure in order to provide standard telephony rather than dial-up Internet access (such as USA Global Link and Qwest) may be caught by the definition, with attendant regulatory implications.

Internet telephony is indicative of the confusion that technological change can create and of its ability to wrong-foot even the most clearly thought out regulatory environment. For example, while the issues relating to the regulation of Internet telephony show the distinction between the regulation of IP based telephony offered as a distinct service from network termination points and the use of dial-up Internet services for the same purpose, how would an IP telephony service which is accessible via a portal to which an individual may connect without subscription or charge (such as the Dixons Freeserve offering) fall to be regulated? It can be seen that the traditional distinctions between infrastructure provision and service provision are breaking down once more.

In addition, there is a second cause of regulatory complexity to consider which is reflective more of the past than of the technological present and future. To the interested observer it is clear that the regulators responsible for the constituent industries involved in convergence bring separate perspectives born out of their regulatory traditions. Historically, each of the industries has been regulated in a different fashion:

(a)　Information technology has been subject to little (if any) sector-specific regulation, with the competition authorities having the principal role in dealing with the abuse of market power, coming to the forefront most recently and publicly in the ruling against Microsoft in the United States relating to bundling of its Internet browser with its application products.

(b)　Broadcasting has historically been the subject of considerable regulation, both of the content that is transmitted and of the means by which it is delivered. Concerns regarding media plurality and the preservation of culture, together with continuing constraints upon terrestrial spectrum, mean that broadcasting remains within state control to a greater or lesser extent within many EU countries.

(c)　Telecommunications services within the EU have undergone a lengthy process of liberalisation with the breakdown of state monopolies and the introduction of competition. Generally, however, regulation has focused upon access to infrastructure and the right to provide services of different categories, rather than upon the content of the services themselves.

(d)　Media regulation has tended to focus on plurality and content and not to emphasise the role of the delivery mechanism.

The effect of these different approaches is that similar activities may fall within different regulatory regimes merely because of the precise circumstances (for example, the network infrastructure) involved in their performance. For instance, the provision of the same 'broadcasting' content by means of terrestrial analogue TV and by means of the Internet will, arguably, be subject to radically different regulatory controls. The means of delivery will be dictating the extent of content regulation rather than the nature or accessibility of the content itself.

In the converging environment many of the reasons for regulation diminish. For example, in the broadcasting sector spectrum scarcity (which was a significant factor behind Government involvement in the sector) becomes of diminished importance, while the interchangeability of telecommunications and other networks for the delivery of content such as broadcasting raises issues regarding the practicality (if not the appropriateness) of content regulation. The important distinction between one-to-many and point-to-point delivery or exchange of content in regulating the substance of that content, and the nature of its arrival in the viewer's home, is breaking down as digital interactive TV enables one-to-one communication via the traditionally heavily content-regulated television.

Some observers have commented, for example, that a natural effect of the process of convergence and the consequent explosion of available content will be that responsibility for making decisions regarding the appropriateness of content will shift away from a regulator towards the individual user, or perhaps the individual parent. Commentators who take this view believe that the sheer volume of content will drive a technological solution whereby content providers will have the opportunity to tag their content electronically with information regarding, for example, the extent of any violent or sexual content. The user will then have the opportunity to screen the content using receiving devices that may be programmed to exclude certain types of content, or any content that is not tagged using the appropriate coding. Such a scheme would be entirely voluntary – the content provider would not have to identify or tag its materials if it did not want to, but not to do so might mean that its audience could not view them with a resultant loss of advertising revenue.

It will be interesting to see to what extent these predictions of a movement towards self-regulation will be realised and who will be the ultimate winners in the battle for regulatory competence, described in more detail at 12.4 below.

12.3   SOME PRESENT REGULATORY CHALLENGES

12.3.1   Fixed/mobile convergence

It is common to focus on inter-industry convergence rather than to examine the extent to which convergence may be taking place within individual industries. For example, in the telecommunications industry there has been a tendency to regard mobile and fixed networks as not being substitutes for each other, given the differences in costs, bandwidth and quality that have hitherto prevailed. The regulation of these two markets has therefore been quite distinct in the past. Leaving aside any of the issues relating to incumbent fixed operators being able to exercise their advantage in the fixed market in the mobile market and/or their advantage in the delivery of combined fixed and mobile services (both represent challenges for the regulators), technological advances in the mobile world will no doubt impact its regulatory position.

The same technology that is driving intra-industry convergence will alter the relative positions of mobile and fixed networks in the medium term. Already we have seen the development of enhanced standards for GSM mobile telephony (for example, GPRS and Edge) that are being implemented in some form or another by mobile operators worldwide to increase the capacity that can be carried using the GSM technology on the frequencies and limited amount of spectrum that is available. What this will enable, of course, is the delivery of multimedia type services (including e-mail, Internet access, etc.)

Of perhaps greater sectoral significance (in respect of bandwidth, and therefore the development not only of new multimedia consumer services but also the provision of wireless infrastructure for corporate LANs and WANs) is the adoption and, at the time of writing, current implementation of the third generation mobile standard in EU Member States. The need for licensing, and thereby concurrent regulation, in the area of mobile telephony is apparent when one considers the global scarcity of radio spectrum that is available for the running of mobile networks and the provision of mobile services.

The so-called UMTS standard is used to describe a third generation system for which a mobile technological standard is being developed in the EU and elsewhere. The expectation that Member States would implement a licensing framework and encourage the development of third generation mobile services was adopted by the EU in the 'UMTS Decision'[6] and has led, in the UK, to an auction of five new mobile licences to which this standard will apply. In addition to conventional voice, fax and data services, it will give enhanced access for mobile users to multimedia services such as Internet access at speeds of up to 2 Megabits per second, services which have hitherto been associated with fixed networks only. Perhaps the most telling indication of the potential value of this recent development in mobile telephony is the number of applicants, and the size of the bids for the UK licences. The final results of the auction generated a £22 billion windfall for the Government.

Some predictions suggest that there will be more mobile lines than fixed lines by the year 2004. As a consequence, mobile operators will control access to a significant percentage of the NTPs on a country's PSTN, and the basis on which other service providers and mobile subscribers may access the networks, and the pricing for interconnection to mobile networks, will become key.

In the past, in order to encourage investment in the infrastructure necessary to establish a mobile network, regulation has been applied with a

---

[6] Council Decision 128/1999/EC of the European Parliament and of the Council on the coordinated introduction of a third-generation mobile and wireless communications system (UMTS) in the Community, (1999) OJ L 17/1.

comparatively light hand, not least because mobile operators in many countries do not yet satisfy the test for SMP (approximately 25 per cent market share) and accordingly are not obliged to offer cost-based interconnection pricing or number portability/carrier pre-selection.[7] One certain development in an increasingly converged telecoms market will therefore be the extension of regulatory obligations on mobile operators, either because their market power increases or as a result of the positive steps of NRAs (for example, Sweden and Austria have designated their mobile operators as having SMP in the national market for interconnection). In the UK, even with the presence of four competing and established mobile operators, which would suggest a relatively competitive environment, OFTEL decided[8] to designate Vodafone and BT Cellnet as having 'market influence' in the market for mobile telephony in the UK. (Both operators had previously been notified to the Commission by the DGT as having SMP in the mobile market under the Interconnection Directive.)[9]

Although the Determination did not go so far as to include fixed services as well as mobile services in the market definition, OFTEL did acknowledge in its explanatory memorandum that substitution of calls between fixed and mobile services does take place (at para. 8). OFTEL has stressed that its strategy is to withdraw from regulation where there is effective competition, and it believes the mobile market will become effectively competitive however, in the meantime, Vodafone and BT Cellnet will have to face the regulatory burden of 'market influence' and its implications in relation to the provision of and pricing of interconnection.[10]

OFTEL instituted a consultation process[11] regarding indirect access from mobile networks in February 1999. During the process OFTEL dealt with a complaint from an indirect access operator, which resulted in two determinations[12] from OFTEL at the end of 1999, stating that both BT Cellnet and Vodafone should provide indirect access to the indirect operator's customers using a short access code. The service to be provided by the two mobile operators to the indirect operator was to be charged on the basis of retail minus. Mobile network operators will be obliged to connect calls from the nearest mobile switching centre to the network of the fixed operator to whom indirect access is achieved.

---

[7] Under the Interconnection Directive 97/33/EC, as amended by Directive 98/61, (1998) OJ L 268/37. See also Chapters 5 and 8.

[8] 'Determinations that Vodafone and BT Cellnet have Market Influence under Condition 56 of their respective licences', issued by the DGT on 28 March 2000.

[9] Noted in OFTEL's February 1998 Statement on the 'Identification of Significant Market Power for the purpose of the Interconnection Directive'.

[10] See 'OFTEL Strategy statement: Achieving the best deal for telecoms consumers', January 2000.

[11] Consultative Document issued by the DGT, 'Customer choice: OFTEL's review of indirect access for mobile networks', February 1999.

[12] *Determination under the provisions of Regulation 6(6) of the Telecommunications (Interconnection) Regulations 1997 of a dispute between Intelligent Network Management Services (UK) Ltd ('INMS') and BT Cellnet*, 2 December 1999.

OFTEL also consulted[13] on whether mobile operators should be required under their licence to provide services required by mobile virtual network operators (MVNOs), those who offer mobile subscription and call services to customers but do not have spectrum, and who therefore require services to be provided by one of the four mobile network operators. OFTEL concluded in October 1999[14] that for the time being, and with the expectation of an increasingly competitive mobile market, in light of the introduction of mobile indirect access, and a likely new entrant in the auction of third generation spectrum, the need for regulatory intervention was not present. However, this serves to show that OFTEL is and will be increasingly requested to consider the regulatory position of the mobile operators, as the mobile and fixed markets for telephony become ever-more converged. The recent launch of a new Internet Protocol for use with mobile telephones, commonly known as WAP (wireless application protocol), is further fuelling the substitutability of the wireless and the fixed markets.

One point to observe, however, is that since this convergence is intra-industry, the regulatory regime already exists in terms of a framework of telecoms Directives, UK specific regulation and the competition rules to police its development. This situation might be contrasted with some of the scenarios discussed later in this chapter.

12.3.2 Convergence and broadcasting

12.3.2.1 The regulation of broadcasting in the United Kingdom The activity of broadcasting in the UK is regulated by a complex and at times overlapping system of statutes. At the highest level, the activity of broadcasting itself is currently regulated by two key statutes, the Broadcasting Act 1990 and the Broadcasting Act 1996. These statutes have been updated and modified, for example to take account of the two Television Without Frontiers Directives, by statutory instruments, of which the key ones are the Satellite Television Services Regulations 1997 (SI 1997 No. 1682) and the Television Broadcasting Regulations 1998 (SI 1998 No. 3196).

In addition to requiring a licence and being subject to the regulatory regimes referred to above, a potential service provider may also fall to be regulated in terms of delivery infrastructure used to convey signals. The two Wireless Telegraphy Acts (1949 and 1998) apply to the use of radio spectrum for the delivery of signals, while for cable companies or others involving a telecommunications network in the delivery of their services (for example an interactive television company) a licence will be required under the Telecommunications Act 1984 for the ancillary running of a telecommunications system and for the provision of telecommunications services (see Chapters 3 and 4). This telecommunications licence may be in the form of a so-called 'class licence' (meaning that no individual application is required), such as the TSL for interactive companies, or it may be in the form of a specific PTO

---

[13] A Consultative Document issued by the DGT, 'Mobile Virtual Network Operators: OFTEL inquiry into what MVNOs could offer consumers', June 1999.
[14] OFTEL Statement on Mobile Virtual Network Operators, October 1999.

licence for cable companies pursuant to s. 56 of the Telecommunications Act 1984 (see Chapter 4).

In relation to active regulatory involvement in broadcasting, s. 2 of the Broadcasting Act 1990 gives the Independent Television Commission ('ITC') the authority and duty to regulate aspects of commercial television in the UK, while s. 6 of the Act *requires* the ITC to do all that it can to ensure the compliance of licensed services with key requirements, including:

(a) that nothing is included in programming that offends against good taste or decency;

(b) that news is presented with due impartiality and accuracy;

(c) that due responsibility is exercised with respect to religious programming; and

(d) the prevention of subliminal broadcasting.

These obligations have caused difficulties for the ITC in seeking to deal with the issues raised by convergence. Additional difficulties arise because the ITC is charged with the implementation of EU law in the area, such as the observance of the quotas regarding European productions imposed as part of the EU Television Without Frontiers regime.[15]

The ITC exercises its authority in two main ways: (i) by the granting of licences for various classes of services, either on a demand basis or competitively where issues such as spectrum scarcity are important (e.g., in 1996 in relation to the digital multiplex licences eventually awarded to ONdigital and S4C);[16] and (ii) by the monitoring of the activities of licensees. This monitoring includes assessing their adherence to the ITC's Codes relating to programming scheduling and content and to the amount and types of permitted advertising. The Codes, adopted by the ITC in compliance with s. 7 of the Act, are the means by which, for example, the ITC polices the so-called post-9 pm 'watershed'. They also impose upon broadcasters the duty, as a licence obligation as well as part of general law, to comply with rules regarding honesty and integrity in advertising.[17]

12.3.2.2 Regulating convergence Convergence has presented perhaps its greatest challenge to the regulation of the broadcasting sector in the UK. Hitherto it had always been assumed that significant, 'fit and proper' (as required by s. 3 of the Broadcasting Act 1990) companies would be licensed by the ITC, who would thereby be able to exercise control over their activities and the activities of advertisers on their channels by the means summarised at 12.3.2.1. This assumption has been thrown into question by technological advances which have made possible convergent or (in broadcasting speak) interactive television services, the basis of uncertain regulatory status.

---

[15] Established by Council Directive 89/552/EC, (1989) OJ L 298/23; as amended by Directive 97/36/EC, (1997) OJ L 202/60.

[16] In 1996 the ITC held a competitive auction for the rights to operate from so-called digital terrestrial 'multiplexes' created by the Broadcasting Act 1996.

[17] The ITC Programme Code and the ITC Code of Advertising Standards and Practice.

It is at an early stage of any analysis that the regulatory issues begin to emerge. What is 'television', and does the ITC have the same authority to regulate the same activities irrespective of the technological means by which they take place? As the following analysis will show, the answers to these simple questions are very far from straightforward.

The ITC is given general authority under s. 2 of the Broadcasting Act 1990 to regulate aspects of commercial television in the UK. Fundamentally it is authorised to regulate 'television programme services'. A television programme service means, amongst other things, a 'television broadcasting service', a 'satellite television service' and a 'licensable programme service'. A 'television broadcasting service' is defined in s. 2(5) and (6) of the 1990 Act as a 'service consisting in the broadcasting of television programmes for general reception in, or in any area in, the UK'. However, it excludes (in s. 2(6)):

> . . . any teletext service or any other service in the case of which the visual images broadcast in the service consist wholly or mainly of non-representational images, that is to say visual images which are neither still pictures nor comprised within frequencies of visual images capable of being seen as moving pictures.

This brings into question the ITC's authority to regulate interactive and convergent services.

(a) The regulation of interactive television as part of a satellite television service   The UK regulation of satellite television was revised under the Satellite Television Services Regulations 1997 (SI 1997 No. 1682). These streamlined the 'old' concepts of 'domestic and non-domestic' satellite services. Now, under s. 43 of the Broadcasting Act 1990, a 'satellite television service' means 'a service which consists in the transmission for general reception of television programmes by satellite' provided, essentially, that the person providing the service is under the jurisdiction of UK regulatory authorities.

The Broadcasting Act 1990 does not define 'television programme'. However, in s. 46, in defining a 'relevant programme' for the purposes of that section, the Act states that a relevant programme means 'a television programme other than one consisting wholly or mainly of non-representational images (within the meaning of section 2(6))'. Accordingly, it seems that the Government had in mind that a television programme *could* consist wholly or mainly of non-representational images, otherwise it would not have been necessary to create this specific exclusion. This leads to the conclusion that it is probably necessary to obtain a satellite television service licence for the transmission of a wide range of material by means of a satellite, including material that might not be regarded as traditional linear television programming, such as WWW-based information.

(b) The regulation of interactive services on cable television   In the UK, companies operating on cable platforms generally have two types of licences.

The first is a 'local delivery services' licence. This is essentially the licence which enables a cable company to operate its delivery system, i.e. the 'pipe' that it provides to the home. The definition of the matters covered by a local delivery service licence is set out in s. 72 of the Broadcasting Act 1990. This section relates to the use of a telecommunications system for the purpose of delivering one or more specified types of services for *simultaneous* reception in two or more dwelling-houses in the UK.

For the purposes of analysing the regulation of the delivery of interactive or convergent services, the key categories of services that would come within the local delivery service licence would be 'television broadcasting services' and 'licensable programme services'. However, s. 2(5) of the Broadcasting Act 1990 (read in conjunction with s. 2(6)) provides that a television broadcasting service does not include any teletext service, or a service consisting wholly or mainly of non-representational images. The effect of this drafting is that it is generally considered that the carriage of teletext on a cable service does not come within the ITC's jurisdiction, at least as regards the cable operator itself.

There is an argument as to whether any Internet service or interactive service would ever be transmitted for 'simultaneous reception in two or more dwelling-houses' within the scope of the licence. It is certainly arguable that each viewer has a unique experience (particularly in relation to the Internet), and therefore that a local delivery service licence is not required.

(c) The relevance of the 'licensable programme service licence' The other key area with regard to the broadcasting of convergent services by means of a cable or other telecommunications system, is the applicability of the licensable programme service licence. Section 46 of the Broadcasting Act 1990 contains the definition of 'licensable programme service'. It is lengthy, but for the purposes of this analysis there are some key elements. The first is that there is a need to have a licensable programme services licence if the information transmitted constitutes 'relevant programmes'. Section 46(5) states that a relevant programme means 'a television programme other than one consisting wholly or mainly of non-representational images'. This means that if the images conveyed by means of the relevant telecommunications system do not consist wholly or mainly of representational images, it is arguable that no licence is necessary. This position has been criticised, because it could have the effect that otherwise licensable material if transmitted at one-eighth screen size instead of full size may fall outside the broadcasting regime (if the rest of the screen consisted of text and background). The result therefore is that it may be possible for providers of combined services, drawing in text, images and sound, to argue that they are not subject to this aspect of regulation.

In addition s. 46(2)(c) provides that a service cannot be a licensable programme service if it is a two-way service, which is defined as

> a service of which it is an essential feature that while visual images or sounds (or both) are being conveyed by the person providing the service

there will or may be sent from each place of reception, by means of the same telecommunications system or (as the case may be) the part of it by which they are conveyed, visual images or sounds (or both) for reception by the person providing the service.

It is arguable that the Internet and the on-line interactive services offered by companies such as Open are inherently two-way services and are therefore outside the scope of the licensable programme services licence.

12.3.2.3   The ITC's response to the regulatory challenges   The preceding analysis is not merely of academic interest. It is an offence to provide a licensable programme service without a licence from the ITC. Licence fees might apply. Operators could be obliged to comply with the regime for content regulation and advertising regulation controlled by the ITC and, just as importantly, at an EU level with the regime established by the Television Without Frontiers Directive[18] regarding the reservation of a majority of broadcasting time to the transmission of European programmes where 'practicable'. These requirements are economically significant.

The ITC is fully conscious of these issues and in 1999 carried out a series of consultations with representatives of the traditional broadcasting industry and those interested parties from 'convergent' companies, in order to consider what the appropriate regulatory environment might be for interactive service providers offering viewers the chance to interact with service providers on a one-to-one basis via their televisions. The process led to a public consultation on the application to interactive services of the ITC's advertising regime on the content and scheduling of advertisements (as set out in its 'Codes').[19]

In its consultation the ITC acknowledged the fundamental sea change that has begun to occur in the broadcasting industry as 'broadcasters' have become 'narrow casters' and individual users are able to receive content by means of unique interaction – as the ITC put it, a movement from 'push' technology to 'pull'. Moreover, the ITC accepted that this process of change would only be accelerated by the introduction of new technologies. For example, the advent of the digital video recorder with a hard drive (such as those marketed under the brand name Tivo) capable of storing up to a year's viewing intelligently by reference to the viewing habits of the owner threatens to throw into confusion traditional concepts of 'scheduling' and the 'watershed', enabling users to order their own television schedules upon demand. The ITC questioned whether in an interactive environment it was possible to impose upon the regulated the obligation to pre-vet advertising in the way that had hitherto applied, given that the viewer's experience would be unique, and proposed a lightening of the regulatory burden by movement towards a 'notify and takedown' (i.e., an *ex-post*) form of advertising regulation.

---

[18] *Supra* n. 15.
[19] 'Interactive Television – the Regulatory Issues', an Independent Television Public Consultation, February 2000. See now ITC 'Guidance to Broadcasters on Interactive Television Services', February 2001.

Nevertheless, the ITC's position and its approach to regulation with a light touch has drawn criticism from some within the industry, not least because of the ITC's continued distinction between 'the Internet' (where the ITC felt that it had no jurisdiction and was conscious of the general agreement at an international level to exercise forbearance in relation to the creation of new laws) and regulated 'interactive services' provided by means of the satellite and cable platforms (where the operator presented a 'walled garden' or selective offering to users). Many have argued that, while recognising the ITC's invidious position in the light of an outdated and confused regulatory regime, the distinction was entirely arbitrary and threatened to undermine a key goal of regulation, namely to establish regulation which is platform neutral and that fixes upon the object and effect of conduct rather than on the means of its actual implementation. The consequence of not establishing such a framework may be that there will be a flight to the jurisdiction that provides the lowest or most convenient level of regulation from which content may be transmitted. In a converged world, local presence for content distribution may become a thing of the past and consumer choice will replace regulatory influence as a filter.

12.3.3   Regulating access to 'gateways'

The issues to be considered in relation to Internet broadcasting are illustrative of the need to refocus existing regulation to deal with technological encroachment upon its efficacy. Convergence also produces other regulatory challenges, however, in the form of new activities from market participants. This is perhaps most apparent in the development of digital television broadcasting and interactive services.

In telecommunications, a key requirement for effective competition is that competing service providers should have access to a unique network termination point, the actual connection to which, at an infrastructure level, will be controlled by a single operator. In digital broadcasting the access point is likely to be an integrated digital receiver/decoder, more commonly known as a 'set-top box'. This box will be purchased (or leased in the case of cable) to enable a subscriber to access the services offered by the network operator and, through him, by other providers of television and interactive services. Access will be provided or restricted by means of an embedded conditional access system (and additional software such as the API discussed at 12.3.4 below).

In order to have perfect neutrality between competing providers of content, in an ideal world it would be envisaged that a set-top box would be capable of receiving a variety of different signals using different conditional access systems (a so-called 'multi-crypt' approach). However, realistically, the entrenched interests of both broadcasters and the owners of the intellectual property rights in the various competing conditional access systems have meant that (although the European common interface is mandated) interoperability has been difficult to achieve.

The result of the above position is that a consumer is required to make an investment when choosing a set-top box/platform for digital television/

interactive television. Given that the consumer may have paid for a set-top box or become familiar with the way in which it works, he or she is likely to be wedded to that technology as a means to receive content. Thus, while the subscriber may want to migrate between competing content providers, the entity that controls access to the set-top box is likely to need to be involved, and as such may have a 'gatekeeper' role.

The possibility of companies emerging as gatekeepers in a converged world has been recognised for some time. In 1995, the European Commission established rules regarding the provision of conditional access services in the Advanced Television Standards Directive (95/47/EC). This Directive, which was implemented in the UK by the Advanced Television Services Regulations 1996 (SI 1996 No. 3151), mandated the provision of conditional access services for digital television on fair, reasonable and non-discriminatory terms. This meant, for example, that a broadcaster that operated its own conditional access services would be prevented from discriminating in favour of its own content either by offering access services at a lower cost, or by refusing to provide services for competing content.

In the UK conditional access services are provided under a class licence, but the regime described above only applies to conditional access services in the context of 'television'. Accordingly, the use of the same technology to regulate, for example, the transmission of software to a set-top box, or Internet connectivity via a set-top box is not covered by the EU Directive. In order to pre-empt the use of technology for these purposes the DTI and OFTEL in the UK acted to modify the regime in the UK to introduce provisions regarding 'access control' services, which essentially mirror those regarding conditional access for broadcasting but do so under the auspices of telecoms regulation. All suppliers of access control services in the UK operate under the class licence for the running of telecommunications systems for the provision of access control services, which was granted by the Secretary of State in August 1999. Access control regulation is also being propagated at the European Union level.

The development of the new UK regime to deal with the potential abuse of this 'gatekeeper' role in the control of access to end-users of digital interactive services has resulted in much debate in the UK. OFTEL, the regulator tasked with enforcing this new regime, published a Statement during 1999 following consultation with the emerging industry and the public, entitled 'Digital Television and Interactive Services – Ensuring access on fair, reasonable and non-discriminatory terms', together with guidelines on the pricing of access control services.[20] Following the familiar hallmarks of telecoms regulation, OFTEL considered and debated the issues of what these 'fair' terms should be which would allow sufficient recovery of investment in the delivery platform built. In addition, OFTEL has had to debate and clarify the boundary between conditional access and access control services – a boundary that is still not always clear to some commentators, or

---

[20] OFTEL guidelines on 'The Pricing of Conditional Access and Access Control Services', issued May 1999.

to those in the industry. A fuller understanding of this regime is likely to develop over time as OFTEL is requested to apply it to the digital interactive television market.

More recently OFTEL consulted on whether Sky Subscribers Services Limited (SSSL) had a dominant position under the terms of its access control class licence. OFTEL then clarified in its draft Decision[21] that it believed that SSSL was dominant in the provision of those 'technical services that enable only authorised digital interactive TV services to be accessed by end-users', and would be for the foreseeable future. The types of services were identified by OFTEL as authentication services, message processing services, access device management services, selection services and subscriber management services. The Decision assumes a particular definition of the interactive services market that is bound to change immeasurably as the fledgling market develops over the next couple of years. Recognition of the speed of change, and indeed of the regulatory challenge, was acknowledged by OFTEL in its announcement of its intention to conduct an early review of the market for access control services.

What of the impending rollout of ADSL technology by BT[22] which has been precipitated by the announcement by OFTEL that it will require BT to unbundle its local loop (the final means of access to the end-user in the telephony network)? The widespread introduction of ADSL modems in the home is likely to have an immense impact on the digital interactive service delivery market, and thereby on access control regulation.

12.3.4   Gateway software

The comments in 12.3.3 above regarding conditional access illustrate that, in a convergent world, the power of so-called technology 'gatekeepers' will be of considerable importance to regulators and market participants alike. Other gateways may arise in relation to different technologies in addition to the conditional access system itself.

In a world in which digital television and personal computers become essentially interchangeable, and both are used as a means to receive and process digital content, two other obvious gate-keeping scenarios emerge. The first is that the owner of the intellectual property rights in the operating system for the reception equipment will exercise its rights so as to prevent or distort competition. In the PC environment we are familiar with operating systems and the almost ubiquitous Windows platform. In the digital television environment the relevant technology is the 'application programming inter-

---

[21] Draft Decision and Statement of reasons on the DGT's intention to determine that SSSL is in a dominant position under the terms of Condition 9 of the Class licence for the running of telecommunications systems for provision of Access Control Services, issued on 31 August 1999, Consultation Document issued by the DGT, April 2000. See now Final Decision, 20 June 2000.
[22] See 'Access to Bandwidth: Delivering Competition for the Information Age', OFTEL Statement, November 1999. See also 'Open Access: Delivering Effective Competition in Communications Markets', OFTEL Statement, April 2001.

face' (API) which is essentially the relevant part of the operating system of a set-top box which processes interactive content, for example, the operation of applets or pay per use software downloaded by means of the broadcasting system.

Concern over the ability of the operator of a broadcast system to use access to the API to provide a competitive advantage has meant that its licensing has been brought within the remit of the legislation regarding conditional access discussed at 12.3.3 above and, in the UK, within the remit of the Advanced Television Services Regulations 1996. However, in practical terms, the analogy with computer operating systems suggests that, in fact, an industry solution to potential problems associated with APIs may be that open standards become widely accepted. In a scenario where, for example, Java is an open standard for delivery of certain types of interactive content to PCs, it may be harder for the operators of broadcast platforms to be restrictive regarding access to their own operating systems if they wish to compete effectively as a delivery mechanism for certain types of digital content.

Lastly, in relation to gateway technologies, both Internet enabled PCs and digital set-top boxes enable users to locate attractive content. In the digital broadcasting area viewers are able to appraise and view content by means of an on-screen-electronic index known as an electronic programming guide (EPG). An EPG provides viewers with information as to programme start times, dates and content. Basic EPGs operate on the basis of a 'now and next' principle; more sophisticated versions (such as that operated by BSkyB) enable viewers to analyse forthcoming programming across more than one hundred channels for a week in advance. In the Internet sector the device that is broadly analogous to the EPG is a browser. The opportunities provided to the party controlling the EPG and a party bundling an Internet browser are broadly, but not completely, similar. The advantage given to the operator of an EPG is the ability to make preferred programming more enticing by means of the provision either of more, or of more interesting information regarding the programming or the placement of the programming in an advantageous position on the EPG (for example the 'start-up' page).

In an interesting example of the way in which convergence has driven regulators of theoretically separate industries together, in the UK, both the ITC and OFTEL have produced Guidelines and Codes of Conduct regarding the way in which an operator of a broadcast system should run its EPG.[23] These Codes provide, for example, that the operator should allocate space on an EPG without regard to the originator of the programming concerned.

12.3.5 Competition law issues in converging industries

At the present time there have been three leading competition cases regarding convergence in the context of broadcasting with applicability to the United Kingdom.

---

[23] See ITC Code of Conduct on Electronic Programme Guides (June 1997) and OFTEL Guidelines on the Regulation of Conditional Access for Digital Television Services (March 1997).

The first key competition case[24] concerned the attempt by three German companies – Bertelsmann AG, Deutsch Telekom and a subsidiary of the Kirch Group – to create a joint venture called MSG Media Service GmbH. The role it was intended that MSG would play was the provision of administrative services in relation to pay television (and other interactive services). The European Commission believed that the joint venture would affect the markets for technical and administrative services for pay TV and other TV services financed by means of subscription in Germany.

What gave the Commission particular cause for concern was that the proposed joint venture involved not only the owners of rights in relation to television programming, but also the former PTO which owned both a monopoly for voice telephony services (at the time) and nearly all of the television cable networks in Germany. The Commission's worry was that the market positions of the companies were so strong that the joint venture entity would obtain a dominant position in the German pay TV market and would foreclose the development of a truly competitive market for the delivery of pay services. This might potentially thwart efforts to liberalise provision of cable television services and infrastructure. Accordingly, the Commission acted to block the proposed venture.

The second leading case[25] concerned the intentions of an entity called Nordic Satellite Distribution (NSD) to transmit satellite TV programmes to cable TV operators and direct to home (DTH) households receiving satellite TV by means of their own dish in Scandinavia.

Again, concerns were raised given the status of the three parent companies involved in the venture. Norwegian Telecoms was at the time the main cable TV operator in Norway with connections to approximately 30 per cent of cable homes. In addition it controlled the satellite capacity on one of two allocated Nordic satellites and had interests in the pay TV distribution sector. TeleDanmark was the largest cable TV operator in Denmark with connections to approximately 50 per cent of homes passed. Lastly, Kinnevik (together with TeleDanmark) controlled much of the satellite capacity on the other Nordic satellite position and, as a media conglomerate, had interests in IV programming print publishing as well as packaging and telecommunications. Kinnevik was the premier provider of Nordic TV programming and the largest pay TV distributor in the Nordic countries, as well as having substantial cable TV interests in Sweden.

The European Commission concluded that the creation of NSD as a joint venture between the companies would have led to the existence of a dominant position in three distinct markets: (i) the market for the provision of satellite TV capacity to the Nordic region; (ii) the market for paid television by means of cable TV networks in Denmark (since the dominance of TeleDanmark would be reinforced); (iii) and the market for the distribution of satellite pay TV and other pay television services to DTH households.

One of the key concerns for the Commission was that the joint venture would be vertically integrated and, therefore, have the potential to exercise

---

[24] Decision 94/922, (1999) OJ L 364/1.
[25] Decision 96/177, (1996) OJ L 53/20.

dominance both at the stage of access to consumers by means of DTH or cable television and in relation to the provision of key 'upstream' elements such as satellite transponder capacity and programming.

On 12 November 1999, the Secretary of State for Trade and Industry asked the Competition Commission to investigate the proposed acquisition by ntl Incorporated (ntl) of Cable & Wireless Communications plc. The Competition Commission reported on its findings on 22 March 2000 and concluded that the merger was unlikely to operate against the public interest.[26] The Competition Commission's investigation is nevertheless of interest in examining the development of the market for convergent services in the UK. While the analysis of the merger turned upon the respective market power of the merged organisation in the market for wholesale pay television – and in particular in relation to the market power of British Sky Broadcasting Limited – the Commission was also required to look at the effects on competition of the coming together of two companies with interests in pay television, telephony and the nascent industry of digital interactive television services, and at the issue of whether the fact that the cable industry is 'closed' (in the sense that third parties cannot require access to unbundled capacity over the networks) was likely to be restrictive of the development of competitive services to those offered by the merged company.

12.4   ESTABLISHING A REGULATORY ROADMAP

12.4.1   Regulating convergence in the UK

The year 1998 saw a concerted effort by regulators and Parliament in the UK to draw some conclusions as to the effects of convergence upon the existing regulatory framework for, in particular, telecommunications and broadcasting in the United Kingdom. The object of the consultations was to take appropriate decisions regarding regulatory policy in order to facilitate the emergence of the most dynamic and competitive market possible, while maintaining social goals such as universal service.

In the period leading up to the publication of its Fourth Report,[27] in May 1998, the House of Commons Select Committee on Culture, Media and Sport held detailed hearings on the process of convergence and debated its implications for the UK economy. Amongst other regulators, OFTEL submitted detailed representations to the Select Committee. In particular OFTEL's Second Submission to the Select Committee, 'Beyond the Telephone the Television and the PC III', dated March 1998, set out its views regarding a future regulatory structure. The Submission, which was extremely prescriptive, was greeted by many as a veiled attempt by OFTEL to obtain competence in the overlapping aspects of a convergent economy.

OFTEL envisaged that the Telecommunications Act 1994 and much of the Broadcasting Acts 1990 and 1996 would be replaced with new primary

---

[26] Competition Commission Report, Cm 4666, 22 March 2000.
[27] Fourth Report of the Culture, Media and Sport Select Committee inquiry into the Audiovisual Communications and the Regulation of Broadcasting, May 1998.

legislation intended to regulate the 'electronic communications' industry. In particular, it referred to the coming into existence of what it called an 'open state'. In OFTEL's opinion the open state would be a converged electronic communications environment in which many of the traditional restrictions giving rise to existing regulatory structure had changed. In particular OFTEL foresaw the erosion of distribution capacity scarcity and the circumstances in which content suppliers would be able to supply services to a variety of customers on a commercial basis by means of different access control systems.

OFTEL's regulatory approach was intended to deal with the situation in which capacity scarcity (which had been the basis for much of existing broadcasting regulation) had been swept away and replaced by competition between content suppliers, who were able in theory to access a variety of consumers by means of alternative networks but who might be subject to restrictions in practice because of the diversity of access control systems operated by the network providers with which they would have to contend.

OFTEL called for a root-and-branch change to the regulatory structure in the UK, stating that 'many established rules in broadcasting and telecommunications regulation will no longer be required and many will, in any case, be ineffective'. Referring to the need for simplification and clarity, and to avoid regulatory overlap, OFTEL advocated that 'additional patching and mending will not deliver a sensible regulatory structure and nor is [it] likely to actually deliver the objectives of regulations . . . a fundamental overhaul of the existing rules and regulatory institutions is necessary to ensure that UK plc maintains, and builds on, its comparative competitive advantage in the sector'. It proposed that the linchpin of economic regulations should be general competition law (in the form of the new UK competition regime). In addition, general consumer protection policies should apply and be supplemented with special rules defined in electronic communications legislation.

In relation to content regulation, OFTEL distinguished between positive and negative content regulation, i.e. the difference between a positive obligation upon a broadcaster (or other supplier of content) to include programming of particular types and a negative obligation not to include programming that is regarded as undesirable (for example, pornography).

Concerning negative content obligations, OFTEL foresaw the development of a voluntary system of content classification which, it anticipated, would generally be adopted by suppliers of content. OFTEL recognised that the voluntary standards would not be universally accepted, but suggested that systems might develop to block all content that was not classified. In relation to positive obligations, it believed that the only way to secure the future of public service broadcasting would be by means of Government funding, with a straight relationship between the sums provided by the Government and the development of appropriate content.

In terms of the over-arcing regulatory structure, OFTEL advocated the development of two principal regulators. These would be a regulator having control over contents/culture (to be designated 'the Electronic Communications Standards Authority') and another regulator who would have primary responsibility for ensuring that economic and social objectives were met, i.e.

that customers were offered competitive supplies of services and that all were able to access appropriate services. The latter regulator ('the Electronic Communications Commission') would exercise many of the powers currently exercised by OFTEL and the ITC.

Not surprisingly, the Radio Authority and the ITC opposed OFTEL's structure, arguing that it was impossible to distinguish between decisions regarding content regulation and decisions regarding wider issues of social policy and economic considerations.

The Select Committee was charged with making recommendations on the way forward. Its report, entitled 'The Multi-Media Revolution',[28] argued that 'we are living through a global revolution which links almost instantaneously any place on the planet with any other place . . . there just seems to be almost no limit to it'. It noted that there was considerable overlap and confusion between the various statutory and regulatory bodies responsible for regulating aspects of the economy involved in convergence. There were approximately 14 different statutory and self-regulating bodies responsible for media and communications. The Select Committee quoted Dr Kim Howells, on the subject of Government policy in the area and, in particular, inter-government departmental cooperation, as saying: '. . . it would be very nice if we had total confidence that there was a completely organised interface between every Department and we were all singing from the same hymn sheet'.

The Select Committee advocated an even more radical solution to the problems of regulation than that suggested by OFTEL. It proposed the creation of a single over-arcing communications regulator, to be termed the 'Communications Regulation Commission'. This body would have overall responsibility for statutory regulation of broadcasting, telecommunications and the communications infrastructure.

The Select Committee suggested that the Communications Regulation Commission should have as its principal duty the regulation of access to communications platforms (including all gateway issues). However, the new body should also be responsible for encouragement of self-regulatory initiatives regarding content and for broadcast content regulation.

The Government published its initial thoughts on the issues related to convergence in a Green Paper presented to Parliament by the President of the Board of Trade and the Secretary of State for Culture, Media and Sport in July 1998. The Green Paper, entitled 'Regulating Communications: Approaching Convergence in the Information Age', was considerably more conservative than the thoughts of the Select Committee. It noted that the debate regarding convergence had polarised between two distinct visions. One group of interested parties argued that convergence was an immediate concern and that, accordingly, a root-and-branch approach was required with the acceptance of radically new regulatory structures. The other camp argued that the *status quo* was sufficient because the real effects of convergence had not yet been felt.

---

[28] Cm 4020, May 1998.

Broadly speaking, the tone of the Green Paper was to push the Government into the second of these camps. The Government argued that while, from the perspective of providers, convergence was a reality, at the customer end convergence had yet to make a real impact (particularly in relation to domestic use of televisions and PCs). The Government concluded, accordingly:

> . . . it seems likely that a spectrum of distinct elements of provision, reflecting established patterns of consumption, will persist for some considerable time to come. At one end of this spectrum there is likely to be a segment that looks much like the universal broadcast television as consumers know it today. At the other there is likely to be a segment with many of the characteristics of the Internet.

The Government argued that 'rather than making a false choice between tearing up our regulatory structures or sticking to the *status quo*, we will follow an evolutionary path'. This evolutionary path suggested placing considerable emphasis on the role of competition law in bringing a non-platform specific, non-industry specific approach to the regulation of common problems in the converging sector. In addition, the Government proposed progressively to lift restrictions on the broadcasting activities of telecommunications companies.

The Government's view was that there was a considerable risk that the UK would move too rapidly to develop a system of regulation around possibly starry-eyed predictions of what the digital world would be like, only to find that the regime that had been created was inappropriate and obsolete almost before it began. However, the Government's faith in the efficacy of existing approaches clashed strongly with the strength of feeling expressed by many before the Select Committee (and the Select Committee itself). The Government also announced that the principal regulators would cooperate more closely, presumably in an atmosphere of brotherly endeavour, which seemed at the time over-optimistic given the vested self-interest of the various regulatory bodies in the choice of direction for regulation.

The Green Paper was intended to form the basis for further consideration of the issues rather than a statement of answers in itself. It posed a series of fundamental questions for consultation, asking, for example, what the impact of current and future regulatory systems might be on the development of new services and the convergent industries generally.

Among the responses to the Green Paper was that of OFTEL[29] which included a reiteration of the view that it was essential that the UK had clear sight of the issues surrounding convergence in order to build on the advantages of the UK's liberalised telecommunications market and creative media sector. Clarity in such a fast-moving market was essential, and an overly prescriptive approach to regulation was inappropriate. A key issue was access.

---

[29] OFTEL, *Response to the UK Green Paper – Regulating Communications: approaching convergence in the information age*, January 1999.

On the supply side, there was the issue of access by service providers to networks and technical information; and at the other end, there was the issue of access by consumers to information and services. The regulatory framework would need to take account of the balance between the two, and inevitably the trade-offs. The regime should reflect the importance of competition, secure the independence of the regulator(s), promote consistency and coherence, ensure transparency and accountability, and rely primarily on general horizontal (competition and consumer protection) laws rather than sectoral rules, where possible. Of the last, OFTEL still recognised the need for some sector-specific rules dealing with issues such as universal service, content and consumer protection. There would also still remain a need for some sectoral rules relating to competition to deal with bottlenecks, interconnection and network externalities such as interoperability. Content regulation, OFTEL believed, should be based on self-regulatory classification of browsable or user-selected content, with reference to content codes drawn up by self-regulatory bodies in consultation with the relevant statutory authority.

The Government issued a Paper setting out the results of the consultation on the convergence Green Paper in 1999.[30] The Government received over 70 written representations from consumer organisations, industry regulators, businesses and others, supporting in general an evolutionary approach to developing regulation. The Paper reinforced the Government's policy aims and its preliminary view of the matter, that convergence was a present reality in the way services were provided to the public but that there was still considerable uncertainty about the speed at which services would be adopted by the public and/or replace or supplement established services. The growth of digital TV, the Internet in the home and as a delivery mechanism for television services, and third generation mobile telephony were all recognised as key drivers of the take-up of new interactive services.

Most respondents saw the existing regulatory structures, the Government said, as sufficiently flexible for the current environment, although an improvement in regulatory practice and particularly cooperation between regulators was still required. Most respondents argued, however, that the regime would require modification as convergence accelerated. Issues such as gateway control, selection services, privacy and data protection were just some of those which could require sector-specific regulation. Self-regulation of content was supported as a general ideal, although there was still much support for the statutory regulation of broadcast, with it being graduated according to the control a viewer exercised over a service.

The Paper also stated that the most widely supported model for a particular regulatory structure was a single content and a single economic regulator, either in one organisation or under an umbrella organisation.

The majority view of respondents, said the Government, was that comprehensive change would not be required for a few years, although it was vital to monitor developments closely. It was therefore surprising that on 3

---

[30] 'Regulating Communications – The Way Ahead: Results of the Consultation or the Convergence Green Paper', DTI and DCMS Statement.

February 2000, the DTI and Department of Culture, Media and Sport[31] announced their intention to publish a White Paper later in 2000 setting out the UK Government's proposals for reform of the framework of communications legislation. The White Paper would be broad in scope, dealing with both infrastructure and content issues, and taking into account the responses to the earlier consultation and the EU 1999 Review of Communications. It would examine objectives, principles and a system for the economic regulation of communications services crossing not only the boundaries of telecommunications and broadcasting, but also touching on the issues surrounding cross-media ownership.

The Government published its White Paper[32] in December 2000, proposing a single regulatory body for the communications and media industries – the Office of Communications (OFCOM) – which would cover telecoms, television and radio. OFCOM would exercise the previous regulators' powers under the Competition Act, and have additional sector-specific powers to promote competition in the consumer interest, covering essential issues such as consumer protection, access and interconnection in relation to companies having SMP. These powers would apply to EPGs and similar new access systems, and would cover the management of radio spectrum. In effect OFCOM would take over the powers of the Broadcasting Standards Commission, ITC, OFTEL, the Radio Authority and the Radiocommunications Agency, including their licensing functions. New universal obligations would include the promotion of widespread access to higher bandwidth services and achieving universal access to the Internet by 2005.

The intention is also to rationalise the system of regulation of broadcasting so that it is coherent across all broadcasters. A new three-tiered structure is proposed, with the basic tier supporting standards across all services and with further tiers applicable to public service broadcasters principally regulated through OFCOM, but with more qualitative elements self-regulated against legal duties but with OFCOM having backstop powers. New rules would be introduced on media ownership (but which do not appear to address cross-media and cross-media/communications ownership).

OFCOM would be a public corporation responsible for economic and content regulation in the communications sector, reporting to two different government departments.

12.4.2   Regulating convergence within the European Union

In December 1997, the European Commission published a Green Paper[33] on convergence, prompted by the obvious overlap in practice of sectors such as telecommunications and broadcasting. In the Commission's opinion, techno-

---

[31] See DTI's summary of the UK Response to the European Commission's 1999 Communications review, 'Towards a New Framework for Electronic Communications Infrastructure and Services: The 1999 Communications Review'.

[32] *A New Future for Communications*, Cm 5010 (London, HMSO, 2000).

[33] Green Paper, 'On convergence of the telecommunications, media and information technology sectors and the implications for regulation' COM (97) 623, 3 December 1997.

logical advancement had resulted in traditional regulatory regimes losing effectiveness in terms of application.

The Green Paper was written, as the Commission put it, as a step on the way to securing the benefits of convergence for European social and economic development:

> . . . the changes described in this Green Paper have the potential to improve substantially the quality of life for Europe's citizens; to integrate Europe's regions better into the heart of the European economy, and to make businesses more effective and competitive on global and national markets.

The Commission described its goal as to establish a wider framework that recognised the need for regulation of the telecommunications and broadcasting sectors in the context of convergence, without creating an environment that would hold back the progress of change.

The first step in developing this framework was a five-month public consultation period followed by three hearings in March–April 1998, which allowed for broad participation and debate, providing a forum for individuals and businesses alike to input their views.

12.4.2.1 The Commission's options   In its Green Paper the European Commission set out five principles for comment as part of the developing debate on a proposed regulatory framework:

(a) regulation should be limited to what is strictly necessary to achieve clearly identified objectives;

(b) future regulatory approaches should respond to the needs of users;

(c) regulatory decisions should be guided by a need for a clear and predictable framework;

(d) regulation should have the object of ensuring full participation in a converged environment;

(e) that independent and effective regulators will be central to a converging environment.

Based on the above principles, three broad regulatory options were put forward for consideration:

(a) *Build on current structures*   This approach would leave current vertical regulatory models in place, and normal principles of interpretation would be applied on a case-by-case basis to resolve questions of where particular activities might fall. In theory the pace of change would be dictated by the speed of innovation and the effectiveness of competition; the regulatory framework would adapt in response to market forces thereby avoiding the need for further deregulation/regulation. This in turn would minimise the need for short-term change and might provide regulatory certainty while avoiding creating unnecessary internal barriers. Coordination at a European level would be necessary to avoid creating significant new barriers between Member States thereby slowing the transition to the Information Society. One negative aspect of the approach was that it might not address certain anomalies (for example, in the treatment of 'broadcasting') that deter investment.

(b) *Develop a separate regulatory model for new activities, to co-exist with telecommunications and broadcasting regulation* Under this model, Member States would establish new services and activities alongside existing regulatory models for telecommunications and broadcasting. The principal difficulty was foreseen as determining boundaries between what may be part of a lightly regulated new service world and what would remain subject to traditional regulation.

(c) *Progressively introduce a new regulatory model to cover the whole range of existing and new services* This would require the gradual adaptation of existing frameworks to promote flexibility, remove inconsistencies, avoid intra- and cross-sector discrimination and to achieve public interest object-ives. Time for migration to a new regime would clearly be required.

12.4.2.2 Responses to the Green Paper In total, 274 parties responded to the five-month public consultation carried out by the European Commission. Initial analysis of the three hearings held in March–April 1998 and the written comments received revealed common themes and concerns. The Commis-sion, in its Working Document of July 1998,[34] summarised the comments it received under the following four headings:

(a) *The nature and pace of convergence* There was felt to be agreement on the reality of technological convergence, but different views emerged as to the speed and scope of its impact on markets and services. Most commentators preferred an evolutionary approach, and many of those expressed a prefer-ence for the first option in the Green Paper, of building on existing structures. There was general recognition of the continuing role of sector-specific rules to assist in securing certain general interest objectives (in particular within the audio-visual sector), even if those rules or the way they were applied might need to be modified to take account of the impact of new technology. Such sector-specific rules would co-exist both with the application of competition rules and with increasing reliance on industry self-regulation.

(b) *The economic and social impact of convergence* Comments on the impact of convergence on growth and employment tended to reflect optimism about the benefits to the broad economy of many aspects of convergence, despite misgiving about the short-term effects of rationalisation and new technologies. Electronic commerce was seen as a positive factor for economic growth. Convergence was perceived as offering both opportunities and risks for the less developed regions within the Union. In addition, the comments indicated the expectation that markets would remain fragmented along

---

[34] Working Document of the Commission – Summary of the Results of the Public Consultation on the Green Paper on Convergence (Sec (98)1204).

national and regional lines for cultural and linguistic reasons, but also because of the geographical scope of certain aspects of the business.

(c) *Barriers to convergence* Generally, many of the issues raised in the Green Paper were perceived as potential barriers. A majority of respondents focused on regulatory uncertainty, availability of content, IPR (intellectual property rights) protection, consumer protection, access issues, pricing, radio spectrum and the manner in which public interest objectives could be achieved. Two additional barriers were identified: the need to overcome 'technophobia', by developing user-friendly access to new services; and the need to avoid new fiscal barriers in the form of new taxes on information or services.

(d) *The future approach to regulation* Most responses agreed with the assertion in the Green Paper that convergence does not question the objectives underpinning sector-specific regulation, but may call for a review of the manner in which the objectives are achieved. There was general agreement that future regulation should be technology and platform-neutral, and that existing rules would need to be adjusted where this was not the case.

There was also a large measure of agreement on the need to ensure a consistent approach to the way in which networks and transmission services were treated, leading many to support a move away from current vertical regulatory divisions to a more horizontal approach. This would ensure a consistent approach to infrastructure, and at the same time allow rules governing content provision to continue to reflect the specific nature of the services concerned. In addition, there was general agreement on the fact that all sectors affected by convergence require a clear, transparent framework to facilitate investment decisions, and on the fact that there was a need to avoid inconsistent regulatory treatment of essentially similar services.

The European Commission believed there was a need for further debate on three issues that were open for response until 3 November 1998:

(a) access to networks and digital gateways in a converging environment;
(b) creating the framework for investment, innovation and encouraging European content production, distribution and availability; and
(c) ensuring a balanced approach to regulation.

12.4.2.3 Results of the second stage of consultation The European Commission received further responses from 80 organisations to the second stage of its consultation process on the Green Paper up until November 1998. The responses were incorporated by the Commission into its Communication to the European Parliament, the Council, the Economic and Social Committee and the Committee of the Regions on the Results of the Public Consultation on the Green Paper.[35]

The Communication is of interest principally for the so-called 'key messages' that it said had come out of the consultation process (and as we will see

---

[35] COM (1999) 108 EN Fin.

below, the Council's reaction to these). The Commission identified a series of principles as arising from the consultation, some of the most relevant being:

(a) '[s]eparation of transport and content regulation with recognition of the links between them for possible competition problems. This implies a more horizontal approach to regulation with homogenous treatment of all transport network infrastructure and associated services irrespective of the types of content carried';

(b) the need for application of an appropriate regulatory regime to new services, recognising the uncertainties of the marketplace and the need for the large initial investments involved in their launch, while at the same time maintaining adequate consumer safeguards;

(c) the need for a balanced solution to be applied to the integration of public service broadcasting to enable public service broadcasters to innovate while maintaining the distinction between public service and competitive broadcasting;

(d) the need for 'effective application of the competition rules; an increased reliance on those rules, accompanied by gradual phasing-out of sector-specific regulation as the market becomes more competitive'.

It will already be obvious from the above that the European Commission has the unenviable task of seeking to find a middle way between the demands of industry for light touch regulation and the social goals of the politicians, with concerns for the maintenance of plurality in media (and especially linguistic mix) and of public service broadcasting. The Commission identified its objectives as being to introduce reform in relation to the regulation of infrastructure and associated services as part of the more general 1999 Review of the communications sector, and to deal with content issues by adjustments to existing legislation or the introduction of new measures at an appropriate time.

The Commission's Conclusions were received by the Council of Ministers and referred to in the Council's Conclusions of 27 September 1999 concerning the results of the public consultation on the Convergence Green Paper.[36] Interestingly, the Council elected to emphasise still further the societal goals of broadcasting policy, taking note 'that a general message with regard to content was the recognition that actions aimed at promoting premium European content could play an important role' and stressing that, in addition to technical and economic aspects, social, cultural and democratic aspects are of great importance for the development of the Information Society, although it did also state that 'self-regulation could usefully complement regulation and contribute to the achievement of the right balance between facilitating the development of open and competitive markets and securing public interest objectives'.

---

[36] (1999) OJ C 283/1.

12.4.2.4   Other developments since the consultation   Two other policy statements from the European Commission are worth mentioning. The first is the Communication from the Commission to the Council, the European Parliament, the Economic and Social Committee and the Committee for the Regions, 'Principles and Guidelines for the Community's Audiovisual Policy in the Digital Age'.[37] This Communication is concerned with the terms on which development will take place and emphasises that separate approaches will be applied to the regulation of transmission infrastructure and content: '. . . services providing audiovisual content should be regulated according to their nature and not according to their means of delivery'. Familiar themes emerge in relation to the goals and strategies for action – regulation should 'be technology neutral' and 'the minimum necessary to meet policy objectives' – with the Commission also suggesting that both a responsiveness of regulation to the degree of viewer choice and control and a greater degree of self-regulation may be appropriate.

The second major policy initiative of significance since the end of the Consultation process was the Communication from the Commission to the Council of 10 November 1999, 'Towards a new framework for electronic communications infrastructure and associated services'. This Communication in fact stems from the results of the so-called '1999 Review', the widespread analysis of the status of regulation of communications in the European Union and policy options for the future. The Communication acknowledges that the process of liberalisation of communications is now over, although compliance issues remain. What is now required is a simplification of the regulatory regime, with an acknowledgement that 'competition law will become increasingly important and replace much of the sectoral regulation once competition becomes established in the market'.

This simplification will be accomplished by reducing the current 20 plus Directives in the area into just five, the process beginning with the introduction of a new 'Framework Directive' which will enshrine consumer rights and establish the general principles by which markets will be governed by NRAs. This Directive will be followed by others aimed at clarifying the regulatory environment in the following four areas:

(a)   authorisation and licensing (including in relation to radio spectrum);
(b)   universal service (i.e., the rights that all should have to basic services and corresponding obligations for providers);
(c)   access to networks and interconnection between operators; and
(d)   data protection and privacy.

The new regime will apply to the use of communications infrastructure irrespective of the underlying networks. Thus communications activities will be regulated in a like manner whether provided by means of a cable TV network, mobile network or fixed telephony.

---

[37] COM (1999) 657 final.

12.5 CONCLUSION

As the preceding sections demonstrate vividly, although progress has been made, considerable debate has yet to take place before a coherent regulatory framework evolves (either at the domestic or at the European Union level) that deals with all of the regulatory challenges presented by convergence. To no little extent this is because fundamental solutions will involve a redistribution of responsibilities between numerous regulators and interested parties. While this is broadly feasible at a domestic level, it has to be questioned whether a sufficient political will exists at the European Union level, where vested interests span not only the interests of the individual Member States, but also those of their own subordinate regulators and of the European Parliament and the individual Directorates of the European Commission itself.

In the absence of political will, and bearing in mind the very valid points made by the UK Government in its Green Paper regarding the state of realisation of the so-called Information Society at the present time, it is to be expected that much of the brunt of the need to exercise regulatory control will be borne by existing and developing competition regimes. Indeed, it would seem that we may have passed the high-water mark in relation to sector-specific regulation for the converging industries, with the emphasis turning towards competition law and, in relation to content issues, towards technology facilitated self-regulation.

Competition law has several merits in that it is not technology or industry specific. Moreover, it does not, necessarily, forbid certain types of conduct automatically but looks, instead, at the practical economic effect of the behaviour of enterprises. However, advocates of this approach may overlook some of the inherent problems with an *ex-post* regulatory regime. Competition law, for example, cannot deal with remaining areas of spectrum rationing and it cannot regulate the externalities applying to the convergent industries or the actual and probable overlaps between regulators foreseen by OFTEL as an 'unsatisfactory patchwork'.

In the short to medium term, competition law compliance is likely to be key to businesses seeking to grasp convergence opportunities, as is the need to tread carefully between adjacent or overlapping regulatory regimes. There are two other key issues, though, that are likely to be of importance to business and individual participants in the converged environment. The first of these additional concerns is likely to be the issue of 'ownership' of the individual subscriber. The previous sections of this chapter have discussed the importance of control of 'gateways'. In addition, access to subscriber information as a by-product of gateway control is likely to become more important. As 'push technologies' become more accepted and sophisticated profiling systems enable businesses to target products and services that they feel may be of interest to individuals, so the rights of individuals to personal privacy and control over their personal data may become of greater regulatory significance. This is likely to make data ownership and data protection compliance of greater importance to companies in the converging industries.

Lastly, there is an overwhelming need for domestic and European regulators to develop an approach to the regulation of the Internet that reflects the fact that it is not an entirely separate phenomenon that supervenes upon existing activities and regulatory regimes, but rather that it is a subset of an increasingly integrated communications environment. For fear of 'killing the goose that laid the golden egg', policy makers are adopting the laudable objective of 'no Internet-specific regulation'; but the risk remains that this will be carried to extremes whereby similar activities over the Internet fall to be treated in the same way as if they were carried out over a telecommunications network or a cable network. Regulation of convergent activities demands flexibility and responsiveness, but above all an approach by which like activities are regulated in a like manner without regard to the technologies involved.[38]

---

[38] The authors acknowledge and are grateful for the invaluable assistance and contribution of Sophie Jackson and Katia Kluglia in the analysis and drafting of this chapter.

CHAPTER THIRTEEN

Lessons from Asia and the Pacific

Lisa Suits[1]

13.1 INTRODUCTION

There is great diversity in the current state of this sector with respect to its regulations, technical and economic development, political institutions, the state of user-driven applications such as Internet and e-commerce, etc. across all of Asia and the Pacific region. Geographic categorisation merely by what one might think of as 'Asia', or Asia/Pacific, is a poor proxy for the range of circumstances to be found. In fact, there is an argument that the area the 'West' calls Asia and the Pacific has less in common among its constituent countries and peoples than have the countries and peoples of Western Europe.

To shed a better light on the vastness and complexity of trying to describe 'Asia and the Pacific', it might be useful to turn briefly to Huntington, who aggregates the peoples of the world not in terms of political and ethnic groupings, but in terms of civilisations. He dedicates quite a bit of his book, which concerns the future of politics as a clash among civilisations, to weighing and discussing various definitions of a civilisation. Perhaps the simplest way to think about a civilisation for our purposes is as 'the biggest "we" within which we feel culturally at home, as distinguished from all the other "thems" out there'.[2] In this controversial work, Huntington divides the

---

[1] The author is Vice President, Public Policy at Cable & Wireless IDC Inc., Tokyo, Japan. The facts and opinions expressed herein are solely the work of the author and do not represent the views of Cable & Wireless IDC Inc.

[2] Huntington, Samuel, P., *The Clash of Civilizations and the Remaking of World Order* (New York, Simon and Schuster, 1996), at 43.

modern world into eight major civilisations, five of which are located either exclusively, or predominantly, in the Asia and Pacific area. The five are the Sinic, Islamic, Hindu, Buddhist, and Japanese civilisations.[3] These are groups of people who have almost nothing in common with members of another group. Any examination of Asia and the Pacific region should be mindful of these distinctions.

These distinctions are vividly present with respect to telecommunications around the Asia Pacific region. (See Tables 13.1 and 13.2 below.) This chapter will address current themes and topics in telecommunications law and regulation, drawing on country examples to illustrate different approaches and policy initiatives. These approaches are conditioned by the relative state of economic development, national priorities and past experiences with foreign powers. The Asia Pacific area is taking up the emergent technologies of the Internet and e-commerce quite rapidly despite, in most cases, significant challenges. Some hurdles are appearing on the horizon for Asia's ability to capitalise to the full extent on these technologies for their economies.

Table 13.1 Asia Pacific Basic Economic Indicators, 1996

Country	*Population in millions*	*GNP US$ billions*	*Avg. annual growth % 1995–96*	*GNP per capita US$ 1996*
Australia	18	387.8	4.0	20,090
Bangladesh	122	31.2	5.5	260
China	1,215	906.1	10.0	750
Hong Kong, China	6	153.3	4.7	24,290
India	945	357.8	6.9	380
Indonesia	197	213.4	7.5	1,080
Japan	126	5,149.2	3.9	40,940
Korea, South	46	483.1	6.9	10,610
Malaysia	21	89.8	8.3	4,370
Nepal	22	4.7	4.6	210
New Zealand	4	57.1	0.6	15,720
Philippines	72	83.3	6.9	1,160
Singapore	3	93.0	7.6	30,550
Thailand	60	177.5	5.4	2,960

Source: The World Bank, *World Development Indicators, 1998*, The International Bank of Reconstruction and Development, Washington, DC (1998), at 12–14.

---

[3] For completeness, the other three civilisations are Western, Latin America, and Orthodox. Huntingdon sides with other scholars in not ascribing a separate civilisation to Africa. See *op. cit.* n. 2, at 47.

Table 13.2   Asia Pacific Telecommunications Indicators, 1996

Country	Telephones per hundred	Waiting list '000s	Waiting time in years
Australia	51.9	0.0	0.0
Bangladesh	0.3	155.2	6.6
China	4.5	812.0	0.1
Hong Kong, China	54.7	0.0	0.0
India	1.5	2,277.0	1.0
Indonesia	2.1	117.5	0.2
Japan	48.9	0.0	0.0
Korea, South	43.0	0.0	0.0
Malaysia	18.3	160.0	0.4
Nepal	0.5	136.2	10+
New Zealand	49.9	0.0	0.0
Philippines	2.5	900.2	2.9
Singapore	51.3	0.2	0.0
Thailand	0.7	821.6	1.2

Source: The World Bank, *World Development Indicators, 1998*, The International Bank for Reconstruction and Development, Washington, DC (1998), at 290–2.

13.2 TELECOMMUNICATIONS DEVELOPMENT AND NATIONAL INTEREST

Despite the rapid changes in the telecommunications sector, and the near obsessive attention we focus on it today, telecommunications was not always the national development priority it is now. It was not always a tenet of economic development that a modern telecommunications network was a key input to overall national economic strength. After World War II, many countries in Asia and the Pacific dedicated national policy attention and resources to rebuilding or improving industrial capacity, and recovering basic public services. As there was no Marshall Plan for Asia and its environs, this recovery effort was necessarily slower and more protracted than in Western Europe. In the late 1970s and early 1980s, however, the 'Asian Tigers' of Taiwan, Japan, South Korea, Hong Kong and Singapore made economic headlines for world-class quality and attendant cost competitiveness in heavy as well as light manufacturing. The focus by the tigers on industries such as shipbuilding, auto manufacturing, and steel, as well as lighter industrial areas such as textiles, tended to configure the national economic structure on securing raw material and semi-finished inputs and not 'invisibles' such as telecommunications. Even the multilateral development banks active in the region, namely the World Bank and the Asian Development Bank, did not historically (nor do currently) put special emphasis on telecommunications infrastructure development in preference to discrete construction projects such as dams, roads, ports and hospitals.

In these circumstances, in many countries national resources for telecommunications development were scarce. As countries were compelled to rely primarily on internal financing for infrastructure, the model of telecommunications service delivery most commonly chosen was the State monopoly. In almost all cases across Asia and the Pacific, telephony services were provided by a government-owned company, in a similar way to other utilities. There was virtually no private sector participation in telecommunications in Asia until late in the post-War period. The two major exceptions were the Philippine Long Distance Telephone Company (PLDT) and the Far Eastern Telegraph Company (what later became Hong Kong Telecommunications), which were both founded as private sector companies.[4] The scarcity of resources for telecommunications development forced governments to take a very pragmatic approach to infrastructure development and the extension of service. Government agencies, state-owned enterprises and wealthy individuals tended to receive telephone service first. As time and resources permitted, urban areas received network rollout, leaving the rural and high-cost areas the last on the priority list.[5]

In Asia and the Pacific today, among the larger and less developed countries, basic national telecommunications infrastructure development is still the first goal of public policy in this area. Given the vast populations and geographical challenges of countries such as China, India, Indonesia, Vietnam, The Philippines and Thailand, network construction will continue to require significant resources for years to come. In the face of such requirements, several countries have adopted innovative solutions to their infrastructure needs. India and The Philippines, which took very different routes in pursuit of similar objectives, are discussed at 13.2.1.1 and 13.2.1.2 below. In each case there were complex issues to be resolved regarding the relationship between State and private capital, fears over employment losses, the acceptability of foreign capital, and how to achieve the delicate balance between receiving a much-needed technological infusion without creating a national dependency on foreign goods and know-how.[6] In addition, like many developing countries, each of these countries faced significant challenges in terms of policy development and formulation, and an inadequate regulatory infrastructure to manage a changing sector.

---

[4] The first British submarine telegraphs cable was laid to Hong Kong in 1871. In 1872, John Pender merged the Eastern Extension and Australasia and China Telegraph Company into what was the forerunner of today's Cable & Wireless in Hong Kong. See *Global from the Start, a Short History of Cable & Wireless*, available from the company in London. Cable & Wireless is also part owner-operator of several national and international telephone companies in the South Pacific Islands, namely Fiji, Solomon Islands and Vanuatu. In many of these cases, ownership is shared with the national government, and represents a private-public sector partnership.
[5] Leidig, Lisa, 'Universal Service/Access Funding Strategies', Connect World Asia, First Quarter, 1999, at 24.
[6] Although not the subject of this chapter, it should be noted that issues of national independence and sovereignty were hotly debated in many countries that had only recently won independence from a colonial power. The conservative view would argue that in key sectors both for the economy and national security, such as telecommunications, foreign investment should be strictly limited.

13.2.1 Meeting infrastructure needs

13.2.1.1 India With the political and economic reform begun by Rajiv Gandhi in the mid-1980s, attention in India inevitably turned to telecommunications as a sector ripe for foreign investment as well as accelerated integration into the national economy which, at the time, was increasingly exposed to the forces of globalisation. The Department of Telecommunications, which performed the roles of policy maker, regulator and operator, had proved itself inadequate to meeting the growing needs for investment in India's telephone infrastructure. The statistics in the mid-1980s were not salutary. The overall national level of teledensity was 1.5 per cent, with some urban areas such as Delhi and Mumbai reaching as much as 15 per cent.[7] These heightened levels of telephone access may be explained by the presence of the national government in Delhi and the commercial centre in Mumbai, which would have received the scarce resources on a historical basis as noted at 13.2 above. In India's 600,000 villages, home to over 74 per cent of the population, teledensity was estimated to be merely 0.2 lines per hundred.[8] The increasing prosperity of India and its growing population were adding numbers to the waiting list at a rate with which the Department of Telecommunications could not keep pace. For example, a high-level study committee chaired by Rakesh Mohan reported as late as 1997, in its India Infrastructure Report, that India needed an additional 52 million lines by 2006.[9] This would require an investment in the order of $52 billion.[10]

India made the initial decision to open up the mobile and value-added services market to private participation in 1991. Mobile was a logical choice, as it was a capital-intensive, urban-focused service and (at the time) one not provided by the State monopoly, the Department of Telecommunications.[11] The four major metropolitan areas, Delhi, Mumbai (Bombay), Chennai (Madras) and Calcutta, were chosen to receive two competitors each. Foreign participation was set at 49 per cent, thus requiring a local partner, and Global System for Mobile (GSM) was named as the preferred technology. In 1994–1995, two licences were awarded for the four cities, involving local industrial groups and their foreign partners such as Bell South (US), Vodafone (UK), AOTC (Australia), Malaysia Telecom (Malaysia), Cellular Communications International (US), SFR (France), France Télécom (France) and Hutchison (Hong Kong).[12]

India took another step towards telecom market reform and opening the sector in January 1995, when it issued tenders to companies registered in

---

[7] World Bank Project Report, Project ID INPE55456, *India – Telecommunications Sector Reform*, April 1998. See http://www.worldbank.org. See also Government of India, Ministry of Finance, *Economic Survey of India* (1997), chap. 9, 'Infrastructure', available at http://www.m-web.com/es009.html.

[8] *Ibid.*

[9] *Ibid.*

[10] *Ibid.*

[11] A few years previously, however, the Department had awarded licences for paging, VSAT and e-mail services.

[12] Mody, Bela, 'Liberalization of Telecommunications in India in the mid-1990s', in Noam, Eli (ed.), *Telecommunications in Western Asia and the Middle East* (New York, OUP, 1997), at 11.

India for the installation, operation and maintenance of basic telephone service on a regional basis.[13] The Department of Telecommunications, which ran the tenders, divided the country into 20 'circles', roughly corresponding to India's states, as the service areas to be bid for. In a secondary categorisation, the circles were grouped into A, B, and C categories, corresponding to the desirability of each group, and hence the expected bid price. States such as Andhra Pradesh, Gujarat and Maharashtra were graded 'A'; Haryana, Kerala, and West Bengal were among the 'B' circles; Bihar, Orissa and Assam were graded 'C', and so on.

The proposition was that the Department of Telecommunications and one other licensee would compete to supply basic local service in that circle. An additional cellular provider would also be awarded on a circle-wide basis. The rationale of the Indian Government was to preserve the most lucrative segments of the telecommunications business, long-distance and international services, for the Department and VSNL, India's international carrier. A further liberalisation of these services would be considered at a later date. These two services were critical sources of revenue for cross-subsidies to the local service, as well as for other parts of the economy. By opening up the local loop to competition, India hoped to attract private sector interest in the part of the network that had historically been the most underinvested, and the most needy of new technology and management expertise. India's goal of 'privatisation' was not to get the State company out of the business, but rather to bring the private sector in for the first time. There would be local loop duopoly – virtually a world first.

Some of the obligations on the new entrants included having to use the Department of Telecommunication's domestic long-distance network to carry traffic out of one circle into another circle. In response to queries, bidders were told that they might bid for and win more than one circle, but would not be awarded contiguous circles, to prevent them 'bypassing' the Department's long-distance lines. The Department required a build-out program to be submitted for the circle bid for, and the rural component weighed heavily in the evaluation process. Annual roll-out plans were to be approved through the Department of Telecommunications following the award.[14]

Despite many unresolved questions surrounding such fundamental issues as interconnection pricing with the Department, tariff regulation of the new entrants, licence fees and the post-award regulatory structure, the response from bidders was enthusiastic. Local industrial and entrepreneurial groups teamed up with telecom stalwarts such as AT&T and Deutsche Telekom, but the tender also drew a response from some less expected players such as the Guangdong PTT and Moscow Telecom. British and French companies were notably absent from the running. As to be expected, the A circles were the most contested and, happily for the Indian Government, no circle was not bid for.

---

[13] Tenders for mobile outside the four cities already awarded were also conducted.
[14] Government of India, Ministry of Communications, Department of Telecommunications, Tender Documents for Provision of Telephone Service, Tender No. 314-7/94-PHC, New Delhi, 1994.

Implementation of the awards was anything but smooth, as it was marred by controversy and policy reversals. As the Department of Telecommunications began to review the bids submitted, it was taken aback by the fantastic amounts that were being offered to run telephone service in India. Quite contrary to the terms of the tender, the Department 'invented certain minimum license fees for each service area', and 'rejected all bids lower than the invented minimum termed a reserve fee'.[15] The Department called for a second round of bids, thinking it might capitalise on a bit of 'India fever' among the foreign investment community. A sad irony occurred here, as the number of return bidders fell from 16 to 11, and some circles received no bids at all. The Government was forced to call for a third round, in which it lowered the reserve price for certain circles, effectively to get what it could. In the end, eight circles went without any interest expressed, leaving the Department of Telecommunications the only service provider and source of investment in those areas. Finally, the Minister under whose care the tenders were run was snared in a financial scandal, causing him to leave office. These events unfortunately served to discredit the Government of India as unable to manage a major international tender, to guarantee that the results would be respected, and to secure India in the mind of the international community as an attractive place to invest.

On the positive side, as the new entrants develop their networks, in urban and rural areas as they are required, the fundamental policy goals of improved distribution of infrastructure will begin to be achieved. Customers will have more choice in both fixed and mobile, and the Department of Telecommunications will be exposed to the rigours of competition. In the same regard, middle-class and business users should be able to purchase efficient services that were previously out of reach, putting the network to work for the economy, and social purposes.[16]

13.2.1.2 The Philippines

The Philippines had many of the same goals as India when it announced its new telecommunications policy in 1993. Overall teledensity in The Philippines was 2.4 per cent. This number varied between the capital, Metro Manila, where there were about ten telephones per hundred, and the outlying areas, where teledensity levels were as low as 0.1 per hundred.[17]

The severe imbalance in infrastructure is the result of several factors. First, the capital generates approximately 30 per cent of The Philippines' gross domestic product, hence it had first call on scarce investment resources.[18] With higher incomes and more economic activity, the revenue per line is

---

[15] Chowdary, T.H., 'Telecommunications in India', in Noam, *op. cit.* n. 12, at 35.

[16] See interview with Planning Commission Member, Montek Singh Ahluwalia, on future steps for India, 'Monopoly in telecommunications is undesirable', at http://www.economictimes.com/150699, 15 June 1999.

[17] Republic of the Philippines, Department of Communications and the Arts, Telecommunications Industry Division, *Telecommunications in the Republic of the Philippines, Infrastructure and Regulatory Environment*, June 1995, at 1.

[18] Barings Securities, *Philippines Telecommunications Review*, September 1995, at 4.

higher than elsewhere in the country, thus focusing construction attention here again. Secondly, PLDT, the incumbent and largest operator, was under no explicit universal service obligation, leaving it to decide where best to concentrate its network build. In 1994, for example, 80 per cent of PLDT's existing 1.03 million lines were installed in Metro Manila.[19] Thirdly, the overall low levels of teledensity in The Philippines can be attributed in part to years of slow economic growth and lack of foreign investment.[20] Fourthly, although the telecommunications sector was far from a true monopoly, the lack of clear interconnection guidelines for PLDT tended to deter investment in the local exchange. PLDT was by far the largest, but by no means the only, local exchange service provider in The Philippines. Owing to the topography of the country, it is almost impossible to have a universal backbone network with local feeder networks off it. In many remote villages, there are small 'Mom and Pop' stand-alone systems with 1,000 or so lines. Typically their link to the outside world is through PLDT, a Government-run, or radio-based backbone. It is fair to say that The Philippines is a patch-work of many networks, of which PLDT's is the largest. Therefore, it is no surprise that most competitive activity has centred on the more lucrative areas of cellular and international gateway services.

The competitive situation at the time of the new policy announcement in 1993 warrants some explanation. The Philippines, long used to private sector provision of service, was at the time one of the most competitive and liberalised markets in all of South East Asia. In 1986, the sector had been substantially opened to competition, with multiple providers existing in multiple sub-markets of telecommunications. Between 1986 and 1993, The Philippines regulator, the National Telecommunications Commission (NTC) had awarded 11 international gateway licences, five cellular and ten paging licences. Each of these was fighting for a slice of the growing market, concentrated in Manila, with little thought to the underserved.

Like India, The Philippines built telecommunications development into its overall macro-economic plans. Acknowledging the importance of the tele-communications sector, and the need to arrest the accelerating infrastructure imbalance, the Government took a number of important steps to reach the long-term goal of a teledensity level of ten telephones per hundred people by 2010. The first step on the road to fulfilment of this plan was Executive Order 59, issued in February 1993, requiring for the first time mandatory intercon-nection of all public networks. Looked at another way, the Executive Order gave all operators the right to use PLDT's national backbone and all extant international gateway facilities. Interconnection agreements were to be bilat-erally agreed on a commercial basis, with the NTC acting as arbiter in the case of failure to agree or a dispute. The Executive Order, although helpful, merely put a legal obligation on PLDT. It stopped short of specifying cost-based rates, outlining terms and conditions, etc. for new entrants, or requiring PLDT to issue a reference interconnect offer. Another Executive

---

[19] *Ibid.*
[20] In the new Constitution promulgated by President Corazon Aquino in 1986, foreign participation in key economic sectors such as telecommunications is limited to 40 per cent.

Order, number 109, issued in July 1993, established the Universal Service Policy. This put fixed investment obligations on international gateway facilities (IGF) and cellular licence holders. The Universal Service Policy was to be implemented by the Service Area Scheme.

The Service Area Scheme divides the country into 11 service areas, typically comprising several remote provinces. Each IGF and cellular operator was assigned one of these areas, which entailed significant local infrastructure installation requirements. IGF licensees were required to install 300,000 local access lines, and cellular licensees 400,000 local access lines over a three-year period. In order to provide some economic incentive, the licensees who were assigned a particularly poor rural service were also given a slice of metropolitan Manila to serve. The three existing licensees, which held both cellular and international gateway licences, were given two regional areas to serve and tasked with 700,000 local access lines. The provincial assignments were not exclusive, allowing a potential third entrant into the service area, if commercial conditions warranted it.

If successful, the new local service providers stood to gain significant share purely based on satisfying the unmet demand outside the metro areas, which was substantial. They also posed, at least in theory, the first-ever alternative to PLDT, which after so many years had been a source of national frustration. In 1993, the national waiting list stood at 700,000. By 1995, it had exceeded 1 million people.[21] Even where individuals could afford the installation fee, and were ready to pay, the average time spent on the waiting list was more than five years. With a three-year window within which to fulfil their local service obligation of 300,000–400,000 lines, the IGF and cellular operators' rate of installation of lines would outstrip any prior performance measure of PLDT. In response, although not subject to the same obligations as the IGF and cellular operators, PLDT launched the Zero Backlog program in 1993 in order to pre-empt the new carriers. PLDT's goal was 1 million new lines between 1993 and 1996. For a while, in the 1993–1994 time frame, it appeared, that The Philippines was going to enjoy enormous investment, a huge technological infusion and healthy competition in telecommunications. At the same time, the Government had also tagged telecommunications as a fundamental contributor to its *Philippines 2000* program, which was to make the Republic an Asian Tiger Cub by the millennium, or soon after.

Depending on when the original licences were awarded, many operators' installation obligations were becoming due in the 1997–1998 time frame. Unfortunately, the record on compliance was quite poor. Almost all of the carriers subject to the Service Area Scheme had to renegotiate their obligations, many of them near default. The failure to complete the roll-out may be assessed as follows:

(a)   Although there was a requirement for PLDT to interconnect with all carriers and *vice versa*, considerable delays hampered the flow of traffic on to the new networks. Whether this was by design or by the sheer number of

---

[21] Government of The Philippines, Department of Communications, *op. cit.* n. 17, at 14.

interconnection agreements that needed to be completed quickly, and all with PLDT, is not clear. For example, the last company of the 11 international carriers to receive interconnection from PLDT was ETPI. ETPI was connected to PLDT in 1999, having been awarded its licence in 1989. The result, however, was little revenue generation by the new carriers, sorely needed to offset the heavy local investment. And without interconnection to the national or international networks, the service offering in the provinces was unattractive to the local people. This became a vicious circle.

(b) The 1997 period onward saw global attention focused on international accounting rates, the fees international service providers charge each other for delivering in-bound traffic to the called party over their network. Traditionally, these fees have not been correlated to costs, and carriers passed these costs on to the calling party, making international service artificially expensive. The inbound revenue then served to subsidise the cost of local service, which, for public policy reasons, was generally deemed to be in the national interest. The Philippine Universal Service Policy was based on an extension and institutionalisation of the cross-subsidy mechanism between international and local, with severe demands being placed on the operators' international revenues to fulfil their local installation obligations. With 11 competitors in the IGF sector, competition was keen and margins low. In a period of pressure on accounting rates as well, the planned reliance on international revenues from settlements to fund the local build proved a flawed expectation.

(c) Lastly, the Asian financial crisis, which hit South East Asia in 1997, all but dried up international capital for major infrastructure projects such as these. The attendant problem of devalued currencies, including the Philippine peso, increased the pressure on the carriers' dollar-denominated debt.

Perhaps inevitably, The Philippines market has seen a consolidation among its telecom participants. In 1999, the First Pacific Co. Ltd, a Hong Kong-based holding company, bought a controlling interest in PLDT and began a merger between Piltel, PLDT's mobile arm, and Smart. Smart is a multiple licence holder in the local exchange, international gateway, mobile and paging areas. Smart was already part owned by First Pacific, with a 12 per cent stake held by Nippon Telegraph and Telephone (NTT). The Smart-PLDT-Piltel group is the largest telecommunications operator in The Philippines. In another merger, Globe Telecom (Singapore Telecom 38 per cent and Ayala Corp. 38 per cent) combined with Islacom, which fell under the control of Ayala Corp. in 1999.[22] Both Islacom and Globe are multiple licence holders as well, the strength seeming to be in their GSM networks, the only two using this technology in The Philippines.[23]

As we have seen, with varying results, India and The Philippines had similar goals of increasing telephone density in outlying areas, both for economic and social reasons, and both devised a mechanism for drawing investment into

---

[22] See Shameen, Assif, 'Lessons from the crisis', http://www.cnn.com/9911/09, 9 November 1999.

[23] See Francisco, Rosemarie, 'Globe Signs Interconnection Pact with PLDT', http://www.totaltele.com/secure, 23 November 1999.

the local loop. India relied on a duopoly structure, setting a fixed licence period, across a fairly wide geographic area, a 'circle', but in the first round at least, allowed new entrants to put their own market value on the proposition. In contrast, The Philippines granted what for their marketplace was a licence in the most lucrative sectors, namely international and cellular, then put fixed obligations on the licence holders for the uneconomic local loop in remote areas. The combination of using the most competitive area where the margins were thinnest to subsidise the uneconomic service area *and* the dependency on international revenues was a recipe for disappointment. India's miscalculation was to assume that foreign investment would flow even in the face of excessive and unrealistic reserve prices. In the first round of bidding, all circles had expressions of interest, which would have resulted in investment even in the poorest regions of the country, thereby advancing India's telecommunications goals. In the second round, bidders behaved rationally and refused to plump for the same circle at a higher price. The net result is that fewer circles have a second carrier, frustrating national development plans.

The two programs are similar in other ways, in that both Governments tried to minimise to some extent the harm caused by competition to the national incumbent. India required the new entrants to use Department of Telecommunications long-distance lines, and The Philippines did not put the same investment obligations on PLDT. (PLDT did, however, initiate its own build program for competitive reasons.)

13.2.2 Build Operate Transfer in Indonesia and Thailand

For reasons of national interest, Thailand and Indonesia did not wish to cede their national monopolies to competitors, and thus chose an alternative route to speeding local network infrastructure investment. The 'build operate transfer' (BOT) model was invented for Indonesia by the World Bank (see also Chapter 14). The general format is that a private sector company is granted a concession in a geographic area, usually on a monopoly basis. The concession holder constructs the required infrastructure, or invests an agreed amount, and over the period of the concession (say, 25 years) retains most or all of the revenues generated. At the end of the concession period, the infrastructure is returned to the host government or government owned provider.[24] One of the concepts behind the BOT idea is the temporary transfer of sovereign central authority to a private entity for the provision of a public service. The arrangement is mostly contractual in nature, rather than by a licensing process, and therefore contains numerous obligations and requirements on the concessionaire.

In Indonesia's case, the foreign operator runs its project as a joint venture with the national incumbent, PT Telkom, in one of five regions.[25] Each KSO,

---

[24] BOT schemes have been used to build roads, ports, airports, toll bridges and other large infrastructure projects.
[25] The five regions in Indonesia are Sumatra, West Java, Central Java, Kalimantan, and East Indonesia. The more lucrative areas of the national capital area, Jakarta, and East Java have been left to PT Telkom.

as they are called in Bahasa Indonesia, paid an up-front fee and invested it in building out the local network in its service area, operating it jointly with Telkom. In return, it receives a share of the revenues generated over 15 years from 1996–2011. All local networks revert to Telkom in 2011. In Thailand, nearly every service, including fixed, mobile and long-distance fibre optic transmission, is provided through the build, transfer and operate mechanism.[26]

BOT does not represent competition to the national operator, but rather should be viewed as a means to utilise private sector financing for desperately needed infrastructure build. It does not represent privatisation either, as the assets are generally returned to the host Government or national operator, Government-owned in these cases.

13.2.3 More developed markets

What may not be fully appreciated in countries outside the Asia and Pacific area is that the first priority of many countries in this region is and will continue to be progress in the spreading of overall and uniform infrastructure reach, and improving levels of service well into the twenty-first century. There are, however, many Asian countries – such as Japan, Singapore, Hong Kong, South Korea, Taiwan and Australia – that compare favourably against the world's best teledensity levels. By and large, telephone networks in these countries reach almost everyone who wants to have telephone service, they employ a high degree of digital technology and exhibit high reliability. The building phase over, national priorities of these countries are now focused on bringing the benefits of the Information Age to their businesses and citizens, for both economic and social reasons. Usually, the common vehicle to achieve this goal is through regulated competition and the stimulation of service deployment with less emphasis on infrastructure.

As an example, in 1984, Japan eliminated through new legislation the monopoly then held by Nippon Telegraph and Telephone (NTT). As the network was largely constructed on a national basis, the Japanese Government initiated limited competition in the Type I market, that is, infrastructure owners and operators. Although this was not explicit in the regulations, the Government informally held back the number of Type I licences it issued in order to minimise the amount of urban disruption caused by 'digging up the streets'. The government also created another type of licence, the Type II, which was for the provision of services over the facilities of a Type I licensee. In retrospect, the logic seems to be that NTT had built a national network, but some carriers might be allowed to improve infrastructure where demand was especially keen. And indeed, the first competitive networks were built along the Tokyo-Osaka industrial corridor, amid the highest population and industrial concentrations. The Type II licences seemed focused on drawing services innovation into the market, minimising as it did the need for capital.

---

[26] The build, transfer and operate scheme is slightly different, in that the property is transferred at the outset to the host government, and the concessionaire operates the infrastructure it has built for a share of the revenues, and a share of the profits in Thailand's case.

This area was much more open to foreign participation than the Type I licences, initially allowing 30 per cent of equity to be held by a foreign firm under the Type II rules. It is important to remember that at the time of the initial market opening, there was no alternative domestic expertise in telecommunications, as NTT had held the monopoly since the end of World War II. Foreign companies, particularly value-added service providers, could set up fairly quickly, without threatening the national hold over vital infrastructure stock. As a matter of policy, the relatively easier entry offered by the Type II service regulations did prompt innovation in the services markets, providing additional stimulus to NTT, the national carrier.[27]

This chain of events, i.e. reaching relatively high teledensity, followed by the initiation of competition in both infrastructure and services, has been followed by several other countries in the Asia and Pacific area in modified form, including Australia, New Zealand, South Korea, Hong Kong and Singapore.

13.3 INSTITUTIONAL CHANGES REFLECT MARKET EVOLUTION

In the Philippine and Indian examples (see 13.2.1 above), the governments had a significant role to play in creating the right incentives to attract foreign investment. The regulators and foreign investment boards know that major telecommunications companies around the world review numerous opportunities to partner or invest every day, and have a range of choices of where to commit their resources. As a result, countries, particularly developing markets, compete vigorously for the pool of available telecommunications funds. One of the market factors investors seek is a stable and reliable regulatory structure. As competition becomes more of a reality throughout Asia and the Pacific, national governments are reforming their national regulators to cope with new entrants, multiple service suppliers and a growing prevalence of international best practice, from which few countries seem to be immune. There have been remarkable changes across Asia and the Pacific in the regulatory institutions that oversee the telecommunications sector.

The Asia and Pacific area has experienced tremendous reform of its telecom institutions in the past 15 years. It is important to bear in mind that as markets evolve and become more competitive, the requirements on the regulator change. As an institution, it must acquire new and more complex skills and expertise in order to regulate the sector effectively. The challenges to regulators are no less than the challenges to market participants. The regulatory principles that apply under monopoly conditions are no longer relevant in a stage of nascent competition, and change again when effective market competition is occurring. Some governments, such as that of New Zealand, have experimented with abandoning telecommunications-specific regulation altogether, favouring the principles of competition law. In Asia and the Pacific, market evolution along these lines – out of monopoly and into the competitive model – has taken, by and large, less time than in Europe and

---

[27] For more detail on Japan, see Pictrell, G. and Okamoto, M., 'Japan', in Long, Colin (ed.), *Telecommunications Law and Practice* (2nd edn) (London, Sweet & Maxwell, 1995).

North America, forcing regulators through their paces in a relatively compressed time period. We will look at the various stages of competition and the regulatory formats that accompany them.

13.3.1 Structure of the incumbent: corporatisation and privatisation

Across the economic chain, from developing to developed markets, governments have begun telecommunications institutional reform through the corporatisation of their national operators. That is, taking what was effectively a government department, often associated with the Communications Ministry, and giving it the legal status of a government-owned corporation.[28] This change in status initiates the evolution in mind-set away from a civil service mentality, and introduces notions of cost control and responsibility to customers. Corporatisation began with companies such as Japan's NTT in the mid-1980s, but accelerated into the early 1990s, with Singapore Telecom, Malaysia Telecom, Korea Telecom, Telstra (Australia) and Indosat (Indonesia), among others, following suit.

The single most common reason for the corporatisation of the telecom operator is the preparation of the entity for a stock sale. The government generally wishes to give the firm some experience as a 'private' company, and to develop a track record, before exposing it to the scrutiny of the markets. The financing and personnel relationships with the government may vary during this period, as almost all of the company's budget will still come from the national ministerial allocation as previously, and the majority of the staff will still be civil servants. This should change over time. The budgetary reliance on the treasury does little to forge competitive instincts and customer focus in the firm, and civil service tenure does generally not look well on new blood and new ideas. Cultural changes can come slowly, and must be managed by the government depending on its objectives and long-term plans.

The sale of a portion of the telecom operator's stock is itself a complex subject, and can be viewed a number of ways. For many countries, in Asia and elsewhere, the telecommunications operator is among the most valuable national assets the government has. Where monopolies exist, there is a virtual guarantee of revenue in a reliably growing industry. As a result, even partial share sales can attract interest, either from individual buyers or from a strategic partner, eager for early entry into the market. Where governments sell a small percentage of a company, as Malaysia did with its initial sale of 25 per cent, this can only be interpreted as a windfall for the government. It is not a privatisation when the government still owns 75 per cent of the company. Neither is it a privatisation when that 25 per cent has been dispersed among local individuals, none of whom has any operational voice or presence on the management board. We must distinguish between a revenue-raising measure and clear, logical steps of a government to divest itself of an ownership and operational interest in the national carrier. In this regard, Asian government policy has generally been the former, in that

---

[28] Such change is frequently accomplished through national legislation. An example is the Nippon Telegraph and Telephone Corporation Law, Japan, 1984.

national treasuries have garnered windfall from external sources, without giving up significant control. A major country in this category is Japan, where the Ministry of Finance is still the largest shareholder with just over 50 per cent of NTT. Other countries that retain majority government ownership are Malaysia, Singapore, Australia and South Korea, despite very visible share offerings on mostly local stock exchanges.[29] In contrast, the Indonesian Government created a new publicly traded corporate entity, Satelindo, and sold 25 per cent of it to Deutsche Telekom. Deutsche Telekom came in as a strategic partner for Satelindo with a large enough ownership share to drive corporate strategy and institute new management practices.[30]

In the case of strategic investors, governments typically offer some form of incentive or exclusive arrangement, whether by geography, period of time or over a certain group of services. The incoming investor's interest is protected through the prospect of a stable market for some specified period. Other protections and comfort-giving solutions include indemnities, or contractual rights covering the perceived risks taken by the strategic partner. The downside to such guarantees is the reduction in flexibility for the government to institute further market reforms and allow subsequent market entry, which in turn could hold back the development of a truly competitive sector. The rapid development of the telecommunications sector worldwide creates pressures on government not to be too generous with these protections.[31]

The above two steps, corporatisation and privatisation, have little to do with competition. Corporatisation can be undertaken without any new entrants on the horizon. It is justifiable alone on the notion that the national telecommunications company should be responsible for its own profit and loss; a new footing will reduce government civil servant ranks and, for the sake of the economy, should be stimulated to improve its market responsiveness. Equally, privatisation, taken in this context as the raising of funds, need not necessarily be accompanied in the near future by competitive market entry. Competition does, in many cases, tend to follow both of these, but it need not. This two-step approach of corporatisation followed by the introduction of competition, was pursued in Malaysia, Singapore, South Korea, Australia and Japan, among others.

13.3.2 Regulatory structures

13.3.2.1 Separation of functions and an independent regulator Along with corporatisation and privatisation (in varying degrees) comes the necessary

---

[29] In January 2000, the Singapore Government announced that it would, effective April 2000, permit majority foreign ownership in public telecom companies licensed in Singapore. Presumably this also applies to Singapore Telecom, where at the time of writing, the Government is the majority shareholder.

[30] Satelindo is a publicly listed company with the right to offer international services along with Indosat on a duopoly basis until 2005. It is owned by Deutsche Telekom (25 per cent), PT Indonesia Satellite Corp. and PT Telekomunikasi Indonesia (30 per cent), and by private investors (45 per cent).

[31] Nimmo James, 'Network Development in Developing Countries', in *Global Communications* (London, Hanson Cook Ltd, 1997), at 101.

separation of, first, the postal operations from telecommunications operations and, more importantly, the structural separation of telecommunications operations from the policymaking and regulatory functions. Structural separation is akin to corporatisation, but corporatisation refers to the corporate legal status of the firm and not its place within the bureaucracy. The separation of telecommunications from post is necessary in order to divide two functions that have very little to do with each other in the modern world, particularly when the telecommunications function is to manage its own financing.

Separation of regulatory and operational roles tends to occur when national plans call for several operators in the sector. The expectation is that the regulator will be able to oversee multiple carriers in the sector in an impartial way. This is perhaps one reason why so many private sector firms entered the Philippine marketplace. There was no structural relationship between the regulator and the largest carrier, PLDT. The Philippines regulator, the National Telecommunications Commission, is a dependent body reporting to the Department of Communications, the policy maker.

Many countries in Asia and the Pacific have accomplished this structural separation, although somewhat later than might be expected. All of the countries mentioned in 13.3.1 above that went through corporatisation, have also completed their structural separation of operations and regulation, although significant ownership stakes do still exist by governments in many of their national operators. Even China in the mid-1990s separated the Directorate General of Telecommunications' operations from the postal function, and corporatised the Chinese operating arm, China Telecom.[32]

Thailand stands out as being behind in this process. The Telephone Organisation of Thailand (TOT), which is responsible for running the local and national telecommunications systems and cellular services resides, within the Ministry of Transport and Communication, and is a 100 per cent government-owned corporation. The Communications Authority of Thailand (CAT), the international operator, is also 100 per cent government-owned and sits within the Ministry. CAT owns the international gateway and is the sole investing carrier in satellite and submarine cable systems. The Post and Telegraph Department forms the third department within the Ministry. Planning for the Thai telecommunications sector is included in the Government's national planning cycle on a five-year basis. The current plan, the Eighth National Economic and Social Plan, covers the period 1997–2001. Numerous plans over time have been advanced for partial privatisation and the reconstitution of the regulatory function, but delay has prevented any concrete action from occurring.[33]

---

[32] For a comprehensive listing of the state of Asian regulators in this regard, see International Telecommunications Union, Telecommunications Development Bureau, *General Trends in Telecommunications Reform, Asia Pacific, 1998*, vol. V (Geneva, ITU, 1998).

[33] For example, see Government of Thailand, Communications Authority of Thailand, 'Proposal concerning Telecom strategies, policies and restructuring of the sector', Regional Telecommunications Development Conference for Asia and Pacific, Singapore, 10–15 May 1993, as evidence of how long Thailand has been considering reform.

The Ministry of Transport and Communications was due to submit a master plan to the Thai Cabinet in 1997, but this process is now severely delayed. The plan was to contain details for comprehensive market liberalisation, including the abolition of the State's telecommunications monopoly. This action would require the amendment of three laws: the Telegraph and Telephone Act of 1934; the Telephone Organisation of Thailand Act of 1954; and the Communications Authority of Thailand Act of 1976. The Government of Thailand has made a commitment to the World Trade Organization to liberalise the telecommunications sector by 2006.[34]

If the market is liberalised, TOT and CAT would potentially be required to operate like any other private carrier. Even if the legislation could be changed to remove the State's monopoly, this new configuration manages to corporatise the two entities while leaving them under the management and ownership control of the State. A proposed new regulatory board would be an improvement, but without ownership reform of the operators, the degree of independence of the regulator would not live up to the standard around the world in liberalised environments. Thailand would find, in time, that it needed to repeat much of the process in order to finish the job. There are also suggestions regarding the full enfranchisement of the BOT concessionaires (see 13.2.2) into carriers, and leaving their operations in place, to provide 'instant competition', but this notion is quite controversial since it does not afford the national entity a chance to find its feet before the introduction of direct competition.

It is quite possible that telecommunications restructuring plans in Thailand (and perhaps elsewhere in the region) have been put on hold owing to the economic downturn in the late 1990s. Two reasons may account for the stall in plans. First is the fear among Asian and Pacific governments that investors from outside the region will capitalise on the economic distress and win what would normally be highly valuable national assets at bargain prices. A delay may bring more returns, should valuations rebound. Secondly, with little confidence in the region at the moment, although it is returning, governments' credibility would be damaged if they put out a tender, or sought a strategic partner, and received little international interest. In addition, Thailand in particular has focused on the restructuring of its financial sector, and like other Asian countries may have greater demands than telecom on its reform agenda.

The natural culmination of the separation of the policy and operational functions is the creation of an independent regulator or telecom commission outside the Ministry, with its own rights and powers to oversee a burgeoning and competitive sector. It should be constituted by legislation or other instrument, have its own charter, and be only loosely accountable to the executive or legislative branch. This is now accepted as international best practice and takes pride of place in the Reference Paper agreed in February 1997 (see Chapter 10, at 10.4.3.1). An independent regulator is seen as vital

---

[34] See US & Foreign Commercial Service and US Department of State, 'Thailand Telecommunications Industry' at www.tradeport.org/ts/countries/thailand/isa.

because investors, both domestic and foreign, seek assurance that the regulator can implement policy and police the sector from a disinterested point of view. The incumbent and the new entrants must have clear expectations of regulatory behaviour, and be confident of consistent and impartial enforcement and implementation of policy. For example, some countries have given the regulator the licensing function, while others have left it with the Minister. An interesting anomaly in this regard is Japan, given the state of its national network and levels of competition. The Japanese Government, through the Ministry of Finance, still retains over 50 per cent ownership share in NTT. The Ministry of Posts and Telecommunications, by its name alone, has not accomplished the structural separation between these two activities, and the Ministry is also the licensing and regulatory authority. Japan is perhaps among the very few of the 29 OECD countries to have its telecommunications institutions so structured.

From a potential entrant's perspective, there is no point taking on the national operator when the government is part owner and regulator at the same time. The risk of bias is accentuated if the government is considering presenting the national operator to the markets for a stock sale. In this situation, the regulator is unlikely to do anything to damage the company's chances of returning to government coffers the maximum possible windfall from the stock sale. Despite all statements of good intentions to the contrary, it is unrealistic to expect a regulator/owner to rule against the incumbent in a dispute. In this environment, foreign interest in such markets is likely to be modest, and at a minimum must recognise that the incumbent's position will remain solid for a long time.

13.3.2.2 Competition regulation versus a sector-specific regulator Some countries have successfully managed effective competition into their telecommunications sectors, i.e. the steady erosion of market share for the incumbent in favour of new entrants, and the increasing pressure of market discipline to govern competitive behaviour among the parties.[35] In most cases, a country at this stage has satisfied its infrastructure needs, has a variety of service providers in most telecommunications sub-markets, such as value-added services, mobile, paging, etc., and has completed most of the steps of corporatisation, privatisation and the establishment of an independent regulator. These are the most sophisticated telecommunications environments and at the moment are still fairly rare in Asia-Pacific. Under some regulatory theories, a regulator's function is to establish effective competition in the market (which is a regulatory task in itself) and then, once it is established, to withdraw from active intervention in the market. As competition becomes the ruling force, there is, the argument goes, less need for specific telecommunications regulation *per se*. Governments can rely instead on the rigorous application of their competition laws to 'regulate' telecommunications operators, much like any other industry or sector. By the late 1990s, some

---

[35] The definition and measurement of effective competition is widely debated in economic and regulatory circles. We have used a shorthand here to introduce the concept.

developed market regulatory bodies completed the move towards a competition law focus for telecommunications, at the expense of powers normally held in sector-specific bodies. Two examples in the Asia-Pacific region are Australia and New Zealand.

In 1995, the Australian telecommunications regulatory structure was modified in line with the national competition policy reform program. The Government merged the Trade Practices Commission and the Prices Surveillance Authority to create the Australian Competition and Consumer Commission (ACCC). The Commission, an independent statutory authority, has a broad remit covering virtually all areas of economic activity in Australia. Its purpose is to enforce prohibitions against anti-competitive behaviour contained in the 1974 Trade Practices Act and the Prices Surveillance Act of 1983, including unfair market practices, mergers and acquisitions review, product safety and liability, and (most importantly for telecommunications) 'third party access to facilities of national significance'.[36] The ACCC comes under the portfolio of the Department of the Treasury, where there is a Minister for restrictive trade practices and pricing policy as well as a consumer affairs Minister. The ACCC works with consumer affairs agencies in the states and territories, which administer complementary consumer legislation.

With its creation, the ACCC has taken over a sizeable portion of the telecommunications-specific regulatory authority that had been held by the telecommunications regulator (formerly AUSTEL), particularly concerning bottlenecks and interconnection, yet its approach is now via competition law. In theory, the principles that it applies to telecommunications infrastructure access could also be used in matters relating to airports, electricity and gas, as its website suggests. An advantage of this approach is that telecommunications is migrated into the mainstream of economic activity and loses some of its specialist mystique. On the other hand, the ACCC and others who follow in this model may lose sight of many of the details specific to telecommunications, and regulate on high-level principles only.

Another statute, the Australian Communications Authority Act 1997, created the Australian Communications Authority (ACA) to take over from the now defunct AUSTEL, and defined its mandate as to focus on mostly technical areas that are not the concern of competition law.[37] The ACA is responsible for licensing carriers and ensuring compliance with those licences. It has responsibility for service performance and quality, which it maintains through consumer safeguards and service guarantees. The ACA administers the universal service obligation to ensure access to basic telecommunications services throughout Australia. It is the ACA that works with law enforcement and the emergency services. Another of its areas is the management of the national radio spectrum resource, including licensing, auctioning certain frequencies where spectrum is either in high demand or scarce, and inves-

[36] See http://www.accc.gov.au.
[37] See generally, http://www.austel.gov.au/authority.

tigating interference complaints. The national numbering plan is also under the aegis of the ACA. The Authority is Australia's representative to international telecommunications bodies such as the ITU (see Chapter 10, at 10.3) and the Asia-Pacific Telecommunity.[38] On 1 July 1997, the duopoly on network infrastructure and limit of three licensees on mobile expired, allowing virtually unlimited entry in all sectors and for all infrastructure types. In the period from July 1997 to late 2000, the number of carrier licences issued by the Australian Government increased from three to more than 50.[39]

The other country that follows a competition law format is New Zealand, but unlike Australia, which still retains a slimmed-down ACA, there is no telecommunications regulator *per se* in New Zealand. Telecommunications regulation is carried out under New Zealand's Commerce Act, which is administered by the Ministry of Commerce. Within the Ministry is the Competition and Enterprise Branch, which looks after competition and the regulatory environment for all business. New Zealand has a Minister of Communications who is the policy maker for the Government. Under this portfolio comes spectrum management and frequency registration, as well as company disclosure requirements, one of the key tools of all corporate regulation in New Zealand.

13.3.2.3 Integration of regulators or agencies in recognition of technological convergence

The above discussion of various regulatory models reviews institutional change largely through a legal approach. Several countries in Asia and the Pacific, including Hong Kong, Singapore and Malaysia, have adopted a technological approach to the organisation of their regulator.[40] Hong Kong and Singapore are often compared as having emerged together in the 1980s among the original Asian Tigers, moving from light and medium manufacturing into services such as international banking and shipping centres. They both have dynamic and well-educated populations, a sound legal structure, open and unburdensome trading and tax regimes, etc. Both Singapore and Hong Kong have extremely well-developed telecommunications infrastructure, necessary as it is to attract international businesses to locate there, as well to bring the benefits and new skills associated with the Information Age to their working populations. Both Singapore and Hong Kong have moved to the next stage of economic development, that is, becoming information economies. Both recognise that the information technology, telecommunications, Internet, mobile and broadcasting sectors are converging into indistinguishable delivery mechanisms for a whole range of services. Malaysia, in contrast, is keen to attract a host of new age technology companies to the country's Multimedia Super Corridor, and must provide the infrastructure to service them. By creating a centre of excellence for software and high-tech manufacturing, Malaysia hopes that outsiders will bring in and transfer the skills necessary to boost the local knowledge base

---

[38] See http://www.aptsec.org.
[39] See http://www.dca.gov.au.
[40] For ease of use, we are referring to Hong Kong as a 'country'. This is not to disregard its status as a Special Administrative Region of China.

and transform the economy. We address each country's regulatory structure in turn.[41]

(a) *Singapore*   In recognition that the Information sector must be viewed as a single unit, that policy matters increasingly overlap, and in order to set coherent national direction and strategy, both Hong Kong and Singapore have merged their various communications policy agencies into a single overseer for the Information 'space'. As a first step, in June 1999, the Government of Singapore renamed the Ministry of Communications the Ministry of Communications and Information Technology (MCIT). The five main areas of responsibility of the new Ministry are: information technology and telecommunications; sea transport; land transport; air transport; and corporate development.[42] True to its past as a trading centre and entrepôt, Singapore has linked the transport sector with the IT sector under the same Ministry to foster a virtual trading post environment via e-commerce. The inclusion of the transport sector sets it apart from Hong Kong. The corporate development mandate included in the MCIT's responsibilities is for bringing small and medium-sized business into the Internet trading environment through financial assistance and training.

The mission statement of the new MCIT is to 'bring about cost-effective world class transportation and info-communications services and gateways to enhance our economic competitiveness and quality of life in a knowledge-based society'.[43] The operative words in this statement are 'gateways' and 'knowledge-based'. 'Gateways' emphasises linkages with the outside world, a hubbing function. A hub also suggests an inflow of new techniques and practices to keep Singapore competitive. Along with techniques and international best practice comes increased global awareness, something the Government of Singapore has had difficulty accepting in the past. Singapore, despite its economic success and high standard of living, has adopted a fairly intolerant stance toward political dissent, extending even to media censorship and individual prosecution. As evidence of a high sensitivity to content, we note that ISPs in Singapore are licensed under broadcast legislation. All these could come under challenge should Singapore truly pursue the hub approach, comprising, as it must, global inflow as well as outflow. The other key term in the statement is 'knowledge-based', referring to the nature of the economy and its key competitive edge. Knowledge acquisition is meant to be a tool, as well as 'a way of life'.[44] In conjunction with its goal to be an information and e-commerce hub, Singapore is pursuing the Singapore One project, the construction of a broadband digital network to provide Internet access throughout the 650 square mile island.

At the sector-specific regulatory level, Singapore has replaced the Telecommunications Authority of Singapore (TAS) with a new board called the InfoComm Development Authority. This is a merger of the TAS and the

---

[41] See Elegant, S. and Hiebert, M., 'Tech Mecca', *Far Eastern Economic Review*, 16 March 2000, at 48–50.
[42] See http://www.gov.sg/mcit/pr.
[43] See http://www.gov.sg/mcit/pr/mission.
[44] *Ibid.*

National Computer Board, and was officially launched on 3 December 1999. The merger of the two bodies is intended to bring an integrated perspective to the promotion of Singapore as a 'world wide digital hub'.[45]

(b)   Hong Kong   For Hong Kong's part, it is well down the route to a complete transformation of its economy. During the 1980s, Hong Kong steadily reduced the proportion of manufacturing in its economy in favour of services, such that 85 per cent of Hong Kong's gross domestic product is now from services.[46] The Hong Kong Government is actively seeking to diversify the service basis of the economy, and has recognised that information technology is both a key input for other services sectors and a significant area of economic activity on its own. As part of its telecommunications policy, Hong Kong has pursued a consistent path towards a competitive model with the triple goals of competitive prices, state of the art infrastructure, and service innovation. As a result, Hong Kong has one of the most vibrant telecommunications sectors in the world given the size of its population. For example, the entire fixed line network is digital, and it extends to 55 lines per 100 population. In addition, 75 per cent of households are covered by one of two broadband networks. Internet subscriptions run at approximately 14 per cent of the population.[47]

With this outstanding infrastructure in place, Hong Kong is well positioned to accomplish its aim of building an information society and information economy. To this end, in 1998, Hong Kong created from other government departments the Information Technology and Broadcasting Bureau to spearhead Hong Kong's positioning in the information world. This Bureau includes the broadcasting and film areas, plus telecommunications and information technologies. The Bureau has two departments that focus on information technologies. There is one to look after the development of infrastructure and applications, and another to set policy and standards for information technology. The telecommunications regulator, OFTA, although independent, is affiliated with this Bureau. Like Singapore, the combination of various government groups into this new agency is intended to serve as a focal point for Hong Kong's efforts to capture a leading position in the global digital trading world. Hong Kong's counterpart of Singapore One is called Digital 21.

There is an attendant government initiative in the area of e-enablement to accomplish many of these goals. In April 2000, for example, the Electronic Transactions Ordinance 2000 became effective, to recognise electronic contracts, giving them full legal status, and providing for the recognition of electronic signatures. The Hong Kong Monetary Authority (HKMA) intends to bring virtual banks into the mainstream. In May 2000 it issued a Guideline

---

[45] 'Singapore: New High-Tech Regulator – Promoter Replaces Previous Telecom Authority' (2000) 3 *World Telecom Law Report* 11.
[46] Speech by Mr M. H. Au, Senior Assistant Director, for Regulatory, of the Information Technology and Broadcasting Bureau, Message From Asia Symposium, Sapporo, Japan, 25 October 1999.
[47] *Ibid.*

on the Authorisation of Virtual Banks to establish an e-banking code of practice.[48] The SAR government is also pursuing the delivery of government services online to the public, 24 hours a day, seven days a week. The government will offer its common information infrastructure to the private sector for the conduct of electronic transactions.[49]

(c) Malaysia On 1 April 1999, Malaysia inaugurated the new Communications and Multimedia Commission. It takes over the functions of several predecessor bodies and authorities, including the licensing and regulation function of the Ministry of Information, the duties of the Department of Posts, and it assumes the new role of Controller of Certification Authorities. The impetus behind the change is Malaysia's desire to recognise and respond to the phenomenon of convergence in telecommunications and computing. Malaysia also has decided to streamline and simplify its licensing process in order to speed network development and create incentives for the deployment of new technologies and multimedia. In a policy review exercise highlighting convergence issues, the Government identified four main markets as convergent markets: networked applications, including content services; network service providing the connectivity for applications; networking facilities, which create the infrastructure platforms; and goods and services used in conjunction with these services and facilities.[50] The new licensing regime only intends to extend licensing and market regulation to networking activities, although it recognises the need to consider the economic regulation of non-networked activities to the extent that they are substitutable, i.e. it will regulate certain areas according to competition law principles.[51]

Malaysia's new licensing system could turn out to be trend-setting in the region. The intention is to make a flash cut to a new system and cut away as much from the old model as possible. The earlier licensing regime involved a rather complex array of types of licences for facilities and services, the distinctions between which are today becoming meaningless. Under the new regime, there will be four categories of licences, roughly consistent with the categories of convergence described above:

(a)   network facility provider licences;
(b)   network service provider licences;
(c)   networked applications provider licences;
(d)   networked content applications provider licences.

Some of these areas are administered by an individual licence, while others require only a class licence. Malaysia intends to attach to certain types of

---

[48] See http://www.info.gov.hk/hkma/eng/bank/, 'Electronic Banking' section.
[49] See http://www.lowtax.net/lowtax/html/hongkong/jhkeleg.html – 'E-Commerce Legislation in Hong Kong'.
[50] Government of Malaysia, National Telecommunications Council Document, 'National Policy Framework for Communications and Multimedia Convergence', November 1997.
[51] In January 2000, the Malaysia Communications and Multimedia Commission issued a pair of documents outlining new regulatory powers to curb anti-competitive practices. Malaysia does not have a strong base of statutory competition law. See Reuters, 'Malaysia Telecom Body Sets Competition Rules', http://www.totaltele.com, 31 January 2000.

licences (such as network infrastructure) a set of incentive regulations commensurate with the undertakings by an operator. In other words, the more an operator plans to invest, or build or deploy, the more lenient the regulatory requirements on that operator will be. Examples of specific undertakings by operators are a universal service commitment, innovation and research, and industry development and training plans. In return for these commitments, the Government would grant certain concessions and preferential treatment. Current operators have the choice to keep the terms and conditions of their existing licences, or opt to convert their licence to a new one under the incentive system. Some of the conditions for the existing licensees are as follows:

(a)   Operators are not restricted from having both a content applications services licence, and a network services licence.

(b)   The regulatory distinction between fixed line and wireless services will be eliminated.

(c)   Those operators who take up new licences will pre-qualify for the allocation of spectrum.

(d)   No existing network licensee will be required to migrate to a new licence, but those who do not will not be eligible for any of the new benefits.

(e)   All current fixed network licensees who take up a new licence will pre-qualify to offer Internet access services.

(f)   If current fixed network operators take up the new licences, they will be able to deploy satellite, wireless or mobile technologies at their discretion.

(g)   Existing mobile operators without a fixed network licence will not be permitted to add fixed network or wireless local loop services, but they may provide satellite services.

Clearly the incentives are for existing operators to move to the new system. The Government is opening the way for operators to enter each other's markets and compete with whatever technology suits the market. If a group of providers is disadvantaged, it would appear to be the prior mobile licensees, precisely the area where the Government had been trying to impose an industry consolidation, but to no avail. These broad licence categories are indicative of regulators' realising they cannot keep up with or channel technological evolution. The Government of Malaysia has opted instead to abolish artificial and limiting regulatory distinctions so as to permit the sector to evolve (and converge) organically. This action is ahead of institutional evolution in most parts of Asia, and certainly North America and Western Europe.

13.4   THE END-GAME: IS IT COMPETITION LAW, AND IS ASIA READY?

13.4.1   Introduction

The examples of Australia and New Zealand suggest that as countries develop effective competition in their telecommunications markets, it is possible for the mode of regulation to shift emphasis from traditional sector-specific law towards competition law (see 13.3.2.2 above). A similar eventuality is anticipated in places such as Hong Kong as well. Organisations like the WTO, the European Union and the US Department of Justice are also driving the application of competition law principles to telecommunications markets on a global basis. It is not a coincidence that competition and antitrust laws, rooted in the Anglo-Saxon legal framework, found their early telecommunications application in Asia in Australia and New Zealand, direct inheritors of this tradition. In order for telecommunications to be governed by competition law and related concepts of abuse of market power, there must be national competition legislation on the books, an understanding by regulators of what market power is, and their acceptance that it can have a negative impact on the establishment of telecommunications competition. These principles are not widely accepted or enforced in Asia and the Pacific. Although some countries are passing legislation in the competition area, developed Asia is well behind developed Europe and North America in the state of their competition law regimes. It remains to be seen how this legal gap will affect the development of telecommunications competition.

13.4.2 How widespread is competition law in Asia?

It is rare to find in Asia and the Pacific the existence of vigorous competition laws and vigorous fair trade agencies acting to bring such principles into the underlying framework of telecommunications business activity. We would submit that this is because antimonopoly rules are inherently in conflict with traditional national industrial policy and administrative guidance designed to increase the market power and presence of national champions. One example of note is Japan. The American occupation forces left behind them in 1952 an Anti-Monopoly Law modelled on the Clayton and Sherman Acts in the United States.[52] The US authorities also established the Japan Fair Trade Commission (JFTC), modelled after the US Federal Trade Commission. When the Japanese Government regained sovereignty in 1952, it relaxed the controls on mergers and reversed the presumption in the law that cartels were illegal. Other statutes specifically gave the Ministry of Trade and Industry (MITI) the power to sanction export and import cartels and small business cartels, and removed the authority of the JFTC to approve or reject business combinations.[53] MITI was firmly in charge of setting and enforcing economic policy during the rebuilding of the Japanese economy in the 1950s and 1960s and, as successes mounted, so did MITI's power and prestige. MITI continues to guide the country's commercial and industrial developments, and today remains one of the most powerful ministries in the Japanese Government. Although the Anti-Monopoly Law remains in effect, enforcement is generally agreed to be weak.[54]

---

[52] See Government of Japan, Japan Fair Trade Commission, 'Overview of the Antimonopoly Law', at http://www.jftc.admix.go.jp.

[53] See 'Antitrust Laws in Countries Other than the United States', at http://www.antitrust. org/law/International/alother.html.

[54] *Ibid.*

One of the possible reasons enforcement has been casual on firms with obvious market power – such as Nippon Telegraph and Telephone (NTT) – is the acceptance in government and in widely-held public opinion that the pursuit of other desirable national goals such as international competitiveness is an acceptable trade-off for a reduction in domestic competition. Unlike the United States, there is no right of private action in Japan of the Anti-Monopoly Law. In the United States, a case of anti-competitive conduct may be brought by private parties tempted by the possibility of treble damages should harm be proven. In Japan, enforcement is solely the responsibility of government, which 'is often more concerned with Japanese firms' competitiveness in the international markets than with competition in Japan'.[55]

Today, the recognition of the concept of dominance in Japanese telecommunications regulation is beginning to emerge. Legislation introduced in the first quarter of 2001 would write this concept into Japanese telecommunications law for the first time. Even though NTT was restructured in 1999 into a holding company – a long-distance company which includes both national and international long-distance, and two regional service companies for local access – it is not clear from the legislation that cross-subsidisation from the dominant businesses (local access) into the competitive ones (long-distance and international), is prohibited. The legislation does not clearly set out the obligations and prohibitions that apply to NTT, which controls over 90 per cent of the local access lines throughout Japan. It is not clear that NTT is forbidden from cross-marketing and bundling products together across business units. It is also not clear whether NTT is subject to tariff controls that prohibit predatory pricing, particularly in international services, a market it has been able to enter only as of 1 July 1999.

As a result, the United States Government, through the United States Trade Representatives Office (USTR) and the Department of Justice continually pressures the Japanese Government to stiffen the content and enforcement of its competition laws. This is to assist not only US, but also other market entrants in many sectors, including telecommunications, as the Japanese economy is liberalised.[56] Indeed, in April 1999, the JFTC and the US Department of Justice signed a cooperation agreement to exchange information on antitrust enforcement and merger activity between the two countries.[57]

In a counter example, Korea has undertaken the increased use of competition law as a tool to *reduce* the level of industrial concentration in that country. Korea, like Japan, relied on large industrial conglomerates, called chaebol, to lead economic development from the 1960s to the 1980s. The household names such as Daewoo, Samsung and LG created national

---

[55] *Ibid.*

[56] See also Melamed, A. Douglas, 'International Antitrust in an Age of International Deregulation', speech before George Mason Law Review Symposium, Washington, DC, 10 December 1997, available at http://www.usdoj.gov/atr/public/speeches.

[57] See US Department of Justice press release, 'United States Announces Substantive Agreement on an Antitrust Cooperation Agreement with Japan', at http://www.usdoj.gov/atr/public/press_releases/1999, 3 May 1999.

manufacturing empires in everything from shipbuilding to automobiles, from household appliances to semiconductors. This relative concentration of national economic power and resources in the Korean economy became a vulnerability during the Asian economic crisis in the late 1990s, as employment, a large fraction of national exports and government tax revenue were put at risk. National policy in Korea is now focused on diversifying ownership of assets, introducing more competition for the traditional chaebol, and moving towards a more services-based economy. Korea is also highly aware of the globalisation trend, and seeks to toughen its international trading sector through the use of international best practice. One of the ways Korea has chosen to do this is to reduce the use of industrial policy and administrative guidance, and to lean more heavily on enforcement of competition law.

In January 1999, the Seventh Amendment of the Monopoly Regulation and Fair Trade Act came into effect in Korea, applying the Act to all sectors of the economy and government activity where it is for profit. The amendment removes several areas of economic activity – such as agriculture, mining, fishery and forestry, plus certain government activity and other monopolies – from previously held antitrust exemptions. In the area of telecommunications, and other specialised and technical areas, authority is shared, albeit somewhat ambiguously, between the Korean Fair Trade Commission (KFTC) and the sector regulator.[58] Indeed, Korea has reformed its telecommunications regulator into the Korea Communications Commission (KCC), modelled on the US Federal Communications Commission, and has reconstituted the Communications Ministry into the Ministry of Information and Communication. This split conforms with the global trend of separation of the policy-making power (held in the Ministry) from the implementation and enforcement authority (located in an independent agency). The KCC is charged in part with preventing anti-competitive activity with respect to access to networks.[59] There are now multiple licensed competitors in every sub-market in Korea except local service.[60] In order to oversee the sector, particularly with increased foreign participation over time, the Korean Government was under pressure to create an independent regulator.[61] This action is in line with the stated aim of checking the power of the chaebol, which are financial backers to some of the second entrants in the sub-markets as well as fixed and mobile equipment manufacturers.

Elsewhere in the Asia-Pacific region, the existence of strong competition law, or anti-monopoly law, is sketchy. Some countries, such as Hong Kong

---

[58] See Lee, Byung-Ju, 'Exemptions and Exceptions to Competition Policy and Law in Korea', http://www.apeccp.org.tw/doc.

[59] This split of authority between the KFTC and the KCC concerning anti-competitive conduct in the telecommunications sector raises interesting questions about the relationship between competition and regulatory authorities. See Submission of the United States, to the Competition Policy and Deregulation Workshop, Christchurch, New Zealand, 30 April/1 May 1999, at http://www.apeccp.org.tw/doc/workshop/w1999/010USA.html.

[60] See Information and Communications Policy Statement for the Realization of an Information Society, at http://www.unesco.org/webworld/observatory/doc_policies/apa_kor.shtml, 1999.

[61] See generally Hyun, D. and Lent, J., 'Korean telecom policy in global competition: implications for developing countries' (1999) 23 *Telecommunications Policy* 389.

Table 13.3 Competition law in the Asia-Pacific area

Countries with a competition law and a Commission to enforce it	*Countries with a family of laws but no enforcement authority*	*Countries with no competition law*
Australia	Hong Kong	Brunei
Japan	Indonesia	Malaysia
New Zealand	Philippines	PNG
South Korea	PRC	Singapore
Taiwan		
Thailand		

Source: http://www.ftc.gov.tw

and The Philippines, rely on a family of laws covering such practices as price fixing, anti-dumping, anti-boycott, and restrictive agreements to accomplish many of the same things. There is, however, no central commission or agency for enforcement or oversight, so it can be weak. And some countries, most notably Singapore, have no competition statute yet. This is keenly felt in telecommunications, since SingTel is not regarded as dominant or regulated any differently from any other carrier. In summary, the state of competition law in the Asia-Pacific area breaks down roughly as shown in Table 13.3.

It is fair to say that some countries in Asia will have difficulty, even the more advanced ones in terms of their legal structure, in adopting to the world trend away from sector-specific law and towards general competition law. Those that have robust competition authorities with some admixture of telecommunications regulators, as does Australia and is developing in South Korea, will create a more stable and predictable environment for market participants. They will attract major international telecommunications companies, which are seeking investments outside their home jurisdictions, and they will keep their regulators and regulatory skills honed with the best international practice. Others will find themselves increasingly the target of demands from foreign carriers, potential investors, trade partners, the WTO and, in time, the ITU, as it endeavours to become more business-friendly.

Telecommunications regulation is converging at the supranational level. The international community of which trading nations form part is becoming more uniform, and standardised in its norms.[62] This is the case in certain areas such as trade practices, market access and the belief in market competition, where international expectations are crystallising. Politicians are no longer able to shield their economies completely from these globalising forces. In telecommunications, the case for competition has, by and large, been made and won. Countries that cannot or will not follow the competitive

---

[62] See Story, Jonathan, 'The Frontiers of Fortune', *Financial Times* (London, Prentice Hall, 1999).

model may be held accountable by their people for thwarting economic development.[63]

13.5 NEW TECHNOLOGIES AND REGULATION IN ASIA AND THE PACIFIC

13.5.1 The coming boom in bandwidth

Although some parts of Asia will be preoccupied with putting much-needed basic infrastructure in the ground, other parts will be coping with a virtual explosion in bandwidth under the sea. Carriers on both sides of the Pacific are planning to lay extraordinary amounts of new fibre optic cable, most of it planned to come on-line by 2001–2002 (see Table 13.4). Much of the demand for this capacity is Internet driven on both the voice and data fronts; and of that Internet demand, much of it is expected to come from China. The Phillips Group, a consultancy, predicts that China will overtake Japan as the heaviest Internet using country by 2005. It predicts that China's Internet user base will be 85 million, or 37.64 per cent of Asia-Pacific total. This compares with Japan's projected base by that time at 33.5 per cent.[64]

The price of trans-Pacific circuits is under severe pricing pressure in the early years of the twenty-first century for several reasons. The globalisation of the bandwidth market will tend to reduce regional disparities. The addition of significant capacity will bring about a decline in the underlying cost per megabit of traffic. The bursting of the bubble on technology stocks in 2000/2001 created severe corporate financial retrenchment. The urgent need for cash flow on the part of many firms creates a buyers' market when prices on some routes are at cost or below. The amount of prospective capacity and

Table 13.4 Announced cable ventures and their expected capacities in gigabits 1999–2001 (selected)

Venture	1999	2000	2001	Total
China-US	80 gigabits			80 gigabits
Pacific Crossing – 1	80 gigabits			80
Japan-US	80 gigabits		320	400
Southern Cross	80 gigabits	80		160
Project Oxygen			1280	1280
				Cumulative total: 2000 gigabits

Source: Communicationsweek International, 4 October 1999, p. 6.

---

[63] For a fascinating account of the evolution of legal systems in Asia and the Pacific, see Pistor and Wellons, 'The Role of Law and Legal Institutions in Asian Economic Development 1960–1995', project report for the Asian Development Bank, 1998.
[64] Totaltel@total.emap.com, 31 October 1999. More information about the study can be found from consult@the-phillips-group.com.

more efficient technologies have the potential to change the cost profile of trans-Pacific international traffic, and to pass significant cost reductions on to consumers.

It is also likely to be the case that there will be a large difference between what the carriers paid per circuit to install this capacity and what they are likely to be able to charge for this capacity when it comes on-line. They will be interested in filling the cables and keeping the traffic flowing. The decline of the international accounting rate system, which is occurring at the same time as the vast installation of capacity, is pushing facilities owners into alternative settlement arrangements, such as volume deals and termination agreements. The net effect of these two forces is to push a significant portion of international traffic (both data and voice) into a wholesale arrangement. Major telecommunications providers – frequently the large national and international carriers who generally are the owners of undersea cables – will be offering much of the capacity on a wholesale basis to other ISPs and telcos. At present, however, few traditional telcos have much experience in the wholesale market; and they may not see wholesale as a core business, and their regulators may be slow to see the benefits for users and other pur-chasers.

It could be difficult for the prospective purchasers of the newly activated capacity, such as new entrants and ISPs, to acquire low-cost international capacity if their regulatory regime does not support a wholesale approach to facilities-based re-sale. The International Telecommunications Users Group (INTUG) published a report in 1999 that suggests that the high prices worldwide for leased lines will retard the development of the Internet and Internet-enabled sectors such as e-commerce.[65]

Cost, and who pays, is much on the minds of Asian ISPs, who want the international Internet community, particularly the US, to adopt a new approach to settlement fees for Internet traffic flows. Under the current system, the average Asian websurfer spends about 80 per cent of his or her time browsing US-based websites. The United States is where the lion's share of web-based content is located, and most users everywhere pass through the United States in an average Internet session. US users do not frequent Asian-based sites as often, hence the traffic is predominantly in one direction. In order to provision their customers adequately, Asian ISPs have taken out leased lines from their international exchange across the Pacific to the United States, which then connects with the US Internet backbone and ultimately terminates at the host site that the user is trying to access. The Asian ISP pays the entire cost of the connection and, it is argued, subsidises the US-based user who wants to surf in Asia. This is the charge that eight major Asian telecoms companies that are also ISPs wrote in a joint statement issued in January 1999. The eight companies were Chunghwa Telecom (Taiwan), the Communications Authority of Thailand, Indosat (Indonesia), KDD

---

[65] INTUG has done a series of studies, the most recent in 1999, of leased-line prices in European countries based on equivalent distances. There is great variance among countries, and an indeterminate relationship to cost. See 'International Leased Lines, National vs. International Costs', http://www.intug.net/surveys/. This may serve as a model for Asia and the Pacific.

(Japan), Korea Telecom, PLDT (Philippines), Singapore Telecom, and Telekom Malaysia.[66] Their statement was immediately endorsed by Telstra (Australia) and China Telecom, bringing to ten the number of those who want to correct what they see as an unjust system. Telstra by itself had already complained to US telecom authorities about the A$40–50 million that it pays to cover outgoing Internet traffic from Australia to the US while receiving no payment in return.[67] The joint statement was forwarded to the major US 'Tier 1' Internet backbone suppliers – PSINet, Sprint, AT&T, Cable & Wireless USA, and Uunet – and circulated to worldwide regulators, demanding that a fairer system for settling Internet traffic be established.

The trend in many parts of Asia is for international Internet traffic to overtake international voice calls, as it already has in Japan and South Korea, and the unwelcome prospect is that the financial burden on Asia ISPs could increase. An innovative proposal coming from the ISPs is for all ISPs to establish and recognise a 'financial mid-point', that is, acknowledging traffic flows in some ratio that both sides agree to bear. If Korea, for example, sends 80 per cent of the two-way Internet traffic and receives only 20 per cent in return from the US, the US ISPs must pay their 20 per cent share of the total traffic. This is a new concept in international settlements and a new concept for the settlement of Internet traffic. One of the difficulties in implementing this proposal is the effective tracing and metering of Internet traffic in a packet switched environment. There will necessarily have to be a tagging system for packets, that can establish each packet's origin and termination and take into account the possibility that packets could transit many countries before arriving at their destination. The installation of such complex equipment and software may pose something of a threat to the cost efficiency and cost advantages that the Internet now has, as well as attract considerable privacy concerns (see Chapter 11). In May 2000, this issue of 'reciprocal compensation' was raised at the APEC ministerial meeting on telecommunications, where the main concern was the future of financing Internet infrastructure.[68]

13.5.2 Voice over the Internet in Asia and the Pacific

In many countries in Asia, there is a fairly relaxed regulatory approach to the provision of Internet access services. It is relatively easy to establish an ISP business and begin providing Internet access for customers in many jurisdictions. Since November 1998, when Internet access service provision was deregulated, the Indian Government, for example, has given out over 100 licences, and the sector is quite competitive.[69] This general approach is replicated in many countries, perhaps motivated by governments' interest in

---

[66] Bickers, Charles, 'Backbone Pain', *Far Eastern Economic Review*, 25 March 1999.
[67] *Ibid.*
[68] Task Force for the Study of International Charging Arrangements for Internet Services, 'Report to the Fourth APEC Ministerial Meeting on Telecommunications and Information Industry', Cancun, Mexico, 24–26 May 2000.
[69] Singh, Sanjit, 'India Paves Way on Net', *The Industry Standard*, at http://www.thestandard.com/articles/display, 2 August 1999.

promoting widespread Internet use and Internet skills in their populations. In Japan, for example, the Ministry of Public Management, Home Affairs, Posts and Telecommunications (MPHPT) reports that there were 3,365 ISPs operating as of March 1999.

Governments have taken a somewhat more careful approach where voice over the Internet is concerned.[70] Two areas of concern are (i) the bypass opportunity afforded by voice over the Internet, in that international settlements are not assessed on the transmission; and (ii) the potential for Internet telephony to be used as a way to end-run restrictions in ISPs' operations. For example, alongside the relaxed licensing atmosphere of India, the Government has quite specifically prohibited speech from being carried by an ISP, as it would violate the voice services monopoly of Videsh Sanchar Nigam Limited (VSNL), India's international carrier. India has indicated that it will stick by the ban until it concludes the formal review of VSNL's monopoly, due in 2004. In the same vein, Taiwan has declared voice over the Internet as equivalent to the provision of a 'fixed line' service, that is, putting it on a par with circuit switched telephony. As such, the offering of voice over the Internet would violate the basic service monopoly of Chunghwa Telecom, the current national provider, whose monopoly expires in 2001. And indeed the Government of Pakistan has banned voice transmission over the Internet under threat of prosecution according to the Telephone and Telegraph Act of 1885, bringing into stark contrast the old and new worlds. These limits are like a red flag to Internet operators, who see a market opportunity to offer an alternative voice service at significant savings.

In a more liberal vein, the voice over the Internet regime in Hong Kong is quite pragmatic. The regulator there, OFTA, has held that basic voice services in Hong Kong may be provided by any technological methods, including Internet, call-back, frame relay and asynchronous transfer mode (ATM), among others. The regulator, in exchange for this flexibility in choice of technology, will license ISPs that wish to offer voice services, and subject them to the same regulations as a traditional circuit-switched telco. The requirements include, for example, contributions to the universal service scheme, paying access charges where applicable, conformity to the Hong Kong numbering plan and reporting of traffic statistics. The regulator has come up with a Solomonic decision, which offers a choice to the consumer of service quality and price, while at the same time putting the Internet telephony providers and the circuit-switched providers on an equal competitive footing, through the sharing of regulatory obligations.

In Japan and in South Korea, the regulators have actively recognised voice over the Internet as a regulatory category and as a fully legitimate service in its own right. AT&T Jens, in Japan, was the first to announce an international Internet telephony offering in conjunction with its traditional Internet access business, and has attracted a considerable following.[71] The partial rationale by the Korean and Japanese Governments seems to be to encourage ISPs to

---

[70] For a discussion of voice over the Internet generally, see Hopkins, M. and Lakelin, P., *Commercial Strategies for Internet Telephony* (Cambridge (Mimeo), Analysis Publications, 1998).

[71] See http://www.attjens.co.jp/index_e.html.

enter the telephony market quickly, while international retail call prices are still high. The ISPs can put competitive pressure on call charges of the more established operators, primarily through their much-reduced infrastructure costs and lack of settlements payments. Routers and gateways, essentially commodities, cost in the tens to hundreds of thousands of US dollars, as compared to millions for a customised network switch for the PSTN network. These initiatives are seen as pro-competitive and indicate that there is room in these markets for call charges, particularly on international routes, to come down. When they do, and in conjunction with the fall in international accounting rates, it will have to be seen whether the Internet voice service providers can still remain viable, as the price of Internet telephony and PSTN charges converge.

13.5.3 China and the Internet: development versus control

Almost all governments in Asia and the Pacific have recognised the tremendous economic potential of the Internet. Yet many feel ambivalent about letting it take hold unfettered in their countries. Perhaps no country exhibits this ambivalence better than China. China's varying approaches to the Internet can be regarded from three angles: (i) the role of foreign firms in the Chinese domestic telecoms sector; (ii) China's efforts to develop a home-grown industry; and (iii) the political dilemma posed by the Internet for the Communist Party.

13.5.3.1 The role of foreign firms   As far back as 1979, China, under Deng Xiao Ping, recognised the overwhelming importance of telecommunications to the national economy, and in the intervening years has invested heavily in its network. In 1985, for example, China's national network, by lines installed, was the seventeenth largest in the world. By 1997, China had the second largest network in the world, including one million kilometres of fibre optic cable.[72] To assist the massive build effort, and to upgrade the overall quality of the underlying technology, the Chinese Government permitted foreign firms to invest in equipment manufacturing joint ventures with Chinese state-owned companies, with the attendant requirement of significant transfers of technology, primarily in the semiconductor, network switching and fibre optic cable areas.[73] In the 1980s particularly, China signed contracts with many of the major Western telecommunications equipment manufacturers, all of them eager to sell into the China market. The list includes Philips, CIT-Alcatel, Fujitsu, Northern Telecom, Nokia, Canada's Spar Aerospace, Ericsson, ITT, and others.

---

[72] Both the 1985 figure and the 1997 figure come from Lawrence, Susan V., 'Telecoms Brawl', *Far East Economic Review*, 30 September 1999, at 69.

[73] In the late 1970s and early 1980s, the spate of joint ventures raised significant concerns in some Western countries about dual-use technologies, such as semiconductor manufacturing equipment and processes being transferred to China. See Vawter, Lisa Allen, 'The Case of Telecommunications in US Technology Transfer to China', Masters Thesis, Massachusetts Institute of Technology, Department of Political Science, 1985.

On the services side, at least officially, foreign firms were not permitted to partner with any of the telephone companies at the national or provincial levels for network operation or service provision. Western, as well as Chinese, eagerness for entry into Chinese telecommunications and information services was so pressing, however, that many firms resorted to an evasion of the rules – a complicated, tiered holding company pattern which became known as China-China-Foreign (CCF). Once the Chinese and foreign companies ally, that company in turn creates a second joint venture with the original Chinese partner, thus creating what on paper appears to be a wholly Chinese company. One Chinese telecoms company, China Unicom, used this method to create approximately 45 joint ventures with more than 40 foreign partners worth a total of US$1.4 billion.[74] The Chinese Government did not actively enforce the ban, although most observers agree it must have been aware of Unicom's activities. The CCF policy applied equally to Chinese Internet and web hosting companies that were all too eager for foreign investment and know-how. Even Internet cafes, although technically illegal, operated in the open, especially in cosmopolitan centres such as Shanghai. In the later part of the 1980s and early 1990s it seemed that Deng's Open Door finally meant 'open for business', and at long last the Chinese telecommunications market could be developed.

In 1999, the open door began to swing shut, as Minister of Information Industry Wu Jichuan announced in September that he would henceforth enforce the ban on foreign firms' investment in the operations side of the telecommunications sector, which includes Internet businesses. Foreign firms began scrambling to recover their investment as Chinese partners served notice that the joint venture had to be wound up.[75] The practice of contract by acquaintance in China, rather than according to a reliable legal framework, removes avenues of recourse for foreign joint venture partners who find themselves out of favour. Potentially millions of dollars could be stranded.[76] The Minister's September announcement indicated that a clarification would be issued by year's end. The status of all CCF joint ventures had to wait. In January 2000, the real concerns of the Chinese Government became somewhat clearer. In a statement, the Government created a previously nonexistent distinction between Internet service providers and Internet content providers. Under a new set of rules, Internet content providers would be held responsible for ensuring that their sites did not reveal State secrets. Content included chat rooms and bulletin boards, suggesting that content providers must actively monitor their sites. All content providers would have to be licensed, and in case of any doubt as to what was a State secret, content

---

[74] See Williams, Martyn, 'Metromedia Dissolving China Project after CCF Ban', at http://www.newsbytes.com.pubNews/99/134488.html, 8 August 1999. China Unicom's partners include Deutsche Telecom, France Télécom, NTT, Sprint and Bell Canada, among others.
[75] Harmsen, Peter, 'China Turns Up Heat on Foreign Firms to Exit Telecom Ventures', at http://www.totaltele.com/secure/view.asp, 27 October 1999.
[76] Following this announcement, many foreign firms that decided to extricate themselves had the unenviable task of re-valuing their initial investment in light of their partner's trading activities, and determining whether any taxes were owed.

providers were invited to apply to local authorities.[77] The new rules were to be retroactive to 1 January 2000, and there was no specific mention of the role of foreign firms in either Internet content or service providers.

This January announcement came just two months after China and the United States signed an agreement finalising China's entry into the WTO. Under this agreement China pledged, upon its accession, to allow foreign firms into the services side of the telecommunications sector, initially value-added and mobile services, and then basic wire line telecommunications services on a 49–51 per cent basis with a Chinese partner by 2006.[78] Still, considerable confusion lingered concerning the extent of permitted foreign ownership, in which services, and the time frame for legitimate entry. In these circumstances, foreign firms would be raising their risks considerably were they to undertake significant market activity in China in the short term, until the situation resolved itself. The Minister's September announcement and the January 'clarification' have not prevented further joint ventures with foreign partners from being announced, though, despite the uncertainty. In June 2000, it was reported in the press that following successful talks between China and the European Commission on China's entry into the WTO, European firms would be allowed to re-invest in China Unicom. This new policy applied to firms such as France Télécom, Deutsche Telecom and Telecom Italia, which were in the process of completing or had just completed the termination of their partnerships.[79]

13.5.3.2 Developing a home-grown industry The fragile state of foreign participation in the Internet and hosting markets in China in no way signals a pulling back from the medium. Indeed, China has taken very clear steps over the years to foster a vibrant telecommunications sector, and now has a lively Internet environment with locally cultivated inputs. The overall telecoms sector is far from monolithic. In 1994, the Government injected some competition into the national market when it authorised the creation of a second national telephone company, China Unicom, to compete with China Telecom, the State-run national service provider. China Unicom was also intended to act as an instrument of reform for China Telecom, which badly needed a competitive challenge. China Telecom, like most incumbents, stalled its rival on issues such as interconnection so as to frustrate the competitor's development. After four years, the Government was not seeing the results it wanted, which were increased line deployment, a bit of price competition and choice for consumers. Given its unwillingness to invite foreigners into the services market, the Government had to seek further reforms of China Telecom. As a result, in 1998, the Government forced the regulator, the Ministry of Information Industry, to separate the operator from

---

[77] 'China Unveils New Internet Regulations', http://www.totaltele.com/secure/view, 27 January 2000.
[78] See 'China's WTO Accession: Trade Interests, Values and Strategy', speech by Ambassador Charlene Barshefsky, US Trade Representative, 4 February 2000, http://www.ustr.gov/speeches.
[79] Nuttall, Keith, 'China OKs foreign re-investment in Unicom' at http://www.totaltele.com/view/asp, 19 June 2000.

the Ministry in order to administer the sector more neutrally. We see with this move recognition on the part of the Chinese Government, like many before it, that in order to promote telecom sector development the regulator must be completely divorced from any operational role.

But the Chinese Government did not stop there. In 1999, it began the process of breaking up China Telecom into three smaller companies, each operating in separate markets, namely mobile, fixed line (domestic and international) and satellite services. In the same exercise, the Ministry required China Telecom to transfer its entire paging business to China Unicom in a bid to strengthen the new entrant. China Unicom, like China Telecom, already provided mobile and Internet access services. In 1999, China Unicom was given the exclusive right to build and operate a CDMA-based mobile network in China; and in January 2000, the Government licensed China Unicom for external facilities-based operations, that is, international services.[80] The Chinese Government perhaps handed China Unicom the paging and CDMA businesses for two reasons. First, these are popular services that if handled correctly could lead to rapid revenue gain for China Unicom and a healthy financial position from which to confront China Telecom in the areas where they compete directly. Another motivation for the Chinese Government lay in the fact that paging and mobile infrastructure are relatively easy and inexpensive to install relative to fixed line deployment. In China Unicom's hands, increased rollout might result in faster access for many of the population to even rudimentary telecommunications services. Nevertheless, the restructuring of the industry between China Telecom and China Unicom, although profound, was not the end of the Government's stimulation of the sector.

The Chinese Government in 1999 created the first new telephone company in five years with the authorisation of China Netcom, licensed to provide high-speed voice, video and data services in 15 cities.[81] China Netcom entered the world with 5,000 kilometres of fibre optic cable and the pooled resources of its founding investors, the Ministry of Railways, the State Administration of Radio, Film and Television, the Chinese Academy of Sciences, and the Shanghai municipal government. The business space this company occupies is the high-speed, broadband services area, which includes video and Internet voice.[82] The network is entirely based on Internet Protocol (IP) technology. China Netcom's principal product offering is Internet-based phone service. It hopes to expand into IP-based corporate networks, when the city links are complete, focusing on data and web-hosting services. China Netcom's chief executive, Edward Tian, is a US-trained Chinese national

---

[80] See Reuters, 'China Unicom gets thumbs up for international service', http://www.totaltele.com/secure/view/asp, 10 March 2000.

[81] See Kynge, James, 'China plans to launch third state telecoms company', *Financial Times*, 27 October 1999, p. 18.

[82] Internet telephony became legal in China in February 1999. Three companies, Jitong, China Unicom and China Telecom, received the first licences. In May 1999, China Telecom launched a nationwide Internet telephony trial in partnership with Jitong and China Unicorn covering 14 cities. See Zhu, Joseph, 'China Launches Internet Telephony', http://www.techweb.com, 19 May 1999.

who has already made a name for himself as the founder of AsianInfo, a software company.

In the spring of 2000, the four licensed data carriers – China Telecom, China Netcom, China Unicom and Jitong – all made announcements regarding increased spending on their networks to respond to spiralling demand for Internet capacity. Indeed, total spending on network infrastructure in the period from 1996 to 2001 was 800 billion yuan, or US$96.4 billion.[83] China's Internet users, who currently number approximately 22.5 million, are expected to increase to 60 million by 2005.[84] As the numbers grow and the users become more sophisticated, their usage patterns, such as downloading software and music files, put a substantial strain on the network.

The Government, despite its actions concerning foreign investors, does wish the Internet to become a mainstay of China's telecom environment, and indeed is trying to make it easier for Chinese ISPs to reach their customers and for customers to get on to the Net. In 1999, for example, the Ministry of Information Industries ordered China Telecom to cut its international leased-line prices, and to reduce by 45 per cent the price of a domestic digital leased-line.[85] It is clear that China wants to have a world-class Internet sector, but one that is home-grown and not reliant on foreign investment or content. China is also looking ahead to the growth of electronic commerce as an economic engine. China has put in place the telecommunications infrastructure in the major city centres to accommodate a growing e-sector, but much work remains to be done in the finance, consumer credit and banking sectors to bring the e-conomy to reality.[86] China also seems ambivalent about the globalising effect such activity would have on the national population.

13.5.3.3 The political challenge of the Internet and the search for acceptable content Every year around the middle of May, in the run-up to the Tiananmen Square anniversary on 4 June, headlines appear in the Western press such as 'China Starts Seizing Satellite Dishes',[87] or 'Police net 300 illegal Web cafes',[88] or 'Shanghai orders clampdown on pager, Internet news'.[89] These are fairly recent additions to the now-expected round-up of dissidents for temporary shelter in custody until the anniversary passes. What is new is the judgment on the part of the Chinese authorities that the human and technological threats are comparable, and that both require action by the State. The events of Tiananmen Square have sensitised the Communist Party at least to be aware of public opinion, but the Party has not reached the point

---

[83] 'China has 230m phone subscribers, 22.5m Net users' at http://www.totaltele.com/view, 11 April 2001.
[84] *Ibid.*
[85] Addison, Craig, 'China Cuts Telecom Rates for Internet Providers', http://www.totaltele.com, 25 October 1999.
[86] See Dougan, D. and Xing, P. (eds), *Scaling the Great Wall of E-Commerce*, China Electronic Commerce Project Report 1999, Washington, DC, Center for Strategic and International Studies in conjunction with Cyber Century Forum, 1999.
[87] See http://www.cnn.com/world/asiapcf, 6 May 1999.
[88] See http://www.scmp.com/news/China/Article, 9 June 1999.
[89] See http://www.insidechina.com, 25 May 1999.

where it will forbear trying to control public opinion and the information that fuels it. The freewheeling world of the Internet, therefore, is viewed rightly or wrongly as potentially destabilising.[90]

For example, since the Tiananmen Square events, the Chinese authorities have been irked by the Fa Lun Gong sect, which reportedly uses the Internet to help organise rallies and spread its message. Part of its message, ironically, adheres to the non-violent political tradition, and so actually does not pose much of a threat. Thus the Government finds itself in a quandary between development and control, between freedom and stability. The economic goals of improved infrastructure and a more efficient economy via Internet technology are directly inimical to the political goals of information control and limiting dissent.[91] As evidence of this, rather tellingly, the clarification on Internet policy that was announced in January 2000 (see 13.5.3.1 above) came from one of the State security directorates, and not from one of the telecommunications and information policy organs. We believe that for years to come there will be a conflict within the Chinese Government between the economic orientated ministries that believe in the development of the Internet, and the security bodies that distrust the medium as threatening.[92]

In the meantime, in order to fuel the continued growth of the Internet in China, the authorities, whether economic or security orientated, will need to agree on a formula for sourcing enough content to keep the sector viable. Perhaps larger than putting enough telecommunications infrastructure in place is the challenge for China of finding acceptable content for Chinese users of the Internet.[93] It would appear the options are either (i) the content can be filtered Western content, which requires direct State censorship, or (ii) the Government can assist in the development of Chinese-based content. In 1996, the Chinese Government created the China Internet Corporation, a company set up to manage content on the Internet in China, effectively a filtering group.[94] The China Internet Corporation, in collaboration with the State news agency, Xinhua, and AOL, for example, have cooperated to

---

[90] See Lawrence, Susan V., 'In Tiananmen's Shadow', *Far Eastern Economic Review*, 27 May 1999.

[91] Holland, Lorien, 'Plugging a Sieve', *Far Eastern Economic Review*, 10 February 2000, at 20–21.

[92] In March 2000 a Chinese website, IT163.com, suffered a hacker attack that shut down the e-commerce site for a period of days. The method of attack was similar to that used during the three-day barrage in February 2000 that crippled several US sites. The hacker bombards the site with so many messages that it cannot respond and becomes overloaded. Events such as this in China will most certainly give weight to those arguing in favour of stringent control over the Internet and content. See Kynge, James, 'Hacker cripples Chinese web site', *Financial Times*, 11 March/12 March 2000, p. 1.

[93] Krochmal, Mo, 'China Sees Huge Demand for Net Content', http://www.techweb.com, 14 May 1998.

[94] Reporters Sans Frontieres (RSF) is a group that reports on blocking, filtering and banning of content by government authorities around the world. In its 1999 report, the RSF singled out China for its monitoring of Internet use and the detention of Lin Hai, 'who was jailed for supplying Chinese e-mail addresses to a US-based dissident site that publishes an e-mail newsletter critical of the government'. See Williams, Martyn, 'Reporters Sans Frontieres Uncovers Enemies of the Internet', http://www.newsbytes.com, 9 August 1999. Lin Hai was released ahead of his two-year term on 23 September 1999.

develop a web-based service that has the look and feel of AOL but conforms to Chinese content laws. China.com selects general Western and business news according to State guidelines, has it translated, and posts it on government servers around the country.[95] Despite the Government support, China.com has not appeared as popular as other Chinese language websites that have sprung up to fill the demand for content, such as Sina.com, Sohu.com, Netease.com, and Renren.com, primarily based in Hong Kong.[96]

As we have seen, China is struggling to develop and capitalise on the best the Internet has to offer, while trying to shield itself from potentially 'harmful' political effects. In the advantages column for the Internet would appear the positive attributes such as a low-cost, efficient technology, with productivity-enhancing potential for China's economy. In the 'harmful' column would appear lack of control over information coming into China, the possibility that communities of interest would begin contacting each other within China, and that organised public opinion would put pressure on the state, all via this new medium.[97] Also in the negative column one might put the threat of entrepreneurship. Young engineering graduates are starting small businesses, mostly centred in the Haidian district in Beijing, and bettering themselves without relying on the State. Their ingenuity and initiative are sending profound signals to a new generation of Chinese that it is possible to succeed without using personal connections, or relying on the extras that come from a Government sinecure.[98] China's trading partners (and international human rights groups) are no doubt hoping that the economic benefits of widespread Internet use in China will compel the authorities to keep the trading and investment channels open to the outside world. Another, equally persuasive view of the future of the Internet in China is not to expect China to do anything that will undermine the stability of the State, whatever the associated economic cost. For several years to come, it is likely that the uncertainty over the role of foreigners and the controversy over acceptable content will hold China back from fulfilling all the optimistic predictions favoured by telecommunications consultants and Western marketing gurus.

13.6   CONCLUSION: TELECOMMUNICATIONS LAW, INFORMATION POLICY AND THE ROLE OF THE INTERNET IN ASIA AND THE PACIFIC

13.6.1   The Internet requires infrastructure

Before countries such as China and others can profit from the information economy, they must ensure that the basic domestic telecommunications and other enabling infrastructures, such as IP-based network or advanced mobile

---

[95] See Krochmal, Mo, 'China Seeking Filtered Content', http://www.techweb.com, 28 May 1998.

[96] See Holland, Lorien, 'Riding The Wave', *Far Eastern Economic Review*, 8 July 1999, p. 78.

[97] Gilley, Bruce, 'Han Hooligans', *Far Eastern Economic Review*, 4 May 2000, pp. 72–75, for an account of the rise of soccer fan clubs, new loyalties and web-based promotions.

[98] See McCarthy, Terry, 'China's Internet Gold Rush', *Time Magazine*, 28 February 2000, p. 32.

systems, are in place. At one extreme, countries such as Nepal and Bangladesh, which face comprehensive development challenges that go beyond telecommunications, will need to invest or attract vast sums to upgrade and expand the basic 'teledensity' of their telecommunications networks. As we have seen in the cases of India, Indonesia and The Philippines, there are several options and financing structures that can be used to help get the construction underway without excessive demands on the national treasury. Many of these financing options will raise domestic considerations regarding the use of private capital, and establishing the proper role (if any) for foreign investors. Traditionally, multilateral development banks, such as the Asian Development Bank and the World Bank, have played a part, but these are coming under heavy criticism regarding their appropriateness and effectiveness.[99]

In addition, much of developing Asia finds itself in the position of managing away from a monopoly structure towards a multi-provider environment. The difficulty is that in a monopoly position, generally there are no other corporate entities in the domestic economy with any telecommunications experience, forcing the government to seek solutions abroad. In this regard, this chapter reviewed examples from Indonesia and Thailand. A typical response in such cases is for the host government to limit the foreign portion of a telecommunications joint venture to around 50 per cent, seeking to strike a balance between attracting a large inflow of funding and expertise while leaving the majority of the venture in local hands. In these days of ever-liberalised markets, however, influenced by an emerging WTO structure, the more conservative countries in this regard will find themselves unable to attract foreign investment, because there are better opportunities presented to foreign investors (including control, management and ownership) elsewhere.

At the international infrastructure level, a significant fraction of network development and its financing originates from outside the Asian region. As an example, construction of undersea networks linking Asian countries with the United States for handling Internet traffic involves extensive participation from outside Asia and the Pacific. Companies such as Level 3 and Global Crossing represent a new generation of network builders that seek to provide Internet capacity to major cities, where demand is booming. In early 2000, Level 3 was among the first non-Hong Kong-based companies to become licensed to land an international submarine cable in Hong Kong. Level 3 is putting in infrastructure to link Hong Kong with Japan, Korea and Taiwan, and then join up with its international IP-based system to take the traffic back to the United States and beyond. Level 3 also operates data centres for corporate hosting services in Tokyo and Hong Kong.[100] For its part, Global Crossing, a Bermuda-based company, is undertaking a phased building approach, which will end by installing capacity from the US to Japan, and

---

[99] The protests at the WTO Ministerial meeting in Seattle and the World Bank meeting in Washington, DC in the late 1999/early 2000 period are testimony to the growing popular distrust of large, and seemingly remote, financial institutions.

[100] Bickers, Charles, 'New Kids in Town', *Far Eastern Economic Review*, 16 March 2000, p. 12.

then to Hong Kong, Malaysia, The Philippines, Korea, Taiwan and China. In addition, MCI/WorldCom (10 per cent) with Telecom New Zealand (50 per cent) and Cable & Wireless Optus (40 per cent) in Australia constructed the Southern Cross Cable network, an undersea cable linking Australasia with the United States. At this point it is appropriate to observe that the demand for Internet capacity in Asia is being met by non-Asian investors. Why does it take outsiders to bring connectivity to Asia?

Another interesting question mark sits over the absence to date of an Asian transnational supercarrier (on the order of AT&T/BT) with interests in several countries that would have the scale and the resources to see to the construction of its own regional network with links globally. We believe that the absence of a regional telecoms power is due to the still high, retained government shares in many of the region's incumbents. Their incentives to invest, form alliances and merge outside their national borders are limited. This may be due in part to the lack of shareholder pressure to deliver competitive returns. A fragmented regional market, where no one company has the scale to be an infrastructure provider to the region and globally, will leave Asian carriers relatively weak and under-represented among the global telecom titans.[101] The takeover of Cable & Wireless Hong Kong Telecom in mid-2000 by non-telco Pacific Century Cyber Works (PCCW) may herald a new era, and may stimulate more cross-border activity in the region.[102] We also note the agreement in early 2001 between Singapore Telecom and Cable & Wireless plc for the purchase of Cable & Wireless's controlling interest in Cable & Wireless options in Australia.

13.6.2   The telecom legal structure must evolve

To the extent that governments have decided that competition is healthy for the telecom sector, they must also put in place the underlying regulatory framework, laws and institutions to support a competitive regime. Some actions involve reforming the national incumbent, and some involve reforming the regulator. Over the last five to eight years, countries in the Asia-Pacific region have taken bold and innovative actions with respect to reforming regulatory structures, even going as far as combining the broadcasting, telecommunications and IT policy-making and regulatory function into one administrative body. There are no parallel moves in other countries to 'converge' the regulators outside this region, which puts some Asian and Pacific countries at the forefront of institutional reform.

In much of the developed world, traditional telecom sector regulation is giving way to competition law, and this chapter has reviewed the state of competition law across several Asian jurisdictions. Some countries, such as Australia and New Zealand, have adopted the competition law approach with vigour; while others, such as Japan and Singapore, have not taken on these concepts convincingly. The lack of competition law will affect the ability of

---

[101] See Wilhelm, Kathy *et al.*, 'Wake-Up Call', *Far Eastern Economic Review*, 16 March 2000, pp. 8–10.
[102] See Gilley, Bruce, 'Shared Gamble', *Far Eastern Economic Review*, 4 May 2000, pp. 38–39.

regulators to resolve carrier disputes, which typically arise in relation to the market power of the incumbent. Without a concept of 'dominance' in local laws, regulators will not have the power to restrain incumbents from anti-competitive behaviour. As global practice and expectations converge around international regulatory norms, which include some competition law principles, new entrants will prefer to compete in markets where these ground rules are better established.

13.6.3   Telecommunications law and the new economy

In Asia, as in the rest of the world, Internet use has moved on from casual surfing to a mission-critical application for both individuals and businesses. With this level of integration of the Internet into daily life and commerce, regulators and legislators are facing up to a whole new range of public policy and legal issues in order to create a predictable and stable electronic communicating and trading environment (see Table 13.5).

At the infrastructure level, growing Internet and e-commerce usage requires robust networks and a very high quality of service. Issues such as local loop unbundling, the installation of xDSL, and the deployment of broadband transmission as policy matters come to the fore. As of early 2000, only a few Asian countries, Malaysia being among the first, and Australia have begun to address how to make incumbent networks available to competitors, or to

Table 13.5   E-commerce essentials

Public policy/legal issue area	*Sub-issues*
Infrastructure	• Internet peering • Local loop unbundling • ADSL availability
Internet governance	• Internet domain name resource • Cybersquatting
Security	• Digital signatures • Authentication • Encryption
Privacy	• Protection of personal data • Spamming
Content	• 'Harmful' content
Commerce	• Applicable law • Taxation and tariffs • Liabilities of intermediaries

debate what pricing structure for that infrastructure should apply.[103] Even the use of leased lines, whereby new entrants rent their infrastructure from the incumbent to offer services on a re-sale basis, is generally not on a competition-friendly footing. Up until 2000, for example, Singapore Telecom was allowed to charge full retail rates for its leased lines, reducing to practically nil any possible margin on the services offered by a third party in competition to SingTel. The regulator can opt to intervene and regulate the price incumbents charge for leased lines and other unbundled infrastructure, and can thereby affect the incentives for new carriers such as ISPs to enter the market.[104] Japan is a noteworthy case, where NTT's per minute local access charges are so high (by some estimates three to four times US and EU averages).[105] These costs are passed on to residential customers who balk at such high rates for Internet access. Potential competitors have little incentive to acquire local access from NTT as a platform from which to offer alternative Internet services.

Australia is one place where the regulator, in this case the ACCC, has compelled the incumbent carrier, Telstra, to grant access to its networks to make sure ISP competition flourishes. Telstra has said it will roll-out ADSL technology in all of Australia's major cities from August 2000. ADSL is a broadband technology that increases the local copper network line speed by 30–50 times, and is considered essential for high-speed Internet access.[106] Telstra has assured the ACCC that it will allow competitors, such as Cable & Wireless Optus and AAPT, access to the network once the technology is installed, so they too may offer the faster Internet services.

Many countries across Asia and the Pacific have also recognised that in order for electronic commerce and trading to flourish, individuals and businesses need to be able to conclude contracts and engage in trade reliably and confidently over the Internet. This requires recognising the legal validity of electronic transactions and contracts, which can be established in local law by legislation. Between 1998 and early 2000, a bow wave of legislation on electronic signatures made its way through parliaments, cabinets and congresses, in countries such as Japan, Malaysia, Hong Kong, Singapore,

---

[103] The use of existing infrastructure by new entrants can take many forms, and is a complex regulatory subject. Among the alternatives are simple leased lines, 'unbundling' network elements for use by new entrants, such as the local loop, certain conditioned circuits of specific capacities, virtual circuits, bitstream unbundling, or other elements of the local network such as switching, signalling, operator and directory services and operational support systems. Malaysia introduced equal access in 1999, a system of accessing competitive carriers by special dialing codes. Hong Kong has also taken a long look at access to broadband networks to further Internet development. See http://www.ofta.gov.hk.

[104] At the international level, the availability of circuits for re-sale is a key method of bringing down calling rates and stimulating international traffic. As of the first half of 2000, only a handful or so of countries had an international re-sale regime: Australia, Hong Kong, Japan, New Zealand, Singapore and South Korea.

[105] See Lazarus, David, 'Cheaper Net Access in Japan?', http://www.wired.com/news/news/businessstory, 17 June 1999; and http://www.nni.nikkei.co.jp, 'Editorial: Costly NTT Local Network Hurts Economy', 23 June 1999.

[106] See Reuters, 'Telstra to start ADSL roll-out in August', at http://www.totaltele.com, 29 May 2000.

Australia, Taiwan, South Korea, India, and others. It is a fairly mechanical, but essential, part of establishing basic operating parameters for the electronic world. In the same vein, some countries, such as Japan, have drafted legislation to establish certification and authentication bodies, authorities which provide a service that verifies the identity of the parties in a transmission and confirms the soundness of the content thereof. Such measures contribute to user confidence regarding electronic transactions.[107]

Electronic commerce issues that relate more to the consumer protection side, such as the treatment of personal data, electronic privacy, fraud and the settlement of disputes arising from a retail electronic transaction, are a whole separate field of policy and law that must, as elsewhere, be addressed across many Asian and Pacific jurisdictions.[108] Hong Kong stands out in the privacy protection area as having developed an industry code of practice for tackling unsolicited e-mail, known as 'spam', and establishing a Not-to-Call list for commercial fax advertisements. The code of practice was announced in February 2000 by the telecom regulator OFTA and the Hong Kong Internet Service Providers Association, in conjunction with the Privacy Commissioner for Personal Data.[109] ISPs, which adhere to the code of conduct against spamming, will be able to display a logo, approved by OFTA, on their site. The Not-to-Call list is intended for advertisers so that they do not send faxes to recipients who have specifically elected to be excluded from such bulk calling lists, the so-called 'opt-out process'. The list is available on the OFTA website and is updated every two weeks, showing a fairly robust commitment to privacy on the part of the regulator.[110]

Increasingly around the world, and in Asia as well, industry associations such as HKISPA are taking responsibility for many concerns in the consumer area and developing codes of conduct and business practices to guide members, suppliers, business partners, etc. in order to give confidence to consumers. It becomes more difficult to determine, therefore, whether official 'policies' exist if no legislation is evident, as such matters may be safely in the hands of industry. Industry codes of conduct can be powerful and convincing alternative tools to assist the development of electronic commerce, and may delay or obviate the need for formal government intervention. On the other hand, some areas, such as the legal standing of electronic signatures, can only be handled by government intervention to enact legislation, resulting in a partnership across the range of issues between industry and government in this emerging area. Further electronic commerce areas ripe for such co-regulation are taxes and tariffs for electronic transactions, applicable law (i.e., how to establish in which jurisdiction a transaction takes place) and what are

---

[107] APEC has an Electronic Commerce Task Force, which is considering the full range of the issues mentioned above, including the interoperability of public key infrastructures used in the 21 member States. See the Task Force website at http://www.dfat.gov.au/apec/ecom.

[108] See also Government of Japan, Ministry of Posts and Telecommunications, 'Interim Report of the Study Group on Legislation of the Privacy Protection Law in the Telecommunications Sector (Summary)', at http://www.mpt.go.jp/policyreports/english/group/telecommunications/PrivacyProtection.html, 25 November 1999.

[109] See http://www.ofta.gov.hk.

[110] *Ibid.*

the reasonable liabilities that should attach to an ISP or hosting entity. Governments and industry can consider these matters together so as not to hinder the growth of the e-market, while at the same time providing a stable and predictable environment for trade.

Mention must be made of the issues of computer security and computer crime in Asia, the region that was the launch pad for the hackers who paralysed several leading e-commerce sites in the United States for three days in February 2000[111] and produced the 'I Love You' virus a few months later. Traced to The Philippines, the virus spread by e-mail. Once opened, it corrupted files and disabled internal computer drives.

Hacking, whether for showcase stunts such as defacing government sites, or data theft and fraud for unlawful gain, is growing in Asia. All forms of hacking are seeing an alarming rise. In Hong Kong, for example, reported cases rose from 13 in 1998, to 238 in 1999. The figure for South Korea tripled over the same period from 158 in 1998 to 572 in 1999. These numbers are approaching US levels, which reached 1,154 reported cases in 1999.[112] In that year, the Governments of Hong Kong and Singapore handed down jail sentences for hackers, for the first time. By March 2000, the Singapore courts had prosecuted nine hacking cases since the beginning of the year.[113] Unfortunately, not enough countries in the region have the anti-hacking laws to make it a crime, or enough resources in the hands of law enforcement authorities to control the rise of computer crime.[114] The denouement of the 'I Love You' hacking story is encouraging nonetheless. The alleged Filipino hacker was traced through the efforts of the Philippines National Computer Crime Centre, one of the more advanced anti-computer crime agencies in the region. Perhaps ironically, however, although Filipino authorities had successfully traced a suspect, they were forced to free him and drop the case because there were not sufficient laws on the books the authorities could use to raise charges.[115] By the end of June 2000, however, the Filipino Congress had rushed through a new computer crime law in order to deter future activity of this kind. Since the suspect could not be charged under the new law, the alleged crime having taken place prior to its passage, he was eventually charged under laws pertaining to credit card fraud and theft.

---

[111] Hackers launched a series of stunning denial of service (DOS) attacks on leading e-commerce sites in the United States such as Yahoo!, eBay, E*Trade and others, shutting some down for hours and others for days. While the hackers themselves are rumoured to have been based in Germany, they allegedly used servers in Australia in part to launch the DOS attack. See Dolven, Ben *et al.*, 'How Safe Are You?', *Far Eastern Economic Review*, 24 February 2000, p. 16.

[112] These data come from Gilley, Bruce, and Crispin, Shawn, 'A New Game of Cops and Robbers', in *Far Eastern Economic Review*, 20 April 2000, p. 50.

[113] See 'Singapore, Hong Kong crack down on teen hackers', at http://www.cnn.com/2000/TECH/computing, 23 March 2000.

[114] As far as we are aware, Hong Kong, Australia, Singapore, South Korea and The Philippines have dedicated computer crime units. Japan is considering legislation that would empower its police force in this area, and Thailand is setting up a larger unit to reinforce its one cyber cop. It is very difficult to generalise on this subject, and omissions are inevitable, given such a rapidly changing field.

[115] See Reuters, '"Love Bug" suspect freed', at http://www.cnnfn.com/2000/06/07, 7 June 2000.

We expect that the computer crime area will be the focus of another wave of legislation that will sweep across Asia and the Pacific in the near term to shore up the region's defences. Public education programs also go a long way towards informing users and companies about steps they can take to increase their own computer security, such as the use of firewalls, and warning of the risks of purchasing stolen passwords. Apparently, the owner of one of the Australian servers used in the February 2000 US attack was unaware of firewall technology, which might have reduced his risk of being used as an unwitting host.[116]

13.6.4 Asia will confront the Internet society

As this chapter has described, there is a telecommunications infrastructure boom occurring in Asia and the Pacific region that will permit all of those countries benefiting from such investments to take advantage of the electronic age, transform their economies, and bring improvements to the quality of life for many. When the new infrastructure is coupled with telecommunications policies and laws supporting liberalisation, competition and restructured regulators, Asia has the opportunity to make significant and lasting economic gains, to recover from much of the damage that occurred in the late 1990s.

Many parts of Asia now stand at a crossroads involving choices that go beyond pipes and statutes – that was the easy part. The information travelling over the Internet has the potential to transform society and, whether by stealth or by design, governments will be challenged to respond. Many governments across the Asia-Pacific region have the opportunity to create consciously a new culture of information where perhaps there was not one before, or to discourage the influx of unwelcome and discordant values, opinions and interest groups. In this chapter, the example of China was used to demonstrate the concern that a cheap public medium such as the Internet can cause to the Communist Party. Each country is free to select its own path and level of degree regarding access to information and use of this medium. Specific choices made today could lead to different outcomes, however, concerning the future development of electronic commerce, foreign investment and technological innovation.

It is too early to tell what will be Asia's overall future with respect to the handling of information and sensitive content, and what expectations will develop between governed and government, but the forces of both conservatism and openness are evident.[117] These anecdotes from recent years illustrate ambivalence over a new and powerful medium:

- *Australia.* On 1 January 2000, the Broadcasting Services Amendment (Online Services) Act (1999) became effective, giving the Australian Government the authority to require Australian ISPs to take down or block indecent or offensive content, hosted within or *accessible from*

---

[116] Dolven, *op. cit.* n. 108.

[117] See Montagnon, Peter, 'The Future of Asia, Catching the Next Wave', *Financial Times*, 28 December 1999, p. 10.

Australia. The practical upshot of this legislation has been for ISPs to furnish their customers with filtering software, so that they may control access to websites.[118]

- *Japan.* In 1998, the opposition Democratic Party submitted a Bill to the Diet, to permit election campaigning over the Internet. It was defeated by the ruling Liberal Democratic Party.[119, 120]

- *Burma.* In January 2000, Burma, also known as Myanmar, introduced rules limiting the country to only one ISP, the Burmese Ministry of Posts and Telecommunications. Internet users must be granted an account by the Ministry, and are banned from posting on *any* website writings detrimental to the current policies and security of Myanmar. Violations of these rules can carry jail terms of up to 15 years.[121]

- *Malaysia.* On 1 March 2000, the Malaysian Home Ministry reduced the publication frequency of *Harakah*, newspaper of the opposition Islamic party, from twice per week to twice per month, only weeks before an election.[122] The Government allowed the Internet version of the paper to continue unrestricted, however, as evidence of a policy commitment not to interfere with on-line information. Then, on 24 May, the Malaysian Government issued new guidelines for Internet content liability, stating that 'anyone spreading false information or lies through the Internet' could be the target of government action.[123]

Australia's case is one where the global reach of Internet infrastructure raised social concerns principally based on children's access to pornography. The tension here is between freedom of expression and protection of minors. The other three examples above reflect political discomfort concerning the role of the Internet in fostering opposition political movements or parties in three very different Asian countries. It is ironic that some Asian governments take pains to protect or restrict one type of information, political opinion, while other information with real economic value, such as corporate data, is left at risk, as has been shown regarding Internet security in Asia.

It may be controversial to suggest that the extent to which Asian societies can co-exist with dissent is linked to how integrated the Internet economy will become in that society. It can be argued that dissent, deviant and non-conformist behaviour are the sources of what makes the Internet and the

---

[118] See Taggart, Stewart, 'Turning the Screws on Content' at http://www.wired.com/news/news/politics/story/20496.html., 30 June 1999. The Australian Internet Industry Association has a discussion of the law at http://www.iia.net.au.

[119] Nakamoto, Michiyo, 'Net worries of Japan's old guard', *Financial Times*, 11/12 June 2000.

[120] It is interesting to note that in May 1999, Japan's Diet passed a freedom of information law, which will come into effect in 2001. It allows individuals to request official documents from agencies, ministries, etc. The Bill was brought to hold bureaucrats' actions up to greater public scrutiny. See 'Japan Parliament passes freedom of information law', at http://www.cnn.com/world, 7 May 1999.

[121] *World Internet Law Report*, 'World's Harshest Internet Controls Introduced', April 2000, p. 4.

[122] See Elegant, Simon, 'Net Gains', *Far Eastern Economic Review*, 16 March 2000, p. 20.

[123] 'Ministries Have Conflicting Views on Internet Censorship', *World Internet Law Report*, June 2000, p. 9.

World Wide Web the chaotic and creative place that it is. It has been developed, perfected and taken to new frontiers by people most of us call 'nerds', who dare to think the unthinkable and view the world from its possible state. The 'Wild West' atmosphere about the Internet and the web are part of its draw, and the source of the feeling that anything is possible, where fortunes are made and lost. New ideas in the new economy sprout from unexpected origins, including people's garages and basements. Wherever they come from, what they may have in common is the freedom (and funding) to 'think outside the box'. Not surprisingly, large-scale bureaucracies, be they big government or big companies, are not the best incubators of creative chaos. Below is one person's view of chaos, dissent and creativity in Asia:

> What distinguishes these marginal individuals on the fringes of the economy is that money isn't everything to them. The restaurant owner who loves food, the engineer who loves gadgets, the stilt-walker who loves to perform, aren't primarily motivated by immediate economic rewards. Most Asian societies have a low tolerance for dissent. Usually seen as a political or cultural issue, this fear of weirdos, trouble-makers and people who don't fit in is also a serious economic issue. This isn't about Asian values versus Western values. This is about producers vs. consumers. Producer-led economies are run like giant suburban industrial parks. Consumer-led economies are run like chaotic, vibrant, colourful cities . . .
>   . . . exporting sophisticated services will be a key source of future growth for Asia's richer economies. Many Asian fortunes were founded on privileged access to a domestic market or cost arbitrage in international markets for commodity goods such as T-shirts and memory chips. That won't work any more. We need more stilt-walkers and fire-eaters.[124]

The comment and illustrations above have more to do with society-wide structures and beliefs, and less to do with telecommunications policy, but the role of the Internet as a social, economic and political force is fundamental to both.[125]

---

[124] Goad, G. Pierre, 'Circus Economics', *Far Eastern Economic Review*, 10 February 2000, p. 52.
[125] See also 'Culture and the Entrepreneurial Climate', http://businessweek.com/bwdaily/dnflash/june1999, 22 June 1999.

CHAPTER FOURTEEN

Telecommunications Reform in Emerging Markets

Tim Schwarz, David Satola[1] & Camilla Bustani[2]

14.1 INTRODUCTION

Significant reform has occurred in the telecommunications sectors of emerging markets and developing countries over the past 15 years. Governments have established new regulatory regimes and institutions, corporatised and privatised their state-owned telecommunications companies (both by way of selling strategic stakes and via initial public offerings (IPOs)), and liberalised their markets by issuing new licences to new entrants. But what was once traditionally and conveniently defined as a sector has witnessed change at a dizzying pace. This change requires flexible, innovative approaches to reform in the context of ever-increasing new challenges posed by convergence, the promise of the Internet and the threat of the 'digital divide'. Convergence and globalisation have ushered in a 'new economy' that has contributed to blurring those traditional, comfortable services- and facilities-based distinctions. Oddly, the very forces that shape this 'new economy' – forces brought about in part through reform in the 'sector' in the developed world and in the 'old economy' (wealth creation, new forms of capital formation, and access to and use of information) – are the same forces creating the challenges of the digital divide. Today, convergence defines the 'sector'. It is no longer a collection of discrete phenomena at the margins. Accordingly, the reform

[1] The author is Senior Counsel, the World Bank. The views expressed are those of the author and not necessarily those of the World Bank.
[2] The authors are grateful for the research assistance of Ursula Schwessinger, trainee with Clifford Chance and a doctoral candidate at Munich University.

'paradigm' needs fundamental transformation to be responsive to these new realities.

This chapter will address the following issues:

- key characteristics of the telecommunications sectors of emerging markets pre-reform;
- principal regulatory concerns of investors in emerging market telecommunications sectors;
- Government objectives for the privatisation and liberalisation of the telecommunications sector;
- the role of multilateral development agencies;
- creating the right legal framework;
- creating the right regulator;
- telecommunications privatisations; and
- telecommunications liberalisation.

14.2 KEY CHARACTERISTICS PRE-REFORM

14.2.1 Combined posts and telecommunications

In many emerging markets, prior to reform, telecommunications and postal activities were combined and provided by the same parastatal or state-owned entity, operating under a government department or ministry, commonly-known as the PTT (referring to 'posts, telegraph and telecommunications').

The trend in most privatising emerging markets is to separate out the postal and telecommunications activities of the state-owned entity, often transferring the telecommunications activities to a newly formed joint-stock company. Postal activities are often transferred to a statutory corporation, frequently a transitional corporate structure allowing the State to retain certain special privileges, such as tax exemption. Finally, a new and independent regulatory body is created.

14.2.2 State ownership

Where the incumbent is state-owned, it will often operate pursuant to a (politically motivated) five-year plan rather than a licence, and enjoy special property rights (such as the use of public property for no, or for minimal, payment), special radio spectrum rights, and special customs duties and tax exemptions. Management of the state-owned incumbent is often unprepared to face the challenges of a commercially driven, competitive environment.

There is usually no accounting or structural separation between the telecommunications and postal activities, and the military often has a significant influence on both. Employees have civil servant status, making internal restructuring difficult. Over-staffing is typical.

In nearly all emerging markets pre-reform, the incumbent telecommunications operator is state-owned. There are a few exceptions, such as in the Caribbean, where in most of the English-speaking islands (the Bahamas being a notable exception) a private monopoly exists in the hands of Cable & Wireless.

14.2.3 Monopoly rights

Pre-reform, the incumbent operator generally enjoys monopoly rights of varying scope and duration. Indeed, in some cases such rights are for an undefined duration. In particular, fixed voice telephony services and telecommunications infrastructure are invariably subject to monopoly rights. In some countries (such as Kenya) call-back is prohibited (thus protecting the monopoly in respect of international voice telephony), while in others even Internet services are covered by the monopoly rights.

Ironically, in the English-speaking Caribbean, where the incumbent operators are not state-owned but private monopolies (with a few exceptions such as the Bahamas), the scope of the monopoly is extremely wide, in some cases covering fixed voice and mobile services, infrastructure, data and value-added services, and Internet and satellite services.

In many of the English-speaking Caribbean islands, Cable & Wireless enjoys a blanket exclusivity (in the case of Dominica, for example, until 2020) which effectively 'future proofs' its licences from technological developments, so that future telecommunications services automatically fall under the monopoly. Furthermore, in a number of these islands, if Cable & Wireless's licences are terminated or expire, Eastern Caribbean governments must buy back its assets, creating a costly disincentive for these governments to interfere with the private monopoly.

14.2.3.1   Zero or minimal service obligations   Prior to reform, the state-owned incumbent is generally subject to no, or to minimal, service obligations, usually resulting in low penetration (often below 1 per cent in sub-Saharan African countries), poor quality of service, long waiting lists for telephone lines, inaccurate and late billing, and a limited range of services. Often there is hidden demand for telephone lines, with waiting lists already so long that no one bothers to add his or her name.

14.2.3.2   Unbalanced tariff structure   The tariff structure of an emerging market telecommunications sector pre-reform is typically unbalanced, with high international and long-distance tariffs (significantly above cost) and cheap, below-cost installation and local call rates. The above-cost revenues generated from international and long-distance tariffs generally subsidise the below-cost local charges, which in turn are often kept low for political reasons.

14.2.3.3   Services to the government, military etc.   Pre-reform, the incumbent operator might well be expected to provide telecommunications services for free, or below-cost, to a royal family, to government ministries or to the military. In certain countries, the royal family or the government might be late in paying, or simply might not pay, for these telecommunications services. The military might also control large parts of the radio spectrum, which must be ceded as part of the liberalisation process.

14.2.4 No independent regulator

Prior to the inauguration of the reform process, to the extent that there is any regulatory function being performed in the sector, it can be characterised by political and industry 'capture'.[3] There is generally no independent telecommunications regulator in an emerging market prior to reform. Instead, the regulator may be located within the relevant ministry, or worse, within the PTT (postal, telegraph and telephone). The ministry might have the power and discretion to appoint and remove members of the regulator, who would be subject to lax or no conflict of interest controls. Where the government is both owner of the incumbent operator and its regulator, this creates an obvious conflict of interest, even though these two functions might be split between two ministries (for example, the Ministry of Finance and the Ministry of Communications).

Several political imperatives might influence the government in its role as regulator of the telecommunications sector, which are not necessarily in the medium- or long-term interests of the sector as a whole. Such political considerations might include setting or keeping local tariffs low and below cost so as not to alienate voters (particularly in an election year), or causing the incumbent to build out its network in certain regions but not in others, for strategic political advantage.

All of these lead to chronic inefficiencies and a bottleneck to development. Lack of access to capital is also a problem.

14.3 PRINCIPAL INVESTOR CONCERNS

14.3.1 Transparency

Investors are concerned about the transparency of the environment in which they are about to invest. A less certain, less transparent investment environment inevitably means risk premiums (i.e., lower prices) being assigned to investments. There should also be certainty about what is being sold (a licence, shares, or management rights). The concern about transparency also extends to matters of transaction process – are the qualification and selection criteria clear and objective? Are they published or publicly available? Is the bidding process public? This section addresses a number of key issues concerning investor certainty.

14.3.2 Lack of an independent regulator

Among investors' main concerns about transparency is the independence of the regulator. In particular, an investor will be worried that the government,

---

[3] See, e.g., Smith, Warrick, 'Utility Regulators – Roles and Responsibilities', *Viewpoint Note No. 128*, the World Bank (October 1997).

as both owner of the incumbent and its regulator, might discriminate in favour of the incumbent *vis-à-vis* new entrants. The government might adopt a tariff policy determined by political imperatives (e.g., low local charges), and which could be subject to arbitrary and politically motivated change. The government might also implement an interconnection policy that favours the incumbent (e.g., through the use of historic cost-based, rather than incremental cost-based interconnection charges) or fail to make sufficient spectrum, property rights and numbers available to new entrants. An investor might also be concerned that the government has a bias towards resolving disputes in favour of the incumbent.

For obvious reasons these concerns are more important to new entrants than to a strategic investor in the incumbent, the latter possibly benefiting from a pro-incumbent bias. That said, there are a number of important regulatory decisions that the government might make that are not to the advantage of the strategic investor. For instance, artificially low tariffs might be necessary from a political point of view, while undermining the financial soundness of the incumbent as a business (and consequently as an investment for the strategic investor).

14.3.3   Unclear/harsh legal and regulatory environment

Investors will be concerned about legal uncertainty and a disadvantageous (and often harsh) regulatory environment. For instance, investors might expect to see a detailed sector policy statement setting out the government's envisaged liberalisation schedule, while the sector policy will in fact be unclear and non-committal.

Strategic investors will be concerned about the lack of clarity in the scope and legal basis of the rights of the incumbent and those of any competitors. The lack of a proper licensing regime might mean that the circumstances triggering licence revocation, modification, suspension and renewal are unclear or draconian. Furthermore, the government might have reserved emergency powers which it can exercise at any time, including, for instance, to seize an operator's assets.

14.3.4   Absence of controls on anti-competitive conduct

The enormous market power enjoyed by an incumbent monopolist will only increase following the injection of capital and know-how by a strategic investor. This, compounded by the incumbent's head start (including, for example, a legal monopoly over basic and other services, and ownership of infrastructure and terminal equipment), results in the potential for abuse.

Cross-subsidies, with predatory pricing to squeeze out potential competitors at one extreme, and monopoly pricing on the other, are one example of abusive behaviour. However, controls on anti-competitive cross-subsidies should be sensitive to the incumbent's need to re-balance tariffs gradually, so as not to jeopardise the company's financial health.

An incumbent may also impose tying arrangements between monopoly and liberalised services, enter into joint ventures with a private operator on preferential or exclusive terms, discriminate between customers, or engage in price-fixing or other collusive behaviour.

Investors, and in particular new entrants, will expect to see controls on such anti-competitive conduct. While the incumbent operator (and any strategic investor in the incumbent) will often have much to gain from weak controls on anti-competitive conduct, new entrants into liberalised segments of the market (such as a second network operator, cellular operators, or value-added service providers) will regard effective controls on anti-competitive conduct as essential, and will often be deterred from entering the market unless such controls are put in place.

14.3.5 Property rights

In many emerging markets, existing property law does not provide adequately for the types of real property rights that new entrants require. For instance, there may be no rules for the acquisition of rights over private property, or for the compulsory acquisition of land or rights of way other than indirectly through the State. New entrants will therefore expect amendments to the existing property legislation or the introduction of new legislation, or alternatively the inclusion in the Telecommunications Act of specific property rights relevant to the telecommunications sector.

14.3.6 Intellectual property rights

Similarly, a lack of clear rules for the protection of intellectual property may deter potential investors from entering markets, especially when their investments will oblige them to import sensitive or proprietary information which may be protected in their 'home' jurisdiction. Players in the telecommunications industry increasingly depend on new, high-technology equipment and services to remain competitive. In the context of telecommunications privatisations, especially where a strategic investment is sought, there is an expectation that the strategic investor will bring with it know-how and technology to make the to-be-privatised incumbent competitive. However, as is generally the case with infrastructure,[4] where intellectual property is not well-protected, investment, innovation and therefore economic growth may be dampened.[5] Accordingly, jurisdictions without robust protection of intellectual property rights can expect either that potential investors will seek assurances of the protection of their intellectual property, or that those investors will discount the value of the investment according to some risk premium attached to the protection of intellectual property. In this regard, countries with emerging legal regimes for the protection of intellectual property rights can look for guidance in the reform process to the Agreement

---

[4] See *infra*, notes 6–14 and accompanying text.
[5] Maskus, K., *Intellectual Property Rights in the Global Economy* (Washington, DC, *Institute for International Economics*, 2000), at 169. And see Braga, C.P., *et al.*, 'Intellectual Property Rights and Economic Development', *World Bank Discussion Paper 412* (Washington, DC, World Bank, 2000) ('Braga I').

on Trade-Related Aspects of Intellectual Property Rights (TRIPS) and its implementation in national law and judicial and institutional reform.[6]

14.3.7 Investor 'self-help' remedies

Investors concerned with the legal and regulatory environment in an emerging market telecommunications sector will often try to obtain contractual regulation, i.e. building as much regulation as possible into the licence itself, in order to compensate for the lack of regulatory clarity in the primary telecommunications legislation.

Investors will often seek to make it a term of the licence that the government will provide financial compensation for any change in regulation, or for the early termination of the licence.

It is also common for agreements to contemplate that arbitration will take place outside the country of the investment, in the event of disputes between the investor and the government or the regulator.

Although it is possible for investors to be involved in or comment on the drafting of new telecommunications legislation in a privatising or liberalising environment, this inevitably raises issues of democracy, as well as the potential for another conflict of interest, with the prospective subject of regulation commenting on the design of the regulatory regime.

14.4 GOVERNMENT OBJECTIVES FOR THE TELECOMMUNICATIONS SECTOR

14.4.1 Attracting foreign and domestic investors

The government will often wish to encourage domestic investors (such as local utilities) to enter the telecommunications sector. It will also generally be seeking to encourage foreign investors, whether as strategic investors in the state-owned telecommunications operator or simply as new entrants, as they bring with them capital, know-how and technology such as wireless local loop technology which can be a relatively cheap way of serving remote and rural areas.

However, national security concerns will be reflected in government caution as to the identity of the strategic investor, to ensure that the investor is not from, or an investor in, another State perceived to be hostile. This often creates some tension during the privatisation process, with the need for transparency and objectivity in assessing bids (on the one hand), and the need to ensure that national security concerns are met (on the other). That said,

---

[6] A full discussion of the TRIPS Agreement is beyond the scope of this chapter. The TRIPS Agreement is an essential piece in the overall WTO architecture, and has common elements with the General Agreement on Trade in Services, such as its embodiment of the rule of law as the basis for the trade system, evidenced, for example, in its dispute resolution mechanisms. But while it provides minimum standards of protection, TRIPS does not go so far as to provide harmonising legislation. The TRIPS Agreement is available at http://www.wto.org/english/tratop_e/trips_e/t_agm0_e.htm. See also Braga I, *supra* n. 5, at 41.

there are examples where the government has permitted a strategic investor from a potentially hostile State.

Governments will generally also impose stringent change of control provisions in the licences of the incumbent operators, to retain some control over future investors and ensure that any change in the identity of the strategic investors does not raise any national security concerns.

14.4.2 Increasing penetration and quality of service

Governments will wish to increase both penetration of telecommunications services and their quality. It will generally be a term of a new licence, or of a strategic investor's purchase of a strategic stake in the incumbent, that networks are built out to predetermined levels or that penetration reaches certain milestones during the first five or ten years of the investment. Notably, Internet access is likely to become a key priority for governments liberalising their telecommunications sectors.

14.4.3 Increasing revenues

Government coffers inevitably benefit from a privatisation. Receipts from the sale of a government stake can amount to hundreds of millions of pounds, and can be used to cover a budget deficit. Licence fees from new licences issued to new entrants can generate substantial revenues, as can radio spectrum fees. In Mauritania, for instance, spectrum fees associated with new mobile licences recently brought the Government US$25 million. Lastly, the government can anticipate increased tax revenues, both from the telecommunications sector and from the rest of the economy (which is likely to grow as the telecommunications sector develops).

However, if the price paid by an investor for a stake in the incumbent or for a new licence is too high, then, although government coffers benefit, ultimately consumers may not. High prices may result in less money being available for investment to improve networks and increase penetration, and in higher tariffs to be paid by users. This was the case in India, for example, where second fixed operator licences were sold for what were perceived to be exorbitant prices in 1996. This meant that projected revenues were modest, and the licence holders had great difficulty in obtaining debt financing for investment.[7]

14.4.4 Bridging the digital divide – the risk of exclusion and the potential for inclusion[8]

Among the causes of slow growth rates is inadequate infrastructure.[9] Infrastructure is an input to all other production, so where it is expensive and inefficient, it affects competitiveness and growth.[10] Increased access to better

---

[7] Wellenius, Björn, 'Telecommunications Reform – How to Succeed', *Viewpoint Note* No. 130, the World Bank (October 1997). See also Chapter 13, at 13.2.1.

[8] Braga, C.P., 'Inclusion of Exclusion?', *UNESCO Courier* (1998). ('Braga II').

[9] *Can Africa Claim the 21st Century* (Washington, DC, the World Bank, (2000), at 1–2.

[10] *Ibid.*, at 137–9.

Figure 14.1   Telecoms and networking are skewed towards the developed world

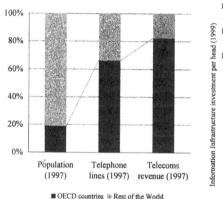

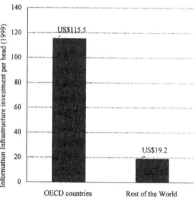

infrastructure in competitive, independently regulated markets with private sector participation will be essential to removing those barriers to competitiveness and economic diversification.[11] Synergies across infrastructure sectors will also contribute to overall growth. Obviously electricity is needed to provide telecommunications and financial sector services. But electricity alone is not enough to drive growth without the financial sector to fund it and the communications sector to transfer essential information and knowledge.

With respect to information and communications technology generally, inefficient and costly telecommunications impede participation in the burgeoning information-based economy.[12] Globalisation and developments in new technologies, especially information technology, offer the potential for developing countries to leapfrog intermediate stages of development and avoid the risk of exclusion from the global economy.[13] In other words, telecommunications is the core of the information infrastructure that developing economies need to compete in the global economy, as well as to assist in the delivery of educational, health, agricultural and even governmental services domestically.[14] Increasingly, the emergence of the Internet-driven phenomenon known as the 'digital divide' is posing further developmental challenges. Governments of developing countries will need to create facilitating regulatory and investment environments, with special emphasis on infrastructure liberalisation, in order widely to diffuse usage and understanding of

---

[11] *Ibid.*, at 4; and see Analysis, 'The Networking Revolution and the Developing World', *info*Dev, the World Bank (2000), Box 1, at vii.

[12] *Ibid.*, at 18. Indeed, it has been suggested that '[From a developmental perspective] in the emerging knowledge-based economy of the 21st century, information and communications technology will likely assume an importance that dwarfs other types of infrastructure' (*ibid.*, at 153).

[13] *Ibid.*, at 132 and 143. See also Mann, C., *et al.*, *Global Electronic Commerce: A Policy Primer* (Washington, DC, Institute for International Economics, 2000), citing Braga II.

[14] World Bank, *op. cit. supra* n. 9, at 147 and 157–158.

the Internet to close this divide.[15] Yet there is also the promise that the digital revolution provides unprecedented opportunities for developing countries to create sustainable growth, enhance good governance and fight corruption through participation in opportunities presented by this revolution.[16] Indeed, bridging this divide within and among countries was given priority at the G8 summit in Okinawa in July 2000, and the World Bank was specifically identified to contribute to formulating and implementing programmes to address the problem.[17] Again, for developing countries to take advantage of the digital opportunities that exist will require appropriate legal and regulatory responses.

As with other 'hard' infrastructure sectors, access barriers to telecommunications and information technology can be removed through better, pro-competition policies and regulations and enhanced private sector participation. Regulation implies the underlying legal basis to regulate. The certainty brought about by legal and regulatory reform will provide the basis for framing an environment conducive to private sector participation.

14.4.5 Regional hubbing

A country with a modern and functioning telecommunications sector in a region still lagging behind can act as a regional hub for transit traffic, resulting in revenues from incoming transit and from directing the traffic onwards to termination points. A healthy telecommunications sector attracts related industries, as well as businesses and industries that rely on telecommunications, including telemedicine, banking, and call centres.

14.5 ROLE OF MULTILATERAL DEVELOPMENT AGENCIES

While each multilateral development institution[18] pursues its own development mandate according to its own constitution, each can play an important

---

[15] Mann, *op. cit. supra* n. 13, at 174.

[16] See, *G8 Communiqué Okinawa 2000* and the *Okinawa Charter on the Global Information Society*, available at http://www.europa.eu.int/comm/external_relations/g7_g8/intro/global_info_society.htm.

[17] *Ibid.*

[18] These institutions are sometimes referred to as 'International Financial Institutions' (IFIs). These include: (i) the members of the World Bank Group (International Bank for Reconstruction and Development (IBRD): International Development Association (IDA); International Finance Corporation (IFC); the Multilateral Investment Guarantee Agency (MIGA); and the International Centre for the Settlement of Investment Disputes (ICSID)); (ii) the European Bank for Reconstruction and Development (EBRD); (iii) the European Investment Bank (EIB); (iv) the African Development Bank (AfDB); (v) the Asian Development Bank (ADB); and (vi) the Inter-American Development Bank (IADB). When referred to in this chapter, the World Bank means the IBRD and the IDA. The European Union, through the PHARE and TACIS programmes, has been involved in telecommunications sector reform. Recently, subregional development institutions such as the Development Bank of Southern Africa (DBSA) have become active in telecommunications sector reform. In addition, there are a number of bilateral donors who have been active in telecommunications sector reform. These include the Canadian International Development Agency (CIDA); the Danish International Development Agency (DANIDA); the Swedish International Development Agency (SIDA); the UK Department for International Development (DfID); the US Agency for International Development (USAID); and others.

role in providing credibility to the reform process and ultimately certainty to investors and consumers of telecommunications services. Some institutions (such as the IFC and the EBRD, for example) will play a role in the reform process by making path-breaking investments in the sector in a country. Others (such as MIGA) can provide comfort to investors by providing guarantee instruments in connection with transactions. Apart from investment activity or otherwise taking a financial interest in operators in the sector, IFIs can also play an important role in sector reform by providing funding for technical assistance in the reform process. This can take the form of policy advice, legal and regulatory reform, privatisation transactional assistance, engineering services such as frequency monitoring, and other regulatory capacity-building for the newly created regulators in the sector. While the World Bank deals almost exclusively with governments and parastatals, the IFC's activities[19] are almost entirely with private sector entities, or entities in the process of being privatised. Like the IFC, the EBRD makes investments in operators, but also provides funds for advisory services in the sector reform process, either as stand-alone legal reform projects, or in conjunction with its investment activities. In contrast, the World Bank's sector reform activities are primarily in providing funding for sector reform advisory services. The World Bank also co-finances projects with other IFIs. The World Bank may be involved indirectly in sector reform (i.e., not providing funding for advisory services) through a structural adjustment operation which has certain conditions or targets involving reform. In such a case, the disbursal of a non-telecoms loan or a credit (even though related to achieving macro-economic objectives) may depend on the government introducing market liberalising legislation or offering for sale a strategic stake in the incumbent, or on other criteria as agreed between the government and the World Bank.

The World Bank's activities over the past five years have focused on the sustainable development of telecommunications sector growth through the competitive introduction of quality services at affordable prices and the promotion of private participation in the operation of networks and the provision of services.[20] The World Bank has reduced its funding for infrastructure investments in telecom operators in favour of playing a catalytic role in sector development, by encouraging governments to create enabling legal and regulatory environments to mobilise private capital and management.[21]

In the context of the policy imperatives outlined above, and in conjunction with its other initiatives, such as alleviating poverty generally, fighting corruption, promoting good governance and comprehensive legal and judicial reform and bridging the digital divide, the sector reform activities of the World Bank are aimed at ensuring the transparency of the enabling environment.

---

[19] The IFC's activities are mainly in the form of making debt or equity investments in operators. The IFC also provides transactional advisory services.
[20] See, e.g., World Bank Telecommunications Sector Operational Policy 4.50, available at http://www.worldbank.org.
[21] *Ibid.*

Moreover, as a Bretton Woods sister institution of the World Trade Organisation (WTO), the World Bank cooperates with the WTO in its areas of competence. In this sense, the World Bank played an instrumental role in providing encouragement and funding (through *info*Dev)[22] to some 20 of the nearly 70 countries that submitted offers on the WTO telecommunications agreement in 1997, assisting them in the preparation of their offers.[23] Since that time, the World Bank has assisted countries in implementing their offers into national legislation. The WTO Reference Paper[24] has proved a powerful policy driver in the sector reform process in WTO member countries and in non-member countries alike.

The World Bank has active projects under implementation in about 60 countries, of which about 25 projects are under preparation.[25] These projects are part of the World Bank's lending operations. In addition, it is involved in a number of non-lending projects, including administering various bilateral and multilateral grant funds such as *info*Dev and PPIAF.[26] In sub-Saharan Africa alone, the World Bank supports activities in the telecommunications sector in 24 countries on a bilateral basis, in addition to the regional initiatives that it supports. In all but a few of these countries, there is a privatisation component to the project.

However, in recognition of the changing communications sector environment, the focus of World Bank assistance is re-orientating itself (based on those same principles of establishing proper enabling environments through pro-competition policy, the introduction of independent regulation (where needed) and private participation), from the traditionally defined telecommunications sector towards a more comprehensive approach reflecting the

---

[22] *info*Dev is the Information for Development Grant programme, a multi-donor grant programme administered by the World Bank, whose purpose is to promote projects on the use of information and communication technologies for economic and social development, with special emphasis on the needs of the poor in developing countries. More information is available at http://www.infodev.org/.

[23] See http://www.wto.org/english/tratop_e/servte_e/tel08_e.htm.

[24] The Reference Paper is available at http://www.wto.org/english/tratop_e/servte_e/tel23_e.htm. The Reference Paper was prepared in connection with the Negotiating Group on Basic Telecommunications, and embodies certain regulatory principles at the core of the so-called WTO telecommunications agreement. Many countries submitted schedules of specific commitments and exemptions to most-favoured-nation treatment pursuant to the Fourth Protocol of the General Agreement on Trade in Services, which contained or incorporated the Reference Paper. See further Chapter 10, at 10.4.3.1.

[25] A list of current projects is available at http://www.worldbank.org. Currently, the World Bank has operational activity (including grants) related to telecommunications reform in the following countries: Algeria, Armenia, Bangladesh, Bosnia and Herzegovina, Burkina Faso, Cameroon, Central African Republic, China, Comoros, Congo Republic, Dominican Republic, Ecuador, El Salvador, Gabon, Georgia, Ghana, Guatemala, Haiti, Honduras, India, Indonesia, Jamaica, Jordan, Kenya Kyrgystan, Latvia, Lebanon, Lesotho, Lithuania, Macedonia, Madagascar, Malawi, Mali, Mauritania, Mauritius, Moldova, Morocco, Nepal, Nicaragua, Niger, Nigeria, OECS States, Panama, Paraguay, Poland, Romania, Rwanda, Senegal, Sri Lanka, Tanzania, Thailand, Togo, Turkey, Uganda, Uzbekistan, and Zimbabwe.

[26] PPIAF is the Public–Private Infrastructure Advisory Facility, a multi-donor grant programme administered by the World Bank, whose purpose is to alleviate poverty and achieve sustainable development through private sector involvement in infrastructure. More information is available at http://www.ppiaf.org.

convergence in the telecommunications and information technology sectors globally, including the Internet and challenges posed by the digital divide.

14.6 CREATING THE RIGHT LEGAL FRAMEWORK

14.6.1 New sector policy

The starting-point for any reform process is to clarify what the objectives are, to articulate them and engage in a consultative process with stakeholders, and to make them publicly available as a roadmap for the reform process. Too often, difficult policy decisions such as timing and the sequencing of market liberalisation are avoided early in the process for political expediency or for other reasons, with the sometimes unspoken expectation that they will in fact be made in the process of preparing the new sector legislation or conducting the transaction. Nevertheless, it may be a condition of World Bank financing (or, for that matter, financing from other IFIs) that the government implements or abides by certain policies in the telecommunications sector, including that it adheres to a liberalisation schedule or complies with terms of licences, or ensures an operator's access to foreign exchange (thus allowing it to obtain foreign financing, whether in the form of capital market instruments or loan financing).

Some countries use their telecommunications law to spell out in detail their sector policy objectives (e.g., to sell a certain percentage of the incumbent operator or to issue a certain number of national mobile licences). Indeed, in some countries the telecommunications law is used to impose an obligation on the government to privatise the incumbent operator and issue certain licences by a certain date. Many investors welcome this approach because it provides them with greater assurance that the sector policy will in fact be implemented, as it will have been embedded in primary legislation. However, governments rarely like to constrain their discretion, and so it is more common for a country to set out its sector policy in a legally non-binding government policy statement, rather than to include it in primary legislation.

14.6.2 New telecommunications legislation

An effective legal and regulatory framework is essential in order to attract private investment into the telecommunications sector of most emerging economies, especially where, as is currently the case, potential investors have a wide range of telecommunications opportunities to choose from worldwide, in developed as well as in developing countries.[27]

14.6.2.1 Establishing a regulator (split with Ministry of Communications) New telecommunications legislation will describe the composition of the regulator and appointment procedures, and allocate responsibilities between the Min-

---

[27] Schwarz, T. and Satola, D., 'Telecommunications Legislation in Developing Economies' *World Bank Technical Paper 489* (Washington, DC, the World Bank 2000).

ister and the regulator. New entrants and strategic investors will wish to see a depoliticised sector regulator, independent from the Ministry of Communications and as independent as possible from the executive branch of government. However in some legal systems, only the Minister will have the constitutional authority to 'issue' a licence. In such cases it will be important to define the Minister's discretion clearly so as to ensure that the licensing decision is made fairly and transparently. This could be done by agreeing predetermined licensing criteria, and criteria on the basis of which licence applications can be declined. An alternative, where constitutionally possible, would be for the Minister to delegate this power to the regulator.

14.6.2.2 Key regulatory powers of regulator New telecommunications legislation will define the powers of the regulator in areas ranging from the licensing regime to the resolution of interconnection disputes between operators, the gathering of the information and the investigating of and imposition of sanctions for breaches of licence terms and the commission of offences. Offences will include the breach of licence terms, unauthorised interference with communications, unauthorised use of radio spectrum, and the connection of unapproved terminal equipment, to name but a few. The regulator will also manage the allocation and use of scarce resources, including numbering and infrastructure sharing, as well as (in the case of wireless telecommunications) radio spectrum.

14.6.2.3 Tariffs and USO funding Tariffs will sometimes be set by the regulator, in consultation with the Ministries of Communications and Finance, according to guidelines set out in the new telecommunications legislation. More often, the Ministry of Communications and/or the Ministry of Finance will have retained this function, given the important political impact of tariff increases and decreases. Particularly in countries where reform is driven by a need to dramatically increase penetration, there may be universal service obligations (USOs), i.e. the obligation to provide reasonable access to telecommunications services to any person requesting it, at a reasonable price and quality. In some countries, a single operator will have this obligation (often the incumbent), financed out of a USO fund administered by the regulator, towards which other operators or service providers will contribute (pursuant to the terms of their respective licences). In other countries, each major licensee will have a portion of the USOs, which may include a network build-out obligation.

14.6.3 New non-telecommunications legislation

From a development policy perspective, the entire legal regime must be borne in mind when envisaging what the telecommunications sector will look like after liberalisation and privatisation.[28] Several areas of law should be considered, including tax, company law, insolvency law, intellectual property law, and data protection and privacy law, as well as the following:

---

[28] *Ibid.*, at 13–16.

14.6.3.1 Antitrust However well-conceived a country's privatisation and liberalisation strategy might be in the telecommunications sector, it is unlikely to succeed fully unless accompanied by strong controls on anti-competitive conduct, including abuses of dominant position, anti-competitive agreements and anti-competitive changes in market structure.[29]

Controls on anti-competitive practices might include dividing services provided by the incumbent into two or more separate and independent entities, e.g., separating international and long-distance operations from local operations, or equipment manufacturing operations from service provision operations. There could be controls on anti-competitive mergers, acquisitions and concentrative joint ventures, possibly requiring prior clearance. The government might also limit the lines of business into which the incumbent may enter (e.g., precluding the incumbent from applying for a cellular licence), or restrict the incumbent from acquiring a stake in the second network operator.

If there is no competition law of general application, the importance of including provisions for fair competition in the telecommunications law is magnified. Even if a law of general application exists, the telecommunications law should address fair competition between operators on certain key technical matters such as interconnection, frequency allocation and the numbering plan, and should include a general prohibition on cross-subsidies among different licensed services provided by the same operator (subject to any allowance granted for re-balancing, as discussed above).[30]

If there is a competition law of general application, a number of substantive and procedural questions arise concerning the interface between it and the telecommunications law. For instance, the mandate of the telecommunications and competition regulators will have be defined so as to make clear which anti-competitive practices fall within the jurisdiction of which regulator.[31]

It is generally preferable that the general competition law apply widely to all types of anti-competitive conduct in the telecommunications sector that are not specific to that sector, and that telecommunications licences contain controls on those anti-competitive practices that are specific to the telecommunications sector (such as numbering, radio spectrum, infrastructure sharing, control of space segment due to signatory status under international satellite agreements, and value-added services).

The telecommunications law should also provide *preventative* controls on telecommunications-specific anti-competitive conduct, such as tariff or price controls, or a requirement that the incumbent obtain the approval of the

---

[29] *Ibid.*, at 9–13. See also Smith, P. and Wellenius, B., 'Mitigating Regulatory Risk in Telecommunications', *Viewpoint Note No. 189*, the World Bank (July 1999).

[30] See Schwarz and Satola, *op. cit. supra* n. 27, at 9–13.

[31] See Ungerer, H., 'Access Issues under EU Regulation and Anti-trust Law: The Case of Telecommunications and Internet Markets', Incidental Paper, *The Program on Information Resources Policy*, Harvard University and the Center for Information Policy Research (July 2000) (available at http://www.pirp.harvard.edu) for a comprehensive discussion of the increasingly important interplay between sector-specific legislation and general competition legislation in the converging telecommunications and Internet markets.

Figure 14.2 Technological development

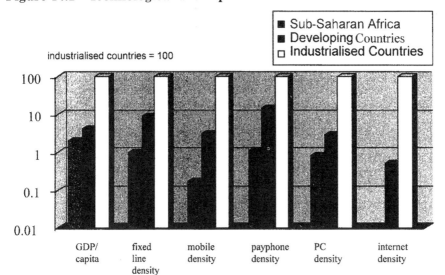

regulator for the standard terms of its subscriber contract. In any event, the telecommunications and competition regulators should liaise closely in relation to the application of their respective powers.

14.6.3.2 'Convergence' legislation The global pace of technological development, especially the emergence of the Internet-driven phenomenon known as the 'digital divide', is posing real developmental challenges, as shown in Figure 14.2.[32] In addition, the telecommunications and broadcasting sectors worldwide are rapidly converging, and it is becoming increasingly unclear whether certain 'hybrid' services (such as video conferencing, cable television, video-on-demand, or Internet broadcasting) should be regarded and regulated as telecommunications services or broadcasting services, or both.

Generally, where a traditional non-telecommunications service (such as broadcast TV) or medium (such as CATV) is used to deliver a telecommunications service, it should be treated under the telecommunications law. It will be important to investors that the interface between broadcasting and telecommunications legislation is carefully crafted. Investors will need to be aware of which regime regulates their activities, including which licences they require.

Governments are increasingly cognisant of the need to create an enabling environment in order to take advantage of the opportunities presented by the 'digital revolution', while bridging the 'digital divide' and avoiding exclusion from this global revolution. One element of this enabling environment is a 'future-proof', flexible legal and regulatory regime that encourages investment

---

[32] *Source*: World Development Indicators, the World Bank.

and the seamless introduction of new technologies, permitting emerging economies to compete in the global economy, as well as to fight corruption, enhance good governance and assist in the delivery of educational, health, agricultural and even governmental services domestically.

Such a comprehensive communications legal framework would include, in addition to 'best practice' telecommunications legislation referred to above, broadcasting, ICT (certification, data privacy protection, recognition of data messages, validity of digital signatures, encryption, with a view toward incorporating applicable provisions of the UNCITRAL Model Law on electronic commerce[33] and the appropriateness of regulation or forbearance from regulation), intellectual property,[34] and competition matters to the extent not otherwise addressed in competition legislation of general application. Where there is already telecommunications legislation, it may need 'future-proofing' with respect to, *inter alia*, regulatory forbearance, technology neutrality, coordination of spectrum management and spectrum-based licensing, licensing (or forbearance from licensing) of service providers (including ISPs), tariffs, interconnection, and the liberalisation of alternate network provision.

14.6.3.3 Consumer protection Consumer protection law is generally applicable to a wide range of sectors. It will be necessary to ensure that it contains specific mechanisms to protect consumers in the telecommunications sector, including such things as an obligation on the incumbent operator to have its standard customer contract approved by the regulator.

14.6.3.4 Property rights As noted at 14.3.5 above, new entrants to a liberalised telecommunications sector in an emerging market will require certain property rights in order to construct, maintain and operate their networks. They will need reassurance that they will enjoy real property rights which are adequate – both substantively and procedurally – to meet their build-out and service obligations under their licences. In any event, new entrants will need reassurance that they are to have the same property rights as the incumbent operator. Indeed, in certain cases, they will expect to have more favourable property rights than the incumbent operator (e.g., a right to share the incumbent operator's infrastructure).

Clearly, the importance of property rights to any particular new entrant will depend to a large extent upon the property rights it previously enjoyed (e.g., a railway company with existing rights of way along its track) and the technology proposed (e.g., new entrants relying on wireless technology will generally have less need for rights of way and compulsory purchase powers than fixed-link new entrants).

New entrants will generally require rights over both public and private land. At a substantive level, three types of real property rights will be important for new entrants (and in certain circumstances, the incumbent as well). Rights of way may be necessary for the installation of infrastructure,

---

[33] The UNCITRAL Model Law on Electronic Commerce (version 1998) ('Model Law') is available at http://www.uncitral.org/en-index.htm.
[34] See §1.3.5 of the Model Law.

compulsory purchase powers may be required for the building of microwave towers, and rights to share in 'bottleneck' infrastructure (e.g., obtaining the right to share the incumbent's ducts or co-locate equipment on the incumbent's premises) may also be required.

Operators may also require rights to cut trees, or to fly lines from state-owned or environmentally sensitive areas. In some cases it may be necessary to coordinate the property rights exercised by different utilities, particularly in respect of network construction, so as to minimise disruption.

At a procedural level, new entrants will expect effective legal mechanisms for obtaining such rights. In particular, they will expect there to be a procedure for obtaining certain essential property rights in the absence of the property owner's consent, or co-location or facility-sharing rights in the absence of the incumbent's consent (in either case against payment of appropriate compensation). There will also need to be a procedure for assessing adequate compensation payable by the new entrant to the landowner or incumbent operator for any physical damage to the property as a result of the exercise of such property rights.

Such procedures may be operated either by the telecommunications regulator or by the courts.

14.6.3.5 Privatisation In some cases it may be necessary to enact specific privatisation legislation, to apply either generally to the sale of State assets, or on a case-by-case, industry-specific basis. The main purpose of the law from an investor point of view is to create a level of certainty about the procedural aspects of the privatisation process. Generally, such a privatisation law will be a framework piece of legislation creating a privatisation agency, providing institutional authority and responsibility to organise and oversee the procedural aspects of privatisation transactions and making recommendations to the government, possibly identifying sectors or industries to be privatised, and even specifying employee preferences. Measures to protect against conflicts of interest by members of the privatisation agency are cornerstones to the creation of public and investor confidence in the privatisation process. Usually, formal decision-making authority, including overall policy direction, is retained by the government, although this can be provided for in the privatisation law. The privatisation agency is usually the main interlocutor with the transaction advisers. The privatisation law can also set certain pre-privatisation obligations on state-owned enterprises (keeping of books and records, valuations, etc.) to ensure their saleability. The law can also determine the transactional modalities (IPO, auction, international competitive bidding, etc.), and even the application of transaction proceeds. In addition, there may be special legal requirements for corporatising parastatals, if it is not possible to accomplish this pursuant to the companies/corporate law.

14.6.4 New main operator licence

14.6.4.1 Clear legal status Pre-reform, licensing or authorising an operator to provide telecommunications services or install a network (and similarly, amending or revoking such licence or authorisation) can often be, or at least be perceived as, discretionary and political. The lack of a clear licensing regime may either prevent operators from entering these markets, or increase the perceived risk of their investment. In the context of a new regulator and new telecommunications legislation, investors will expect their legal position to be governed and protected by the licensing regime contained in the legislation, and often in the terms of their licence or authorisation as well.

14.6.4.2   Investor friendly (e.g., modification, revocation)   Investors in emerging markets are highly sensitive to the regulatory risk of unilateral licence modification, suspension or revocation. However, it will often be politically imperative for the Minister to retain the power to modify, suspend or revoke licences unilaterally where it is 'in the public interest' (subject to fair procedural controls such as reasonable notice) and in order to take account of unforeseeable changes in market conditions which may occur during the term of a long licence.

This is particularly relevant in the fast-changing world of telecommunications, where the pace of technological convergence can render regulatory controls ineffective in a matter of months. A compromise can be reached by protecting certain licence conditions from modification for a fixed period (e.g., for five years), or by requiring the assent of both the Minister and the regulator for unilateral modifications, revocations or suspensions on grounds of public interest or public policy.

14.6.4.3   Clear interface with primary legislation   In general, the easier unilateral licence modification is, the more investors will insist on having details of their rights and obligations built into the primary legislation on the basis that the primary legislation is more difficult to modify than licences. In general, robust protection for the investor will be included in the legislation, with much of the detail being dealt with in the licences.

14.7   CREATING THE RIGHT REGULATOR

14.7.1   Different models

Even in developed markets with fully competitive telecommunications sectors, there is a wide range of regulatory models (see also 1.7 and 8.4.2 above). In the United States, for instance, the Federal Communications Commission (FCC) is essentially a rule-making body which is fully independent from the Government; while in the UK the Office of Telecommunications (OFTEL) is a quasi-independent issue-specific advisory, investigative and enforcement body with strong links to the Government.

In much of continental Europe, the regulator is located within the relevant ministry, separated only by 'Chinese Walls'; while in New Zealand there is no regulator specifically for the telecommunications sector, full reliance for economic regulation in the sector being found in the general antitrust legislation, the New Zealand Commerce Act 1986.[35] Despite this variety in developed markets, investors into emerging markets will prefer as independent a regulator as possible, as they will be less familiar with, and less trusting of, political and policy-making processes in these countries.

Regardless of the regulatory model, a functioning transparent regulatory regime in a competitive market will reduce transaction costs, enhance the efficiency of operators in the market, and (it is hoped) encourage new entry and competition and remove barriers to capital flows.

14.7.2 Independence-enhancing mechanisms

An independent regulator increases investor confidence in the objectivity and stability of the regulatory process, and therefore leads to greater foreign and domestic investment in the telecommunications sector. This begins the virtuous circle whereby increased investment stimulates economic activity, in turn leading to increased tax revenues for the State. The main disadvantage of independence (from the point of view of the government) is the loss by the government and the relevant ministry of some influence over the running of the economy and over some decisions which will affect voters (e.g., keeping local telecommunications prices low rather than re-balancing them pursuant to the terms of a post-liberalisation licence).

14.7.2.1 Financing Independence will be enhanced if the regulator is financially autonomous from the ministry, relying primarily on licence and other fees for its revenue, rather than on a large budgetary allocation. Furthermore, the ministry should not have decision-making power over the level of remuneration of individual commissioners, so as to avoid indirect ministerial influence on commission decisions and policy directions.

14.7.2.2 Commission or single regulator The use of a committee structure (e.g., three commissioners) as opposed to a single individual as the regulator reduces the risk of arbitrary and subjective regulatory decisions being made, though it may also slow down the decision-making process. The trend is towards commission-based regulators. Indeed, prior to 1998, 70 per cent of new telecommunications regulators were headed by a single individual, whereas among the nine regulators created from July 1998 to August 1999, seven were established as commissions of between five and 11 members.[36]

---

[35] At the time of writing, the issue of whether to create a sector-specific regulator in New Zealand was under consideration. See Kerf, M., and Geradin, D., 'Controlling Market Power in Telecommunications: Anti-trust vs. Sector-Specific Regulation – An Assessment of the United States, New Zealand and the Australian Experiences' (1999) 14 Berkeley Technology Law Journal 3, at 919 *et seq.*, for a comparative analysis of different approaches to economic regulation, including the sector-specific approach under the FCC model, the general antitrust approach adopted in New Zealand, and the blended approach adopted in Australia.
[36] International Telecommunications Union, *Trends in Telecommunications Reform: Convergence and Regulation 1999* (Geneva, ITU, 1999), at 6.

14.7.2.3 Composition   Despite the independence ideal, government ministers will usually retain some influence, at the very least in nominating individuals to posts within the new regulatory authority. Sometimes government officials will be appointed as commissioners to the regulator as of right on an *ex officio* basis. Although useful where an independent appointment authority is difficult to find, such an arrangement can potentially undermine the regulator's independence and immunity from political influence. This can be mitigated, however, by ensuring that such *ex officio* commissioners have reduced voting power, or simply representative status, on the board of the regulator. In addition, *ex officio* commissioners can come from such organisations as the Chamber of Commerce, the Law Society, or a group representing consumer interests.

A telecommunications regulator usually needs at least 30 professional staff with expertise in such fields as engineering, accounting, pricing, law and administration. Where (as is common in emerging markets) the regulator is also responsible for managing radio spectrum, this number is even higher.[37]

14.7.2.4 Appointment and removal   Commissioners should be appointed on the basis of their professional qualifications rather than political allegiances, by someone other than the ministry (such as by the country's top executive or by a cross-party Parliamentary committee), and only if they meet certain predetermined appointment criteria. Ideally, commissioners' terms should be staggered so as to reduce the influence of any one government over their appointment, and to encourage policy continuity and preserve institutional memory.

14.7.2.5 Conflict of interest   Conflict of interest provisions (applicable to both commissioners and their direct families) can serve to improve the perception of independence, though these should not be so wide as to prevent skilled and experienced individuals from being selected. This will be a particularly difficult balance to achieve in a country lacking a pool of experts in the field of telecommunications, and indeed in many cases the staff of the regulator and possibly some of its board members will have come directly from the incumbent.

14.7.2.6 Licensing   The choice as to which functions should be the responsibility of the minister and which should be the responsibility of the regulator will be a political one, and will vary from one country to the next. However, the ministry will usually retain responsibility for decisions concerning overall liberalisation policy, and will often be responsible for the final approval and issuance of major licences or, in a system which adopts a 'class' licensing regime, the issuance of so-called 'individual' licences. The minister's discretion can be somewhat circumscribed if the regulator designs and manages the tendering process, or if the minister's approval of licensees (and revocation of licences) is made subject to a (binding or non-binding) recommendation from the regulator, where the grounds for the exericse of the ministry's

---

[37] Smith and Wellenius, *op. cit. supra* n. 29.

discretion not to approve a licence or licensee would be strictly limited to procedural matters regarding the selection and evaluation process.

The regulator, meanwhile, could retain the responsibility for the modification of licences, on the basis that it is best placed to judge whether modification is necessary in light of market developments. The regulator could also remain responsible for licence renewal (which should in any event be automatic provided the licensee has not breached the licence terms), since the regulator will generally be responsible for monitoring and enforcing compliance with licence conditions.

14.7.3 Strong enforcement powers

14.7.3.1 Information The regulator should have robust information-gathering powers which, together with sanctions available to it, will give it teeth as a regulatory body. The type of information-gathering powers which a regulator will have will depend on the institutional and legal framework of the individual country, though they might be 'benchmarked' to the information-gathering powers of another national organisation (such as another sector's regulator, or the High Court). If there is no entity with sufficiently robust information-gathering powers against which the regulator can benchmark its own, specific information-gathering powers will have to be written into the telecommunications law.

14.7.3.2 Sanctions Sanctions typically include fines, suspensions and revocations of licences, and the award of damages to third parties. The regulator's enforcement powers should be consistent with those of other regulators such as the competition regulator, particularly where the two enjoy concurrent power (e.g., over anti-competitive conduct in the telecommunications sector). The regulator should have at its disposal not only robust sanctions, but also a variety (or armoury) of sanctions which can be applied in a graduated way depending upon the seriousness and frequency of the licence breach or offence. At the same time, sanctioning powers should not be overly draconian, and so should not include seizure of network and equipment without compensation, or imprisonment of officers of telecommunications operators found in breach of licence conditions.

14.7.4 Cross-sectoral regulator

By far the most widely adopted approach in emerging markets is to create a single-sector regulator, though a number of countries have established or are in the process of establishing a cross-sectoral regulator (notably Bolivia, Jamaica, Panama and El Salvador, though the number and type of sectors covered varies from country to country).[38] If a cross-sectoral regulator is chosen, the first decision will be which sectors will be covered, and in

---

[38] Kerf, M., and Smith, W., 'Privatising Africa's Infrastructure: Promise and Challenge', *World Bank Technical Paper No. 337* (Washington, DC, the World Bank, 1996).

particular how responsibility for competition regulation will be allocated. From a telecommunications point of view, however, the overriding concern, whichever institutional structure is adopted, will be to ensure that sufficient technical expertise exists to carry out what are often sophisticated, complex technical functions, such as the analysis of interconnection disputes and radio frequency management.

A cross-sectoral regulator can help to avoid the rule-making process being captured by industry-specific interest groups, though a dominant industry interest group may still be able to capture the regulator, resulting in its influence across several industries as well as its own.[39] Similarly, while a cross-sectoral regulator might be more immune from political capture by the relevant government ministry, a dominant industry might succeed in exerting its power over the regulator and, by extension, over sectors under the aegis of other, weaker ministries.

Although a cross-sectoral regulator could reduce regulatory uncertainty for investors (as a decision by such a regulator on such issues as price cap regulation in respect of one sector is likely to be replicated in respect of another), there is a risk of inappropriate application of common decisions across sectors. This could, however, be mitigated through sector-specific departments underneath a central decision-making body.

In terms of personnel, a cross-sectoral regulator could benefit from economies of scale in professionals such as lawyers, economists and financial analysts (especially in the early stages of liberalisation where there might be a scarcity of skilled personnel). On the other hand, this could result in the dilution of sector-specific expertise. Similarly, economies of scale in respect of administrative and support services could reduce the costs of regulation (and ultimately result in more affordable basic services), though the risk is that administrative failures cannot be easily contained to a single sector.

Economies of scale could also result in respect of rules and procedures (such as licensing and dispute settlement), thus avoiding needless replication and market distortions. Such a set-up would facilitate the sharing of regulatory know-how between regulators responsible for different sectors, particularly important where a country has limited experience in regulation or a scarcity of skilled personnel.

Given the quickening pace of convergence, a cross-sectoral regulator would also seem better equipped to adapt to the changing regulatory requirements in related sectors (such as telecommunications and broadcasting), to regulate the provision of bundled services (e.g., telecommunications and electricity provided by one company) and to coordinate regulatory requirements between sectors (e.g., over the digging up of roads to construct networks). In addition, issues of convergence such as access to Internet facilities require a regulatory response based on both technical sector expertise and competition law principles.[40]

---

[39] See Smith and Wellenius, *op. cit. supra* n. 29. See also Schwarz and Satola, *op. cit. supra* n. 27, at 30–34, for a general discussion of the advantages and disadvantages of the multi-sectoral and single-sector approaches, as well as strategies for implementing a multi-sectoral approach.
[40] See Ungerer, *op. cit. supra* n. 31.

However, government ministries will generally oppose the concept of a cross-sectoral regulator, and the diversity of their interests could make the operation of such a regulator difficult and slow. Ironically this is the very political capture that such regulatory arrangements are intended to overcome. The design of the legal framework for such regulators will be complicated by the fact that the pace of reform in different sectors occurs at different speeds. Also, one sector may have a regulator or regulatory function and others may not, leading to inevitable debates about whether the mandate of the existing regulator should be expanded to accommodate other sectors, or whether it should be disbanded in favour of creating a new institution and transferring the competencies of the existing regulator to it. It will inevitably be difficult to design the legal framework for such a regulator, and in particular to allocate functions between the different ministries and the regulator. Where the relevant ministry or regulator previously carried out a regulatory function, the merging of existing regulatory functions in one sector with others could be problematic. In sum, setting up (and running) a cross-sectoral regulator could produce potential delays to the reform process.

The position may be different in more developed markets. These markets are mature and have an evolutionary history. There is generally also a high degree of confidence in the legal and judicial systems in those markets to resolve disputes impartially. There is a history of 'independent' regulation, i.e., there is no difficulty in conceiving of an entity that is independent of the government and the political process, despite being part of the governmental complex. In most cases in the developing world, not all of these other enabling environment factors supporting and sustaining multi-sector regulators can be taken for granted. The United States has had multi-sector public utility boards at the state level for many years, often covering telecommunications, natural gas and electric power supply. In other jurisdictions a single regulator may be responsible for transport and broadcasting, as well as telecommunications.[41] In these more developed markets, where technological innovations originate and are quickly marketed, the speed of convergence, particularly between telecommunications and broadcasting, and the increased incidence of utility operators expanding into the telecommunications sector all point to a case for a single, multi-sector, regulator.[42]

Table 14.1 below illustrates the variety in the functions of the telecommunications regulators across several emerging markets.

14.8 TELECOMMUNICATIONS PRIVATISATIONS

Participation by the private sector in the formerly State-dominated telecommunications sector can come in a variety of forms, including the licensing of private operators, the opening of the incumbent to private ownership or

---

[41] For instance, in Malaysia, the telecommunications, broadcasting and computing industries are all grouped together under one regulator. See ITU, *op. cit. supra* n. 36. See Chapter 13, at 13.3.3.3.
[42] See Smith, P., 'What the Transformation of Telecom Markets means for Regulation', *Viewpoint Note No. 121*, the World Bank (July 1997).

management, or a combination of both. As with the establishment of independent regulatory functions and institutions, one objective of industry privatisation is to remove government and political considerations from management in order to make the operator more commercially responsive and market-orientated. In the period from 1997 until the present alone, there have been announced or concluded in some 90 countries transactions to privatise (in whole or in part) incumbent telecommunications operators, of which nearly 80 have been in countries with transitional or developing economies.[43]

Table 14.1   Functions of Telecommunications Regulators: selected countries

Country	Regulator	Created	Reports to	Functions
Angola	Direcção Nacional de Correios e Telecomunicações	1985	Ministry of Transport and Communications	Frequency allocation.
Ghana	National Communications Authority	The National Communications Authority Act 1996. Began operations in 1997.	Ministry of Communications	Licensing, numbering plan, tariff approval and establishment of licence fees together with the sector ministry, interconnection rates together with the ministry and the operator, technical standards, frequency allocation, type approval and monitor service quality.
Egypt	Telecommunications Regulatory Authority	1998	Commission (11 members) reporting to the Ministry of Transport and Communications	Numbering, tariff approval, standards setting, frequency allocation, type approval, monitoring service quality, licence fees.

[43] The list includes the following countries, literally from A-Z: Albania, Algeria, Armenia, Australia, Bangladesh, Belgium, Bolivia, Bosnia and Herzegovina, Brazil, Bulgaria, Burkina Faso, Cameroon, Central African Republic, Chad, China, Colombia, Comoros, Congo Republic, Croatia, Czech Republic, Denmark, Dominican Republic, Ecuador, Egypt, El Salvador, Estonia, Finland, France, Gabon, Georgia, Ghana, Greece, Guatemala, Haiti, Honduras, Hong Kong, Hungary, India, Indonesia, Ireland, Italy, Japan, Jordan, South Korea, Kenya, Kyrgystan, Kuwait, Latvia, Lebanon, Lesotho, Lithuania, Macedonia, Madagascar, Malawi, Mali, Mauritania, Mauritius, Mexico, Moldova, Morocco, Nepal, Nicaragua, Niger, Nigeria, Pakistan, Panama, Paraguay, Peru, Poland, Portugal, Romania, Russia, Rwanda, Saudi Arabia, Senegal, Slovakia, Slovenia, South Africa, Sri Lanka, Switzerland, Tanzania, Thailand, Turkey, Uganda, Ukraine, Uzbekistan, Venezuela, Vietnam and Zimbabwe. This list does not include multiple offerings or tranches, issuing wireless licences to second or third operators or other means of introducing private participation in the market, even though in some countries, for example, the authorisation of a private party to use frequency (a scarce national resource) may be considered a form of 'privatisation'. *Cf. supra* n. 25.

Country	Regulator	Created	Reports to	Functions
Bulgaria	State Telecommunications Commission	1998	Commission (5 members) reporting to the Ministry, Council of Ministers, and the National Radio and Television Council	Licensing (including radio and television, upon decision of the National Radio and Television Council), numbering, developing spectrum management, policies for civil services, frequency coordination, standards.
Venezuela	Comisión Nacional de Telecomunicaciones (CONATEL)	Decree No. 1.826, began operation in 1991.	Ministry of Transport and Communications	Licensing, tariff approval (with the Ministry), technical standards, type approval, frequency allocation, monitor service quality, establishing licence fees.
Mexico	Comisión Federal de Telecomunicaciones (CFT)	Federal Telecommunications Law. Began operations in 1996.	Secretary of Communication and Transport	Numbering plans, tariffs, technical standards, interconnection rates, frequency allocation, type approval, monitor service quality, establishing licence fees.
Singapore	Telecommunications Authority of Singapore	Telecommunications Authority of Singapore Act 1992	Ministry of Communications	Policy-making and developing legislation for sector, regulation including licensing and managing radio spectrum, ensuring compliance with licence terms and international agreements, tariffs and price control, promoting competition, dispute resolution, interconnection and access charges principles, monitoring service quality, consumer complaints, development of technical standards, technology selection and equipment approval.

Country	Regulator	Created	Reports to	Functions
Philippines	National Telecommunications Commission	1979	Department of Transportation and Communications	Licensing and managing radio spectrum, tariff regulation, monitoring operator activities, service quality and ensuring compliance, administration of numbering plan, tariffs and price control, standard setting and equipment type approval, setting guidelines for interconnection.

Source: Drawn from ITU, *General Trends in Telecommunications Reform 1998 – World* (Vol. 1), at 28–9, 31, 48–9, 81–2, 98; ITU, *General Trends in Telecommunications Reform 1999*, at 7.

14.8.1 Separation of posts and telecommunications

The trend in most emerging markets is to separate out the postal and telecommunications activities of the state-owned operator. In some countries the legal aspects of separating the telecommunications, postal and regulatory activities of the operator (including the transfer of assets, and the establishment of new corporate bodies and the new regulator) are addressed in the general telecommunications law. However, a number of countries have preferred to address these aspects of the separation in discrete legislation, on the basis that these issues are 'one-off' (i.e., with little relevance once the separation has taken place).

14.8.1.1 Employees (telecommunications preference) There may be a potentially adverse effect on the independence of the new regulator by transferring into it 'lock, stock and barrel' personnel who previously worked in the state-owned operator, though this might be inevitable if there is a lack of relevant national expertise.

14.8.1.2 Corporatisation of telecommunications (generally not posts) The telecommunications activities are often transferred to a newly formed joint-stock company. Rather than transfer the operator's telecommunications activities directly into a joint-stock company governed by ordinary company law, some governments decide, as an initial step, to transfer the telecommunications activities into a statutory corporation established under special legislation which can serve as the legal basis for reserving to the State certain rights which may not be available under ordinary company law, and also confer special privileges on the statutory corporation (e.g., exemptions from taxation and from legal liability for deficient performance). The postal activities are generally transferred to a statutory corporation.

14.8.1.3 Transfer into regulator (independence implications) The regulatory activities of the state-owned operator are generally transferred to a new regulatory body. The approach in some countries historically has been to deal with the regulation of the postal and telecommunications sectors in the same law, possibly even with a single regulator for both. However, separation of the two sectors will reveal significant differences between them which provide a case for two regulators. In particular, the postal sector may well be loss-making and remain state-owned (at least in the short term). It may be subject to different pricing controls and a different licensing approach than the telecommunications sector, and generally be subject to slower liberalisation than the telecommunications sector.

Furthermore, the postal sector raises particular legal and regulatory issues that are not directly relevant to the telecommunications sector (such as postal banking activities and e-mail regulation) and *vice versa* (including interconnection, equipment approval, radio frequency allocation and leased-line provision, to name but a few).

14.8.2 Different privatisation techniques

'Privatisation' is used generally to refer to the opening of the share capital of the incumbent state-owned operator to ownership by private parties (through a share sale to a strategic partner or through a flotation of shares). Alternatively, private parties may be permitted to manage the incumbent (e.g., through a management contract). Regardless of the type of transaction, one overriding consideration is the transparency of the process.

14.8.2.1 Strategic sale (majority/minority/management control) Initially, the State will own 100 per cent of the shares in the telecommunications joint-stock company, but will then often 'privatise' by selling a stake to a 'strategic investor'. Strategic investments are particularly important in high-technology industries such as telecommunications, where a national carrier is unlikely to be able to afford the research and development costs necessary to compete globally.

The stake sold may be a majority stake, or a minority stake accompanied by a degree of management control.[44] Where the government sells a controlling stake, bidders are likely to offer a 'control premium' for the block of shares[45] (see Figure 14.3). There may be political opposition to foreign ownership of the national telecommunications operator, in which case the government may arrange a consortium of domestic and foreign strategic

---

[44] In the following transactions involving a strategic stake of less than 50 per cent, the seller made significant control concessions: Deutsche Telekom's 35% acquisition in Croatian Telecom (1999); OTE's 35% acquisition in Rom Telecom (1998); NTT's 35% acquisition in Sri Lanka Telecom (1997); SBC/Telecom Malaysia's 30% acquisition in Telkom South Africa (1997); KPN/Swiss PTT's 27% acquisition in SPT Telecom (1995); and Telefónica de España's 35% acquisition in ENTEL Peru (1994). In the case of Telkom South Africa, full management control was transferred for the period of exclusivity (see Figure 14.3 below).

[45] As Figure 14.3 demonstrates, the percentage of shares sold and the level of control transferred varied from deal to deal. The list is illustrative only (*cf. supra* n. 42).

investors, as was done in the privatisations of both the Mexican and Argentine national telecommunications operators. In some emerging market countries the State may then also dispose of a tranche of shares through an IPO.

What constitutes 'management control' will therefore vary from deal to deal. Consequently, the meaning of a transfer of management control should need to be viewed together with the percentage of shares sold, and within the particular context of each deal. Management control is usually focused on finance, operations, marketing, technical and even day-to-day functions of the company. Factors affecting what the 'context' is include, but are not limited to:

(a)   the competitiveness of the sector and the company's position in the sector;
(b)   the size, financial health and operational and management capacity of the company;
(c)   the composition of the investor consortium;
(d)   the premium attached by investors to attaining control;
(e)   the corporate/companies law of the jurisdiction (including special rights or protections, if any, for minority shareholders, respective voting requirements of shareholders and directors, and general corporate governance concerns);
(f)   the perceived political risk of the jurisdiction; and
(g)   the capacity of and confidence in regulatory processes and the judicial system.

In this sense, transfer of control can vary qualitatively from case to case. What is clear is that, in each case, the interaction between investors and sellers will determine what level of management control, together with what percentage of shares for sale, will be necessary to secure the transfer of control. In many instances, attempts at privatisation have failed where the seller did not respond adequately to the needs of the buyers in this regard.

Figure 14.3   Privatisation by strategic sale

Country	Target	% Equity Acquired	Management Control Transferred (F = Full Management Control)
Europe			
Belgium	Belgacom	49.9%	F
Denmark	Tele Danmark	48.3%	F
Hungary	MATAV	67.2%	F
Poland	TPSA	35% (plus option on 16%)	F (IPO preceded strategic sale, control will shift to strategic investor)
Slovakia	Slovak Telekom	51%	F

Country	Target	% Equity Acquired	Management Control Transferred (F = Full Management Control)
Americas			
Argentina	Telecom Argentina	60%	F
Brazil	Embratel	75%	F
Mexico	TELMEX	20.40%	F (until end 2000 subject to Mexican Law on controlling shareholder provisions)
Africa			
Ghana	Ghana Telecom	30%	F (for the period of the licence; for key issues, at least one vote from Telecom Malaysia)
South Africa	TelKom SA	30%	F (for at least the period of exclusivity)
Uganda	UTL	51%	F
Middle East			
Jordan	JTC	40%	Company operations will be handled by a seven-member 'Operation Committee'. Five of its members will be investor executives, while the other two will be from the Government.

To ensure transparency in the strategic sale context, best practice indicates a simple two-staged process. The first stage is qualification. The criteria established to qualify or pre-qualify bidders should be published and objective, for example setting minimum threshold, pass/fail tests such as financial criteria or numbers of subscribers. If these are not pass/fail tests then the criteria should be weighted, and bids publicly opened. Then selection should be similarly objective and typically limited to a financial offer, against an agreed set of transaction documents. Financial offers should be publicly opened.

14.8.2.2   IPOs – local and international   Alternatively, the government may sell its stake in the incumbent telecommunications operator through an IPO. The IPO will frequently take place on both local and international equity markets, often with a domestic retail offering and both foreign and domestic institutional offers. Thus, an IPO allows retail and institutional investors to participate in the privatisation. IPOs may also allow the general public to participate in the privatisation of a national telecommunications operator, a potentially politically important factor. Indeed, in developed markets, domestic retail shares (including shares issued to employees of the privatising entity) are often slightly cheaper than those offered to institutional investors or a strategic investor.

However, telecommunications is a sector which requires high levels of capital investment and consistent technological development. Indeed, often it is the lack of such investment and the obsolescence of networks and equipment which provide the final impetus for privatisation. An incumbent operator lacking such investment and updated technology, and probably with a revenue stream reflecting low levels of penetration, may not be highly valued in anticipation of an IPO. Thus, selling its stake before engaging a strategic investor may not maximise the government's revenues, or, for that matter, provide any assurance that the necessary capital and technological investment in the incumbent will take place. In addition, speculation on the secondary markets can inflate share prices of a privatised telecommunications operator after an IPO, making a subsequent strategic investment more costly and therefore less likely.

14.8.2.3   Timing – successive strategic stakes plus IPO   For these reasons, an IPO is more usually made subsequently to one or more strategic investments. Strategic investors bring capital and technical and management expertise to the companies in which they invest. After a period of, say, 18 months, the company will have benefited from the capital injection and the improved management, and will probably have begun to meet some of the government's service penetration and quality requirements.

At this stage, the company will be worth more than it was when the strategic investor initially came in, and the government may decide to make an IPO of its shares (or part of its shares) to realise this increase in value. In the privatisation of Teléfonos de Mexico (TELMEX), for instance, the Mexican Government first sold only 20 per cent of its interest to a strategic investor in 1990, for the price of US$1.8 billion. In 1991 and 1992, it sold another 31 per cent through two IPOs, for the price of US$4.5 billion, representing an appreciation of 70 per cent per share.[46] However, the recent experience in Poland[47] stands in stark contrast to that generally accepted convention of transaction structure and sequencing. The Polish national

---

[46] Wellenius, *op. cit. supra* n. 7.
[47] See *supra* n. 44. The discussion regarding pricing of TPSA's shares does not take into account the effect that exchange-rate fluctuations, inflation or other such factors may have had on pricing or timing, but these are obviously factors that would need to be taken into account by financial advisers in structuring a transaction.

operator, Telekomunikacja Polska (TPSA), was first privatised through a public offering of 15 per cent of the shares of TPSA in 1998. Subsequently, the Government launched a tender for a strategic investor. Eventually only one bidder emerged, a consortium led by France Télécom, which purchased 35 per cent of TPSA's shares for US$4.3 billion, plus an option for an additional 16 per cent of TPSA's shares.

14.8.2.4 Management contract Under a management contract, a contractor will take over the management of a state-owned enterprise for a determined period. A management contract may also involve the acquisition of a minority stake in the incumbent. Management contracts with major capital expenditure (without an equity investment) are rare in the telecommunications sector (only eight awarded by 1998, five in Thailand and one each in Indonesia, the Lao People's Democratic Republic, and the Ukraine). Management contracts without investment commitments are even more uncommon, the only ones currently being in Kiribati and Mongolia.[48] In these situations, since the contractor does not take any investment risk, the management contract must contain incentives for good performance such as penalties or bonuses.[49]

Management contracts are particularly useful where there is political opposition to divestment, allowing the government to retain full ownership while importing management expertise. However, the contractor may manage the enterprise in such a way as to precipitate privatisation, at which point it would hope to be in a privileged 'insider' position for the purpose of bidding.[50]

14.8.2.5 BOT (concession) A 'build operate transfer' (BOT) contract is a form of concession. Under a BOT contract, an investor (or a consortium of investors) will be granted the rights to build a telecommunications network and to operate it pursuant to the terms of the concession, usually sharing a portion of the revenues with the State. This arrangement has been used in India, Lebanon and, in a slightly different form, in Indonesia.[51] At the end of the concession term, the network will be transferred back to the State.

Less common but also in existence are 'build transfer operate' (BTO) contracts. Under BTO contracts the investors build the network and transfer title to the government, but continue to operate the network and share revenues from its operation with the State. Technically, the State retains control over the network and remains responsible for the provision of the service. One example of BTO contracts is in Thailand, though the Government is currently undertaking the conversion of the BTO arrangements into licences.[52]

---

[48] Izaguirre, Ada Karina, 'Private Participation in Telecommunications – Recent Trends', *Viewpoint Note No. 204*, the World Bank (December 1999).
[49] Kerf and Smith, *op. cit. supra* n. 38, at 43.
[50] *Ibid.*
[51] ITU *op. cit. supra* n. 36, at 45.
[52] *Ibid.*

Table 14.2 illustrates the different approaches to privatisation taken by a selection of emerging markets.

14.8.3 Advisers

The government will often choose its path to privatisation with the help of a variety of advisers. Once it has made its choice, it will require the services of these advisers to assist it in designing and implementing its strategy. The government may find it convenient to tender for the following advisers as a single consortium, or it may prefer to hire them separately.

14.8.3.1 Investment bank   There will typically be an investment bank advising the government. Along with the legal and accounting advisers, the investment bank will prepare a due diligence report for the government, assess potential investor interest, have overall responsibility for the drafting of the prospectus or information memorandum and (in the case of a strategic sale) any pre-qualification and pre-selection documents and the transaction documents (such as the shareholders' agreement, or any purchase or management contracts, for instance), and be responsible for advising the government about regulatory issues impacting the transaction, such as the operator's licence or interconnection agreement. Investment banks will also recommend a sales strategy and transaction structure, and advise the government on the timing of a sale. As well as preparing the information memorandum, the investment banker is responsible for marketing the transaction and conducting other 'market-conditioning' functions. These may include an information or communications campaign to the investor community alerting them of the investment opportunity, but equally to wary governmental officials, trade unions or labour organisations and consumers. Typically the investment bank assists with the bidding process and negotiations or sales completion. Where there is a domestic tranche of an IPO, it may be a legal requirement to engage a local investment bank, who will in any case be more familiar with local market issues. Lastly, in an IPO, an investment bank will often underwrite and sell the government's shares in the privatising entity. Brokers will market and sell the shares to interested investors.

14.8.3.2 International and local accounting firms   These advisers will undertake audits prior to the sale, and assist the investment banks in valuing the privatising company, either for a strategic sale or for an IPO.

14.8.3.3 Tariff, interconnect, spectrum advisers   Technical experts with specialised industry know-how may be required to advise on key technical issues relating, in particular, to tariffs, interconnection and spectrum.

14.8.3.4 International law firm   Different stages of the reform process require different inputs from legal advisers. Best practice would indicate that before privatising, the legal and regulatory framework for the market would be put in place first. Lawyers would typically be hired to prepare the basic

Table 14.2 Method of privatisation: selected countries

Country	Privatised company	Strategic sale	Year	Buyer	% sold	IPO	Year	% sold
Armenia	Armentel	yes	1997	Hellenic Telecommunications Organisation (OTE)	90%			
Czech Republic	SPT Telecom	yes	1995	TelSource (KPN, Swiss Telecom)	49%			
Poland	TPSA	yes	2000	France Télécom (consortium)	35%	yes	11/98	15%
India	MTNL					yes	1994 1997	34% 8.6%
Israel	Bezeq	yes	1990	Cable & Wireless	10%	yes	1991* 1997	12.5% 13%
Senegal	SONATEL	yes	1997	France Câble et Radio	33.33%	yes	1997	27.66%**
Guinea-Bissau	Guiné-Telecom	yes	1989	Portugal Telecom	51%			
Peru	ENTEL Peru	yes	1993	Telefónica de España	35%			

Source: Drawn from www.worldbank.org/html/fpd/telecoms/gif/; ITU, *General Trends in Telecommunications Reform 1998 — World* (Vol. 1), at 86, 113.

* Private placement to Merrill Lynch US.

** 10% of this was sold to employees, the remainder to domestic investors.

texts and instruments for the legal and regulatory framework, including the new telecommunications legislation, regulations or subsidiary legislation and new licences. At the transactional phase of the reform process, lawyers will generally be responsible for managing the due diligence, which must be carried out prior to the sale. They will advise the government on legal aspects of the privatisation, including regulatory issues affecting the transaction and international best practice, and will typically be responsible for identifying legal constraints to the transaction and drafting the transaction documents. Generally, transactional lawyers are familiar with basic corporate governance principles, and in this sense can be valuable assets in structuring and managing selection and bidding processes to ensure fairness and transparency.

14.8.3.5   Local law firm   A local law firm may be required in addition to any international telecommunications transactional legal expertise, in order to advise the investor and/or the investment bank on local law aspects of the transaction. Often, it will work together with the international law firm to ensure that any new legislation, licences or even transaction documents, are constitutional and legally enforceable under domestic law. In the event of a local share offering, the local law firm will also assist the local investment bank in preparing the necessary documentation for the local listing authority. Equally important from a developmental perspective is the knowledge transfer and local capacity-building that comes from involving local lawyers in the various stages of activities. Working with experienced, international firms will provide a unique opportunity for local lawyers to learn about the industry and prepare themselves to represent operators in a competitive environment. It is likely that privatisation of the incumbent will occur only once, and after the international lawyers have gone home, the local market will need experienced advocates.

14.8.3.6   World Bank involvement   Generally, the World Bank acts as an 'honest broker' in the selection of advisers. It should be noted that the advisers, even if funded by the World Bank, are advisers to the government. Where the World Bank is providing funding for the government to hire advisers, the World Bank procedures[53] for selecting and engaging advisers will apply. Depending on the contract amount, advisers can be selected according to a number of methods, including international competitive bidding (ICB). ICB is aimed at assuring a transparent and competitive process, where selection criteria are usually weighted in favour of technical expertise, to ensure that the government benefits from cost-effective, competent and experienced advisers. Even where the World Bank is not funding the advisory engagements, governments may want to use World Bank procedures to ensure transparency. In other cases, the 'honest broker' role of the World Bank in itself can add credibility to the transaction. Because the World Bank

---

[53] *World Bank Guidelines for the Selection and Employment of Consultants by World Bank Borrowers,* January 1997 (as amended), available at http://www.worldbank.org/html/opr/consult/guidetxt/intro.html.

does not have a financial interest in the transaction, and because of its global reach and depth of experience in the sector, it can, through its supervision activities, provide valuable policy and best practice support throughout the reform process.

The selection of advisers is not an end in itself but part of a broader process of local capacity-building, good governance and transparent procedures. Most governments have never been through a process like this before. Having qualified, experienced advisers in place is an important part of the process of establishing fair, transparent and objective transactional criteria and processes.

14.8.4 Steps in a strategic sale

14.8.4.1 Sector policy statement The hallmark of a competitive tender is certainty for investors. This is accomplished through the development of a coherent policy, ideally embodied in a legal framework. As discussed at 14.6 above, sectoral policy may be incorporated into primary legislation, though often a government will wish to retain some flexibility and will publish its sector strategy in a legally non-binding policy statement. Such a policy statement will typically include the following key elements: competition for the provision of services, regulatory separation, incentives to private (and probably foreign) investment, plans to enhance the reliability and utility of telecommunications services, all while ultimately balancing the public interest and private profit.

14.8.4.2 Adjust legislation As discussed throughout this chapter, legal reform, including the drafting and enacting of sector-specific legislation, competition legislation and (perhaps) privatisation legislation, will be among the conditions that will attract private investors into the telecommunications sector. The telecommunications regulatory regime must be made open, fair and transparent. Often it will be necessary to amend existing competition, tax, company or other legislation as well, in order to provide the necessary regulatory security for investors. Some countries (particularly in civil law jurisdictions) prepare a general privatisation law defining the rules of the privatisation programme. While this may be helpful in promoting transparency in jurisdictions with weaker institutions and law enforcement, it could also prove inconvenient if the privatisation procedures need to be changed, amended or added to, as this would require ratification.[54]

14.8.4.3 New licences, interconnection agreements The newly privatised telecommunications operator will operate under the terms of a licence which, along with the newly drafted telecommunications legislation, will contain the terms and conditions of operation. Interconnection agreements will be necessary when new entrants enter the marketplace, whether as second fixed

---

[54] Welch, D. and Frémond, O., 'The Case-by-Case Approach to Privatisation: Techniques and Examples', *World Bank Technical Paper No. 403* (Washington, DC, the World Bank, 1998).

operators or as new mobile operators and providers of value-added services, such as ISPs.

14.8.4.4 Valuation The method of sale will determine the level of detail required and the methods to be used in valuing a privatising company. Generally speaking, a strategic sale will require less precision than an IPO. While in a strategic sale valuation is usually based on discounted cash-flow projections of future earnings and comparisons of similar firms' market prices, in an IPO valuation is usually based on a stock market valuation. In either case, the valuation will be overseen by a financial adviser (an investment bank), often selected through a tender process, who will prepare the terms of reference for a financial audit of the company. Together with the audit, the financial adviser's own due diligence will determine the valuation of the company. This due diligence will usually consist of gathering information on the company's past performance, projections, proposed management team, finances and balance sheets, organisation and international standing, as well as on the company's operating environment (e.g., the regulatory and taxation regime).

14.8.4.5 Structural changes As described at 14.8.1 above, posts and telecommunications will need to be separated, with the creation of a telecommunications joint-stock company into which the assets of the state-owned incumbent will be transferred, ready for privatisation. At this stage, the government may also engage in some balance sheet strengthening and organisational changes such as divesting non-core operations, closures or workforce reductions, in order to make the target more attractive to investors.

14.8.4.6 Information memorandum (plus licence, etc.) A call for tenders will announce and describe the investment opportunity, and describe the selection process and timetable, providing details on bid opening and evaluation procedures. Selection criteria will also be described, and a draft of the licence, shareholders' agreement or other relevant document will be attached. An information memorandum will address such things as dividend policy, any environmental issues, the regulatory regime, management of any government residual shareholdings (whether active or passive), and the government's intentions towards the incumbent operator and the industry. The information memorandum is the principal sales tool, but is only one aspect of the marketing and market-conditioning activities of the transaction process. Typically investment bankers will conduct 'road shows' to market the investment opportunity. As discussed at 14.8.4.1, it may also be necessary to conduct a 'communications' strategy to explain the objectives of the government and the benefits of privatisation to the economy as a whole. The communications strategy can also be targeted at stakeholders (labour unions, opposition political parties, consumer groups) who might object to and delay the process, and in that sense can be a cost-effective way of removing transactional obstacles.

14.8.4.7 Investor due diligence A prospective investor will conduct a thorough due diligence of the company based on materials made available to it, usually in a data room at the offices of the law firm representing the investment bank. The depth of scrutiny of the incumbent will often be in proportion to the interest being bid for. In other words, if the proposed investment is a fixed-term BOT-type arrangement, the investor's risk is already somewhat circumscribed as an exit strategy out of its investment is guaranteed. On the other hand, if the investor is proposing to purchase a large minority stake, or a majority stake, in the incumbent, it will need to know precisely the existing and contingent assets and liabilities of the target company, and to be more fully familiarised with the domestic legal and market environment. It is at this stage that investors decide whether or not to put forward a bid, and the results of such due diligence will determine the price at which the bid is entered.

14.8.4.8 Pre-qualification Based on their due diligence, interested investors will submit expressions of interest. At this stage, applicants will be identified who can proceed to the selection phase. Public pre-qualification criteria, which should remove discretion in the selection process, can include minimum financial performance characteristics, operating experience, and minimum coverage and service quality requirements. In order to maximise transparency, these criteria are published and weighted. Short-listed bidders sign confidentiality undertakings with the government and obtain access to more detailed information on the target.

14.8.4.9 Bids and selection At this stage interested investors submit a binding offer and a deposit. Bids are opened in public, and evaluations of the bids are published. Selection is objective, and typically based on a financial offer. There is often a public ceremony to announce the selected bidder. Finally, once the bidder is selected, it will enter into negotiations with the government for the sale of the strategic stake. It is at this stage that the minutiae of the transaction will be determined.

14.8.4.10 Negotiated sale An alternative to the open bidding process described above is a negotiated sale, often used when there is only one bidder, or where one bidder is significantly preferable to another.[55] The government negotiates a tailor-made agreement with the chosen investor which reflects the interests and concerns of both government and investor.

14.9 TELECOMMUNICATIONS LIBERALISATION

14.9.1 Relationship with privatisations

14.9.1.1 Before Rebalancing is a keystone of liberalisation. As described at 14.9.2.3 below, the failure to rebalance tariffs in Argentina ultimately under-

---

[55] *Ibid.*

mined the financial position of the incumbent. In contrast, prices for most telecommunications services were substantially rebalanced in Uganda prior to the award of the second licence in April 1998, with the result that in the following year the number of telephone lines (including cellular) increased by almost 50 per cent.[56]

14.9.1.2 After It is possible to take the approach of allowing prices to be rebalanced through the competitive pressures exerted by a new entrant or new entrants. The success of this approach will depend on the new entrants' ability to challenge the incumbent's dominance in respect of artificially low-priced local services.

14.9.1.3 Simultaneously Liberalisation of the market for telecommunications is easiest in the early stages of reform. This is partly because of high unmet demand for telecommunications services, which provides growth opportunities for both the incumbent and any competitors. Furthermore, challenging the incumbent's advantages early on (long-standing customer relations and market recognition, ownership of infrastructure, knowledge of the market, etc.) may prevent it from consolidating its dominance to the eventual detriment of consumers. This strategy was followed in Uganda, where a second licence for local, cellular, domestic long-distance and international telephone services was issued just as the State monopoly, Uganda Telecommunications Ltd (UTL), was being privatised.[57]

14.9.2 Exclusivity of main operator

14.9.2.1 Scope The broad trend in many emerging markets is to leave the incumbent operator with a monopoly over 'basic' services (e.g., voice telephony between fixed points, telex, telegraph), or international long-distance services, and the corresponding network infrastructure. Most other market segments (e.g., terminal equipment, data and value-added networks and services) will be opened up to competition immediately, although limits will typically be placed on the number of mobile cellular licences issued due to radio spectrum constraints.

14.9.2.2 Duration The initial exclusivity period is generally three, five or seven years. In a few emerging markets, such as Ghana and Uganda, a more radical approach has been taken to the liberalisation of 'basic' services, where licences for a second network operator have been awarded prior to, or at the same time as, the sale of a strategic stake in the incumbent operator, leaving the latter with no exclusivity period. Meanwhile, in Latin America, the benefits of full competition were evident, with connections growing twice as quickly in Chile (where the Government retained the right to issue competing licences at any time) as in Argentina, Mexico and Venezuela (where incum-

---

[56] Smith and Wellenius, *op. cit. supra* n. 29.
[57] *Ibid.*

bents enjoyed monopoly privileges for six to ten years). Chile also enjoyed higher rates of private investment and rural penetration.[58]

14.9.2.3 Rebalancing, preparing for competition Although it is important to grant the incumbent a period of adjustment during which it can gradually eliminate cross-subsidies between its services and rebalance its tariffs so that they reflect true cost, this period should not be allowed to be excessively long. In Argentina, partly thanks to the adoption of a currency board making indexation for inflation illegal, it took the incumbent and the Government over six years to resolve the issue of rebalancing. During this period, the price of long-distance calls was up to 50 times cost, and international calls were four times more expensive than in other countries in Latin America. This stimulated the use of foreign call-back and calling card services, resulting in a fall in Argentina's international telephone revenues of about 25 per cent. In Chile, on the other hand, rebalancing has been 'institutionalised' by the 1982 Telecommunications Law, which requires dominant operators' prices to be revised every five years using marginal cost pricing, and to be indexed between revisions.[59]

Rebalancing will often be a condition of further competition being introduced into the sector, such that delays in achieving rebalancing simply hinder the reform process. Although it may be difficult to identify the operator's true costs (and so establish the rebalancing level at which tariffs should be set), international benchmarks from competitive markets may provide some guidance. Once competition is introduced, these tariff levels are bound to fall further.

14.9.2.4 Financing USO As noted at 14.6.2.3 above, USO is often financed through the establishment of a USO fund, into which all major telecommunications operators and service providers may be required to contribute. The privatised incumbent is usually the party with the USO, though if new entrants are introduced early on in the liberalisation process they may share this obligation.

14.9.3 Tilting regulatory framework towards new entrants

14.9.3.1 Controls on anti-competitive conduct The incumbent will be at a natural advantage by virtue of market and brand recognition, as well as an existing subscriber base. In addition to the introduction of general antitrust regulation as discussed at 14.6.3.1 above, in some cases it may be necessary to limit the scope of an incumbent's licence to exclude certain services or products. For instance, an incumbent's market dominance can be limited by preventing it from applying for cellular licences, as was the case in Brazil.

14.9.3.2 Accounting/structural separation The terms of the privatisation of an incumbent usually include a restriction, if not a prohibition, on cross-

---

[58] Wellenius, *op. cit. supra* n. 7.
[59] Smith and Wellenius, *op. cit. supra* n. 29.

subsidisation between, for instance, local and long-distance services. This tariff rebalancing is critical if new entrants are to be able to compete effectively with the incumbent in the market. For instance, a privatised incumbent which continues to use its above-cost revenues from long-distance services to subsidise a below-cost local telephony service will make it very difficult for a new local telephony service provider to use cost-based pricing. New entrants are unlikely to be attracted to a market where rebalancing is not a term of the incumbent's new licence, and consumers are unlikely to benefit unless competition can be effectively introduced.[60]

14.9.3.3 Interconnection pricing (incremental versus historic cost)   In order to compete viably in the liberalising marketplace, new licensees will need to interconnect their networks to the incumbent's. The incumbent's interconnection obligations (including pricing and technical terms) will need to be spelled out in its licence or in the new legislation, and to include dispute settlement procedures if interconnection negotiations should fail. Without the right to interconnect to the incumbent's network (and so to terminate a call originating on the new licensee's network on the network of the incumbent, and *vice versa*), a new licence may be near worthless. Historic cost pricing tends to benefit the incumbent to the detriment of the new entrant seeking interconnection. If the government's policy is to provide significant incentives to new entrants, it will be preferable that interconnection pricing is based on long-run incremental cost instead, which more accurately reflects the true cost of interconnection to the incumbent.

14.9.3.4 Independent regulator   As discussed at 14.2.4 above, in many countries prior to reform the regulator and the national operator are often one and the same. The disadvantage to the new entrant in such circumstances is obvious and creates the need for an institutionally separate operator. Particularly as the national carrier is often an important and politically potent national symbol, the chances of impartial regulation are likely to be higher if the new regulator has some independence from the government. The more independent the regulator from the political process, the more a prospective new entrant is likely to be attracted to making an investment in the local telecommunications market.

14.10 CONCLUSION

Telecommunications reform can lay the foundations for the reform of other sectors of the economy, attracting new (foreign and domestic) businesses, facilitating transactions and reducing transaction costs, and fostering the dissemination of information, to name but a few positive effects. As such it can be one of the most important factors in the economic development of an emerging market.

---

[60] It should be pointed out, however, that some see the integration and bundling of services (and consequent limited cross-subsidisation) as important to the promotion of digital convergence. See ITU, *op. cit. supra* n. 36, at 24.

Successful reform, however, will ultimately rely on there being the requisite political support at the highest levels of government. From the point of view of the emerging market, privatisations invariably attract domestic criticism, and the sale of part or all of a government's stake in the national telecommunications operator will bring a variety of pressures on to a government. As mentioned above, consumer groups may be concerned about higher prices (which may result, at least in the short term, due to tariff rebalancing) and object to the selling of the 'family jewels', while the Minister of Telecommunications might be nervous that he is ceding his power to a newly created regulator. A government must ensure that it is capable of dealing with these and other pressures, and of completing the task of reform.

From the point of view of investors, the recent wave of third-generation mobile licensing in Europe has redefined the rules for investments in the 'telecommunications' sector. The third-generation licences forced some difficult investment choices in the global telecommunications investment market, showing on the one hand that the telecommunications investment capital markets have also experienced their own globalisation, but also that capital resources for investment are not limitless. The third-generation phenomenon also proved that the investment community sees value in the wireless segment of the market. Interest in traditional strategic investment stakes in wireline incumbents, even those with healthy balance sheets, is dwindling. These new realities, coupled with globalisation and the demands of the 'new economy' brought about by convergence, mandate innovative approaches to telecommunications reform and especially the privatisation paradigm.

Index